✔ KU-773-152

ECOGEOGRAPHY AND RURAL MANAGEMENT

A contribution to the International
Geosphere–Biosphere Programme

Jean Tricart and Conrad KiewietdeJonge

EDINBURGH UNIVERSITY LIBRARY
WITHDRAWN

Longman
Scientific &
Technical

Copublished in the United States with
John Wiley & Sons, Inc., New York

Longman Scientific & Technical,
Longman Group UK Limited
Longman House, Burnt Mill, Harlow,
Essex CM20 2JE, England
and Associated Companies throughout the world.

Copublished in the United States with
John Wiley & Sons, Inc., 605 Third Avenue, New York, NY 10158

© Longman Group UK Limited 1992

All rights reserved; no part of this publication
may be reproduced, stored in a retrieval system,
or transmitted in any form or by any means, electronic,
mechanical, photocopying, recording, or otherwise
without either the prior written permission of the Publishers or a
licence permitting restricted copying in the United Kingdom issued by the Copyright Licensing
Agency Ltd, 90 Tottenham Court Road, London W1P 9HE.

First published 1992

British Library Cataloguing in Publication Data
A catalogue record for this book is available from the British Library

Library of Congress Cataloguing-in-Publication Data
Tricart, Jean.
    Ecogeography and rural management : a contribution to the International Geosphere–
Biosphere Programme / Jean Tricart and Conrad KiewietdeJonge.
        p.   cm.
    Rev. and enl. English ed. of the author's: L'éco-géographie et l'aménagement du milieu
naturel.
    Includes bibliographical references and index.
    ISBN 0–470–21812–6
    1. Agricultural ecology.   2. Land use, Rural–Environmental aspects.   3. Physical
geography.   4. Agricultural geography.   5. Landscape ecology.   6. Geomorphology.
7. International Geosphere–Biosphere Program 'Global Changes" I. KiewietdeJonge,
Conrad, 1920–   .   II. Tricart, Jean. Eco-géographie et l'aménagement du milieu
naturel.   III. Title.
S589.7.T77   1992
333.76 – dc20   91–29212
                                                                                                        CIP

Set in Linotron 202 9/11pt Times u/lc

Produced by Longman Group (FE) Limited
Printed in Hong Kong

CONTENTS

LIST OF FIGURES

LIST OF PLATES

PREFACE

A first edition of this work was published in France in 1979 by François Maspero, now Editions La Découverte, Paris. J. Tricart's co-author was J. Kilian, a pedologist of the Institut de Recherches Agronomiques Tropicales (IRAT). J. Kilian declined to participate in a completely revised and enlarged second English edition. If his original contribution is still evident in his specific research done in West Africa and Madagascar, much of his written text has been modified by the present authors. J. Tricart offered the co-authorship to C. KiewietdeJonge, a long-time collaborator, translator of two of his books, and a member of the 'Comité de Patronage et de Lecture' of the *Revue de Géomorphologie Dynamique*. C. KiewietdeJonge served for ten years as a photo, field and subsurface geologist for the Royal Dutch/ Shell Group in Venezuela, Canada and New Mexico, and has taught physical geography, geomorphology and aerial photograph interpretation at San Diego State University for 27 years. The typescript of this book was read by Professor Ian Douglas, University of Manchester, who offered many valuable suggestions for which the authors are very grateful and wish to express their sincere thanks.

Most of the illustrations were drawn at the Centre de Géographie Appliquée, now at the Atelier de Cartographie Thématique Appliquée (ACTA), directed by Ing. Claire Beller, incorporated in the Centre d'Etudes et de Recherches Eco-géographiques (CEREG, FA to the CNRS) of the Louis Pasteur University, Strasbourg. Some of the charts were made at the draughting section of the Department of Geography, San Diego State University. The authors are grateful to Annie Bouzeghaia and Christophe Sirat in Strasbourg and to Barbara Aguado in San Diego, California, for their professional skill, and to Ing. Claire Beller for her technical guidance and leadership.

FOREWORD

The importance of safeguarding natural resources against reckless exploitation and misuse is at last coming to be generally acknowledged. The issue now arouses such strong feelings that whenever there is an industrial accident on the scale of Schweizerhalle on the Rhine near Basle, or an oil spill at sea, all the media give it front-page treatment. More encouragingly, media attention is no longer confined to disasters and spectacular accidents: the public is also informed about events and phenomena that are less conspicuous but equally important on account of their insidious effects. I refer to

- overuse of chemical fertilizers resulting, for example, in eutrophication of lakes and rivers
- chronic air and water pollution
- the rapidly worsening condition of our sea-shores and coastal landscapes, and more especially of marine life
- the uncontrolled dumping of dangerous and toxic wastes and the scandalous practice of shipping them abroad
- the way in which areas of natural beauty are carved up to make room for more and more highway networks, industrial estates and recreation facilities
- harmful agricultural and forestry techniques.

We must be under no illusions: while real progress has been made in a number of areas including the treatment of sewage and gas emissions and the protection accorded to certain threatened wildlife habitats, the situation of Europe's natural heritage is still a matter of grave concern, as we know from the immense amount of research the Council of Europe has done on the subject. For example, in Europe today

- 102 species of freshwater fish out of a total of 200 (more than half) and
- 46 species of reptiles out of 102 (45 per cent) are *threatened with extinction.*

For the invertebrates, the situation is scarcely more encouraging: for instance, 102 of the 380 European species of Rhopalocera (butterflies) are threatened.

Human behaviour takes a heavy toll among the plant species as well: 22 per cent of the 1,100 vascular plants mainly southern European varieties and endemics, seem likely to become extinct in the years ahead.

Taking the biosphere as a whole, what makes the situation still more alarming is that in the countries of the Third World human onslaughts on the natural environment are frequently more aggressive than in Europe. One has only to recall the means employed to exploit – massacre would be a better word – the Amazon Rain Forest. The sheer scale of these operations adds considerably to their impact upon the natural habitats: whole ecosystems are disturbed, with considerable loss of animal and plant life; not to mention the soil, which becomes degraded to the point of sterilization. What is more, the majority of tropical species are not even known to science. We are wrecking a capital asset whose volume and characteristics we do not even know: what unbelievable insouciance!

It is essential therefore not only to arouse public opinion, but also to ensure that the right answers are clearly explained, so that everyone concerned knows what they are. I use the plural deliberately: far be it from me to wish to keep the natural environment strictly intact, or advocate a return to ancestral farming techniques. No, humankind's creative ability must be used to the full, but used intelligently. Like all the other creatures of the biosphere, human beings are entitled to make use of the environment, provided that the changes they make are consistent with a long-term policy of conservation rather than short-term profit. Leaving economic considerations aside, there is no moral justification for knowingly contributing to the extermination of any species.

This book will help in no small way to foster the kind of understanding that is needed. It is immediately clear from the title that the authors have undertaken and pursued their task with ecological considerations constantly in mind. Their subject of study, the rural environment, is, as it always was and I believe always will be, essential to the life of every human community: the land is, after all, the basis of humankind's food supply. But that is not its only function: it permits the development of numerous recreational activities such as hunting, fishing and tourism, and assumes major ecological significance chiefly by the presence of running waters. Soil fertility, an essential feature, is directly dependent on human intervention on the land.

The rural environment is more sensitive than first appearances suggest, and before interfering with it one must get to know its characteristics and how the different components interact. There is nothing static about the countryside: on the contrary, it is constantly changing.

In Part I the authors consider the natural environment, chiefly from the standpoint of ecogeography, explaining clearly how our knowledge of the workings of the rural ecosystems has progressed and the means which science offers for improving that knowledge. Remote sensing techniques are being used more and more widely, although the findings of traditional geomorphology and pedology are still invaluable. It is vital to know about the hydrologic cycle and the water budget. Each of these aspects is presented and analysed with careful attention to detail.

In Part II, the possible ways of improving and managing the countryside are discussed, with particular reference to agriculture. Here too, the authors supply a wealth and variety of information: their topics ranging from salinization in irrigated regions to cartographic survey procedures.

In short, this study is an indispensable tool for anyone wishing to gain a deeper insight into the geomorphological and ecological aspects of the rural environment, or to make use of the land for farming or any other purpose. The book will also appeal to non-specialists, and give them a good idea of the current state of knowledge in this field.

The authors are to be congratulated on the immense amount of work that has gone into this study and the quality of the finished product. Let us hope that their efforts are rewarded by wide readership. In welcoming this, they will be joined by ecologists everywhere and by all those eager to see some improvement in the management of the world's natural resources.

Jean-Pierre Ribaut
Head of the Environment Protection
and Management Division
Council of Europe
Strasbourg

ACKNOWLEDGEMENTS

We are grateful to the following for permission to reproduce copyright figures and tables.:

Centre de Géographie Appliquée for plates 1–52, Professor Wieneke for fig. 16.

Whilst every effort has been made to trace the owners of copyright material, in a few cases this has proved impossible and we take this opportunity to offer our apologies to any copyright holders whose rights we may have unwittingly infringed.

INTRODUCTION

Environmental problems today are posed on the political plane under pressure of public opinion. For example, in the 1970s a Bavarian chemical firm in Markolsheim, Alsace, hoping to receive a government grant for the construction of a factory that would have caused considerable pollution from the by-products of mercury, had obtained the support of the local Prefect. Stricter German legislation had previously prevented the installation of the factory in the Federal Republic. Both Alsatians and the people of Baden, on the German side of the Rhine, then got together and convinced the French government to scrap the project. In another case the people of Plogoff, in Brittany, led by their mayor, revolted in order to prevent a technical study by Electricité de France, the object of which was the construction of a nuclear power plant at Pointe du Raz, one of Europe's most beautiful coastal sites. The mayor emphasized that he did not have the necessary competence to respond to the out-of-date procedure of *de comodo et incomodo* of the investigation and that such questions should be debated in the Parlement, which in fact happens in Sweden, in the UK and in other democratic countries.

More recently many problems have arisen at the international level concerning the disposal of dangerous industrial wastes, as some firms shirk their responsibilities or others try to make fast profits, while there is insufficient control by the authorities. The toxic wastes of Seveso, Italy, were illegally put into barrels and shipped to France, eventually to be 'exported' to Germany, when they were discovered in a former butcher's warehouse. Other dangerous wastes are exported by specialized Italian concerns to the Lebanon, where, owing to the chaotic political situation, there is no effective control. Some African states, especially the poorest, have accepted millions of dollars (Guinea-Bissau $140 million annually) in return for allowing toxic wastes to be dumped on their national territories. Several of these states have struck back at this dumping, generally under false pretences, of west European shipping organizations (e.g. the Norwegian ore ship *Banya* trying to dump the ashes of domestic trash of the City of Philadelphia in an abandoned bauxite quarry on Kassa Island, offshore from Conakry, Guinea). Since May 1988, however, any dumping 'contract' was formally forbidden to members of the Organization of African Unity (OAU). Another international decision, at an earlier date, had already prohibited the uncontrolled dumping of toxic wastes at sea, as was commonly practised, for example, by specialized Dutch shipping.

The reactions in France in the mid-1970s and the more recent ones of some African governments are demonstrative of two aspects of our present crisis of civilization; a crisis that involves rich and poor as well as capitalist or socialist countries. The first aspect is the growing fear of the well-informed, educated public *vis-à-vis* the increasing danger resulting from unrestrained technological development. The second is a reflection of the unequal standards and living conditions of the 'developed' and 'underdeveloped' world. That the problem of the 'export' of toxic wastes arose in the poorest countries of Africa is significant, as development has practically ceased there for a decade or more.

But these are only a few aspects of a much larger environmental crisis in which humankind has to deal with acid rain, polluted rivers and beaches, chemical leaks, record temperatures and severe drought (summer of 1988 in the USA), the beaching of seals, and other induced phenomena deleterious not only to fauna, flora and soils, but also to humans.

Our institutions, the types of administration they have created and the power of decision that result from them are no longer in tune with our present needs, particularly the protection of the environment and the proper use of natural resources.

The first edition (1979) of this book was well in advance of the then current scientific opinion. Nevertheless, the authors were not predicants in the desert. Shortly after its publication a new current of thought began to form, which resulted in the adoption of the International Geosphere–Biosphere Programme (IGBP) at the twenty-first General Assembly of the International Council of Scientific Unions

Plate 1 Losing our past
Ph. JT CDIV-17. Romanesque church of Sasabe, Catalonia, Spain, being buried by torrential alluvium, result of unrestrained runoff caused by the abandonment of the watershed.

(ICSU) held in Berne, Switzerland, in September 1986. This programme was defined in the following terms:

The central aim of the IGBP is to describe and understand the interactive physical, chemical and biological processes that regulate the Earth's unique environment for life, the changes that are occurring in this system, and the manner in which they are influenced by human actions. . . . A deeper understanding of the coupled processes that govern the Earth's environment will provide the basis for more rational management of resources and will improve the forecasts of significant global change.

The object of the IGBP is to evaluate the evolution of our terrestrial environment in the 'mean-short' term, of some one hundred years. But to achieve such an objective, it is necessary to reconstruct changes of longer duration of the recent past during the millennia that have elapsed at least since the last cold maximum, some 18,000 years BP (before present). All scientific techniques developed by the various disciplines should be used in a convergent approach.

Knowledge of the past is essential to the tasks of understanding the present and of predicting the future. The IGBP is envisaged as a program of cooperative efforts of varied disciplines with biospheric interactions as the focus and discriminator in setting priorities and in establishing principal emphasis. In concentrating on the interactive areas of the physical, chemical, and biological realms the program is truly focused and uniquely defined.

(Rutter and Faure 1987: 3–4)

These quotations clearly demonstrate our position as precursors at the time of the first edition. The manuscript of this second edition, completely revised and enlarged, was, for its major part, already written when the IGBP proposal became public. The present book is presented as a contribution to the IGBP. Our task is identical, as our approach follows the same philosophy. Nevertheless, because of our personal experience, we shall, in our study of the interdependence of the various environmental components in a system's approach, combine our scientific investigations with a practical orientation relative to the ecological environment, its constraints and its rational development and management.

The myth of unlimited growth, a convenient invention of irresponsible economists, is questioned: the Club of Rome, which is not a minor left-wing organization, promotes the idea of 'zero growth'. This is another extreme position acceptable only to the well-to-do, which is denounced in underdeveloped countries as a hypocritical way of safeguarding acquired positions. A zero growth solution would permit a reduction of the shocking inequalities of the present world only by a redistribution of wealth, by taking from some and giving to others, which would provoke much resistance. Zero growth would preclude a solution to underdevelopment, a problem affecting three-quarters of humanity.

The reasoning is false; the problem must be posed in different terms. We must return to more sober concepts. Increased production cannot be an end in itself, but should improve the conditions of life, to enable everyone to eat one's fill, to buy clothes, to acquire shelter, to be protected from illness, to have a decent life. The narrow vision of econometry cannot apprehend all this correctly. The GNP is incapable of properly measuring economic growth (for example, it increases with the number of fatal automobile accidents).

We should distinguish *three* levels of organization in the world that surrounds us – our environment:

1 the level of the organization of matter, characterized by the arrangement of the particles that compose it
2 the level of the organization of life, which entails an aptitude to reproduce, accompanied by a tendency towards forms of increasing organization, the reverse of material things
3 the level of social organization, which is based on an awareness that creates forms of social and economic organization within the framework of a culture.

Each of these levels is characterized by structures supported by specific forces. People of the least technological societies are fully aware of them: this awareness is a fundamental element of culture. Because of it they admit a certain harmony of things towards which they pledge the greatest respect. This harmony is based on interdependencies: interdependence between the elements of Nature, interdependence between humans, and interdependence between humans and Nature. Those who fight for the preservation of the environment have rediscovered these interdependencies and want to safeguard their harmonious working. We are at the level of philosophical concepts: the problem is therefore a problem of civilization. We do not pretend to resolve it. But the problem constitutes the framework in which our action, whose object is the improvement of the natural environment takes place.

First, a false problem must be got rid of: that which consists of opposing Man and Nature. Those who believe in this viewpoint try to rediscover a virgin Nature, intact, not modified by humans, that would serve as a reference. This is the search for a terrestrial paradise. To fall from here into a Rousseauist Manichaeism, according to which Nature is good and humankind bad, there is but a very small step. But this attitude extends all the way to the rational development of the natural environment: it leads to a radical conservation, dreaming to cover the Earth with reserves allegedly completely protected from the effects of human society. Such positions are untenable: between 1880 and 1980 the carbon dioxide content of the atmosphere rose 15 per cent and may reach 25 per cent by the year 2000. How can such integral reserves be protected from this rise? Atomic explosions since 1945 and a nuclear power plant accident have incorporated into the atmosphere a certain number of radioactive bodies such as strontium and caesium. The rate of diffusion of strontium can be calculated from its precipitation on the Antarctic ice-sheet, whereas caesium is currently used to date very recent lake sediments and to determine their present rate of accumulation. Can such integral reserves be protected from them? We cannot hope to find a virgin landscape that humans have not affected. Humans, like all living beings, are part of Nature with which they are connected by innumerable interdependent ties. Like plants and animals humans are incapable of assimilating solar energy directly to produce their tissues and must feed themselves by drawing food from the various levels of the food chain. Humans are an integral part of ecosystems, without which, not being a primary producer, they could not exist. The primary producers, starting-point of the food chain, are those organisms that are capable of producing living tissues with the use of solar energy through photosynthesis. Only green plants are primary producers. Humans belong to the second level of organization, that of living beings, from the moment they were differentiated as a species, several million years ago, well before the advent of economists and the GNP!

All forms of social organization depend, by way of life itself, on this fundamental fact. *Ecogeography* is a point of view which recognizes this. It studies how humans are integrated into ecosystems, and how this integration is diversified as a function of terrestrial space. This integration of humans into ecosystems assumes two important aspects:

1 The *demands* humans impose on the ecosystems in which they participate and on the physical environment (use of the air, water and minerals).

2 The *modifications* humans impose, voluntarily or not, on the ecosystems, including the physical environment: creation of artificial ecosystems (agriculture, including stock rearing) and pollution of all kinds.

Humans modify the functioning of ecosystems in two fundamental ways. An important part of the second aspect is that humans are decisive agents of *ecodynamics*. But the social and economic structures influence the kind of modification and, even more, the geographic distribution of the demands made upon the ecosystems and the adverse effects that frequently result from the alteration of the ecodynamics.

Over against the scandalous inequalities that exist between humans on the biological plane and the rapid contemporary demographic explosion, the dilapidation of finite Earth resources, such as soils, is a manifestation of criminal blindness. Not demanding more than they can provide is the only acceptable moral and rational attitude if ecosystems are not to be degraded or destroyed. This objective safeguards the future and is in harmony with the fundamental manifestation of Life, to provide for the perpetuation of the species. We rediscover here the basic laws that all living beings respect. For Christians and Jews the despoliation of the environment is an infringement of the First Commandment, that is against God and His creation, and is therefore punishable. Other major religions hold equivalent views on the natural environment. We thus acknowledge a deep preoccupation of public concern, already expressed at the beginning of this introduction.

To make a judicious, responsible demand on ecosystems without causing a degradation, without exceeding the threshold of their sensitivity, is not a simple matter. Jean Tricart has experienced this on five continents during his professional life; he has made mistakes, tried to correct them and to improve his understanding in order to be of greater social usefulness. This book is guided by this experience, which explains its basic methodological orientation. Both authors hope that by the presentation of this book and through its instrumentality they can save the time and effort of others. Our goal is practical: to help realize an improved use of the natural, rural environment. The Earth is diverse, each environmental intervention must take account of it. It must, above all, adapt itself to the enormous diversity of ecosystems, whose first characteristic is its unequal sensitivity to human activities.

Part I is concerned with the elucidation of the *ecogeographical point of view*. It begins with a presentation of other approaches that have been proposed to acquire an integral knowledge of the natural environment, or (as we now say) the ecologic environment. Our approach is based on the energy flows that actuate and structure ecosystems and determine their dynamics, and therefore their sensitivity.

Part II deals with the rational management of the natural environment, mainly the part formed by ecosystems transformed by human beings to provide their sustenance, the emphasis being on the relationships between agronomy and the ecosystem.

The entire work corresponds to a particular point in the evolution of our thoughts. We are aware of its transient character, which is bound to be exceeded. And the sooner this happens, the more satisfied we shall be that this publication will have been of some use. The book is not only provisional, but also incomplete. We voluntarily stop at the production of food and fibre after the environment has been properly developed and protected. We therefore skip all aspects of geographical distribution and of the benefits derived from the improvement of the land. This task, mainly its socio-economic aspects and their political implications, is left to others. Our task is to provide the necessary scientific and technical preliminary knowledge.

PART ONE

ECOGEOGRAPHY: THE STUDY OF THE NATURAL ENVIRONMENT

INTRODUCTION

Since the nineteenth century (that is for altogether too long), scientific research has favoured the analytic method to an excessive degree. The result has been a proliferation of specialties, ever more narrow, ever more esoteric, and ever less capable of responding to the preoccupations of public opinion, which takes a broad view of the deterioration of the quality of life every time a questionable 'development' takes place. People demand protective measures, actions that will *improve* the quality of life. They are tired of the consequences of irresponsible actions taken in a fragile and complex environment.

Unfortunately research has insufficiently addressed these questions of environmental quality. The state of our knowledge often trails behind the demand. The first attempts of a comprehensive apprehension of the natural environment did not appear until the end of the Second World War. They were static, however, of the 'inventory' type.

But our ecologic environment is in a constant state of flux. It is characterized by the dynamics of a certain number of interacting elements. We must understand these mechanisms, take them into account in order to make better use of the environment, to produce more food, fibre and timber, to protect the land against the degradations that would destory its capacity to provide for human beings' biological existence. Every intervention modifies the dynamics and affects the interactions or interdependencies. And so does every development. In order to attain the required goal, development should take full account of these dynamics and interdependencies. It should insert itself harmoniously into their fabric. It cannot be based on a mere inventory of all the objects, which is a static approach. A comprehensive understanding of the environment, required for its proper use and conservation, should first be that of its dynamics. Only in this way can we appreciate the degree of sensitivity of the environment, that is its tolerance *vis-à-vis* our ever-increasing complex, even insidious, interventions, the result of rapid technological progress. Such is the problem that is addressed in Part I.

We shall first analyse the methods that have been used to attain a comprehensive understanding of the natural environment and its resources. Next, we shall demonstrate that the demands of a rational management of the environment can be understood only through a knowledge of its dynamics. Leaning on our professional experience, we shall adopt a point of view that is both ecological *and spatial* and therefore geographical. We propose the term '*ecogeography*' to designate it.

The study of energy flows, which ecologists/ biologists have applied only to the inner workings of biocenoses (organic communities), will be extended to the ecologic environment. It will show that most of the energy available to ecosystems is used not by the food web but by the dynamics of the environment. An ecogeographic study able to respond to the demands of a rational land use therefore must begin with the physical geographical phenomena, especially the morphogenic processes. An account of the new concepts will provide researchers with a methodological approach for research with a practical end.

1 APPROACH TO AN INTEGRATED STUDY OF THE NATURAL ENVIRONMENT

Australians made the first major endeavour to revive the old concept of the unity of Nature since the day the concept was lost sight of. The initiative came from the Commonwealth Scientific and Industrial Research Organization (CSIRO) during the Second World War. The method has had considerable success. Outside Australia and New Guinea it has also been applied in Nigeria, The Gambia, Tanzania, South Africa, Botswana, Lesotho and Japan. It was 'discovered' by the UN Food & Agriculture Organization (FAO), which tried to apply it in Argentina, but without tangible results in spite of the considerable means at its disposal. The method therefore deserves to be examined and its scientific and practical value discussed.

Subsequently we shall discuss the concept of 'landscape' (*Landschaft*) and the more recent concepts of landscape ecology and systems analysis which allowed a marked progress in the global apprehension of the natural environment as developed since the 1960s, particularly in the Soviet Union, the former German Democratic Republic and France.

LAND SURVEYS OF THE CSIRO (AUSTRALIA)

The first survey of the Australian project was applied to the Katherine–Darwin area of Australia's Northern Territory starting in 1946; its report appeared in 1952. The time of its execution is important to appreciate its value.

Principles of the method

Knowledge of its object helps understand the principles of the method. In 1945 much of Australia was still an empty continent. The Japanese

bombing of Darwin in 1942 and their assault on New Guinea produced a reaction in the struggle for life which did not manifest itself on the battlefield only. It made Australians realize the urgent necessity of accelerating the development of their country, which was also at the origin of a new immigration policy adopted shortly after the war.

If Australia was an empty continent, it was also not well known. Thousands of square kilometres remained to be explored. Its characteristics, many endemic, are very different from those of the other austral continents. The composition of its plant formations, the originality of its deserts (actually semi-deserts), its geology and physiography, its soils, in short its resources, all had to be made known for their eventual exploitation or development. Detailed, large-scale studies were out of the question. Time was of the essence. Enormous areas had to be charted and prospective areas further investigated for a rapid exploitation of their resources with few hands and small investments. Success was important in order to attract pioneer settlers.

The war had shown the importance and developed the techniques of aerial photography. The CSIRO (a federal government agency), used a specially created division to produce 'land systems' of the least known parts of the continent with the help of air photographs. A scale of 1:1,000,000 was chosen, later reduced to 1:500,000 and even 1:250,000, but the method is applicable specifically to small scales. Occasionally the Land Surveys Division applied the method to already developed areas. Later the work was expanded to Papua New Guinea, then under Australian administration and at the gates of Indonesia and Asia. Obviously, East and South-East Asia are of major importance to Australia, which remains an important exporter of raw materials and lacks capital, while Japan, a banker to the United States, is a big importer of all kinds of minerals and agricultural products.

The method of the land surveys is physiognomic. Its object is to delimit 'types of country'. With aerial photographs and accessibility in mind sample areas are chosen and transects planned to establish the 'land elements' and their interrelatedness as well as the relationship between land patterns. The introduction of the helicopter at this time greatly facilitated the work. Information is gathered on plant species, soils, superficial deposits, weathering profiles, rocks and geologic structure. Samples are taken and, if necessary, levelling is carried out to measure minor elevation differences in lowlands. Attention is paid to morphodynamics as revealed by micro-relief and ground surface details, which may indicate deflation, sheet erosion, soil sealing, sand accumulation around plants, etc. Once back in the office all data are collated, completed with library information and put on maps by means of symbols. Boundaries are drawn and the land systems are given geographic names from typical regions (Mabbutt and Steward, 1963).

Results are presented in the form of two types of complementary documents:

1 A text that describes the essentials of the area studied, especially the characteristics of the mapped units with block diagrams that show the relief and, where pertinent, geologic structure or surficial formations, occasionally also distribution of plant formations or even soils, but this is by no means the rule.
2 A map of the natural units selected and defined in the text. A certain evolution of the work is observable during the course of time. Initially only a map of land systems was presented. Later, separate maps of vegetation, soils, occasionally of distribution of rainfall, and even so-called 'geomorphological' maps (and others) were added. Such an evolution is quite demonstrative of the artificial nature of the initial land systems maps. They lacked a satisfactory criterion for integration and were rejected by various specialists, who procured maps of their own in conformity with their needs, disregarding the needs of others, which is the opposite of *integration*.

The taxonomy adopted by the CSIRO is simple. In its most elaborate version it includes only three categories:

1 The types of country called *land systems*, which are at the highest level. They are chorographic units that correspond to what has generally been called 'natural regions', however poorly defined. They are determined by climate and palaeoclimate, lithology and geomorphic history; for example, a plateau region capped by a ferruginous cuirass more or less dissected, or a

coastal plain with barrier islands, lagoons, small deltas and relict shorelines.
2 *Land units* are subdivisions of the land systems. They are more homogeneous and recur repeatedly. They may be too small to be mapped individually. For example, in the case of a dissected cuirassed plateau the units are: plateau surface remnants, the valleys dissecting the plateau, and the buttes flanking it.
3 *Land facets* are at the lowest taxonomic level. They have not been strictly defined and are not generally used. We have noted that they correspond to the elements of a landform; for example, the escarpment of a valley-side or its colluvial slope.

The taxonomy does not pretend to fit the elements which it distinguishes into a genetic whole. It is purely descriptive.

Pure description is the object of the land systems. Block diagrams of land systems show the patterns of land units, identified by numbers. The general characteristics of each land system are described under *discrete* headings such as climate, geology, geomorphology or drainage. A concise description of the land units is given in tables. These indicate, for each one, in separate columns their approximate area in square miles, the kind of landforms, soils and vegetation. Each column later became the specific matter of a thematic map. Supplementary information, such as soil analyses, and lists of species of the plant formations, is provided in the main text in corresponding chapters. An example of these maps and block diagrams is reproduced in Figures 1 and 2.

Critique

The method of land surveys of the CSIRO is very empirical. It may be explained either by a certain mental attitude common to the English-speaking peoples or it is a characteristic of a certain intellectual isolation of the continent, which is indisputable and deeply felt by resident research scientists. Whatever it may be, it is interesting to note that the Australians have hardly preoccupied themselves with a critical examination of their method, exposed and discussed its principles, and confronted it with outside currents of thought. Nevertheless, modifications of the method have gradually been introduced into their publications, the *Land Research Series*. The main one has added a series of more specialized thematic maps, such as land surface or surface drainage maps, to the land systems map. Nowhere (as far as we know), has this change been the object of a published methodological discussion.

Figures 1 and 2 are taken from the CSIRO's study of the land systems of the Mitchell–Normanby area of the Cape York Peninsula (Galloway, Gunn and Story 1970). This report gives an example of the multiple speciality maps arrived at by the CSIRO at this time. The change, however, is noteworthy. It consists in the abandonment of the initial postulate on which the method is based, that is the contention that affirms the areal identity of the landforms, soils, vegetation and drainage units, a position that implicitly admits that the outlines of these various landscape components necessarily coincide. Our own experience intimates that this is not always the case. Coincidence is frequently realized, perhaps 80–90 per cent of the time, sometimes more when the limiting factors are simple and very compelling, sometimes less when other factors, which have not been taken into account, intervene. According to this wry statement, 'something usually looks simple when it has not yet been investigated', the less known the area explored, the easier it is to force the coincidence of the limits of its different natural features. Moreover, frequently, a gradual modification of an ecologic factor coincides with an abrupt change in vegetation (Zonneveld 1974). In short, the problem is similar to that of a statistical scatter. It is passed over in silence, while the study of correlation ratios offers a perfectly adequate instrument for its study. Indeed, the degrees of coincidence in the spatial extent of different types of phenomena (or the aspects they create, to remain in the descriptive perspective of the CSIRO) express correlation ratios between these very phenomena. We have here a research problem of the first importance, not only for the study of a natural system, but also for the eventual development of the land, for such studies are indispensable in order to be able to predict the cascading changes that an intervention may bring about. The problem is similar in remote sensing, and statisticians are proposing various solutions to calculate 'coincidence ratios' for the limits of units resulting from the numerical treatment of magnetic tapes.

It seems that as studies progressed the Australians sharpened their perception and realized that the outlines of the various natural units do not always exactly coincide. As a result, but faithful to tradition, they then retained the land systems map as a pious relic resulting from a more or less happy compromise but without taking it too seriously, as

various specialists drew their own outlines. But what has now become of the value of the land systems map? Worse, what has become of the value of the method? Why not squarely face the problem of coincidence? This is all the more surprising as English-speaking geographers are the most inclined to quantification and mathematical formulation in the name of the 'new geography'.

In truth, there is no need to be surprised. The questions that we have posed in the preceding paragraph are the consequences of a methodologic position. Let us examine this point more closely.

The CSIRO approach is based on aerial photograph interpretation. We have made too much use of aerial photographs ourselves to slight this method, but we are much aware of its limitations. Aerial photographs, especially on the rather small scale of 1:50,000 or 1:60,000, as are common in Australia, lend themselves better to description than to an analysis of dynamics. They permit a *direct* observation of the landforms in stereoscopy, and of the vegetation. Many years after the CSIRO, the ITC, a Dutch institution specializing in aerial photograph interpretation as a help to development, published a multi-volume textbook for integrated surveys. The basic materials are aerial photographs and the procedure and concepts used are basically similar to those of the CSIRO. The main difference is the inclusion of hydrological maps. The other aspects of the natural environment, that is, soils lithology, geologic structure and even the present morphogenic processes, are deduced from the preceding by interpretation. Frequently, as was the case of the CSIRO surveys, the available material, the urgency of the studies, sometimes the political decisions, the precarious and insufficient level of knowledge precluded a more elaborate investigation. This is the reason why the UK Ministry of Overseas Surveys adopted, with only a few insignificant modifications, the CSIRO land system approach. In any case, description is imperative during the initial phases of exploration, but becomes insufficient later. A criticism that can be addressed to the Land Survey Division of the CSIRO is that it remained too empirical, that it failed to change its concepts and its method at the opportune moment for lack of sufficient introspection.

Indeed, around 1940–6, geomorphology in the English-speaking countries was little process oriented. W. M. Davis's influence, in which recourse to observation was subordinate to that of 'imagination', remained overwhelming. Dynamic geomorphology was born later and spread slowly in the Anglophone world (which often disdains

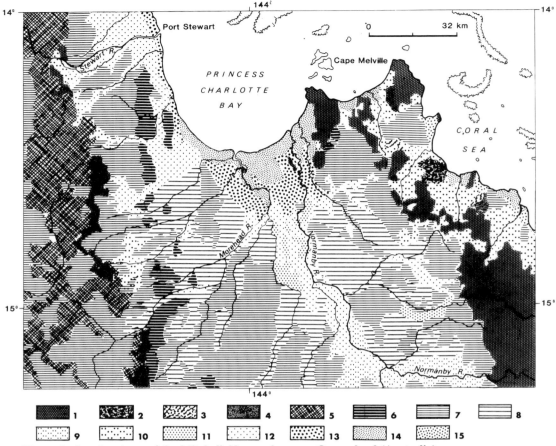

Figure 1. Land systems of the Mitchell–Normanby area, Queensland (Australia)

Mountains and hills on resistant volcanics, granite, and sediments

1 Starcke (6,560 sq miles)   Mountains on volcanics, granite, greywacke, and other sediments, deeply dissected plateaux on quartz sandstone; shallow rocky soils; ironbark or mixed eucalypt woodland

2 Rumula (320 sq miles)   Mountains on granite, greywacke, and other sediments; uniform fine-textured soils and structured red loams; vine forest

3 Maytown (3,560 sq miles)   Closely dissected low hills on volcanics, greywacke, and other sediments; shallow, gravelly soils; ironbark woodland, some box woodland

Undulating to hilly country on fairly resistant metamorphics, granite, sediments, and basalt

4 Hodgkinson (930 sq miles)   Undulating to hilly country on greywacke and other sediments; shallow, gravelly soils; ironbark woodland

5 Arkara (5,670 sq miles)   Undulating country and low stony hills on metamorphics and granite; massive earths and uniform sandy soils; bloodwood-stringybark or ironbark woodland

Plains and lowlands on weathered terrestrial sediments

6 Koolburra (1,500 sq miles)   Plains and low plateaux on weathered Tertiary sandstone; sandy red earths; bloodwood-stringybark woodlands, some paperbark woodland

7 Balurga (13,320 sq miles)   Extensive plains on weathered terrestrial sediments; sandy red and yellow earths and uniform sandy soils; bloodwood-stringybark woodland, some paperbark woodland

8 Mottle (4,890 sq miles)   Extensive plains on weathered terrestrial sediments, siltstone, and alluvium; massive earths; paperbark or bloodwood-stringybark woodland

Plains on older alluvium and colluvium

9 Leinster (4,330 sq miles)   Extensive, uniform old alluvial plains; leached grey and brown massive earths with hardpan; paperbark or bloodwood-stringybark woodland

10 Ninda (1,160 sq miles)   Colluvial and alluvial aprons and fans; texture-contrast soils; mostly paperbark woodland but very variable

Plains on younger alluvium
11 Radnor (1,520 sq miles)   Stable alluvial plains largely above flood level; texture-contrast soils; grassland or savannah
12 Cumbulla (2,890 sq miles)   Alluvial plains in part actively forming and largely flooded in the wet season; texture-contrast soils; paperbark woodland

Plains and dunes on young coastal sediments
13 Inkerman (1,180 sq miles)   Coastal clay plains with low sandy beach ridges; saline-alkaline cracking clay soils; grassland, some mixed evergreen scrub
14 Battersea (890 sq miles)   Coastal mud flats; saline-alkaline cracking clay and uniform fine-textured soils; patchy salt-marsh vegetation; alternating with large bare areas
15 Flattery (280 sq miles)   Dunes largely stabilized by vegetation; uniform sandy soils; evergreen mixed scrub

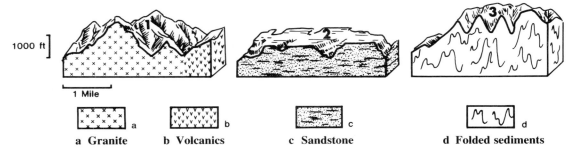

1000 ft

1 Mile

a Granite   **b Volcanics**   **c Sandstone**   **d Folded sediments**

Figure 2. Starcke land system (6,560 sq miles)

Example of a definition of a land system in the Mitchell–Normanby area, Queensland (Australia)

Mountains on volcanics, granite, greywackes, and other sediments; deeply dissected plateaux on quartz sandstone; shallow rocky soils; ironbark or mixed eucalypt woodland.

Land Unit	Area and Distribution	Land Forms	Soils	Vegetation
1 2 obs.	40% Mainly in south	Mountains on granite and volcanics; 2,000–4,000 ft above sea level; extremely rocky with extensive outcrops; narrow valleys with little or no alluvium	Mainly rocky land and shallow rocky soils, Mungana; small areas of shallow sandy soils, Cardwell (Uc4.2), with abundant gravel	Outcrop with some deciduous scrub (*Petalostigma* present), elsewhere ironbark woodland (*E. shirleyi, E. cullenii, E. brevifolia, Callitris*, shrubs, *Xanthorrhoea*, in east with *E. alba*) over *Themeda australis, Schizachyrium*, some spinifex
2 4 obs.	35% Mainly in north	Dissected sandstone plateaux; local relief 200–1,500 ft; restricted summit surfaces locally with ironstone gravel caps; rocky benches and cliffs on upper slopes; very restricted sandy alluvial foot slopes in narow valleys	Mainly outcrop and shallow rocky soils; shallow gravelly red and yellow earths, Brooklyn (Gn2.11, 2.24), on summit surfaces; shallow uniform sandy soils, Cardwell (Uc2.21), on foot slopes	Mixed eucalypt woodland, evergreen mixed scrub, or paperbark woodland; shrubs common, short or mid-height grass; some lancewood scrub
3 2 obs.	25% Mainly in centre	Dissected mountains on folded sediments and metamorphics; local relief 300–2,000 ft; restricted colluvial foot slopes, stony in upper part, subject to gullying and sheet erosion	Mainly shallow rocky soils, Emu (Um4.1), with stony surface strew and minor outcrops; minor areas of texture-contrast soils, Stewart (Db2.43), on foot slopes	Ironbark woodland (*E. cullenii*); foot slopes, box woodland with *M. viridiflora, E. cullenii*, and bloodwood; both over *Themeda australis* and both with some *E. alba* in the east

* Similar to Wairuna, Ortona, Torwood, and Leichhardt land systems of the Leichhardt–Gilbert area.

foreign-language publications). The only geomorphology available to the pioneers of the CSIRO was of a physiographic type, which was restricted to the description of landforms influenced by geologic structure and the stages of a would-be 'cycle of erosion', with an excessive attention to peneplains. In this way progress was hardly possible. But the then current methods, scantily demanding from the point of view of rigour, accommodated themselves readily, mainly by default, to the practice of aerial photograph interpretation. The vicious circle was closed. And such vicious circles have an uncanny capacity to survive, for example Davis's 'cycle of erosion' in the United States. A similar methodological shortcoming occurs in two other concepts of American origin: that of climax in ecology and of catena in pedology.

In the latter connection it should be noted that the relationships between soil and landform, as they are held by the land systems of the CSIRO, are based on the catena concept. This concept allows an easy correlation between morphographic and pedologic units. It is a pity that a certain intellectual endemism impeded the CSIRO Land

Survey Division researchers to take account of the work that produced changes in these concepts. This is all the more regrettable as the very pedologists of the CSIRO have played a major international role in the study of the relationships between soils and geomorphological phenomena. It might have been the result of an administrative compartmentalization.

This critique, which is concerned with the insufficient evolution of the methods applied to the land systems, should not cause an important point to be overlooked: the surveys not only have drawn the attention of geographers to the use of aerial photographs (which they had previously much ignored), but also inaugurated interdisciplinary work, based on small teams composed of a geomorphologist, a botanist with an ecological inclination, a pedologist, and occasionally a geologist, a forester, a specialist in pastures, or an agronomist.

Another important point must be stressed: the land systems were conceived for the reconnaissance of areas that were practically uninhabited, *terra incognita* from the scientific point of view, and for the making of small-scale maps. But with time

Plate 2

Plates 2, 3 An example of what the Land System approach neglects
Ph. JT CCLXXII-13 & 14. Wind destruction of the regolith, Mereddin, Western Australia. Regolith truncated as deep as the 'pallid zone' of Tertiary ferrallitic weathering. Deflation caused by cultivation. The wind-blown material is being accumulated in the acacia thorn forest in background. The field was 'gained' on this type of forest, which was an excellent phytostabilizer.

these conditions changed and problems appeared in Australia itself. They remained benign, however, owing to the acquired empirical know-how. But once this was not available, the increased difficulties produced a set-back. This happened at great cost to the FAO in Patagonia (Argentina) with a large team composed, nevertheless, of Australians only. But in the presence of entirely different conditions to which they were not accustomed their intuition failed them. The method proved wanting. In another connection, it is not surprising that the method, based essentially on aerial photograph interpretation, and capable of being applied at an elementary level, was adopted by the International Institute for Aerial Survey and Earth Sciences (ITC) at Enschede, Holland (Zonneveld 1979), which, however, increased the rigour of the procedures. In Canada, in a study of the forested zones around Lac Saint-Jean, the method had to be considerably modified. Paradoxically the method was adopted outside Australia, notably by the FAO and the Ministry of Overseas Development in London, the moment it needed to be improved in order to remain effective.

Let us now examine another approach based on the concept 'landscape'.

ANALYSIS OF 'LANDSCAPES'

Another approach to the comprehensive study of the environment has been developed in Europe. Its origins are remote and predate aerial photographs. There is a continuity between the great naturalists of the nineteenth century and contemporary thought. The method is that of the analysis of landscapes and was developed in central and eastern Europe. The term is but a translation of the

Dutch term *landschap* (due to painters), whose German equivalent, *Landschaft*, is already part of the scientific vocabulary. Through F. von Richthofen the concept is linked to the explorers of the nineteenth century. This great German geographer published a small book on the methods of observation for scientific travellers (1886). In the tradition of A. von Humboldt he was interested in the various aspects of Nature and their interrelationships. In Russia, V. V. Dokuchaev, the founder of a scientific pedology, believed in the same concepts. He adopted the term *Landschaft*, which was incorporated into the Russian scientific language. He put soils back in their context, the entire natural environment, and frequently qualified soil terms with names of vegetation, such as tundra, forest and steppe, which characterize them. Through his impulse the origin of pedology was integrated into physical geography, and so it remains to this day. Because of him there is a tendency to insist on the zonality of soils, a characteristic that derives directly from the zonation of natural vegetation in the lowlands of Russia and the west of Soviet Asia.

It is also worth noting that in Spanish or Portuguese, particularly in America, the same landscape term usually has a combined meaning including topography, vegetation and climate, and ultimately soil and the modifying influence of humankind. For example, a *paramo* in Venezuela, Colombia and Ecuador is a very high gently undulated surface with certain types of small trees, shrubs and endemic plants ('frailejones'). Or *lomas* in the foggy coastal desert of Peru are hills where the saturated atmospheric water of the trade wind condenses directly on a special type of vegetation also called *lomas*, allowing a transhumant pastoralism and even some cultivation. Similarly, in west Africa, where for the Toucouleur peasants of the Senegal Valley the various types of soil, combined with the time and duration of flooding and a cropping system, have their proper designation. Of course, such a concept is absent in Australia, where the Aborigines did not practise agriculture and the convicts and other European immigrants did not have the least knowledge of the nature of the continent.

The concept *landscape* approximates that of a natural region: it is characterized by an association of features (relief, climate, vegetation and soils) and it is physiognomic. It is the concept that the Australians of the CSIRO rediscovered in the method of 'land systems', while at the same time ignoring it. But the methodological perspective is rather different, and the Australians would have

profited by taking it into consideration. The preoccupation of early geographers to systematize observations, to link the different aspects of the landscape together by causal relationships, is evident from the beginning. This orientation is also reflected in the concept of zonality introduced from the start into pedology by V. V. Dokuchaev.

This explains a series of facts. First, that the Soviets have been interested in the method of land systems. They were prepared for it by their own way of apprehending the landscape. Moreover, it meets analogous practical needs: the rapid occupation of most of Soviet Asia, still poorly known, very sparsely inhabited, difficult to develop, and for geopolitical reasons akin to those of Australia at the time of the Second World War and which appear clearly in an 'explosive' manner since 1989.

Second, the Soviets pattern their research on a scientific tradition that does not exist in Australia. They analyse the landscape as a *system* and attempt to measure the degrees of correlation between its various components, applying modern mathematical tools. The system is called a *geosystem* by V. B. Sochava. It differs from an ecosystem in that it also takes into account physico-chemical interactions (such as weathering), man-made changes, and has a definite spatial and vertical (such as climate) extent. A geosystem is investigated by means of transects, stationary measuring sites, laboratory analyses, statistical and graphic methods, modelling, and large-scale mapping resulting in a theory of geographic dimensions. Such research, on various scales, leads to the recognition that besides the existence of basic homogeneous areas, called *geomeres* (*geotopes* when mapped), there are above all heterogeneous spatial units (*geochores*) of greatly different size and composition, consisting of assemblages of 'topologic' (geomeres) building blocks. A geomere in a continuously changing landscape is an area of similar structure and function and, therefore, with a uniform material system. In it, according to K. Herbs et al. (1975), values measured at field stations along transects drop at a uniform rate regardless of their absolute or relative range. On the contrary, boundaries are zones of steep value gradients. In time processes work towards homogeneous or towards heterogeneous landscapes. Homogeneity tends to decrease in higher taxons. Thus there is a whole taxonomy of geomeres and geochores, each with their own name, 'fitted into' three major spatio-temporal dimensions: topical, regional, and planetary (Sochava 1977). These categories are interrelated but are also, up to a point, autonomous. This depends on the object of research; for example, the evaluation of climate as an ecological factor is based on regional and not on planetary factors. The taiga, a zone of planetary dimension, can be subdivided into parts that have a topical autonomy, which is of direct practical importance in land use planning.

Third, research is conducted in a similar vein in Poland and in the former German Democratic Republic (GDR). East German publications have dealt with this *Landschaftsökologie*, or landscape ecology, since 1962 (Neef 1962, etc.). East German workers, however, work only on the topological plane. They speak of *geocomplexes* rather than of geosystems, which remain to be worked out. Like the Soviets, they study the vertical relationships between the elements of a biocenosis and their spatial distribution. They take into consideration the flow of energy and materials (ecology concept) and changes in time, whether periodic or aperiodic, indicating a certain evolution. According to Haase (1967) a reconnaissance should be made first, followed by a qualitative analysis of the phenomena, which is later quantified by drawing up a balance sheet. This leads to a revision of the physiognomic classification. The defined units can then be mapped. East German workers go as far as to measure the flows of material down to the level of ions along transects, an enormous task, the *in situ* results of which are still unknown and which, therefore, have not led to any cartographic expression. Haase's style is arduous, far from lucid, but his preoccupations stand out clearly.

There is a large gulf between the work of the CSIRO and that of the East Germans. In northern Australia large areas have been covered on a small scale without too much reflection on the method used and without worrying about what is being done elsewhere. The work has become increasingly routine, a danger that always threatens organizations of applied research. On the contrary, hairs have been split and application has been neglected in the former GDR. In both cases there is the same shortcoming: the concept is static. The most interesting studies from the fundamental as well as from the practical point of view are those of the Soviets, but all of them have a great merit, as they try to relate ecology and the study of its support, the physical environment.

In France, the word *paysage*, as a geographic expression, came into use much later than the German *Landschaft* concept. The emphasis, through Vidal de la Blache, was on *pays*, often combining small regions with rather uniform natural and cultural characteristics with historical names. It was not until A. Cholley, on the eve of the Second World War, in his classes at the Sorbonne, drew attention to a more rational approach to regional studies that the term *paysage* received a more scholarly meaning. At the same time as A. G. Tansley, he insisted on interactions occurring in the midst of 'geographic complexes' reflected in the landscape. His approach was that of a non-quantitative systems approach, although the word 'system' was not used except in the expression *systèmes d'érosion*, by which he coined what J. Tricart later called 'morphogenic systems'. From that moment on the common meaning of the word landscape may be compared to the emerged part of an iceberg, whereas the scientific meaning of the term also includes the invisible submerged part (to use a somewhat worn but effective metaphor). Old concepts, however, die hard, and, as in the Soviet Union and the GDR, substantive work did not appear until the 1960s. The studies of the French researchers of the Centre d'Etudes Phytosociologiques et Ecologiques of the CNRS in Montpellier are in the same vein as those of the Soviets and the East Germans. Particularly interesting is the work of J.-P. Deffontaines and of G. Bertrand, who are not far apart.

Deffontaines (1982) now uses the landscape concept as a means of studying land management. He defines 'landscape' as 'a portion of land or space that contains both visible and invisible phenomena and actions, of which at a given moment we perceive only the "global" result' (1973). It exists for a more or less long period of time and poses questions that otherwise would not be asked. It has certain dynamics: 'Everything changes in a landscape, each element according to its own pace and rhythm, which itself changes with time' (1982: 17). 'The unity of the landscape is a common level of articulations between natural phenomena and Man's interventions' (1982: 19). In an agricultural landscape the notion of a system of production (including technical and socio-economic factors) must be added. Thus for Deffontaines as for Cholley, the landscape is an indicator of all the supporting factors of the environment. Deffontaines's viewpoint reflects Cholley's key ideas and, not by chance, some of his favourite terms, such as 'combination'. The landscape is a physiognomic unit in which 'the various combinations between factors present a certain homogeneity'. The only difference (and progress) with Cholley is that Deffontaines uses an explicit systems approach. The object of the systems analysis is to identify the constraints that affect agropastoral production, to suggest changes in the system of production, or adoption of a new system of production.

G. Bertrand defines the landscape as

a portion of space characterised by a combination of dynamics, therefore unstable, of different geographical elements (physical, biological, and anthropological) that by reacting dialectically upon one another produce an integrated 'geographical whole' that evolves as a unit through the effects of the dynamics between its constituent elements as well as through the effects of the dynamics of each of its elements separately considered.

(G. Bertrand 1970: 197)

This definition, which also follows Cholley's views, is that of a system, in our view a *natural system*. Each unit is characterized by its own structure, which coincides with this network of interactions. The whole is different from the sum of its parts: it has its own specific organization. A large number of multicoloured stone pieces is not a mosaic . . .

G. Bertrand distinguishes three successive orders in landscape units: the physical environment, the ecosystem, and human intervention. The addition of a temporal dimension (a dynamic evolutive perspective), presents no problem. In that regard, G. Bertrand (1968) leans on Erhart's (1967) theory of bio-rhexistasy, distinguishing 'geosystems' in biostasy, which are stable, and geosystems in rhexistasy in which morphogenesis 'counteracts pedogenesis and plant growth'. Some geosystems are in a steady state, morphogenesis assuming a certain intensity related to the characteristics of the physical environment, and, being associated in the system, to a certain type of plant cover, itself considered to be climactic. Others are the result of an anthropic degradation and are said to be 'regressive'. We shall return to these concepts later, as they play an important role in our own research.

G. Bertrand's (1968) 'landscape units' are organized into a hierarchy. (His terminology differs from that of Soviet and East German authors; where his terms are the same, they sometimes have different meanings.)

1 The *geotope* is the smallest unit. It covers a few square metres and corresponds approximately to the space occupied by a microclimate in the sense ecologists give to this term. It provides specific ecologic conditions, producing what some ecologists call a niche. Examples are a ledge on a slope, a crevice on a rock face, the mouth of a spring, a karstic sink. They harbour or provide refuge to specific biocoenoses, sometimes endemic or relict.

2 The *geofacies* has a homogeneous physiognomy over a distance of a few hundred to a few thousand metres. A floodable bottomland in an alluvial plain, the face of a slope oriented in a certain direction, a plateau segment, or a vale can serve as a support to a geofacies as long as they are occupied by a homogeneous plant association. From the lithologic point of view it is frequently heterogeneous and, consequently, also from the point of view of pedology. But the soils are classified according to certain criteria and form a sequence or catena. Farmers for centuries have exploited the attributes of geofacies and respected them in determining their field patterns. In France a geofacies has often been the subject of a division into parcels that observe the characteristics of the land and is shown on cadastres as a *quartier*.

3 A *geosystem* is still larger. It may cover tens to hundreds of square kilometres. For example, in mountains it corresponds to part of a climatic altitude zone, uniform from the lithologic and topographic point of view. A geosystem groups together different geofacies; for example, the sunny or shady sides of a valley (G. Bertrand and Dollfus 1973b). It provides a framework for settlement and, as such, lends itself to analysis of the human impact on nature, as we have indicated above.

G. Bertrand has given examples of the application of his system in areas as different as Cantabric Spain (G. Bertrand 1972) and Nepal (G. Bertrand and Dollfus 1973b). The method can be applied to regions being scientifically explored and is much broader than that of the 'land systems' of the CSIRO, which allows it to be adapted to the needs of land management. Some complementary efforts, however, are required to understand better the structure of the natural environment.

INTEGRATION OF THE DYNAMICS

Good land management consists in redirecting or replacing the existing dynamics by others. A static, descriptive vision of the natural environment is therefore insufficient. It should be able to take into account the sensitivity of the environment *vis-à-vis* human intervention. This perspective has been formulated by certain ecologists. It is of paramount importance.

Progress in knowledge of the environment induces us to attach great importance to its degree of stability. Humankind, which is familiar with technological upheavals and unprecedented demographic explosions, exerts an enormously increased pressure on the entire environment. A catastrophe is not excluded. To be able to evaluate the capacity of resistance of the environment is essential. The environment has also undergone major changes during the course of time for which humans are not responsible. Only 12,000 years ago (the recent geologic past), the last Glaciation still reigned in Scandinavia, Scotland and the vicinity of New York and Saint Petersburg: our ancestors hunted the reindeer.

To regard the present environment as being in a 'steady state' would be a major deviation from the truth: it is in the course of adaptation to entirely new conditions. Depending on the kinds of phenomena, the adaptation, more or less rapid, is more or less complete. But the problem of adjustment must be posed. There are many legacies and features of the environment, such as landforms, which have ceased to be formed and which survive the conditions under which they were created. This has a considerable influence on the degree of sensitivity of the environment *vis-à-vis* our interventions. To differentiate between fundamental knowledge and applied research would be artificial: the problem concerns both aspects of our intellectual activities.

Integration based on dynamics must be preoccupied with two aspects:

1 The *present dynamics*, which determine certain aspects of the environment and interfere with certain ecologic resources that are being exploited or that we would like to exploit, and which also may threaten the structures that we build. They must be taken into account with every development.
2 The *past dynamics*, which functioned before the present during rather short periods of time relative to the geologic time scale. They have left behind legacies in the environment which we utilise and are part of our ecologic framework. The succession of these various dynamics set in motion mainly by changes of climate is a decisive explanatory factor of the present situation. Indirectly it affects the problems of development, the susceptibility of the environment *vis-à-vis* the impact of humankind.

Erhart (1967; 1st edn 1956) in his *theory of bio-* *rhexistasy* has proposed an explanation of the characteristics of sediments that is related to climatic changes. He visualizes periods of *biostasy*, during which land masses are covered by dense vegetation, which permits the migration only of ions in solution toward the sedimentary basins. Rocks then weather and pedogenesis reigns without interference. Sedimentation is of a chemical, biochemical and organic nature. With a climatic change to less humidity a period of *rhexistasy* is introduced. The vegetation suffers, thins and ceases to provide a good protection to the soil. Morphogenic processes begin to exert important mechanical actions and surface runoff strips the soils previously formed. Rivers entrain the materials, which are deposited in sedimentary basins. Another detrital type of sedimentation occurs.

This theory drew attention to the importance of biocenoses on sedimentation, a fact that contemporary geologists ignored. Nevertheless, it is too extreme and should be criticized.

First, the combining form 'bio' is improperly used, as it implies *all* living things – not only plants, but also animals. It is mainly plants that impede morphogenesis, as the uprooting of trees by wind promote it, and so it is preferable to speak of *phytostasy*, rather than of biostasy. The concept should be used in a *dialectic manner*, which means that it includes contradictory elements. Animals are usually factors of instability, for example, termites, ants and earthworms that stir the soil and upper subsoil, while at the other dimensional extreme elephants and livestock pack it, and thus accelerate the detrital flux.

Second, deposits hundreds of metres thick, as western Europe's Permian and Lower Triassic formations of 'Germanic facies' cannot result from a catastrophic stripping of a former soil. . . . They are the result of a steady state that lasted some tens of millions of years and which was characterized by simultaneous pedogenesis (or, better, weathering) and export of its products into sedimentary basins.

The concept is schematic. It is of catastrophic inspiration, in the tradition of Cuvier and in that of Davisian geomorphology. Nevertheless it has the merit to provoke thought, notably with certain geologists too inclined to attribute an intercalation of a few centimetres of sand in a shale member to a tectonic event. . . . Even so, it remains valid on condition of qualifying it. The mobilization of a thick regolith provides a sedimentary basin with more sediment than soils, which are always thin. The distinction should be made, although pedologists sometimes seem to ignore it. (There is confusion in the earth sciences concerning the definition of certain terms. For us and for most geologists and geomorphologists the soil is part of the regolith, which is synonymous with mantlerock and overburden. The materials of the regolith may be either in situ weathered material or material transported from elsewhere by fluid agents, glaciers or simple gravity. These materials are in fact sediments, which is admittedly confusing. Another useful expression is 'surficial formation', but this is also ambiguous, as a 'formation' for a geologist is a mappable rock stratigraphic unit.) It must be admitted, in conformity to what is observed, that pedogenesis and morphogenesis do not alternate as the theory of biorhexistasy would have it. Pedogenesis and morphogenesis frequently coexist and then interfere with one another. To analyse this interference, to record its modalities, to understand its effects is certainly more complex than to admit their alternation and their exclusive reign during successive periods of time. That this thought had not first sprung to mind is comprehensible, but now it is time to reflect on it in order to better understand the natural processes.

We must now proceed to examine the structure and dynamics of the terrestrial system, followed by an attempt to classify environments according to their degree of stability.

Organization of the system and flows of energy and materials

Let us recall the structure of the Natural System of the Earth (Tricart 1987a). We have constructed a flow chart (Figure 3) around the interface lithosphere/atmosphere, which is split into two parts in the presence of water bodies (approximately 70 per cent of the Earth's surface), namely the two interfaces lithosphere/hydrosphere and hydrosphere/atmosphere. There are three major inputs of energy (Tricart 1972d):

1 Extraterrestrial energy in the solar system, that is solar radiation and Newtonian attraction producing the tides.
2 Energy originating inside the Earth, producing earthquakes, crustal movements and vulcanism,

Plate 4 Contrast of environments with different stabilities
Ph. JT CDXCIV-5cn. Pardinella, Catalonia, Spain. In foreground bare argillites; very hard when dry, seeds cannot germinate on them. In the small valley in background, colluvium is being deposited, water is more abundant and trees are able to grow. The opposite valley slope is a 'glacis', where incipient degradation in the form of bare soil patches can be observed.

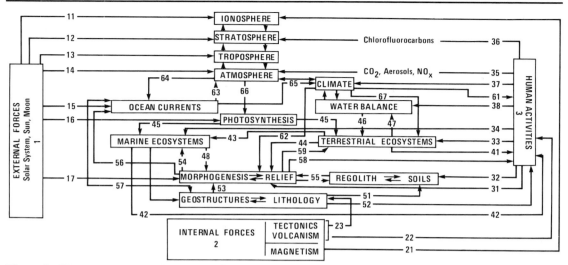

Figure 3. The natural terrestrial system: flow chart of energy and materials

expressions of tectonic activity. This energy is the result of changes in the structure of matter produced by radioactivity, which produces heat and changes of volume in the mineral matter.

3 Human activities, which use the raw materials of the environment (minerals, living beings), and have to protect themselves from certain natural hazards (earthquakes, hurricanes, etc.), resulting in ever more waste, whether solid, liquid or gaseous. These wastes are pollutants and affect the dynamics of the environment.

Clearly, the first two inputs predate and occur independently of the presence of humankind. They affect the other planets, even if their efficacy is different from that of the Earth. For instance, there are no tides on Mars, as a result of the total absence of water. The quantity of energy involved in these two inputs is enormous, so that human beings cannot modify it. They can only influence the mechanisms that result from it.

The third input, 'human activities', is of a different nature. It is the result of the technology invented during historical time and which is used unequally on the Earth's surface according to the technical level and socio-political and economic organization of human societies. In the USA an Amish, a Navajo, and a manager in this 'Silicon Valley' do not use the same technology, and what they extract from the environment as raw material and introduce into it as waste is not the same. The main flows of energy and material are shown in Figure 3 to give an overall view of the interactions that characterize the structure of the Terrestrial Natural Environment.

Let us now focus more specifically on a part of the interface, the one between the lithosphere and the atmosphere. This interface is particularly 'alive' in comparison to the other solid planets. Apparently unique in the universe, it is the locus of the interaction between external and internal forces and gravity in the presence of H_2O in the liquid state, and Life: plant, animal and human. The result is a 'water planet' with extraordinary resources and a constantly changing 'face', either by natural forces over geological time or by civilized humankind during historical time. In the natural process the rocky surface of the Earth at the contact of the atmosphere is broken up by weathering and transformed into soils in the presence of flora and fauna, which make possible all agricultural activities in the broadest sense of the word, that is including all forms of animal husbandry and forestry, that sustain humankind. This unique environment, generally in balance between enormous forces, can easily be upset by modern humans. To preserve its qualities becomes increasingly important with the unceasing growth in technology and the demographic explosion.

The energy that operates the system, itself composed of matter, is introduced into the environment in two ways.

First, part of it comes from outside, from the solar system, and a tiny part, including cosmic radiation and meteorite impacts, from even further. It represents the so-called 'external forces'. Most of it is solar energy in the form of radiation. At the top of the atmosphere this energy is equal to $1.4 \, \text{kW/m}^2$, which is considerable. Of secondary importance, as far as we are concerned, is the gravitational attraction caused by the Moon and the Sun, which produces the tides and, in turn, sets in motion important currents in narrow seas and plays an important role in the shaping of coasts. These flows of energy have been conventionally indicated on the flow chart by arrows coded 1 (11–17). The 'terrestrial tides' which causes some small deformations of the solid Earth surface have the same origin.

Second, the remaining part comes from inside the solid matter of the Earth's interior, the source of the 'internal forces'. Rearrangement of electrons produces heat through the transformation of matter, which is responsible for vulcanism, crustal deformations, sea-floor spreading and plate tectonics. The very mass of the Earth itself also exerts a Newtonian attraction, which produces the force of gravity. Schematically the tectonic forces produce irregularities in the surface of the lithosphere, such as deep sea trenches and mountain ranges, while the flow of material set in motion by gravity tends to reduce them. Materials are mobilized on uplifted regions while part of them is finally deposited in the form of sediments in depressions occupied by seas and oceans. The persistent juxtaposition of land and sea throughout the course of geologic time is the consequence of

the ever continued deformations of the Earth's crust. For better intelligibility the main aspects of the Internal Forces are listed in the lower box that is magnetism on the one hand and the twin aspects of tectonics and vulcanism on the other. Flows of energy generated by them are indicated by arrows coded 2 (21–23). The input of or effect on 'human activities' are indicated by arrows coded 3 (31–38).

Now let us take a closer look at the flow chart (Figure 3):

The input of 'internal forces' (coded 2) results in three flows:

21 represents the effect of terrestrial magnetism on the ionosphere (Van Allen Belts), resulting in a deflection of most alpha and beta ionizing particles.
22 indicates the influence of vulcanism and tectonic movements on human settlements and activities: lava flows, ash-falls, earthquakes, diastrophism.
23 substantiates the effect of tectonics, including the specific aspect of vulcanism, on the characteristics of the upper Earth's crust, that is geostructures and the correlative nature of the rocks (lithology).

Plate 5 Effect of external forces
Ph. JT CDLXXXVIII-7. Very unstable environment caused by runoff, near Tulancingo, Hidalgo, Mexico. There is no more 'soft' regolith. Runoff is maximum.

Plate 6 Effect of internal forces
Ph. JT CDXX-19A. Valley incision caused by
tectonics in the Cordillera Oriental of Colombia.
Valley sides are fashioned by episodic slumps on
folded Mesozoic sandstones and shales with some
limestones. Forest climax. Marked contrast
between the partly cultivated summital
palaeotopographies and the sharp incision caused
by the Plio-Quaternary orogeny of a river
descending toward the Llanos. Dissection is too
recent to be affected by the geologic structure. On
the left, road towards Villavicencio.

The third input (coded 3) consists of 'human
activities'. This designation was chosen as it is
clearly restricted to the *behaviour* of humankind
towards Nature, *without* an examination of the
internal complexity of human societies. This box is,
in part, a 'black box', as it fixes the limits of the
flow chart. It could be completed on its right by
another box that would analyse the interactions of
the socio-economic and cultural characteristics,
which determine the activities of societies, with the
natural environment. For better legibility only the
main flows are shown:

31 consists of the human influence on landforms
and morphogenic processes. The main factors
are the intensification of wind and water action
on soils, conservation practices such as terracing
or building containment walls, topographic
alteration by public works in urban areas
(undercutting of slopes, fills . . .), mining and
generation of morphogenic processes as a result
of the disequilibrium caused by such alterations:
mass movements, gullying and alluviation (see
Plates 1, 2 and 3).

32 indicates other aspects of soil degradation such
as salinization, chemical impoverishment,
deficiency in organic matter, pollution by
pesticides, etc., which result in a decrease of
ecological potential, affecting yields and
phytostabilization.

33 refers to the modification of terrestrial
ecosystems by humankind. It includes changes
of animal and vegetal populations as a result of
hunting and gathering and much more drastic
changes such as substitution of natural
ecosystems by artificial ones: pastures,
afforestation, cultivation, urbanization. By
'ecosystem' is meant the association of a
biocenosis with its environment.

34 is the equivalent of 33 for marine ecosystems.
The main action of humankind on these
ecosystems is fishing and seaweed gathering, but
aquaculture, especially oyster and mussel
breeding, is increasing in spite of the thorough
transformation of the environment it requires.
The ocean too has become humankind's main
rubbish dump.

35 concerns the emission of pollutants into the
atmosphere, principally carbon dioxide, sulphur
dioxide, nitrogen oxides, and liquid and solid
aerosols, which drastically modify the
transmission of solar radiation to the lower
atmosphere and the Earth's surface. Some of
the gases, mainly carbon dioxide, produce a
'greenhouse effect' (Tricart 1988a), which
eventually will produce catastrophic
environmental changes. Photochemical
processes provide the energy needed by many
complex chemical reactions that, for example,
result in acid rain, very damaging to both
terrestrial and marine ecosystems.

36 consists mainly in the destruction of ozone in
the stratosphere by chemical reactions with
chlorofluorocarbons. A vertical circulation,
both upward and downward, exists throughout
the atmosphere, so that the products of
photochemical reactions, which are at their
maximum in the stratosphere, can be elaborated
from pollutants introduced into the lower

Plate 7 Careless cultivation increases the effect of tectonics
Ph. JT CDXLVI-7. Tectonic instability resulting in regressive incision of gullies. Incautious cultivation of grain on marl substratum, Nekor watershed, Rif Mountains, Morocco. Absence of terracing or buffer strips causes violent runoff and gullying, destroying the fields. A dammed reservoir built downstream was entirely filled up with sediment ten years after its inauguration!

atmosphere and, conversely, can get down to the ground as acid rain.

37 represents direct changes of weather and climate as a result of human activities, causing changes in albedo, which affect ground temperature. Bare ground and structure of all kinds drastically modify the heat balance, the bare surfaces heating more when the sun shines and cooling more rapidly after sunset. The temperature regime looks more 'continental' with increased range. A dense plant cover with green matter has the opposite effect. These effects also affect evaporation, interdependent with temperature.

38 consists, in part, of this direct influence of ground features on evaporation and condensation. But other aspects also play a role: canals and artificial reservoirs present free water bodies to evaporation, while drainage of swamps and wetlands diminish evaporation.

The central part of Figure 3 depicts the main

interrelationships that occur at the interface of the atmosphere and the water and land surfaces. Plants are typical of this interface, as most absorb the mineral elements from the soil with their roots and use the radiant energy of the Sun to elaborate their tissues by photosynthesis. Most aquatic plants and some terrestrial epiphytes, however, extract the minerals they need from the solutions in the ambient water or directly from aerosols. All biotic phenomena are represented by code 4.

41 refers to human use of the terrestrial ecosystems as a resource, or subjection to them through the presence of parasites, pathogenic agents, vectors of endemic diseases, and epidemics (Sorre 1947).

42 is symmetric to 41, but relates to marine ecosystems, which essentially yield resources.

43 indicates the very important input of organic products and solutions from terrestrial ecosystems (rivers, lakes, lagoons . . .) into the marine environment.

44 symbolizes the influence of living organisms on morphogenic processes: on the one hand phytostabilization, on the other bioturbation.

45 focuses the dependence of ecosystems on radiant solar energy.

46 and 47 represent the relationships between waterbalance and terrestrial ecosystems. Waterbalance is one of the most decisive environmental factors determining the metabolism of plants and the behaviour of the plant cover, but through transpiration plants provide water vapour to the atmosphere; the quantity emitted, when there is enough water in the soil, is proportional to the temperature. Vaporization is an endothermic process, that is a process that consumes energy in the form of calories and causes a drop in temperature of the evaporating surface. By this means plant leaves remain at a temperature inferior to the lethal one, at which cells are destroyed.

48 is more or less symmetrical to 44. Nevertheless, the influence of marine ecosystems on morphogenesis and landforms is somewhat different to that of terrestrial ecosystems. In both cases there is phytostabilization and bioturbation, but marine ecosystems produce much more biotic sediment than terrestrial ones (e.g. most limestones) and are able to build very specific landforms such as coral reefs, including barrier reefs and atolls.

There are other components of the Terrestrial System on each side of the interface: on one side, the upper part of the Earth's crust (coded 5) and on the other, the lower part of the atmosphere in contact with the ground (coded 6).

51 indicates the dependence of regolith and soils on the characteristics of the upper crust, mainly the nature of the rocks, possibly modified by tectonics, as included in box 'Geostructures ⇌ Lithology'.

52 is quite different, it refers to mineral resources that can be used by humankind, including deep-seated ground-water and geothermal energy.

53 corresponds to what is usually called 'structural geomorphology' (the influence of geologic structure on landforms), already recognized in the last third of the nineteenth century (Tricart 1968d).

54 alludes to the effects of morphogenesis on water ecosystems. These effects are quite diverse, ranging from the subsidence of extinct volcanoes on the development of atolls to the extinction of lakes as a result of sedimentation, as morphogenesis generates a flow of mineral matter (the flow of organic matter, a product of terrestrial ecosystems, is indicated by arrow 43). This matter is a source of nutrients in the form of solutions, but it can also be a nuisance, as suspended matter obstructs the penetration of light in water and thus diminishes the depth to which photosynthesis is possible.

55 recalls the very narrow interdependence between, on the one hand, morphogenesis and transported regolith, referred to as 'correlative deposits' by W. Penck (1924), and morphogenesis and soils, as formulated in Tricart's concept of the 'morphogenic–pedogenic balance' (see Chapter 2, pp. 67–72).

56 indicates the influence of submarine relief on ocean currents. For example, the chain of deep-sea troughs along the Pacific coast of South America from the vicinity of Antarctica to the Equator allows a progression of cold Antarctic waters as far as the Galapagos Islands and the 'very cold' upwelling of water that characterizes the Humboldt Current, resulting in one of the most extreme discrepancies of regional from planetary climate known on Earth: a desert 5° south of the Equator (arrows 65 and 62).

57 depicts the feedback of ocean currents on geostructures. Currents participate in sedimentation and are able to accumulate great quantities of material transported over long distances by turbidity currents. These sediments can by their weight induce a downward movement of their substrate. Such a positive feedback promotes the continuation of sedimentation: a continuous downward movement of the crust, roughly equivalent to the rate of sedimentation, can result in an enormous column of sediments even though the sea is shallow.

58 refers to the constraints that morphogenesis and landforms have on human activities, such as sedimentation of reservoirs, wandering of river channels, mass movements, gullying, siltation of harbours, rough topography, etc. The morphogenic–pedogenic balance is heavily in favour of morphogenesis.

59 records that instability resulting from active morphogenesis is a constraint on biocenoses, only a few species possessing anatomic or, better, metabolic adaptations permitting their survival. Such biocenoses are characterized by a low number of species. The ecosystem is dominated by dynamics that drastically restrict the population of a biocenosis and its variety. The opposite occurs when a thick and permanent plant cover restrains the activity of

the landform shaping processes. Such a situation is called phytostability.

In the lower atmosphere, at the contact of the interface, the following flows are shown in Figure 3:

61 refers to the influence of climate on human activities: necessity of clothing, heating or air-conditioning, seasonal rhythm of agriculture and animal husbandry, recreational activities; extreme events like typhoons, heavy snowfalls, droughts, excessive rains, triggering floods, mass movements, and so on. The price of climatic constraints is enormous, and climate-induced catastrophes are among the most costly in human lives and property damage.

62 the direct influence of climate on landform shaping is obvious although more restricted than the indirect one, expressed through the intermedium of biocoenoses. Examples are glacial, periglacial (e.g. the Arctic barrens), and desert conditions in which vegetation is practically eliminated (that is the scanty vegetation that can exist does not exert any appreciable influence on morphogenesis; this is the case of lichens and micro-organisms, which have been identified even in the most severe environments of Antarctica). The study of the influence of climate on landforms is the task of climatic geomorphology (Tricart and Cailleux 1972).

63 the influence of ocean currents on the atmosphere is well known, as demonstrated by examples of the Humboldt Current, already noted, of the Labrador Current, of the Gulf Stream, etc. Some have world-wide effects, as El Niño of 1982–3.

64 the feedback is the influence of the temperature of the air on that of the superficial water, the effects of wind, as that of the trades, on ocean currents, and of extreme variations of atmospheric pressure on the sea level, which induces surges of water in coastal areas. These generally go hand in hand with wave cyclones or hurricanes and can cause severe floods, as of the Dutch polderland in 1949, or drastic changes in

Plate 8 Sedimentation in a reservoir
Ph. JT CCLXXX-28. The Castillon Reservoir in the French Alps is used to generate electric power. At the time of the photograph (April 1962) it was nearly empty, revealing a huge quantity of mud spread over its floor. A prograding delta, in background, consists of shingle. The 'useful life' of this reservoir is obviously limited.

landforms, in particular barrier islands, as along the Atlantic and Gulf coasts of the USA.

65 climate being defined as the succession of characteristics of the atmosphere at ground level, obviously the influence of ocean currents on the lower atmosphere determines important climatic phenomena, such as the difference between 'oceanic' and 'continental' climates, the difference between the climate of the British Isles and the Labrador, at the same latitude.

66 solar radiation reaching the green matter of plants has passed through the entire atmosphere. The ability of the atmosphere to let the radiation reach the ground, called its 'transmittance', is a function of atmospheric quality, as carbon dioxide, water vapour, dust and ozone determine the transmissiveness of the atmosphere at different wavelengths. Pollution plays a major role in the concentration of most of these, but this concentration is also influenced by photosynthesis itself (carbon dioxide) and other natural mechanisms such as evaporation and transpiration (water vapour).

67 corresponds to the well-known influence of climate on ecosystems, mainly terrestrial ones, on which there is no buffer effect as in the ocean.

In a broader perspective the terrestrial environment is a subsystem in a larger, more inclusive system. The same is true of the solar system in relation to the galaxy. The natural system therefore is an *open system*: it receives energy from outside but also emits energy in the form of infrared radiation emanating from the Earth's surface. This readily explains a certain *instability* of the environment during the course of time, particularly the pronounced and repeated climatic changes of the last 3 million years since the Villafranchian Stage. But even before then the terrestrial climate underwent major changes. The Palaeozoic glaciations were at least as important as those of the Quaternary, which, in contrast to those of the Palaeozoic whose interest is mainly geological, still have an important influence on the present environment. The Quaternary climatic oscillations produced temperature changes that affected the entire Earth; for example, it has been determined that during the last glaciation (Würm of the Alps, Weichsel of northern Europe, Devensian of Britain, and Wisconsin of North America) the temperature dropped 5° to 6°C near Bogotá, Colombia, in the Equatorial zone, which proves that the temperature fluctuations were caused by a change in the balance of radiation (Tricart 1975a).

An understanding of the nature of solar energy at different wavelengths is helpful in the study of the natural environment. It may be useful to recall that the shorter the electromagnetic waves, the more energy they carry. For example, there is seven to eight times as much energy in a quantum of blue than in a quantum of red. The shortest waves – gamma rays, X-rays and ultraviolet (UV) – are quite lethal to life, but are wholly or partly screened out before they reach the Earth's surface. The long waves, on the other hand, are harmless; the far-infra-red are emitted as sensible heat from the Earth's surface, heated by the Sun. These radiations are also far less intense per unit area than the light radiation of the Sun. The latter is still called short wave and carries just the right amount of energy to break up in the presence of chlorophyll molecules of water and carbon dioxide to unite them into molecules of carbohydrates, releasing oxygen in the process called photosynthesis. This energy is so strongly concentrated in the green, however, where it peaks, that it is reflected by the plants, which accounts for their green colour. This remarkable process produces all green plants and *food* at the base of the food chain (arrows 16 and 45, Figure 3).

The very short wave radiation also has a positive aspect, at least for us. Not all of this radiation is deflected by the Earth's magnetic field (arrow 21) or absorbed (arrow 12) in the ozone layer (the UV); there is some collision of alpha and beta particles with atmospheric nitrogen (arrow 11) and with C and O, which produces the radioisotopes ^{14}C, ^{13}C, and ^{18}O. The first two are used for dating organic matter and carbonates, while ^{18}O is used to determine the temperature at which carbonates, such as of shells and certain bones, were formed; these are two very important techniques in the temporal study of the environment.

The flow of radiant energy from the Sun to the stratosphere and the troposphere, that is to the atmosphere as a whole, is shown by arrows 12, 13 and 14. Part of this short wave, 'visible' energy is absorbed by the atmosphere and re-emitted as infra-red radiation, the same type of re-emission that occurs at the Earth's surface, and is perceived as heat. The atmosphere receives most of its sensible heat and all of its latent heat from this long-wave infra-red radiation. However, at certain wavelengths, called 'windows', this radiation is not absorbed by the atmosphere but passes through it and can be recorded by airborne or orbital remote thermal sensors, which thus can provide a new 'dimension' to the physical environment.

It is important to note that under optimum

laboratory conditions photosynthesis uses on average 20 per cent of the incident short-wave solar energy (27.5 per cent in the extreme blue and 15.7 per cent in the extreme red): this percentage is clearly less under natural conditions. There remains a lot of energy not used by plants that can be exerted on other things, such as the water of the ocean. Part of the radiant solar energy not absorbed by the atmosphere directly reaches that water and warms it unevenly, which results in differences of density, which helps generate oceanic currents. The properties of the superficial marine waters (arrow 64), like those of the land surface, are also affected by the temperature of the atmosphere, winds, and even precipitation (box 'climate').

The long-wave infra-red energy, for its part, raises the temperature of the aerial parts of plants. But while scorching of the plants is prevented by transpiration, as water is extracted from the soil and circulated through the plants in the form of sap, returning it to the atmosphere as vapour, photosynthesis reduces the amount of energy reaching the ground. This flow of sap, which furthermore always entrains that of minerals, certain of which are dissociated at the contact of the roots, parallels and conjoins the less complicated evaporation of water from the soil.

Living strictly on the lithosphere–atmosphere interface, plants therefore play an extremely important role in the natural environment: first, they trap part of the energy radiated by the Sun in the process of photosynthesis, and second, another part, mainly in the infra-red part of the spectrum, is absorbed. Its use increases the water content of the air through respiration, moisture conditions in the root zone permitting.

Plants thus modify the micro-climate at ground level and in the soil. This climate generates weathering and pedogenesis. The need for a study of the natural environment according to this perspective is therefore easy to understand, as land improvement almost invariably affects the plant cover.

The intervention of plants in the flow of energy and materials, however, is not limited to this aspect, no matter how important. Part of the carbohydrates produced by photosynthesis is destroyed by respiration. But there is an excess of carbohydrates stored in the vegetal matter, where it is associated with mineral matter extracted from the soil. This stored material is set free after a certain length of time, a summer in the case of mid-latitude deciduous plants, longer for their woody parts. The tissues die and fall to the ground and the mineral elements return to their place of origin, initiating a cycle. The carbohydrates provide energy to creatures such as insects, earthworms, rodents, and especially micro-organisms, which release most mineral elements incorporated in the tissues. During the course of these transformations, certain bodies enter into solution and are carried through the soils, whose profile and properties they determine. They produce the humification of the organic matter and what pedologists call the 'mineralization' of the humus. The downward migrating solutions are gradually modified by micro-organisms that extract their food from them, changing their properties and causing the horizonation of the soil. Similar mechanisms occur in the subsoil, down to the bedrock; they generate the weathering of the rock. The subsoil is influenced by the superficial soil, but through an important feedback it also influences the soil, being its parent material. Soils owe their very existence to biotic actions through the availability of vegetal matter and its decomposition at the ground surface. Like plants, soils are intrinsically part of the lithosphere–atmosphere interface.

Our account at this point, however, suffers from an oversimplification. We have restricted ourselves to a single dimension, the vertical. We are in an impoverished intellectual situation of a pedologist huddled up in a hole. There is another dimension that should also be taken into account: the tangential down-slope flow of material that takes place parallel to the ground, to the interface.

The soils of the Earth are varied: their horizons have not only their own chemical but also physical characteristics, notably a certain *permeability*; the subsoil, too, is heterogeneous, frequently composed of different layers; finally, below, the bedrock varies from place to place. Besides, this superposition of materials of different properties is usually not horizontal; it approximately follows the relief composed mainly of slopes, down which water migrates along the most permeable layers. This migration, or *hypodermic flow* (Tricart, Maine and Cloots-Hirsch 1981), which is a more accurate expression than 'throughflow', is not composed of pure water, unknown in Nature; it contains mineral matter, mainly in solution, but also, in part, mechanically entrained (see Figure 13, p. 117). Hypodermic flow produces a flux of material that must be taken into account in the one-dimensional scheme presented above. It affects pedogenesis and weathering and also landforms, that is the geometry of the interface. There is an output of material here, an input there, reflected in a footslope cuirass. Compaction or changes in the chemical or mechanical properties of the materials may result. Sometimes piping occurs. If within reach of the roots, water circulation influences plant growth, thus affecting the ecologic environment. If slow, it may produce a waterlogging. It may change the properties of clayey materials; if the liquid limit is reached it could trigger a mass movement, a geomorphic event. All such changes occasioned by the flow of material are more or less rapid. They interfere with pedogenesis by modifying the conditions of its actions. Slow, down-slope movements disturb the soil horizons. Rapid movements entrain the soil and, depending on the depth affected, the subsoil. After such events, the soil-forming process has to start afresh. Such a case, an extreme example, has a certain similarity with the theory of bio-rhexistasy, but is part of a greater variety of cases.

Finally, all the water does not infiltrate. If a soil with a slow rate of infiltration is saturated, rainfall may be sufficient to cause an excess of water, which then runs off. But more frequently the mechanism is more complicated. A shower indeed contains a certain amount of kinetic energy, whose origin goes back to the radiant energy of the Sun. This energy has introduced a certain quantity of water vapour into the atmosphere through evaporation and plant transpiration. But the atmosphere is not stable, air masses move over the irregular face of the Earth because of the unequal distribution and absorption of solar energy by the atmosphere, which affects the relative humidity and the possibility of condensation. When condensation occurs and drops reach a certain size, gravity causes their fall. The friction of the air slows them, but, in any case, they reach the ground with a certain kinetic energy, causing *splash erosion* (see Plate 31, p. 127). Splash erosion breaks up the soil aggregates, freeing fine soil particles which, after a leap, fall to the ground and are entrained by the running water. As long as they are not too abundant, they accompany the water that infiltrates into the ground, tending to block up the soil pores. If the shower lasts long enough or, what amounts to the same, if the impacts are more violent, the pores are closed, the soil smoothed and 'glazed' by clay and fine silt, even if the soil is still dry at depth. A *sealing crust* has come into existence, which increases the runoff, slope permitting. On a level surface the water gathers into puddles. On a slope rills form and the fines are entrained by water that has become muddy.

Splash erosion, for one, is a function of the violence of the impact of raindrops. These reach the ground at the terminal velocity of free fall, at least when there is no wind. This velocity varies depending on the size of the drops, the smallest remaining suspended in the air, producing mist. The others reach their terminal velocity after a fall of only some 9 m for the largest. At impact the size of the drop determines the kinetic energy, which it transmits in two ways: by means of its mass and by means of its velocity, which itself is a function of mass. But, still dealing with water, the mass is directly a function of the size of the drop. The effect of the size of the drops, which depends on the weather (condensation), is therefore important.

The impact of raindrops is particularly severe with convectional rain, especially common in the intertropical convergence zone, and orographic rain, both of which are generally more intense than the rainfall of the wave cyclones of the marine temperate lands. However, we should not reason as if we were in a desert. The energy transmitted to the ground by a rainstorm is proportional to the product of its intensity and duration only on bare soil; for example, between the plants of a clean tilled crop, or after ploughing before the seeding of a crop. In other cases the plant cover should, of course, be reckoned with.

With a continuous plant cover the impact of the raindrops occurs not on the ground but on the aerial limbs of the plants. The kinetic energy, therefore, is dissipated there. Nevertheless, after a while, depending on the nature of the leaves, branches and bark, the water that wetted them begins to flow and concentrate into *aerial streamlets* to drop again. When encountering new obstacles these streamlets may reform at decreasing levels. Cascading aerial streamlets pose complex problems. Indeed, if their drops fall from lesser heights than those falling from the free air, their size is usually larger. But, as a whole, the energy exerted by rain splash is less the shorter the trajectory of the drops. Furthermore, there is a limit to the growth of the drops; it is reached after one or two cascades. Also, to further complicate matters, the aerial limbs of the plants are situated at variable distances from the ground. In any case, a basic principle may be derived from this: the soil is not protected by large trees, but by smaller plants, especially grasses and, to a lesser extent, shrubs. Thus, splash erosion and surface runoff occur under a forest lacking undergrowth, such as a eucalyptus forest on a glacis, which is actually being fashioned by these processes, as observed in Australia by Tricart. (The word 'glacis' has been in use in France for centuries to designate the flat, gently sloping area left completely bare at the foot of a fortification in order to fully expose an approaching enemy to the guns of the fortification. A scientific meaning, perfectly compatible with this original one, is currently used in geomorphology. Cholley, as early as 1943, consecrated the word in the *Annales de Géographie*. A glacis is a flat and smooth surface at the foot of a hill or mountain, or any higher and steeper terrain, which even may, during the course of time, have been completely eroded away, producing an inversion of relief; the glacis' head then is shaped as a cuesta, overlooking the lowland excavated from the former higher relief. Glacis may be fashioned from basement rocks or built by accumulation of sedimentary materials. The term is more objective than the American 'pediment', which is tied to strict genetic hypotheses, which differ from author to author in the English-speaking world and in France as well.) Other factors, some of which are interdependent, intervene. Among them compensations may occur; for example, measurements in Colombian coffee plantations have shown that aerial streamlets from shade trees have increased the kinetic energy of the drops falling on the ground. On the other hand, the abundant litter produced by these trees caused the energy to be dissipated without producing any splash erosion. Furthermore, by favouring the nitrification of the soil, the litter improved the soil itself as well as its permeability. So while an assessment made at an intermediate level (slightly above the ground) proved negative, another assessment made after completion of the process turns out to be very positive. This is a good example of the methodologic difficulties involving good rural management. The role of aerial streamlets depends, of course, much on the type of plants. The diversity is infinite. Sometimes they form at a high level so that their drops pelt the ground at terminal velocity. At other times they form at such a low level that their kinetic energy is negligible, which is the case of grasses.

Splash erosion is also a function of soil structure: the initial roughness of the soil, the size and kind of aggregates and free particles and the mechanical resistance of the aggregates. (Pedologists call this 'stability', which is not immediately understandable to the uninitiated. This is explained by the fact that pedologists use various laboratory procedures to destroy these aggregates and to analyse their components. To speak of the 'stability of the aggregates' is like confusing 'thermometer' with 'temperature'. Such abuse of language is unfortunately common.) Aggregates vary considerably according to soil as a function of climate, parent material, and supply of organic matter. The cropping system has an influence on

the latter and on the permeability of the soil, and therefore on the rate of infiltration. The mechanical resistance of the aggregates depends on the nature of their cement: if carbonate or organic matter, it is high, if salt, quite low. Agronomic practices influence the amount of organic matter and can modify the concentration of carbonate by liming.

Finally, splash erosion is a function of the duration and intensity of rainfall. Splash erosion may be prevented by a good cover of dead leaves, a humic horizon, a dense grass cover, or by mechanically resistant soil aggregates well cemented by clay associated with iron or organic matter, all of which cause the dispersal of the kinetic energy. The litter is a function of vegetation or agronomical practices and also of the activity of decomposers.

Furthermore, a certain proportion of the rainfall, up to 5–10 per cent of a shower, flows down tree trunks spreading at their base without any impact occurring, except for a very high intensity cloudburst. But if aerosols have been deposited on the plants' limbs prior to a shower, they are 'leached' and their soluble components are brought down to the ground surface, whose chemical characteristics they may alter, as is the case in the vicinity of Nouakchott, Mauritania (see Chapter 8, pp. 216–17).

Precipitation of rain and snow that wets or covers the plants but never reaches the ground but evaporates is referred to as *interception*. It may reach as high as 30–35 per cent of the annual precipitation in snowless humid regions, such as the Banco Forest, near Abidjan, Ivory Coast. Stemflow is a kind of byproduct of interception. It amounts to only a few per cent of the total rainfall and is difficult to measure, so that quantitative knowledge is quite limited. Its geomorphic action consists in the delivery, at the foot of the stem, of a small quantity of concentrated water, which can, if the soil is bare, form a rivulet and mobilize a small quantity of fine material (see Chapter 3).

Surface runoff, lastly, produces an important flow of material. It entrains particles set free by splash or torn loose by strings of running water. Also humus, organic remains, and solid fertilizers recently applied are washed away. In short, its effect is a generalized removal of the surficial part of the soil in one area and an accumulation in another, for example along a decreasing slope where the entrainment of particles is no longer assured and colluviation takes place. Such morphogenic mechanisms interfere with pedogenesis. The fine particles of the soil too play a particularly important role in the agronomic properties of the soil: they determine their water retention ability, known as *storage capacity*, on which plants depend between showers. The clay fractions also determine the base exchange complex, that is their ability to retain base cations, very important as plant nutrients. Surface runoff, for its part, causes a surficial impoverishment of the soil and even an ablation, while the soil continues to develop at depth. Thus splash erosion and surface runoff have important agronomic repercussions that should be taken into account in proper ecological land management.

The various factors of interception, splash erosion, and surface runoff together form a dialectical confrontation and, as such, should be investigated in the form of a balance.

To understand the soil, splash erosion and surface runoff must be taken into account. To set them side by side in the form of a balance-sheet is instructive. The result is the *morphogenic–pedogenic balance* (Tricart 1965a), a flexible instrument that applies to a generalized geomorphic process that affects an entire area, as does the soil-forming process.

The morphogenic–pedogenic balance varies with time and space (see Chapter 2, pp. 67–72). Morphogenesis, specifically by surface runoff, is favoured by an 'aggressive' climate with violent downpours, by soils with a poor structure, and by a sparse plant cover; soils then develop with difficulty and remain skeletal (lithosols, regosols). Inversely, pedogenesis is favoured by a continuous plant cover with a low stratum forming a particularly good protection, by gentle slopes, by a slow decomposition of the organic matter, and by moderate rainfall; morphogenesis is then peacefully slow. The balance is in favour of pedogenesis, the opposite of the previous case.

Either balance is subject to change. The cause may be climate. This possibility is not merely academic considering the importance of geologically recent climatic oscillations. The question then is to know exactly when such a radical change took place. But the vegetation and the structural stability of the soil also play their part. They may be rapidly modified by human intervention. Here again we are faced with problems of rural management, of the insertion of human activities into the natural environment (see Chapter 6, pp. 180–8, and Figure 23, p. 201).

It has not been our intention to give a complete analysis of the system that is the natural environment. We have only tried to justify our concepts with the help of some examples, which show the relationship of ecogeography to ecology and, in particular, offer a more rational approach to the problems of development, improvement or management of our ecologic environment.

We shall now turn our attention to the second stage of our analysis, to define types of environments subject to development or improvement as a function of this dynamic point of view.

Types of environment subject to development

Morphogenic processes, a cause of instability, are activated not only by solar radiation, but also by gravitational attraction, in part functioning owing to relief differences produced by internal forces, whether tectonic or volcanic. Every natural slope modification implies a displacement, a 'flow' of material, which generally counteracts the soil-forming process and, in most cases, the growth and reproduction of plants. Similarly, constructions such as roads and railways, industrial plants, housing and hydraulic structures may destabilize hill or mountain slopes. Also ash falls, such as those that have accompanied the repeated volcanic eruptions of Mount Usu, Japan, have for years maintained an environmental instability, impeding pedogenesis and keeping plant communities in a pioneer stage (Kadomura et al. 1983). Eventually increased plant growth tends to stabilize the environment and even prevents most mechanical mass wasting processes. Conditions of *topostability* occur when morphogenic processes are of minor import or after ash falls have totally ceased. The environment therefore should be viewed in terms of its stability and susceptibility *vis-à-vis* human interventions.

A classification of environments according to degrees of stability, however, presents certain difficulties, concerning a chronologic perspective and a morphodynamic perspective.

Chronologic perspective

A chronologic perspective based on a temporal taxonomy of the dynamics is necessary. To be correctly appreciated actual phenomena should be placed in this perspective: it requires the use of a time scale of thousands of years. The main fact is the major climatic change of which the end of the last glaciation is but one aspect. It is demonstrated by a good knowledge of ancient vegetation, mainly based on study of the pollen assemblages of marshes, lakes, peat bogs and even soils in areas far removed from one another. The regolith and types of landforms associated with it, for their part, reveal changes in the dynamics of the environment that can be correlated with changes in plant associations. Lastly, palaeotemperatures of water bodies obtained from ^{18}O isotopes in organic carbonates are another lead that have revealed a 5° to 6° C drop in temperatures in the oceans of the equatorial zone. But some precautions are in order; for instance, a bone of a mammal would be unsuitable, for it would reveal the temperature of the body of the mammal itself. What is needed are organisms that do not control their own temperature and that are small enough so that their temperature is roughly that of the environment. A good example are Foraminifera, Protozoa that are actively used for this purpose. Another important precaution is to make certain that the organisms lived in shallow water, whose temperature is close to that of the air, as it may be assumed that the temperature of the ocean surface is approximately equal to the mean annual temperature of the air in low latitudes or on an essentially tropical Earth as existed before the build up of ice. Notwithstanding, it must be kept in mind that ocean currents almost wholly control the temperature of surface waters, like, for instance, the Gulf Stream or the Labrador Current today. But, at the same time, they influence the air temperature close to sea level. These interactions are shown on the flow chart (Figure 3). This method, therefore, provides excellent crosschecks with the preceding ones.

The last method has demonstrated the existence of periods during which temperatures were lower than at present all over the earth. Already in the first third of the nineteenth century it was known that the glaciers of the Alps once had a much greater extent and that huge glaciers had covered northern Europe and northern North America in the not too remote past. This period was quickly referred to as 'Glacial' or the 'Ice Age', and when more such periods were identified near the end of the same century, they were called 'Ice Ages'. It would be more accurate, however, to speak of 'cold periods' or 'colder periods', as these expressions can be applied also to areas where no glaciers existed, such as Amazonia and Indonesia (which were also drier).

A rapid and important universal warming up, although discontinuous and interrupted by a short return to cold weather, occurred between 12,000 and 8,000 BP. It was preceded by the last, now well-known, cold period during which glaciers were widely spread not only over North America and Europe, but also as smaller icecaps in Siberia, the

Andes of Patagonia, and Tasmania, not to mention the mountain glaciers of the intertropical zone. The atmospheric circulation was then quite different from that of today. It can be reconstructed, in part, from the orientation of relict dunes and other aeolian deposits. Most climates of the Earth then differed considerably from the present ones. The Sahara was less arid: fluvial outwashes can be seen in areas not reached by floods today and palaeosols of Mediterranean and tropical varieties have been discovered in various locations. On the whole, the last glaciation there corresponds to a more humid period, traditionally called 'pluvial' in the northern Sahara. (We give only the broad features. In fact, things are more complicated. The periods referred to have subdivisions and environmental changes that differ somewhat from place to place. Nevertheless, a general phenomenon is the result of physical laws: as temperature was lower, so was evaporation, and for the whole Globe the amount of precipitation was lower than at present. Even so, the hydraulic balance could be favourable where the reduction of precipitation was lower than the decrease in evapotranspiration.) But a zone south of the present desert was drier than at present. Indeed an arid climate with immense dune fields extended in the Sahelian and north Sudanese zones from Senegal to the neighbourhood of Khartoum. It was as if the whole Sahara had shifted southward with the climatic belts. However, after the end of the Pleistocene the tropical part of the desert became relatively humid, as evidenced by the remarkable rock pictures of prehistoric people in the Tassili-n-Ajjer of south-eastern Algeria. Cattle then grazed in regions where today dromedaries can be used only with great care. This Neolithic period has been radio-carbon dated (from the ashes of camp sites) 10,000–3,200 BP. This relatively humid period allowed the establishment of human settlements on the shores of now dried up lakes and, of more direct interest to us, of the formation of palaeosols on the aforementioned dunes. In Senegal, Niger and Nigeria these relict soils are used today for the massive commercial cultivation of groundnuts. But this type of environment is particularly sensitive to degradation. The soils, which are very siliceous and poor in organic matter, are quickly exhausted and have a poor structure (the way soil particles are held together to form lumps called aggregates). As their productivity drops, surface runoff and especially wind attack them with force. As a result much land has been abandoned after several years of continuous cropping, as in the case of northern Senegal, for example around Louga, an area that as a result has become overpopulated and 'exports' people to the 'virgin lands' of eastern Senegal.

This example demonstrates the importance of palaeoclimatic conditions. They are the origin of certain, frequently fragile, relict phenomena. The soils of the ancient dunes of Louga have a poor structure because the parent sands are almost wholly quartzose. Hardly possessing any alterable minerals, they are rapidly leached to become acidic. They owe their cohesion only to the organic matter, which is scarce given the semi-arid climate and quickly destroyed by the effects of cultivation. The re-entrainment of the sand by wind is easy given its origin. Emplaced by wind, it is easily blown away by it owing to its favourable texture. The importance of its legacy is obvious. It defines certain conditions that should be observed in good land management, that is proper land use combined with conservation. The object of an ecogeographic study is to define these conditions.

This example also serves to define a second time scale, a much shorter one, expressed in years, of the order of a human life. It concerns degradational phenomena. Virgin land, such as west of the Mississippi, in the nineteenth century, exploited without regard for the next generation, can rapidly be worn out to the point of abandonment in less than a lifetime. The now cultivated short grass prairies of Oklahoma fell prey to the wind in the 1930s, raising dust clouds that reached as far as New York. The virgin lands of northern Kazakstan have shown an even greater susceptibility of the environment, unfortunately perceived too late. In Colombia, in the vicinity of Villa de Leiva, at an elevation of 2,500 m, hills covered 50 years ago with wheat fields and pastures have been transformed into sterile badlands. Such phenomena, unfortunately frequent in a world much of which is short of food, help understand the expression 'accelerated erosion', which in other respects is subject to criticism as it is insufficient from the conceptional point of view. The chronologic perspective also results in the establishment of a taxonomy. Mechanisms of degradation, which may be rapid, should be placed in a framework that takes account of palaeoclimatic legacies.

We are therefore led to ask ourselves, in the case of each environment, if it is the result of presently functioning dynamics or of different, ancient dynamics that long ago ceased to function. And in the latter case since when? This leads to the distinction of a currently stable environment, with a minor mechanical morphogenic component, that was previously unstable. The Louga area again serves as an example: it demonstrates (and this applies generally) that such an environment is very susceptible to certain types of degradation that result from the reactivation of processes that caused its instability in the past. If an environment has been stable for a very long time, this management problem does not exist. While certain environments are currently unstable as a result of a recent, induced degradation, others are so because of a change in morphoclimatic system. Their characteristics are very different, so that their management poses the problem, difficult to resolve, of materially altering the natural dynamics.

Morphodynamic perspective

A morphodynamic perspective is equally necessary. To make this clear, a few principles of geomorphology should be recalled. Landforms are the result of complex mechanisms. Not only should these be analysed, but also their mutual relationships examined. A good approach is to consider them as systems, as morphoclimatic systems, on the level of climatic domains, or as morphogenic systems, on a subordinate level due, for instance, to differences in lithology. A morphogenic system is composed of a number of interdependent processes that fashion the land. They, of course, produce 'flows' of material and consume energy. Transport processes such as runoff, mass-wasting, or aeolian transport are the essence of a morphogenic system. But these transport processes cannot move all loose materials. Their energy produces work only if it is applied to movable materials. A fluid, under certain conditions, can move particles of a certain dimension and mass only. The maximum size and mass of movable particles define the fluid's *tractive competence*. Frequently, mobilization is possible in unconsolidated rocks if the particles are inferior to the competence, but this is not always the case, as cohesion also plays its part. The case is different for consolidated rocks. These are formed by masses separated by planes of discontinuity such as bedding planes and joints. These masses are usually superior to the competence of the agents of transport. To be mobilized they must first be broken down to smaller sizes. We call this the *preparation of the material*. It is brought about by various processes that function at the contact of the atmosphere: variations of temperature, particularly across the freezing point, and of humidity. The first produce dilatations and contractions of the rock and therefore tensions that cause shearing. The efficacy of frost is considerably increased when there is water in the voids of the rocks, as ice has a lower density than water and, therefore, a greater volume. Variations in humidity activate chemical processes such as alteration of certain minerals, causing the breakdown of the rock, for example through granular disintegration in the case of granite.

A morphogenic system usually associates processes of preparation of the material with processes of mobilization-transport over a certain distance. The relationships between the ones and the others should be studied carefully. They are influenced by various factors, the most important of which are gravity, as determined by the degree of slope, and the plant cover. The latter favours chemical and biochemical actions by a direct attack of the roots and the decomposition of organic matter. In other respects plants help the cohesion of the soil by the ramifications of their roots: even strong currents produced by a river in flood have great difficulty in incising grassland. Plants, too, produce a certain roughness at the ground surface, which slows down the movement of fluids and creates turbulence, which disperses a certain

amount of energy. This principle is put to use in windbreaks which exert an ecologic effect on a width of land twelve to eighteen times the height of the tree screen. The soil is then protected from deflation, or its entrainment by the wind. The influence of vegetation on a morphogenic system is enormous. These examples have a general value.

From the point of view of rural management it is necessary to make a careful analysis of the morphogenic system. The limiting factors, those that fail to make adjustments between the various components of the system, should be well understood. For example, the preparation of the material under a continuous plant cover by weathering and pedogenesis may be intense and produce more loose material than can be mobilized by the slow-moving transport processes, a situation that corresponds to Erhart's biostasy. (This term does not properly reflect reality. The stabilizing role is almost wholly provided by plants, while animals, the other element of the biosphere, are a source of instability. Suffice to recall burrowing, trampling under foot, and, especially, the activities of invertebrates such as ants, termites, and earthworms that stir up huge quantities of soil (10

Plates 9 & 10 Examples of the chronologic perspective in land stability
Ph. JT CDLV-14. 15 km W of S. Pedro, Rio Grande do Sul (Brazil). The forest has been cut and replaced by pastures on 'soft' siltstones and sandstones. Result: increased runoff, although there is no overgrazing. Running water cuts deeply into the gentle slopes of the glacis and the very open valley bottom.

Plate 10 Ph. JT CDLXV-7. These Quaternary relict dunes in Rio Grande do Sul, Brazil, are being reactivated due to poorly managed pastures, generating intense runoff and burial of the vale bottom by fresh sand.

to 100 t/ha/yr by earthworms alone in field crop parcels and market gardens). We shall therefore use the term 'phytostasy' except when referring to Erhart.) A potential danger, however, which good management should take into account, is inherent in such a situation. The environment *must be* managed in such a way that the action of the transport processes is not intensified. Usually the best solution is to adopt a farming system that includes a good plant cover. To determine it requires interdisciplinary work between physical geographers, pedologists and agronomists. There are also other solutions such as field strip cropping, the use of buffer strips, or the planting of plant screens along contour lines to reduce surface runoff by increasing infiltration. But before making a choice it is advisable to have recourse to pilot schemes based on a good understanding of the environmental dynamics.

If the study of morphodynamics is essential to understand the constraints of the environment on rational land use, an evaluation of the susceptibility of certain types of land use to the risks of degradation is equally important. The succession of different morphogenic systems is often evident from the presence, in the natural environment, of

relict features, many of which are useful. The conditions of their persistence and, hence, the measures to be taken to ensure their preservation can be determined by establishing their succession, which brings us back to the chronologic perspective.

The dynamic classification of the natural environment, therefore, should be based on the combination of two perspectives, as formulated in Table 1 (pp. 38–47). By specifying categories of stability and modes of instability based on morphogenic systems, we dispose of an effective instrument of ecodynamic integration.:

1 The degrees of stability depend on all the morphogenic conditions: amplitude of the relief, intervention of internal forces, direct climatic influences, that is where the agents of the weather act directly on the ground without the interposition of plants, and indirect climatic influences acting through the medium of the plant cover and soils.
2 The chronologic influence is reflected in types of relief, which are the result of a more or less long morphogenic evolution, occasionally in soils, and even in types of vegetation, which too may be

relict. Thus among the stable environments we distinguish those that have been so for a more or less long period of time. It is indeed mainly among them that legacies from the past are important; they are unimportant in unstable environments in which legacies have little chance of being preserved.

3 Morphogenic stability is favourable to pedogenesis and to climax plant formations. Taking it into account helps the understanding of these two important components of the environment.

Finally this approach enables the study of the natural environment to be conducted in a way that answers the needs of ecologic development and the conservation of natural resources.

We shall be satisfied merely to expound our classification here. Its integrating aspects, already presented at a higher level, will be examined in detail in Chapter 2.

We shall consider two extreme cases, comparable to Erhart's biostatic and rhexistatic conditions. They are the stable (A) and the highly unstable (C) environments. But to limit ourselves to these two conditions and to oppose them schematically is not enough. There are transitions that are very gradual or multiform, and as they are the most common and widespread on Earth important to us. We shall call them *intergrade* environments (B). But if we design our classification in the form of a table, it is only to make things as clear as possible. Nevertheless, concern for a clear display, as is every instructional effort, is necessarily largely schematic and, therefore, does not exactly correspond to reality. We would be better served by a colour spectrum that includes all the intermediate situations.

Stable environments are characterized by morphogenic systems with few mechanical components. Weathering is mainly chemical and flows of material are mainly in the form of solutions. Migrations of detrital material are minimal. The kilometric tonnage of gravel, pebbles, and even sands is small in comparison to the size of the area considered. This paucity of detrital flow corresponds to Erhart's biostasy. The composition of the material transported to the sea indeed is mainly in the form of solutions. Some of these are precipitated directly on the sea floor to produce sediments, but more often they are used by organisms to make shells, skeletons, calcareous

Plate 11 Instability caused by bioturbation
Ph. JT CDLV-10. 'Ploughing' by ants in uncared-for pastures in Rio Grande do Sul, Brazil. This example countervails H. Erhart's theory of bio-rhexistasy.

algae, and so on, which after the death of the organisms produce biogenic sediments, most of which are eventually transformed into limestones.

The paucity of the flow of detritus means a very slow evolution of the relief, which is very favourable to plant life. There is no morphodynamic constraint whatsoever on the plants. And the same applies to the soils, which develop under optimum conditions, taking into account the seasonal or constant input of biotic matter. The morphogenic–pedogenic balance is then so overwhelmingly in favour of pedogenesis that it can be ignored.

Nevertheless, the chronologic perspective should be considered. We should ask ourselves if the present dynamics have existed long enough to preclude the presence of relict features relating to, especially, mechanical morphogenic processes. Most regions of the Earth indeed have experienced alternations of periods of stability and of instability during the Quaternary. Changes in atmospheric circulation during the last cold period went hand in hand with larger thermal gradients between the middle and lower latitudes. It seems that as a result the weather was more extreme. A greater morphodynamic instability and a greater activity of the morphogenic processes are indeed evidenced by the landforms and by the transported materials associated with them. Stable conditions should therefore be subdivided into *long-term* and *recently stable* environments. The formulation is admittedly vague; chronologic data are necessary to increase its precision. The main criterion, important on the interdisciplinary as well as on the practical plane, is the presence of inherited phenomena produced by dynamics other than the present ones. If legacies are common, the present stability is of relatively recent date. If they are absent, the stability is ancient. But, of course, strict definitions should be avoided. There are transitions that assure a continuous typological variation between two extremes. With sufficient observations such intergrade environments can be included into the classification. In any case, they should not be overlooked even if our perception is insufficiently precise to attempt well-defined subdivisions.

Unstable environments are more complex. The causes and characteristics of their instability should simultaneously be taken into account. They are the basis for their subdivision. Before examining these topics, let us first explain the concept. Unstable environments are characterized by notable landform changes, whether frequent, seasonal, chronic or catastrophic, due to an important flow of material, mainly coarse, but not necessarily so; for example, the runoff of badlands may move an abundant suspended load in terms of weight per km^2. Also mudflows, as the name indicates, are composed of materials rich in clay. Whatever the case may be, the geomorphic process is a limiting ecologic factor, impeding the normal development of vegetation. A case in point: a landslide or mudflow completely destroys the vegetation, leaving behind a bare scar that heals more or less quickly thanks to the growth of pioneering plants, different in species from the previous plant cover. But things may be more complex; for instance, in the high Queyras of the French Alps a distinct vegetation grows on the conic run-out zone of chronic avalanches. On the track itself, where the sweep of the process is most acute and frequent, there are no plants whatsoever. On the margins, where the action is less, some shrubs grow between the disturbed rubble. They bend with each avalanche. A bit further on there are flexible willow saplings, followed by birches. Both try to grow into trees, but their growth is interrupted by major avalanches at about 1 to 1.5 m above ground, at mid-winter snow level. The result is stunted forms. Ground or dirty avalanches, that is, those that scrape the ground, and other mass-wasting processes and even surface runoff also have consequences on the soils. They are more or less lacerated or even completely swept away. Their formation is thereby impeded or brutally interrupted. Together with pioneering plants they have to restart from the mineral subsoil, in the worst case from the bedrock. The concept morphogenic–pedogenic balance may be applied, depending upon the situation.

Unstable environments may have various causes; let us examine the principal ones: internal forces, relief and bioclimatic conditions.

First, the internal forces. Strong earthquakes trigger landslides, mudflows, snow and ice avalanches (see Chapter 2, pp. 80–3) and produce crustal dislocations. Volcanic eruptions produce lava flows, lahars, or ash falls temporarily, partly or completely, destroying the environment, creating unstable conditions for a more or less long period of time. Lava flows are the most thoroughly devastating, causing a complete interruption of all environmental processes. Lahars, which are 'mudflows' on the flanks of a volcano, are almost equally destructive, especially when caused by the ejection of the water of a crater lake in a volcanic eruption, which in that case may be followed by an ash fall too. The latter are, of course, less common but more extensive and destructive than the former. The eruptive lahar of Mount Kelud (Java),

Table 1

Major categories of geodynamic environments	Geomorphological characteristics	Types of morphogenic influences on pedogenesis	Principles of integration of the morphogenic factor in the pedologic classification
I	II	III	IV

| | 1 *Stability realized a long time ago:* Slow, barely perceptible, superficial evolution of landforms in equilibrium with present bioclimatic conditions similar to those having existed for several hundreds of thousands of years. Result: *climax landforms* realized on the one hand in regions with strong biotic influence, on the other in regions of minor aggressivity of certain mechanical processes such as the foggy coastal deserts of the Pacific coast of South America. Dissection should be minor. The external geodynamic characteristics, to a certain extent, may neutralize rather active internal geodynamics, as on the same coast. | Weathering and pedogenesis proceed with a minimum interference from agents of transport. Their products remain in place or are subjected to slow removal. They may reach a high degree of evolution, variable according to bioclimatic conditions. The latter determine the rate and kind of evolution. In regions of slow evolution the weathered mantle and soils may be thin and poorly evolved, although developed over long periods of time; for example, the dust-like regolith of the foggy Pacific coast or the moist, peaty soils of certain tundras in NW Canada. | The classic classifications of soils have been devised by taking into account these conditions (of III), which are the simplest and most intradisciplinary for pedologists. The evolution of soils proceeds within a steady state. The concept of *catena* is valid. An important point is the length of time these conditions and their corresponding pedogenesis have existed. |

A
Stable environments
A slow, barely perceptible evolution, in 'equilibrium', approaching a *climax* situation. Such conditions are realized in regions with minor internal geodynamic activity and with low intensity of the mechanical processes of the external geodynamics.

The pedogenic-morphogenic balance is strongly in favour of pedogenesis.

Extreme case corresponding to Erhart's *biostasy.*

| | 2 *Relatively recent stability:* A more common and widespread case than the preceding case because of Quaternary climatic oscillations. Usually the approximate stability under present conditions has been realized only since the beginning of the Holocene, about 10,000 years ago. *Relict and inherited forms* of paleoclimatic origin associated with active climax forms of the preceding types. They may be of different types, belonging to several successive generations, which introduced variants that may be very complex.

The relief, which then is *polygenic*, is characterized by successive readjustments under the influence of climatic oscillations. This evolution usually produces a degradation on upper slopes and a correlative aggradation on lower slopes and low land. A more complicated situation arises | An association of soils has resulted from soil-forming processes of different type and age, which, moreover, have been subject for a longer or shorter period of time to certain transformations. The ancient soil serves as parent material to the new soil.

A definition of present soil-forming processes is indispensable to determine the nature and importance of legacies from the past. *Truncations* of ancient soil horizons are the rule in all regions where the previous periods of instability have not been too intense, otherwise the ancient soils have been removed entirely. The truncation of ancient soils sets free pedogenized materials that are reworked into the regolith especially on colluvial slopes. Pedogenesis of stable periods affects, on the one hand, truncated soils, producing *superimposed soils* of different ages and, | Most soils are *polyphased*; they have different histories.

A double principle of classification should be introduced:
(a) as a function of the initial type of pedogenesis, possibly as a function of the succession of different pedogeneses that have taken place;
(b) as a function of the degree of evolution, of *transformation*, caused by recent pedogenesis.
  1 Truncated polyphased soils to be classed as a function of:
(a) type of truncated soil,
(b) level of truncation,
(c) later transformation by renewed pedogenesis whose type and intensity should be taken into account;
  2 Buried polyphased soils to be classed as a function of:
(a) type ⎱ of overlying
(b) thickness ⎰ soil
(c) transformations |

Lithologic influence on		General consequences for conservation VI	General agronomic consequences VII
morphogenesis Va	pedogenesis Vb		

Decreasing importance of the lithologic influence with time in geomorphic as well as pedologic aspects: 'ageing' of landforms and soils. The products of weathering become as thick and generalized as the bioclimatic conditions permit. They tend toward a certain homogenization; for example, the products of ferrallitic weathering. The character of the products influence in a determinant way morphogenesis, pedogenesis, as well as the hydrology. Their study is of the utmost importance.		The equilibria assuring the stability, the vegetation among others, should not be disturbed. The vegetation is frequently the result of a long evolution resulting in the appearance of endemic species very sensitive to a change in ecologic conditions; for example, the 'lomas' of the Peruvian littoral desert.	The common occurrence of ancient soils means an excessive leaching in humid climates and the development of highly consolidated cuirasses and crusts in regions with pronounced, usually seasonal, dry periods. Nevertheless fertilizers and various improvements are rendered effective by the stability of the environment. Once realized they remain so as long as the techniques used permit it.

Important lithologic influence if there is exposure by stripping of the regolith.		Maintain a plant cover of equivalent density to the climax vegetation to avoid degradation. If not, degradation may be very rapid and have serious consequences because of the mantle of friable weathered products common to these environments. This type of degradation corresponds to Erhart's *rhexistasy*.	Same aspects as above, but the conditions vary much in space, whence the necessity to work more subtly by paying attention to interpolations, which should have a well-founded basis. Extrapolations are very dangerous and should be proscribed.
Variable lithologic influences according to the morphoclimatic system. Notwithstanding, the lithologic influences are reflected through the regolith. Knowledge of the soils is indispensable for the understanding of the morphogenic processes.	The lithological influence is limited to the initial soil-forming processes. During phenomena of transformation they interfere indirectly through the medium of the old soil that has become parent material and through the medium of drainage at the base of the profile. However, the influence is not so much of the rocks themselves as of the characteristics of the products of weathering.		

Major categories of geodynamic environments	Geomorphological characteristics	Types of morphogenic influences on pedogenesis	Principles of integration of the morphogenic factor in the pedologic classification
I	II	III	IV
	if aeolian processes intervene. During periods of stabilization materials in transit on the slopes are immobilized wherever they are, in whatever topographic location. The Pampa Deprimida of Argentina is an excellent example of such a case. The materials that remained in place at the beginning of the present period of stability constitute the present regolith of the region and the parent material for the present soils.	on the other hand, transported regolith (coluvium or wind-blown material) partly supplied by weathered or pedogenized material that is undergoing *transformations*. On aggradation sites soils of periods or episodes of stability are *buried* under the transported regolith of periods of instability. When the burial is shallow they undergo a transformation as a result of the new conditions under which they have been placed. The fossilizing material, in this case, has usually undergone a certain amount of pedogenesis before transport and has also been affected by transformations. Regions of minor relief subjected to alternations of aggressive climates and periods of phytostability, the type of which is the Argentine Pampa Deprimida, are especially favourable to such a complex evolution.	undergone after burial and caused by it; 3 Polyphased soils that are both truncated and buried: Combine the criteria of 1 and 2.
B *Intergrade environments* The present dynamics are characterized by interaction between pedogenesis and morphogenesis. The pedogenic–morphogenic balance is slightly in favour of pedogenesis or of morphogenesis depending	Morphogenesis and pedogenesis proceed simultaneously and interfere with one another. We are in the central part of a continuum. Intensities are roughly equal, which gives much importance to short-period climatic fluctuations. Successions of more humid or drier years, or colder winters, may tip the balance in one direction or the other, which is important for agronomy and conservation. Interactions between morphogenic and pedogenic processes play an important role; for example, the properties of soils affect morphogenesis, which in turn, through feedback influence pedogenesis. Such very coherent natural systems should be taken into account in conservation and	1 If pedogenesis prevails somewhat over morphogenesis, the balance moves all the closer to the preceding case (A) as the pedogenic–morphogenic balance is favourable to pedogenesis. However, the intervention of morphogenesis slows down the evolution of the soil which, even under climax conditions and during a long period of time, does not attain the highest degree of evolution. The same holds for weathering; for example, illitic alterations of the granitoid rocks forming the steep/abrupt slopes, subject to chronic sliding, of the *selva nublada* of the Venezuelan Andes. The soils undergo a kind of permanent more or less effective rejuvenation	1 The very sensitive pedogenic–morphogenic balance here varies not only in time during short periods, but also in space as a function of site. The catena concept is valid on condition to give it not only a merely topographic but a dynamic significance. The results are an association of soils, usually with intergrades, which are characterized by different degrees of evolution, possibly also of hydromorphism, when the lithologic influences do not play a role. The mosaics should be analysed by taking into account the morphodynamic factor.

Lithologic influence on morphogenesis Va	pedogenesis Vb	General consequences for conservation VI	General agronomic consequences VII
		The conservation of a continuous vegetal cover or the improvement of this cover is essential. If the cover is degraded a swift liquidation of the soils and passage to C-I results. In the opposite case, i.e. improvement of the cover, evolution is favourable and toward A-I. Successions of ecologically unfavourable years are often critical and trigger degradational episodes that later are difficult to curb. Strict measures should be taken during such periods.	Agronomic conditions are increasingly unfavourable as the balance shifts in favour of morphogenesis. Cultivation usually promotes the morphogenic processes. A consecutive number of ecologically unfavourable years are especially dangerous. The morphogenic processes impoverish the soil in fine and soluble materials, and even in organic matter, as humus is entrained by surface runoff. Improvement of yields is conditioned by a greater morphodynamic stability. Agrotechniques must help it and consider it as a preliminary. Wrong practices produce positive feedbacks: the margin of tolerance of the environment is very low.

Major categories of geodynamic environments	Geomorphological characteristics	Types of morphogenic influences on pedogenesis	Principles of integration of the morphogenic factor in the pedologic classification
I	II	III	IV
on the case. When clearly in favour of pedogenesis the balance grades towards a stable environment; when clearly in favour of morphogenesis towards an unstable environment. The various cases form a continuous series in which steps are arbitrary.	restoration. Certain agronomic practices can change them and reverse the evolutive trend; for example, the stability of the aggregates influences pluvial erosion and diffuse surface runoff and, as a consequence, runoff or infiltration, gullying or mass movements; but it may be increased by agronomic practices, such as use of mature or addition of lime.	depending on the intensity of morphogenesis. 2 If morphogenesis prevails somewhat over pedogenesis, two cases should be distinguished: (a) Superficial morphogenesis, i.e. pluvial erosion, diffuse surface runoff, and soil creep. The soil is subject to superficial removal but grows at the base. One of the most demonstrative cases of the application of the concept of the pedogenic–morphogenic balance.	2 Morphoydynamics play an even greater role, which leads to the distinction of two cases: (a) Here too the pedogenic–morphogenic balance varies as a function of site. But poorly evolved soils are more common in sites where the balance is in favour of morphogenesis. The mosaics should also be analysed as a function of the morphodynamic factor. There is also, on the whole, approximate compensation between superficial soil removal and penetration in depth of pedogenesis. But the compensation is more or less well realized as a function of the variations of the pedogenic–morphogenic balance from site to site. This should be made apparent in the analysis of the mosaics.
		(b) Morphogenesis by shallow mass wasting, generalized or localized (two variants), i.e. laminar or lenticular solifluction. The entire soil profile is affected.	(b) The differentiation of horizons is hampered, even completely hindered, where there is movement. A mixture of horizons is possible. In the case of localized phenomena there are mosaics of diversely affected soils, including little or not affected soils in areas of local stability.
			Predominant influence of morphodynamics, determining a twofold classification: 1 Intense, sporadic, localized phenomena.

Lithologic influence on		General consequences for conservation VI	General agronomic consequences VII
morphogenesis Va	pedogenesis Vb		
Very high influence determining landforms of various orders of magnitude: very fine stream network in poorly consolidated rocks of arid regions with sporadic stream flow. The mechanical properties of the material are the most important.	Intervenes all the more as pedogenesis cannot attain a high degree of evolution.	Critical environment very difficult to preserve: the forest does not prevent mass movements. These develop in an argillaceous material apt to gullying, whose development must be prevented, but without increasing infiltration. Buffer strips should be proscribed. Increase of water use by the vegetation does not occur during very wet periods. Thinning of the vegetation may favour landslides through the formation of desiccation cracks, which increase infiltration.	Plants with deep roots such as trees, even small trees, are mutilated and deformed by mass movements. A permanent pasture is the most adequate use, on condition that it is lush. It favours a morphogenically inactive runoff, but decreases the time for its concentration and intercepts less water than a forest. This should be compensated by small hydraulic works. Excessive trampling underfoot by animals should be avoided, as well as terracettes, which may produce soil slips.

Minor consequences because the diversity of the materials permitting mass movements is limited. Calcium carbonate, which causes flocculation, and sodium chloride, which causes dispersion, play a particularly important role in morphogenesis as well as in pedogenesis.

| Determinant. In dissection sites the aptitude for material to entrainment is decisive; for example, their mechanical properties and the | Very great: the incipient pedogenesis depends narrowly on the properties of the present material. Raw mineral soils are common. | The entire category is composed of *very sensitive environments*. Agronomic utilisation is more or less marginal. It is more a matter of conservation in order to *protect* the land downslope and the water resources than to produce crops. | |

Major categories of geodynamic environments	Geomorphological characteristics	Types of morphogenic influences on pedogenesis	Principles of integration of the morphogenic factor in the pedologic classification
I	II	III	IV
C *Highly unstable environments* Strong predominance of morphogenesis over pedogenesis			They destroy the soils. Pedogenesis, when it is possible, restarts from scratch on raw material. Result: a soil mosaic characterized by a double differentiation determined by the duration of pedogenesis (monogenic) and the lithology. Transitions exist with B-2-b and A-2. Main cases: mudflows, alluvial digitations such as fans, outwashes, and natural levees.
			2 Frequent, recurrent, localized phenomena. Pedogenesis is not possible; result: lithosols, regosols, or raw mineral soils. Pedogenesis takes place only on intermediate sites benefiting from a certain stability for a minimum of time. The mosaic is *heterodynamic*. Two opposed evolutive tendencies are possible: (a) Increasing instability: islands of relict soils are progressively destroyed by ablation, dissection, or burial. (b) Increasing stability: decrease in the frequency and intensity of the morphogenic actions, recolonization by the vegetation. Soils develop on sites that are being stabilized. Transition with B-2.
	Intense morphogenesis whose causes, which may be compounded, are the following: (a) 'aggressive' bioclimatic conditions, such as extreme climate, with high, irregular variations deleterious to the vegetal cover and	Are closely subordinated to the morphogenic processes but not very important. In the case of an anthropic degradation, liquidation of the soils. In the case of a steady-state situation, regosols or lithosols.	(a) On ablation sites the main process is runoff with incision of gullies whose network increases to eventual formation of badlands. Generalized stripping of soil as in the case of C-3. In the extreme, badlands may

Lithologic influence on		General consequences for conservation VI	General agronomic consequences VII
morphogenesis Va	pedogenesis Vb		

availability of water for mudflows.
 	
    In accumulation sites the properties of the material, such as fluidity of lavas and texture of alluvia, determine the landforms.
		It is very difficult to contain the triggering of such phenomena. Afforestation, for example, does not prevent mass wasting, even sometimes promotes it.
		    An attempt should be made to prevent increased degradation, for example by gullying in an area affected by mass movements, for gullying cannot be controlled except by increasing the risk of mass wasting.
			Strong agronomic limitations make this land *marginal* for cultivation. Improvements are costly and precarious, as soils are poorly evolved or even absent.
			    Limitations to the use of the land should be very strict, of the same type but more severe as B-2. It is essential that the risk of irreversible degradation should be taken into account, especially for neighbouring areas.

They determine the intensity and the kind of morphogenic processes and the course of evolution. The structural stability of the soils is critical as far as runoff is concerned. If the incision of gullies, for example, reaches a different subjacent material, there may be, depending on the case, either an acceleration or a slowing down and a stabilization of the gullying process.	As in case C-1	Attempts should be made to favour evolution toward stability, which may be difficult.
		    In the case of torrential processes the following techniques may be combined:
		(a) Remedial works intended to temporarily slacken the torrential processes.
		(b) A revegetalization that profits from the respite provided by the remedial works. It should relay the latter before they require expensive rebuilding.
		    A succession of plant associations should be planned to ensure an ever-increasing stabilization. A natural route or revegetalization may be auspicious and should be helped along.
			The land is *marginal*, inapt for profitable cultivation. Vegetalization cannot be justified by a direct economic yield. It is no more than a step toward stabilization. This stabilization may be imposed by the character of *neighbouring areas*.
			    Once begun, stabilization can progress only owing to severe, strictly observed methods of protection, which impose narrow limitations on the utilization of the environment.

Very great influence, producing a sculpturing whose texture, down to details, is closely related to the attributes of the lithology.			

Major categories of geodynamic environments	Geomorphological characteristics	Types of morphogenic influences on pedogenesis	Principles of integration of the morphogenic factor in the pedologic classification
I	II •	III	IV
	transmitting a great deal of energy. (b) A bold relief with long, steep/abrupt slopes and intense dissection. Considerable recent internal geodynamics, such as uplift or vulcanism, are favourable factors. The present active dynamics prevent the survival of legacies from the past. Reconstruction of the past for lack of evidence is of minor interest.	These characteristics apply to environments of dissection as well as to environments of aggradation. The migration of the detritus from the ones to the others is rapid.	also be considered as entering the C-3 category.
			(b) On accumulation sites raw mineral products are encountered. Depending on frequency of occurrence and more or less wide distribution, there is a transitional series between cases C-1 and C-3.
			3 Chronic, rather intense, generalized actions; for example, stripping by runoff or aggradation on a floodplain. Areas of ablation and aggradation should be kept apart:
			(a) Ablation areas. Mosaics of lithosols, regosols, and of embryonic soils. Transition with case B.
			(b) Aggradational areas. Aggradation is rather slow, an embryonic pedogenesis is taking place before influx of new materials. A homogenization by biotic intermixing occurs in areas rich in organisms. In certain areas poor in organisms intermixing occurs owing to mechanisms of cryoturbation, hydroturbation, or haloturbation.

Lithologic influence on morphogenesis Va	Lithologic influence on pedogenesis Vb	General consequences for conservation VI	General agronomic consequences VII
The texture of the material determines the forms of the deposits: talus cones, alluvial spreads, aeolian or colluvial deposits.	Strong influence of the texture of the material on embryonic pedogenesis.	A morphogenic stabilization is an indispensable prerequisite. Protective containments should be carefully studied and permit deposition under propitious conditions outside of the protected sector. If not, ever more serious ruptures of the embankments shall take place. It is necessary to act on the source of the detritus.	Once stabilization is realized, the problem is to plan a succession of crops tolerating raw mineral soils at the beginning and helping their gradual improvement later. The water balance plays an essential role and should be taken into account with the economic development of the land.
Influences the greater or lesser morphodynamic instability			
Influences the rate of morphogenesis and determines the forms of relief.			As in case C-1
Decisive influence of the kind and texture of the deposits on the relief and the soil-forming processes.			
			As in case C-2-b

Plate 12 Catastrophic instability caused by a lahar
Lahars, like other mudflows, and ash falls cause a long period of interruption of vegetative growth, but not as long as lava flows. Depicted is one of several lahar tongues descending from Mount Kelud (Keloet, alt. 1731 m), East Java, as a result of that volcano's eruption on 19–20 May 1919. 30 million m³ of more or less hot water were ejected from the volcano's crater lake. The lahars spread as far as 38 km destroying all highly cultivated land, 104 villages, and taking 5,110 lives. From *Vulkanologische Mededeelingen*, no. 2, 1921, Weltevreden, former Netherlands East Indies.

in 1919, not only destroyed 130 km² of mostly paddy rice fields but also wiped out 104 villages and cost 5,110 lives. The 'mud', which actually consisted mainly of sand, gravel and scattered boulders, was 1.5 m thick on the lowland at Blitar, 24 km from the crater. Eruptive lahars on Mount Kelud have occurred at least six times since 1800. After the last eruption, a tunnel was dug through the crater rim to keep down the level of the lake. The morphogenic readjustment is less here than on ash slopes of stratovolcanoes because the lowland at the foot of the volcano is much flatter owing to the very processes that have produced it (Kemmerling 1921). Ash falls are more or less serious depending on their quantity and on the temperature of the ashes as they reach the ground, red hot in the case of *nuées ardentes*. At least, they kill the lowest stratum of the vegetation, the most influential from the morphogenic point of view. For a few years after the last ash fall, there is, on all slopes, intense morphogenic activity as ashes are scored, talwegs swept clean, and pedogenesis is

prevented. In the case of the Mexican volcano El Chichón, which erupted in March–April 1982, the ashes, which did not exceed 50 cm in thickness at most, were quickly washed away by rain, particularly heavy and abundant because the dust particles of the eruption itself created additional condensation nuclei at the beginning of the rainy season. The rain began by forming an impermeable crust, which immediately increased the coefficient of runoff, but later pierced the crust and eventually washed away the friable underlying ashes. The former soil was then exhumed and the grass began to grow again, the soil having been fertilized by the dissolution of soluble minerals in the overlying ashes. In these three cases vulcanism caused an extensive change in the environment followed by a period of readjustment or instability. Normal, stable conditions return, climate permitting, with renewed plant growth or cultivation and resumption of pedogenesis. The succession is analogous to that of a stable region previously affected by destabilizing climatic conditions, except that the length of time involved is not at all the same. In the case of a climatically relatively stable region that was previously unstable, the change took several thousands of years; often it spans the end of the last cold period and the Holocene, or some 15,000 years. On the other hand, the changes in dynamics caused by a volcanic eruption take several months or years to heal, even centuries for extremely massive lava flows very slowly conquered by vegetation. There is analogy in the sequence, but the length of time involved is of a different order of magnitude.

Second, relief which is the result of several million years of evolution also plays a role. Processes set in motion by gravity increase as a function of the sine of the slope. Morphogenic processes, particularly surface runoff and creep, are especially active in mountains with steep or abrupt slopes. Slope processes are triggered only when slopes pass a certain minimum gradient or a specific threshold. This is the case of rockfalls, landslides, mudflows and avalanches. The slope gradient, of course, is a very important factor in morphogenesis in the instability of the environment. This factor is certainly not the only one; a continuous plant cover can counteract its influence. For example, surface runoff remains inefficient at 800–900 m on 30° slopes in the Vosges Mountains (Alsace) under a dense forest and luxuriant undergrowth on soils with a thick humic horizon. This is the case, on granites, on the north flank of the Champ du Feu. But forest does not prevent the triggering of slumps or mudflows. Such phenomena are common in the forests of the Hawaiian islands, the South Island of New Zealand, or the mighty forests of New Guinea, the Venezuelan Andes, and the Amazon versant of the Peruvian Andes. They sweep away the forest and produce scars that are later invaded by secondary vegetation. From another point of view forests even favour slumps and mudflows, as they overload the ground and help infiltration. In general, slope increases the risks of instability, hence its emphasis in the American land-capability classification. The morphogenic–pedogenic balance tips in favour of morphogenesis with every increase of slope, so that mountain slopes are generally characterized by thin, undernourished or, to use an old expression, 'skeletal' soils, a term actually more objective than the expression 'little evolved' which has replaced it. The vigour of the relief, of course, results from the intensity of dissection, which itself is a function of tectonic upheaval. Dissection, according to the nature of the rocks and climatic conditions, follows with a certain delay upon the initial upheaval, but also continues once uplift has ceased. Such hystereses, or phase differences, come to light with reconstruction of the morphogenic evolution.

Bioclimatic conditions are the third cause of instability. Climatic irregularity, in general, is a serious limiting ecologic factor. Vegetation adapts itself less well to episodic rainfall, occurring at irregular intervals with droughts of variable duration, than to moderate rainfall or definite periodicity. Morphogenesis, in contrast, profits from irregular meteorological events without strict periodicity. Depending on their violence and destructive capacity, such phenomena may be included in the concept of 'catastrophic' events. A protracted drought, such as has afflicted the Sahel on and off since 1968 gravely affects a marginal ecologic environment, where plants compete for the available water. The losers die, thinning the plant cover, also overgrazed, thus reducing its stabilizing effect. This zone, more than 5,000 km long, is for the most part composed of ancient dunes stabilized since the beginning of the humid Neolithic. This stabilization is now threatened in the long term, which should be taken into account in a programme of restoration. The effects of short-term climatic fluctuations, which are minor elsewhere, are amplified by resonance in a transitional climatic zone such as the Sahel. The evolutive sequences are shortened, which introduces intergrade conditions between a presently unstable zone (Sahara) and a formerly unstable zone that has become stable (Sahel–northern Sudan). A steady state, or climax, characterized by a mediocre pedogenesis and a rather active surficial morphogenesis, mainly surface runoff, can therefore exist within the framework of long-term climatic oscillations (which, moreover, occur frequently). The sands and finer materials are rapidly entrained as soon as they have been prepared by weathering. Soils remain embryonic for lack of fine material and cannot develop no matter how long their evolution. There are, therefore, regions with sparse vegetation where steady-state soils are embryonic or remain more or less composed of raw mineral matter because of the instability of the environment. Analogous results under more favourable natural conditions may occur in cultivated lands. Especially in Mediterranean regions, the rate of soil ablation on cropland is frequently faster than pedogenesis, so that the rocks, when unconsolidated, or the parent material is cultivated.

The classification of unstable environments should therefore take into consideration the nature of the morphogenic processes in space as well as in time. Generalized morphogenic processes (see Chapter 2, pp. 64–66), affecting entire areas with frequency, constantly strip them of fine materials by surface runoff or deflation. They tip the morphogenic–pedogenic balance strongly in favour of morphogenesis. This is frequently the case in semi-arid environments. The steady state situation is characterized there by a near absence of soils, which worsens the ecologic conditions. The only inherited regolith in the Sahel is that of some desert varnished talus at the foot of highlands, as in southern Mauritania and in the bend of the Niger, in Mali. In dissected regions where this steady state has reigned for a long time, palaeosols and the friable weathered mantle have disappeared completely.

A variant of this subtype occurs in regions of high anthropic degradation. Ploughing to level the ground affected by deep rilling promotes the action of generalized morphogenic processes. Cultivation also, at least temporarily, leaves much soil exposed, especially under dry-farming practices. In a region of unconsolidated rocks this regime, if practised long enough, finally ends up cultivating the rocks themselves, the soils having been stripped away. If this trend is recent but on the increase, patches of residual soils temporarily persist and an intergrade situation exists with an infinite number of intermediate stages.

The two preceding cases have been chosen in regions of dissection. They have their equivalent in regions of deposition such as valley bottoms, outwash plains, or colluvial piedmonts. Pedogenesis is interrupted by influxes of mineral matter, resulting in 'poorly evolved' soil. Actually, they are essentially sediments.

The generalized morphogenic processes just described do not fit into Erhart's concept of rhexistasy. Except for the case of a sudden acceleration of anthropic degradation, there is no entrainment of pre-existing pedologic materials. We are in the presence of a steady state. But even in the case of a worsening degradation, it would be improper to speak of rhexistasy, as the length of time involved is totally different.

Localized morphogenic phenomena produce dispositions in the form of a mosaic. They occur at a given moment on a restricted area only and are therefore associated with a different type of dynamics. Conditions of penestability, even of stability, persist between the areas affected. An example is a slope subject to slumping. The slumping process should be examined from the point of view of frequency: if it is chronic, the entire slope will eventually be affected. The result is a juxtaposition of more or less old slumps in different stages of pedogenesis and recolonization by plants. The mosaic is characterized by the work of a single process, but having functioned at different times; it is *heterochronic*. In another case, that of ravines dissecting a terrace, the evolutive trend should be taken into account: when the ravines are functioning, a regressive incision takes place, which is reflected in a deepening and spreading of the ravines at an exponential rate at the expense of the terrace. Evolution is toward an ever-increasing proportion of unstable land. It has been calculated that in the Ukranian–Russian steppe the area occupied by ravines of anthropic origin increased at an average rate of 5 per cent per annum in approximately one hundred years since the middle of the nineteenth century. The high rate is explained by an aggressive climate, thick loesses, easily undercut, and poor land management. The exponential increase ceases after a certain period with the decrease of space between the ravines, but the land is then irretrievably lost. Attempts to contain the process should be made before the exponential increase but after the determination of the evolutive trend and its rate. Persistence of stable islands during the course of destruction provides a transition to penestable environments. We are then in the presence of a *heterogenic* mosaic, as it associates areas of very different dynamics; but it is also heterochronic, since the two types of dynamics are not synchronous. This case corresponds rather well with Erhart's rhexistasy, but, again, the time involved is not the same.

Penestable environments form an intergrade between stable and unstable environments. Characterized by an approximate balance between the morphogenic and pedogenic processes, they can be differentiated from the two extremes only by gradations. In such poorly contrasted situations nuances are numerous and should not be eliminated for the sake of simplification. The consequences of the processes are often amplified in relation to their effects, for example, through resonance. Modifications that appear to be minor may play an important role, such as modifications produced by short-term climatic fluctuations. We have mentioned them in connection with the recent Sahel drought. We insist here on the general importance of this type of phenomenon, mainly in zones of climatic transition, whether semi-arid or subarctic.

Minor modifications in the morphogenic–pedogenic balance may have an important consequence: they often cause a positive feedback that accelerates the phenomenon and contributes to the effects of resonance, as in the case of the structural stability of soils and their ablation by splash erosion and surface runoff. If the structural stability diminishes, infiltration decreases at the expense of runoff; the plants supplied with less water provide a lesser cover, splash erosion increases, and so on; the dynamics become increasingly destructive and evolution is toward instability. On the contrary, if the structural stability of the soil increases or if the plant cover provides an increased protection, the plants receive more water and vegetal output is less influenced by the irregularities of rainfall; production then increases together with the stability of the environment. Thus the margin between the two types of evolution in a penestable environment is quite narrow.

Human intervention, too, may be particularly delicate; it is a corollary of the preceding events. Stability of the aggregates and resistance of the soil to splash erosion are mainly a matter of agronomy, that is of the input of manure, lime and of the cropping practices. The same is true of the protection offered by the plant cover. Through pilot projects, that is experimentation, type of crops and tilling methods should be determined in order to better protect the soil or to withstand critical periods of the weather.

The management of penestable environments, therefore, is particularly delicate and requires reliable methods based on adequate research by an interdisciplinary team. Penestable environments are the rule in Mediterranean regions, former steppes, and in tropical lowlands with a long dry season particularly favourable to agro-pastoral exploitation. Care is needed; we must think of the morrow, which will come all too soon.

Regions with steep relief but with favourable bioclimatic conditions that allow the vegetation to restrain the morphogenic processes also enter into the penestable category; for example humid, not too cold mountains such as the northern Alps and parts of the Andes. But a combination of certain lithologic and climatic conditions may cause a serious risk of rapid degradation: ill-advised public works, particularly road construction, may induce landslides, which are difficult to counteract. A case in point is the highway between Trujillo and Boconó in the Venezuelan Andes, which cuts into the decomposed granite on slopes of 30°–40°. Landslides caused by it jeopardize its maintenance, destabilizing large slope segments. The scars opened up do not heal and evolve alternatively by sliding and by gullying with every new storm.

The various factors favouring instability intervene to a degree that varies considerably within short distances. They include slope, lithology, undercutting by streams, and certain types of land use. Risks of degradation and degrees of instability vary accordingly. Such factors may produce complex mosaics. Only reference to detailed geomorphic maps (see Chapter 2, p. 73–83), showing the locations of different dynamics, allow a clear understanding of the risks and can thus provide the basis for a rational, in this case delicate, intervention.

Two principles of classification should be combined into these two types of intergrade environment to organize the observations and to make a correct diagnostic:

1 The concept of the morphogenic–pedogenic balance should be used in the case of generalized morphogenic processes. A continuum is thus provided between stable and unstable environments. If inherited phenomena exist, the length of time that the present dynamics have functioned since their inception should be taken into account. This situation, of course, applies only to relatively stable environments, subdivided chronologically.
2 The double intensity–frequency criterion should be used in the case of localized morphogenic processes. Particular climatic conditions may trigger processes that are not part of the climax morphogenic system. They may cease to function after several years and leave behind only a few relict features. Depending on how quickly the climax morphogenic system re-establishes itself and on the frequency of the processes that are not a part of it, all transitions between unstable regions affected by localized processes and stable regions previously unstable are assured. The main processes in question are slumps, avalanches and torrential floods. It should be noted that the return to stability is not necessarily simultaneous for all processes. In this case, too, there are phase differences. For example, during the exceptional spate of the Guil River in June 1957, avalanches of half-melted snow caused the appearance of slope scars that have since been recolonized by plants and, for the most part, stabilized. They are becoming inherited forms. On the other hand, the dynamics of the river itself have been completely changed. A series of obstructions by tree trunks, by sediment masses of affluent torrents, and the rupture of some of these obstacles, especially bridges, that caused jams of tree trunks, have

EDINBURGH UNIVERSITY LIBRARY
WITHDRAWN
UNIV. EDINBURGEN.

caused the deposition of extensive gravel beds in the valley bottom. Pastures have disappeared and the stable bed with a single channel has been replaced by braided channels. They still persist but are gradually being stabilized where the bed has been neither cleared nor diked in. A pioneering vegetation, mainly of willows, has grown on the gravel beds. These are residual forms that still function, but at a much reduced rate, becoming decrepit. The stabilization of the valley bottom is therefore lagging behind that of the mountain sides. The morphogenic system that existed prior to the spate has already been re-established on the slopes, while the dynamics of the Guil are still different from what they were before 1957. To take such phase differences into account is of the utmost importance in the development of the land. A vast sum of money could have been saved in the reconstruction of the roads had this been admitted by the engineer in charge of road and bridge construction (Tricart 1961a; 1974d).

CONCLUSION

Our intent in this chapter has been to show the progress that has been made in the concept of an integrated study of the natural environment. The method of the 'land systems', as practised by interdisciplinary teams of the CSIRO, is a physiognomic description that has not received sufficient reflection to escape a certain routine empiricism, which limits its usefulness. It can be applied only to reconnaissance, on a small cartographic scale, of little known regions, so that it does not fit the needs of a rational, rural land management.

The concept 'landscape', as forged by naturalist geographers, has gone through a juncture of atomization of scientific thought in eastern Europe. When the time came it proved capable of incorporating the ecologic approach and thus could be used in an integrated analysis of the environment. In this way it provides a framework for research in the universities of the Soviet Union, the former German Democratic Republic, and Poland. In France certain biogeographers such as Deffontaines and G. Bertrand have worked along similar lines. G. Bertrand and Dollfus (1973a) have shown that the analysis of landscapes can be done from the stage of reconnaissance onwards in countries that remain to be explored on the scientific level, such as Nepal. This method, which, like those of eastern Europe, has recourse to systems analysis, is clearly more elaborate than that of the CSIRO, for which it can be substituted.

The link between the study of the physical environment and ecology permits a further progress through a unification of concepts and methodologic approaches. We have attempted to do this by considering the *natural environment* as a system within which the various types of phenomena that are the object of specialized disciplines are but subsystems. Ecology, as observed by Labeyrie (1975), is not a specific science. Like history and geography it presents a point of view applicable in various branches of knowledge. 'Ecologic research by nature is interdisciplinary; its field is transdisciplinary.' Our object is to combine both ecologic and geographic 'points of view' in a single *ecogeography*. We make use of the tools forged in physiology: balance sheets and flows, which structure the ecosystem and determine its dynamics; and we apply them to the natural environment in the same way as they were originally applied to biocenoses.

The characteristics of the environment, an interface between the atmosphere and the lithosphere, should be based on the manner it undergoes changes, that is on its degree of stability. This conception leads to the rediscovery of the common denominator of the fields of ecology, pedology and physical geography. Changes in the interface reflect the interactions of the internal and external forces. Our conception permits the raising of ecogeography to higher taxonomic levels, as required by a scientific approach. By adopting this orientation, we hope to make a contribution to the ambitious International Geosphere–Biosphere Programme.

The dynamics of the environment, governed by the interactions of the internal and external forces, first of all involve the morphogenic processes. Indeed, the energy by which they are induced has its source both within the Earth and without it in the solar system. These morphogenic processes interact with the other components of the natural system, mainly the pedogenic ones. We shall now study them in some detail to understand their interactions.

Plate 13 Spontaneous tendency towards phytostabilization of gullies
Ph. JT CDLXXXVII-11 cn. Between Talca and San Fernando, Chile.

2 THE GEOMORPHOLOGICAL APPROACH

The object of geomorphology is the study of the terrestrial relief and its explanation. That every modification of this relief implies a flux of material is self-evident. Some of the forms are enormous and account for the differentiation of the Earth's surface into continents and ocean basins. A contracting or an expanding Earth, isostasy, continental drift, plate tectonics and sea-floor spreading are so many hypotheses that try to account for the geophysical and geological observations. These theories, which attempt to explain the major traits of the Earth's relief, are of interest to geomorphology, but are not its main object. Their study must needs be interdisciplinary. The differentiation of relief that results from crustal movements is, because of the pull of gravity, one of the main sources of energy in morphogenesis. The characteristics of the material that is moved and deposited reflect on the morphogenic processes. The external dynamics, which begin with weathering, manifest themselves by flows of material highly influenced by the *biosphere*. Study of these flows, indispensable in geomorphological studies, is not their exclusive domain either. Interdisciplinarity is the only attitude possible that can resolve the contradiction between the unity of natural phenomena and the division of knowledge into separate disciplines.

Study of the geomorphological aspects of the dynamics of Nature assures the link between phenomena studied by the Earth and Life sciences. The reasoned description of the relief normally follows the measurement of its geometric features and its examination on aerial photographs. This aspect, which remained static owing to the epoch of its implementation, is the basis of the method of 'land systems' of the CSIRO, which proceeds from the physiography. Since then, progress realized in the study of processes permits further improvements. The static aspect of physiography remains valid but, presently, insufficient. It should be supplemented by a dynamic approach, which permits a better understanding of Nature and, moreover, is the only one adequate for the rational development of the land. We have shown how such

a conception can provide an integrated method of study of the natural environment. Regardless of the considerable progress in methodological concepts and knowledge since about 1950, the place of the phenomena studied by geomorphology remains the same; it is the starting-point of inventories of ecologic resources and basic to the knowledge of natural systems.

In this chapter we shall study the modern concepts of geomorphology, its methods of research, and how the contributions of this science fit into ecogeographic studies.

BASIC CONCEPTS OF GEOMORPHOLOGY

For a long time geomorphology was a split discipline, which hampered its development. This stemmed from two currents of thought that ignored each other too long. Civil engineers, and later foresters, called upon to intervene in natural phenomena have routinely made observations preliminary to their actions. Occasionally, they even made generalizations. Leonardo da Vinci drew a relationship between the size of valleys and their streams. M. Brémontier, observing dunes, developed a biological method to stabilize them. A. Surell, a civil engineer during the reign of King Louis-Philippe of France, by repairing roads washed out by torrents gathered observations that allowed him to formulate principles dealing with the action of torrents. However, geologists, from the birth of their discipline, were led to look for the agents responsible for the accumulation of deposits and the particularities of their disposition. At the end of the eighteenth century the Genevan H. B. de Saussure and, during the course of the first half of the nineteenth century, L. Agassiz, another Swiss, deduced from the identification of moraines an ancient extension of the glaciers of the Alps – a feat later repeated by Agassiz in North America, where the disparity with present glaciers is enormous. The concept of 'glaciation' was born. Sir Ch. Lyell, the great Scottish geologist, in the same epoch, writes about weathering phenomena in his *Principles of Geology* and formulates the concept of 'actualism' that only actually observed phenomena should be applied to geological explanations; therefore, that reference be made to currently observable dynamics. Half a century later, in France, the collaboration of a topographer, General G. D. de la Noé, and a geologist, E. de Margerie, resulted in a model of structural geomorphology based on the plateau and folded Jura Mountains. A little later, at the end of the nineteenth century, W. M. Davis, who had started out with studies in meteorology, botany and astronomy, elaborated a body of doctrines in geomorphology in the framework of geology. His 'cycle of erosion' proceeds from the observation of an angular unconformity that separates the base of a sedimentary series from the structure of an old, truncated, folded mountain range. He thereby positioned himself squarely in a geological time framework. Although he recommended the confrontation of phenomena by application of his trilogy: structure, process and stage, the excess of theoretical speculations, helped by his eloquence, prevailed catastrophically over the careful observation of processes, which are admittedly not very evident. The second term of the trilogy was neglected. Thus is explained the physiographic conception of geomorphology, that is its regional application, as perfectly expressed in W. W. Atwood's *Physiographic Provinces of North America* (1940) and E. Raisz's extraordinary hand-drawn, small-scale physiographic diagrams of the United States and other parts of the world.

During the same period, in central Europe, research generally followed a different course. If W. Penck plunged into wild imaginations as theoretical as those of W. M. Davis, the majority of German geographers remained naturalistic. S. Passarge, who was a medical doctor, a geologist, and became a geographer, was the most eminent of them; he was an indefatigable traveller, excellent observer, and an original and deep thinker. His regional descriptions include narrations of processes that have not aged with time. In 1914 he published a geomorphological map, on a scale of 1:25,000, of the neighbourhood of Stadt-Remba, in Germany. Based on conceptions that are valid today, it was much ahead of its time but unfortunately ignored. This tradition was kept alive by a large number of scholars, such as A. Penck,

H. Mortensen and C. Troll, who published a remarkable study on periglacial mechanisms in 1944. On the whole, German geomorphology was opposed to the Davisian schemes, which had a great effect in France and spread as far as New Zealand, and concerned itself with a 'climatic geomorphology', relating morphogenis to climate. Its principal advocate was J. Büdel (see KiewietdeJonge 1984). Even though, in the beginning, the direct influence of climate on landforms was overestimated, and specific correlations were drawn between climate and certain minor forms, for example, polygons caused by diurnal rather than by seasonal freeze–thaw cycles, this approach presented the great merit of lending itself to integration with the natural sciences, especially ecology, and contributed to the birth of 'landscape ecology'. Seminal interdisciplinary links were thus established which was not the case in American geomorphology, which remained physiographic and somewhat hampered by inclusion in geology departments where it played a minor role.

This historical summary helps understand the present situation. Geomorphology has recently gone through a period of rapid mutation, reflected by a great variety of attitudes on the part of its practitioners. While some have tried to work with more or less satisfactory mathematical formulas, thereby furthering the practice of theoretical speculation, others have had recourse to experimentation, the most successful of which has been the frost splitting of rocks. In the United States important work has been done in fluvial dynamics, establishing statistical relationships between river bed geometry and discharge. Also field measurements and laboratory methods have become increasingly frequent. Still others, as in the related natural sciences, insist on observation, trying to improve its methods, as, for example, in geomorphological mapping, which, for them, is an incomparable means of analysis that not only records the facts but also permits them to be fitted into an ensemble at a higher taxonomic level. Laboratory analyses confirm the mapping. It is only after completion of this work that the information is digested and correlations are made with other phenomena. Although such different approaches and working methods have disturbed specialists of neighbouring disciplines who wish to collaborate with geomorphologists, the broadening of the spectrum has helped forge narrow links with some of them through the use of similar techniques. This demonstrates that geomorphology has been orienting itself in proper fashion on the conceptual as well as on the methodological plane, and that the 'splendid isolation' of Davisian geomorphology is now a thing of the past.

By recalling, in part, one of Davis's best ideas, but which he never put into practice – the trilogy 'form, process, and stage' – we have constructed the triangular sketch of Figure 4. The angles of the triangle correspond to landforms, processes and materials.

1 The *landforms*, the specific object of the discipline, may roughly be classed into forms of *dissection* (the only ones considered by Davis) and forms of *accumulation* (which he completely ignored).
2 The *processes* fashion the forms and are indispensable to land use management: for which reason civil engineers were interested in them even before the advent of the discipline. This aspect of geomorphology is called *dynamic geomorphology*. And, in so far as the processes are influenced, directly or indirectly, by climate, *climatic geomorphology* is a subdivision of dynamic geomorphology.
3 The *materials* are bedrock or transported regolith. The dissectional forms form mainly from the bedrock, whose properties, to be understood, should be examined. The transported regolith forms in close association with morphogenesis, whose *correlative formations* they are. The dissectional relief in the bedrock is the object of *structural geomorphology*, the aspect of geomorphology that stresses the influence of lithology and geologic structure on morphogenesis.

Figure 4 illustrates the interdependence of these three characteristics, which are only the different faces or, better, aspects of the same object, geomorphology. The triangular shape of the figure has an important logical significance. It allows the data of two different domains (angles of the triangle) to be confronted with the third domain, which permits a *verification*, which is indispensable to avoid a *petitio principii*, to be locked in a vicious circle, as in Davisian geomorphology in which gently rolling forms are automatically attributed and explained by the old age stage! This new conception allows stress to be put on flows of energy and materials, in a positive or negative balance, on work performed by energy inputs into the system and, therefore, on the performance of the system. This puts us on an equal footing with ecology. The integration of the natural environment is therefore possible.

The definition of a geomorphic unit in terms of

Figure 4. Logical structure of geomorphology

The two 'babuchka' triangles depict the causal relationships between landforms, whether aggradational or dissectional; processes may be either aggradational or degradational and the material either solid rock or regolith. With an adequate knowledge of two angles the third may be deduced.

form, process and material in fact only formalizes an attitude adopted, in certain cases, of everyday speech; for example, a dune is not just another hill, but a hillock built by the wind and normally composed of sand. But in most cases things are not that simple. Some processes such as soil creep or embryonic runoff are so slow that they cannot be seen. Others act sporadically, for a moment, without definite periodicity, after which they are inactive for a long period. This presents difficult problems, including those of measurement (to which we shall return).

But let us have a closer look at the three corners of the triangle or, better, their corresponding terms: landforms, processes and materials.

Landforms

Landforms have been represented on topographic maps since the *Carte de Cassini* (of the whole of France – scale 1:86,400) finished in 1789. They have materially contributed to the birth and development of geomorphology. Progress has been made since, nevertheless a topographic map still leaves much to be desired by the geomorphologist, who should complete it with another map, the geomorphological map, which will be examined below. Another, more original, procedure is that of morphometry.

Morphometry is the measurement of land forms. Supplementary information put on topographic maps to indicate spot heights, as on top of hills or scarps, are morphometric data. The Austrians had much recourse to morphometry around the turn of the century. A renewed interest was shown in it by the Serb Jovanovitch at the end of the Second World War. Since then it has received little attention, except as regards drainage networks. The idea was to invent indices and complex modes of treatment that were supposed to explain the landforms. The technique was unsuccessful for two reasons: first, whatever landform description, even quantitative, no matter how sophisticated, remains but a description. It does not go beyond the phase of a physiognomic study, which is only a form of apprehension, lacking any explanatory ability. Second, to determine a correlation between two morphometric characteristics of a landform is not an explanation either: it is still physiognomic. The use of a computer certainly eases the calculations, which previously took a long time, but this is only a minor aspect of the problem, as the result of the operation is inconsequential. Tricart experienced it when applying Jovanovitch's procedure to the eastern part of the Paris Basin. His mistake was not to have called attention to it in a publication.

Another common, and very useful, morphometric procedure is the making of slope maps from the contour lines of topographic maps. Such maps are valuable not only to developers but also to geomorphologists, as they provide information on gravitational energy in morphogenesis. The best way to express the value of a slope is in degrees from the horizontal. If desired, the sine or the tangent can be obtained from it by using a logarithmic table. Unfortunately, many pedologists give slope values in percentages, that is by means of the tangent of the slope angle. If allowable for gentle slopes, it is a necessity for very gentle gradients, such as those of large rivers, which are of the order of 1 per cent, but for usual hillsides it is inappropriate: a gradient of 45° means a slope of 100 per cent, while steeper gradients have values that increase exponentially.

Processes

The processes are more difficult to study than the forms. Only some of them are clearly visible: in general they are catastrophic, violent, but infrequent phenomena such as landslides, torrential mudflows, or major floods that change the course of a river. Many processes are hardly visible, insidious. Nevertheless they function and their cumulative effects over long periods of time may be as important as those of catastrophic effects over the same period. The sporadic nature of many of them constitute a major difficulty in measurements, as they imply a series of very long observations. Moreover, if the movements are infinitesimal, they require great precision of measurement difficult to make without upsetting the very area under study. Reliable numerical data are rare, which impedes

Plates 14–17 Examples of forms and processes
Ph. JT CDXXXIX-61. Mudflow at La Coma, Pedra i Coma, Catalonia, Spain. It can be seen from top to bottom. The density of the mud was such that it stopped on a still rather steep slope. It was generated by torrential rains in October and November 1982. Note the ridges around the tongue.

quantification and, therefore, the application of graphic techniques or a mathematical analysis of a geomorphic system. Formulating hypotheses or introducing arbitrarily chosen values into the process of mathematical processing to get around such deficiencies is dangerous; subjectivity is great and the representation one has of the phenomena is often simplified to excess. So then, what is the advantage of the procedure?

It may be well here to pause for a moment on discontinuities of all sorts in Nature, a notion exactly opposite to that of W. M.Davis, in which everything links up perfectly without a hitch in a well-oiled mechanism. Herein lies the whole difference between a rational, mathematical mind and a natural phenomenon subject to statistical frequency–intensity analysis such as the classed discharge curves of streams. (The object of a classed discharge curve is to show the discharge of

Plate 15 Ph. JT CDIII-14. Compound landsliding in marls containing salt, Romania.

a river (on the *y*-axis) during a certain number of days of the year: e.g. 10 days, 6 months, 365 days (these reflect, respectively, the characteristic discharge of high, average and low stage) shown on the *x*-axis (from 0 to 365, or represented in percentages: 0 per cent being higher than the highest discharge measured during the period considered). The discharge may be measured in m^3/sec, $1/sec/km^2$, or as a coefficient of the discharge, i.e. the ratio of the period of discharge over average (annual) discharge. The lowest discharge class ends at 100 per cent, its inferior limit. In other words, the curve is cumulative and shows the probability, for a certain period, that each discharge class, or a higher one, should be attained. Discontinuities suggest questions on work performed, about output of available energy. For example, a flow of dissolved products in a weathered, granite mantle of the humid tropics does not necessarily produce a modification of the relief. The morphogenic work performed is minimal. The rocks lose a lot of matter through dissolution, but their volume remains unchanged, as is indicated by the survival and disposition of joints, veins, and weathered crystals: they are as they were in the fresh rock. Such weathering is said to be *isovolumetric*. The loss of ions in solution,

however, is reflected by a decrease in density. As a whole, the mechanism of weathering, including the neoformation of argillaceous minerals (e.g. kaolinite), modifies the physical and chemical properties of the rocks. The result is a *preparation* without immediate effect on morphogenesis but that later, after a more or less long period, permits the mobilization of the regolith by mass movements, piping, and even by superficial processes such as creep and runoff. The temporal discontinuity is clear. The morphogenic system associates successive processes offset in time; preparation is followed by mobilization. In a stable environment, with reference to processes of mobilization, the difference in time is considerable, so that the weathering front can proceed in depth to separate itself ever more from the ground surface. The energy balance of morphogenesis is therefore very difficult to obtain, as can be understood from this example.

To apprehend now the rate of sporadic, discontinuous processes, measuring devices or reference marks should have been installed during the past century, which, of course, was not done, as our current problematics were then unknown and the sophistication of our present instruments lacking. But it is now high time to develop our

Plate 16 JT CDLXXIX-69. Fluted slip-off surface of a landslide, Galicia, Spain.

observation and to put our instruments into place, even though only future generations will profit by them.

Thus the obstacles that at present stand in the way of the direct study and measurement of processes explain why geomorphologists often have recourse to *sedimentological studies*, particularly of correlative formations. They provide an indirect way. Sediments abandoned by streams or deposited by wind present characteristics that are the result of the processes, mainly of transport, that have acted upon them: the *surface texture* of the particles (e.g. glossy or 'frosted'), their *texture* (size), *form*, and *disposition*, to mention only those that are most frequently studied. Part of the recent progress in geomorphology results from studies investigating how these characteristics have been acquired. Their study, taking into account an inevitable margin of error, permits deductions to be made concerning the processes that have caused them. Some attributes are rapidly acquired and provide information on, sometimes, fleeting phenomena – for example, the texture, which depends on the dynamics of the fluid at the very moment of the

abandonment of the particles at a specific depositional site. The fashioning of sand grains, usually quartz or feldspar, by mechanical action is acquired very slowly: under a binocular microscope it is still negligible after 100 or 200 km of fluvial transport, but can be recognized by its surface texture with an electron microscope. Once acquired, however, such an attribute is quite lasting. It may serve not only to characterize present high-energy environments such as beaches subject to heavy swell, but also to recognize evidence of ancient processes. In Senegal, along the lower valley of the Senegal River, sands, reworked during the Quaternary, have preserved the character that was bestowed on them at the time of their deposition during the Ordovician Period, 400 million years ago. Like chemists, we have at our disposal many reagents; our task is to use them advisedly. These methods, of course, apply to the regolith as a whole, transported or not. Study, too, of the weathered mantle may be revealing. Comparison with the parent rock will show what has been lost and what has been gained *in situ* by neogenesis and by transformations. Geochemists do not work differently.

The study of processes, therefore, is in large part carried on by use of sedimentological and geochemical methods. They provide an indirect approach which enables the reconstitution of phenomena that are difficult to observe. Such reconstructions are based on correlations determined by field observations, on the results of other disciplines, and occasionally on experiments. For a long time experimentation has played a key role in the mechanics of fluids. In geomorphology experiments are made with meaningful results only on elementary processes free of complex interactions, mainly weathering processes, such as the crystallization of salt, the effects of freeze–thaw alternations, and the percolation of various solutions on rock fragments. Actually, such experiments test only the efficacy of simple factors whose value changes while others remain the same. Obviously a large number of samples should be tested and the results analysed statistically. But when mechanisms are intricate or complex difficulties arise owing to the artificial conditions inherent to a laboratory. Examples of this are experiments that apply the law of similitudes to scale models.

Materials

The materials, part of the geologic structure, should also be studied and their properties *vis-à-vis*

Plate 17 JT CCLXXXIX-24. Upheaved toe of a slump, Mérida, Venezuela. The Pan-American Highway, bypassing the city, has been upheaved. The pavement has been torn up into slabs and rubble, which testify to the surficial movement of the slump.

the morphogenic agents defined. Geologic maps, particularly of the European type, stress the stratigraphic point of view, therefore the *age* of the rock units, which occludes the lithology, except for igneous and metamorphic rocks, which do not contain fossils. In contrast, in the United States, the stress is on lithology, that is on rock stratigraphic units rather than on time stratigraphic units. They furnish the criteria for the definitions of 'groups', 'formations' and 'members'. In geomorphology what is important are rock stratigraphic units. Age is less important than the physical and chemical properties of the rocks, which affect their weathering and their eventual mobilization, that is, ultimately, their dissection. The joints (visible to the naked eye) and fissures (microscopic) even of crystalline rocks are as important to weathering as the nature of the crystals and the proportion of their various minerals. They are, therefore, important to geomorphologists. These also should make use or adapt methods developed by others, especially engineers. Thus the Atterberg limits (plastic and liquid limits), classical in soil mechanics, provide useful information on the greater or lesser aptitude

of a slope material to start flowing, to produce an earth or a mudflow. But these limits are always determined with the use of distilled water, unknown in Nature. The team of the Centre de Géographie Appliquée, working in the Queyras of the Alps for the Direction Générale du Génie Rural was thus confronted with a contradiction. The material supporting a village was theoretically stable, while slowly flowing material was moving the village and dislocating its wooden structures. There was no denying the contradiction, after rechecking the procedure. Tricart then decided to use the irrigation water that fed the material, permitting its movement. The new Atterberg limits then obtained confirmed the instability of the material: once again we see the importance of replacing laboratory methods in the context of the natural environment.

Modern conceptions of geomorphology therefore require adoption of working methods similar to those of the other sciences studying Nature, including the borrowing of techniques from other disciplines, especially sedimentology, geochemistry, and soil mechanics. The results obtained thus become easily comparable and useful to closely related sciences, and progress toward an integrated knowledge of the environment becomes a reality.

INTEGRATION OF GEOMORPHOLOGY INTO ECOGEOGRAPHY

Geomorphology is integrated into ecogeographical studies in two ways: through the flow of materials and through the flow of life-giving water.

The flow of materials, and their effect on the environment, is often a limiting ecologic factor, as the example on avalanches (in Chapter 1) has already demonstrated. Another example of this integration is the adaptation of the reproductive processes of particular plants to the local morphogenic processes. Certain plants that are able to survive when buried or uprooted in the highly unstable environment of active dunes have an enormous advantage over others. When their

stems, part of underground rhizomes, become exposed by the wind, they transform themselves into leaves that perform photosynthesis. The reverse also occurs. Their survival is guaranteed. Actually the instability of the regolith is to their benefit. Of course, only a few species, even of different families, in each floristic domain are capable of such adaptations: we shall mention only the *oyats* (*Elymus arenaria*) of France, the *helm* (*Calamagrostis arenaria*) of the Low Countries, the marram grass (*Ammophila arenaria*) of the British Isles, and the American beach grass (*Ammophila brevigulata*). In each case the plant community is reduced to a small number of species. The flow of material at or near the ground surface of course interferes with the soil-forming process. It upsets the soil, lacerates, strips or buries it. Truncated or buried soils are more common than formerly believed. Their study should have recourse to geomorphology. These aspects of the interactions between plants, regolith, and geomorphic processes are of a dynamic nature. They were not perceived at the time when geomorphology still had a static, physiographic vision of the terrestrial relief. They

Plates 18 & 19 Preparation of the material for removal
Ph. JT CCCXII-39. Foggy coastal desert at Punta Chala, Peru. Differential granular disintegration of granite due to salt crystallization (haloclastism). Resistant quartz veins and thin aplitic dykes stand out. Corestones fall; the weathering process is continued on them.

Plate 19 Ph. JT CCCVII-37A. Granitic slope in a subarid climate, Chongoyape, Peru. Granular disintegration, exfoliation (producing rubble), and unconcentrated runoff washing away the fine material and causing rubble-creep are all participating in the degradation and fashioning of the slope.

enter into our integration of the natural environment based on its dynamics.

The flow of life-giving water in the regolith (part of which is the soil) includes infiltration to the water table, hypodermic flow, superficial waterlogging and surface runoff, and is also the concern of other disciplines: hydrology and pedology. Geomorphology contributes certain descriptive elements necessary to an interdisciplinary approach. This is not new, it was recognized and applied to the 'land systems' of the CSIRO. Every modification of the relief being necessarily caused by flows of materials (solid and fluid), geomorphology is concerned with the surficial materials, which may be the result of ongoing processes or relate to a remote past in the case of presently stable environments. To understand their formation is an *indispensable* preliminary to pedologic study, the dating of soils (mainly to determine the length of the present period of stability), and the mapping of soil units.

The integration of geomorphic events and the biosphere into a system was also, at least in part, attempted by Erhart in his theory of bio-rhexistasy, which schematically opposes living beings (bio) and

soil erosion (rhexistasy). In fact, the detrital flux is mainly slowed down by plants, as most animals, from termites to elephants, accelerate it as a result of stirring or packing the soil. As to 'erosion', it is hardly limited to the soil. Erhart's theory, therefore, characterizes to excess a major opposition between living things and mechanical morphogenic processes. With the above reservations, we shall borrow this idea, underscoring its dialectical nature. Proceeding from geomorphology, which plays a predominant role in the various degrees of stability–instability of the natural environment, it will serve as a starting-point to expose other basic concepts that govern ecogeographic integration.

The dialectic opposition biocenosis/morphogenesis

Because of its basic nature, we have already taken this concept into account in the flow of energy and materials and the dynamic classification of environments of Chapter 1. At this point we have to develop the concept, stressing the dialectic opposition between biocenoses and morphogenic processes.

The activity of biocenoses is characterized by two main aspects: biochemical and mechanical. The most general and visible form of the biochemical actions is the soil-forming process: by definition, a soil, in its edaphological sense, exists only owing to the presence of living things. They are the cause of its differentiation from the parent material. The soil is therefore a specific material as regards the morphogenic processes. The litter and the subjacent humus are totally, or almost totally, composed of carbohydrates, not of minerals. Only this material is mobilized as long as the entrainment of material remains sufficiently moderate. Its presence is a factor of stability. Some decomposers feed on it and transform it into soluble products, which modify the composition of the percolating solutions. As these trickle down to the mineral matter, they react with it. Also, various micro-organisms that live in the soil incorporate certain products, such as iron, permitting their migration. The presence of organisms and of dead organic matter modifies the chemistry of the infiltrated water and, therefore, the kind of weathering of the subjacent rocks. For example, the karstifying process, an elementary chemical, geomorphic process, is different when the limestone is covered by soil and when it is not. Other decomposers, such as earthworms, ingurgitate a mixture of mineral and humic matter as they burrow. They assimilate most of the humus and reject the remainder and the mineral matter toward the surface. Their turreted casts are therefore rich in fine mineral matter that comes from a certain depth and that are then incorporated into the humic horizon when they are decomposed by weathering or rain splash. Some of this mineral matter migrates with the morphogenic processes, such as creep, more seldom runoff. Indeed, earthworm burrows considerably increase the porosity of the soil, therefore the infiltration of water, which counteracts runoff.

This *bioturbation* (see Plate 11) or stirring of the soil by living things, is even more important in the tropics in the case of termites. These insects build structures of various forms with volumes of several cubic metres, even a hundred and more! They dig galleries in the soil from which they obtain the fine materials to build their nests. The voids left behind, as those of earthworms, permit the circulation of air and water, important for pedogenesis and in hydrology. But, like human dwellings, termitaries do not last for ever; they cease to be maintained

and become the victim of pluvial erosion. Runoff spreads its materials in the form of small fans around them, burying the upper soil horizon. The material is of different texture and chemical composition than the original soil because of selection and addition of cement due to secretion.

Another manifestation of bioturbation is windfalls. If during a storm the wind breaks trees, especially when covered by ice, the phenomenon is one of economic concern. But when a poorly rooted tree topples over, raising the mass of soil and rocks in which it was rooted, a windfall becomes of geomorphological importance. The newly exposed material then, like abandoned termitaries, becomes subject to the direct effects of the weather, which rework and spread it. The process, however, is faster because there has been no induration by cementation. It is surprising to find that windfall sites are not haphazardly distributed but located as a function of local winds and material that does not permit deep rooting, and that, in spite of this, agents of the French Office National des Forêts after each windfall always replant the same conifers, which are destined to become new victims before becoming exploitable. What has happened to the naturalist foresters of the time of N. Brémontier?

The complexity of such intricate actions and retroactions require a hierarchical ordering according to taxonomic level in the system and its subsystems. Firm, absolute assertions are seldom correct.

As to the effects of growing plants on morphogenesis, they have been sufficiently analysed in Chapter 1 (pp. 20–31), where we have seen that the mechanisms producing splash erosion and surface runoff are very complex, in fact, much more so than supposed by Horton in his pioneer works, in which only saturation of the soil was considered in the triggering of runoff.

In conclusion, the number and variety of parameters dealing with interception, splash erosion and surface runoff preclude any attempt at mathematical modelling. At best, the effects of rainfall may be summarized in terms of the factors of the energy balance of splash erosion:

1 *Positive factors*   intensity and duration of rainfall, poor mechanical resistance and little initial roughness of the soil surface, poor soil porosity, high free fall of the water drops, allowing them to reach their terminal velocity (absence of low ground cover).
2 *Negative factors*   the inverse of the preceding, including interception by the plant cover,

stemflow, dispersion of the kinetic energy of the water drops on the litter, and a humic horizon.

It is clear that if plants help to arrest mechanical morphogenesis, to play a phytostabilizing role, there are also inverted cases in which they promote morphogenesis. Their effects should be studied from a dialectical point of view, in the form of a balance-sheet, which on the whole is favourable to phytostabilization.

Certain adaptations therefore result from the dialectic opposition biocenoses/morphogenesis. The object of this analysis has been to show the influence of certain aspects of biocenoses on morphogenesis. But there are also cases corresponding to a link of inverse causality, such as the adaptation of a biocenosis to a geomorphological instability resulting from an intense and frequently repeated mechanism ('*intensity–frequency*' concept, to which we shall return). We have already given a rather detailed example of this in Chapter 1, as regards the struggle of plants to survive in avalanche tracks. This example illustrates the usefulness and the logical efficiency of classifying natural environments as a function of their degree of stability. It also shows the often determinant role of morphogenesis in this greater or lesser stability. Let us now examine other fundamental aspects of morphogenesis: the spatial distribution of the dynamics, their frequency and succession in time.

Spatial distribution of morphodynamic constraints: localized versus generalized phenomena

This problem has been discussed because the art of map-making does not tolerate any blank spaces. There is therefore no better mental guide to the spatial aspects of morphodynamic phenomena than to try to map them. Some authors use the term 'areal' to designate phenomena that affect a certain area; we think the term 'generalized' is more appropriate and contrasts well with 'localized'. Thus a gully is a localized manifestation of runoff, whereas soil creep affects an entire slope in a generalized manner.

A generalized phenomenon is mappable if sufficiently intense to produce distinct morphological characteristics: it is the *determinant factor* of the relief. It imposes itself as a geomorphological constraint in the ecodynamics of the affected area; a constraint that may be more or less important at the level of the ecosystem,

depending on the nature and intensity of other constraints, as determined in a systems analysis. Let us examine some common generalized phenomena.

Weathering, as well as pedogenesis, is a generalized phenomenon in its very essence. Even though weathering changes as a function of parent material, exposure, and plant cover, it is a widespread phenomenon. The differences, if the level of perception is too high to delimit each and every unit, can be represented by a mosaic pattern (i.e. a patchwork, a unit characterized by its structural heterogeneity; with a larger scale the components can be 'isolated' and mapped as separate units of a lower taxonomic level). Soil creep, too, is an easily understood generalized process. On the other hand, other processes pose delicate problems. Many geomorphologists have been the victim of incorrect inductions: having observed the generalized effects of a process, they have concluded that it functions in a generalized manner. To better understand the problem let us take the simple example of screes, the basic origin of which nobody disputes. Along a relatively straight escarpment with minor indentions they form a continuous deposit. Nevertheless, nobody pretends that rockfalls occur along its entire length at precisely the same time. No, they occur intermittently at different locations. The forms scree slope and escarpment are the cumulative result of so many rockfalls over a certain period of time. There is, therefore, a *statistical space–time integration*. To borrow an expression from physicists, 'everything occurs as if' the process were a generalized phenomenon. Nevertheless, a true perception of the process requires the observation of different individual rockfalls. At a higher level of perception the object of the study is the form *as a whole*. The individual events are integrated into a space–time that permits its statistical treatment: slope of the components of the morphosequence (escarpment = zone of departure; upper scree slope = locus of transport; lower scree slope = site of accumulation), rate of escarpment retreat, and progression of the toe of the scree on to the terrain it buries.

The case of surface runoff (overland flow) is identical. After a sealing crust starts to form due to rain splash, puddles develop in slight depressions between plants, where the impact of the raindrops has produced fine materials. *Embryonic runoff* starts to form as the puddles overflow, producing rills of water that are lost as they reach the emplacements of shrubs that have protected the soil from the beating rain. The result is that the whole area becomes criss-crossed by strings of water that do not meet to form a network. They form a (spatially) *discontinuous runoff*. With continued rain the work of splash erosion spreads, gradually reducing and even eliminating previously spared areas. The rills no longer vanish by infiltration. They now meet obstructions such as stumps, stones, tracing roots, etc. They split at their encounter, and, losing part of their energy, drop their entrained load behind the obstacles. But slightly further down they meet again, finally forming an anastomosed network. The runoff has become continuous. Exerting some energy it produces a generalized entrainment and removal of material. And 10, 50 or 100 years later, 'all other things remaining equal' (to borrow another expression from physicists), the same microprocesses, the same patterns still repeat themselves. But – for there is a 'but' – the spots protected by the shrubs have moved, some shrubs have died, others have grown where there were none before. Tracing roots are no longer in the same location, stones, too, are in different locations as a result of splitting, upfreezing, creep, solifluction, or the actions of humans and animals. The small outwashes behind the obstacles, the slight incisions lower down now occur elsewhere. In short, the rill network has been redrawn. The same microphenomena occur as before, but their effects have shifted. A repeated localized phenomenon can, given enough time, produce a generalized fashioning as long as it shifts location. Again, 'everything occurs as if' the land underwent a generalized fashioning process. The integration space–time is therefore justified. Is it necessary to insist on the importance of these phenomena on land management? A small amount of energy is involved in this example of *rillwash*: it is easily contained and the area stabilized. But this is no longer the case when the flow of water has sufficiently converged to incise a gully.

The incision of a gully is one of the phenomena that creates instability in the natural environment. Like a slump, it has a different temporal structure. Beyond the head of a gully there always is a non-gullied area, swept by rillwash, just described, that serves as the watershed of the gully. This watershed has a certain surface-area, function of the intensity and duration of rainfall, the degree of slope, the kind of ground cover, and the porosity of the regolith. If that area is sufficiently large the *surface-area threshold of channelled runoff* is reached. It can be determined statistically from large-scale aerial photographs supplemented by ground checks. Its existence is confirmed by a minor

statistical dispersion in a uniform area. Gullies spread rapidly given sufficient slope, poorly consolidated, rather impermeable materials and a favourable climate, especially semi-arid. They spread by regressive incision and ramification at the cost of the original land until its surface has been sufficiently reduced to produce enough runoff to continue the process. The concept surface-area threshold of channelled runoff then reappears. The extension of the gullies is exponential owing to positive feedback. The gullies indeed promote runoff, speeding it up, which increases flood crests, whose energy is at a maximum, as the dissipation of energy by ground friction decreases with the concentration of runoff. In humid climates, deforestation may trigger the formation of gullies in the regolith and/or a favourable substratum, consuming the available area in one or several decades, depending on the size. Once developed we are in the presence of generalized gullies. The terrain is practically useless, even as pasture, so that the French pioneers occupying what is now South Dakota in the second half of the nineteenth century called them *mauvaises terres*, later translated into 'badlands', which has become a generic term. There are, therefore, transitions from localized to generalized phenomena without any change in process. This clearly illustrates the importance of the time factor.

The transition gully–badlands is discontinuous in time. By definition the stream flow of gullies is torrential, narrowly dependent on the time of rainfall. But it functions only when the rain has a certain intensity–duration, allowing the shower-threshold of runoff to be passed. Plants play a role in this. On the non-dissected land they produce a *buffer effect*, which is practically absent in the gullies, where there are few plants. The coefficient of runoff in the gullies is therefore higher, which increases runoff frequency and discharge, which in turn increases gully deepening and headward incision. Gully development, therefore, is subject to many positive feedback effects that allow it to proceed, as noted, according to an exponential law.

In analysing the development of gullies we have made a statistical transposition. We have considered an ensemble of gullies globally. If we change our level of perception and observe individual, specific gullies, things are even more complex. For example, a particular shower has caused runoff in some gullies but not in others. In the case of a thundershower, whose intensity and duration varies over short distances, this occurs frequently. Furthermore, the degree of ground cover and the nature of the soil frequently change in the watershed. The frequency and intensity of runoff consequently varies from gully to gully and, with it, the growth ratio of the different gullies.

The various parameters of gullying have been considered in W. H. Wischmeier's 'universal soil-loss equation' (1959). But as the equation is a simple addition of parameters, it excludes all interactions and feedback effects, which makes it too crude, invalidating its universal use. As the feedback mechanisms become increasingly important with time, the 'universal soil-loss equation' is close to reality only when applied to very short time intervals: a straight line can be confused with an exponential curve only at the point of tangency.

Other examples of forms produced by generalized phenomena are alluvial fans and plains, deltas, and aeolian deposits, all of which are built, or mainly built, at intermittent times. Most geomorphic processes, whether localized or generalized, are spasmodic, many are seasonal, such as mudflows, floods and avalanches; some that occur seldom and are of exceptional intensity are termed 'catastrophic'. They include floods and torrential mudflows due to exceptional weather conditions, including hurricanes, particularly large landslides, rockfalls, or ice avalanches like the ones that destroyed Ranrahirca in 1962 and Yungay in 1970, both at the foot of Nevado de Huascarán, Peru. These events, because of their catastrophic nature are obviously important considerations in proper land use, especially on the village level, in critical areas. Thus it is well to recognize localized or generalized external geodynamics and understand their periodicity.

Relationships between different processes

Even prior to the Second World War and twenty years before von Bertalanffy's 'general system theory' became popular, Cholley spoke of 'systems of erosion' in his classes at the Sorbonne. The word 'erosion' in this expression certainly and, regrettably, is used in the Davisian sense, but let us not dwell on it. For this reason Tricart, a student of Cholley, started to use the expression 'morphogenic system' as early as 1955, in keeping with Cholley's definition that the various processes working in a particular region interact with one another. In examining these interactions we must keep in mind two reference planes: space and time. Most reliefs indeed require a very long time to form.

Incompatibility and mutual reinforcement of processes

To speak of incompatible processes in the same morphogenic system appears to be paradoxical. Not, however, if the time factor is taken into account.

Let us begin with gullying and slumping, two processes that, in principle, are incompatible, as a gully is the work of running water and a slump is usually triggered by an extreme infiltration of water. Yet, frequently both processes affect the same location. A sufficiently deep and abrupt gully-head may be transformed into a scar left by a slump that fills the gully and, because of its narrowness, spills over its edges. This may happen after a long rainy period or a considerable snow melt on a slope with slow but persistent infiltration. Eventually the mass of water reaches the threshold that causes the shear stress to pass the force of friction, which triggers the event. The gully is slowly cleared by regressive incision unless the slumped materials reach its lower end. Then, if the obstruction projects over the gully edge, a new drain tends to form along its margin to eventually form a new gully. Thus the two fundamentally incompatible processes alternate in time as a function of circumstances, mainly meteorological. Their containment and the stabilization of the slope, for example to protect a road or a settlement at its base, is particularly delicate because of this very incompatibility. Any attempt to contain the gullies by channel-type terracing or construction of small earth dams in the gullies increases infiltration, therefore the risk of more slumps. To prevent them is well-nigh impossible. Even afforestation is of no use, as the role of the water uptake by the trees does not function during protracted precipitation, and that, when large, the weight of the trees is an additional burden that tends to reduce the slippage angle, which eases the triggering.

Antagonistic processes, as in this example, occur frequently. In deserts there is the case of sporadic channelled runoff and the effects of the wind. If abundant the sand of the beds of washes or wadis forms aeolian accumulations between floods. If somewhat incised, the channels trap the sands blown in their direction from the surrounding desert. The obstructions they form temporarily back up the water of the next flood before clearing them away. In this fashion aeolian sands may migrate down stream quite a distance.

Let us now examine a diametrically opposed situation in which two processes reinforce one another. This also happens in deserts with running water and wind. Salt flats, or sebkhas, for example, are closed depressions where water accumulates, but they also dry up. As the water evaporates, the materials in solution become increasingly concentrated. If sodium sulphate predominates, gypsum is precipitated on the bottom, cementing it into a hard crust. But if marine salt predominates, the salt crystallizes between the fine particles cementing them into aggregates. At the same time the crystallization produces a kind of churning that softens the material, as can be felt by walking on it, causing the foot to sink a few millimetres into it. The wind produces a certain amount of deflation, especially during daytime, because the salt increases the albedo contrast between the salt flat and its surroundings. Ascending whirlwinds form during the hottest part of the day, sweeping up the dust. These 'dust devils' contribute to dry haze, producing a light blue or even a whitish sky, whereas it is blue, often dark blue, when the air is clear. At night, the high thermal range of arid lands produces a high relative humidity. The suspended salt crystals then absorb much moisture, which weighs them down. And as the wind usually drops during the night, they settle on soil and plants, covering them with a veneer of sodium chloride. The next rain dissolves the salt and part of it returns by runoff to the salt flat or flats. Evaporation, in turn, concentrates it, and so on. Another part consisting of finer particles is transported away in the form of *aerosols*, and at night when the temperature drop increases the relative humidity, they become heavier and are deposited on the plants and on the ground, which becomes salty. But there is more. Part of the aggregates are too heavy to be sucked up by the whirlwinds. Instead, the wind sweeps them by rolling and saltation to the downwind side of the salt flat. There, the rim itself and a little vegetation increase the ground roughness and cause the deposition of the aggregates, the size of coarse sands (called 'pseudo-sands' by pedologists). A crescent-shaped ridge, termed 'lunette' by Australians, is built up. The salt in this marginal landform is, of course, again dissolved by rainwater and returned with the water to the salt flat, where again it will be precipitated by evaporation and so on.

These two fluxes are each characterized by a mutual reinforcement of the three major mechanisms that produce them: the crystallization of salt, deflation and the more or less distant aeolian transport, and runoff toward the salt flat. In the case of lunettes, we are dealing with an almost closed system. There, because of the barring

lunette less salt returns to its locus of origin but to other salt flats, if present. In Mauritania, where the trade wind blows from the same direction (the north-north-east) during the entire dry season, the salt dust blows from one sebkha to another in the direction of the wind and sprinkle with salt vast tracts of land located hundreds of miles downwind. They salinize the skimpy soils and accentuate the effects of drought by impairing plant life. This mechanism has had its part in the disastrous desertification that has afflicted the Nouakchott area and even the Trarza down to the Senegal River.

What is the ultimate origin of this salt? Part of it comes from ocean spray, quickly evaporated and transported by the wind. In Mauritania, this process is relatively unimportant for two reasons: the winds, at best, are parallel to the coast, but more frequently blow slightly from the interior, and the air of the immediate coastal zone, about 10 km wide, is humid because of cold water upwelling caused by the Canaries Current. In contrast, in Western Australia, where the wind blows seasonally from the north-west, almost normal to the coast, this salt of the ocean spray plays an important role, the more so as the rocks of the salt flat region are crystalline. (Why Australian pedologists refer to this salt of marine origin as 'cyclic salt' is not clear to Tricart, who paid a visit to the pedologists in the field.) The remaining salt, according to CSIRO pedologists, would be derived from the deep horizons of an ancient ferrallitically weathered mantle and the decomposition of soda-lime feldspars of the outcropping crystalline basement. Frequently, as in the chotts of Algeria and Tunisia, some of which function according to the sebkha mechanism, most of the salt, notably sodium chloride, comes from the folded, uplifted, and highly dissected Neogene rocks that surround the closed depressions, themselves of tectonic origin.

Finally, let us examine the relationships between two much more important and also different processes: pedogenesis and morphogenesis. They could have been examined under the present heading, but because of their exceptional importance we shall devote a separate section to them.

The morphogenic–pedogenic balance

Certain morphogenic mechanisms produce a generalized fashioning of the relief. Pedogenesis, too, is a generalized phenomenon. The two can be related. This is the object of the concept of the morphogenic–pedogenic balance; the following facts should be understood.

1 Pedogenesis proceeds *vertically*, from the ground surface down: for this reason the soil is characterized by a succession of horizons, parallel to the surface. This vertical development is shown by vertical arrows in Figure 5.
2 Morphogenesis, in the case of generalized processes, proceeds down the topographic surface and may be qualified as being *tangential*. It has been shown by arrows drawn parallel to the ground surface.
3 Pedogenesis and morphogenesis are much influenced by a common factor, the plant cover: no soil without vegetation; concept of phytostabilization. In general, the plant cover has an opposite effect on pedogenesis and morphogenesis: it is a condition of the one and it slows down the other.

Only intense and localized morphogenic events, often of the catastrophic type, more or less fit the scheme of Erhart's bio-rhexistasy: a lava flow, a landslide, a gully or a karstic collapse.

The very principle of this balance is based on the fact that the soil develops downward, without however passing a certain limit (2–3 m for the thickest monogenic soils), while morphogenesis affects the surface by ablation, reworking or by accumulation. Gradually, during the course of its evolution, the soil acquires well-differentiated horizons and, sometimes, particular characteristics. This will be examined in greater detail in Chapter 3 when dealing with the pedogenic approach.

The morphogenic–pedogenic balance varies according to morphodynamic sites. First, on a *level surface not subject to accumulation*, for example on a plateau, detrital fluxes are nil. They therefore cannot prevent plant growth or pedogenesis. Good drainage is assured if the substratum remains permeable over the first few metres. The soils then evolve without constraint and, after a certain period, depending upon the case, acquire their modal, that is their 'typical' or 'normal' characteristics, which correspond to the statistical mode of a frequential analysis. Nevertheless, a certain mixing of the soil by earthworms, by windfalls in forested regions, especially on exposed sites, such as a plateau margin, and, in the tropics, by termitaries and their evolution may take place. Also in cold, periglacial, regions geliturbation produces a thorough and generalized mixing of materials.

Second, on a *slope subject to export of material*

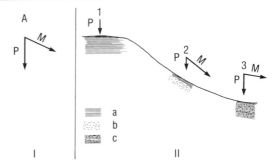

Figure 5. The morphogenic–pedogenic balance

I Principle of the balance
  A hypothetical slope is shown by a fine line. At some point, A, the balance is represented by two vectors whose lengths are proportional to the forces involved.

M stands for morphogenesis which works down the slope
P stands for pathogenesis which works perpendicularly from the ground surface downward

II Illustration: types of balance along a catena
  a Upper soil horizon with organic matter
  b Lower, mineral soil horizons
  c Poorly differentiated soil horizons

In 1, on the plateau, the absence of slope eliminates runoff, soil creep, etc. Aeolian deflation is the only process that could occur, but the vegetal cover prevents it. Transport by a morphogenic process is therefore non-existent, consequently no M vector. A deep soil with well-differentiated horizons forms as a result of pedogenic factors unimpeded by any morphogenic factor.

In 2, on the slope, morphogenesis becomes important, as shown by a long M vector. A good part of the water runs off and therefore does not participate in the soil forming process; the vector is therefore short. The balance tips in favour of morphogenesis. The soil is not very thick and its horizons are thinner than on the plateau; it is also less evolved, which the diagram is unable to show without colours. Morphogenesis produces a certain amount of superficial truncation of the soil, which may proceed to the complete elimination of the upper horizon during periods of heavy runoff, but which reforms later during periods of stability.

In 3, at the bottom of the slope, affected by colluviation, morphogenesis remains intense owing to input of materials by runoff from above. But the gentle slope favours the infiltration not only of rainwater but also of surface runoff, which in turn favours pedogenesis: the P vector is long, longer than under the plateau. But the soil, although thick, does not show a good differentiation of horizons because colluviation (morphogenesis) interferes with pedogenesis. During episodes of heavy runoff the soil on the upper slope is truncated down to the mineral horizon, which, reworked, forms part of the colluvium. During periods of less runoff, the input of material on the lower slope is mainly of organic origin (such as fragments of litter), which is deposited on the previously accumulated material. In that way organic matter is intermixed with mineral matter along the entire profile. An important fraction of this soil has undergone an initial pedogenesis on the slope, followed by transport and a renewed pedogenesis after deposition.

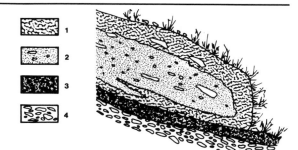

Figure 6. Burying of a soil by a solifluction lobe, Chamberton Massif, French Alps

1. Entrained A horizon of the lobe
2. Entrained and kneaded C horizon of the lobe
3. *In situ* A horizon
4. *In situ* C horizon

The soil, a high altitude ranker (Kubiena classif.), is mainly composed of a humic horizon, *in situ* ahead of the lobe and entrained on top of the lobe, which has not been deformed. The slow movement of the lobe does not prevent the ranker to form, as herbaceous vegetation grows at its surface (the site is at about 2200 m elevation, above the tree line). The mass of the soliflucted material undergoes a kneading as it moves forward and eventually overturns, burying the *in situ* soil and producing an inversed ranker between two ranker profiles.

Lautridou J-P (1984) *Le Cycle périglaciaire pléistocène en Europe du Nord-Ouest et plus particulièrement en Normandie*, PhD thesis, University of Caen, Centre de Géomorphologie du CNRS, Caen. Reproduced in Pissart A (1987) *Géomorphologie périglaciaire*, Belgische Franqui Leerstoel. Rijksuniv. Gent, Fak. Wetenschappen.

there is removal of the upper part of the soil and frequently mixing. The modalities of the one or the other depend on the acting processes and, to a large degree, on the amount of gravitational energy, factor of the slope angle. Some authors believe that the gravitational energy is a factor of the sine of the slope, but this remains to be demonstrated. Soil creep, which proceeds at a rate of a few centimetres per year and affects a decimetric layer only, decreasing with depth, is responsible for a slow beheading of the soil, particularly effective on slow-forming soils. Runoff, too, frequently affects the litter and sometimes the humic horizon below. In both cases the result is a reduction of organic matter, the cause of pedogenesis. The soil-forming process is thereby reduced, the horizons thinned, and the profile impoverished. Depending on the balance being examined, the B horizon may be slowly transformed into A horizon, producing a 'polyphased' aspect on top of the 'old' B horizon. On slopes lacking organic horizons, rillwash beheads the mineral horizons and, often, rapidly liquidates the entire soil. The balance, then, is strongly negative from the pedogenic point of view. Solifluction affects pedogenesis in a more complex way, as it is less generalized, frequently even localized. In cold regions solifluction tongues and lobes, for example, push their leading edge over organic soil horizons, which fold under as a rug (Figure 6). Such organic, peaty horizons are quite old and evolve very slowly: some in the Canadian Arctic have been dated as being 4,000–5,000 years old. In temperate climates solifluction lobes and slumps mix horizons to the point that soils are no longer soils in the 'classical' sense, but pedogenized materials lacking horizonation.

Third, on a site of *accumulation at the foot of a slope*, colluvium is deposited. The materials, fine by definition, have been entrained by creep or runoff from the surficial horizons higher upslope,

which as a result have been truncated. The material, depending on the depth reached by ablation, consists either of litter or of a mixture of litter and organic matter and, if the truncation is deep, of leached mineral matter from the A_2 horizon. In extreme cases the B horizon is also affected; in that case there is little or no soil left on the slope. The upper part of the soil at the colluvial site has therefore been enriched by a more or less rapid and abundant influx of a mixture of pedogenized and mineral materials, which are further mixed by bioturbation. Such conditions are unfavourable to the development of horizons and, in extreme cases, such soils have much in common with plateau soils subject to considerable mixing. If the influx is less diversified and composed of litter and humus only, there is much enrichment of organic matter in relation to that which is provided by the local vegetation. The humic horizons are then excessively developed but poorly differentiated in relation to the modal soil. The abundance of the organic matter induces the proliferation of decomposers, especially earthworms, which again increase bioturbation. This analysis shows that the concept of the morphogenic–pedogenic balance is an enrichment of the catena concept. This enrichment results from replacing the static concept of topography by the dynamic one of morphogenesis.

Fourth, on sites of *aeolian or fluvial accumulation* the situation is different because the influx of material from sometimes very distant locations (hundreds and even thousands of kms) does not include vegetal debris or organic matter. We shall leave out dunes and the beds of stream channels, loci of intense dynamics ever subject to the reworking of materials, where there is no time for pedogenesis. Here we again meet the case analysed at the beginning of this section (and in Chapter 1) when we demonstrated the shortcomings of the theory of bio-rhexistasy. We shall deal only with generalized, recurrent accumulations, such as the deposits of floodplains, of aeolian loess, and of more exceptional volcanic ashes. Tricart has shown, however, that the ash falls of the eruption of Chichón, Mexico, in 1982, in a mountainous humid tropical climate, were entirely washed away by runoff in the following weeks and that the 'old' soil surface had been re-exposed (Tricart, Lopez Recendez and Cervantes Borja 1983). Nevertheless, in the meantime the soil had been chemically modified by the penetration of solutions containing ions dissolved by the water in the overlying ashes before they were liquidated. In most cases, however, volcanic ashes form a new, in this case, geologic material that killed the existing vegetation and from which the pedogenic process has to start again from zero.

Floodplain deposits as well as the loess deposits

Plate 20 Colluviation
Ph. JT CCCXLVIII-23 cn. Sierra de Guadarrama, Spain. A deeply, spheroidally weathered granite has been washed clean down to the corestones and weathering front. The colluvium resulting from this morphogenesis has been deposited in the small basin. At one time it was cultivated, but present socio-economic conditions (higher standards of living) have caused its abandonment. The evolution is the result of a climatic change from wet, warm enough to allow a deep weathering, to a periglacial cold, without phytostabilization, allowing the ablation of the material by a generalized runoff. These conditions prevailed for a long time and affected, in part, pedogenized materials; they do not fit H. Erhart's theory of bio-rhexistasy.

Plate 21 Tor
Ph. JT CDVI-2. A tor in Monts de la Margeride, Auvergne, France. The weathering front has been exposed. The cluster of boulders coincides with more resistant granitic material, probably because of wider jointing. These former corestones became rounded not as a result of fluvial transport but of spheroidal weathering. Some are still *in situ*, others on the surface of the pile have slid a few decimetres.

of the cold phases of the Pleistocene, for their part, relate to chronic phenomena. Floodplain deposits accumulate because of a decrease in hydraulic radius and the roughness produced by the vegetation, both of which slow down streamflow because of increased friction once the water has gone overbank. The dragged and saltating sands are thus deposited on the natural levees, while the finer material in suspension settles out beyond, the silts first, and then the clays during the waning flood when water starts to stagnate in pools. They are mixed with organic debris provided by the plants, whose productivity has been increased by the abundance of the water, and, frequently, by the nutrients it brings. From the pedogenic point of view the situation resembles that of colluvial slopes: there is an enrichment of organic material and more or less argillaceous silts in relation to the modal soil developed on 'pure' alluvium. But the differentiation into soil horizons is hampered, even totally prevented by bioturbation and the influx of materials. Pedogenesis, therefore, has little time to proceed before it is interrupted by a new flood. The morphogenic–pedogenic balance is definitely

tipped in favour of morphogenesis. As to loess, its deposition during the cold phases of the Pleistocene in central Europe, for instance in Hungary, was favoured by a continental climate with warm summers in comparison to the marine regions of western Europe (e.g. Normandy). Thus, the morphogenic–pedogenic balance was periodically modified with subordinate fluctuations in climate. With each cold oscillation, deleterious to plant life, but favourable to deflation, the balance tipped in favour of morphogenesis. On the contrary, with each warm oscillation promoting plant growth, pedogenesis, producing humic horizons and a leaching of calcium carbonate precipitated lower down into the voids left by the roots of steppe plants, proceeded ahead. About a dozen such palaeosols have been recognized in these loesses over a period of some 40,000–50,000 years. Such alternations of loess deposition and pedogenic phases also have been discovered in the very much thicker loesses of north-east China. Those of the early Quaternary, completely oxidized and including enormous 'loess dolls' throughout their profile, hardly resemble the loesses of central

Europe (Tricart 1985c). The large-scale scattering of wind-blown dust has actually been observed by T. L. Pewé (1955) in Alaska during the month of August. Violent winds at that time cause intense deflation on the emerged bars of the very broad, braided Yukon River. The dust cloud swiftly rose to an altitude of some 2,000 m. When the wind dropped, the dust settled in a generalized way over the subarctic forest.

Finally, the concept can also, with profit, be used *in relation to major climatic oscillations*, as, for example, on the lowland of the Pampa Deprimida of Argentina. This is a particularly demonstrative but complex case. Tricart (1972b), working for the FAO, showed that during the last dry period, contemporaneous to the last Ice Age and marine regression, brown soils of the previous humid period (pedogenesis of the last Interglacial) were truncated down to the argillic B horizon (B_t) and irregularly covered by a thin veneer of aeolian silt with a high salt and alkaline content (morphogenesis). The percolation of water during this dry period resulted in the salinization–alkalization of the upper part of the truncated B_t horizon, transforming it into a solonetz or soloth, depending on the type of soluble ions that had migrated (pedogenesis). The impeded drainage of the B_t horizon and the absence of slope (slopes of only 0.2 per cent draw attention as being 'steep') makes impossible, under present predominantly pedogenic conditions and a humid climate, any leaching out of the salt and alkali. This character, together with the adverse hydrological regime, has an important effect on land use. It impedes the penetration of plant roots deeper than 10–15 cm, which means that the land, which is used for pasture, is very susceptible to degradation. Two rainless weeks is all that is necessary to cause a shortage of cattle feed, and therefore a financial loss, to occur. This evolution, much abridged here, has been reconstructed by geomorphological investigation. Combining field and air photo work, a geomorphological map at a scale of 1:50,000 was made and later used as a basic document for a field soil survey and agronomic evaluation. As the study was carried out in 1968, no remote sensing imagery was then available.

The elaboration of the above concepts has been closely related to research in large-scale geomorphological mapping. Mapping is an irreplaceable method for the spatial analysis of the environment, but prior to it, the making of a legend has required a greater taxonomic effort than had ever been undertaken before.

Geomorphological mapping

The past misadventures of geomorphology explain an incredible fact: that the practice of geomorphological mapping took so long to appear. While mapping in geology, pedology and biogeography started as soon as they became individualized as fields of research, it took until after the Second World War for detailed geomorphological mapping to become organized. This happened, moreover, partly because of external needs, such as rural developments and the preoccupations of UNESCO concerning the acquisition of knowledge about the ecologic environment. Even today, most geomorphologists continue to ignore more or less totally the practice of geomorphological mapping and the contribution it can make to the progress of knowledge and of the environment. Geomorphological mapping is mainly carried on in Europe: in Poland, the USSR, Germany, Hungary, Romania, Belgium, the Netherlands, Spain, France, Italy and Switzerland. From there the method has spread to Argentina, Brazil, Canada, Chile, Mexico and Venezuela. American workers are almost completely wanting in this domain, while Europeans also work in Africa, South America and Asia. In China Tricart has recently seen a draft of a map at the scale of 1:500,000 for agricultural management purposes, a ridiculously small scale for such an overpopulated country with fields the size of a handkerchief. Another 1:1,000,000 scale map planned for the whole country has been under publication since 1964. In Brazil there are very few maps at a larger scale than the country-wide map of RADAMBRASIL/IBGE completed in 1982 at a scale of 1:1,000,000.

The International Geographical Union for twelve years has maintained, with support of UNESCO, a Committee of Applied Geomorphology that included a subcommittee concerned with geomorphological mapping. After many meetings this subcommittee worked out a doctrine adopted by most interested researchers. Some committee members thought of compiling a universal legend and to impose it world-wide. In fact, to normalize all signs and symbols is an error, as complex and extremely varied phenomena must be represented. To catalogue them all is impossible: new discoveries of forms and processes keep on occurring and will for a long time. Furthermore, signs and symbols cannot be multiplied *ad infinitum*. Adoption of a more detailed subdivision of certain predominant phenomena for a map sheet or group of maps may be useful, while, on the contrary, several varieties of less widespread and less typical phenomena are reclassified for greater clarity. What is needed is flexibility in the symbolization of phenomena. The choice of signs and symbols is less important than the conception of the map itself, its object, its contents, and the method used to make it. These points determine the kind and quality of the information to be found on the map, therefore, in the last analysis, its usefulness and its justification. That the subcommittee reached a conclusion concerning these matters was important.

Conception of a geomorphological map

A geomorphological map is the result of direct field observation combined with the use of aerial photographs and various types of remote sensing images. It is therefore the result of original research specially undertaken for its elaboration. It is a first-hand document that contributes to basic scientific knowledge in the same way as geological,

pedological, biogeographical and other maps. Such maps should not be confused with schematic maps illustrating the ideas of authors, which are not the result of specially conducted surveys.

A geomorphological map should provide an explanatory description of the geomorphological aspects of the terrain, placing them in their genetic context, which allows their understanding.

Content of a geomorphological map

A geomorphological map should present information on the following aspects:

1 *The geometry of landforms:* it is provided by the topographic base if it exists. Even in that case, it is not always satisfactory and therefore should be completed. For example, the following morphographic (qualitative) and morphometric (quantitative) data should be incorporated: the incision of small stream courses, the height of stream banks, terrace edges, escarpments, rock benches, and dunes. Such data are particularly

Plate 22 Interaction of pedogenic and morphogenic actions
Ph. JT CCCLXXXVIII-45 cn. Glacis dissected into terrace, near Novelda (W. of Alicante), Spain. The glacis surface is strewn with limestone float derived from higher grounds. This helps prevent the concentration of runoff, thereby delaying the dissection of the glacis by gullies. The glacis becomes a terrace above the braided stream which actively undercuts the terrace edge.

necessary on maps without topographic base made directly from aerial photographs.

2 *The kinds of landforms*, linking them to the processes that fashion them. Identification of landforms is made by stressing the relationships between forms, processes, and material and by having recourse, whenever necessary, to laboratory techniques.

3 *The kind of material:* regolith and substratum. The substratum is characterized by its lithology, degree of cohesion, structural attitude and, if the rocks are friable, by their texture. Stress is put on the regolith pertaining to morphogenesis, that is products of weathering, alluvia, slope materials, etc.

4 *The age of landforms and of materials* pertaining to morphogenesis. Landform sequences should be clearly featured, taking into account Quaternary climatic oscillations mainly. The same applies to the regolith, particularly if transported. On the other hand all the stratigraphic aspects of geological materials are omitted, as they appear on geological maps.

Making geomorphological maps

A geomorphological map, considering the complexity of the field of geomorphology, which studies a world-wide interface, is a complex document. Devising graphic legends for them is difficult and very time consuming. Making use of previous efforts of systematization, it took the Centre de Géographie Appliquée (CGA), in the framework of a 'Recherche Coopérative sur Programme' (RCP no. 77) of the Centre National de la Recherche Scientifique (CNRS) fifteen years to complete the legend of the Detailed Geomorphological Map of France. Success was finally achieved thanks to sustained efforts of various working parties and cooperation with the subcommittee of the International Geographical Union (IGU).

In the preparation of the legend it was necessary to use, in the most rational way possible, the various means of graphic treatment tailored to the object pursued. Inevitably different solutions were reached as to use of colour, tone, conventional signs, and recourse to special symbols. Whatever the results, the most important thing was to be able to dispose of an efficient and flexible instrument.

The various field parties each made their own legend. In that way they could emphasize problems they considered major and adapt their surveys to the particular aspects of the environment under investigation. The large-scale Geomorphological Map of France (RCP legend) went very far in this respect. Its legend has been the object of a particularly exhaustive effort, organizing observations hierarchically, dissecting the various aspects of the objects studied in the field, and then recomposing them graphically on the map. The legend is based on precise criteria of identification adapted to field-work. It offers a guide to research and an intellectual rigour beneficial to the progress of the discipline. Lastly, the legend is accompanied by a numerical code that permits data processing. This effort proved very useful when pedologists decided to define with greater precision the environment of soil profiles in the compass of interdisciplinary work. (The working party of the Délégation Générale à la Recherche Scientifique et Technique (DGRST) 'Pedology and data processing', which later grew into the International Association of Data Processing and Biosphere, 105 ter, rue de Lille, 75007 Paris.) They were swiftly provided with the data they requested.

The RCP legend is flexible. It grants each author freedom to include on the map data that are particularly relevant to him, but which were not originally foreseen. For example, on some Normandy sheets, Yvette Dewolf has made a distinction between calcareous and non-calcareous aeolian silts, or on maps of a dry region of the Venezuelan Andes, the CGA has shown several degrees of intensity of embryonic and discontinuous runoff.

Colours are used to indicate major *morphogenic systems*, such as littoral, fluvial, dry periglacial, dry temperate, dry tropical, and humid tropical for the Narbonne area of southern France. *Processes* and *forms* of these systems are represented by symbols, most of them scale drawings, some conventional, to indicate particularly important minor forms. This solution was adopted because symbols can be multiplied more easily than colours, patterns or tones; because it was expedient to apply them to the type of information with the largest variety; and because it provides a maximum flexibility and permits the introduction of new symbols whenever necessary. Symbols as for creep, unstable runoff, generalized or lobed solifluction, or scree have been so conceived as to give a certain plasticity to the map; they are placed, depending upon the case, parallel or perpendicular to the contour lines. They thus visually underscore the topographic base or make up for its absence. The *materials* of the transported regolith (e.g. alluvial silts, colluvial silty-sandy gravels) are shown by patterns in the colour of the morphogenic system that emplaced them, and the *substratum* in neutral colour patterns (grey, brown) to bring out the morphostructural units. When the regolith is less than 75 cm thick the symbols and patterns are overprinted on the substratum, otherwise they appear by themselves (see Narbonne 3–4 sheet in RCP no. 77, 1971). Symbols may be used to show a partly dismantled or very thin regolith (<25 cm) as, for example, the scattered siliceous rock fragments on the surface of the limestone plateau north of the Morvan (central France). These thicknesses apply to France, taking into account that soils usually have a thickness of 75 cm or less. This type of mapping provides pedologists with valuable information on parent materials.

Thus conceived, a geomorphological map is a basic document. It is not specifically designed for the needs of neighbouring disciplines or for development programmes. That is not its function. It constitutes a first step in a scientific inventory, which, if needed, is followed by a second step, that of applied research with a specific goal.

Nevertheless, geomorphological maps (especially those prepared by the methods developed at the CGA or by the RCP no. 77) offer a direct aid to pedologists. They provide information on conditions of pedogenesis and gather together all the physiographic data pedologists require; they also provide data on the kinds of parent materials and the processes that act or have acted upon them in the remote past. For example, a terrace is represented by the materials that compose it, its age, and its subsequent evolution, such as burial by colluvium, dissection by ravines, or refashioning by glacis. Each of these phenomena has influenced the soil-forming process. In the beginning, soil has started to form on the remaining original depositional forms right after the end of alluviation. Where, however, colluvial materials cover the terrace, pedogenesis may have interfered with the period of colluviation, after which it proceeded unimpeded. The precision of such a type of map is much superior to a physiographic map. Indeed, not only are the geomorphic units inventorized, but also their evolution is followed step by step from the period of their initial formation down to the present. Their morphogenesis is reported in detail. The processes have been analysed and the morphogenic system determined.

The first detailed French geomorphological map appeared in 1954. It was surveyed in the Senegal Delta by a team of the Centre de Géographie Appliquée at the request of the *Mission d'Aménagement du Sénégal* to help pedologic studies in the framework of a programme of agricultural development (Tricart 1956; 1959b). Geomorphological maps provide excellent information on the stabilty of the environment. They are basic to the method of dynamic integration presented in Chapter 1.

Geomorphological and pedological observations may also be associated to delimit units characterized by certain types of relationships between morphogenesis and pedogenesis, as characterized by the morphogenic–pedogenic balance. The results are morphopedologic maps (discussed in Chapter 3).

For the needs of good land management, specifically conservation, geomorphological observations may be presented in a special way different from straight geomorphological maps. The latter, of course, are very complex and include types of information not applicable to interventions; action requires greater precision on certain particular aspects. To satisfy specific demands, special maps are required, based on standard topographic maps when they exist, in the same way as geological or mining maps, but their legend, their degree of precision, and their scale are different. For instance, after the flood disaster of June 1957 the valley bottom of the Guil River in the French Alps was remapped, using newly made aerial photographs at a scale of 1:10,000, for the reconstruction of the main road and the reconditioning of the river bed. The same was done, at a later date, of the 110 km of the Soummam Valley in Algeria for land recovery, irrigation and channel stabilization (CGA – Coyne & Bellier 1973).

Justification of geomorphological maps

Such maps are justified mainly in two cases: for soil and water conservation and for protection against natural phenomena.

For soil and water conservation

The danger of degradation of cultivated land is more than a matter of slope and surface runoff. Splash erosion and heavy runoff may occur on slopes of only 1° to 2°, as is common in the clean tilled cotton fields of the irrigated perimeter of Repelón, Colombia. Similarly, near Machiques, western Venezuela, overgrazing causes severe sheet erosion on the soils of early Quaternary terraces when these reach a gradient of not more than 3°.

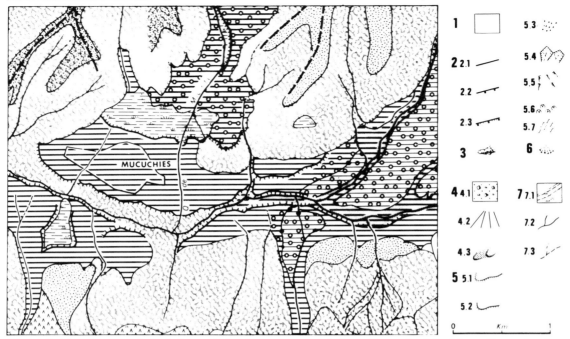

Figure 7. From geomorphological map to land use recommendations. Example of the Mucuchies region in the Venezuelan Andes

7(a). Mucuchies, Venezuela, geomorphological map

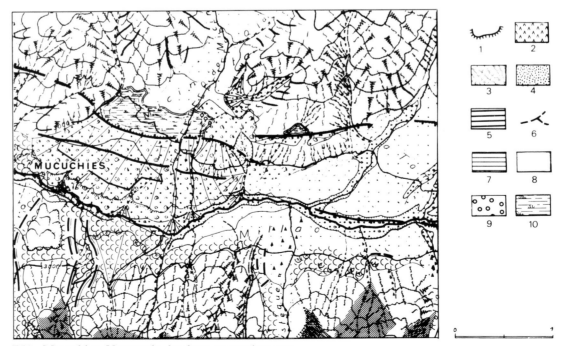

7(b). Mucuchies, Venezuela, land use constraints map

7(a). The contour interval is 100 m.

1 Lithology: granite; its resistance depends on its degree of weathering. The decomposed rock is very light grey, the still rather fresh but highly fractured granite is shown by hatching, and the fresh rock by rocky scarp signs and closely spaced dots (3).

2 Tectonics
    2.1 Fracture without visible throw
    2.2 Observed fault, down thrown block on barb side
    2.3 Observed fault with scarp, barbs on down thrown side

3 Scarps in fresh granite

4 Fluvial depositional forms
    4.1 Terrace, coarse material: sands and gravels
    4.2 Fine colluvium, may rest on coarse terrace materials (in which case there is superposition of two symbols)
    4.3 Mudflow deposits, rich in boulders

5 Fluvial dissection forms; mass movements
    5.1 Terrace edge, height > 10 m
    5.2 Terrace edge, height < 10 m
    5.3 Gullies, usually anthropic
    5.4 Badlands
    5.5 Stripping by stable runoff
    5.6 Soil slips
    5.7 Solifluction

6 Talus (scree)

7 Hydrologic data
    7.1 Marshy depression (of tectonic origin)
    7.2 Perennial or seasonal runoff
    7.3 Sporadic runoff

Moraines, rich in boulders, are indicated by half circles open to the right

7(b). A minimal number of symbols have been retained to give the map a maximum plasticity and legibility

1	Steep terrace edges, to be protected from gullying
2	Rocky and semi-rocky steep slopes, partly usable for afforestation and grazing
3	Friable formations (moraines, weathered mantle), steep slopes usable only if phytostability is assured (controlled grazing or, better, afforestation)
4	Fine material, danger of gullying; maintain in a state of phytostability
4 & 3	Superposition of the two symbols: discontinuous layer of fine material on an irregular, partly rocky, substratum; serious danger of degradation; protective afforestation necessary
5	Detrital deposits rich in stones hamper cultivation: only non-mechanized agriculture possible; gardening or arboriculture possible
6	Convex, penestable ridge crests, minor morphogenesis
7	Detrital, partly torrential, partly morainic deposits, but composed of fine surficial material, suitable for mechanized agriculture
8	Same type of environment, but subject to flooding (additional constraint)
9	Same type of environment, but well drained, porous material, suitable for irrigation from wells
10	Marshland, drainage necessary

To understand the risk of degradation, *all* ecodynamic phenomena should be studied in an integrated fashion.

    The American method of soil conservation implies that the only danger is the removal of soil particles by runoff. Authors speak unceasingly of 'erosion', seldom of deposition (e.g. B. D. Blakely et al. and W. S. Chepil in USDA's *Yearbook of Agriculture*, 1957) nor of deflation, in spite of Chepil's otherwise good work on 'wind erosion'. Thus the USDA has recommended the use of 'channel terraces', a somewhat brutal method that destroys soils and often causes widespread damage. Seldom do channel terraces, especially after several years, prevent overflow during heavy showers. They concentrate the runoff, which rapidly cuts gullies. At other times the water, infiltrating, causes argillaceous materials to reach the liquid state, triggering destructive mass movements, as Morocco, in the Rif Mountains, as well as Tunisia, sadly experienced, having adopted the method soon after independence.

The Wischmeier09soil-loss equation only treats of runoff. But frequently wind action is added to that of water, as in much of the Middle West and West of the United States. Tricart observed the effects of both runoff and deflation on Quaternary palaeosols in Mali (between 14° and 15° N and 5° and 7° W). The entire tilled A horizon (about 30 cm thick) had been washed or blown away during a single sorghum or millet-growing season. In places this sandy–loamy material was trapped by the fences of cut branches with which peasants protect their fields from wandering cattle, sheep or goats. Slopes of only 2° were suffering from incipient, discontinuous gullying. The cause of such high susceptibility to entrainment is that we are dealing here with a palaeosol with a B horizon that lacks pore permeability and hardens so much that a pickaxe is needed for sampling.

With regard to soil conservation, maps should, besides slope angles, provide information on lithology, certain soil characteristics, especially sealing, and morphogenic processes. If pertinent, they should also show the provenance of sediments capable of filling-in a reservoir. In that case, they should be completed with the location of in-transit deposits, that is sediments temporarily stored along stream courses by interruption of the flow of material, but to be eventually re-entrained by future spates, as has been done by the Centre de Géographie Appliquée in the study of the Soummam Basin (mentioned above).

The importance of a detailed geomorphological map in connection with soil conservation and proper land management is shown in Figure 7, in which the geomorphological map serves as a base for a land use constraints map. After the fall of strongman Pérez Jiménez (1958), the democratic government of Venezuela inaugurated a policy of agrarian reform and rural development. Tricart was called upon to propose new methods of land use and to teach them to Venezuelans in the high Andean area of Mucuchies. This place was chosen to grow fruits and vegetables to replace imports and to enable small-time peasants to make a living. Up till then sharecroppers grew wheat on the mountain slopes, causing intense degradation. Yields dropped to 0.3–0.4 t/ha! The maps, extracts

of which are shown here, are part of this investigation (Tricart 1964).

The object of the detailed geomorphological map is to understand an area whose use is to be improved; the original is in colour. Transcription in black and white, unfortunately, has forced elimination of the colour discrimination of successive generations of landforms or processes (actual, Holocene, Wurm, Riss, old Quaternary), but the lithologic data and morphodynamic aspects remain, which is essential.

The constraints map begins with objectives set by the government: development of fruit and vegetable minifundia. It represents an evaluation of the possibilities offered by the environment for the realization of the objectives by combining negative aspects, constraints and resources to be used for simple and inexpensive developments within reach of the peasants without any experience in market gardening. A stop must be put to the degradation of the mountain slopes in order to be able to cultivate the alluvial fans and terraces freed from the menace of torrential floods. Climatic conditions require complementary irrigation to increase the number of harvests per year and substantially raise yields. Special symbols indicate areas where peasants can dig shallow wells and equip them with motor-driven pumps, permitting low-cost irrigation.

For protection against natural phenomena

A good knowledge of natural processes also includes improvement of watercourses to combat channel migration and floods that threaten the destruction of cropland. Such fluvial actions can be controlled. Detailed geomorphological mapping in small watersheds on scales of 1:10,000 to 1:5,000 and even 1:2,500 provides much of the required basic information. Accompanied by sedimentological studies, specifically grain size curves and petrographic spectra, detailed mapping permits analysis of what happens during floods. Such maps show the exact disposition of alluvial bars, their material, plant cover, if any, channels, and live and sapped banks. This information is valuable to hydraulic engineers to plan their structures and in the preparation and adjustment of scale models.

The Guil Valley of the high French Alps offers a particularly demonstrative example of the importance of detailed geomorphological mapping, as the steady-state Holocene morphodynamics of this valley were extensively deranged by a two-day catastrophic flood in June 1957. An exhaustive

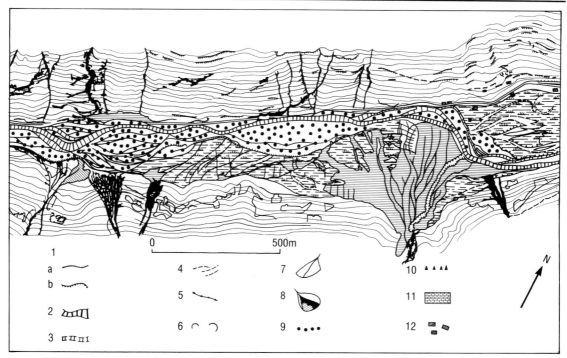

Figure 8. Restoration of the Guil Valley after the flood of June 1957

8(a). Segment of Guil Valley

1a Major undercut banks
1b Minor undercut banks
2 Incised river bed strewn with boulders
3 Abandoned incised river bed
4 Traces of channels having functioned during the flood
5 Gulch and minor stream incisions (in SW)
6 Slump (in SE)
7 Fans, partly covered by more recent alluvium, grown over by trees and grass
8 Fans; dense hatching when covered by mudflow deposits
9 Gravel beds
10 Deposits of boulders 1–2 m in diameter (in braided channel near W margin)
11 Limestone ledges (in NE)
12 Dwellings that survived the flood

geomorphological, sedimentological, and soil mechanics study of the valley soon after the event was made by the Centre de Géographie Appliquée at the request of the French Ministry of Agriculture (Tricart 1958; 1961a). Suffice to say here that numerous villages built on tributary alluvial fans inactive since the end of the Pleistocene (the New Tundra, to be exact) were destroyed and that three-quarters of the highway (RN 547) serving the valley was swept away and much of the rest damaged. With help of pre- and post-flood aerial photographs (scale of 1:40,000 and 1:20,000 respectively) the deposits and forms produced by the flood were mapped at a scale of 1:10,000 with a contour interval of 5 m, provided by the Institut Géographique National. The morphogenic processes set in motion included avalanches (the highest or north-facing slopes were still snow covered), soil slips, intense surface runoff and stream surges, the latter causing sapping of banks in unconsolidated deposits, and these again triggering, sometimes staggered, slumps. These processes uprooted larches, produced debris jams, some against bridges, and new surges when they gave way. New materials were piled up on the tributary fans; when sufficiently abundant, they forced the Guil against the opposite bank, impounding the water, causing it to drop part of its

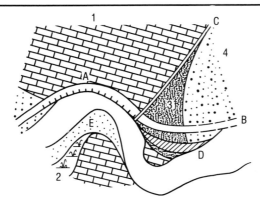

8(b). Petite Balme Gorge proposed scheme

1 Limestone	A Semi-tunnel and embankment road
2 Terrace	B Reconstructed road
3 Alluvial fan (dots)	C Channelized torrential stream bed
4 Scree	D Concrete flood evacuation channel
	E Alluvium of the June 1957 flood to be cleared away and used as construction material

bedload, producing braided channels, as happened downstream from the village of Aiguilles (on the east margin of Figure 8a), sparing part of the old valley bottom and its vegetation. The result was that coarse materials previously prepared by weathering and swept down from the valley sides, together with others already present in the Guil River bed, were irregularly spread or redistributed over the valley bottom. Many are unstable and their sites hazardous for development. Their type and distribution is important to know for the reconstruction of roads, villages and other structures.

Figure 8(a) gives an example of the detailed mapping of the deposits and forms of the Guil River bed and its tributaries with their fans over a distance of 2 km between Aiguilles and Ville-Vieille along RN 547. Figures 8(b) and 8(c) are examples of recommendations made for the restoration of the valley structures. They are based on the reconstitution of phenomena that occurred during the flood, on field observations, and on sedimentological studies. The geometry of the sketches is not accurate, as they were drawn in the field without help of a land-surveyor.

Figure 8(b) proposes a solution for the reconstruction of the National Highway (RN) 202, completely washed out in the gorge of the Petite Balme, about 8 km downstream from Château-

Queyras (km 6–6.2). The highway had to cross the lower extremity of the very active alluvial fan and to be protected from the sapping action of the Guil.

Figure 8(c) concerns the villages of La Rua and Ville-Vieille, built on the Aigue-Agnelle Fan, which in the remote past had been subjected to torrential mudflows. About 40 per cent of the fan's surface was devastated, both villages having become uninhabitable. The figure shows where, very close to their original sites, they could be reliably relocated. It was a preliminary project, but the recommendations have been accepted and so far the results have been good, no overflow or infilling of the tributary channel having occurred.

Also in planning new roads, irrigation canals, high tension lines, or the building of new settlements, factories and other structures a good understanding of the degree of stability of the land through detailed geomorphological maps is necessary. It is a matter of safety, sound investment and minimizing maintenance costs. To move vast amounts of earth at a site that may be subject to mass wasting processes spells danger to development projects, for means to contain them are few and, frequently, costly. Knowledge of the possible hazards is therefore an important factor in decision-making. If alternatives are out of the question, risks may be reduced by taking certain precautions as work is in progress and by the use of certain structures. Failure to do so may lead to abandonment of a road or canal under construction that has already given rise to considerable costs. Making a geomorphological map (of course, with help of aerial photographs) that covers a sufficiently large area will reveal past and present degradational geomorphic processes that affect a certain region. In Venezuela millions have been spent on Andean roads even before they became usable, as the landslides they triggered in deeply decomposed granite got out of control. Furthermore, they fed enormous masses of debris, mainly sand, into streams that spread the material over the piedmont plains below, burying the land in the process.

Regions subjected to earthquakes present special problems. Earthquakes cannot be prevented. The *direct* effect of the tremors can be only lessened, seldom eliminated, by better architectural design and building materials and by moving to safer sites. Only the latter is our concern. Safer sites are related to geological and geomorphological factors. Geomorphologists are mainly concerned with the *indirect* effects, whether immediate or delayed, of earthquakes that set in motion certain, frequently destructive, morphogenic processes, and with the

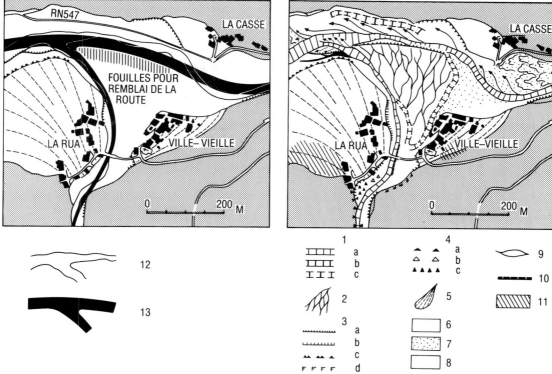

8(c)I. Guil and l'Aigue-Agnelle development scheme

8(c)II. Reconstruction of Ville-Vieille and La Rua

1 Incised beds
  a boulder beds
  b gravel beds
  c abandoned
2 Braided channels
3 Undercut banks
  a 0–1 m high
  b 1–5 m high
  c older bank >5 m
  d in bedrock
4 Boulders
  a 0.3–1 m in diam.
  b 1–2 m
  c >2 m

5 Old alluvial fans
6 Sand
7 Pebbles
8 Valley-side slopes
9 Scree
10 Gabion wall
11 Site proposed for reconstruction
12 Present stream bed
13 Proposed straightening of stream bed

fouilles excavations for road embankment

stability of certain landforms in relation to their materials and water content. As an example we have taken the case of the major Peru earthquake of 31 May 1970. In the framework of aid to the afflicted country by the French government, the Centre de Géographie Appliquée was called upon with members of the Institut Français d'Etudes Andines in Lima to make a study of the phenomenon in order to provide recommendations as to where to rebuild the destroyed settlements (Tricart 1973a).

The main *immediate* indirect effect of the earthquake was a formidable ice avalanche that in less than a minute came cascading down the top of the Nevado de Huascarán, the third highest (6,654 m) mountain in the western hemisphere, destroying the town of Yungay and affecting the length of the Santa Valley all the way down to the Pacific, a distance of some 160 km. This valley is replete with surficial deposits derived from the surrounding mountains. Besides simple slope regolith, these deposits, generally of Quaternary age, are of glacial, alluvial (including huge fans), and of lacustrine origin. Most of them have been

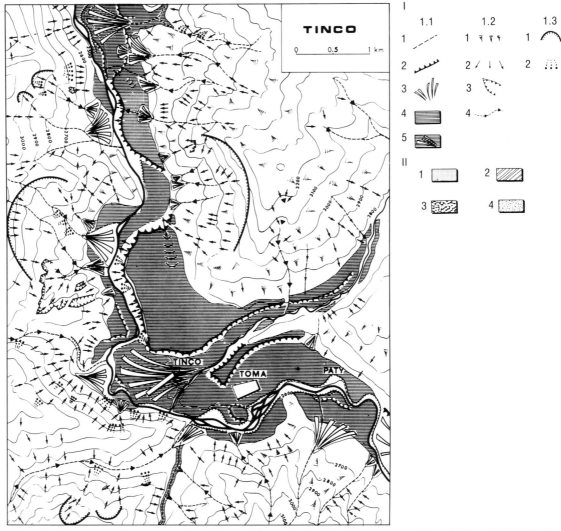

Figure 9. Tinco area, Peru: example of determining safe sites for the reconstruction of villages in the Santa Valley of Peru after the earthquake of 31 May 1970.

1 LANDFORMS
    1.1 Fluvial forms
        1 Incised stream bed
        2 Actively undermined terrace edge
        3 Fan
        4 Terrace
        5 Fan-terrace (fan symbol on top of terrace)

2 PHYSICAL LIMITATIONS TO DEVELOPMENT
    1 Serious, latent imbalance: high risk of mudflows
    2 Potential moderate imbalance: recent slumps ready to function again
    3 Permanent imbalance: niches and mudflows, intense gullying
    4 Minor risks: few isolated gullies, soil ablation by unstable runoff, minor lacerations. Areas left white are stable.

1.2 Effects of slope runoff:
    1 Unstable runoff, generalized soil ablation
    2 Small gullies, localized gullies
    3 Badlands
    4 Major individual gully

1.3 Effects of man movements and debris falls
    1 Slump scarp
    2 Scree

incised or terraced during a recent phase of the geomorphic evolution. They are frequently the result of catastrophic events, common in mountains. Ice avalanches are not necessarily triggered by earthquakes, but simply by overloads of glacial ice and a season of exceptional melting, as occurred on the same Nevado in January ('summer') of 1962. Elsewhere, high altitude lakes are in precarious positions, being blocked by glacial tongues or moraines, which for one reason or another may suddenly give way. . . . Either such débâcles or the glaciers themselves during the last cold period may have, in places obstructed the Santa Valley, impounding temporary lakes. The Santa Valley, more specifically the Callejón de Huaylas, has had a complex, unstable, geomorphological history. To assess the stability and safety of the landforms as possible settlement sites, the French undertook to map, with help of pre- and post-catastrophe aerial photographs, topographic maps on 1:25,000, and a helicopter, to the bottom of the Callejón, at 2,500–3,000 above sea level over a distance of 140 km and a width of several km from points below Huaylas to above Recuay, a simplified extract of which is reproduced in Figure 9.

At this point it may be useful to recall some elementary factors concerning the stability of geologic materials. Sands and gravels are poor transmitters of seismic waves, they are not very elastic and compressible and, therefore, like crystalline basement rocks, do not amplify tremors. They constitute relatively safe terrains. On the other hand, silty and clayey materials are elastic and amplify shocks besides being subject to compaction when moist. If interbedded with coarser materials (non-compressible), the whole mass becomes subject to extremely dangerous differential movements, especially when below water table. Along scarps, for instance on terrace edges in fluvio-lacustrine materials, as at Recuay, they may help trigger *delayed* slumps and earth- or mudflows, particularly in the presence of open ground cracks and in the rainy season. At shallow depth, as in coastal lowlands, differential compaction by shaking may locally lower the ground surface by ejection of the water, causing ponds (see Plate 46, p. 193). Deformation of the ground surface then causes walls to pivot on their base and crumble, as occurred in Chimbote, partly built on lagoonal deposits, whereas homes built on aeolian sands remained stable.

Settlements built on terraced fans at first sight appear safe from ice avalanches or the catastrophic emptying of ice-dammed lakes. The fans were built mainly at the end of the Pleistocene and incised later. Nevertheless, the ice avalanche of 31 May 1970, transformed into a mudflow at its distal end, overtopped the fan-terrace on which Yungay was built, burying nearly all of it below a layer of unsorted debris, although spared in 1962. Such locations are unsafe depending on the physical geographical conditions in the highland above.

The map of the Tinco area shown in Figure 9 (simplified for financial reasons) gives an example of the mapping method and illustrates other factors not mentioned in the text. The original map is in black, blue and red: black for geomorphological data, blue for hydrological data (e.g. areas susceptible to flooding owing to sediment compaction), and red for hazards related to terrain instability. The information on Figure 9 whose code begins with 1 describes the natural environment the day after the earthquake, that is morphogenic processes and types of landforms. The notations beginning with 2, corresponding to an evaluation of the potential stability of the environment with regard to sites for the reconstruction of settlements, originally in red (decreasing in intensity with diminished danger), are superimposed on areas coded 1.

CONCLUSION

Geomorphology participates in different ways in studies of ecogeography and the improvement or development of the environment:

1 it provides basic information with thorough photo interpretation
2 it allows the soil-forming processes to be situated in their dynamic framework
3 it defines constraints that must be taken into account by developers
4 it offers a principle of integration in ecodynamic studies that consists of defining types of environments as a function of their degree of morphodynamic stability. This facilitates the study of the other components of the natural system and allows a better integration of human activities.

3 THE PEDOLOGICAL APPROACH

To defend our position in regard to the concept of soil, its study and management, it is necessary to go back into the history of soil science and review the value of various concepts.

BASIC CONCEPTS AND HISTORICAL REVIEW

Although the concept of soil is an old one, the science of pedology is relatively new. The word 'pedology' comes from the Greek *pedon* (soil, the terrain we tread). But the soil is not just a surface, it extends downward a certain distance. How far? Soil scientists have often displayed a certain intellectual imperialism, which led them to consider the whole weathering profile as the specific object of their investigations. Such an annexation is unacceptable, as weathering is much slower than pedogenesis, and may not even reflect the same environment. The weathered mantle is in most places much thicker, especially in the humid tropics. On the Atlantic seaboard of Brazil, from Recife to Santos, and even further south, it commonly reaches 40 or 50 m, even 100 m. Also, the milieu in which it forms is different. For us (based on observation) the soil layer is the uppermost layer of the solid Earth, located at the interface of its solid matter and its gaseous or liquid envelope. Soils are closely associated with the distribution and evolution of the bulk of the biosphere. The flora depends on them, and the fauna on the flora. This definition reflects these observations:

The soil is the surficial layer of the lithosphere at its interface with the atmosphere and hydrosphere, significantly modified by living organisms.

This definition

1 includes subaqueous soils, recently discovered

2 focuses on the fundamental relationships between the pedosphere and the biosphere, drawing attention to the soil's ecologic aspects, including those which depend on humans (agriculture, animal husbandry and forestry)

3 includes the links between pedogenesis and ecodynamics and permits the integration of pedology into the study of the dynamics of the environment, its development, its management and its degradation.

The development of soil science

This definition of 'soil' reflects the concepts of V. V. Dokuchaev, the true founder of modern soil science, with a view toward its applications. At the end of the nineteenth century (before Dokuchaev's work) the study of soil was part of the field of *agrology*, whose object was to increase agricultural production. Its vocabulary was still crude, as it was that of a peasant, in which soils were 'light', 'heavy', 'medial', 'thin', and so on. Because of progress in the knowledge of fertilizers and the increasing spread of their use since the 1840s, agrology was for a long time solely interested in increasing the soil's chemical fertility. This was made possible by the work of J. B. Boussingault in France (plants obtain their carbon, oxygen and hydrogen mainly from the air and rain), Baron J. von Liebig in Germany (minerals), and Sir J. B. Lawes, founder of the Rothamsted experimental farm, in Britain (nitrogen comes from the soil; superphosphates). Simultaneously modern geology came into being. W. C. H. Staring in Holland and Ch. E. Risler in France pointed out the relationships of soils to geology. Their high point was Risler's four-volume *Géologie agricole* (1884–97); he classified the agricultural characteristics of soils in relation to stratigraphy rather than to lithology. His student, H. Lagatu, modified this to mineralogy and the consistency and porosity of soils. The work of these pioneers, trained as geologists (in its most elaborate form) at the time of Dokuchaev, resulted in agro-geological maps and regional descriptions of soils. In fact, this was not yet soil *science*, but a competition between agricultural technicians, geologists, chemists and physicists who had their own exclusive conceptions of soils and did not communicate with each other. There was no broadening of scope, so that the soil classifications and the criteria on which they were based never went beyond the chemical, physical or geological framework and were therefore unable to provide a basis for a comprehensive classification. The concept that the soil is a natural body with an independent existence, the result of specific processes, but belonging to the geographical environment, although surmised a number of times, did not become generally accepted until the work of Dokuchaev, beginning in 1879.

V. V. Dokuchaev, professor of geography at the University of St Petersburg, was ordered by his government in 1877 to study the soils of the Ukraine, then experiencing a severe drought. The object was related to practical purposes, but Dokuchaev observed the soils from a new angle, introducing three basic ideas:

1 The soil is a *special medium*, the result of a continuous process or *pedogenesis*.
2 The influence of *climate*, reflected by major types of vegetation (such as boreal conifer forest, mixed forest, steppe) is predominant in pedogenesis.
3 The main characteristics of soils can be derived only from the study of pedogenesis.

These ideas spread slowly. In western Europe they eventually replaced the concept of 'agricultural geology'. The First World War and the October Revolution paralysed for years research on soils in the USSR. Under Stalin agriculture was relegated to the field of politics, with its bloody collectivization. Later, the obligation of scientists to support T. D. Lysenko's erroneous theories were unfavourable to the resumption of Dokuchaev's geographic concept of soil science. This had to await until after the Second World War, under the aegis of Academician I. P. Gerasimov, another goegrapher.

The Russian pedological concepts, however, quickly reached Germany and the United States owing to K. D. Glinka's own German translation in 1914 of his Russian text on soil science and to the English translation of that text by C. F. Marbut (1927). The transmission of ideas was slower in France, in spite of many Russian *émigré* pedologists, but these were sent to Africa. It was only in 1952 that A. Demolon conceived the idea that the soil, situated at the interface of the atmosphere, lithosphere and biosphere, is the result of their interactions.

Practical necessities have played an important role in the United States. After the extraordinary boom of agricultural exports during the First World War, the drop in prices, caused by reconstruction in Europe, exposed the degradation of land caused by careless speculative farming. The Dust Bowl of the early 1930s helped enact Roosevelt's New Deal, resulting in programmes of agricultural diversification and soil conservation. Soil science was no longer considered as a minor academic discipline. The Department of Agriculture created programmes that led to the concepts and principles embodied by the Bureau of Reclamation (see pp. 107–10). But, at the same time, Davisian geomorphology reigned unchallenged. Its erroneous concepts had repercussions on the Land-capability classification, in which there is exclusive reference to 'erosion' and surface runoff (rillwash). The danger of land degradation is determined by the topography, that is the degree of slope. This empirical experience is at the origin of the *catena* (Latin for 'chain') concept (which became *toposéquence* in French). A catena is a soil sequence whose character changes as a function of relief. For example:

1 *Plateau*   water infiltrates, pedogenesis is intense.
2 *Flanking slope*   there is more runoff, therefore less infiltration because of the slope: pedogenesis is reduced. Later, the concept of 'lateral drainage' is introduced; a preferable expression is 'hypodermic flow'.
3 *Lowland at the foot of the slope*   again level terrain, infiltration, effective pedogenesis; possibly insufficient drainage, leading to hydromorphism.

A catena, as the name indicates, is based on the role of the relief, and the relief only. Its role is therefore *static*. But the relief is not given, unalterable. It is 'alive', changing, owing to processes it engenders itself and interfering with pedogenic processes. The catena concept, as such, is also based on another abusive simplification: it does not integrate differences in the soil's parent materials, whether bedrock or transported regolith. It actually represents a set-back from the 'agricultural geology' of the late nineteenth century. The agricultural geology was an intellectual product of western Europe, ignored in the United States, where the catena concept was born. The restricted vision of pedologists and their unfortunate tendency to ignore progress made in ' other disciplines are particularly evident in this concept.

The catena concept was improved during the Second World War by the aerial land surveys of the CSIRO. The soils were fitted to the physiographic units of the 'land-systems', charted by photo interpretation and later field checked. Although still static, this approach at least integrates the nature of the soil's parent material. While there is no progress on the conceptual level, it eliminates a major practical defect. This stagnation on the conceptional plane is due to the fact that the approach is entirely *dependent* on a single preponderant, virtually exclusive, source of information: aerial photographs. But these have their limitations: the mapping of soils from aerial photographs becomes the prisoner of these very photos. The same holds true for remote sensing studies, even if the information provided is more diverse (Girard 1986). The work, in essence, of the Netherlands ITC suffers from the same limitation, as its specific object is photo-interpretation and, by extension, remote sensing studies. On the other hand, the repetitiveness of remotely sensed recordings, by comparison, allows, another, *dynamic*, approach.

While the Division of Land Surveys of the CSIRO practised this physiographic approach, the Division of Soils launched a more novel approach under the leadership of B. E. Butler. This approach takes into account important elements of the morphogenic evolution and studies the soil in relation not only to its parent material but also to its *site*. The soil profile may display time units in the form of successive 'K' 'cycles of pedogenesis'. Furthermore, soils may be destroyed by ablation or by burial, by a regular influx of material, or a constant ablation can bring about a 'situation of equilibrium' (Butler 1959). Setting aside Davis's aberration of the cyclic concept, let us now inquire what is new about this conception:

1 The concept of *morphogenic–pedogenic interaction*, as restated by Tricart at about the same time, but in the more systematic form of a 'balance' (Tricart 1965a).
2 The concept of *steady state*, expressed, somewhat schematically and too theoretically, as a 'situation in equilibrium'.
3 The concept of *pedogenic duration*, still ignored by too many present pedologists, as well as by the American soil classification (the Seventh Approximation).

Butler (1958) developed his thoughts in a somewhat specific study of the Australian Riverina alluvial plain, where climatic oscillations have produced alternations of depositional events (of soil burial) and of incision of the previously deposited alluvial spreads (when pedogenesis is much influenced by drainage conditions, themselves dependent on the characteristics of the alluvium, especially its texture). Butler can justly be regarded as the founder of a new school of pedology, which may be called *pedostratigraphical*. His conceptions have demonstrated their usefulness when they were applied to environments different from alluvial plains by other Australian pedologists. Digests of these researches are found in the 1983 volume of the Divisions of Soils (CSIRO). Mulcahy (1961; 1967), in particular, has shown that soil types and their distribution in Western Australia are determined by the morphogenic evolution in the framework of physiographic units. A colloquium, 'Symposium on geochronology and land surfaces in relation to soils in Australasia' (1962), allowed the ideas and results obtained to be confronted. Although its title unequivocably states that soils are formed under the dependence of landforms (recalling the previously noted catena concept), the papers show that the physiographic units are only an evolution framework in which morphogenesis and pedogenis interact. In this perspective of the stratigraphic relationships of soils, Firman (1969a) and Stephens (1967) insist on their inclusion in the morphogenic sequences, just as Butler had done in the case of terraced alluvial plains.

This approach was later, or simultaneously, adopted in other countries. A case in point are the studies of Zinck (1970), a former student of Tricart, in Venezuela. It is also noted in the studies of ORSTOM pedologists, particularly as reflected in the introduction of a 'Group of reworked soils' in Aubert and Ségalen's soil classification (1966), in Boulet's (1970) and Kaloga's (1966; 1977) studies in Burkina Faso, in Boulvert's (1971) studies in the Central African Republic, in which the geomorphic units and soil types are juxtaposed in the described sequences, and in Ségalen's (1967) study of the Cameroon. The changes in climate of temperate Europe are the main stratigraphic reference points for Boulet (1975), Boulet, Bocquier and Millot (1977), for Fritsch et al. (1986) and for A. Billard (1987).

In Britain this approach has been rediscovered and recommended by Catt (1986). With exclusive examples from Britain, Catt draws attention to the importance of Quaternary climatic changes in frequently determining the characteristics of the parent material of soils and in influencing pedogenesis and the geomorphic processes. The latter, when depositional, in turn bury the soils and, when erosional, truncate them. They are able, too, to disturb them and to upturn or mix their horizons.

The same, pedostratigraphic approach, was independently discovered by R. V. Ruhe (1965; no Australian works cited). He notes the deposition of acidic colluvium during marine regressions, while calcareous shells, later producing neutral soils, were deposited during transgressions. He indicates, as the Australians, that, based upon the age of the topographies on which they have formed, the duration of soil formation is variable. This assertion reveals the limit of Ruhe's thinking: he is a step behind Butler, as he does not take into account the interaction between morphogenesis and pedogenesis. The landforms are for him an unalterable, dead, framework, as in the case of the catena concept. As to Walker, Hall and Protz (1969), they, for their part, add the influence of ablation in their study of soil series on loess in Iowa. Pollen analyses have been made by Riezebos and Slotboom (1974) to date more accurately successive sequences. Thus, in Luxemburg, soils with an argillic B horizon have formed during a period of topostability during the Subboreal under a climate with dry summers. Above it, the A horizon is not very distinct and poorly developed. It was formed, during the Subatlantic, in colluvium whose provenance was the truncation of the B_t horizon during the Subboreal. Thus the contribution to knowledge of the pedostratigraphic viewpoint is far from negligible. Nevertheless, certain pedologists, such as Duchaufour (1983; 1988) continue to ignore it.

Others, in contrast, have introduced some dynamic elements, which enable them to see more or less vaguely the importance of the interaction between morphogenesis and pedogenesis. This is the case of the Israeli D. Yaalon (Wieder and Yaalon 1985; Dan and Yaalon 1986) or of Gerlach (1976). The Brasilian Neto (1984) correctly remarks that 'the study of an isolated profile, in fact, represents an artificial segment' (coupure, p. 105). But a slope is a continuum: 'the delimitations proposed between soil units are divisions (coupures), which symbolise or suggest discontinuities that do not exist in Nature' (Neto 1984: 105). What the author does not indicate is that the continuum is the result of morphogenesis.

The same concept has been used by Johnson and Watson-Stegner (1987), who oppose two antagonistic tendencies in soil evolution. The first, a 'progressive' one (P) results in a better

differentiation of the soils into horizons, of the deepening of the horizons, and in an accentuation of their characters. The opposite, 'regressive' one (R tendency) consists of soil truncation, in a slowing down in the development of their characters and in haploidisation.

This progress in the evolution of thought results in a better, more complete, integration of pedology and geomorphology, of the soil's parent material (the physiographic, static aspect), of the temporal framework of its formation (the pedostratigraphic aspect), and of the interaction, past and present, of the two, morphogenic and pedogenic, dynamics. Tricart (1965a) has explained the fundamental concept of the morphogenic–pedogenic balance, determined by various degrees of topostability. Tricart (1968b) used this idea in a regional monograph on the soils of the Pampa Deprimida (Argentina), integrating it with the two other aspects. In doing so, in the framework of the FAO, he provided the ground work that made possible, under remarkably efficient and economic conditions, and the mapping, on the scale of 1:50,000, of the soils in an area of 148,000 km², prior to commencing agronomical experimentation. Hervieu (1967) adopted a similar method concerning the soils of Madagascar. Bottner (1972), following the same trend, showed that, in the south of France, resistant limestones, in which ancient karstic forms had developed, have for a long time been topostable, allowing the development of polyphased soils. These soils have recorded the successive changes in pedogenesis as a function of the recent climatic oscillations. Inversely, the morphogenic instability on the poorly resistant, marly or chalky, limestones has not permitted the formation of young, recent, Holocene soils. Palaeosols are the exception. Weathering rapidly penetrates into the porous rocks, so that present pedogenesis takes place on the weathered mantle. Dewolf (in her doctoral thesis 1978), has applied these concepts to a large area west of Paris. An important part of this methodological evolution took place in Morocco, where as early as 1962. Raynal understood the necessity of combining the pedogenic and morphogenic factors, followed by Belaid and Belkhodja in Tunisia in 1967. Another interesting case of complex interactions is reported by Conacher (1975) from the York-Dawson area of the Western Australian wheat belt. Noting that the surface occupied by salt-bearing soils on slopes of only 1.2° to 3.5° increased by a factor of 2.2 in fifteen years, he showed that the salt was brought in by hypodermic flow from surficial sandy formations covering a cuirass. This salt (called

Plates 23 & 24 Examples of pedogenic/volcanic/morphogenic interactions
Ph. JT CDXXII-21. Recurrent interruptions of topostability by sporadic ash falls have interfered with the formation of a clayey prismatic soil. Near Madrid on autopista to Medellín, Colombia.

'cyclic salt' by Australian authors) has an aeolian origin. The hypodermic flow into the lowlands feeds shallow ground water into the colluvium that covers the rather impermeable alluvium. Land clearing, causing reduced transpiration, has sufficiently raised the water table in the valley bottoms to cause evaporation, resulting in the precipitation of the dissolved salts and in the extension of the salt bearing soils.

Such an evolution of concepts is typical in France. Early in the 1970s a 'Comité de classification des Sols' was founded. It worked under the predominant influence of overseas soil scientists, mainly of the IRAT (Institut de Recherches Agronomiques Tropicales et des Cultures Vivrières) which elaborated, for applied purposes, the morpho-pedologic approach (see below). Unfortunately their work was ignored by metropolitan pedologists. Nevertheless, the ideas mentioned above spread and were adopted in the mid-1980s by the Service de La Cartographie des sols, a government agency, assisted by M. Jamagne, a Belgian soil scientist who for years had

been mapping soils in the north of the Paris Basin. This Service created a committee with the task of making a guide for soil investigations and a new classification. With the help of Tricart, who was invited to participate in 1988, the Committee created a draft, called the *Référentiel Pédologique Français*, which states that soils must be studied in the framework of a 'landscape', the 'soil landscape', which includes geomorphology, vegetation, land use, agronomic practices, etc. A final approximation is scheduled to appear starting in 1991. It will be broken down according to the world's great climatic zones and include various appendices, including one by Tricart on soils and geomorphology. The work will be truly collective in the sense that all contributions will have been circulated and criticized. The first part to be published will deal with the soils of the temperate zone, to be followed by those of cold environments.

The *morpho-pedologic approach* is basically a cartographic approach. It was carefully defined at the IRAT in the early 1970s thanks to a narrow cooperation between G. Gaucher, an agronomist and pedologist, J. Tricart, and IRAT pedologists. Its basic principles are as follows:

1 The physiographic units are, simultaneously, the starting-point of pedogenesis, providing the parent material, and of morphogenesis. As static phenomena, they are cartographically represented as part of the base map. Aerial photographs and remote sensing images can be used freely to map them.

2 What counts are types of pedogenesis: they have a higher value than soil types, which, being static, are of little use to the agronomist. A chart may be made to show the juxtaposition of pedogenic types and soil types according to the classification in use.

3 Morphogenic mechanisms and processes are represented and combined cartographically to types of pedogenesis, specifically in the form of a morpho-pedogenic balance.

The morphogenic–pedogenic concept having been examined, it should now be clear that an understanding of the interactions involved, and of the constraints, whether morphogenic or pedogenic, can enable effective protective or conservation measures to be taken, and agronomists to determine how to best use, manage and even improve the land. IRAT pedologists have published many papers using this method, which has been successfully applied, especially in Africa (Gaucher 1972; Brouwers and Latrille 1974; Kilian 1974; Raunet 1974; 1979; Tessier 1974; Thibout 1974).

A concept similar to the morpho-pedologic approach, and integrated with the pedostratigraphic concept, has been applied in Poland to the study of the palaeosols of Quaternary dunes (Manikowska 1983; Kaminska et al. 1986). The present trend is to go beyond the morpho-pedologic approach toward an ever increasing integration of the soils into the natural environment. The result is the *ecodynamic approach*, of which Anthony (1985) has given an example dealing with the Sierra Leone littoral.

This historical and methodological review helps to understand pedogenesis, the principles of which we shall now examine.

Plate 24 Ph. JT CDXXII-23 cn. Same location. Mass wasting has deformed the same type of material without scrambling the various layers. Recent pedogenesis, some 50 cm deep, affects the top of the material which has not suffered any deformation, an indication that mass wasting occurred under conditions different from the present.

The mechanisms of pedogenesis

According to Duchaufour (1983), specialist of the organic matter of soils, the three main mechanisms of soil formation are as follows:

1 Weathering of the bedrock, producing the parent material.
2 Input of organic matter produced by the vegetation implanted in the soil in progress of formation. A steady state is reached more or less rapidly, depending upon the case when the organic influx is compensated by the destruction or vegetal matter ('mineralization').
3 Translocation of soluble and colloidal elements by water circulation from one part of the soil profile to another; such migrations produce empoverished upper (A) and enriched lower (B) horizons.

This vertical differentiation of the soil into 'horizons' is labelled downward from the surface with capital letters in alphabetical order. The horizons, in turn, are subdivided by means of numbers, in the same order. Some are labelled with letters, indicating their particular character; for example, B_{Ca} for a calcareous horizon, or B_t for a B horizon said to be 'textural', that is clayey. The material directly below the soil is commonly called the 'C horizon'. This horizon is the locus of all misunderstandings concerning the lower limit of the soil. Some pedologists even go so far as to subdivide it, as if it were indeed part of the soil. The only logical solution, in accord with the definition of soil we have adopted, and with Gaucher (1968), is to consider the contact between the B and C horizons as the *pedogenic front*; that is the base of the soil is that of the B horizon. The C horizon is not part of the soil, at best it is the *parent material*. We say 'at best', because, frequently, the base of the soil corresponds to a change of material, which has prevented the further penetration of the soil-forming process. With topostable conditions the pedogenic front does not proceed downward indefinitely. With time, it tends to stabilize under given bioclimatic conditions. Which means that the various soil horizons, for their part, tend toward a certain thickness, called *modal*, whose statistical population, classed according to frequency, is a Gaussian curve. The modal thickness of the horizons, and of the entire soil, corresponds to the maximum of this frequency curve. The same condition is realized in a steady state situation, that is if the rate of downward progression of the pedogenic front is exactly equal to that of the generalized surficial ablation taking place at the expense of the soil. Such an adjustment, however, is somewhat theoretical, as it is seldom realized. The morphogenic–pedogenic balance is seldom such that a steady state is realized during a sufficiently long period of time. The balance over the course of time is successively tipped then in one direction then in the other at a particular site and, during the same period, from one site to another.

It is therefore necessary to add to Duchaufour's three 'essential mechanisms' of pedogenesis a fourth: the *morphogenic–pedogenic balance* (see Chapter 2, pp. 67–72).

The 'flow' of organic material, as indicated in our definition of soil, plays a determinant role in pedogenesis: it differentiates the soil from whatever surficial mineral formation. At the origin of this flow are living things (providing the dead organic material), which also determine its characteristics. The chemistry of the soil, specifically, is organic rather than inorganic. Better still, it is a biochemistry, as living things, especially micro-organisms (bacteria, fungi), play a determinant role. They feed on the organic material, modifying its physical characteristics and molecular structure, generally imperfectly represented by chemical formulas. In fact, there are no valid chemical formulas for certain organic compounds, which reveals not only the complexity of the phenomena, but also their variability, and our insufficent knowledge. Somewhat esoterically, pedologists refer to these modifications of the organic matter and its final destruction as '*mineralization of the organic matter*'. A strange expression, whose equivalent while drinking a bottle of beer would be 'vitrification of the beer bottle', which leaves behind but an empty bottle. The most important example of these complex and difficult to define mechanisms is chelation, which dissolves part of the organic matter and thus permits its migration from the litter to the B horizon. But oxygen is a 'competitor' of micro-organisms, for in its presence the organic matter is transformed by oxidation. In particular, the humic compounds of iron, transformed into insoluble oxides, are precipitated. They then form concretions in the B horizon of certain soils. A waterlogging prevents their oxidation, as the content of oxygen in the water is considerably less than that of the air, thus permitting the preservation of the organic matter. This occurs in peat-bogs, in swamps, and, to a lesser degree, in so-called 'hydromorphic' soils, which owe their character to permanent or seasonal waterlogging. Iron occurs there in *reduced* form, that is not oxidized (ferrous oxides, sulphides), in a

Plates 25 & 26 Morphogenic destruction of soils
Ph. JT CCLXXIX-38A. Soil truncation and colluviation of a ploughed field. Lacustrine proglacial silt of the Dombes (north of Lyon), France. The field is ploughed downslope to somewhat improve the drainage of the impervious material, the furrows channelling the runoff. The photograph was taken at the beginning of April, before sprouting. Colluvium can be observed in the foreground. After the next ploughing no localized ablation will appear. The loss of soil in the upper and the gain of colluvium in the lower part are equal. A generalized truncation and a generalized colluviation have taken place. The pedogenic–morphogenic balance is negative in the upper part (exportation site) *and* in the lower part as well (accumulation site); here for ablation, there for *too rapid* accumulation.

grey or greenish colour, whereas iron hydroxide is yellowish, brown or reddish, depending upon the degree of hydration. If the materials are sufficiently permeable, alternations of reducing and oxidizing phenomena occur in the zone of a swinging water table. But, in that case, one cannot speak of pedogenesis, as the phenomenon is a physico-chemical one without the intervention of the biosphere, although certain bacteria are able to assimilate iron and to abandon it at their death.

The swings of the water table are responsible for many ferruginous cuirasses of the intertropical zone. To attribute to them a pedologic origin is a mistake, although a knowledge of the chemistry and biochemistry of iron is indispensable to their understanding, as in the case of soils. Both iron hydroxides and clays and silica have different electrical charges, enabling them to attract one another. Iron and manganese, whose structures are quite similar (they are both bi- and trivalent),

migrate in the form of organic compounds, mainly owing to biochemical processes. Destruction of the organic matter, putting an end to organic life, causes their precipitation. The attraction of clay and silica then comes into play. The iron and manganese hydroxides penetrate into the crystalline structure of the quartz, colouring its discontinuities (fissures, crystal faces), which weakens them potentially, as the oxides can be reactivated more easily than the silica: all that is necessary is for the organic matter to enter into contact with them. The removal of the oxides leaves the microfissures wide open and causes the separation of the crystals previously welded together: the material, as a consequence, disintegrates. This specifically happens to quartzite. The same hydroxides, like paint, adhere to the surface of clay crystals. They are then said to be 'adsorbed'. The precipitation of these hydroxides characterizes the exit from the 'pedogenic domain', as it results from the cessation of the biochemical actions, determined by the complete consumption of the organic matter by the micro-organisms. Their renewed mobilization, on the contrary, in the form of organic compounds and/or through the intervention of specialized micro-organisms enters into the framework of pedogenic mechanisms. Far from making subtle distinctions, we are trying to get to the heart of the matter for a better understanding. All this conforms to the basic concepts of Gaucher (1968: 13–14) that the soil is

1 a *natural milieu* formed independently of humans but in which humans may intervene
2 an *autonomous milieu* produced and modified by specific mechanisms and according to its own laws, which are discovered and formulated by several disciplines, to which pedology must have recourse
3 a *continuous body*, the locus of complex, superimposed or successive mechanisms, which

impart it with a certain evolution, in a given direction.

Because of these principles the subdivision of the soil into horizons is somewhat *formal*. It is useful only if we eliminate the inconveniences resulting from this formality, that is if we adopt a flexible attitude in a genetic, therefore dynamic, perspective. Unfortunately the attitude of most present pedologists tends to be increasingly formal, resulting in an ever-increasing subdivision of the soil horizons. For example, in the A horizon:

- $A^°$ and $A^{°°}$, both formed by the litter, that is by the vegetal debris falling on the ground and to be consumed by 'decomposers'
- $A^°$ is formed by relatively 'fresh' debris
- $A^{°°}$ is formed of debris transformed into humus, in which only a few woody remains are still recognizable
- A^1, A^2 and sometimes A^3 do not contain any organic matter and have a lighter colour; they

Plate 26 Ph. CDXCIX-28. Pedogenesis disturbed by surficial mass movement, between Tlaxco and Chignahuapán, Mexico, alt. 2800 m. Colluvium deposited under periglacial conditions in the small valley during the last cold period is at present stable; pedogenesis acts exclusively, generating a good soil under cultivation. On the steep slope underlain by fresh basalt the soil is thin. A hydrological discontinuity located at the weathering front generates a hypodermic flow. Heavy rains prior to the taking of the photograph (July 1986) saturated the regolith, which passed the liquid limit and was dragged down the slope. The soil has been disturbed, horizons scrambled, the characteristic profile lost.

represent a zone of removal ('leaching') of the mineral elements, each subdivision determined by the kind of elements removed

- B^1, B^2, . . . are horizons of accumulation, subdivided in the same way, but inversely, that is according to the kind of mode of deposition of the elements. These notations, as noted above, may be accompanied by others, in letters: B_t and B_{Ca}, respectively indicating an accumulation of clay and of calcium carbonate. These letters are placed slightly below the B, whereas the numbers are placed as exponents. The two notations can therefore be combined.

This example clearly shows the excess of formalism, often more descriptive than genetic and explanatory. The same tendency occurs in *classifications*. Most of the time and effort of pedologists are spent in classifying soils, as was the case of botanists two centuries ago.

The time difference is significant, as is the multitude of classifications: all the main national and international groups of pedologists have their own, different from the others and frequently incompatible. This simply means that *pedologists are presently incapable of correctly classifying soils*. Thus agronomists politely say to pedologists: 'Yes, make your classifications since it allows you to make a living, but do not bother us with them, they are of no use to us . . .' For this reason the IRAT, an agronomic organization, has adopted the morpho-pedologic approach, in which soil classification does not intervene, except as an annex, as a free bonus. These classifications, first, are based on physiognomic criteria, horizons and profiles, which tend to be multiplied without restriction, and second, on the analytic characterization of the horizons, which is descriptive and therefore physiognomic. The extreme example of this intellectual attitude is the American classification. The soil is examined in total isolation. It is taken out of its ecological, chronological and dynamic context. The pedostratigraphic point of view and the morphogenic–pedogenic balance are totally ignored. The length of time the processes have exerted themselves and, consequently, the time of response of the different characteristics of the soil to the modifications of the pedogenic environment, are not taken into consideration, except in a single case, when it is written that oxisols, in general, result from a rather long evolution. This is all. Indeed, 'polyphased soils', as used by French authors, are numerous. They include various types of inherited features of several ages, which

generally persist for a long time, and are more or less difficult to correct or to eliminate. The entire agronomic problem of the Pampa Deprimida (Argentina) is one of inherited alkalinization, very difficult to eliminate owing to the absence of an integrated drainage network. These physical geographical phenomena result from the geomorphic evolution as determined by tectonic subsidence. To label these soils does not explain why they are there, what is the cause of the problem, and in what direction to seek a solution to reduce the severe ecologic constraints they pose to cattle-raising.

The sole object of the following presentation of soil classifications is to enable readers to extricate themselves from the welter of ideas in publications.

Soil classifications

The object of soil classification is twofold:

1 as in every classification, to group 'objects' into definite categories according to principles that claim to be scientific
2 to provide pedologists with the practical means of mapping soil units defined by the classification.

Such a classification includes a taxonomy and a pyramidal type of hierarchy of the objects with which it is concerned. At this point, two opposing attitudes are possible: is the hierarchy to be of a genetic or of a physiognomic nature? The progress of knowledge of every science is reflected in an increase of the part of the genetic aspect, while the physiognomic aspect tends to be no more than an index, increasingly recognized as being deceptive and, therefore, insufficient. In geomorphology an increasing importance is attributed to phenomena of convergence, that two 'aspects', landforms and surficial formations, are analogous but have different origins. Their different geneses *converge* toward the same result.

Although early classifications were exclusively based on a single factor such as colour, texture or parent rock, a more comprehensive point of view, including the influence of vegetation and climate, was developed by E. W. Hilgard (*Soils*, 1906) in the United States, but had no lasting effect. E. Ramann, in Germany, as late as 1917, still maintained the geological point of view (see Whittles' translation 1928). It was left to the Russians, in whose country bioclimatic zonation is particularly evident, to develop a *zonal* pedology that was going to revolutionize the study of soils world-wide. Dokuchaev not only linked soils to bioclimatic and other environmental factors, but also for the first time took account, in the classification of soils, of the *soil profile*, assuming that it is the resultant of an evolutive process. This led him to divide all soils into three (now well-known) orders, later called 'zonal', 'intrazonal' and 'azonal' by his chief follower, N. M. Sibirtsev. The zonal soils being dependent on bioclimatic factors, the intrazonal soils upon factors of site related to drainage (e.g. hydromorphic soils) or to a specifically influential parent rock (limestone), and azonal soils, the 'immature' soils of alluvium, aeolian sands, moors, or steep rocky slopes. These concepts, eminently applicable to Russia, had to be qualified in other countries, notably in Mediterranean regions. In the United States, in 1912 G. N. Coffey was the first to recognize that soil is an independent natural body. Although he believed and Marbut (1927) insisted that soils should be classified on the basis of their properties, an enhanced zonal classification by Baldwin, Kellogg and Thorp (1938: 979–1001) prevailed. In it the higher units, including the 'great soil groups', were supposedly determined on the basis of the 'soil characteristics', which, in fact, were defined as 'due to the effects of climate and biological action', while 'many of their subdivisions owe their distinctive characteristics to parent material' (Byers et al. 1938: 949).

While the zonal concept was in full swing, new attempts were being made to make a taxonomic classification based on chemical processes: that of Gedroiz (1929) on the absorption complex and cation exchange capacity, and that of Pallmann (1947)

in which an insoluble, practically immobile, *filter* fraction is distinguished from a *percolate* fraction comprising entities transported in solution or suspension, the direction of movement, the chemical make-up of the filter and the properties of the percolate being used to define the successive hierarchical level of classes, orders, associations, and types.

(Duchaufour 1982)

All this is much removed from the natural environment.

A more useful and successful classification has been devised by the Polish pedologist Kubiena (1953). It is based on differences in hydrological regime, morphological characteristics (colour, texture, profile, porosity, compactness, etc), reflecting and integrating the evolutive process, and on diagnostic horizon sequence (e.g. ABC soils,

AC soils, B/ABC soils, i.e. with surface crust, etc.). There are three major soil 'divisions':

1 *terrestrial*   e.g. rankers, rendzinas, terra rossa
2 *semi-terrestrial*   e.g. alluvial soils, high moor peats
3 *sub-aqueous*   divided into two classes: peatless and fen peat.

This system has attracted much attention in Europe and was adopted in Germany by Mückenhausen (1962). In the Australian classification of Stephens (1953) units are differentiated by morphology according to characters that have genetic implications.

In the diversity of classifications, it should be remarked, however, that there has been a recent tendency towards convergence. Differences in concept are fewer and the nomenclature is increasingly synchronized. We shall pay further attention here only to the American (1960; 1975), French (1967) and FAO (1974) classifications, which are all the result of team-work on an international level and are in wide use at the present time.

The American classification

This classification, called the Comprehensive Soil Classification System (CSCS), was made by the Soil Survey Staff of the Soil Conservation Service of the US Department of Agriculture under the direction of G. D. Smith and with assistance from a Belgian team of the Institut pour l'Encouragement de la Recherche Scientifique dans l'Industrie et l'Agriculture at Ghent, under the leadership of R. Tavernier. Started in 1951, it went through seven drafts or 'approximations', the last one of which, the seventh, was considered to be final. It was further improved with input from European pedologists with tropical experience, thus providing an enhanced version in 1975. The Seventh Approximation was first presented by G. D. Smith at the Seventh International Congress of Soil Science at Madison, Wisconsin, in 1960 and again expounded at the International Symposium of the Classification of Soils in Ghent in 1962.

The units of the system are defined as a function of soil properties according to the following principles:

1 Soils are the object of the classification, not the factors of soil formation such as climate, landforms or geography.
2 Soil units must be defined objectively, so as to

suit all pedologists. Genetic interpretations are subjective, as they depend on the opinion of the classifiers.

3 The use of genetic definitions precludes the classification of soils whose genesis is not known.

The object of the system is to select a certain number of properties which can be used to define soil units, the selection to be based on

1 concrete properties only
2 properties that result from pedogenesis or that influence pedogenesis
3 properties that are 'measurable, visible, or tangible'
4 a genetic point of view, as apprehended by the direct effects processes have on the soil.

Thus the different stages of the evolution of a soil are not ordered in a single taxon, but soils are classified according to the 'marks' dominant processes have left on them.

These concepts have led first, to a broadening of the concept 'profile' to that of a (preferably) hexagonal soil column, called *pedon* (1–10 m^2 in area), which permits the characterization of an irregular or interrupted soil profile, and secondly, to the definition of *diagnostic horizons*, which permit, except for Aridisols and Vertisols, the differentiation of soil orders at the highest taxonomic level. The pedon is the smallest unit that can be called a soil. Pedons are grouped together into *polypedons* that are bounded by 'not-soil' or other polypedons to form a classifiable soil. The diagnostic horizons are defined in the most rigorous terms and are divided into three groups:

1 Surface horizons, or *epipedons*, which correspond to the old A horizons. Examples: mollic (soft) epipedon, umbric (dark) epipedon, ochric (pale) epipedon.
2 Subsurface horizons, which are the most significant, as they are not as easily destroyed as epipedons. Examples: argillic, oxic, cambric (change) horizons.
   These horizons, especially the lower ones, serve to define the highest units, the orders and suborders.
3 Secondary or particular horizons. Examples: calcic, gypsic, albic (white), duripan and frangipan (brittle) horizons, which serve to define the great soil groups and the lower units.

According to G. D. Smith, these already numerous and complex definitions will become even more complicated and more precise with increased knowledge and mapping. The road charted by

American pedologists is therefore clear: to avoid genetic aspects, to abstract the soil from its environment, which influences its genesis, and to increasingly formalize its physiognomic characteristics. This approach is diametrically opposed to ours. Aware of it, the American classification in use by the Directorate of Hydraulic Works of the Ministry of Public Works of Venezuela was abandoned in favour of a more naturalistic approach in a combined study of land and water resources.

The French classification

The French classification started in the 1930s was interrupted by the Second World War. It is a collective work of the Comité de Pédologie et de Cartographie des Sols with participation of ORSTOM pedologists. It is constantly being revised and improved and occasionally republished, as in 1967. At the present a new version is being prepared under the leadership of a soil scientist of the INRA (Institut National de la Recherche Agronomique). The most significant changes to be adopted are the expression *couvertures pédologiques* (pedologic covers), which has the drawback of a possible misunderstanding, as a 'cover' is different from the substratum, and a reference to the environment by the expression *paysage pédologique* (pedologic landscape), which is not well constructed, as it depicts something difficult to define (see Chapter 1). The basic principles of the classification are those of G. Aubert, presented at the International Symposium of the Classification of Soils held in Ghent, Belgium, in 1962. They include the principles of homology, the subordination of characters, and the ideas of parenthood and filiation. The classification is general, that is it permits the classification and mapping of all existing soils, at whatever level of study. It is designed to be workable in the field and to take care of all observable features. Lastly, the classification aims to be of agronomical interest.

Although the concept of parenthood is made use of, the classification is focused on the soils themselves, not their genesis. At the level of the highest units, classes and subclasses, soils have the following common characteristics:

1 a certain degree of profile development, as indicated by the appearance of a B horizon
2 a degree of mineral alteration, which increases from immature soils to soils of the mid-latitudes to those the tropics, as defined by the nature

of the sesquioxides and the dominance of certain types of clay

3 a composition and distribution of organic matter capable of influencing the soil's evolution and its differentiation into horizons

4 certain factors in the soil's evolution that become dominant; for example, hydromorphism or halomorphism, on condition that their intensity completely modifies the soil's evolution and profile.

In the lower taxonomic units, the *groups* are defined by the morphologic characteristics of the profile caused by evolutive processes, and the *subgroups* either by the intensity of these processes or by secondary processes. The genetic characteristics become subordinate. These units help the mapping process. The basic taxonomic mapping unit of the Service de la Carte de France is the *série*, subdivided into derived series, variants, and phases. Belong to one and the same series 'all soils having the same succession of genetic horizons developed in a parent material of the same nature and presenting an analogous hydrologic economy' (Jamagne 1967). The *série* is thus defined by the combination of two elements: the lithologic element, or parent material, and the type of pedogenesis, which determines the profile, as related to drainage. Identification of the *série* is the preliminary step toward its genetic interpretation. Thus the starting-point is the observation of the profile and the prior search for identification criteria. The soil remains the basic object to map.

The FAO/UNESCO classification

The FAO/UNESCO soil map of the world on a scale of 1:5,000,000 was started at the recommendation of the International Society of Soil Science in 1956. Objectives include appraisal of the world's soil resources, establishment of a general framework for more detailed investigations in developing countries, and to promote international cooperation in the study of soil science, which eventually may lead to an internationally accepted nomenclature and classification. But faced with a multitude of national and regional classifications, the FAO initially found itself in a delicate position on the technical as well as on the political level. Use of a single classification would have aroused endless polemics, the first consequence of which would have been the complete ignoring of a document produced at high cost. The need for a legend, the

definition of soil units, and a nomenclature resulting in a system independent of the various schools of thought was obvious if the objective, certainly laudable, was to be attained. The classification proposed was approved at the Ninth Congress of the International Society of Soil Science held in Adelaide in 1968. This achievement was all the more difficult as the basic principles of classification were different. Nevertheless, if opinions differed, a certain convergence of minds appeared at the level of the 'great group'. Work therefore centred on synchronizing the different groups by giving them new definitions, rather than on trying to find criteria for a new classification. This final regrouping into 26 soil units 'defined in terms of measurable and observable properties' succeeded by imposing itself in spite of the many criticisms levelled at it. 'The differentiating criteria are the essential properties of the soil itself', in keeping with a natural system, and the units are classified according to increasing degrees of weathering and profile characters, from Fluvisols to Ferralsols. The categories are defined by geographic rather than by morphologic criteria. Traditional names have been preserved as much as possible, and each unit is further subdivided according to specific characteristics such as orthic, mollic, and gleyic for Solonetz. The classification is therefore relatively simple and non-hierarchical. It makes wide use of the American and French classifications and of the vocabulary of the CSCS.

Comparison and critique of the American and French classifications

Our object is not to provide a detailed critique of the multiple aspects of the two classifications, we would never get through with it, but to see, by an examination of the concepts and cartographic methods, if the classifications can be of use to our pursuit, which is the study of the environment with an eye to its use.

In both classifications priority is given to the morphologic characters of the soils: the soils themselves must be classified, not the factors of their formation. Pedogenesis, of course, is taken into account, but only in so far as it leaves marks in the soil profile. Emphasis is on physiognomy, not genesis.

In **the American classification**, the principle stated above is most clearly affirmed in the CSCS. For example, a soil on chalk can be classified as a Rendoll (Rendzina) only from its characteristic profile. If disturbed by ploughing, it cannot be identified as such, as the profile is not evident. To reconstruct it would be a subjective interpretation, not an observation. The concern for objectivity is such that it explains the importance given to diagnostic horizons, specifically the lower ones, out of reach of the plough. The properties identifying soils must have a degree of permanence and should be visible or tactile. The most useful are those that can be measured or estimated quantitatively in the field. Genesis does not figure in the definition, as it cannot be observed or measured. The characterization of the soil in the field, therefore, is made without an analysis of the pedogenic milieu and, *in extremis*, without taking into account the environment of the profile. The time factor is included, but in an aspect that could be qualified as negative; only the measurable marks that one or more processes, whatever the length of their duration, have left behind on the soil are identified. Thus an appreciation of the evolution becomes impossible. What matters is the act of classification, nothing more: hence, a certain intellectual dissatisfaction.

All aspects of this approach, however, are not to be rejected. A certain discipline of appraisal is instituted, which helps the standardization of the observations and the making of comparisons. A certain explosion in diversity has thus been avoided, which was probably the intention of the authors. Nevertheless, the excess of quantification produces a rigidity which reflects on the incapability of the system to apprehend the complexity of the environment. If, on the practical level, the codification facilitates the task of the field-worker, it does not provide a good perception of the total environment. In the last analysis, the place of the pedologist could be taken by a good technician who, with a thorough knowledge of the code, would apply it without hesitation. In that case the mapping could be done in the office. This indeed is what Tricart has experienced south of Lake Maracaibo, in Venezuela, where government pedologists, reduced to simple technicians, defined soil profiles in pits unbearable under a blazing zenithal Sun, while American consultants made the classification in an air-conditioned office. It is doubtful that if the declared objective of the method, to improve soil mapping for practical purposes and for the benefit of agiculture, is thus effectively attained.

The recourse to permanent, low, diagnostic horizons, undisturbed by cultivation can also be criticized. Most are of minor importance to agriculture. In other cases, such as the duration of waterlogging for hydromorphic soils (classified as −90, 90–180, and +180 days/yr), the pertinent criteria are inapplicable. Any naturalist knows that such data are wanting, and also the duration of waterlogging may vary over a distance of only a few decimetres. The soil for agricultural use is only one environmental component among others; isolated from the others, it has no value, for, agricultural management, in conformity with system theory, makes use of the various components by affecting those that are most readily changeable with the technical and socio-economic means at our disposal.

The French system, although formulated a quarter of a century later, has remained faithful to the catena concept. The classification, although somewhat less than the American, is also essentially physiognomic, as the genetic viewpoint, although not entirely excluded, is only marginally tolerated. The main difference that distinguishes the French classification of Aubert and Duchaufour (1956) is that it is based on the genesis and properties of *virgin* soils. This was quickly noticed by the Americans at Ghent. It therefore ignores truncated soils with a BC profile. Aubert's position was that in that case a non-truncated profile should be looked for in the vicinity in order to complete the identification of the incomplete profile. If that is not possible, other methods permit the profile to be ascribed to other taxonomic units, at whatever level. Aubert was educated as an agronomist and was first of all a theoretician. Because of this, the IRAT (Institut de Recherches Agronomiques Tropicales) was not satisfied with the classification of the Comité de Pédologie et de Cartographie des sols, and even less with some of its procedures. As a result it looked for solutions in a different direction, whose originality has been expounded at the beginning of this chapter. The latter approach is basically a cartographic one which aims to provide agronomists with the data they are in need of.

THE CARTOGRAPHIC APPROACH

The objective of this approach is to describe the ecologic environment in terms of its dynamics. This means that the components of the environment should be analysed in their various interactions as part of a system. The systems approach, by its very nature, is dynamic. It strives to discover an evolution and to analyse its mechanisms. Static elements form only a framework, which must be taken into account, but not for their own sake. The method is diametrically opposed to the intellectual approach of the authors of the American and French classifications. The genetic aspects are less rigorously excluded from the French classification, but as they are tolerated at different taxonomic levels, they do not have their proper place, so instead of being useful become a source of confusion. This attiude should be categorically rejected and no attempt made to find a compromise, which would be vain and ill-advised.

Rather than juxtaposing the different aspects of the environment, each apprehended by a specific discipline having its own store of knowledge and its own preoccupations, that is rather than assuming a sectoral approach, it is pertinent to recognize as the main theme of research the whole, that is the environment with its own unity and, as such, different from the sum of its sectoral parts. A system is not the sum of its components, but is endowed with specific properties. These should be recognized. Certain scholars, ignoring the vocabulary of systems theory, were aware of it, using other terms to express it; for example Cholley (d. 1968) spoke of geographic 'complexes', while others in France used the term 'global'. In the meantime more than twenty years have passed since L. von Bertalanffy published his popular scientific work on systems theory, which should be used to unify our vocabulary. In Chapter 2 we have shown how dynamic geomorphology is integrated into ecogeography. Now we shall show how to integrate it into mapping. But, first, we examine how pedology can be integrated into ecogeographic studies.

The integration of pedology into ecogeographic studies

We have discarded the physiognomic approach of both the American and French classifications, whose object does not serve land use planning and management. The right approach consists in proceeding from the *conditions of pedogenesis*. What is mapped are soils characterized by the same pedogenic regime, not the extent of soil units as defined by their physiognomic characters. As the intensity of these regimes varies as a function of other factors, such as lithology or morphogenic processes, the maps should also show the variations

of this intensity. This is possible if we apply Gaucher's concept of the *pedogenic milieu* (1968), which is both the *spatial framework* of pedogenesis and the condition of its *regime*. The pedogenic regime is the result of the influences, actions or constraints opposed to the various pedogenic factors. It is also the framework of their interactions. It readily allows the introduction of the geochemical components, whether internal or external, at a level of perception corresponding to the scale of the map. According to Gaucher, it is more important to be familiar with the way a podzol forms than to have a minute description of a podzol, for a podzol is a *type* of soil; the definition of a type is the result of an abstraction: two podzols are never exactly the same. A particular podzol should be apprehended as a part of a 'landscape', in relation with other landscape elements, which allow it to be better understood, if needs be, in connection with its proper use of its eventual improvement by fertilizers or cultivation methods. (Some twenty years later the soil scientists of the INRA and the Soil Survey of the French Ministry of Agriculture are rediscovering Gaucher's concepts and now are discussing the 'pedologic landscape'. Their committee meetings were not attended by soil scientists of the IRAT. Tricart is currently trying to encourage members of the committee to make use of the morphogenic–pedogenic balance concept and environmental dynamics to improve the understanding of soils.) To separate in a calcareous region on the pretext of different profiles well-developed rendzinas from degraded, truncated soils occludes their common origin: a *calcimorphic milieu* in which a secondary differentiation has taken place, often attributable to poor soil management. In our system these two subdivisions are made evident cartographically. In a similar way, the Oxisols of the CSCS would have a much larger, rational, distribution than that provided by a definition based on an extremely strict diagnosis: the presence of a plinthite ('brick') at a depth of less than 30 cm. A consequence is that space is less cut up into a multitude of cartographic units whose filiation is not always easy to recognize.

Working with the pedogenic milieu also makes possible a differentiation between past and present pedogenesis, which is not always possible if soils are solely classified according to a too strict diagnosis. Each soil, whether truncated, buried, or having been subjected to a superposition, preserves, in variable degrees, traces of its history; the dynamics of each soil being conditioned by those of the past. Pedogenesis, to recall the thinking of Gaucher, is a succession of phenomena that follow one another in time and space. It is therefore important to distinguish present pedogenic regimes from inherited soils, making it possible to trace the soil's evolution. For example, is it logical to classify as ferrallitic soil a present pedogenic regime characterized by a tall grass cover, inducing an accumulation of dead organic debris and a mobilization of organo-mineral substances totally different from the processes that function under forest and favour ferrallitization? Even if deep-seated weathering remains of the ferrallitic type, the new pedogenesis functioning at the surface on a material that preserves traces of its past is totally incomparable to that which functions at some distance under forest. The structure of the surface horizon is different, the A horizons become thicker, permeability increases, and the character of the B horizon changes. Even the evolution of the relief changes. Such a situation is typical of the middle-west of Madagascar, where a steppe replaced the forest more than a thousand years ago. The economic development of these, generally favourable, areas is different from that of the same climate still under forest.

The concept of pedogenic milieu and that of the pedogenic trend, which derives from it, therefore permits the integration of pedology into ecogeography, to view the soil not by itself but as a component of the natural system. In the field, rather than focusing the attention on details in isolation from one another, it is preferable to practise steadily a dialectic oscillation between detail and the whole and between the whole and detail, which mutually enlighten one another, as a detail can exist only in the framework of the whole and the whole only as a result of the interactions of its components. When other components are discovered, the chances are that the diagnostic must be modified. The integration of factors proceeds from the base upward in successive steps at the same time as our knowledge and understanding increase. J. B. Lamarck understood this when he wrote in his *Philosophie zoologique* (in 1809) that 'the true way to know an object, even in its smallest details, is to begin by viewing it as a whole'.

Devising maps

Our objective is to devise a set of maps that will provide a synoptic view of the landscape whose improvement or development we have in mind. To this effect three large-scale maps are necessary: a morpho-pedological map, a constraints map, and a proposed land use map.

The morpho-pedological diagnosis: at a comprehensive level of perception

The objective is to determine, that is regionalize, *morpho-pedologic units* in space and in time. In this we shall again lean on the work of Gaucher, who was one of the world's foremost pedologists, but much indebted to the French school of geomorphology.

Soil units exist within the framework of structural and climatic geomorphology, the basis of which is the taxonomic classification of Tricart (1952; Cailleux and Tricart 1956; Tricart 1965b: 79–98). It consists of temporo-spatial 'scales', that is a dimensional and temporal hierarchy of physiographic units, including seven orders of magnitude, the first order being the largest and most durable (division of the Earth into continents and oceans), the seventh order the smallest (microforms) and most recent in age. (The term 'scale' is really not satisfactory, although frequently used in this sense. A preferable expression is 'level of perception'. True, a map scale offers a certain level of perception, but it is no more this level of perception than a thermometer is the temperature.) These units form a hierarchy of interdependent units. They situate the conditions of occurrence of geomorphic phenomena and form, mainly from the third to the sixth orders, a structural framework for the pedologist. The classification has a larger number of units than the morphoclimatic classification because geologic structure and lithology exert a more local influence on landforms than climate. These criteria, therefore, allow a further breakdown of soil units than is possible by climate alone. The largest units (1–4) are determined by tectodynamics, the intermediate (5) by differential denudation and deposition, the smallest (6–7) by lithology and morphogenic processes. An eighth order is at the level of micro dimensions (mm–microns) and applies particularly to the study of sediments and soils. This taxonomy thus integrates all the positive elements developed in pedology since the nineteenth century: the bioclimatic domains of Dokuchaev, the lithologic influences of the 'agricultural geology' of Risler, the pedostratigraphical approach, the morphogenic–pedogenic balance. Each of these approaches, although valid, is incomplete or partial. Instead of 'choosing' between them and thus accepting the shortcomings of any one of them, we combine them in an enhanced systems framework.

In France, according to Gaucher, the fourth order corresponds to the 'pays', framework of pedological studies and, usually, of Ministry of Agriculture interventions. This is significant and satisfactory both from the scientific and practical points of view. The morphopedological units are subordinate to the 'pays', and therefore belong to the fifth (kilometric) and sixth (hectometric/decametric) orders. In a quite different region, that of the Senegal Delta (Tricart 1961c), the ensembles formed by the palaeodunes, the Senegal floodplain with its distributaries, or the reaches of the *Continental Terminal* belong to the third order. ('Continental Terminal' is a current geological expression for the terrestrial sediments deposited at the end of the Caenozoic in subsident regions of western tropical Africa by running water or in swamps. They consist of weathered products, including clays, sands, hydrated iron oxides that can be precipitated in the form of 'laterite', gravels, etc. On the whole, they are poorly to moderately well-consolidated rocks of low fertility.) They can be mapped on a medium scale (1:200,000 or 1:250,000). The bottomlands (*cuvettes*) and natural levee clusters of the floodplain fit the fourth order, while their subdivisions, such as the crevasse deltas of the *cuvettes*, the various levees and their intermediate depressions, as also, in the sand seas, the various dune patterns belong to the fifth order, which corresponds to the pedogenic milieux or morphopedologic units, used in land use planning. A scale of 1:25,000 is appropriate. The published geomorphological map at 1:50,000 (the scale of the aerial photographs – a recent detailed map did not exist at the time) shows the units of the fourth order of magnitude.

Yet another example may be taken from a slightly rolling till plain in the State of Indiana, divided into an irregular pattern of very shallow depressions and subdued divides, of the sixth order of magnitude. Whereas nearly black, poorly drained Aquolls characterize the depressions, the divides feature slightly better drained, light-coloured, Aqualfs; the light colour being due to truncation down to the B horizon (Birkeland 1984: 182). Other morpho-pedologic units may be caused by exposure (aspect) or by pedostratigraphic conditions (Morrison 1967). A scale of 1:25,000 is adequate for this level of perception. This example shows how our approach is independent of soil classification systems. It is as appropriate in Indiana, where pedologic studies have been made in the framework of the CPCS, as in the Senegal

Delta, where no previous soil classification had been made, but where geomorphological mapping served as a framework to pedological studies. These, as a result, were made more easily and rapidly and materially benefited the cost–benefit ratio of the entire land use study. In fact, the morpho-pedologic approach had its origin in this experience. This approach, as emphasized by Gaucher and IRAT pedologists, facilitates the localization of soil pits as a function of the units determined by field observation and the use of aerial photographs.

The determination of transects is important during this preliminary phase. Some, in an alluvial region, should be along the longitudinal axis in the direction of deposition, while others should be transversal, normal to the first, thus intersecting an old bed, its levees and the neighbouring bottomlands. This method was followed in Mali, in 1988, in the area of Kogoni, by Tricart and Blanck, consultants for the IRAT, which was in charge of providing the necessary diagnostic for a programme of rehabilitation and the extension of rice paddies for the Office du Niger, financed by the World Bank. R. Bertrand, who was responsible for the intervention of the IRAT, was able to convince this organization of the recommended procedure. However, resistance to the new method nevertheless caused the IRAT to proceed with a costly and unnecessarily dense quadrangular network of pits. Habit and thinking in geometrical terms are not easily overcome. On the other hand, the Malian pedologists, in particular their leader, the Engineer B. Keita, were easily convinced. Because a morpho-pedologic unit is characterized both by a type of geomorphology and a type of pedology, it is particularly suitable to serve as an area of agricultural experimentation. The results of the experiments can then be applied to other similar units of the same region at a minimum cost and lapse of time. The struggle for rational agricultural development is urgent. In Mali, in particular, the Office du Niger should be able to fill the role it was assigned: to contribute to the self-sufficiency in food of the country and to guard against drought.

The morpho-pedologic approach not only enables the intrinsic – and costly – approach of digging pits according to a chequered pattern, whose density is automatically a function of the adopted scale for soil mapping, to be abandoned, but also gives a dynamic orientation to pedology: a palaeosol is of necessity associated with an *inherited landform*, while an inherited landform suggests a palaeosol. Our trend of thought intersects here with degrees of topostability, defined in our discourse on the geomorphological approach. Truncated palaeosols appear if complete topostability is wanting. Levels of truncation and their location are related to the geomorphic processes that have functioned since the formation of the palaeosol; their characteristics and age should be determined by geomorphic study. The palaeosols, followed by the weathered mantle, disappear with increasing topo-instability. Gradually, the landform itself starts to change. But during the course of such an evolution a spatial differentiation takes place, so that, cartographically, the result is a *mosaic* of subunits. They are usually *heterochronic* (composed of elements of different age) and *heterogenic* (produced by different processes or mechanisms). To define them requires a pedostratigraphic approach, whose equivalent in geomorphology has been used since the origins of the discipline ('stages' of W. M. Davis, 'generations' of J. Büdel).

Traditional pedologists are generally satisfied with a very elementary perception of the relief: convex or concave slopes, undulating or flat relief, etc. When trying to be more precise, they provide only the values of the slopes, which, according to them, determine the potential use of the land. A slope of less than 2° does not require any 'anti-erosive' precaution. If more than 10°, it is doomed to an irrevocable destruction. Some indicate slope values in percentages, which is as inconvenient for abrupt slopes as the Mercator projection is unusable in the polar regions. All this reflects a total ignorance of the most elementary geomorphology. For example, a slope of less than 2° on bare marls, without organic matter, may be the locus of intense surface wash, whereas in a same climate, on a slope of 15°, under dense forest, the surface runoff coefficient is nil. On the other hand, such a slope is occasionally affected by mass wasting. Exposure (aspect) by modifying the surficial water balance (desiccation or, on the contrary, persistent moisture, snow) considerably influences pedogenesis as well as morphogenesis. Exposure and lithology, on the one hand, and vegetation and soils, which much depend on them, on the other, modify the threshold limits of the various pedogenic and morphogenic processes. Much research remains to be done in this domain, which has been poorly explored. But these problems are not resolved by adopting obdurate slope values, defined as arbitrarily as the chequer density of soil pits. What is needed is a little more *esprit de finesse* and less *esprit de géométrie*.

Our approach simultaneously permits the following.

1 A better use of the means available: improving results at lower cost.
2 To encourage workers to think, instead of transforming them into a kind of machine, as results from the use of the CSCS. Such workers enhance themselves instead of developing a complex of frustration. This, too, is important for the quality of the results.
3 To show the interdependence of the various components of the environment by using a systems approach: a more refined tool than the previous approaches, which ignored it.
4 To list uncertain or insufficiently known phenomena in the text accompanying the maps. This approach was followed by RADAMBRASIL in its recommendation maps, whose legends include an item called 'areas where problems are insufficiently known and where decisions should be preceded by more in depth studies'.

Making the maps

The morpho-pedologic diagnosis leads to the making of detailed maps. What has to be determined now is the extent of the area to be studied and the object of its improvement or development. The level of perception corresponds to what agricultural engineers demand for a development project. It implies a large scale for the three maps that we recommend. However, in conformity with our approach, pre-established standard scales, like the density of soil pits, are out of the question. Two determinant factors should be considered:

1 The specific 'grain' of the region, that is as on aerial photographs, the size of the objects to be mapped. As in remote sensing, depending upon the quality of the resolution, objects of a certain size appear, or not, on the recordings. Thus a scale should be chosen so that all objects significant in the particular study appear sufficiently clearly delineated to be taken into consideration.
2 The object of the development: the limiting factors of course differ depending upon the case. Vegetable and fruit crops are much more sensitive to topoclimatic constraints than hay fields or silviculture. Agribusiness requires large and, as much as possible, homogeneous, regions, for which heterogeneity is a serious handicap. A

less detailed level of perception, here, is satisfied with smaller scale maps.

The text of the accompanying report may of course reveal contradictions between opposed demands.

Morpho-pedological maps

Usually, a scale of 1:25,000 or 1:50,000 is satisfactory in relation to what has been discussed above. Occasionally a scale of 1:10,000 may be preferable. It should of course be remembered that every increase in scale increases the cost per unit area. Outside of other considerations, therefore, the smallest scale possible should be adopted. Larger scales, however, increase the possibility of using particular symbols for specific dynamics according to 'Meccano' (erector set) principles: with more parts, the more complicated the assemblage. On the other hand, a greater degree of variety becomes possible. To help the map user, these assemblages should be shown in the map legend. The golden rule is one of common sense: is the game worth the candle? Never should the legibility of the map be sacrificed for an excessive abundance of information, and even less when part of the information is redundant. The main object is to represent clearly the kind and intensity of the interactions, which determine the dynamics of the units.

The lithology   In contrast to the geological aspect, our object is not stratigraphic or chronologic. Fossils are of no avail to us. Risler's work is passé. What is important are the types of rocks, the lithology, not the geology. Their physical and chemical properties condition the kind and rate of weathering, their morphogenic and pedogenic behaviour, in other words, the basic characteristics of the morpho-pedogenic units. Particular attention is therefore directed to texture, consistency, permeability and jointing. These properties affect the penetration of roots, the water regime, and the water balance, that is the ecodynamic environment. The lithologic information of the morpho-pedologic maps is also found on the ecodynamic maps. Static and descriptive, it provides the base colour of the map, on which the other, dynamic, elements are superimposed by symbols of different colours. Seen in this light, the lithology is not limited to the bedrock, but includes all surficial materials serving as parent material for the soil and as a medium for morphogenesis. Their thickness is of little import: practically nil on an outcropping slab

of fresh quartzite, devoid of soil and weathered products, carrying only a few lichens, but reaching some one hundred metres into the regolith of the wet tropics or in the residues of deep karstic phenomena. There may be a more or less important disjunction between the deep-seated, essentially chemical, weathering at the weathering front and the kind of evolution near the surface, influenced by biotic processes. Their products, produced simultaneously, are different. Much cartographic research remains to be done to find clear and expressive modes of representation of such complex combinations. A change of climate, vegetation, or morphogenic processes may modify the superficial pedogenic milieu without notably affecting the processes active at the weathering front, or only after a long time of response. Our observation of what happens at the weathering front is of course difficult, so that our knowledge of it remains quite insufficient. Nevertheless, the principle is clear: a surficial formation that is not currently being formed at the level of the soil should be considered as the parent material of that soil, and should therefore be apprehended as being static. On the other hand, a surficial formation in the course of transformation should be cartographically represented from the dynamic point of view, just as an inherited soil currently being transformed is called a 'polyphased soil': the nature and trend of such a transformation should be analysed and its extent mapped. Such is the case, for example, in Ndzuani (Anjouan), in the Republic of the Comoro Islands, of the thick, ancient ferrallitic weathered mantle, on volcanic rocks, which presently is undergoing pedogenesis of the brunifying or andic type, according to the French classification. These soils have a positive reaction to sodium fluoride, a low density, and a poorly developed structure, characteristic of Andosols. There is, therefore, a marked transformation by present pedogenesis of the ancient, inherited, 'dead', ferrallitic mantle. To include this regolith into the 'lithology', emphasizes the contrast between the two successive dynamics and the inherited character of the ancient ferrallitic mantle. To make this distinction is of importance not only to the management of these ancient fragile soils, but also in the use of the land, which will require adequate conservation measures.

Morphogenesis   There is no intention of superimposing the contents of a geomorphological map on to a pedological map: each of these are the business of specialists and have their specific objectives. The result, moreover, would be too confusing to be usable. As the contour lines of the topographic map provide information on the geometry of the land, all that is necessary is to show landforms that are dominant or that provide important explanatory information. In the absence of a contoured base map, it is very helpful to sketch in some characteristic landforms, which give a certain plasticity to the map and make it more readable.

The geomorphological component basically consists of

1 the degree of topostability, which influences pedogenesis and the morphogenic–pedogenic balance
2 the processes which interfere with pedogenesis, as to their nature and intensity.

Thus, in order to remain readable, degrees of topostability (stable, penestable, unstable) are selected from among other choices to be put on the morpho-pedologic map. As to the various geomorphic processes and their intensity, which interfere with the soil forming process and tend to destroy the soils by removal, burial or mixing, they are ecodynamic constraints, which pertain to the constraint map. It should be clear, however, that the pedologist have recourse to this map too in order to fully understand the pedogenic processes.

Pedogenesis This is approached from the angle of the pedogenic milieu, not from that of the formal classification of soils. This does not exclude the examination of profiles, necessary to identify the pedogenic trend. Profiles are not an end in themselves, only a means, an instrument. The classification itself is not rejected, but it is not indispensable. A column may be provided for it in the map legend, where the soil types of the classification, used as a reference, are indicated, facing the morphopedologic units in which they occur. But the main object is the identification of the pedogenic mechanisms and the appreciation of their effects. This leads to the identification of legacies and the transformation of soils. The nature of these, their chronologic succession, the effects of climatic oscillations, taking into account the lithologic framework, and the successive and changing interactions with morphogenic processes should be defined. As the object of the map is to show the dynamics of the environment and to explain them, this map does not necessarily indicate all the characteristics of the soil in which agronomists are interested; they should further consult the constraints map.

In practice, each group of phenomena of the same nature can be shown on the map by different hatchings or dots of the same colour. For example, on the morpho-pedological map of Ndzuani (Anjouan) lithologic features appear in brown, pedologic data in black, and morphogenic phenomena in red, that is in contrasting colours. In that way morpho-pedologic units are not delimited: they appear automatically as a result of the combination of patterns. Any arbitrary formalism is thus avoided. What is shown is the degree of coincidence between the various phenomena. It is up to users of the map to appreciate it according to their own point of view. We do not hold them to our own position, as would be the case if we drew limits to the units. Such limits would be traced according to our own criteria, which are not necessarily those of other users. In this we are happy to satisfy, for once, one of the preoccupations of G. B. Smith.

Constraints maps

These maps show the various types of constraints, as determined by the type of development decided upon. They are inherent to the physical environment, therefore independent of human beings. For that reason we shall examine them first, for to make a map of 'potentialities' or, worse, 'vocations', means a higher degree of complexity, as human phenomena are involved. Farmers or peasants must earn a living. True, they do it as a function of the natural environment, but also, more often, as a function of their productive capacity, closely linked to agricultural techniques, technological progress, available credit, interest rates, extension services and prices, which in turn depend on social structure and political decisions (taxes, subsidies, customs duties). The farmer's income depends on cost and selling prices, as mentioned, but these depend on trade relations, taxes, transport costs, and the purchasing power of the consumers. All this is once again determined by political decisions, whether in the liberal economy of free countries or the planned economy of 'socialist' states. The daily press stands witness to it. All this is beyond the domain of naturalists who, nevertheless, cannot ignore it, but have no power of decision over it. The opening of a road, a decrease in taxes or of customs duties, the creation of a cooperative, or more favourable credit rates cause profits to fluctuate. Production is subject to a very wide range in profits even in ecologically favourable areas. The profit margin, depending upon the case, may make an ecologically marginal

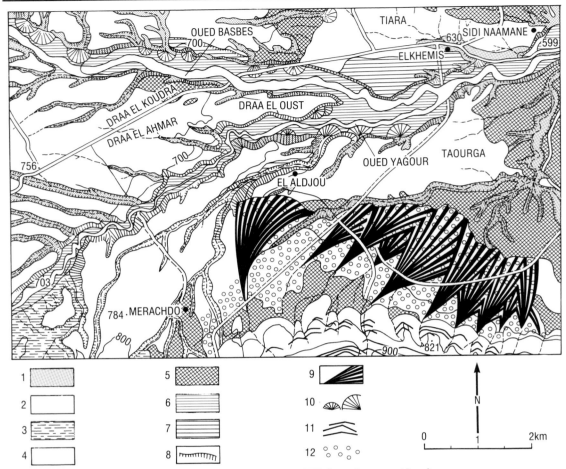

Figure 10. A morpho-pedologic map: extract from map of El Omaria area, Algeria
Source: M. Rannet (1973) IRAT—SOOLTEG.

1. Calcareous ss, cgl & sh. 2. Albian-Aptian qtzt & sh. 3. Marls & marly ls. 4. Glacis, surficial material oxidized. 5. Incrusted, degraded glacis. 6. Recent terrace. 7. High terrace. 8. Incision in the glacis. 9. Glacis-fan. 10. Small fans. 11. Main quartzitic strata. 12. High surficial stoniness, up to boulder size

MORPHO-PEDOLOGIC UNITS

Unit no.	Morphogenesis	Pedogenesis	Constraints for agricultural development
1	*Landform*: Much structural influence (steep slopes, ss scarps, structural benches). *Present dynamics*: Wandering runoff eventually concentrated in gullies (high anthropic influence).	*Thick brown calcareous soils* predominant. Oxidation inherited. Coarse texture due to lateral drainage. Decalcified, truncated soils poor in organic matter.	Steep slopes (benches excepted). Generalized ablation. Limited soil water and chemical reserves.
2	*Landform*: flysch facies: steep concave slopes, E-W hogbacks, Scattered quartzite boulders. *Present dynamics*: generalized surface runoff in spite of a certain phytostability (*maquis*). Fans at the mouths of small, very steep watersheds.	Heterogeneous lithomorphic soils: *brown hydromorphic* or *vertic fersiallitic soils*, lithosols on qtzt, discontinuous calcareous crusts; colluvial, stony, non-calcareous soils, occasionally vertic at depth.	Steep slopes. Stoniness (boulders at shallow depth). Argillaceous, often vertic soils.

Unit no.	Morphogenesis	Pedogenesis	Constraints for agricultural development
3	*Landform*: highly dissected, steep slopes, narrow crests randomly oriented. *Present dynamics*: gullying, generalized ablation by runoff. The destruction of the maquis induces badlands.	*Crude erosional, incipient soils* (lithosols). But the poorly consolidated rocks allow trees to take root.	Bold relief, intense 'erosion' accelerated by the disappearance of the plant cover. Absence of soils.
4	Landforms inherited from the middle Quaternary. Denudation glacis on clays or stony materials. Oxidation to a depth of 0.5–2 m. Minor present dynamics.	*Oxidized chestnut, isohumic soils*, argillized at depth. Calcareous crust at depth 0.5 m. Absence of active calcium carbonate.	Very argillaceous soils hampering root penetration. Occasionally very stony.
5	Degraded landforms inherited from early Quaternary. Laminated calcareous crust, depth 0.5 m, grading downward into shales slightly indurated by calcium carb. precip. Some rillwash.	*Brown calcareous soils* or *anthropic rendzinas*. Very abundant active calcareous material. Many buried stones exposed by anthropic 'erosion'.	Shallow, very calcareous stony soils, very sensitive to drought.
6	Several m thick Rharbian silty deposits. The lower zones are subject to flooding. Undermining of banks cause slides and debris falls. Small tributary fans.	Thick silty, stoneless, *brown calcareous soils* rich in active calcium carbonate.	Very good soils, but threatened by active calcium carbonate.
7	Remnants of Soltanian terraces 10–20 m high forming several levels. Generally reworked and stony at the surface.	*Modal isohumic chestnut soils*, occasionally vertic at depth, very stony, absence of calcium carbonate.	Very stony.
8	Linear incisions, shredding the glacis. Much runoff and regressive incision. Colluvial veneer.	*Slightly evolved soils* on non-calcareous, very stony colluvium, grading downward, at variable depth, into shales.	Very stony. Abrupt slopes.

crop rewarding, or, on the contrary, non-profitable an ecologically well-adapted crop. All this in spite of the prognostications of economists, which are as uncertain as weather forecasts. In referring to 'potentialities', we mean 'pedologic' or 'ecologic potentialities'. It is a question of prudence and honesty. We thus class the constraints into edaphic, morphodynamic and hydrological.

Edaphic constraints   Stoniness, want of soil depth, poor drainage and various chemical toxicities. Heterogeneity, that is the very small dimensions of land with a minimum of homogeneity, are frequently also a constraint. Sometimes the constraints are innumerable, such as in Ndzuani (Anjouan), where overpopulation forces land that elsewhere would remain idle to be cultivated. To crowd the map with all the constraints identified would only make the map illegible and produce a fatalistic attitude among the authorities: what is the use of attempting something when there is no way

out to begin with? The solution, has been to grade the constraints and to map only those important from a practical point of view, that is those that can be contained. Edaphic constraints are shown in black.

Morphodynamic constraints   These are the morphogenic processes, such as surface wash, mass movements, wandering stream courses, and alluviation on valley bottoms. The process is generally identifiable and should be mapped, as well as its intensity. Quantification is usually illusionary and fallacious, so that a qualitative scale (high, medium, low) is generally more useful. It may be necessary to grade the constraints and show only the main ones, as in the case of the edaphic constraints in Ndzuani (Anjouan). Photo interpretation, sequential comparisons of second-generation satellite recordings, SPOT in particular (10 m resolution of the panchromatic band), are indispensable tools, especially when the vegetation is discontinuous or sparse. Often, excellent results are obtained by combining pedologic and geomorphic observations, as on the glacis of Mogtédo and Bittou in Burkina Faso (Upper Volta), where centimetric benches indicate an intense and chronic soil truncation by the unstable runoff of major storms. A layer of scattered, small, friable aggregates on the surface of 'vertic' (cracked) soils is the sure sign of the partial removal of a fine fraction by surface wash. Similarly the height of accumulation of vegetal debris, or even humus, on the upslope side of grass tufts, tree trunks or termitaries is an indication of the intensity of runoff. The diagnosis of such processes provides objective information as to the need for protective measures, which slope maps with limiting values identical from Greenland to Tierra del Fuego would not do. Indeed the functional thresholds of the various processes vary in a complex manner as a function of the lithology, the quality of the soil, and the nature of the plant cover, and are still far from being known. Morphodynamic constraints are shown in red.

Hydrological constraints   Their analysis should explain the water balance and its limitations on agriculture. An example of a hydrological constraint is persistent hydromorphism, either as the result of the relief (artificial drainage is then possible), or of chronic hypodermic seepage, or, still, of a slowly rising water table. Protracted submergence is another example. The areas affected are mapped in blue (usually) hatchings.

The constraints map provides a useful framework for agronomic experimentation. The various shortcomings of the physical environment help define research problems. Representative sites may be chosen for carrying out the experiments, such as methods of cultivation, modes of planting devised to contain or restrain the constraints, remodelling the land parcels by contour ploughing, buffer strips, terracing, or by installing wind breaks. The effects of runoff may be assessed under the various conditions. Successful results can then be applied in other regions where the same conditions obtain.

Proposed land use maps

Regional land use planning and development frequently depend on political decisions dealing with socio-economic matters. These are outside the realm of the technicians of the natural environment. The latter, however, should provide the former with information favouring good decisions. Not participating at the level of final decisions, the technicians cannot impose their views. For this reason, this last map, sequel to the two others, cannot be but a formulation of *proposals*.

The area under consideration on the constraints map is divided into several classes whose possibilities of development are defined as a function of the constraints and the results of agronomic experimentation. The resultant units are therefore dependent on the natural conditions and their limiting factors. We cannot propose a general system of land capability, for if it is easy to put together such a system for a given region, its generalization is inexpedient, as it may require local modifications that would completely transform the original system. This is the case, for example, of the very elaborate Land Capability Classification of the Soil Conservation Service of the USDA, which, although well suited to the United States, would hardly be applicable to the wet tropics. This classification defines a hierarchy of constraints. (A brief presentation of it is given on pp. 107–10.)

On the original coloured map, the restrictions to development are all the greater as the colour is dark. The various agricultural possibilities and the different types of development for each defined class are explained together with their advantages and disadvantages.

Under certain conditions a simplified method of representation may be used, as in the case of a recent study by R. Bertrand (1986), of the IRAT, in Senegal. He had to examine the possibility of using for irrigation part of the water of the Senegal River in a canal planned to supply the water needs of Dakar. A morpho-pedological map was prepared over a distance of 210 km from the Lac de Guiers, at a scale of 1:200,000 (assembled from field maps at 1:50,000), a medium scale, appropriate for an overview to be used to make decisions. A legend of eight columns includes, besides the standard features (morpho-pedological units, landforms, materials, water regime, and soil types), a column for morphodynamics (morphogenic processes) and a column for constraints and suitability for irrigation. The inclusion of a column listing the soil types of the current soil classification is to facilitate communication with more traditionalist edaphologists.

Plates 27–29 Complex pedogenesis
Ph. JT CDV-17 cn. Alternating periods of morphogenesis and pedogenesis. Servainza, Galicia
(Cantabrian Mountains), Spain, alt. 2,100 m. Decomposed granite. First, a humic soil formed on the
truncated regolith. This soil was buried by sandy colluvium generated by the same granite exposed on
higher slopes. Short centimetric beds indicate a very gentle runoff, unable to concentrate, so that the
fossilized older soil is not gullied. We interpret this type of colluvial deposition to have occurred on a
frozen soil under periglacial conditions during the last cold period (Wisconsin, Devensian, Weichsel,
Wurm). Later, a new pedogenesis began under topostable conditions presently interrupted by wheat
cultivation, which has caused an induced colluviation of 'raw' granitic weathered products.

CONCLUSION

We are convinced that this transdisciplinary
approach, with recourse to systems theory, is an
improved way to understand the problems of a
rational land use, be it for agricultural, pastoral or
forestry uses. It has been developed to enable
agronomists to make better use of the scientific
progress made by pedologists and, especially, by
geomorphologists. The IRAT, which has
participated in its elaboration, has applied it
successfully in many countries, especially in Africa.
It answers some of the preoccupations raised at the
highest international scientific level, in the
framework of the International Council of
Scientific Unions, resulting in the creation of the
International Geosphere-Biosphere Programme.

APPENDIX: THE AMERICAN LAND-CAPABILITY CLASSIFICATION

The American Land-capability Classification is a
remarkable, comprehensive system of rational land
use planning (also for non-agricultural uses) on the
local (farm) and, indirectly, on the regional and
national level. It came into being as a result of the
creation of the Soil Conservation Service in 1935.

The classification is coded and is based on
permanent land and climatic characteristics; for
example, degree of slope, soil texture,
permeability, water-holding capacity, type of clay
and, to begin with, whether the land is suitable
(classes I–IV) or not suitable (classes V–VIII) for
cultivation. These two major *divisions* are broken
down into eight land-capability *classes* based on the

degree of suitability of the land to various uses, that is in regard to their limitations: class I having the fewest, class VIII the most limitations. These classes, in turn are subdivided into four *subclasses* based on the **kind** of limitations or hazards, except for class I, which does not have any serious limitations. The four kinds of limitations are

1 danger of 'erosion' (e), except for class V
2 excess water (w)
3 soil limitations (s) (e.g. shallow depth, low moisture-holding capacity, stoniness, salinity, nutrient deficiencies
4 unfavourable climate (c) (e.g. too dry, frost pockets, low temperatures and short growing season at high elevations).

Danger of erosion (e) is related to soil losses and degree of slope, whose maximum limit varies with each soil or group of soils. Lastly, the subclasses are composed of an assemblage of basic units,

called *land-capability units*. These are regions, not necessarily corresponding to soil units, that, for all practical purposes, can be used and treated (managed) in the same way. They are the basic mapping units. In farmland they are accurately delineated on field maps of 4 inches to the mile (1:15,840), reduced to 8 in/mi for later use; on ranchland: 2 inches to the mile (1:31,250). These capability units are generally designated by adding an Arabic numeral to the subclass symbol (e.g. IIe-5). Although a certain degree of standardization may be possible, the units have no standard definitions, but differ from one district to another. For example, in California the land-capability units are

0 Sand and gravel in the substratum.
1 Erosion hazard.
2 Wetness caused by poor drainage or flooding.
3 Slow or very slow permeability of the subsoil or substratum.

Plate 28 Ph. JT CCCLXXV-72 cn. Colluvial soil on gentle slope, Lebrija, Colombia. The substratum consist of poorly cemented sandstones and siltstones of the Formación Girón, which has suffered an intense leaching of its iron oxides, transforming it into a bleached loam. On the upper right an early Quaternary weathered material older than the incision of the vale is exposed. Its texture is that of a clay loam, source of the loamy colluvial material blanketing the lower vale slope, most of the finer fraction having been entrained further down. It is characterized by a marked polygonal structure, caused by desiccation, and was later cut by an induced gully. Each type of surficial formation and soil is characteristic of a morphogenic stage and cannot be understood or mapped without an adequate geomorphological reconstruction.

Plate 29 Ph. JT CCCIII-17 cn. Soil genesis on No. 4 (churchyard) Terrace, Pest-Lorinz, Hungary. The alluvium has been geliturbated with deep 'congelistatic' pockets at the contact of which calcium carbonate has precipitated due to differences of permeability. This is possible only in a seasonally very dry climate, different from the present one. Red clayey weathered material in the pockets probably dates from the last Interglacial (Riss-Wurm). The gelifluced pockets are truncated by an aeolian deflation pavement ('reg') on which finer material has been transformed into a Holocene brown soil. A dry late-Glacial period with wind action (loess) and a climate during the last Interglacial warmer than the present one have been firmly reconstructed in southern Central Europe. These periods can be applied to this particular outcrop. Nevertheless, the precise nature and genetic conditions of the post-reg material affected by Holocene pedogenesis remains undetermined for lack of laboratory investigations.

4 Coarse texture or excessive gravel.
5 Fine or very fine textured soil.
6 Salts or alkali.
7 Cobblestones, stones or rocks.
8 Nearly impervious bedrock or a hardpan.
9 Low fertility or toxicity.

(USDA 1973: 93)

As to the eight land-capability classes, they are, in their briefest form:

I Few limitations. Wide latitude for each use. Very good land from every point of view.

II Moderate limitations or risks of damage. Good land from all-round standpoint.

III Severe limitations or risks of damage. Regular cultivation possible if limitations are observed.

IV Very severe limitations. Suited for occasional cultivation or for some kind of limited cultivation.

V Not suited for cultivation because of wetness, stones, overflows, etc. Few limitations for grazing or forestry use.

VI Too steep, stony, arid, wet, etc. for cultivation. Moderate limitations for grazing or forestry.

VII Very steep, rough, arid, wet, etc. Severe limitations for grazing or forestry.

VIII Extremely rough, arid, swampy, etc. Not suited for cultivation, grazing, or forestry. Suited for wildlife, watersheds, or recreation.

(Hockensmith and Steele 1949)

This system is in wide use in the United States today: it has obvious qualities. Nevertheless, it is unfortunate that it was developed at the time of static physiography, before much attention was paid to geomorphic processes and geomorphic systems. It suffers from some of the same shortcomings as the Seventh Approximation. The word 'geomorphic' is seldom or never used, there is constant talk of 'erosion', 'water erosion' or 'runoff', without specification. It is also limited by the dearth of modern local and regional geomorphological studies and detailed geomorphological maps, by the limited use of the time factor dealing with frequencies and intensities, to say nothing of the use of palaeoclimatic factors. The system assumes a moderately high level of management and is really not adapted to human groups with 'exotic' social and cultural characteristics and, therefore, to world-wide use. Apart from that the system has the merit of precocity and proven usefulness in the United States.

REFERENCES

Hedge, A. M., Klingebiel, A. A. (1957) The use of soil maps. *Soil: Yearbook of Agriculture.* USDA, pp. 400–11.
Besides two sketch maps (for a farm and for a ranch) soil and capability units are shown and described for two conservation plan sketch maps.
Hockensmith, R. D., Steele, J. G. (1949) Recent trends in the use of the land-capability classification. *Soil Sci. Soc. Amer. Proc.,* **14:** 383–88.
Account of the Land-capability classification and its usefulness.
Klingebiel, A. A. (1958) Soil survey interpretation-capability groupings. *Soil Sci. Soc. Amer. Proc.,* **22:** 160–63.
The classification, granted assumptions, evaluation of capability groupings and their uses.
Klingebiel, S. A., Montgomery, P. H. (1961) *Land-capability classification.* SCS, USDA Agric. Handbook 210, 21 pp. (reprinted 1966).
More detailed than the above ref.
USDA, SCS (1952) *Land-capability classification guide, Pacific region.* 30 pp., USDA.
Explanation of the system.
USDA, SCS, Forest Service et al. (1973) *Soil Survey, San Diego Area, California,* Part II. 118 pp., USDA.
Example of a specific regional survey.

4 WATER RESOURCES

Water is unique matter that is a primary characteristic of the Earth's environment when compared to other planets. Water is found in large quantities not only in liquid form, but also as gas and as a solid; it is more or less mobile, depending on its state, but most of it is in permanent storage. It is superabundant as standing water in oceans, seas and lakes, as ice in glaciers above, and as ground ice in permafrost below the Earth's surface. Water is also in storage in the pedosphere, the decomposition sphere (subsoil), in aquifers, and even enters the composition of minerals. In the biosphere water molecules predominate over all other bodies, frequently making up 80 per cent of the weight of animals, and even more of that of plants. In the atmosphere, water is abundant in the form of clouds and all kinds of precipitation or simply as vapour, and besides plays an important role by absorbing part of the solar radiation and reflecting it as diffuse light.

Water flows, in a 'material flow system', in and between these water bodies and 'spheres', as it is set in motion, with a greater or lesser amount of other materials, by solar energy or gravitation, including that of the Sun and the Moon (tides). The soil returns it to the atmosphere through evaporation, and the plants, which extract it from the soil, through transpiration. Water is the vehicle of dissolved products on the surface and in the subsurface of the Earth. Interstitial water modifies the mechanical properties of the regolith, permitting its deformation and mobilization on slopes, producing soil slips, landslides, mudflows and solifluction. Runoff, overland and in streams and rivers, is the main instrument of morphogenesis, except in glacial and formerly glaciated regions, in non-deltaic coastal zones, and in regions where the action of the wind is presently predominant. Without doubt, the hydrosphere, in three states, puts its stamp on the originality of the natural environment and all creatures in it, large and small, as water enters into most metabolic processes and mechanisms that transform the natural environment and characterize its dynamics. Water indeed characterizes *this* planet, which led

J. Y. Cousteau to remark that a more appropriate name for the Earth would have been the 'Water'.

THE STATE OF KNOWLEDGE

The omnipresence of water in Nature has had a negative effect on its study in the framework of traditional, excessively analytical research. The more comprehensive viewpoint professed by teachers at the dawn of the twentieth century has not been maintained.

Precipitation

From the beginning climatology has associated the measurement of rainfall to that of temperature. However, in spite of the existence of very long series of observations in certain countries, our perception of the nature of rainfall still leaves much to be desired. We know little, often very little, of the two most important characteristics of a rain storm: its intensity and its duration. These are, precisely, of the highest importance in an integrated study of the environment, for on them depends the energy transmitted by the rain to the ground, and the behaviour of the water on the ground. The intensity and duration of rain storms are basic, irreplaceable data for the study of morphogenic processes, problems of land and water conservation, the soil water regime, and other hydrologic phenomena. (We demonstrated this in previous chapters in regard to interception and splash erosion.) Unfortunately, gaps in our knowledge are not limited to these alone. Rain gauges are generally poorly sited and distributed, forming too loose a network. They allow only the making of coarse maps on a medium and, more generally, a small scale. The precipitation map of

France on a scale of 1:1,000,000 is valid, but the mapping of precipitation on the climatological map of 1:200,000 is based on many interpolations, which are more or less satisfactory depending upon the experience or dexterity of the authors. The making of climatological maps at a scale of 1:25,000 or 1:10,000, that is at the scale of other components of the environment, is nearly always out of the question. Too coarse a perception leaves out the effects of exposure and landforms on precipitation. In France, for example, it is impossible to know whether it rains more on the west or on the east flank of a peak of the Vosges Mountains, on the backslope or on the faceslope of a cuesta in Lorraine, or on the sunny or shady side of a valley in the Alps or the Pyrenees. Even the establishment of an accurate precipitation gradient between the Rhine Valley and the summits of the Vosges is not feasible.

Furthermore, precipitation in the form of rain and snow is only part of the water resources benefiting the natural environment. Other occurrences of weather phenomena are still insufficiently known, to say nothing of being recorded: a hailstorm is reported by only a limited number of weather stations and is usually not the object of any measurement, such as its duration, the size of the hailstones, or its rainfall equivalent. Better informed are insurance companies, but they do not divulge their information. Various forms of condensation (such as dew, rime and fog) are sometimes known as 'occult precipitation', a risible expression, bringing to mind the 'occult sciences'. A good fog, hoarfrost or a heavy dew are quite observable, and could be measured. To ignore them is all the more regrettable as their role is important in ecology. Certain life forms, such as the 'lomas', or episodic pastures, which attract transhumant flocks in the coastal desert of Peru exist only thanks to fog and the condensation it produces. But the rain gauges record only 'traces' of precipitation! At Lachay, north of Lima, the rain gauge recorded a mean of 168 mm from 1944 to 1954. Nevertheless, a transhumance was developed by the Incas, perhaps even earlier, from the Andes to these 'lomas' during the southern winter, when the high pastures of the puna are subject to nocturnal frost. The flocks were then brought down to the verdant rolling, even tree-growing, 'lomas'. During the same decade the average precipitation rose to 488 mm under casuarinas and to 676 mm under eucalypti. In 1949, a humid year, an official rain gauge recorded 204 mm, while 1,240 mm were recorded under eucalypti! In 1954, a dry year, the values were 121 and 756 mm respectively. The fog condenses more on the trees than on the ground, and aerial streamlets form from the branches. But whereas the site of Lachay is only moderately arid, grassy lomas and thick-set shrubs grow in a more genuinely arid climate, where rain gauges sited on sand receive less than 100 mm per annum.

Are these phenomena surprising? The observations at Lachay were made by ecologists, not by climatologists. This is often the case, as in the rainforest of Banco, near Abidjan (Ivory Coast), where a vertical profile of insolation, temperature and precipitation was made through the various strata of the vegetation, which helped explain the development and life of insects.

The research of climatologists has also been too independent of that of meteorologists. They have exclusively sought to establish a world-wide inventory on a small scale. While the use of a recording time-span of 24 hours results in observations that are too coarse, the presentation of data in the form of monthly or yearly averages inordinately cuts down the importance of individual weather phenomena. The results are abstract data, which certain climatologists elucidate with studies on types of weather. This, however, does not fulfil the requirements of husbandmen, hydrologists or ecologists actually concerned with the weather and its consequences. Why not, as in hydrology, make frequency-intensity analyses, similar to the curves of classed fluvial discharges? The data are available. They would show the frequency of a certain amount of daily precipitation; for example, <10 mm, 10–30 mm and >100 mm. Correlatively, frequency tables of periods of x, y or z consecutive days without precipitation could be made.

There is also the question of instrumentation. The cost of rain gauges is minimal compared to many other modern meteorological instruments. Why not introduce them systematically in critical areas? It is done by most agencies concerned with hydrological studies. Finally, other instruments should be improved, as those that measure dew. Is it impossible?

Evaporation and transpiration

Our knowledge of the output of water through evaporation and the transpiration of plants, usually grouped under the term 'evapotranspiration', is as wanting as our knowledge of the input of water through precipitation. Both evaporation and transpiration return water vapour to the atmosphere, whose moisture content they feed, which helps renewed precipitation. But it is not this logic that is at the origin of the word 'evapotranspiration'. Quite the contrary, the term is misleading. Indeed, whereas the transpiration of plants is not subject to direct measurement, plain evaporation is not readily calculated. What has been associated is not a blind man and a paralytic, but a one-eyed man and a blind man.

Much research has been done on potential evapotranspiration, that is on the maximum value of transpiration. All calculations are dependent on formulas that take account of various climatic parameters. Unfortunately, each formula is valid only under certain biogeographic conditions. Moreover, many of them include parameters that are seldom measured, such as solar radiation. So, it must be admitted that the results obtained are rather approximate. Under these circumstances recourse to the simplest formulas, such as the aridity index (in fact a humidity index) of Emm. de Martonne in 1926 or the ombrothermic diagrams of Bagnouls and Gaussen (1957), both of which make use only of precipitation and temperature data, has much in its favour. However, evaporation and actual transpiration remain to be measured, but the required instruments are still deficient. One, the Colorado tank, has been devised by American irrigation technicians. A yard long (0.914 m) and half a yard deep, and theoretically insulated from the ground, a steady water level is maintained in it at ground level by means of a siphon. A gauge measures siphon inflow, while a pluviometer allows rainfall input to be subtracted. The resultant quantity is considered to be equal to the evaporation. This device has the following liabilities:

1 Insulation of the bottom and sides is always insufficient, so that the water heats or cools with the ground temperature.
2 The size and depth of the tank are insufficient to eliminate reflected radiations from the bottom and sides, which distort the measurement.
3 The maintenance of such tanks is delicate and often deficient. Some years ago, the tank of the Mediterranean Agronomic Institute of Zaragoza (Spain), an international and specialized research organization, filled with algae and contained frogs and toads, while measurements were still being made.
4 There is no comparison possible even between a field irrigated by submersion and a Colorado tank, and even less between this tank and non-submerged crops. The tank might seem to measure the height of the column of water evaporated at the surface of a reservoir if the currents, the unequal depths, often substantial, did not considerably modify the energy reflections of the bottom. At best, the tank can provide a vague order of magnitude.

Another method to measure atmospheric evaporation is by means of a Piche evaporimeter. (The Piche evaporimeter uses an inverted graduated cylinder of water with a filter-paper seal at the mouth. Evaporation takes place from the wet filter paper and thus depletes the water in the cylinder, so that the rate of evaporation can be read directly from the gradations marking the water level.) But results only approximate reality. Several corrective measures have been proposed, but these only demonstrate that the method leaves much to be desired.

Thus evaporation is most often *evaluated* indirectly. Together with the transpiration of plants, which is not measurable either, it shares in the runoff deficit, which is the difference between the amount of water which has fallen on a basin and that evacuated from it during the same period. This deficit not uncommonly reaches 90 per cent in small basins covered by tropical rainforest (e.g. in French Guyana). This method, too, is not without problems.

1 A small basin has the advantage of uniformity and easy gauging, but is it representative? It is subject to catastrophic, often poorly gauged, flash floods with crests that stagger observers. Yet such floods form an important part of the annual runoff.
2 Even in a small basin, a fortiori in a large one, there are phase differences between pecipitation and runoff. To record them and to take account of them is difficult. An extreme case is one in which surface and subsurface basins do not coincide, for example, because of aquifers, karstic circulations, or runoff divides in discord with subsurface partings. Both the runoff deficit and coefficient are then perverted.
3 Lastly, the measuring of discharge itself, whether by mechanical or chemical gauging, entails a non-negligible margin of error. To obtain a result that is 90 per cent accurate is a veritable feat.

We must admit that outside of very small basins precipitation as well as runoff is known only to within a margin of 10–20 per cent. Runoff coefficients, therefore, reach deviations of 20–33 per cent approximately. The same holds true of the runoff deficit, which is obtained by subtraction.

Consequences

The want of precision of measured data, the insufficient representativeness of the sites where the climatic measurements are made, and the considerable annual variation of hydroclimatological data justify the recourse to statistics, in this case almost exclusively to *averages*. But an average value is a very simplistic, mediocre instrument. Recourse to *medians* is still rare, although adopted by some geographers. The advantage of a median is to divide a series of numbers in increasing order into classes of two equal parts, or numbers. In other words, for our purpose, the median corresponds to a probability of one year out of two. Quartiles are calculated in the same way (75 and 25 percent), deciles, etc. The quartile corresponding to the lowest values of the series of numbers arranged in order of increasing values means that the probability that this value may be attained or exceeded is three years out of four; the first decile nine years out of ten; and the last decile only one year out of ten. The discharge of a river corresponding to the ninth decile is that of a ten-year flood, which in France is an administrative norm to distinguish 'normal' from 'catastrophic' floods. Construction is in principle allowed only on land that floods less frequently than once in ten years. If a flood does occur, the action taken falls into the category of events termed catastrophic. The method can, of course, also be applied to meteorological and climatological data. Unfortunately researchers who want to apply this type of simple and effective treatment do not benefit from any help, must do everything themselves and buy the data at a heavy price.

Climatology and hydrology have traditionally had recourse to averages. Because of the mediocrity of the data, the procedure has been to apply the law of large numbers, to lengthen the statistical series. Thirty years is considered 'normal' for precipitation, at least twenty in hydrology. This has serious consequences on planning. What decision-maker, what politician can accept a time lapse of twenty to thirty years before approving a land use project? If such a record is not available because of lack of time or installations certain precautions have to be taken. A large margin of security must be provided, which means building extra large structures, such as dams, which in turn mean higher costs. Seldom, in spite of many efforts, have countries established sufficiently dense hydrometric networks in the 1960s and 1970s to provide a chosen basin with the necessary data to

plan a certain development. This certainly applies to France. The solution of oversized structures results, depending upon the case, in a certain amount of extra or insufficient industrial capacity. France offers examples of both. If·certain pressure groups, in the first case, impose the building of extra large structures, a wastage results; in the opposite case, nothing is built, and the result is underdevelopment. Thus while technology progresses and should be able to make better use of the natural environment, and while, also, the demographic expansion continues to increase human needs, there is less rather than more environmental management, and the development that takes place is increasingly risky. We are in a state of contradiction, of illogicality. Meanwhile the list of technological catastrophes lengthens at an increasing rate.

The traditional approach, therefore, needs to be changed. Is there another way?

THE NATURALISTIC APPROACH: THE FUNCTIONING OF A DRAINAGE BASIN

J. Tricart has created a new term, *hydromorphology*, to designate the various forms the water takes in the natural environment. These will be examined in a systems framework, as used throughout this book. Because of the great complexity of the problem, we shall use Descartes's principle: to examine the components (of the basin) before examining the whole, which is at a higher level.

The basin as a system of energy and materials

The flow chart (Figure 11) is limited to the main interactions characterizing the functioning of the drainage basin.

1 The two 'motive elements' are physiography, that is the relief and the regolith, and climate, specifically precipitation and relative humidity. At this very general level we are satisfied with 'physiography', as we omit the genesis of the relief. Similarly with climate, we stress precipitation and relative humidity, as these two components determine the water balance. Certainly, temperature also intervenes, aside

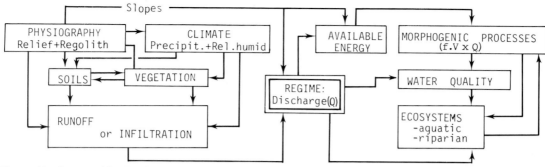

Figure 11. Systems idealization of a drainage basin
V – velocity
Q – Discharge

from its role in relative humidity; for example, in the form of a temporary snow cover. But, not to complicate things, we shall limit ourselves to the essential.

2 Physiography and climate affect soils and vegetation. We have purposely left out the feedback of the soils on morphogenesis, since we have adopted the concept 'physiography', which eliminates morphogenesis. Similarly, the feedback vegetation → climate has been omitted – one of its main aspects being the transpiration of plants. Physiography and climate intervene indirectly as well as directly. Both effects converge on the *alternative 'runoff/infiltration'*, which is a major determinant of the fluvial regime. The other determinant is the *slope*, on which depends the velocity of runoff.

3 Slopes are usually divided into *hill* or *mountain sides* and *longitudinal drainage lines*. They intervene, as just noted, in the fluvial regime. How? During the *time of concentration* (of hydrologists), that is the time water takes from the arrival of raindrops or the liberation of water from the fusion of snow at various points in the drainage basin to the passage of that water at a gauging station lower down. The time of concentration is therefore a determining factor of the regime, that is, of the variations of a stream's discharge as a function of time. The *unitary hydrograph* is a curve $Q = f(t)$, Q being the discharge, t the time. Its object is to show how discharge varies at a gauging station as a function of the time elapsed since the storm that produced the spate. The less the time of concentration, the shorter the duration of the maximum discharge, or, in other words, the more 'pointed' the curve. This is what characterizes, but less precisely, what is meant by a 'torrent' and also the expression 'influenced regime' (influenced by the precipitation).

4 The slopes affect not only the 'regime', but the energy of stream flow, the result of the transformation of gravity. This energy is a function of both the velocity and the abundance of the water, which depend on the gradient and the discharge, as shown by two arrows. The two factors are interdependent, for, in a given bed, the larger the discharge the greater the current velocity energy loss by friction of the water against the bed is comparatively less.

5 The *regime* is placed in the centre of the chart, as is proper, since we are dealing with the structure of a drainage basin. It is at the end of the arrows coming from the 'black boxes' at the left, which show the origin of a stream's regime. It is also at the origin of the arrows pointing to the boxes at the right. The discharge determines the available energy: a drainage basin, indeed, is not only a natural unit carrying flowing water (hydrologic point of view), but also an *energy system*, part of which, let us not forget, can be transformed into electricity. In Nature, this energy system produces *morphogenic processes* that are a function of the product of the current velocity and its discharge: $f(V) \times Q$. To simplify, we have voluntarily eliminated the fashioning of the relief by the morphogenic processes, which should have been shown by an arrow: morphogenic processes → relief.

6 Regime and morphogenic processes determine, in a convergent manner, the quality of the water and the ecosystems, which depend closely on them. The silts, muds and ions mobilized by the morphogenic processes affect the quality of the water, as well as all pollutants produced by human activities. Aquatic and riparian ecosystems are dependent on the quality of the water, on the greater or lesser stability determined by the morphogenic processes and, also, directly, on the variations in discharge

which cause portions of river beds to be then dry, then submerged. These ecosystems themselves, by feedback, influence the morphogenic processes: this is only one particular aspect of the general concept of phytostability.

The integration in this flow chart of a component of the natural environment (a drainage basin) in the system 'natural environment' having been examined, we now can look deeper into the subsystem 'drainage basin' without fear of being led astray. We shall continue to apply Descartes's good principle and to proceed from the simple to the complex, from the part to the whole.

Water flow of a drainage basin

Figure 12 is limited to the flow of water in a drainage basin. Respecting the law of gravity, the main movement of the molecules of H_2O, known as 'water', is from high to low places. This is translated in the disposition of the flow diagram, which should be read downward.

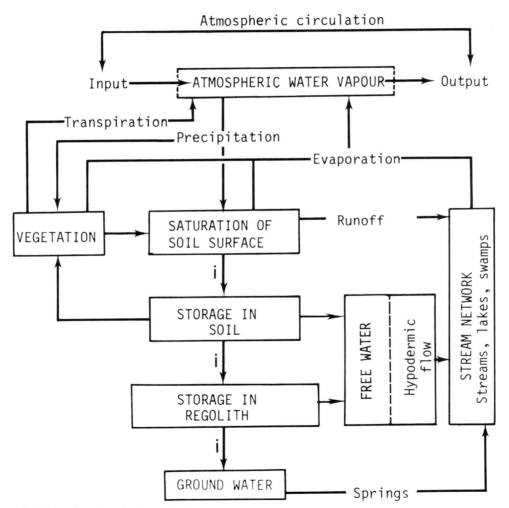

Figure 12. Water flow in a drainage basin

i = infiltration (gravity flow)

We have omitted the capillary rise of ground-water into the regolith. Each box may be thought of as a 'reservoir', storing a certain amount of water; for example, in plant tissues and on the surface of leaves and branches, in the case of vegetation. Such an assimilation is at the origin of reservoir models of hydrologic phenomena.

The *atmospheric circulation* is the starting-point. It produces a generally horizontal movement of air masses, which is shown in Figure 12 by the terms 'input' and 'output', which apply to the space occupied by the drainage basin. The inputs and outputs are those of atmospheric water vapour. Part of the water vapour is precipitated directly by condensation on plants, as in the extreme example of the Peruvian 'lomas', but most of the precipitation is in the form of rain and snow falling either directly on the ground or indirectly through the plant cover. The water then can go in various directions once the superficial layer of soil has been saturated: the flow chart, although somewhat simplified, shows this clearly.

1 In the left centre, vertically superimposed levels in which the water penetrates by infiltration (note the letter 'i') have been shown, each level representing a 'reservoir'. They are successively the soil, from which part of the water taken up by plants returns to the atmosphere through transpiration, and the regolith, sometimes also penetrated, as the bedrock and its aquifers, by roots. This has not been shown for the sake of simplification.

2 On the right, the soil surface, sealed by splash or saturated, is subject to a certain amount of evaporation of the water, which stagnates in puddles or has infiltrated a few decimetres. This evaporation, together with that which takes place after a shower on plant leaves and occurs on water bodies, again feeds the atmosphere with water vapour. But the water that is not evaporated on the ground feeds runoff on a sloping surface and then reaches the drainage network formed by streams, marshes and lakes. When the water infiltrated into the ground reaches a somewhat impermeable layer that impedes further percolation, it courses down dip of this layer as hypodermic flow (see definition on pp. 28–9). Figure 13 shows how it works. It is called 'free drainage' by hydrologists in contrast to the 'confined drainage' of aquifers, which is under pressure in a permeable bed or formation capped by impermeable material. The attitude of the beds is not determined by the topography, as in the case of hypodermic flow, but by the geologic structure. Hypodermic flow necessarily ends at the base of the slope in a valley, where it feeds the drainage network.

The ground-water of the geologic materials, which is the specific object of hydrogeology, is in communication with the drainage network: it supplies it with the water of springs, and is itself

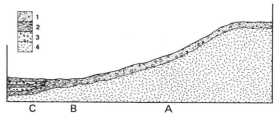

Figure 13. Hypodermic flow

1 Coarse weathered slope material, pervious
2 Finer colluvial deposit, less pervious
3 Alluvium, gravel lenses between finer material
4 Compact, impervious crystalline rock

A Throughflow (hypodermic) in the coarse, pervious material of the slope.

B Arriving in the less pervious, finer alluvium (2), the hypodermic flow becomes more difficult, slows down, saturates the material, and seeps out of the surface in the form of springlets

C The poor permeability of the colluvium impedes the transmission of the hypodermic flow into the alluvium. Were it not for the silty colluvium, the hypodermic flow would contribute water to the alluvial aquifer.

fed by infiltration of surface water. The slow migration is affected by a response delay of many months, currently years, and even thousands of years as in the case of the 'fossil' aquifers of Algeria and Libya. This explains the regularity of the regime. The slow pace, together with hypodermic flow, but with more abundant reserves, ensures an uninterrupted streamflow even during drought, albeit at base flow. The hydrograph then takes the form of a hyperbolic segment becoming gradually, with time, tangent to a straight line parallel to the x-axis, the y-axis indicating the discharge. At the point of tangency, the water input into the stream is by ground-water only. Shortly prior to that, it still received hypodermic inflow. The form of this runoff hydrograph has special significance in hydrogeologic research as well as in the understanding of water resources and their management. Aquifers are mainly fed by streams especially during high water stages when lowlands are flooded. The current is then slow, the flooded zone extensive, which compensates for the slowing of infiltration into the superficial layer of overbank silts that are being deposited. The deep aquifers of the Paris region, namely in the Jurassic and the Lower Cretaceous, are thus fed by floods of the Meuse River in the Barrois and of tributaries of the Seine in the Humid

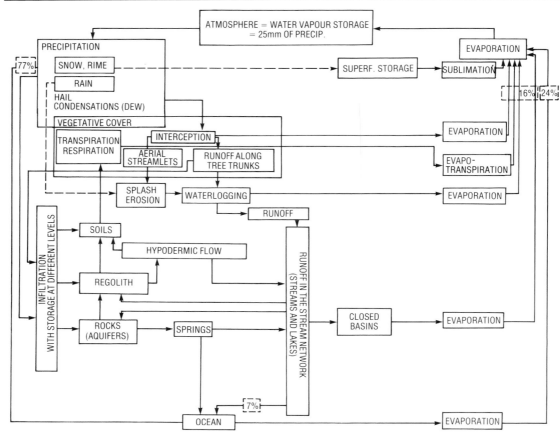

Figure 14. Water flow in the ecologic environment

Champagne, in which regions these rock systems outcrop. Infiltration from stream beds, too, occurs when they are not sealed by muds and permeable rocks outcrop below coarse alluvium. Also interchanges between a river bed and its floodplain contribute to the regularization of discharge. They lower non-overbank high water stages and sustain low water stages by restitution. A deeper infiltration explains why certain rivers dry up completely at 'low water' when all the water infiltrates into the most permeable sectors.

The hydrological cycle in the ecologic environment

Now let us return to these concepts to reach a more comprehensive, indeed more complicated view, as represented in Figure 14. We again find the subsystems presented above, but they are no more isolated and their mutual relationships with other elements have been stressed. This also has made

possible the presentation of a balance sheet at the global level. Its various characteristics are as follows.

First, the role of the oceans is strongly predominant, even beyond what could have been expected, considering they cover more than 70 per cent of the Earth's surface. They indeed receive 77 per cent of the Earth's precipitation, which is explained by the vast areas of the Indian and Pacific oceans situated near the Equator. Plate tectonics influences the water balance. Evaporation, for the same reason, is more than proportional to the size of world ocean, accounting for 84 per cent of the total. The remaining 16 per cent is provided by the soil, the surface of wetted plants, endorheic water bodies, and the transpiration of plants. The input of fresh water into the ocean from submarine springs, rivers and glaciers amounts to only 7 per cent of the total, which is little in comparison to the 16 per cent of the precipitation that does not reach the drainage network. This fact should be kept in mind, as the hydraulic developments designed to increase our –

vital – water resources rapidly reach their limit, the more so as the irrationality of economists, financiers and politicians who depend on them further limit the possibility to realize them because of high interest rates caused by the budgetary laxity of certain countries.

Second, the group of 'black boxes' assembled in the larger box *vegetative cover* takes on an importance that is both fundamental and practical. Let us look at it closely. The object of the partial overlap of the two large boxes, 'vegetative cover' and 'precipitation' is to recall the direct condensation of fog on plants, not only on the Peruvian 'lomas', but also, in much larger quantities, on the cloud forests of mountain ranges, especially in the intertropical zone, such as in the Venezuelan and Colombian Andes or the highlands of East Africa. These cloud forest zones provide the best environment for coffee shrubs. One of the direct effects of the vegetation is its metabolism, indicated by the box 'transpiration–respiration', impossible to separate and, therefore, regrouped as 'evapotranspiration'. The other main direct effect is *interception*, long disregarded and still poorly appraised today. Because of their needs, climatologists have decreed that rain gauges must be installed in open areas, therefore away from trees, which intercept the rain. As the eliminated interception is not measured, it is as if it does not exist, which reminds one of the old proverb: 'he who wants to kill his dog claims that it has rabies'. The rain that falls on foliage begins to wet it. The quantity necessary varies enormously according to the configuration of the foliage, specifically the surface area of the leaves, difficult to measure, and the quality of the upper epidermis (smooth, rough). At the end of the shower, the moisture disappears by evaporation. The quantity is less if the wind blows, and it is not the same for rain and for snow. The problem, from the start, is highly complex. These questions concern the hydrologic aspect of interception. They are not the only ones: there is also an energy question of the impact of raindrops and the splash erosion and runoff they cause, already examined in Chapter 2. As 16 per cent of the Earth's precipitation returns to the atmosphere without passing through the drainage network, it is clear that the use and improvement of water resources depends more on humankind's management of the plant cover than on hydraulic engineering works. The one, however, does not exclude the other – far from it! Splash erosion and surface runoff indeed provide most of the fluvial load in suspension, which, itself, deleteriously affects hydraulic engineering works by irremediably causing the siltation of reservoirs, irrigation canals and ditches, and impeding the drainage of the land. Interdependence . . .

We have up to this point treated the 'plant cover' as a whole. We shall now restrict our perception by examining the relationships water–soil–plants, which are at the centre of preoccupation of applied ecologists or agronomists.

THE SOIL WATER REGIME AND PLANT PRODUCTIVITY

The rational development of the land and the exploitation of its resources are necessarily closely related to agricultural productivity. This productivity is much dependent on the availability of water and the quantity of water transpired by plants to prevent wilting. The circulation of water (sap) in the plant also permits the spreading into the plant tissues of the mineral elements extracted from the soil and of the carbohydrates elaborated by photosynthesis in the chlorophyll.

Peasants, from earliest historic times, have developed schemes to ensure a proper water supply to their crops. These schemes include not only the cropping of floodplains after the seasonal flood, as along the Nile or, later, the Senegal and middle Niger rivers, but also the reclamation of marshlands, ponds and small lakes (as in poljes), common for centuries in the Mediterranean Basin. Other, simple, traditional practices, such as cropping on mounds or raised rows, or downslope ploughing allow excess water drainage on the scale of the parcel. Dry farming, too, was developed very early – at the time of the Phoenicians.

The understanding of and control of the water regime of cultivated lands has been patiently mastered and prudently managed by the cultures of all traditional agrarian systems. Presently, given favourable economic conditions, the progress of technology allows human beings considerably to increase their mastery of the water regime. In many developed countries, like parts of Switzerland, rich in lakes, irrigation is used even though the climate is humid in order to ensure, regardless of the weather, maximum yields year in and year out. But this mastery of the water regime does not apply to other parameters of the ecologic environment. Against excessive solar radiation not much has been accomplished, for example, to protect certain crops such as coffee, except for the growing of shade trees. To counteract low temperature, extensive use of greenhouses or nylon sheeting to grow fruits and vegetables, as in the Westland of the Netherlands, is necessarily limited by economic and other factors. To guard against ravaging winds, rows of trees or hedges have been incorporated into certain well-known agricultural regions, such as the lower Rhône Valley, battered by the mistral, or the High Plains of the United States, where in a semi-arid region, they help reduce evapotranspiration of the cultivated land and provide additional moisture in the case of snowdrifts accumulating adjacent to the shelterbelts. But although agronomists are convinced of the usefulness of these techniques, their use is far from being as widespread as the techniques of water supply.

Mastering of the soil water regime will continue to play a major role in land use; appreciation and instantaneous knowledge of the regime through measurement of its fluctuations and their consequences on crop yields remain a major preoccupation. This enormous water problem will not be developed here, but it will be relevant to recall briefly some fundamental physiological concepts on which the water balance depends, and to review the fundamental criteria and techniques of measurement on which it is based. A few examples will serve to show how particular water regimes can be studied in order to improve regional productivity.

The utilization of water by plants

Water uptake

First a few facts: in Tunisia, maize requires an uptake of 340 g of water to produce one gram of dry matter; peppers 800 g (Yankovitch 1956). In France (Versailles), under experimental conditions, in a ten-year average, with care to prevent any water excess, wheat required 130 g after sprouting, 2,700 g at granulation, or an average of 300 g during its vegetative cycle (Demolon 1968). But this consumption increases rapidly if the water input is increased and reaches very high values in permanently moist soils. The amount of water needed by a plant to produce one gram of dry matter is designated by the expression *coefficient of transpiration*. The water content of a plant varies with age and time of day. It may be as high as 90 per cent in young plants and as low as 15 per cent

in the tissues of old plants. Water is also necessary to nitrogen-fixing bacteria, which carry on a process of natural fertilization.

Water is therefore an important factor of growth and, for humankind, the production of food or fibre. As early as 1920 E. A. Mitscherlich showed that the yield curve increases rapidly with moisture, passes an optimum, and then decreases with further increase in water content as a result of a decrease in aeration, which is also indispensable to plants. The optimum amount varies with plants and soil. Shortages in phosphorus, potassium, sulphur, calcium, magnesium and trace elements in decreasing order of importance, increase water need, but adequate fertilization decreases it, as demonstrated by Kilian and Velly (1964) in Madagascar.

The agronomic management of a crop has repercussions on the use of water. A primordial task of agronomic experiment stations is to determine optimum water needs. The right amount should be provided at the right time. The period *maturation* is a particularly critical moment, as a shortage of water prevents the formation of the grain. The circulation of the sap varies depending on whether dehydration at the time of maturation is slow or fast, as emphasized by Demolon (1952). In a cereal the migration of mineral solutions followed by drying is very active during the pithy stage that precedes, by only several days, the maturation of the grain. If there is an excess of moisture during this period, the quality of the grain suffers; in contrast, with a shortage of water (no rain, a dry hot wind) a scalding occurs. In the absence of irrigation, plants are particularly sensitive to the time and quantity of rainfall during such *critical periods* of their development, which also include growth of the stem before granulation and earing (Azzi 1954). Crop yield is in direct proportion to soil moisture during these periods; for example, the yield of pluvial rice is seriously compromised if there is a water shortage during the growth of the stem prior to granulation. Similarly, the date at which cereals (millet and sorghum) are sown in the northern Sudanese and Sahelian zones of Africa is of the utmost importance for the completion of the vegetative cycle during the last critical periods (maturation in particular). In the temperate zone, winter weather is decisive, as shown by Demolon (1952) in the region around Paris: if the December, January and February precipitation exceeds 100 mm with a mean temperature above 4°C, an excess crop is most unlikely. In contrast, high yields correspond to cool, dry winters ($P < 100$ mm, $t < 3°$). Such conditions, of course, never occur in intertropical mountains, such as the Venezuelan Andes, where the wheat grown at Mucuchies under the conditions of a 'colonial' pact to feed Cuba yielded only a maximum of 4–5 quintals/ha, barely 50 per cent more than the seeds. The straw was abundant, however, and was reserved for the landowners to feed their working bulls, while the tenants cultivated by hand.

Thus it is important to know the soil water regime, which expresses the soil water content as a function of input and output over time, whether the land is irrigated or not; it allows us to situate the role of the water at critical periods and to forecast plant growth and ultimate crop yield. And, as the mineral nourishment of the plant is a function of the circulation of the water in the plant, it is also important to have a detailed knowledge of the organs that ensure the plant's nourishment; their observation in the field often provides simple answers to defects in growth or, simply, to non-adaptations of a cultivated plant to its environment.

Moisture absorption

As early as 1801 J. A. C. Chaptal, Count of Chanteloup (1823) remarked that during certain dry years the humidity of the air has a notable effect on the enlargement of grapes. He believed that moisture could penetrate the grapes through the epidermis of the bunch's stalks and, especially, the leaves. A certain amount of water can penetrate through the leaves' stomata and even their epidermic cuticle. Furthermore, it has long been known that atmospheric moisture, that is water vapour pressure, which is variable, has an influence on the osmotic pressure of the leaf sap. Although minor, this water intake is not negligible; whether in the form of early morning dew, often considerable in dry tropical climates, or as a result of residual moisture after rainfall in a semi-arid climate, the efficacy of such intake is likely, although measured data are few. It is probably important in the foggy deserts of the Pacific coast of South America, where a constant onshore, saturated breeze produces up to 60 mm of measured annual precipitation. Under such conditions certain plants, such as *Tillandsia stratinea* (a bromeliad), prosper practically without roots on the desert floor 'absorbing the moisture of the fog through its leaves'. Their growth, of course, is very slow and their tissues are quite woody. Other bromeliads, a family rich in epiphytes, grow on the telephone and power lines of the cloud forests of Venezuela. This type of water intake is by osmosis, like that of roots, especially rootlets and hairs in close contact with the soil. Osmosis is the ability of a weak solution to pass through a very fine porous membrane into a stronger solution. In plants this process is associated with the circulation of water by the process of transpiration, which, through the consumption of oxygen, provides the energy required by breaking down the molecules of carbohydrates previously produced by photosynthesis. The *osmotic pressure* is all the higher as the sap is rich in dissolved matter. A high osmotic pressure reflects an adaptation to drought. The input of minerals from the soil is distinct from that of the water, as the plant extracts only those required for its health. Osmotic pressure is very high in certain cacti, which are typical xerophytes. The osmotic absorption of water by a rootlet reduces the moisture content of the soil to within a radius of about 10 cm, inciting an influx of moisture from the surrounding area, thus providing continued nourishment. Nutrients such as nitrate, sulphate, calcium and magnesium that are not strongly adsorbed to the clay minerals more readily participate in the osmotic process than strongly adsorbed elements such as phosphorus and potassium. (Adsorption is the electrostatic attraction (adhesion) of base cations (positive charge) to clay minerals with a negative charge.) Osmosis is most efficient where the root system is dense and spread out. So, whenever possible the root system merits detailed examination as it conditions plant growth and, to a certain degree, explains it (Hénin, Gras and Monnier 1969).

Root development

Roots increase by lengthening and thickening, and new roots develop from older ones. Daily growth is variable, ranging from 1 cm in most grasses to 6 cm in maize. Plant growth is closely related to that of its roots, which itself is highly dependent on the physical and chemical properties of the soil and, especially, on its moisture content.

Influence of the physical and chemical properties of the soil

Root depth and spread are primarily conditioned by soil structure and profile. In a loose, relatively homogeneous soil the root system spreads throughout the profile and assumes its natural preordained form, whether fibrous, tracing, or as a taproot. The nourishment of the plants in water and mineral nutrients is then assured with maximum efficacy.

Variations in soil profile affect this development and may explain the character of the aerial parts of the plant. Soil structure, associated with texture, plays a major role, affecting root penetration. The loose, sandy soils of the temperate zones provide the least mechanical resistance; root systems can develop in them without restraint. The texture and consistency of these soils also play their part: too much coarse sand, for example, is an unfavourable factor, as well as too compact sands, which are never cultivated. Most favourable to free, in-depth penetration is a loose, lumpy soil. The most common obstacles are of a mechanical nature: stoniness is most unfavourable to taproots, which are forced into circumventions; on the other hand, a gravelly soil may provide a good medium for grasses and cereals, even increasing soil water storage capacity, as research in tropical West Africa has shown. Similarly, coarse pyroclastic parent materials in the humid tropics do not affect the productivity of cacao and ylang-ylang plantations: their root systems adapting perfectly to the soils, which provide sufficient aeration and moisture. (Ylang-ylang is a small tree whose flowers produce an oil that is the main crop of the Comoro Islands, which through distillation yields an extract used in perfume.)

In contrast, soil compactness, whether natural or artificial, is a major obstacle, as well as hard and compact clods, which restrict the volume exploited by roots. A sudden increase in compactness from one horizon or bed to another is probably the major obstacle to normal root development and may even determine the depth to which roots penetrate. In the Pampa Deprimida of Argentina the presence of a hard, impermeable solod horizon (American 1938 classification) 10 to 15 cm below the surface is a severe limitation to cattle husbandry: the grass roots cannot penetrate it, and as soon as there are some eight rainless days the grass begins to dry and the cattle to lose weight. On the contrary, rainfall exceeding 50 mm saturates the ground, and if it rains again, the lowest areas, without slopes, are flooded, with disastrous consequences on the livestock. All such obstacles impede root growth or cause root deformations, abnormal extensions, harmful circumventions, narrowing, or necroses adverse to plant life. Lastly, certain peculiarities of the soil profile such as cavities, crotovinas (concretions formed in former burrows excavated by rats and other small rodents; a term current in pedology) and abandoned termite galleries may cause a preferential development of root clusters.

Roots are particularly sensitive to the chemical composition of the soil, regardless of its organization. The abundance of nutrients or, on the other extreme, the presence of toxic elements influence root spreading. In Amazonia the rainforest on sandy soils has a very shallow root system that does not go deeper than 20 to 30 cm. The extreme poverty in mineral nutrients forces trees 20 to 40 m high to immediately recycle their own minerals liberated from the litter at their feet before they have a chance to migrate further down. Inversely, if the nutrients are concentrated at the base of the soil, that is where maximum root development will be. The influence of the concentration of nutrients on the development of root systems at a specific level is particularly noticeable in certain tropical floodplains cultivated after the waning flood; the poorly evolved alluvial soils formed by the superposition of beds of variable texture, the result of sedimentary rather than pedologic processes, always show that root development is maximum, even exclusive, in the fine textured, more humid beds rich in exchangeable cations. However, a sudden discontinuity, whether physical or chemical, between, for instance, an argillaceous and a sandy bed, may cause a necrosis or simply a sharp deflection of the roots. The pH too may influence root growth: an excessive acidity causes the liberation of toxic ions such as manganese and aluminium, which slow growth. On the east coast of Madagascar, many banana plantations on peaty soils have failed after several years of production. The yellowness of the leaves suggested a lack of phosphorus to be the main cause; but Kilian (1970) showed that the degeneration was in fact caused by the liberation of free aluminium as a result of a high increase in acidity resulting from the too rapid drainage of the original peat swamps. The presence of excessive aluminium ions produces a coiling of the roots compounded by nanism. By introducing large doses of phosphorus the pH was raised and the production of free aluminium arrested, an effect that can also be obtained by an influx of calcareous fertilizers. The same is true for soils with a too high pH. An excess of calcium provokes the well-known phenomenon of chlorosis through an increase of alkalinity, preventing the absorption of iron by the roots. A deficiency of manganese, for its part, may cause roots to be attacked by saprophytes.

Lastly, the soil atmosphere intervenes in root development. The content of carbonic gas should not exceed certain limits, which would be of the order of 1 per cent according to Hénin, Gras and Monnier (1969). The content of oxygen also has an important influence: 'for each species oxygen has a lower limit beyond which roots cease to grow and an upper limit at which growth is optimum', according to Demolon (1968). A good aeration of the soil profile favoured by structure and good permeability is therefore essential to a well-balanced diffusion of the gases. Aeration, too, is under the strict dependence of the degree of moisture, which is another basic factor of root development.

The influence of moisture

To a certain degree the root system adapts itself quite well to the moisture content of the soil; its volume augments with increased moisture until a slowing down occurs owing to a decrease in aeration, causing asphyxiation. In contrast to mineral concentration, which does not produce a preferential attraction (there actually is no real chemotropism, but rather a greater development of rootlets in the richer horizons), the rootlets are attracted by the more humid horizons, whether situated laterally or deeper. On the other hand, roots always stop abruptly at the top of the water table. They abundantly exploit the capillary fringe above it, which is always better aerated. These hydrodynamics explain the extreme variations observed in the root systems of a particular cultivated plant (cotton, tobacco) in waning flood cropping systems. The form, length and disposition, as well as the volume occupied by roots, are all dependent on the depth of the water table. Root development also may be affected by the past vicissitudes of the deposition of the alluvial materials, that is on the geomorphological history of the floodplain. Such causal relationships are not without interest: indeed, a good knowledge of the fluvial landforms (e.g. different generations of natural levees, crevasse deltas, channel fills, point bars, bottom lands) leads to a better agricultural use of the alluvial sediments.

Knowledge of the dynamics of the soil moisture regime is essential to obtain a sufficient understanding of the evolution of the root system during the course of the vegetative cycle. A very common observation in dry tropical Africa can serve as an example. Cross-sections, or profiles, at low water stage sometimes show an abundant, finely structured and well-distributed root system in a mass of dry, compact, well-cemented material,

indicating that the soil is periodically wetted and, at certain periods of the year, constitutes a porous, aerated, permeable milieu permitting a homogeneous penetration of roots, proof of a temporary or periodically satisfactory soil water regime.

A plant, therefore, can to a certain degree adjust or modify its root system as a function of the mechanical, chemical or hydrological conditions of its milieu in spite of the morphologic properties of the species. According to Demolon (1968), 'the root system constitutes a *deformable system*', and 'is defined simultaneously by its own development ... and by its topographic distribution, that is, the volume of soil it exploits'. These two factors reflect the adaptation of the plant to the milieu it tries to exploit as best it can. For this reason our approach pays particular attention to the physical environment and to an examination of the root profile in whatever soil, cultivated or not. Such an examination should provide a better understanding of the *present* pedogenic milieu, a basic factor in our approach.

Examination from an agronomic point of view of the state of the aerial as well as subsurface parts of wild plants can provide valuable information of the likely behaviour of cultivated plants on the same support. The role of horizons, soil structure, compactness and impermeability, which are so many constraints on root development and crop yields, may thus be estimated. Furthermore, information should be obtained on the dynamics of the soil moisture regime prior to making indispensable measurements, which, in turn, can then be reduced to an absolute minimum. For example, if more or less rotten roots spread evenly in the mottled, sandy or argillaceous horizon of a bottom land, it may be deduced that they have been developed in a well-aerated soil that was gradually waterlogged by a slowly rising water table. The bottom land is therefore subject to a water table regime whose present fluctuation levels can be defined approximately.

With regard to cultivated land we shall make use of Hénin, Feodoroff, Gras and Monnier's concept of the *cultivated profile* (1960), defined as 'the succession of soil layers formed by the intervention of farm implements, plant roots, and natural factors'. This approach, in comparison to similar but non-cultivated soils, offers an understanding of the changes brought about by farming practices. The cultivated profile thus may be considered as the upper part of the pedological profile evolving under the influence of human and mechanical factors. The two concepts should not be viewed competitively; the information obtained is complementary, and the examination of the cultivated profile, as indicated by Hénin (1976), is 'essentially made for the adaptation of agricultural techniques'. Its periodic observation may contribute to a modification or improvement of farming techniques if these produce a degradation of the upper soil layers. This concept, based on a rigorous and logical method of observation, is important to us, as it provides a means to analyse the morphogenic–pedogenic balance at the levels of the upper horizons affected by the farmer. To a certain degree, therefore, it constitutes a link that allows a closer understanding of the interactions between the physical environment and agricultural management; it offers an opportunity to improve interdisciplinary work.

Analytical observations thus reveal a number of relationships between the state of the physical environment and a particular plant, relationships that were perceived here through the medium of the root system.

Soil water

This section is concerned only with basic principles related to moisture uptake by plants, thus limiting our account to aspects of soil moisture, movement of soil water, soil moisture profiles, and the soil water budget.

Aspects of soil moisture

Soil moisture, by definition, is the proportion of water contained in the soil. It may be of direct atmospheric origin (rain, snow, dew) or indirectly so by way of a temporary or fluctuating water table. The most common method of measuring the proportion is to oven-dry a soil sample to 105° C until a constant weight is attained, and then measure the difference in weight. The moisture is expressed in grams of soil, in reference either to dry or moist soil. But, for a given quantity of moisture, the soil properties may vary considerably depending on texture. With an equal moisture content, a sandy soil, for example, always appears more moist than an argillaceous soil, which, on the other hand, retains its water more effectively. This difference is expressed in the concept of *capillary potential*, basic in agronomy; it expresses the suction force, or pressure, 'that must be exerted on equally moist soil to begin to extract water from it' (Hénin, Gras and Monnier 1969). This energy (or

pressure) is expressed as the height of a column of water, as measured in centimetres. As the water used by plants may be extracted at very high pressures (16 atmospheres) stated in large numbers, the logarithm of the number, the pF, is used for simplification; for example, a moisture content of 20 per cent at pF 3 means that if a pressure equivalent to 1,000 cm of water (1 atmosphere) is exerted, the residual soil moisture will be 20 per cent.

The following soil moisture conditions are particularly important to plants.

1 *The maximum soil moisture capacity* corresponds to a soil completely saturated with water; it is equal to its total porosity and remains constant as long as water lost by gravity percolation is replaced by incoming water.

2 *The moisture retention capacity* after water input ceases, the soil progressively dries out by gravity percolation and evaporation to attain after two to four days a moisture content called *retention capacity*, which from then on evolves very slowly. This moisture to a large extent occupies micropores and is not affected by the downward pull of gravity; its quantity is narrowly dependent on soil texture and structure. Measurement of the retention capacity may be made directly in the field on a soil sample taken two to four days after a good rain. The value obtained, however, is slightly larger than the actual retention capacity, for it also contains some water percolated from above; for this reason the quantity has been termed *field capacity* (Richards and Wadleigh 1952). The measurement can also be made in the laboratory by submitting the soil sample to a determined atmospheric suction force of pF 3 (normal gravity); this value, called *equivalent moisture*, does not always correspond to the field capacity, as formerly believed. A field measurement should be carried out conjointly to obtain the pF value corresponding to the true field capacity. Another way to estimate soil moisture is by the neutron scattering method (Bell and McCulloch 1966; Eeles 1969).

3 *The wilting point* when the soil ceases to receive water, it progressively dries out to a point at which the root suction force is no longer sufficient to extract moisture from the soil; the wilting point is then reached and the plant begins to wilt, irretrievably. The wilting point corresponds to a pressure, or suction, of 16 atmospheres, that is a pF of 4.2. It is closely

related to soil texture: the finer it is, the higher the field capacity pF value, because fine materials, like clays, hold water with greater energy than coarse materials like sands.

4 *The quantity of moisture available to plants*   this quantity is equal to the difference between the field capacity and the moisture content at the wilting point; it may be expressed in volume or in mm of water, taking into account the apparent density of the soil sample.

5 *The soil moisture reserve*   it takes into account the quantity of moisture available to plants and the depth of the root system. This reserve is expressed by Hénin, Gras and Monnier (1969) as follows:

$$R = p \times d(C-F), \text{ in which}$$

R is the soil moisture *reserve* in mm
p (profondeur) the root depth in dm
d the apparent *density* of the soil sample
C and F the amount of moisture in per cent of dry soil corresponding, respectively, to the field Capacity and the wilting point (Flétrissement).

Many irrigation specialists believe that this soil moisture reserve, called 'usable reserve', is not entirely available to plants, especially when evaporation is very high. Under such conditions plants could be subject to temporary wilting. The concept 'readily usable reserves', which is equal to one-third of the total reserve, has been used to express the quantity of water easily taken up by plants, but although much used in irrigation is contested by certain agronomists.

Movement of water in the soil

In the preceding section we discussed various aspects of soil moisture that could be called static. We shall now examine the dynamic aspect, that is the movement of water in the soil. This movement takes place in both the liquid and the gaseous state. The gaseous circulation is linked to many parameters, one of which is soil temperature; their effects are difficult to gauge and take place mainly in the upper part of the soil. We are concerned with movements in the liquid state only.

The movement of water in the soil may be affected by gravity, but not necessarily; while the dynamics are different, both methods contribute to the moisture uptake by plants, and therefore, to agricultural production. We shall briefly examine both and then give a few examples of practical applications in which the moisture regime of a landscape has been figured out so that adequate cultivation methods can be proposed.

Gravitational movements of water

Input of water into the soil by precipitation or a flood is subject to the law of gravity. First, in the strict sense, it 'infiltrates' into the soil. Next, 'infiltration' is continued by 'percolation', which takes over after a certain moisture ratio has been attained; its rate is determined by the characteristics of the soil, mainly its texture and structure, and is a reflection of the term 'permeability'.

Infiltration   Water penetrates into the soil from the surface and gradually moistens it. The demarcation between the wetted zone and the dry zone beneath is called the *wetting front*. The dynamics of infiltration, in the broad sense, have been studied in France in particular by Feodoroff (1961; 1962). The regularity of the front depends, in the first place, on the heterogeneity of the soil profile: in relatively homogeneous soils the front is more or less parallel to the ground surface. The rate of infiltration depends on the rate of input by rain, irrigation, and so on. According to Feodoroff, 'after a short period of time during which penetration is rapid, the rate diminishes and becomes constant, but it is all the more rapid as input is high'. After a certain volume of input the water replaces the air in most of the soil pores (in about nine-tenths of them); a waterlogging then occurs, which brings about a stagnation of the water on the surface. 'The intensity limit of water input producing a puddle is called the *maximum infiltration capacity of the soil*' (Hénin, Gras and Monnier 1969). This capacity is variable and closely dependent on the characteristics of the soil, mainly its structure and permeability. An unstable structure, especially if rain is violent, rapidly produces a compact surficial layer, which impedes infiltration; even if input eventually decreases, the compactness of the 'puddled' layer will persist and retard infiltration, thus producing puddles or a superficial sheet of water.

Puddling, that is the sealing of the soil, is particularly important in cultivated fields, as it impedes water infiltration even when the soil beneath the crust is dry. The soil moisture reserve then cannot be replenished by rainfall, so that even if the climate is humid, ecological conditions are' dry.

A moisture ratio higher than the field capacity

Plates 30 & 31 Surficial waterlogging and rainsplash
Ph. JT CCCXCVIII-13 cn. Surficial waterlogging in 'bocage' landscape, Pinay (Aube), France, 30 December 1965. Gently rolling relief mainly on pastures. The oceanic climate is characterized by long-lasting cyclonic winter rains which saturate the soil, as they cannot infiltrate into the impermeable substratum of the Lower Cretaceous marls and sandy clays of the Champagne Humide. A very slow hypodermic flow occurs in the lower soil horizons and seeps out in the ditch at the foot of the slope. Photograph taken from a road embankment (left foreground).

may be attained with infiltrating water. The extra water replaces the pre-existing water, producing an output of excess water. The water then is said to be saturating; under such conditions the rate of outflow (the volume of water flowing through a soil layer for a given amount of time) is subject to Darcy's law:

$$Q = K \frac{(H + L)}{H} \times S, \text{ in which}$$

Q is the discharge per section unit
L is the constant height of the water level above the ground surface (maintaining a saturated state)
H is the column of wetted soil
S is the basal area of the column.

The *permeability* of the soil (in the strict sense) is the greater or lesser aptitude of the soil to percolation; it is formulated as the *rate of filtration over a unit of slope K*. This coefficient is equal to the height of an infiltrated column of water per second, when the height of the water level above

the ground (L) is zero. K is expressed in mm/h. Its value varies with the nature of the soil, more as a function of structure than texture. For a given texture, all factors, in particular the organic matter, influencing the stability of the structure, favour permeability. Sandy soils in certain cases may not be very permeable, as, for instance, fine, clogged sands poor in organic matter. The K factor for a given soil is relatively constant, but may vary with the kind of water percolating through the soil; for this reason, it is very important to work with the water that will be used for the exploitation of the land (notably for irrigation) when permeability measurements are made.

Permeability   Permeability may be measured in the laboratory on a reworked sample (Hénin, Gras and Monnier 1969); the special object of this method is the evaluation of the stability of the soil structure. It may also be made on a non-reworked sample by the *Vergière method*, which consists in subjecting a lump of soil to the infiltration of water under constant pressure. The *Muntz method* may be used in the field on a fresh, moist sample; it consists in measuring the height of water infiltrated in one hour into a cylinder under constant pressure (3 cm) using a Mariotte flask. This measurement is not unlike the measurement of the rate of infiltration from the ground surface mentioned above. The *Porchet method* consists in measuring the time necessary for a given quantity of water to flow into a cylindrical hole dug into the soil; this method gives a better appreciation of the permeability than the Muntz method but does not take place under constant pressure. Moreover, it gives a more global value that at once integrates vertical percolation and lateral flow; the obtained permeability figure, lastly, depends on the most permeable horizon traversed by the hole and on the soil moisture ratio at the time of the measurement, so that it may vary with the season. For all these reasons measurements should be numerous and oft repeated in space as well as in time. In any case,

they provide only orders of magnitude that should not be taken at face value.

Measurements should be more rigorous in the presence of a water table close to the surface, as they are carried out in a saturated soil atmosphere. Under such conditions the auger hole *method of Porchet–Hoghourt* consists of digging a hole, whose bottom is at a certain distance below the water table. The water is pumped out, and the time it takes to refill is measured. This method is currently used in drainage network calculations.

Non-gravitational movements of water

These dynamics are different depending on whether or not the water table is close to the surface; in both cases ascending capillary movements occur. They are also called *per ascensum* in contrast to gravitational movements that are referred to as *per descensum*.

Movements without water table   Such movements

Plate 31 Ph. JT CCCXCIV-41 cn. A key to the alternative 'runoff/infiltration': splash erosion near Dakar, Senegal, December 1970. Soil 'puddling' in a millet field on a loamy soil on basalt. The climate is of the tropical type, with scanty rainfall, most of it in high intensity showers. The present splash erosion is the result of the last storm of the previous rainy season (June–October). A crust has formed as a result of the surficial concentration of the fine soil fraction. When dry it cracks. Quite likely the crop will fail as a result of drought, intensified by lack of water infiltration caused by the sealing action of puddling.

are the most difficult to apprehend and, because of it, are the most debated and sometimes controversial. They lead to the *drying out* of the soil. After the stage of moisture retention capacity of the soil is reached and all gravitational movement has ceased, drying out is mainly caused by evaporation and moisture absorption by roots, which means a loss through transpiration.

The rate of evaporation from the soil, which is rapid and relatively constant when the moisture content is above the retention capacity, drops notably as soon as that capacity is reached. The upper soil horizons then dry faster than the soil as a whole, and

when the moisture content at the ground surface approximately reaches that of soil dried in the air, a regime of *slow evaporation is reached*. The less the water migrates the deeper the reach of evaporation once the moisture content at the surface reaches that of air dried soil.

(Hénin, Gras and Monnier 1969)

In other words, the more a soil dries out, the slower it yields its moisture; evaporation becomes minimal, but does not stop (about 1 mm/day). The soil then very slowly tends toward a hygroscopic moisture content if no new input intervenes. The period of rapid evaporation is prolonged if the soil is plant covered. Other processes too cause a loss of soil moisture, such as various biological syntheses using water, as well as hydration reactions of mineral substances, according to Gaucher (1968).

Movements tied to the water table   The dynamics of drying out are much modified under such conditions. The quantity of moisture evaporated at the ground surface depends, in the first place, on the depth of the water table, which means that the soil starts to dry as soon as the quantity of moisture lost by evaporation is no longer compensated by input through capillary action from below. The drying out process is therefore closely related to capillary rise, the water table remaining stable (Gaucher 1968). The capillary rise and the zone it affects, called the 'capillary fringe', has been studied systematically by Keen (1931). In the most favourable materials the rise *does not exceed 2 metres*, and then the quantity of available water is insufficient to sustain plant life. The quantity of moisture reaching the surface, in the second place, depends on soil texture, which affects the capillary rise. According to figures provided by Keen, the rise would vary from 35–40 cm in coarse sands to 120–150 cm in argillaceous soils.

The thickness of the capillary fringe depends also on other factors. Intense evaporation accelerates the loss of water not compensated by capillary rise; the moisture front may therefore descend to a depth dependent on texture. The height and ease of the capillary rise may also be affected by the heterogeneity of the soil profile, particularly its discontinuities.

Studies of the alluvial soils of the rivers of western Madagascar by F. Bourgeat, M. Damour, F. de Casabianca and J. Kilian between 1963 and 1971 have thrown light on a certain number of facts concerning such capillary movements. These poorly evolved alluvial soils, called 'baiboho', are among the most fertile of the island. They are cultivated following the waning flood during the dry season, which, depending on the year, extends from April or May to October or November. Plants then tap the capillary fringe at a depth of 1 to 3 metres. Productivity and quality of the crops depend on the level of the water table at the time of sowing, on the rate of descent of the capillary fringe, which follows the water table, and on the moisture retention capacity of the soil. Because of the regional importance of these soils, an experiment was made in the area of Ambato-Boeni by the IRAT in 1963. Results obtained (de Casabianca 1968) have shown that in the best soils, of average texture, capillary rise slows down and decreases with a descending water table, and that it seems to depend also on the suction force of the roots of the tested plants (maize and peanuts). The rate of descent of the water table depends on the texture of the materials (it is, therefore, related to past fluvial morphodynamics). The rate of descent as a function of these parameters varies from 18 cm to 40 cm per month.

The depth of the water table at the time of sowing is also an important factor of productivity. For example, for peanuts, it is unwise to sow when the water table is deeper than 120 cm. On the other hand, a doubling of yield can be expected when the water table is at 80 cm. In other respects many field observations have shown that a sandy bed of more than 25 to 30 cm thickness causes a sudden discontinuity in capillary rise. Such beds, therefore, are important to map. Installation of piezometers, enabling a recording of the vagaries of the water table, is strongly recommended for certain crops whose success depends largely on the time of sowing.

These results, although fragmentary, demonstrate how important it is to know the soil water regime, whether or not influenced by the water table. For good land management the hydrodynamics of the soil should be observed and measured. For this reason we attach particular importance to soil moisture profiles.

Moisture profiles

A moisture profile is a curve that indicates the moisture ratio according to depth. Over time it provides an evaluation of the water regime. The graph should be designed as a function of the soil horizons, whose characters have a strong influence on their response to water. The moisture ratio is shown on the x-axis and depth on the y-axis. Examination of the profile, therefore, permits an evaluation of the moisture percentage at the time of measurement and for a given depth in relation to the soil's moisture constants (moisture retention capacity, moisture content at the wilting point, and various pF's), which can be shown on the graph. These indications can be completed by others provided by the soil water budget.

Soil water budget

Water reaching the ground surface splits, classically, into three fractions: one evaporates, the other runs off, and the third infiltrates. Only the last concerns us here. In that connection, we favour Gaucher's definition of the soil water budget: it 'represents the spread of water penetrated into the soil among its several destinations: water drained, water retained, water evaporated, and water used by plants' (1968: 233). In this way, according to this soil scientist, the soil water budget may be represented by the equation: infiltrated water = water retained, plus water drained, plus water evaporated, plus water consumed by plants.

To find strict limits between these various destinations is difficult, if not impossible or illusory. Thus, according to Gaucher (1968), the budget may be viewed in several ways: it may be calculated in a global fashion for the soil as a whole or studied separately by horizon; or it may be calculated globally for an annual cycle or period by period. The information sought varies with the objective. 'Whatever the method used, the result is always approximate, providing an order of magnitude only.'

Insertion of these different fractions into the environment has already been dealt with above. Suffice to say that the soil water budget may be estimated by using a lysimeter, which is a concrete basin in which the soil profile is placed as carefully as possible. Holes in the bottom allow the drained water to be gathered.

The circulation and distribution of water in the soil and the modes of rooting are thus the basic phenomena to know in regard to planning a cropping system in a certain type of environment expressed on a morphopedological map. We shall now provide a typical example with the following geographic study.

The soil water balance: a practical application in Casamance (Senegal)

The 'grey soils' of Casamance are found between the recent (Nouakchottian) terrace and the footslopes of a low plateau (not over 50 m high) along parts of the Casamance River and its main northern tributary, the Sangrougrou. This lowest terrace is reed covered and floodable; some parts of it are used for the cultivation of rice. A slightly higher, 'middle' (last Interglacial) terrace is occupied by a more or less dense wooded savanna, where not cleared. The soils on these terraces are grey because of more or less severe hydromorphic conditions. According to a preliminary study of G. Bertrand in 1970, the middle terrace has highly hydromorphic, slightly humic soils with thick gleys on a sandy parent material, while upslope slightly hydromorphic, ferruginous soils on colluvium grade into ochre soils on the side-slopes of the cuirassed plateau. Traditionally, where cleared, the lower portions of this terrace have been used for cultivating rain-grown rice, in spite of the apparently unfavourable physical (very coarse texture) and chemical (very poor in nutrients) properties of the soil. Investigations since 1962 have disclosed, in several locations, in the wet season, the presence of a water table close to the surface that, apparently, is favourable to the growing of rice. Continued research by IRAT and other agencies, including the local Centre de Recherches Agronomiques of Bambey, led to the selection of five geographically representative sites in the Bounkiling area of the Sangrougrou River to

1 characterize the pedogenic milieu
2 determine the fluctuation of the water table
3 estimate the input from the water table and its capillary fringe on the growth of rice plants
4 evaluate possible influxes of salt water
5 provide a possible extrapolation of the results.

Instrumentation and measurements

Piezometers were placed along a line of maximum slope extending somewhat beyond the outer limits of the zone of grey soils; a secondary line was placed perpendicular to it; furthermore, rain gauges were set up and recording stream gauges installed on the water-courses. The influence of the water table on rice yield was tested on experimental plots paralleling the main piezometer line; and several other crops were tested for an eventual diversification of the cropping system. The piezometers were read three times per week at the break of the 'monsoon' (at the beginning of the experiment) and then once per week. Water table profiles were made periodically by auger sampling. Lastly, the water was regularly tested for salinity.

Results

Present pedogenesis on the grey soils   The grey soils constitute a morphopedologic unit in so far as it is defined by strong interactions between pedogenic and morphogenic processes, as is the case on the middle terrace, whose surface, from the geomorphological point of view, is a glacis. This unit consists of an association of soils, which, as we shall see, is useless to subdivide.

Detailed study of the toposequence at all five representative sites shows that the grey soils of middle Casamance are of a very light grey colour, possess sandy horizons that are bleached throughout, and have a particular structure. Therefore they upslope and in their upper horizons have the appearance of completely deferruginized hydromorphic soils. In contrast, downslope, at the base of the toposequence, zones of iron accumulation, even iron pans, are frequently encountered. The upslope part of the toposequence therefore seems to represent an eluvial horizon, which gradually passes into an illuvial horizon at the lower end of the toposequence. A complete profile is thus represented by the *entire* toposequence; in this context, only study of the toposequence taken as a whole leads to an understanding of the pedogenic milieu and its dynamics; to divide the terrace surface into so many types of soil according to horizon diagnostic is therefore a vain exercise, the more so as transitions down a slope are frequently diffuse. If only a single profile were observed, the grey soils would be classified as poorly evolved hydromorphic colluvial soils, but looking at the entire profile of the toposequence, they are very evolved soils undergoing a hydromorphic pedogenesis of exohydromorphic type. They are, then, grey hydromorphic soils, completely referruginized with their illuvial horizon at the low end of the toposequence. This method of study makes more sense as it characterizes a landscape unit whose genesis, dynamics, and filiation links can be clearly understood. It also recasts the absolute role held by the 'identification criteria' at the level of horizons, which differ with each classification and lead to various subdivisions into cartographic units. Similar observations have been made in other parts of West Africa, notably in Benin (Kilian 1972) and in the Ivory Coast (Kilian and Tessier 1973).

Fluctuations on the water table   Study of the water table by R. Bertrand (1973) led him to discover that it is fed by hypodermic flow from infiltration of rain water on the very permeable thin, gravelly soils that cover the ferruginous cuirass of the plateau, an observation that was confirmed and further demonstrated by Guillobez (1974). During the dry season this ground-water merges with that of the sandy 'Continental Terminal' Group that underlies the cuirass. The water surplus of the rainy season thus produces the hypodermic flow causing the rise of the water table and its capillary fringe in the grey soils. The fluctuations of the water table have been recorded by the piezometers: it begins by rising slowly after the first rains in July to about mid-August, after which it rises abruptly by more than a metre in a few days at the end of August. After that, to the end of the rainy season, the water table fluctuates little about its maximum level. Its decline coincides with the end of the rains, proceeding at a slow, regular rate of approximately 1 cm per day.

Consequences of the fluctuations of the water table on the cultivation of rice   This study of the grey soils has led to the recognition of three zones that correspond to three distinct topographic positions.

1 In upslope positions, right below the ochre hillside soils, the water table is continuously depressed even during an exceptionally rainy season; the roots of the rice stalks are unable to reach down to the capillary fringe; rice must be rain-grown and is therefore subject to climatic accidents; in 1970, for example, a water deficit at the end of the growing season reduced yields down to 15–20 q/ha.

2 In the middle zone, the water table is close to the surface even with low rainfall; it is encountered at a depth of less than a metre and the capillary fringe reaches the soil's upper horizons; under these conditions rice prospers even during drought and yields are reasonable: 35 q/ha at Kandiadiou and 27 q/ha at Inor (see Rép. du Sénégal: Carte Routière et Touristique 1:500,000);

3 In downslope positions, just above the aquatic rice fields of the low terrace, the water table is very close to the surface at the beginning and during the whole critical period of rice growing, extending from mid-August to harvest, generally at the end of October. Drought is no problem and yields are high: 48 q/ha at Kandiadiou, with quick-growing rice varieties and good cultivation techniques, otherwise around 35 q/ha, as at Karsia, on the Casamance River, and also at Kandiadiou.

Criteria for identifying grey soils appropriate for rice growing have been defined by R. Bertrand (1973), taking into account the depth of the water table after the rains and the use of indicator plants. In the mean time R. Bertrand proposes a simple method based on the rate of descent of the water table and its maximum depth during the dry season. This rate, as we have seen, and as indicated by measurements, is of the order of 1 cm per day. As to the depth of the water table, it should not be deeper than a metre at the time of harvest. If prospecting is done with a soil auger after the last rains, soils appropriate for rice growing can be defined as having a water table situated at a depth of 100 cm + y cm, in which y is equal to the number of days elapsed between the last effective rainfall and the date of sampling. Later, during the course of the dry season, the water table drops too low to be reached by auger, and this simple method, available to peasants, can no longer be used.

Nevertheless, if a large part of the grey soils is always suitable to rice cultivation, other factors, such as quick-ripening varieties and immediate sowing with the first rain, at the latest during the first week of July, are also important. The largest extent of grey soils is in middle Casamance, between Diana Malari and Kolda, where they are developed on wide glacis alongside the Casamance River. They become discontinuous along the creeks of upper Casamance. Based on the mapped morphopedologic units, the area of grey soils suitable for rice growing even in dry years is some 20,000 ha. The total area of 'grey soils', including those of the high, sandy, rice fields of maritime Casamance, is estimated at approximately 100,000 ha.

This relatively inexpensive assessment of the agricultural potential of this well-defined environment thus enables a further rational development of it in a region of rapid demographic growth. Having examined the utilization of soil water resources by plants, followed by that of crops at the level of soil units, we shall now raise ourselves to the higher dimensional level of watersheds, or drainage basins.

HYDROMORPHOLOGICAL MAPS

A good preliminary knowledge of hydrological conditions is required for the construction of hydrological engineering works, particularly in agriculture. Usually it is insufficient, as governments have not made the necessary investments in time to obtain satisfactory inventories of their natural resources. This is the case in France, where valid hydrometric networks have been set up only recently in a number of hydrographic basins. It is not so long ago that the only discharge data available for the Seine River were those obtained by the works of E. Belgrand in the reign of Napoleon III. The First World War interrupted the installation of gauging stations on many rivers; during the Nazi occupation the stock of yearbooks in which hydrological data had been published was destroyed. Such data, except in some countries, like the USA or Canada (or parts of them), are generally incomplete and insufficient in most regions of the world for the installation of hydrological engineering works.

Traditional methods of gathering information rely on the statistical processing of generally not very accurate or representative data, so that precipitation–discharge correlations are characterized by a high dispersal of adequate recording stations. Recourse should be had to a long series, of twenty to thirty years, from which averages can be calculated. But such delays are hardly acceptable when a development is being planned. The Centre de Géographie Appliquée (CGA) at the request of the Génie Rural, of the Ministry of Agriculture, has done research to try to arrive at more satisfactory precipitation–discharge correlations through a better knowledge of the

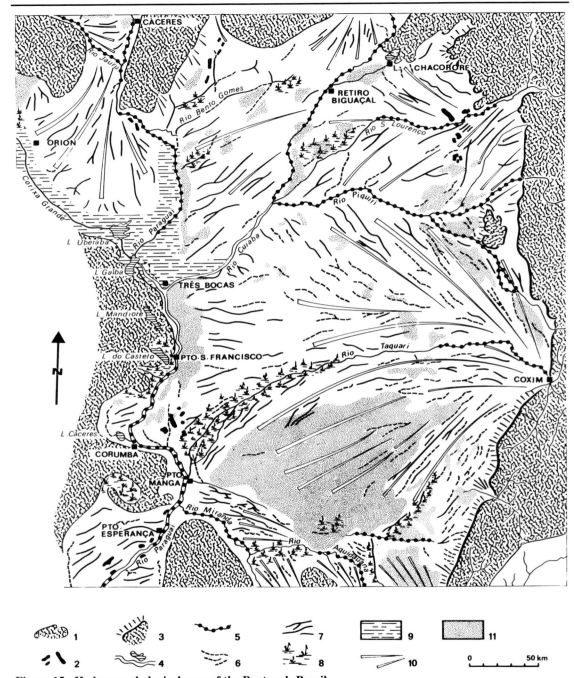

Figure 15. Hydromorphological map of the Pantanal, Brazil

The Pantanal is still a region poorly known from the scientific point of view. The map presented here was made by J. Tricart from remote sensing imagery, mainly the radar mosaics of RADAMBRASIL on the scale of 1:250,000, secondarily from a number of LANDSAT images, including colour composites.

Figure 15 cont.
The main use of the Pantanal is cattle-ranching. At the request of RADAMBRASIL, Tricart examined the possibilities of hydrological management and environmental improvement of the region, whose herds periodically suffer enormous losses due to uncontrollable and extensive floods, the last and worst of the century so far occurring in April–May 1988. The making of the preliminary, small-scale, hydrological map illustrates the considerable difficulties of a rational development on account of the geomorphological conditions, particularly the immense Taquari River Fan. The amount of work and cost of controlling the floods have shelved such a project in favour of smaller, more profitable projects (see Tricart, Pagney and Frécaut, 1984).

Legend of the map
  1 Outcrops of pre-Quaternary substratum
  2 Permanent lakes
  3 Structural escarpments and colluvial piedmont slopes
  4 Perennial rivers and lakes of variable dimensions
  5 Meandering streams (impossible to map to scale)
  6 Stream beds with flowing water during floods only
  7 Stream beds fed by shallow ground-water of the alluvial material
  8 Seasonally flooded marshes with swamp vegetation
  9 Swamp vegetation in permanently flooded wetlands
  10 Axes of Quaternary outwashes
  11 Quaternary outwashes dotted with numerous shallow depressions partly occupied by swamp vegetation. The depressions are the result of deflation during the last cold period.

movement of water in the natural environment. Similar research has been carried on simultaneously in Poland by the Institute of Geography of the Polish Academy of Sciences. The idea is to map the different ways in which water occurs in the geographical environment, hence the name *hydromorphological maps* that Tricart has given to these documents, an expression preferred to that of 'hydrological maps' used in Poland, which is too vague and already used to designate other maps, such as maps of hydrological networks, hydrometrical installations, and maps showing the discharges of rivers and so on (Figure 15). We shall now discuss the conception of these maps and their utilization.

Conception of hydromorphological maps

Hydrologic phenomena in the natural environment do not occur in isolation; they are only one aspect of the dynamics of that environment and, as such, are interdependent with other aspects. The behaviour of water on the land–atmosphere interface is influenced by the plant cover notably through the medium of interception. But, in return, the water uptake of plants has to be subtracted from runoff and may produce a runoff deficit. The kinetic energy of a shower may change the

mechanical properties of the soil, among others, clog, by sealing, a soil that is not waterlogged; the mechanism depends not only on the intensity and duration of the shower, but also on the mechanical resistance of the soil aggregates, that is on their 'stability'; frequently it affects runoff, a hydrological phenomenon. Runoff repeated with a certain frequency produces traces in the micro-relief: a surficial concentration of the coarser particles, identifiable by granulometric curves, deposition of materials behind obstacles (tufts of grass, tracing roots, stumps), incisions by strings of water, sometimes passing into rills, etc. In some cases infiltration produces hypodermic flow, depending on the permeability of the materials superimposed close to the surface; all that is needed is a rather impermeable layer underlying one that is more permeable. Hypodermic flow, if frequent, as for instance in moors or in loams and silts under semi-arid climates, like those of the western Great Plains, takes the form of piping; in other cases it causes mass movements. Such phenomena are not accidental or episodic and consequently of little interest, but oft repeated and characteristic of a certain regime. Migrations of water in the natural environment, studied as such, are the object of hydrology, but they also produce phenomena studied by geomorphology; furthermore, they fit into a more general level in a natural system, which helps us to understand the interdependencies existing between objects that traditionally have been studied by different disciplines and that do not specifically belong to any one of them.

Hydromorphological mapping is based on this conception. Its object is to present the behaviour of water in the geographical environment according to significant observations.

Many observations, or indices, of the behaviour of water are geomorphological. Rills, gullies, a stream bed, a gravelly outwash, pediments or glacis are geomorphological objects and, as such, are shown on detailed geomorphological maps. But they are also manifestations of a certain hydrological regime and of certain types of runoff. They are not specific to one or the other discipline. The surficial formations (regolith), the various types of rocks are also taken into account in a geomorphological study; they are shown on geomorphological maps. The importance of the texture of non-consolidated rocks and the density and disposition of joints in consolidated rocks are stressed on French geomorphological maps (RCP 77). These characters determine the penetration of water into these rocks and its migration. Not surprisingly, therefore, geomorphologists in Poland as well as in France were the first to devise hydromorphological maps (Klimaszewski 1968). To make geomorphological and hydromorphological maps simultaneously stands to reason as about 75 per cent of the observations made for a hydromorphological map are also made for a geomorphological map.

Hydromorphological maps, however, should not be mistaken for simplified geomorphological maps; the object is different. Common observations are made in a different context, determined by that object. The materials of a slope, for instance, are examined from the point of view of morphogenesis on a geomorphological map: attention is on the processes that have produced them, their age and their relationships to landforms. From the hydrological point of view, the only thing that matters is the permeability, which determines the rate of infiltration of water into the materials. Their age and genesis are not important except that they may serve to map their extent. In contrast, what must be observed is the moisture content of the materials, taking into account climatic antecedents. Furthermore, traces of hypodermic flow and of infiltration of water as recorded by entrained clay particles or by precipitates of soluble minerals should be looked for. From common features

observation is sharpened in different directions to identify different phenomena.

A legend reflecting all scientific and practical requirements was, after many years of trial and error, put together by a team of the Centre de Géographie Appliquée. It is based on a distinction of three regions: surficial, hypodermic and phreatic.

Surficial regime

The surficial regime, shown in conventional blue, includes the various manifestations of runoff in talwegs, classified according to frequency as sporadic, seasonal, and perennial, which requires repeated field observations at specific times, possibly completed by inquiries. There are also distinguished runoff between banks in a topographically defined bed and runoff that has not fashioned a bed, that is which occurs through the plant cover or flush over the surface, as is common in tropical water courses that are but a string of ponds in the dry season, and which the French call *marigots*. The type of bed is taken into consideration, as is also, when justified, its dimensions, that is width and depth. Floodable terrains, such as marshes, are also indicated by conventional signs, always in blue.

The map also shows the types of runoff on interfluves: slopes swept by embryonic runoff, incipient forms of concentrated runoff, incisions into gullies and ravines. When justified, areas of puddled soils are indicated. Field observations may be completed by tests on the stability of the aggregates and, in certain cases, permit introduction of quantitative classes.

Hypodermic regime

The hypodermic regime is shown in violet, a colour intermediate between the blue of the surficial regime and the red of the phreatic regime. Depending on lithology and field observations (made at appropriate periods), several categories of hypodermic regimes are distinguished as a function of depth, that is the thickness of the surficial formations in which they occur, and of the rate of movement. If the rate of filtration can be determined in the laboratory, it only provides a not too accurate order of magnitude, the dispersal of the results being rather important. This is the main

Plate 32 Flooding of a glacis
Ph. JT CCCLXXVI-15A. Active glacis near Paraguaipoa (north of Maracaibo), Venezuela, September 1967 near end of the tropical rainy season. Vegetation destroyed by goats in the vicinity of a settlement. This lower part of the glacis is coated with clayey material inhibiting the water to infiltrate. During flood more fine material is deposited, which increases the imperviousness: an example of positive feedback.

obstacle in the way of representing these quantitative data on the map.

Also mapped are the influence of the terrain on hypodermic flow (high or low retention capacity), the springlets and seeps fed by it, the subsurface flow that occurs in alluvial materials, and the alluvial ground water in equilibrium with a river.

Phreatic regime

The phreatic regime, or ground-water regime, is shown in red. Its detailed study is the domain of hydrogeologists. Far be it for us to attempt to emulate their expertise, even less to go beyond our competence. We shall limit ourselves to mapping rock masses having a deep ground-water circulation and by indicating the type of circulation; for example, as resulting from jointing or bedding planes, or simply a diffuse migration in sands or gravels. Also mapped are springs fed by deep

aquifers and, of course, manifestations of karstic hydrology. In contrast, the geometric aspects of aquifers, their rates of transmission or the regimes of the flow of water will not appear on the maps unless there is an input on the part of geologists.

The information provided by the French maps is not very different from that of the Polish maps, although the latter include more hydrological data, notably the depth of the phreatic water, and the location and characteristics of wells. This is justified in a country where most aquifers are in Quaternary materials and at shallow depth.

Use of hydromorphological maps

The object of hydromorphological maps is to represent an aspect of the natural environment based on the possible coincidence of observations otherwise made within the framework of separate disciplines. The approach is different from that of statistical and mathematical hydrology; it supplements it. Hydromorphological maps are used at two different stages of hydrological investigations: establishment and utilization.

During the establishment of a hydrometric network

A hydromorphological map displays different types of drainage regimes (surficial, hypodermic, phreatic) and their extent in a given watershed. To be most effective it should be supplemented by a map of slope gradients and another map of the plant cover, at the same scale, so that they can be superimposed. With such a set of maps the watershed can readily be divided into regions, whose surface areas can be calculated with a planimeter.

After this preliminary work, the most

representative of the affluent basins of each regime that are at the same time the most apt to be gauged are selected. A compromise is thus realized between the convenient practical factors and a rationalization of the measurements in contrast to the traditional procedures in which the practical aspects were too often predominant. Simultaneously, the emplacements of climatic stations are chosen by examination of the maps, supplemented, if needed, by a rapid biogeographical reconnaissance and local inquiries. The locations of these stations, too, should be representative. Recourse to recording instruments, widely used in France, for example, by Electricité de France, avoids such practical constraints, as does the recruiting of essentially voluntary observers. Because of such constraints the climatological network of the meteorological service includes numerous *non-representative*

Plate 33 Subsurface flow
Ph. JT CCCLXVI-39 cn. Subsurface flow (inferoflux), Puna de Atacama, Chile. In the background a volcanic range at the foot of which a glacis has been fashioned. The glacis is underlain by dark coloured ignimbrites which have been dissected into canyons. The glacis has been dated early Quaternary by both its geomorphic position and its degree of weathering. A recent and present aeolian aspersion of sand covers both the glacis and the canyon slopes and bottom. Phreatophytes in vale stand testimony to the subsurface flow of water seeping from the range.

stations, in particular regional ones located at airports and secondary ones located in villages, which, when situated in mountains, are generally in privileged sites. Eventually a biogeographic reconnaissance can be made to identify, on the basis of plants and insects that have well-defined exigencies, the existence and extent of climatic nuances otherwise hard to come by.

Such a network can obtain much more representative measurements of the natural phenomena. Correlations between precipitation and stream flow are improved, which means that more accurate results can be obtained during an equally long period of observation or equally precise results in a shorter period, which is usually preferred for practical reasons.

Another advantage of this procedure is that most stations are located in small basins of several square kilometres, or tens of square kilometres, at sites where discharges are low. The installation of gauging stations, therefore, is easier and the quality of the measurements higher. Other stations at the outlet of larger and more heterogeneous watersheds supplement these stations, providing measurement checks. The instrumentation of the representative basin of the Bruche River, in Alsace, by the Hydrologic Section of the Centre de Géographie Appliquée was planned according to these principles. It also provides a calibration for remote sensing recordings designed to perfect the use of a remote sensing method concerned with water resources.

During the utilization of the hydrometric data

Hydromorphological maps enable a better analysis of hydrometric data, as they display the factors controlling the drainage regime. Study of small representative basins enables the characterization of elementary regimes that are the components of a larger, more heterogeneous watershed. This approach, called the 'synthetic hydrogramme method', was applied by engineers of the Parisian firm of Coyne & Bellier to the Soummam Basin of Algeria, using a hydromorphological map on the scale of 1:200,000 made by teams of the Centre de Géographie Appliquée. In this case a rational hydrometric network was not available, but only episodic measurements, often taken in not very representative basins. This demonstrates that hydromorphological maps render a valuable service even for the utilization of old, not very satisfactory hydrometric data prior to a rationalization of the

network. Stations located at the mouths of rather extensive basins serve as a check on the hypotheses and parameters used for the construction of the synthetic hydrogrammes.

Hydromorphological maps therefore permit a better utilization of not very rational traditional hydrometric networks and of a series of incomplete measurements, the result of circumstances, as is typically the case of the Soummam Basin. They therefore make possible an evaluation of the existing documentation. Results are of course better with a rationally devised hydrometric network based on hydromorphological maps or improved from them. The accuracy of the synthetic hydrogrammes is therefore greater.

In passing, it may be noted that this procedure, based on a better appreciation of the representativeness of specific measuring sites, is applicable in many other technical domains. It is valid every time the measurements to be made are costly and/or long, and therefore cannot be multiplied, and deal with a heterogeneous surface, a very common case in Nature. Specifically, the same approach is applicable to the problems of agricultural experimentation.

Our method is flexible and allows an approach by successive approximations. After several years certain stations may be closed or replaced by others that are more representative or of better quality. The network may also be adapted to changes in land use in order to account, for example, for the appearance of cultivated land, abandoned land, or new forest. Pluviographs may be replaced, after a certain time, by pluviometers, or preferably supplemented by them. In the latter case it was possible to record showers with a certain areal extent in the Bruche Basin of the Vosges Mountains. Study of local differences in such showers is done by comparing the results obtained by associating pluviographs with a larger number of pluviometers. This method was adopted because of the scantiness of research funds available.

In an integrated study of a fluvial basin it should be recalled that hydromorphological maps are readily associated to maps of the presently functioning morphogenic processes. Hydromorphological maps, on which are also shown lithological phenomena, and on which the emphasis is on contemporary processes, are but a variant of geomorphological maps. Mapping of lithological data is useful for both types of maps, even if lithology is differently appreciated in each case. As to the processes, they too include an important common factor: all the manifestations of runoff, overland flow as well as stream flow. But while the concept 'work' appears on geomorphological maps, this is not the case of hydrologic manifestations. Surface runoff may play an important role in terms of volume but without notably contributing to the solid load of a river, as, for example, across a dense prairie. To observe such a phenomenon is important for the managememt of valley-side slopes, the soil conservation of which is then easily understood. Intense, clear water surface runoff produces abundant but episodic water flow of a torrential character; this implies water conservation through construction of expensive dams. In compensation, the reservoirs will be relatively free of sedimentation as long as conservation practices are followed, as through the maintenance of a dense grass cover. In rocky terrains, too, runoff may be intense and the water rather clear if the material is resistant to weathering. Also in such a case the construction of dams to reduce the torrential character of runoff may be considered as a protection against floods and in order to dispose of more water during droughts. To undertake as integrated a study as possible of the natural environment is always preferable when preparing basic maps for the runoff management of a watershed. A frontal attack on hydromorphological and geomorphological mapping is recommended. Different confrontations and convergent phenomena favourable to a rational land use are thus possible. But runoff is not the only water resource of interest to land management. Soil moisture, at shallow depth, is also an important ecological factor which must be taken into account.

CONCLUSION

Water is one of the most important constituents of the ecogeographic environment. It permits the transport of particles and dissolved products and is an agent of morphogenesis and of the metabolism of living beings, especially plants. Moreover (voluntarily or not) it carries the wastes of human activities: the heat transmitted to cooling waters by thermal and some nuclear power plants and blast furnaces, the chemical products of all kinds dumped by industrial plants and mines, the used waters of human settlements, and the excess of fertilizers and pesticides. The volume of water actually consumed is small in comparison to that of

the polluted water. The degradation is also generally reflected by the lengthening of the water's natural pathways, as, for instance, in the case of irrigation water, which infiltrates into the soil and returns to a water course in a circuitous way that may take several months. But it is also true that part of that water returns directly and swiftly to the atmosphere through evapotranspiration.

The management of water is very complex. Human intervention modifies the water's pathways, which may at certain times of the year cause local or regional maladjustments. Demand is always higher during periods of shortage, as during drought or summer low water stage; conflicts between consumers are then at their peak. A regular flow of water can be obtained by creating dams and reservoirs; but reservoirs may be subject to high, even very high losses by evaporation. Also huge stocks of water behind dams may present a serious danger in unstable regions affected by earthquakes, volcanic eruptions or even landslides. Reservoirs interrupt the transit of fluvial sediments; their longevity, which determines the cost amortization of the engineering works, depends on the rate of sedimentation and on the precipitation of dissolved products concentrated by evaporation. Subsurface waters constitute a type of reservoir that is not subject to these effects, as long as they are not too close to the surface and subject to evaporation. The recharge of ground-water, especially by irrigation, is a solution to many developments. But the intrinsic coherence of the hydrologic cycle in the natural environment should not be forgotten, otherwise its degradation, for instance, through salinization or hydromorphism, may be induced.

The rational management of water is of the utmost importance in regional land use. In some cases special organisms have been created to this effect in certain basins or for certain rivers, as the well-known Tennessee Valley Authority, or the Compagnie Nationale du Rhône, the Compagnie Nationale d'Aménagement du Bas Rhône Languedoc, and the Organisation des Etats Riverains du Fleuve Sénégal. They can attract and coordinate the participation of specialists of various disciplines to plan a rational utilization of the water for the generation of energy (power stations), for the production of food and fibre (by irrigation), and for industry and transportation. But the water 'resource' is limited by constraints, especially the flux of materials, which in Nature accompanies the water: dissolved products, suspended matter, and bed load; the concentration of salts sterilizes the land; the solids in transit fill the reservoirs and make channels unstable, which hampers navigation and installations on its banks. One of the most important preliminaries of any improvement in the regional management of water is to restrict this flux, which entails the morphogenic stabilization of the watershed, mainly by plants (concept of phytostasy). One of the objects of agronomy is to protect crops to ensure good yields, the best possible conditions of phytostasy, and the least waste products.

Plates 34–36 Traditional hydraulic techniques
Ph. JT CCCXCVIII-17 cn. Water wheels equipped with buckets ('norias'), Homs, Syria. They use the current to lift the water up to an aqueduct.

Plate 35 Ph. JT CCCXCIII-7 cn. Well with horse or donkey merry-go-round to pump water into an irrigation canal, Valdemosa, Mallorca, Spain.

Plate 36 Ph. JT CDXCVIII-12 cn. Impluvium on roofed water tank, Kerkenna Island, Tunisia. No runoff and very few wells on this archipelago force the population or fishermen to catch rainfall and stock it in underground tanks, where it is protected against evaporation and pollution.

Plate 37 Mudflow sediments
JT CCCXLI-9 cn. Section through mudflow deposits in coastal Peruvian desert, below Moquegua. The site is presently hyper-arid with a few showers per hundred years. The material was deposited during a 'pluvial' period with sporadic rainfall in the mountains. As floods spread over the surface, water is quickly infiltrated or evaporated, leaving behind centimetric layers of fine grained deposits. These are cut by gravelly channel fills (half the height of the photo). Such outwashes when not affected by too violent floods, but providing sufficient water, can be used for cultivation, as, for instance, traditionally has been done in southern Tunisia.

Plate 38 Water pollution
Ph. JT CDXX-9A. Río Bogotá, downstream of the city. On the river bank, gauging station and homes, whose dwellers *drink* this 'water', in fact, an emulsion.

Plate 39 Equipment of an experimental catchment
Ph. JT CDII-16A. An experiment of low-cost stabilization of gullies, DICOREN experimental watershed, Casablanca, Chile. A staircase of small dams has been constructed in the gully in order to disperse the energy of the streaming water. Debris which have already accumulated behind the dams testify to their efficacy. The material used, small branches and bushes, can be obtained locally without any other cost than its collection, and can be easily replaced when necessary.

5 REMOTE SENSING AND ECODYNAMICS

Technical progress, initially accelerated by the bellicose rivalries of the Great Powers is tending to become a source of commercial profits. In the United States the Reagan Administration has turned over NASA to private enterprise, to EOSAT, the Earth Observation Satellite Company. In France the rates charged by SPOT-Image are so high that they may well eliminate all studies other than by research organizations supported by large contracts. (Nevertheless, some commercial competition is engaged between EOSAT, SPOT-Image, and the SSSR. Users can obtain lower prices under conditions to be examined and eventually 'bargained' in each specific case.) Even so, remote sensing provides ecogeographic studies with considerable, irreplaceable information, which technological progress does not cease to increase and diversify. The recordings include aspects of the ecologic environment that are outside our sense perception (infra-red and radar wavelengths); those scanned from orbiting satellites almost instantly span large areas and may be repeated more or less frequently; they produce not only inventories at specific dates, but also a *continuum* of observations, which is seldom the case in aerial photography; they can be used for *diachronic comparisons*, that is to study changes, periodic or not, to *analyse evolutionary trends*. Our objective in making morpho-pedological maps was to map the interactions between morphogenesis and pedogenesis as a basis for agronomic development and land management. Such maps are based on the concept of topostability, which may be more readily discerned with help of remote sensing owing to its repetitiveness. Remote sensing also provides information, often sequential, on other aspects of the environmental dynamics, which should be taken into account in rational land utilization. The concept of morphopedological maps can therefore be enlarged by extending it to all environmental dynamics and the making of *ecodynamic maps*.

This chapter will therefore recall (in a manner easily understood by someone of good education but ignorant of the subject) some of the basic principles of remote sensing together with an elucidation of the technical aspects of the recordings and how they are used. Lastly, we shall explain what we mean by ecodynamic studies and their cartographic expression.

WHAT IS REMOTE SENSING?

Remote sensing is remote recording of electromagnetic radiation reflected or emitted by objects. For example, our ears or eyes are mechanisms of remote sensing that transmit the waves they receive or perceive, the brain resolving the nervous message and identifying the corresponding objects.

Emitted radiation is exceptional on Earth; it is seldom recorded, as, for example, the rumblings preceding a volcanic eruption. In contrast, it is of invaluable use in astronomy, which identifies celestial bodies by their spectral signatures in visible, infra-red, microwave, and radio wave lengths. Medicine, too, by measuring the heat energy radiated by organs can tell whether they are diseased. Medical doctors at the Louis Pasteur University in Strasbourg have made much progress in early identification of breast cancer through use of thermographs and methods of treatment developed by the Laboratoire des Applications Electroniques de l'Ecole d'Ingénieurs Physiciens. Natural radiation ('passive' remote sensing) and artificially emitted radiation ('active' remote sensing), that is radar, are used in remote sensing the natural environment. Special types of emitted energy used in geophysical prospecting, such as seismic and even radio waves and electrical currents triggered at the Earth's surface or at depth, do not enter into the definition of remote sensing. In most cases what is recorded in passive remote sensing is the radiation reflected by natural objects, especially light waves, the near infra-red (or photographic infra-red, for it may be recorded on special photographic film), and part of the far or 'thermal' infra-red, which our senses perceive indistinctly in the form of radiant heat, as that coming off an electric heater. Another part of the thermal infra-red is also *emitted* by terrestrial objects, such as the heat released in the early part of the night by a stone wall or an asphalt road exposed to the Sun during the day. A law of physics indeed states that the heat radiation absorbed by an object is always emitted later at a wavelength longer than that of the incident radiation. This delay is important in the interpretation of thermographs, that is the recordings of thermal infra-red radiation.

A *remote sensing system* is composed, as in the case of our senses, of three elements:

1 *A sensor*   which receives radiation from the environment within a narrow spectral range, called 'band'. The same vehicle, in this case either LANDSAT or SPOT, can juxtapose several sensors functioning in different bands and operating simultaneously on the same 'scene', that is on the same portion of the Earth's surface.
2 *A platform*   on which the sensor is located: an aircraft or a spacecraft; which allows it to move and aim at the scenes that it is to record; which provides it with energy and, on occasion, with specific instructions (e.g. for oblique sightings, as regards SPOT); and, lastly, enables the transmission of the recordings.
3 *A transmitter*   required on non-inhabited platforms. The remotely sensed data, in the form of electrical signals and converted into digital numbers, are recorded on magnetic tape, 'memorized', and periodically transmitted by radio to ground stations, where they are prepared for processing, that is for use. The available energy on board satellites with solar antennas does not allow the use of powerful radio transmitters; the transmitters function only when the vehicle is closely overhead to a receiving station, which itself is equipped with long antennas capable of receiving low energy signals over a distance of hundreds of miles. Moreover, in order to save power and reduce weight, the recordings made on satellites are 'compressed' to a maximum, which means that they must be 'decompressed' at the receiving stations, so that they can be used by computers in the form of *computer compatible tapes* (CCT). After transmission of the data, the magnetic tapes are demagnetized for reuse. In case of defective transmission, the data are lost.

With inhabited platforms, such as aircraft, the Space Shuttle, or space stations, it is not necessary to have a radio transmitter, the recordings remaining on board until brought back to Earth; they may even be directly treated on board, as in the case of most radar recordings. (The serious problems recently inhibiting the full use of the Space Shuttles resulted in a strong predominance of the USSR space stations from which, for instance, are taken numerous photographs of excellent resolution on sale through foreign subsidiary firms, as in Finland and Germany.)

The various radiations utilized by remote sensors are part of the *electromagnetic spectrum*; they are defined by physicists according to frequency or wavelength, characteristics that are mutually interdependent. For simplicity's sake, we shall refer to wavelengths. Electromagnetic waves used in remote sensing, by definition, have to traverse the entire thickness of the atmosphere in the case of satellites, or most of it in the case of aircraft, which usually fly at high altitudes. The trajectory is double with radiation reflected by terrestrial objects. The crossing of the atmosphere, depending on the one hand on its properties and on the other on wavelength, is more or less unimpeded; for example clouds, atmospheric dust, and minute water droplets (aerosols) diminish visibility, even reduce it to zero; depending on the conditions, they exclude aerial photography. Physicists use the more abstract, therefore, more general term *transmittance*. When it is good, the radiant energy crossing the atmosphere is hardly diminished, but when it is bad, it may be absorbed or reflected in all directions, making it diffuse, as happens to light in a grey sky.

Transmittance is affected by various atmospheric bodies, especially at certain wavelengths; for example, clouds (water vapour or minute ice crystals) affect light waves but have no effect on radar microwaves of specific wavelengths. In contrast, other wavelengths are reflected by raindrops and used by meteorologists for remote sensing of rainstorms ('meteorological radars'). Much cloudiness in the Darien region of Panama made it impossible to obtain a vertical photographic coverage in spite of the facilities of the American bases of the nearby Canal Zone; but with the help of a side-looking airborne radar system, developed for military purposes, an experimental survey was made of this eastern part of Panama in 1968 that proved highly successful and was the first to be declassified. This enabled a number of American corporations to sell their services to other countries desiring a similar coverage for their territories. In 1970 radar mosaics were made of Venezuelan Guayana, of a small area in the Venezuelan Andes, and of the lowland south of Lake Maracaibo. In 1972 Brazil contracted several American companies to produce radar mosaics for an area covering 4 million km^2, including all of Amazonia, the North-east, and part of the State of Bahia, and in 1975 decided to do the remaining part of the national territory. The radar coverage has made possible the making of planimetric maps, the revision of topographic maps and, especially, the making of an inventory of the natural environment and its resources (geomorphology, geology, soils, and plant formations), and a list of environmental management problems entrusted to RADAMBRASIL. Publication of the achievements in the form of abundantly illustrated reports and maps on the scale of 1:1,000,000 in the framework of the International Map of the World was finished in 1984. (Tricart first used radar mosaics in a study of the eventual development of the lowland area south of Lake Maracaibo and was named scientific adviser to RADAMBRASIL in May 1975. He took part in the methodological aspects of the work of this organism in Amazonia and in other areas of Brazil until the termination of the radar surveys in 1982. 'RADAMBRASIL' stands for Radar-Amazon-Brazil, a huge government sponsored aerial radar survey that started in the Amazon Basin and was ultimately extended to the entire country.) Similar inventories have been made of Colombian Amazonia and Gabon. All of Nicaragua and of Peru have been covered by radar mosaics, as well as other areas of South America, totalling some 12 million km^2, much of which suffered from a want of satisfactory topographic maps and good quality vertical aerial photography.

The chart of Figure 16 shows in relation to the entire electromagnetic spectrum which major subdivisions can be used for remote sensing the terrestrial environment: the visible, the infra-red, and the microwaves. Atmospheric transmission in the infra-red, however, may be more or less completely blocked through absorption by water vapour, carbonic gas, or ozone (as shown in black below the scales). It is only at certain intervals, figuratively called *windows*, that radiation is let through (the white intervals).

Airborne *platforms* as well as sensors determine the type of recordings. *Aircraft* have the advantage of flexibility as recording flights may be made along freely chosen itineraries and altitudes, but they are more or less dependent on the weather, except for aircraft that can fly above it, at 10,000 m as did the radar-carrying Caravelles over Brazil, or the U-2, which can fly at 19,000 m. Repetitiveness depends on the carrying out of successive flights, often handicapped by want of stable and sufficient financial support at the right time. Traditional recordings, like photographic surveys, are made at a particular time only. This excludes studies of seasonal variations, so important on the ecodynamic level, as well as the establishment of a sequence for a particular event, seasonal or not, such as the progressive flooding, followed by waning, of a river. For example, the annual flood of the Interior Delta of the Niger directly determines the possibility of subsistence of 3–4 million people in Mali. The SLAR (side-looking airborne radar) surveys of Brazil, like aerophotographic surveys, were made in the form of parallel equidistant flights matching the surface of topographic sheets in a west–east or north–south direction, depending on the predominant strike of the relief, such as to provide a most effective visual rendition of the land.

Light aircraft offer many possibilities, but also limitations, in the mounting of sensors (space, power, instalment of hatches). They may be very useful, being less expensive and more readily available, if not adaptable. The Centre de Géographie Appliquée (CGA/UA) (i.e. Unité Associée au CNRS, previously known as 'Laboratoire Associé 95', whose remote sensing activities are integrated in the Groupement Scientifique de Télédétection de Strasbourg (GSTS), which, since January 1983, includes the old Groupement de Télédétection de Strasbourg et Consortium de Traîtement d'Images de l'Université Louis Pasteur) frequently makes use of them, that is as much as meagre budgetary funds allow. This enables the periodic observation of certain 'target areas', such as the small Baschney Basin (2.5 km^2) at Grendelbruch in the Vosges Mountains, which, moreover, is permanently monitored by a climatological and a limnological station with several measurement transects. This basin is used to calibrate complex remote sensing recordings of the Champ du Feu Massif, intended for evaluation of water resources: thickness of the snow cover, rate of fusion, and water stored in the regolith. The significance of the vertical and oblique panchromatic and colour infra-red photographs will be examined later. The ITC (Enschede, the Netherlands) has experimented with very light

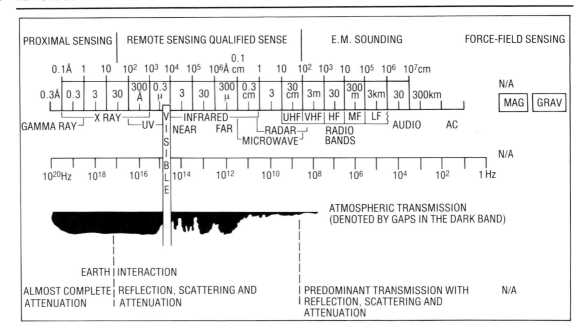

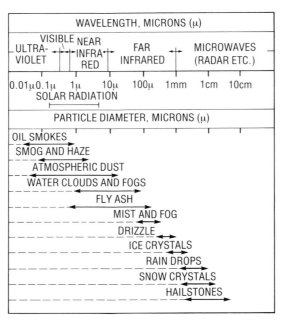

Figure 16. Wavelengths and windows used in remote sensing.

Source: F. Wieneke (1988) *Münchener Geogr. Abh.*, A **38**, p. 7.

Å = angstrom; μ = micron; E.M. = Electro-Magnetic; AC = Alternating Current; n/a = no attenuation; MAG. = Magnetism; GRAV. = Gravity.

The atmospheric windows, of necessity, appear tiny on the chart and are not labelled by capital letters, as is the convention. They are most useful in ecodynamic studies. Their wavelengths and characteristics are as follows.

A corresponds to the visible spectrum and the near IR, ranging from 0.36 to approximately 1.2 microns. It is used by LANDSAT, SPOT, METEOSAT and the HCMM satellite (see below).

B ranges from 1.5 to 1.8 microns.
    The **A** and **B** windows are separated by an interval of high absorption of water vapour.

C ranges from 2.0 to 2.4 microns.
    Bands **B** and **C** are used by LANDSAT 4 and 5.

D in this window the radiant energy emitted by Sun and Earth are about equal, so that for studying Earth surface features this window can be used effectively only at night.
    There is an **E** window at approximately 4.9 microns; it is seldom used, for it is too narrow and a poor transmitter.

F this window, ranging from 8 to 14 microns, is intersected by a band of high ozone absorption around 9.6 microns, which interferes with observations made from satellites but not from airborne radiometers, as aircraft fly well below the ozone layer. This window is used by LANDSAT 4 & 5, METEOSAT, and the HCMR (Heat Capacity Mapping Radiometer) carried on board the HCMM (last M for Mission) satellite (1978–80).

aircraft, with open cockpit, from which the pilot takes photographs with a hand-held camera. The implement is cheap and can easily be repeated, but its use is restricted by air traffic regulations. Anyhow, it is not within the realm of remote sensing but within that of aerial photography.

The use of *satellites*, whose numbers and variety are on the increase, is more general. In the 1960s the first (Mercury, Gemini, Apollo) took spectacular oblique, coloured photographs of specific parts of the Earth, while the meteorological TIROS and Nimbus series produced TV and scanner images covering huge land areas; they served instructional purposes rather than research. LANDSAT-1 (originally called ERTS, acronym for Earth Resources Technology Satellite), first of a series, was launched in July 1972. This began almost uninterrupted recordings of most of the Earth by a multispectral scanner. LANDSAT-4 (1982) (suffered from various technical problems and inadequate fund allocations) and LANDSAT-5 (1984) were also equipped with other sensors: a Thematic Mapper, which has seven instead of four spectral bands and a radiometer for the F window. LANDSAT-4 and LANDSAT-5's transmission system is also different, as it retransmits its data through geostationary telecommunication satellites above different points of the Earth, a change that has caused serious trouble and for a long time has delayed use of the recordings (Figure 17).

The orbit of the LANDSAT is slightly inclined on the Equator (81°), thus effectively excluding the polar regions (above lat. 81°) and causing the images to be lozenge shaped rather than square. Due to the Earth's rotation each successive orbit is shifted westward 2,875 km at the Equator, but the following day, after fourteen orbits, the tracks are adjacent to (159 km from) those of the previous day, filling the 2,875 km gap in eighteen days (sixteen for LANDSAT-4 and -5), after which the

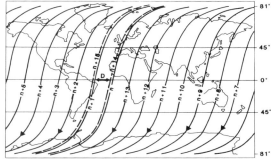

Figure 17(a). Successive tracks of a Sun-synchronous satellite above the Earth. LANDSAT-1.
    Source: NASA *Users' Handbook*.

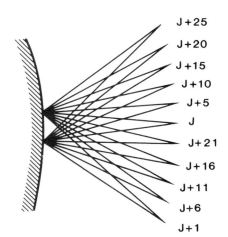

17(b). SPOT imaging system using the possibility of oblique sensing in order to increase repetitiveness: the example given corresponds to a latitude of 45°.
    Source: SPOT *User Hand Book*.

process is repeated (NASA 1976). Images of two adjacent orbits have an overlap of 14 per cent at the Equator and 85 per cent at 81° N or S. At certain times two LANDSAT have functioned simultaneously, in such a way as to halve the return interval of eighteen days, producing a *theoretical repetitiveness* every nine days. Actually, taking into account cloud cover, saturation of the on-board memory, and hitches in the functioning of the sensors this frequency is much lower: from 1972 to 1978 none of the three first LANDSAT made a recording of the Solomon Islands; the CGA/UA 95 practically had to abandon its attempt to keep track of the snow cover of the Vosges Mountains and the floods of the Interior Delta of the Niger using LANDSAT data. As to the HCMM launched in 1978, it does not carry a memory on board, so that its observations can be recorded only in 'real time', that is through direct reception of a station with which the satellite has contact at the very moment the recordings take place, which considerably reduces the areas that can be covered. SPOT (launched February 1986) on the other hand has fixed (so-called 'push-broom') sensors that do not have a scanning mirror. Each recording consists of a strip of a certain width (ground-swath) normal to the orbital track, so that successive strips are automatically juxtaposed owing to the forward movement of the vehicle. This simplification allows the array of detectors to be given an inclination of up to 26° from the vertical, as directed from the ground. In that way a side-looking coverage of up to 60 per cent of the recordings made by successive orbits is possible, enabling stereoscopic analysis, greater repetitiveness (which remains a function of latitude, but may amount to several times per week), decrease in blind spots caused by clouds (for example, by aiming obliquely at an off-track longitude with no or few clouds, while the on-track zone is hidden. The life-span of SPOT-1 was originally estimated at two years. However, in spite of a few incidental defects, it was still functioning in 1990. In the mean time, a SPOT-2 of the same type and performing a complementary service, like some of the LANDSATS, has been launched. The SPOT series will be continued and improved, SPOT-3 being devised with other sensors.

Other satellites are *geostationary*, that is they are positioned at a fixed point above the Equator from which they do not move. This is the case in particular of the five meteorological satellites, including METEOSAT (European, on the Greenwich Meridian) and GOES (American, one at 65° and the other at 135° W longitude) that gird the Earth. From their lofty positions at a height of 36,000 km each scans the entire visible part of the Earth, that is almost an entire hemisphere. Their repetitiveness, therefore, is much more frequent, even at night with a thermal infra-red sensor in the F band. This fulfils the needs of meteorology.

Satellites such as LANDSAT and SPOT are sun-synchronous, that is the plane of their orbits always forms the same angle (37°) with the plane passing through the Sun and the Earth, so that their recordings, above whatever location, are always made at the same solar time. Time discrepancies in the orbital passage above the same terrestrial point do not exceed a few minutes at most – a perfect timekeeper. The local time of each pass depends on latitude: LANDSAT-1, -2 and -3 cross the Equator at 9:42 a.m. mean local solar time; the Sun is then oblique, which produces shadow effects beneficial to the visual examination of the images, but which are detrimental to the mid-latitudes in winter and complicate the numerical processing of the recordings in mountainous regions because of changes in the quantity of reflected energy. Geostationary satellites, in contrast, make closely repeated recordings: every half-hour for METEOSAT and GOES for data received during the 26 minutes that precede the 4 minutes needed for transmission. In this way it is possible to keep pace with changes in temperature of the air masses, modifications in the cloud cover, and to obtain accurate kinematics of the atmosphere. The educated public stands witness (also on television cloud cover pictures) to the progress made in weather forecasting thanks to the considerable technological investments.

The altitude of the satellite orbits is enormous, always well above the terrestrial atmosphere, which would slow down the spacecraft, causing it to fall, to heat up by friction, leading to its destruction: 191 km for Apollo 9, approximately 900 km for LANDSAT-1, -2 and -3, 800 km for SPOT, and about 35,000 km for the meteorological geostationary satellites. Such enormous distances mean that objects of a certain dimension only can be discerned ('resolution'). Inconsiderate enlargements are futile, as common sense tells us that details cannot be observed from huge distances.

Also other airborne platforms besides aircraft and satellites have been used: missiles by the British, stratospheric balloons by the French (Centre National d'Etudes Spatiales – CNES), and especially the American Space Shuttle. The Shuttle, in a way, is intermediate between satellites that go into orbit and aircraft that are flown and return to Earth and dispose of plenty of power and a large cargo bay, permitting many activities on board. For example, the subsequently unfortunate *Columbia* carried a radar system (SIR-A experiment) whose eight hours of recordings were transformed into images on board, in like manner as on the Caravelles over Brazil. Spacelab, of the European Space Agency, on board the same Shuttle (1983) carried a large-format camera (LFC) similar to the one carried by a number of Soviet Soyuz satellites (MKF 6), producing coloured photographs of extraordinary quality.

The *resolution* of the recordings is of fundamental import. It corresponds to the 'grain' of a photograph. Newspaper photographs, transmitted by telegraph, have a coarse grain composed of dots of different shades of grey visible to the naked eye. To enlarge such reproductions would be futile. The grain of photographs, whether aerial or not, is minute; a powerful lens is required to see it. Study of aerial photographs is therefore much enhanced by considerable enlargements. On the other hand, radiometric sensors on board satellites have, of course, a lesser resolution due to distance. The bundle of radiant energy reflected by the Earth's surface and received by them at a distance of hundreds of kilometres originates from a surface that measures hundreds of square metres, even with a sensor having a very small scanning angle. This area determines the resolution of the sensor. In LANDSAT 1–3 recordings, this *pixel* (or 'pictorial element') measures approximately 80×80 m on the ground, 30×30 m for the Thematic Mapper of LANDSAT-4 and -5. The resolution of METEOSAT is of course less: 2.5×2.5 km for the visible and 8×8 km for the thermal at the Equator; they are insufficient for ecogeographical studies. That of SPOT is much better: 10×10 m for the panchromatic band and 20×20 for bands 1–3. The resolution corresponds to a kind of grid pattern arbitrarily superimposed on the Earth's surface, as the military grids on certain topographic maps. Its disposition is totally independent of that of the landscape units. A pixel is practically always heterogeneous and associated, in variable proportions, to different objects; for example, for LANDSAT 1–3: a house, parts of a garden, of a street, and perhaps of a wood or ploughed field. Furthermore, it is impossible exactly to locate the pixel on the ground. The composition of the cocktail cannot be determined. The only way out is to work with groups of pixels having the same radiometric characteristics, a minimum of 9 disposed in a square (3×3), which becomes increasingly difficult with decreasing resolution and accounts for the meagre results

obtained from METEOSAT. This is not surprising considering the number of different objects and the significance of these differences in an area measuring 2.5×2.5 km at the Equator.

With this background we shall now examine the various types of information that can be obtained from remote sensing technology.

WHAT REMOTE SENSING HAS TO OFFER

We shall first show what kind of ecogeographic information can be obtained from various remote sensing systems and then examine by what methods they can best be studied.

Types of information provided by remote sensing

The way to proceed is to subdivide the electromagnetic spectrum into channels usable by remote sensing (cf. wavelength and window chart).

Thermographs

The F window is the most expedient, for it measures the heat radiated from the upper few centimetres, or 'epidermis', of the Earth and the objects on it. The D window provides the same type of information but only at night, as during daytime there is interference with reflected radiation. But this window is approximately three times as sensitive as the F window.

To understand thermographs a few basic principles are in order. During daytime the sun heats the Earth's epidermis. This input varies as a function of its absorption capacity, which depends on its surface characteristics, including colour: black absorbing much, white very little. The radiation then penetrates more or less quickly and deeply according to thermal conductivity. The quantity of calories stored depends on the specific heat of the objects; for easy understanding, this storage capacity may be compared to that of the water retention capacity of soils. The air, whose specific heat is very low, cools swiftly after cessation of the incident solar radiation. The specific heat of the solid matter and water of the

Earth's epidermis being higher, they cool more slowly. This emission drops more or less rapidly during the night as a function of the quantity of heat absorbed the preceding day, and thermal conductivity. Cooling, which correlates with thermal emission, is differential after a certain time (t_n) of emission, depending on the ecogeographic characters; it therefore allows their study. Water, because of its high specific heat, warms and cools very slowly. It, too, is a poor conductor. At dusk water bodies radiate much less heat than solid materials such as bare rocks, especially when dark in colour. But later in the night, especially at dawn, water still emits much heat while the rocks have cooled down to the temperature of the air and have ceased to radiate. Humic soil horizons and the vegetation, poor conductors that retain water and air as in a network, heat up slowly, the vegetation even fighting heat by transpiration. At night they slowly release a small quantity of energy. Their thermic behaviour is closer to that of water than to that of bare rocks.

Thermal remote sensing of the Earth's surface or cloud cover can be done either from aircraft or from spacecraft. Its most useful application, thanks to its repetitiveness, is by meteorological satellites, whether orbital or stationary, whose use of the visible is ruled out at night. Their information, aside from the cloud cover, however, is of little use to us, as the spatial resolution is much too coarse.

One of the first studies made by the Institut Géographique National in France revealed, because of differences in water temperature, karstic springs offshore from the cliffs of the Pays de Caux in Normandy. In another case, the Groupement de Télédétection de Strasbourg revealed an outflow into a number of streams of ground water from the Rhine alluvial plain in the area of the volcanic massif of the Kaiserstuhl, not far from the Fessenheim nuclear power plant; it provided important supplementary information on the hypodermic flow of water in an area whose ground-water has been studied for a long time and is one of the best known in Europe. Indeed, the temperature of the ground-water varies less during the course of the year than that of the surface water because of the thermal inertia of the alluvial materials. As in a cave, temperature is cooler in summer and less cold in winter than the outside temperature, the disparity being greatest during a very warm summer and a cold snap in winter. The circulation of the water close to the surface and its emergence are therefore picked up by a radiometer because of the temperature differences.

In general airborne thermal sensing of the environment can provide important information on soil moisture contrasts due to differences in the thermal inertia of moist and 'drier' regions, which indirectly may also reflect differences not only in the texture of the surficial materials, very fine materials retaining water longer than coarser materials, but in soil structure: soils with good structure retaining more water than soils with poor structure. But sequential thermographs are needed to be of greatest ecogeographic and, especially, of ecodynamic profit.

Near (photographic) infra-red

Special films in black and white or in colour, usable in whatever camera, but which must be kept at a low temperature, are able to record the infra-red radiation reflected by the Earth's surface. They are used on manned platforms (aircraft, Spacelab, Soyuz). With special processing analogous images are obtained from three bands recording in the visible and the near infra-red (MSS bands 4, 5 and 6 or 7 of LANDSAT 1–3). SPOT bands are calculated in such a way that they can be 'added' to obtain a pseudo-infra-red image.

Colour infra-red images provide the most information. They are made by a 'shift' in the sensitivity of the three superimposed layers of a colour photographic film, in such a way that the colours obtained on the prints are completely different from the natural colours perceived by our eyes. For this reason they are called infra-red *false* colour images (IRFC), and more and more frequently infra-red colour for short (IRC). For example, the green matter of plants, when in a healthy physiological state and effectively performing photosynthesis, appears in purple-red (magenta). When the leaves turn yellow or brown by wilting, as during autumn, the colour changes to green. Water appears as dark Prussian blue, almost black: IR radiation does not penetrate it, but when murky or salty shows up in an increasingly light sky blue. Mineral matter appears as a very light, whitish, sometimes slightly bluish tint, even if it is basalt or a ferruginous cuirass. The 'code' is not the one to which our sight is accustomed. Like thermographs IRFC images show places where there is soil and where it has been eliminated, or where the bedrock is exposed; they are very useful, even indispensable, in inventorying degraded land. Of even greater utility is that they provide indications on the metabolism of the plant cover. Early or late frosts that 'burn' leaves, that stop photosynthesis, show up by changes in colour.

Photographs taken at the right time enable the mapping of afflicted areas and identification, for example, of the effects of inversions of temperature in valleys and the localization of cold air flows along the hillsides. Also the shortage of water, after reaching a certain critical point, triggers wilting, which causes the cessation of photosynthesis; IRFC documents thus enable the afflicted areas to be identified. In the Baschney pilot-basin, which is the object of continuous climatological and hydrological measurements, IRFC images are taken periodically and at increased intervals during certain critical periods. The hypodermic water reserves, normally abundant in the decomposed granite, were exhausted at the end of August and beginning of September 1983, in spite of showers and melting of snow that earlier, in March, April and May, caused serious spates in north-east France. Small plants with shallow roots were the first to wilt, followed by deciduous trees, especially beeches, in spite of their deep-seated roots. Stages in the downward drying of the soil can thus be followed and compared in different geomorphological sites, such as ridges and cradle-shaped vales, valley bottoms, and so on. Finally, IRFC photographs also enable detection of flows of suspended matter in rivers, lakes and reservoirs, and coastal regions more clearly than on bands 4 and 5 of LANDSAT. In arid regions intense salinization of temporary lakes, salars and sebkhas, occasionally of reservoirs, is identifiable, as, moreover, the presence of aquatic vegetation, whether floating or rooted, in particular the plague that is the water hyacinth: *Eichhornia crassipes*, so abundant, for example, in the Pantanal matogrossense (Brazil). All this is valuable.

Bands in the visible and near infra-red (LANDSAT MSS, SPOT)

Two basic concepts should be remembered when utilizing bands in the visible spectrum. First, that short waves penetrate deeper into water than long waves, so that, band 4 of LANDSAT and band 1 of SPOT are most effective. The penetration of the near infra-red of band 6 is very small, while that of band 7 (3 of SPOT) is practically nil. Bathymetric indications may be obtained by comparing the sea bottom visible on different bands; for example, the depth of a reef or of a sand bank, on condition, however, that the water is calm, clean and does not produce light reflections. Its transparency can be determined with a Secchi Disk during remote sensing. If the near infra-red is useless in the detection of shallow submerged forms, band 7 of LANDSAT and 3 of SPOT are the best for tracing river banks and shorelines, a task that is very difficult, sometimes impossible, on bands 4 and 5 (1 and 2 of SPOT).

Second, atmospheric transmittance varies in the opposite direction: it is most transparent to long wavelengths. Often, layers of haze or flimsy clouds blot out parts of band 4 imagery, but do not disturb that of bands 6 and 7. Because of the kind of information provided by bands 4 and 5 and also by bands 6 and 7, which are not very different, bands 5 and 7 are to be preferred over the other bands in a rapid preliminary survey. Relief, usually, is not clearly, or not at all, visible on bands 4 and 5 because of low atmospheric transmittance, while it appears distinctly on band 6 and, especially, on band 7 of LANDSAT.

In general, bands 4 and 5 are good for the identification of extensive plant covers, which, at these wavelengths, are poor reflectors and therefore appear in dark tones; of mineral matter, whether in suspension or exposed at the ground surface, which, in contrast, is highly reflective and therefore appears in light tones; and of shallow submerged forms, if the water is calm. Comparison of bands 4, 5 and 6 give an idea as to what depth waters are murky with suspended matter (mud, silt, very fine sand). Bands 6 and 7 best portray the relief, which is fundamental. The plant cover, when green, is a good infra-red reflector especially in band 7, for which reason it does not 'hide' the relief. These bands, therefore, do not lend themselves to the study of vegetation. As to mineral elements, they are not identifiable.

As noted, the data provided by the various spectral bands of the MSS of LANDSAT complement one another. To combine them on a single document, equivalent to an IRFC photograph, therefore has advantages. Work is more precise and detailed than that derived from a visual comparison of three separate images. Such colour composites are made by projecting each given band through a particular filter, normally bands 4, 5 and 7, or created directly from the original data on to photographic film via computer. This is why SPOT has only three spectral bands, corresponding to these three bands of LANDSAT's MSS. The 'freed' band is then utilized for panchromatic recordings, similar to those of aerial photographs.

Radar images

Most radar surveys are flown by aircraft. Nevertheless, several radar carrying satellites are scheduled to be launched in the early 1990s: those of the European Space Agency, Japanese, and American–Canadian. Aircraft radar surveys covering more than half of South America were made with equipment emitting in band X at a wavelength of 30.2 mm. A few minor surveys in Colombia have used a wavelength of 8.6 mm, but the data obtained from them are meagre in comparison. Airborne radars have antennas that produce wide angle beams: in Brazil between 13° and 48° from the vertical, producing a broad image swath (40 km) but considerable relief distortion. Convex ridges appear sharp crested; hill or mountain sides facing the imaging system return good reflections but appear compressed ('foreshortened'), or even 'laid over' when steeper than the look angle, whereas the sides facing away are poorly 'illuminated', receiving little energy and reflecting even less, so that they show up in dark tones, preventing their analysis. The relief displacement thus produces a chevron pattern pointing towards the imaging system. Use of radar imagery requires considerable experience to prevent misinterpretation. Distortions resulting from the wide angle beam preclude the use of radar images for the making of contour maps. The radar installed on the Shuttle Columbia (SIR-A) is better in that regard, as it has a very small angle beam (6°). Airborne radars, however, have an excellent resolution: 20 m in Brazil, and a detection ability of specific objects down to 2 m under the most favourable conditions. Excellent planimetric maps, including the toponymy, can be made from the mosaics mainly in flat regions, where distortions are negligible. Comparison of the radar mosaics with the 1:1,000,000 map of Brazilian Amazonia published in 1972 is startling: the courses of some important rivers are so inaccurate on the map that they cannot be identified on the radar images.

Band X has certain advantages. First, most of the microwave energy passes through the plant cover. The Amazon rainforest, for example, shows up as tiny black dots, whereas on aerial photographs it completely blots out the ground surface, including the trace of small watercourses. Because of it Tricart used radar imagery, on a scale of 1:100,000, rather than good aerial photographs, in a study of hydraulic developments south of Lake Maracaibo, the photos showing only tree tops, making it impossible to draw the stream network and drainage divides.

Second, certain types of vegetation have a high radar reflectivity therefore appearing in a very light tone on the images. They include plants belonging to widely differing families, suggesting a cause probably related to different leaf pigments. Although empirically demonstrated by RADAMBRASIL, there is no scientific explanation for this high reflectivity so far. What is known is that the plants are always amphibious, whether floating Amazon or Pantanal prairies, mangroves of Guayana or Nicaragua, flooded palm savannas, or Amazon forest standing in several metres of water. These plant associations cannot be mutually differentiated on the imagery, but they do reflect a certain type of ecologic environment, which is valuable.

Third, recently ploughed fields, burnt over land, even several months old, show up well: they do not reflect radar microwaves, or very poorly, therefore appearing in black or very dark grey on the images.

Fourth, relief shows up well: directly, in hilly or mountainous regions, with the distortions alluded to, or indirectly through the medium of vegetation in other regions. For example, in Amazonia, the present and recent alluvial plains of the meandering Jurua and the confluence of the Solimões and the Japurá (Caquetá in Colombia) show up in a spectacular manner (Tricart 1979f). Radar microwaves do not penetrate the water and, owing to specular reflection, are not reflected to the antenna, so that the recently abandoned channels, still flooded, show up clearly. Other abandoned channels have already been invaded by the aquatic vegetation with high reflectivity. Lastly, the lofty selva grows on the most emergent natural levees, stopping abruptly, like a wall, where the ground becomes too permanently waterlogged. Such forest edges 'react' like stone walls, depending on their orientation in relation to the incident radar beam, showing up either in a very light tone, in black or in various shades of grey, but always in contrast with the tree tops. They therefore underscore the disposition of the natural levees.

Landforms are therefore the aspect of the natural environment that shows best on radar imagery; for this reason they are the starting-point of the study of that environment, the clue to geological, pedological and plant geographical investigation, which depends on the physiographic units and the links between them and other components of the landscape. But the inability to penetrate water and to provide particular signatures for soils and various rock types preclude the use of radar images for the study of land degradation, flow of detrital material, in short, of the present dynamics. The contribution of radar images is basic to physiography and to hydrology, but indirect to other ecogeographic components.

Tricart also has had the occasion to study the radar images of SIR-A (Shuttle Imaging Radar) recorded over Mali (November 1981). They were made in band L, the same as that used by SEASAT, of a wavelength of 23.5 cm. These images are not easy to use, the more so that simultaneous observations on the ground were not possible. The main facts recorded are the roughness of the vegetation and of the micro-relief. The degree of roughness of the amphibious vegetation of the Interior Delta of the Niger unfortunately varies greatly with the stage of plant growth, about which there is no recorded observation, which does not help the identification of the plants. An advantage of this orbital radar, which operated at an elevation of approximately 250 km with a far range depression angle of 37°, is a much smaller distortion. Meant for oceanographic studies, SIR-A cannot be used in ecogeographic studies except at the cost of long and expensive research. The means to carry this out, even to programme it, were unfortunately refused (i.e. a type of research contract of limited duration and funding requested by Action Thématique Programmée (CGA/UA 95) on a special interest theme selected by the CNRS (in this case: 'remote sensing of the environment'). This rejection was accompanied by the incredible argument that such research requests should not include field-work, i.e. ground truth!).

UTILIZATION OF REMOTE SENSING RECORDINGS

Remote sensing recordings are available in different forms. The most accessible is the photographic image, with which, through aerial photographs, we have become well acquainted over the years. But although aerial photographs were used by the military during the First World War, they were not used by many researchers (outside of the military) until *after* the Second World War. It was also during that war that infra-red photography came into being. At present, SPOT provides panchromatic images with stereoscopic capability, exactly as aerial photographs, except that they

cover very much larger areas, which is a considerable advantage over aerial photographs which have to be assembled into mosaics, a tedious undertaking. The resolution is slightly inferior, but nevertheless 10×10 m, which is not a major handicap. As with most radar recordings, they have been transformed into images already on board the Space Shuttle for SIR-A, so that there are no tapes. On the contrary, SIR-B tapes are available.

Photographic processes aside, remote sensing recordings consist of quantities of energy received by the sensor, converted into numerical values that are recorded on magnetic tapes. The organizations operating remote sensing systems provide users with

1 computer compatible tapes (CCT) on which are recorded, in proper order, numbers corresponding to the quantity of energy received
2 images, obtained by transforming, by means of a mechanism containing a photoelectric cell and a photographic film, the numerical values into a scale of greys, ranging from black to white.

The images are therefore extracted from the magnetic tapes. They allow an immediate pictorial viewing, which, through the practice of air photo interpretation, benefits from a long experience and enables a broad use of the subconscious. This step should not be neglected; only a stubborn neophyte would skip a first viewing of the data before undertaking the numerical processing on the computer. True, it is incontrovertible that the scale of greys obtained corresponds to a certain loss of information, to an impoverishment of the initial numerical values. Theoretically, it is possible to have recourse to a scale of 256 shades of grey, but the eye can differentiate only a fraction of them. Easy access to the information more than compensates for this limitation. Furthermore, recourse to numerical processing is not always justified. Visual examination and optical processing are often sufficient, sometimes even more efficacious. In case numerical processing is justified, it should be so because of a preliminary visual examination, which determines the kind of processing; it should, therefore, be done with circumspection.

If images made from negatives derived from magnetic tapes are ordinary photographic prints, it is nevertheless improper to call them 'photographs'. This would confuse them with real aerial or space photographs as taken from Apollo or by the mapping ('metric') cameras of Soyuz or Spacelab. Magnetic tapes exist and can be used, whereas a photograph or radar imagery, whose magnetic tape has been destroyed immediately after producing the images, must be *digitized*, that is transformed from shades of grey into numerical values, which is a long and costly procedure necessitating sophisticated equipment and specialists, who are to be found only in competent remote sensing laboratories.

Images are usually enlarged. Those of the various bands of LANDSAT (MSS) from 1:1,000,000, on request of the user, to 1:500,000 or 1:250,000. The information, of course, remains the same, but the enlargements may facilitate visual examination, the making of tracings, and a comparison or superposition with maps. The negatives themselves, on a transparent support, may be acquired and *colour composites* made. Similar facilities are offered by SPOT-image, that is enlargements at 1:200,000, and 1:50,000 and various types of corrections, whether radiometric or geometric. IRFC images of popular books may serve as examples. With a small photographic laboratory two images of the same band but of different dates can be compared and used to make a single colour print. All that is necessary is to have recourse to filters to transform the images into complementary colours; for example, image A in red and image B (more recent) in blue. If the object occurs both on A and on B on the print, it will appear in red plus blue, that is in violet, the tones of violet varying with the respective importance of the red and the blue. Pure red indicates an object visible on A only, and a pure blue another visible only on B. This simple manipulation may serve, for example, to compare a flooded area at two different dates by using band 7, or broadleaf vegetation in summer and winter by using band 5, allowing a discrimination of summer green and evergreen plants.

There are various ways, different from those that are standard and mass-produced, in which IRFC composites can be made: either by diversely associating positive and negative images, or by attuning the iris diaphragm and time of exposure of each image. D. Blumenroeder, at the CGA/UA 95, has succeeded in bringing out differences in a virgin evergreen forest in the south of the State of Bahia, Brazil. They possibly correspond to facies changes in the Pliocene detrital substratum, for the relief is a uniform plateau. Unfortunately it has not been possible to obtain ground confirmation so far (Tricart and Blumenroeder 1979; 1981).

As images are the result of optical and *numerical processing*, the latter may be manipulated to advantage. The digital numbers of the magnetic tape can be classed into a certain number of groups by computer, as is done in the preparation of standard imagery. Another procedure, called *density slicing*, is to use only those values that are above a certain value, or threshold, and to vary the limits of the statistical classes, an operation that is more complex than the mere transformation of digital numbers into shades of grey. The computer displays the result of this 'supervised' classification, each pixel being represented in a colour assigned to the statistical class to which it belongs. Such operations are carried out by *computer programming*. Having adopted a tentative classification, the operator displays the results, examining them at ease and seeing to what extent they meet the objective and correspond to what the operator knows about the terrain. If not satisfactory, the operator can modify the classification and thus, by trial and error, improve it. This process is sometimes referred to as a 'dialogue' with the computer. Unfortunately such an expression attributes to it an intelligence that it does not have, as it is strictly limited to execute statistical manipulations: such a system is called *interactive*. This threshold and classificatory procedure may also be bypassed. The computer can easily and quickly make more complex calculations, such as of ratios between the numerical values of pixels in various bands, additions, subtractions, square root extractions and multiplications. The ease of manipulation, however, creates the danger that some workers indulge themselves into data processing for sheer pleasure, losing sight of the physical reality of the landscape, which was the object of the recordings. But, if we lament this technocratic bent, we also recognize the essential value of viewing the results of data processing on the screen, which enables one to proceed by trial and rectification whatever the complexity of the calculations and to make *comparisons with the terrain*.

For a time it was thought possible to rely almost entirely on computers and to bring about an *automated cartography*. Magnetic tapes would be introduced into the computer, which would follow a programme, and the desired map would appear on the screen or, even better, come out of the printer. In short, some hoped to proceed as with machines that automatically bag a raw material, condition it into a uniform product, and enclose it into a standardized package. Study of the natural environment, unfortunately, is somewhat more complex than the canning of beer. Excessive confidence in computer programs and automatic feeding of orders to the Stock Exchange resulted in the October 1987 crash. The danger of this procedure is now recognized: it is exactly the same, or worse, when studying Nature. Some authors commit a grave error by continuing to use the erroneous and mystifying expression; rather one should speak of 'computer-assisted cartography'.

Computer-assisted cartography is dependent on the judgement of the operators, who choose the thresholds, the limits of classes (which are in part a function of the number of classes, themselves subject to technical constraints), the colours to represent them, and the calculations on the numerical values, using programs chosen by themselves. (The word 'operator', in fact, designates a small team of workers, which at the CGA/UA 95 was composed of a data processor (Mme Engelman), a research specialist, who, besides, is a pilot (J. Trautmann), plus other researchers working on a particular project or region.) The input of operators adds a personal coefficient into the operation: their field knowledge, their way to approach problems, their manipulatory dexterity (e.g. choice of programs), and their critical sense vis-à-vis the results of the inputs. Research, here as elsewhere, is characterized by this personal input, which distinguishes it from standard mass-production on an assembly line where robots take the place of humans. Computer-assisted cartography, therefore, is necessarily based on a number of operations that include a previous knowledge of the terrain, choice and examination of training sites, and interpolation from training areas and assisted cartography.

radiometers, such instruments are expensive and, therefore, limited in quantity. Difficulties increase when recordings are made from satellites. Dates and time of overpasses are precisely known ahead of time, but the recordings are extremely rapid (the 'period' – the duration of a single orbit of LANDSAT-1 – was 103 minutes, that of the other LANDSAT and SPOT is the same within 5 minutes), so that in one minute thousands of km^2 are being recorded. The difference between this duration and the time-span of changes in natural phenomena (hours for tides, days for floods or a snow cover, seasons for other phenomena) is enormous. Observers cannot be everywhere at the same time. Moreover, if the data on the passage of the satellite is well known, nothing is known about what the atmospheric transmittance will be. In short, whether the recordings will be usable is not known in advance. To risk much for possibly nothing is the situation: the problem is not easily resolved. Recourse to permanent recordings and observations at specified ground locations is the only solution, which is what has been done in the Baschney and the Bruche basins of Alsace. The series of measurements enables us to know the situation at the time a usable LANDSAT recording has taken place. An automatic station has been acquired by the GSTS at great expense, but one is not enough. Previous field knowledge, of course, should be supplemented by published information and the visual examination of imagery (aerial photographs, LANDSAT, SPOT, etc.).

A previous knowledge of the terrain

A previous knowledge of the terrain, to bring out and define problems related to the objectives of the research and the character of the terrain should include accurate observations whose aspects are conditional upon the type of recordings used (e.g. with band L the roughness of the interface) and the momentary characteristics of the landscape at the precise time of recording. Observations should be as synchronous as possible to the recordings: while this is highly desirable, it poses problems that are difficult to resolve. In the case of small areas surveyed by aircraft, several teams, working simultaneously in a standard fashion with the same type of instruments, can be deployed in various parts of the terrain. At the time of the thermal infra-red recordings of the Fessenheim area, temperature measurements of the water surface were made by teams in canoes, but this requires personnel and instruments. In the case of

Choice and examination of training sites

The ability properly to select and delimit areas representative of the research problems depends on previous acquaintance with the field; for example, a particular landscape unit or an area affected by a certain type of dynamics. The quality of the resultant processing will depend on the degree of representativeness of such an area and the quality of our knowledge of it. The selected sites are used as training areas, to test the spectral characteristics of the landscape components. A critical evaluation of each test depends on a thorough field knowledge. To what extent does the testing faithfully reflect the characteristics of the landscape relevant to the research objectives? A process of trials and improvements by successive manipulations is entered upon. Sometimes, when the experience of the operator is wanting, a certain type of processing must be abandoned in favour of another. Field knowledge, too, for its part, may prove to be insufficient, in which case new outdoor observations must be carried out. A dialectic between ground data and processing is thus engaged in.

A return to the field to improve or complete previous observations as a function of computer data processing implies practical or financial impediments in the case of stable ecogeographic components, such as lithology. But when the components are unstable, such as the meteorological conditions at the interface, the state of the vegetation, or the water balance, the complications are serious. To find out, months later (in France, delivery of LANDSAT recordings may take six months and more, while SPOT deliveries take days only – for those who can afford them), what was the anatomical and physiological state of the plants, the soil water balance, or the water level of a swamp is well-nigh impossible. As to continuous recordings, they can be carried out only in small areas and on certain aspects of the landscape. Improvement of this dialectic approach is an urgent task on which the efficacy of the remote sensing of the natural environment depends. Unfortunately few executives have been convinced on this score.

Interpolation from training areas and assisted cartography

An entire study area is ready for examination once the representativeness of the training areas has been found to be adequate and the processing and classifying procedures have been synchronized. The way to proceed is to tackle the space between the training areas, progressing from what is most like the one or the other training area to that which is most unlike. This procedure, in fact, is the same as the one we described earlier when defining intergrade environments. It may lead to the creation of new divisions and units.

A practical operation remains to be carried out after this work is completed. It consists in taking colour photographs of the television screen of the image portions that have been processed successively. Interactive systems prevent action on the entire image, whose limits, moreover, seldom coincide with those of the study area. A mosaic of photographs, each affected by the distortions caused by the bulging television screen, is thus obtained, so that the photos must be rectified to produce a controlled mosaic based on geodesic points. SPOT-image makes geometric corrections at various precision levels as well as radiometric

corrections, which can be combined. The only problem that remains to be solved is the cost – a detail of major importance.

Automatic cartography is still far off. For the present it is computer assisted: the computer, by data processing, provides a valuable service from the point of view of output, time and reliability. Nevertheless, the initiative rests with the operator, a team of researchers. Such is the state of the art. Thanks to the techniques of remote sensing, the CGA/UA 95 team has been able to make important progress in ecodynamic studies.

REMOTE SENSING AND ECODYNAMICS

The types of dynamics of the natural environment have been reviewed in the preceding chapters: the morphogenic and pedogenic processes, and the water balance. We have emphasized the interactions between them. Of these the morphogenic and pedogenic interactions in the framework of physiographic units are shown in the morpho-pedological maps made through the collaboration of the CGA/UA 95 and the Service de Pédologie of the IRAT; they show to what degree agronomists are free to develop agricultural production and a sound soil management. The conception of morpho-pedological maps goes back to 1970–3 (just before the availability, through study contracts signed with NASA at the end of 1972, of the first LANDSAT recordings). Also at that time (1973) J. Tricart had the opportunity, in Brazil, to commence work on the radar mosaics of RADAM (Radar Amazonia) and to study LANDSAT imagery for the Institut Français du Pétrole in relation to aspects of structural geology. Research in ecodynamics of the CGA/UA 95 was therefore undertaken before the availability of satellite imagery in the form of preliminary studies of the area of Ste Maxime (Var) in the south of France and, later, of the Maradi area, in Niger, thanks to a research contract ('The struggle against aridity in the tropics') with DGRST (Délégation Générale à la Recherche Scientifique et Technique). The purpose of the Maradi study, coordinated with work of the IRAT, was to define the various types of degradation of the natural environment caused by the Sahelian drought in the early 1970s in order to undertake experimental agro-silvo-pastoral operations under representative conditions and, later, to delimit regions where each one of these types of intervention would be applicable.

It was during this initial stage of methodological reflections that J. Tricart broadly defined what is meant by ecodynamics; more recently (1978) he has initiated an exploration of what could be the contribution of remote sensing in this domain. Let us examine these two points.

What is an ecodynamic study?

'Ecodynamics' is the dynamics of the ecological environment. We have already indicated that the concept of ecosystem suffered from an imbalance from the start, as the environment in which the biocoenoses develop was considered to be stable, as is confirmed by such terms as 'toposequence' or 'ecotope'. The main preoccupation at the CGA/UA 95 was to develop a study of the ecologic environment based on a systems or dynamic approach involving flows of energy and materials, exactly as the study of the biocoenoses themselves. The conception of morpho-pedological maps was a first step in that direction; but the approach to the problem was still incomplete. Ecodynamic studies are broader and constitute an enrichment, which also benefits practical applications, specifically as concerns the rural management of the natural environment.

Ecodynamics is concerned with the various processes and mechanisms that cause changes in the ecologic environment. It studies how they function in space and in time, which are inseparable one from the other. As a result of the nature of things, it also examines their mutual interactions, conformable to a systems approach. The flow of material, more directly observable than the flow of energy, and which, moreover, is a manifestation of the available energy in the natural system, permits the characterization of the structure of the system. Reference to space and time is essential, as it enables the study of its successive changes in time (evolution) and in space (different combinations at a given time; different evolutions during a certain period of time). Certain characteristics, changing very slowly, at a different pace, constitute a kind of framework that can be thought of as being stable and not hampering research or causing practical complications.

The present state of knowledge and the means available for research nearly always limits studies to a qualitative assessment of fluxes, whether of mineral or of organic matter. While measurements of the movement of fluvial bedloads is very difficult, so that valid data are extremely rare, information on the transport of matter in solution or in suspension is better, but also practically non-existent outside of fluvial data. Measurements of material transport by surface runoff or by creep are nearly always carried out in small runoff plots, so that results cannot be extrapolated to the breadth of the land. The discharge of rivers is better known, but we are handicapped by dearth of valid, measured and significant data, relative to the surficial and hypodermic runoff that is going on to the slopes of the surrounding country. Cosandey's (1983) excellent thesis demonstrates this clearly.

At the present state of research, it is better to have a good qualitative study than a cascade of computations susceptible of abusing users by giving them a false impression of rigour and precision. A qualitative study, which reveals the inadequacy of our knowledge, constitutes a preliminary step toward organizing carefully thought out measurements. In an ecodynamic study, first we define and map the different morphogenic processes, describing their characteristics, their intensity, the degree of topostability resulting from them, and their interactions; whether they are interfering with each other (e.g. surface runoff and solifluction) or working together, combining their effects to produce results superior to what would be the sum of their effects taken separately. Second, we define and map the circulation of water, conceived in the same manner as on our hydromorphological maps. The water-retention capacity of the soils, their matrix potential (the logarithm of the suction force necessary to extract water from the soil by osmosis), and their rate of filtration are the object of tests in the field and in the laboratory, which enable the water regime and the water balance of the soil and the surficial formations to be defined.

These various components were defined in the study of the Maradi area and mapped at the scale of 1:25,000. During more recent research (Tricart, Trautmann, Gomes, et al. 1984) of the southern part of the coastal plain of Rio Grande do Sul, Brazil, a Franco-Brazilian team (CGA-Dept of Geography of the Instituto de Geosciencias of the Universidade Federal do Rio Grande do Sul) studied flood water regimes, that is permanent or temporary flooding in the form of free standing water or marshland, a supplementary aspect of the dynamics of the ecological environment and a manifestation of constrained instability.

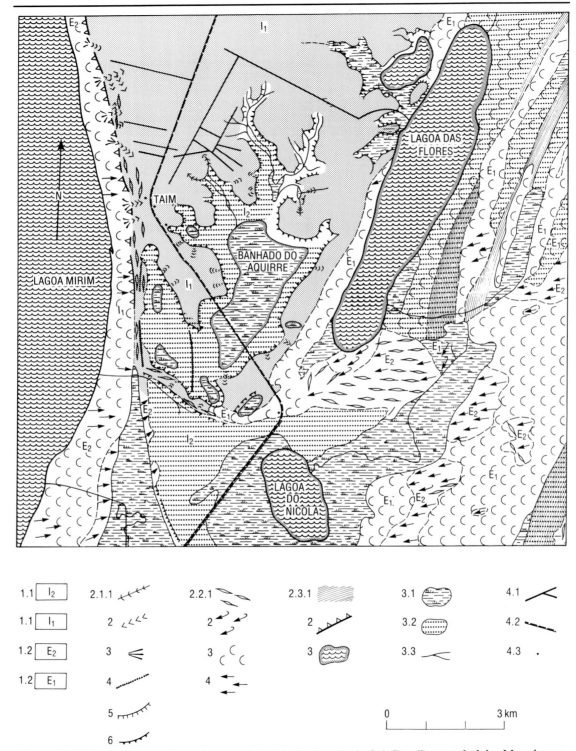

Figure 18. Extract of the ecodynamic map of the Rio do Grande do Sul (Brazil) coastal plain. Map drawn by C. Sira. Shown here is the area of the Taim Ecologic Station (see Tricart, Trautmann, Gomes 1984).

Figure 18 cont.
Legend:
1. Genetic environment
    1.1 lacustrine deposits: 1_1 old, 1_2 recent
    1.2 aeolian deposits: E_1 old, E_2 recent

2. Landforms
  Land forms
    2.1.1 vales
       2 V-shaped canyons
    3 fans
    4 alluvial levees
    5 smooth scarps
    6 steep scarps

  Aeolian forms and dynamics
    2.2.1 active sand dunes
       2 cover sand
       3 hummocky sand accumulations
       4 deflation areas

  Littoral forms and dynamics
    2.3.1 relict coastal sand bar
       2 active lacustrine cliff
       3 shifting lake shore

3. Hydrology and hydrologic regime
    3.1 swamps (*banhados*)
      2 areas subject to flooding
      3 perennial streams
4. Man-made features
    4.1 canals and ditches
      2 road
      3 villages, farms . . .

Banhados, except for a slight difference in spelling but with the same pronunciation, is a term common to both the State of Rio Grande do Sul and the region of Rio de la Plata (Spanish: *bañados*). They are shallow, permanently or near permanently, flooded depressions with a dense vegetation into which cattle and horses can wade. This term represents a hydrological, biological, and geomorphological (settling of suspended materials and, especially, slow decomposing organic matter) unit.

Merit of remote sensing in ecodynamic studies

The merit of remote sensing in ecodynamic studies is considerable. First, remotely sensed recordings in a very short, almost instantaneous, lapse of time cover enormous areas: a LANDSAT image measures 185 km on the side and covers 34,300 km^2, that of SPOT 120 km^2 and 14,400 km^2 respectively. We can omit the very much broader field of view of the meteorological satellites, whose resolution is generally insufficient for our purposes. A homogeneous recording made at the same moment over vast areas under the same meteorological conditions is an enormous advantage, which cannot be provided by aerial photographs. The latter, weather permitting, take hours, more frequently days to make, during which changes in natural phenomena occur. The synchronism of LANDSAT recordings has been put to profit by the FRALIT team (France-Littoral,

a project under the responsibility of F. Verger, executed during the probative period of ERTS (LANDSAT-1) and sponsored by NASA), in order to make an original study of the shore dynamics of the oceanic littoral of France. The remotely sensed satellite recordings provide an instantaneous 'view' of the extent of a flood or, on the contrary, of a low water stage, phenomena which have been put to profit in the study of the amphibious lowland of the coastal zone of Rio Grande do Sul, Brazil (Tricart, Trautmann, Gomes, et al. 1984, see Figure 18).

Second, another use of remote sensing is offered by J. R. G. Townshend's investigations at Reading. Numerical treatment of various remotely sensed reflected wavelengths by vegetation results in an evaluation of the 'green stuff' activity, that is in the picking-up of the visible radiant solar energy used for primary production. At present, the state of the art does not go beyond a qualitative assessment, which, nevertheless, allows the discrimination of healthy and ailing plants under stress, whether by pests or weather (drought, frost, hail). Determination of the date of the calamity will be all the more accurate as the repetitiveness of the sensor carrying vehicle is more frequent; the better the resolution, the more accurate the identification of the type of plants affected. But at present, no orbiting sensor is able to identify individual plants: this is possible only with aircraft.

Third, the repetitiveness of satellite remote sensing recordings is another advantage. An aerial photographic coverage may not be repeated for years, even in France, where, in principle, the Institut Géographique National (IGN) repeat photographic flights over the same area every ten years. It happens, of course, that for various reasons, special flights are made from time to time, but these are sporadic. In any case, years pass before an area is rephotographed. The situation is worse in many countries: in Africa, for example, the most recent aerial photographs may be more than twenty years old. Another disadvantage is that most photography is carried out in the dry season when the cloud cover is least and the transparency of the atmosphere is tolerable. In Senegal and in Mali photographs are made in December–January, during low water stage; it is impossible to use aerial photographs to record the extent of the seasonal floods of the Senegal and Niger rivers, although they are a most important event to the people of these countries and their neighbours. The repetitiveness of orbital recordings may leave something to be desired too; nevertheless it is infinitely preferable to photographic surveys. It can be improved thanks to technological progress, as the difference in the conception of the sensors of SPOT and LANDSAT demonstrates.

Fourth, a greater variety of wavelengths and, in the visible, a narrower range can be used by remote sensors than by panchromatic aerial photography. We have mentioned the types of information these various spectral bands can obtain from the Earth's epidermis. The wealth of this information is unquestionably greater than that provided by panchromatic photographs. SPOT provides panchromatic imagery with stereoscopic overlap, thus associating the advantages of aerial photographs to those of remote sensing (synchronous recordings of a vast area and repetitiveness) at the cost, to be sure, of a lesser resolution, which is, however, sufficient for ecodynamic studies.

Fifth, remotely sensed recordings can be subjected to optical and numerical processing that increases the quantity of information that they otherwise furnish. Aerial photographs can be subjected only to densitometer analyses, which are delicate, relatively expensive, and of infrequent usage. The various bands, in contrast, can be subjected not only to equal treatments, but also to many others, which depend only on the dexterity of the operator. There is here a veritable mine that remains to be prospected. The information obtained from the various segments of the electromagnetic spectrum may be combined to an infinitely variable degree by optical and, even more, numerical techniques. The time elapsed is enormously smaller than that required for field observations, at the cost of very expensive equipment and supplies, as demonstrated by the use of IRFC composites and the diachronic comparisons that J. Tricart and collaborators have made from the LANDSAT tapes of the high and low water stages of the littoral lowlands of southernmost Brazil. Rapid progress in remote sensing is the result of the pace of technological advancement during the past few decades, especially in electronics, much fuelled by the arms race. Research (by Tricart) in the use of remotely sensed imagery in the form of IRFC composites, some scanned from aircraft, others from stratospheric balloons, goes back to 1969. Use of the latter enabled the Centre National d'Etudes Spatiales (CNES) to offer the opportunity to a number of researchers to initiate themselves in ecogeographic studies eventually to be made from LANDSAT recordings. Only seventeen years later SPOT was in orbit. Furthermore, it should not be overlooked that much more sophisticated spaceships with classified equipment in the service of the military are presently orbiting the Earth. Sooner or later, as with the case of airborne radar, that technology will be declassified. One should therefore be optimistic: remote sensing increasingly opens new doors to research in ecodynamics.

Finally, remote sensing technology can detect phenomena which are very difficult to observe by traditional methods, such as ground or water surface temperatures. At large scales, satellites are unsuitable for this task, as the ground resolution of their sensors is insufficient. The only recourse is to aircraft, in spite of their lack of regular repetitiveness. An excellent example, from a methodological as well as practical point of view, is given by Lemieux et al. (1988) in Canada. Growing cranberries is the main source of revenue around the shores of Lac Saint-Jean in Quebec. These plants (*Vaccinium*) need well-drained soils but are affected by early killing frosts, occurring shortly before the harvesting season. They are cultivated on sandy glacial outwash, reworked into low dunes and including kettles, some dry, others occupied by ponds. The highland, overlooking the lowland, is covered by coniferous forest. At St Nazaire, 600 ha of cranberry fields have been used as a training area. The object of the research was how to decrease the damage caused by autumnal temperature inversions producing a build up of freezing air, down to $-8\,°C$, on the lowlands? Remotely sensed temperature recordings, in the 8–14 micron window, were made from the air, at an elevation of 7,620 m, on 7 September 1982, 2 October 1983 and 7 June 1985. The size of the pixel was $15.7\,m^2$. In comparison, similar observations on the ground would have required 218,000 thermometers plus thousands of observers, with a proportional risk in human error. Ground control was carried out simultaneously by means of selectively placed smoke-producing devices and wind vanes, to record the direction of air movement at ground level, which is beyond the capacity of instantaneous thermography. A provisional model was made on the basis of the 1982 and 1983 thermographs. It was checked on 31 October 1985 by a light airplane equipped with search-lights and a dense ground network of sophisticated anemometers, of a special type, whose luminescent panels produced a visualization of the direction and velocity of air currents at ground level. The effects of certain forest clearings were investigated. Measurements made soon after sunset, from 5:45 p.m. to 7:30 p.m., enabled verification of expected temperature differences at various sites: dunes and sandy rises storing the day's heat, while tree hedges and copses, which absorb less heat, remain relatively cool. Passageways were cleared through tree barriers south of the cranberry fields to allow the evacuation of the cold air, reducing the temperature inversions. The cold air coming from the north to north-east over a distance of about 10 km, one of the passageways was oriented north–south, the other north-east–south-west. The check of October 1985 demonstrated their efficacy. The decision was therefore made to profit from the test by opening up other breaches in the obstacles to the outflow of cold air, particularly tree barriers. The cranberry farmers, whose economic stake in this development was considerable, were very cooperative in the operation. Similar research was conducted by the Centre de Géographie Appliquée, in cooperation with Electricité de France, by Trautmann (1981), to determine the location of surfacing ground water and its

accumulation in a sector of the Alsace-Baden Graben.

In these examples thermal remote sensing has enabled phenomena to be studied directly, but this is not always possible. For example, it would be useless to try to identify schools of fish in a lake or sea from an air or spaceborne platform. Nevertheless, it can be attempted with recourse to a systems approach, as we shall now demonstrate.

The drought that has afflicted Mauritania since independence has compelled a courageous people to make a major effort to survive. Traditionally, the Moors have been stockbreeders and, until desertification destroyed their subarid pastures, nomadic herders. One of their tribes, however, the Imraguen, is specialized in offshore fishing, north of the capital, Nouakchott. The government has decided to help these people make greater use of their ichthyological resources, which, of course, have not suffered from the drought. The cold Canaries Current follows the coast in a southerly direction and causes cold water upwelling on the margin of the continental shelf. Rich in dissolved nutrients, it favours the development of plankton, which, in turn, feeds the fish. The mechanisms are identical to those of the Humboldt Current, off the west coast of tropical South America, albeit to a lesser degree. Using METEOSAT thermographs, it has been possible to measure the temperature variations of the surficial offshore waters and, thus, to determine accurately the seasonal regime of the cold upwelling water, whose nutrients together with solar radiation permit the development of phytoplankton, at the starting-point of the food chain. Next, on this chain, are schools of fish, heavy consumers of this primary food, followed by humans at the end of the food chain. Besides these well-known phenomena, the thermographs permit the determination of the shifts and intensity variations of the cold upwellings as a function of the meteorological situation, revealed by the same satellite. The Ministry of Fisheries thus can properly equip small fishing ports and advise the fishermen about the most prospective fishing grounds. The example, notable for its simplicity, demonstrates the usefulness of the systems approach in ecogeographic studies.

Remote sensing is a veritable mine, much of which remains to be prospected. But we should not forget the essential. The domestication of the horse, the automobile, the aircraft did not make walking obsolete. As new techniques are added to old, the old should not be eliminated. We must have mastery over them, that is consider them as an enrichment, and use them advisedly where they prove to be the most effective, by harmoniously adding them to other procedures, also adapted to new conditions. This is the case, in particular, of remote sensing of the natural environment, which reveals its secrets only if we persistently practise a rigorous dialectic between observations and field knowledge and the wise utilization of remotely sensed recordings. If not, the fiasco will be in proportion to the sophistication of the techniques employed.

PART TWO
THE MANAGEMENT OF THE RURAL ENVIRONMENT

INTRODUCTION

In Part I we presented the ecodynamic aspects of Nature. In so doing we have tried (in contrast to traditional trends in research) to demonstrate the unity of the environment, home of living beings. To the ecology concept of biologists we have opposed the ecodynamic concept, also in the framework of a systems approach. In so doing we have caused problems to lovers of labels and to bureaucrats who are used to classifying their materials according to standard methods. Taking a broad view, the study of the aspects of Nature on the Earth's surface is part of physical geography, while ecology is the science of the association of living beings in relation to their environment. Whatever the opinion of traditionalists, we are convinced that in order to understand Nature we must understand its unity over and above the artificial division of the traditional disciplines that avoid it. The aberrant separation of physical geography and ecology, as well as the equally aberrant union of the entire field of geography to the social sciences, can be explained only by historical circumstances, which have varied depending on the schools of thought. This attitude prevented transdisciplinary work and the training of the young for the proper management of the natural environment and thwarted the availability of competent professionals. It has delayed, sometimes irremediably, the improvement of the restricted land on which we live. We are convinced we are on the right track, a track that leads directly to the problems of good land management if we reconstruct the study of the natural environment in a manner symmetrical to that of ecosystems. Having proposed a new approach to the study of the natural environment, we shall now discuss the problems of its rational use.

The rational use of the natural environment is mainly concerned, on the economic level, with agro-sylvo-pastoral activities, but is far from being limited to them. In many countries the farming population has dropped to 15–20 per cent or even less of the total active population. On the other hand, non-farming people have been invading the countryside, whether farmed or not, with residential developments, secondary homes, camping sites, and other recreational and touristic activities, not infrequently arousing the ire of the established rural population. Result: the traditional difference between urban and rural landscapes is becoming ill defined. Nevertheless, the agricultural land remains our ecologic support. Plants, regardless of artificially harnessed solar energy, remain the only effective means of trapping and storing solar energy, transforming it into food for humans and animals and into raw materials for industry now as in the past. Coal and oil are solar energy stored for millions of years.

In the 1960s an incredible aberration of 'expert' technicians and politicians has had the public believe in the illusion of a food surplus (the 'green revolution') and in France has caused the shutdown of coal mines in favour of oil consumption and construction of oil-generated thermal power plants rather than of harnessing waterfalls. These blinker-wearing visionaries have lost; their miscalculations are now manifest; the truth revealed. The increase in world population has been much faster than the increase in resources. The real problem is to produce more food and fibre under proper social and economic conditions without despoiling the environment and to utilize energy more efficiently, available in limited quantity, in the process. The planet's soil and water resources are invaluable; it is not, in spite of the enormous cost, the sending off of astronauts to the Moon or to Mars that will change this state of affairs. These celestial bodies, even less than the bottom of a mine, can be transformed into an ecologic environment.

It is not surprising that NASA itself at the very beginning of the 1960s began to consider the degradation of the terrestrial environment by atmospheric pollution. During the 1970s and 1980s 'greenhouse' gases became much blamed as a serious cause of the problem. Of course, NASA's involvement played in its own favour, as satellites are among the most efficient available tools for monitoring the environment, including the transmittance of solar radiation through the atmosphere, and carbonic gas, which is responsible for absorbing an important fraction of the IR radiation re-radiated from the Earth. Nevertheless, the proposal is scientifically sound, even if things are not quite as simple as NASA would have them. The ICSU (International Council of Scientific Unions) adopted the International Geosphere–Biosphere Programme (IGBP) which emerged from the first NASA proposals. The object of the IGBP is to determine what are the mechanisms of human-induced changes in the environment and what are their effects, as a sound basis for recommendations to governments in order to minimize and, as far possible, reverse these trends and their dangerous consequences. For our part, we support such a programme in our own field in this book.

In Part II, which is, in fact, a comprehensive conclusion of Part I, we shall approach the problems of land and water management, valued as ecologic resources, as the basis for vegetal and animal production profitable to humankind. We shall bypass the problems caused by the expansion of cities, towns, and superhighways, as well as those caused by recreation and tourism.

First, we shall re-examine certain concepts previously discussed, especially the concept of the dynamics of ecogeographic units, by stressing their importance from the point of view of land use. Chapter 6 will show how vastly different is the susceptibility of different types of environment to human intervention depending on their degree of stability. In light of this, the concept of rational land management can be understood, that is a management that uses the ecologic resources without causing a degradation, that safeguards the future. In some cases even natural conditions can be improved! Such a concept enables the resolution of a number of crucial points, particularly the concept of *constraint*, which is more adequate, because more objective, than that of *potential*. A practical method of approach has been developed from this standpoint.

Before explaining it, we shall examine the role of experimentation. This role is important because of the complexity of the phenomena involved, the number of causes that produce them, and the difficulty of apprehending and measuring most of them. Nevertheless, a more thorough knowledge of the natural environment can improve the experiments by making them more representative. The often considerable disparity of the results obtained on an experimental station and those obtained on ordinary farms can be reduced. This problem will be examined in Chapter 6.

Made increasingly representative, agricultural experimentation can be closely associated to the approach proposed in Chapter 6. It is characterized by a gradual, progressive transition from basic knowledge to proposals of practical solutions. The discourse of researchers is followed by that of politicians and administrators so the latter may make their decisions and choices in the most objective way and with full knowledge of the facts. The use of the professional studies by the decision-makers poses difficult problems, which, in general, are far from having been resolved. Most frequently pedologists make maps of crop suitability based on their soil studies. This method is deficient because it overlooks the human, social and economic factors, which often play a determinant role. A change in price, a modification of commercial routes, of credit conditions, or the introduction of a crop that originally was not profitable suddenly means profits. Pressure groups form to get their hands on them. This is all the more speculative the more complex the societies. Such factors cannot be ignored. But they are not within the province of studies of the natural environment. Our approach is based, strictly, on the particular constraints of the environment. It relies on experimentation in order to determine up to what point and according to which practices the constraints may be overcome or reduced. The study ends with land use or land management recommendations that clearly define up to what point human intervention can go without causing a degradation of the environment, taking into account its susceptibility and what precautions should be taken to this effect. Experimentation permits these precautions to be defined and to estimate their cost. It also helps determine the qualifications to be acquired by the farmers to apply the recommended measures. Various decisions will have to be made, as a rational land use not only entails specific work that may be carried out by outside firms, but, necessarily, too, the participation of the local inhabitants, a participation that should be voluntary. To obtain it, certain economic, social, cultural, and political conditions have to be met. The various experiments harmonized to the natural and human conditions of the area enable problems to be posed. Then, once a decision is made, it can be executed, smoothly, by providing the basic, elemental instructions to the work force.

Plate 40 Poorly conceived, useless conservation practice
Ph. JT CDLXV-10 cn. Useless conservation planning, Serra do Mar between Caxambu and Juiz de Fora, Brazil. These slopes were planted with coffee trees during the nineteenth century and converted to pastures during the Great Depression. To protect the highway, reforestation has been undertaken and trees planted along contour lines. Unfortunately, this practice increased the infiltration of water and triggered mass movements in the deeply weathered gneiss. Centre background shows a typical amphitheatre caused by a slump. A fault plane, approximately perpendicular to the highway delimits the edge of the slumped mass (August 1978).

6 THE RATIONAL USE OF THE RURAL ENVIRONMENT

The variety of rural land uses on Earth is enormous, although there has been a trend to uniformity in certain types of modern farming. To try to classify them or to conjure up a taxonomy of them is difficult. Certain techniques successful for centuries, even millennia, in a given environment have had catastrophic consequences in another. For example, ploughing, effective in Europe, has proved disappointingly inadequate in the wet or wet-dry tropics when used indiscriminately or without due precaution. Most chemical fertilizers, effective in the temperate zone, are too rapidly soluble and with little effect in the humid tropics. Cultivation techniques and cropping systems must be adapted to the environment in which they are applied. This is what we call 'rational land use'.

Rational land use is based on a thorough knowledge of its object, without which it cannot be properly adapted to the particularities of the environment. Consequently the techniques and the very concept of a rational land use are bound to evolve as a function of technological progress and also of understanding of the environment. As a whole, for more than fifty years, technological progress has been faster than the improvement of our knowledge of natural environmental conditions. This imbalance has been detrimental, the cause of many degradations and even irremediable despoliations even before the age of bulldozers, as in the coffee plantations of the Paraiba Valley of Brazil (chronic landslides and mudflows) or the Piedmont of South Carolina (monstrous gullying). Recently, investigations by Tricart, in the framework of the Centre d'Etudes Mexicaines et Centre-Américaines (CEMCA), in the region of Lake Zacapú (Michoacán) have shown that Purhepecha (Tarasc Group) settlements had to be abandoned in the period from the eleventh to the thirteenth century after a complete devastation of the environment resulting, in good part, from repeated wood cutting for ceremonial fires. Combined geomorphological and sedimentological work has demonstrated that the morphogenic–pedogenic balance remained roughly in equilibrium, except for an occasional truncation

of the humic horizons during violent floods, from the sixth to the eighth century, but then turned highly negative, the soils and even the subsoils having been swept away entirely. Cultivation then became impossible and the people left the area for another lake 70 km away. This migration is confirmed by a corpus of oral traditions constituted soon after the Spanish conquest. But since the 1930s bulldozers and other power machines have created unlimited havoc all over the Earth. An engineer at a loss for a better answer in reply to one of us who drew his attention to the danger of indiscriminately reworking the alluvium deposited in the Alpine Guil Valley during the June 1957 flood replied: 'In any case, it reassures the population that something is being done'. This 'something' is the very problem.

Up to what point and how is an intervention possible without triggering a degradational process that may be difficult to arrest? To determine this threshold, in fact, is to define the criterion of a rational land development. It amounts to defining the degree of sensitivity of a natural system to various types of possible interventions. What type of crop, what kind of cultivation methods should be adopted on a certain piece of land without risking a soil impoverishment or causing its dilapidation by morphogenic processes? What quantity of phosphorated products can be discharged into a lake without causing its eutrophication? What type of engineering works will be more efficient without causing hazardous environmental imbalances? These are simple examples of the application of the concept of sensitivity of the natural environment. The development of the land, however, generally concerns a higher level of complexity. The eutrophication of a lake, the pollution of a watercourse, the degradation of the soils of a hillside are only the partial effects of a regional activity, whatever the seriousness of their consequences. Soils washed away by surface runoff produce muddy streams that damage the floodplains on which their suspended load comes to rest. Their entrainment modifies the conditions of runoff, therefore the regime of the streams, which

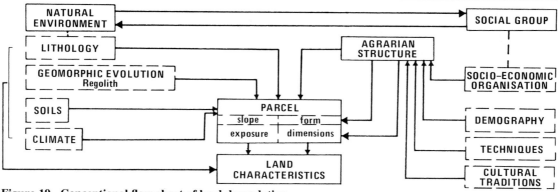

Figure 19. Conceptional flow chart of land degradation

becomes more torrential: water resources will shrink during periods of drought, and spates, more violent, cause greater damage. A sectoral, partial, apprehension of reality avers to be insufficient. In the rational land use concept every manifestation of the environmental dynamics is relegated to its proper place, as the concept is based on the integrated ecodynamic aspects of the environment.

In this chapter we shall show how a rational development of the land can be conceived: based on the principle of dynamic integration (explained in Part I) a principle that takes into account the degree of stability of the environment. Later, we shall give an insight into the interdependence of the various types of land use at the level of heterogeneous regions. We begin by analysing in a systems framework the impact of agricultural activities on the natural environment.

A SYSTEMS APPROACH TO THE IMPACT OF AGRICULTURAL ACTIVITIES ON THE NATURAL ENVIRONMENT

A land parcel, defined as a unit of agricultural production (one crop, uniform cultivation), is the basis of our approach. Accordingly, we have placed the land PARCEL in the centre of a flow chart (Figure 19). Four aspects of the PARCEL are specified as having special importance. Two, on the left, characterize natural features: slope and exposure. The other two, on the right, reflect, in a broad sense, the culture of the social group as inscribed in the agrarian pattern of the land, that is, the form and dimensions of the parcel.

On the right of the flow chart, the different social factors are indicated, as black boxes, under the heading SOCIAL GROUP, that is socio-economic organization, demography, techniques and cultural traditions; together they determine the AGRARIAN STRUCTURE. On the left, in a symmetric arrangement, the main features of the natural environment are recalled under the heading NATURAL ENVIRONMENT, that is lithology; geomorphic evolution, with its consequences: surficial material and landforms; soils in the edaphic sense; and climate. NATURAL ENVIRONMENT and SOCIAL GROUP are linked together by interactions. The various components of the NATURAL ENVIRONMENT, also treated as black boxes, determine the characteristics of the land PARCEL and a somewhat more general element, the LAND CHARACTERISTICS.

Two more flow charts (Figures 21 and 22) analyse how different types of land degradation occur and the successive steps they go through. On the left of the top diagram we proceed from two of the headings already encountered on the first flow chart: LITHOLOGY and CLIMATE. On the right, a third starting-point: the EDAPHIC PROPERTIES; their relationship to lithology, if any, is not shown on the chart for better clarity. For the same reason the two main aspects of degradation, mechanical (1) and biochemical (2), have been kept separate. A single flow chart could have been made, but its size would have been unsuitable for publication and its greater complexity would have made its use more difficult. The links between these two degradational aspects are shown in a third flow chart (3) in Figure 20, which focuses on the relationships between the natural environment and the practices of land management.

The cascading processes of degradation, in the

1. Mechanical transfers

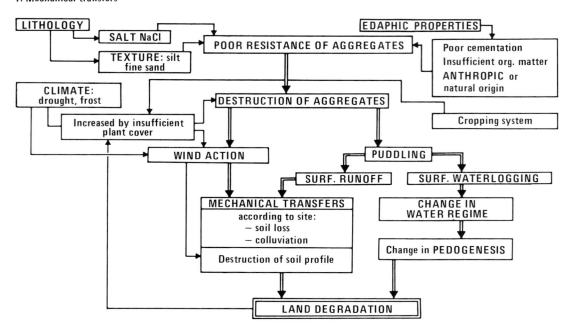

2. Biochemical changes

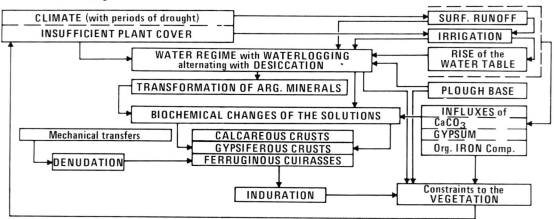

3. Types of land degradation resulting from poor land management

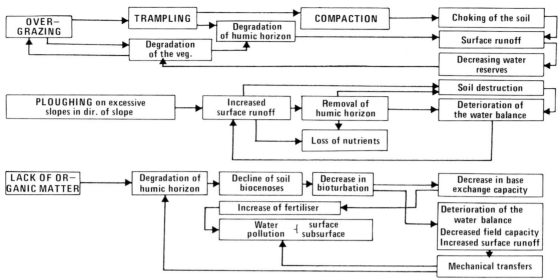

Figure 20. Flow charts of degradational mechanisms of the ecologic environment. (1) Mechanical transfers, (2) Biochemical changes, (3) Types of land degradation resulting from poor land management

strict sense, have been emphasized by a double line arrow in the Mechanical transfers diagram in order to draw attention to them, the other arrows being simply elements of explanation. The entry 'Cropping system' offers a link with the third diagram on the left side of which are indicated, as a starting-point, its three main aspects.

It is important to notice that the feedback mechanism reaches the 'plant cover' in both parts of the second diagram. This is significant as it demonstrates that the evolutive trend is self-accelerating, thereby increasing instability through the gradual, ever more rapid, elimination of phytostability. Thus a stable environment is quickly transformed into an unstable one.

In the third flow chart are reconstructed three types of degradation resulting from poor land management. The first two are proverbial: overgrazing and harmful ploughing. The third, a deficiency of organic matter, is the result of either the one or the other, but mainly of improper cultivation; it is subordinate to the former two. Particular attention should be paid, in any one of these degradational flow charts, to the very strong feedbacks. As already noted, the consequences of bad land management always result in a reinforced mechanism leading to the destruction of the land as a support of rural activities. Frequently, however, the disastrous effects of land despoliation are not restricted to the rural environment. Its effects on the hydrological regime in turn produce a

degradation of the water resources destined for urban and industrial uses. This degradation, in the form of an increased sediment load, reduces the quality of the water, so that expensive purification plants must be built. In other cases reservoirs silt up at unanticipated rates, reducing their life expectancy.

Land degradation eliminates stable environments. This should be kept in mind when examining problems of land management according to degrees of environmental stability.

DEVELOPMENT OF STABLE ENVIRONMENTS

Problems of development mainly concern stable, non-arid environments. In deserts the stability of the environment generally depends on lithology, as outcrops of consolidated rocks cannot be cultivated, even when irrigated, while fine-grained materials, such as argillaceous silts, resistant to deflation can be transformed into oases, on condition, however, that their setting is taken into account. In Libya, for example, newly irrigated areas on hamadas have been choked by migrating sands. But the main danger is the salinization of the water and land. In other types of stable environments the stability is due to plants. Development problems, therefore, should pay particular attention to the relationships between vegetation, soils, and morphogenic processes.

Problems of salinization in irrigated regions

The very idea of irrigation is to prevent a soil water shortage by an artificial influx of water to produce a crop or to increase crop yield. *Irrigation is justified* in areas where a chronic water shortage is an important factor limiting agricultural production. A consequence of this shortage, of course, is high evaporation, which in turn causes a concentration of dissolved products in the water. Phenomena of salinization can occur in valleys even if the rocks provide few soluble ions. (In fact 'alkalinosalinization' would be a better term, to differentiate between soils enriched in sodium chloride and those enriched in bases – alkalinization – with a pH higher than 7.) This is the case of the appropriately named Rio Salitre in Brazil, which drains an area of Precambrian granite and gneiss of the Gondwana Shield in the north of the State of Bahia, where mean annual temperatures are around 25°–26°C and rainfall 400–600 mm. In its lower course the river flows very quietly on a broad valley bottom, where intense evaporation causes the precipitation of salts mainly provided by potassium and soda-lime feldspars. This example shows that even acidic rocks can cause an alkalinization of the soil if the water shortage is sufficient. It is a question of concentration by evaporation. The mechanism is, of course, all the more effective as the rocks contain more soluble ions, later combined into chlorides and sulphates. This may be the case of pyroclastic materials, especially fine, porous ashes. Their leaching produces important quantities of salts.

In Chile the nitrate deposits of Norte Grande were accumulated in closed depressions of tectonic origin at the foot of the high volcanoes of the Andean Cordillera, which produced enormous quantities of pyroclastic materials during the Pliocene and the early Quaternary. They are the result of a concentration by evaporation of the waters of the ephemeral streams coming down from the volcanoes and debouching into the *salars* of the closed depressions. In other, coastal deserts the evaporation of sea spray fills the air with microscopic crystals of marine salt, which may be

transported long distances by wind, sprinkling the ground with salt. A flux of this type is favoured by the trade winds, while a high temperature range producing considerable changes of relative humidity at night weighs down the very microscopic salt crystals, causing their precipitation. In this way condensation of a salty dew occurs in the south-west of Mauritania in January, and especially in February, causing the salinization of the soils and the entrainment of the salt by surface wash, which feeds the playas. A number of soils of the Senegal Delta, as well as the Idjil Sebkha in northern Mauritania, near F'Derick, the old Fort-Gouraud, would thus have acquired its salt (Tricart 1956).

By recalling such natural phenomena we can appreciate the seriousness of the risks of salinization through irrigation. Nevertheless, alkanilization may occur as a result of irrigation with deficient drainage even with water extremely poor in dissolved ions, such as the Niger water of Mali. The Niono Perimeter of the Office du Niger, in a subhumid climate, has experienced such an alkalinization, so that a programme of rehabilitation financed by the World Bank is being investigated. River Niger water has extremely little sodium chloride and no more than 2–3 ppm of dissolved silica. An investigation by Kabirou N'Diaye, an engineer of the Office du Niger, has shown that the alkali (thenardite, etc.) resulted from complex chemical reactions in waterlogged soils.

Irrigation is practised mainly on alluvial plains, whose minor relief favours the construction of irrigation canals. The water used most frequently comes from exotic rivers originating in more humid areas. Upon arriving in a drier region, the waters contain only a small concentration of ions, which, however, increases downstream owing to evaporation. Alluvial plains are generally porous; the materials that compose them, sands and gravels, allow a subterranean flow of water, or inferoflux, that, at a depth of a few metres accompanies the stream flow. This flux, in fact, is but the drainage of the upper part of the ground-water, which in time of drought persists longer than the subaerial stream. It can feed phreatophytes, whose existence reveals its presence in the midst of a desert if stream flow is not too long interrupted.

Irrigation water modifies the natural hydrodynamics: it infiltrates the alluvial materials, recharging the ground water and thereby increasing its flow. Downstream the alluvium becomes finer and less porous with a diminishing gradient, and the rate of flow decreases. A kind of subsurface waterlogging occurs, which raises the water table until it reaches the surface. The water is then subject to evaporation, which concentrates the dissolved products, part of which are precipitated, resulting in a salinization of the plain (Figure 21). In some cases the effects may be felt in a few years only, causing a degradation of the ecologic conditions. In the coastal valleys of northern Peru the following stages have been observed in the lower reaches of the valleys:

1 subsistence farming on small lots prior to the rise of the water table
2 abandonment of the cultivated land, substituted by pastures and accompanied by emigration where the ground water table reaches the surface
3 degradation and abandonment of the pastureland caused by salinization and transformation of the land into a salt marsh.

Before the agrarian reform movement, enacted in 1969, the water of this region belonged to the landowners. These, whose estates not uncommonly covered tens of thousands of hectares in the more sunny piedmont zone, have diverted most of the water to irrigate their vast sugar cane plantations. Water was used in profusion in order to prevent the salinization of the land. Because of it cane sugar yields reached world records. However, by considerably increasing the water input of the alluvial ground water, the *latifundistas* caused the ruin of the lower reaches of the valleys where peasants, driven back on heavier soils in a less sunny climate, used the excess water. If an honest

balance sheet of the entire region is drawn up instead of that of the latifundia only, one is forced to recognize that the outcome has been negative on the environmental as well as on the social plane. Because of it the stream waters were nationalized by the agrarian reform.

Similar mechanisms also occur in less arid climates, as, for instance, in the irrigation perimeter of El Cenizo, at the head of the Río Motatán delta, south-east of Lake Maracaibo, Venezuela. This area receives less than 1,000 mm of rain per year, and its mean temperature is 27°C. There is therefore a soil water shortage. It was the site of one of the first modern irrigation projects planned in Venezuela since the Second World War. Unfortunately, the studies made by foreign firms turned out to be quite deficient, as the geomorphological aspects were totally neglected. The main feeding canal was dug through a system of very porous, coarse-grained natural levees in the axis of the head of the delta. Groups of irrigated parcels were established on the delta flanks, in lateral depressions underlain by finer sediments, and further downstream where the materials are less porous. Problems have plagued the project since its inauguration, more than thirty years ago. Although serious, we shall leave aside those on the human and social plane. The water losses in the main feeding canal have been enormous. Water intake installations had to be altered to increase input and, subsequently, a number of canal sections had to be waterproofed. But it all proved to be

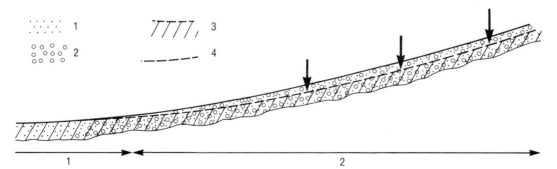

Figure 21. Mechanisms of salinization or alkalinization by evaporation of subsurface flow

1 Sands and silts   3 Ground-water (inferoflux)
2 Gravels   4 Water table

The vertical arrows indicate water input, generally caused by irrigation.

The sketch shows the longitudinal profile of a coastal valley in the north of Peru.
    Reach 2 is irrigated. Excess water percolates into the gravelly alluvium and feeds the ground-water, which drains downstream underneath the river bed (subsurface flow). Soluble products reach the ground-water. Reach 1, where the material is finer and the gradient less, does not have the same transmissibility. Inferoflux is slowed down. The water table rises to the surface where evaporation causes the precipitation of salts, which salinizes or alkalinizes the soil, depending on the composition of the salts.

either insufficient or too late. The ground-water had augmented to such an extent that artesian outflows occurred in the fine alluvial materials of innumerous parcels and, owing to heavy evaporation, caused the salinization of the land, which renewed the vengeful aggressiveness of the settlers.

Desalinization of the land, unfortunately, is very difficult. It takes much longer than its salinization. To leach out the salts by increased throughflow requires much water, more than is generally available; it can impoverish and physically damage the soils. Moreover, the finer the materials the more difficult the removal of the salts, as water does not flow in clays flocculated by salts. In some cases gypsum is used, as it reacts with sodium chloride and calcium carbonate, thus preventing the flocculation of the clays by substitution of sodium by calcium cations in the base exchange complex, but this technique is expensive, especially when the source of the gypsiferous or calcareous materials is distant. In fact, all too often a degradation by salinization must be considered to be practically irreversible at the present time.

It is therefore better to take preventive action. Such action consists in carefully controlling the quality of irrigation water, the soil water balance of the land to be irrigated, the land downstream from it, and to examine if the excess irrigation and drainage water can reach an outlet without causing damage. A careful geomorphological study should be made first, prior to the establishment of an irrigation system: that of the El Cenizo perimeter made by the Centre de Géographie Appliquée was too late; it could no more than explain the cause of the problems encountered, not how to remedy them. The object of such a type of research is to know precisely the configuration and grain size of the alluvial materials. The work should result in a detailed map, helped by microseismology and reconnaissance drilling. The object is to provide the basic information that determines the flow of shallow subsurface water. It should go hand in hand with a hydrogeological study. Drill sites may be equipped with piezometers and pumping experiments may be undertaken to determine the transmissibility of the sediments. The data gathered enable the localization of areas where there is a risk of recharging the ground-water and areas where recharged ground-water may surface or come close to the surface.

Equipped with this kind of information, engineers in collaboration with naturalists can avoid the localization of irrigation canals in areas where high losses can be expected or, where

necessary, waterproof them. They can also regulate the input of water as a function of the characteristics of the geomorphological units, which may entail certain restrictions in the choice of crops. Furthermore, it is possible to improve the drainage of the parcels where a waterlogging can be expected and to arrange for the evacuation of the water. At Niono, Mali (Office du Niger) no rational planning had ever taken place in spite of the recommendations of the sponsor of this irrigation project, the Engineer Belime. Just before and during the Second World War irrigation canals were built, but the ability to drain the water was underestimated. The used waters were directed into old channels active during the Neolithic, when there was more water. But, in the mean time, these channels had suffered some degradation and infilling with aeolian sands. Vegetation grew in them because of more ground water. Their disturbed gradient and high hydraulic roughness hampered an effective drainage of the irrigated lands, causing their alkalinization. Almost one-third of the irrigated land had to be abandoned, while the yields of the remainder dropped dramatically. This is the exact opposite of a rational land use in which the quality of the environment is safeguarded.

Problems in environments with enduring stability

Environments with enduring stability are characterized by few inherited features. Their evolution has been that of a *steady state* over a long period of time. We prefer this expression (used by physicists) to *climax* (used in ecology). Indeed, a certain finality colours the word climax, making it less appropriate. The steady state concept suits us perfectly, as it conveys a gradual evolution according to a definite curve. Determinant factors remain the same in stable environments, producing increasing effects with time; thus soils develop gradually, tending toward clearly defined characteristics.

Stable environments are characterized by a minor flux of surface particles, as surficial morphogenic processes perform little work. In some cases this results from insufficient input of energy into the natural system due to the moderate impact of meteorological phenomena, or to lack of slope. In other cases available potential energy is not negligible, but does not do any morphogenic work because of the screening effect of the plant cover and its litter (phytostatic conditions). It is then tempting to make use of the ecological resources, but that requires precautions. Development of the land must respect the phytostatic effect of the plant cover; if not, rapid and intense degradation may follow. The example of the first rubber plantations of the Ivory Coast is instructive. Complete forest clearing, exposing the soil, resulted in an intense mobilization of the soil, producing gullies and ravines that were cut by only a few showers. From then on rubber trees have been planted without destroying the primitive vegetation, clearing only the immediate vicinity of the new trees.

Traditional methods, in this case in West Africa, were arrived at empirically; they include a fifteen-year rotation during which forest reoccupies the land, permitting an accumulation of minerals in the tissues of the plants, which suddenly, by fire, become available to the crops. Clearing respects the biggest trees, which produce a certain amount of ecologically favourable shade and serve as a source of seeds during the fallow period. Their shade also helps the growth of secondary forest, which produces a denser cover above the ground than the climax forest. A periodic return to a forest condition is of considerable phytostatic importance. The land is cultivated with implements that do not overly disturb the soil, except in the case of the yam, hoed with the 'daba' and planted on raised rows. The digging stick allows the seeding of three or four grains, or the placement of a slip, in a small hole. The soil around it then keeps its consistency and structure, thus better resisting rain splash; only fire harms it. Finally, plant species of different sizes and shapes, forming several tiers, are mingled in the fields, thus causing a maximum dispersion of raindrops and a minimum of splash. Nevertheless, such practices also cause problems: grubbing leads to rapid surficial degradation, which necessitates long fallow periods, while weeds spread rapidly, reducing crop yields. As a result, weedkillers are increasingly used; their negative effects are still being studied.

One of the main problems of agronomy is to maintain original phytostasy while increasing productivity; in other words, to develop cropping systems that properly protect the soil. This frequently leads to the common practice of cultivating only one species on large parcels, a practice that is not ecologically sound. Ecosystems of a single species are very unstable, resulting in massive attacks by parasites. This calls for an abusive use of pesticides and a triggering of lethal pollution mechanisms, which spread from one feeding level to the next. This type of cultivation,

moreover, leaves the soil bare for a more or less long period of time at certain seasons. Sometimes even clean tilled crops, that poorly cover the ground, are cultivated.

Clean tilled crops in the mid-latitudes include vineyards and certain orchards. On hillsides they permit considerable soil ablation. In vineyards north of the Alps it is increased by downslope ploughing to improve drainage. In the past, the soil accumulated at the base of the parcels by surface runoff was periodically carried back upslope, usually in baskets strapped to a man's shoulders. Cereals, especially in countries with cold winters, do not play a phytostatic role between autumn tilling and the end of spring. They do not prevent a morphogenically very active melt-water runoff in spring. Autumn sowing somewhat reduces this danger. The soil loss caused by melt-water in western Germany is as high as that caused by the heaviest summer thunderstorms. It is even worse in the former steppe lands of southern Russia. In lowlands, the loosening of the soil by cultivation, especially when its structural stability is poorly maintained, can also give free rein to the wind. The storms of the Dust Bowl of the south-central United States in the early 1930s have much contributed to the development of soil conservation practices and programmes of crop diversification of the New Deal. Also southern Russia and the Ukraine are regions of intense induced deflation that spread dust several times per century over vast areas of eastern Europe.

In the humid tropics sugar cane provides an excellent soil protection except during the first months after planting, as several cuttings, up to eight, spread over as many years, may be obtained from a single planting. The plants assure a near complete protection from rain splash. However, certain modern practices encourage a more frequent replanting, even every year, which lengthens the critical time during which the soil is left unprotected. Indeed yields are highest at the first harvest and can be further increased by a profuse use of fertilizer, but the effect of such practices (which also require more labour) on the soil and its conservation have not been sufficiently studied.

In contrast, efforts of agronomists to associate forage crops with oil palm plantations produce a stabilization of the environment. Experiments have been carried out for several years by the Institut de Recherches des Huiles et Oléagineux to associate forage crops with coconut and oil palm plantations, especially in low yield, low profit regions. It seems that this practice is possible in plantations with normal tree spacing, that is 144 trees per hectare, and with one animal for every two hectares. An important consideration is the effect of trampling on the tree roots.

In general geochemical phenomena have been intense in enduring stable regions where the soil has been leached. But the kind of leaching and its intensity differ depending on lithologic and climatic conditions. In certain cases leaching results in a desaturation, which reduces the stability of the soil aggregates, which then depends more on the content and kind of organic matter. The resistance of aggregates to the impact of raindrops of course determines the intensity of splash erosion and the effects of sealing and of surface runoff; together with the phytostatic effect it plays a very important role in the stability of the environment.

Certain practices, such as harrowing or hoeing, cause the destruction of the sealing crusts resulting from puddling, allowing renewed infiltration with the next rains; the technique is remedial and consumes energy, whether muscular or mechanical. It is possible only with certain cropping systems, uncommon in developing countries. The breaking up of the soil and the preparation of the seed bed may be risky if the soil has a poor structure, as the fine particles of the upper horizons can be easily entrained by the next rains. In many parts of West Africa an inconsiderate ploughing and preparation of the soil, perhaps at an unfavourable period of the year, have caused serious problems.

Maintenance of the structural stability of the soil aggregates is an essential agronomic imperative. It conditions the permeability of the soil, therefore, its continued genesis and nutrient uptake by the plants. It reduces splash erosion and surface runoff, which are manifestations of morphogenic instability, destructive of soil. Conservation of the soil's structural stability is all the more necessary as crops form a poor cover or as clean tilling is practised. At the present time there is no satisfactory technique of conservation or of restoration of the stability of soil aggregates outside of the use of manure. Chemical fertilizers have no effect. Experiments carried out with chemical coagulants have failed. Unfortunately cattle raising is excluded in many parts of humid tropical Africa where trypanosomiasis is endemic; there is therefore no manure. Cultural traditions and related social structures in West Africa have widely prevented the association of crop growing and cattle raising. But as a result of the protracted drought things have changed during the last twenty years. Now the peasants of the colonization villages erected by the Office du Niger (Mali) regularly cut

the savanna grasses and store them beside their dwellings on small homemade platforms supported by rough poles 2 m above the ground, out of reach of rats, sheep and goats. They are used during periods of want. Not anticipated by village planners, scandalized bureaucrats opposed this useful practice. In the early 1960s nobody believed that the African peasants would accept this technique. But necessity made them 'reinvent' what has been common practice in Europe for centuries. Nevertheless, manure remains scarce. On the other hand agronomists have developed the technique of green fertilizers, but it is frequently difficult to convince peasants that it is profitable to grow a crop to plough it under. In many cases, too, the means or the land are not available to grow such crops.

Furthermore, it should be noted that feedback is common in a natural system in which the maintenance of soil stability conditions the effectiveness of fertilizers. If the stability disappears as a result of cultivation, the effect of fertilizers is reduced, as they are partly entrained by runoff. Stability maintenance, therefore, is of primary importance. To preserve it agronomy has two important methods available: maintain the phytostatic effect to a maximum and safeguard or improve the soil's structural stability. The uptake of water by plants, an important factor in their productivity, is thereby increased as a result of a positive feedback. Based on their knowledge of the ecogeographic environment, agronomists should adapt their choice of crops to methods of cultivation and fertilizers.

Finally, it should not be thought that an ancient and permanent topostability is necessarily favourable to primary production. Topostability indeed promotes leaching in hot and humid climates. A deep regolith forms, which on granitic rocks may be tens of metres thick. All elements having suffered an intense chemical decay, the soil is altogether deprived of soluble elements. Quartz, frequently decomposed into loam and silt, is the main component. Nutrients which are dramatically lacking are a very severe constraint on agricultural development, which could take advantage of the high radiation energy received from the Sun. An extreme situation appears to have been attained in the State of Rondônia, Brazil, the main area of rapid, recent immigration into the Amazon Basin. Here, southwest of Pôrto Velho, along the former Madeira-Guapore (now Pôrto Velho) railway, built before the Second World War, a RADAMBRASIL field party (including J. Tricart) found not a single tree was growing in 1975 on a regolith of Archaean rocks, which would have revealed a trend towards the reconstitution of the original rainforest, destroyed in the 1920s to fuel the locomotives of the railway. In the Ivory Coast rainforest species reappear in the secondary vegetation some fifteen years after deforestation. The situation is even worse along the Amazon River in central Amazonia, where the soil's parent material is not basement rock but detrital Neogene material consisting of weathered products reworked by water. Mineral poverty reaches an extreme. The rainforest survives only as long as the environment can recycle, immediately, the minerals freed by the decomposition of the dead organic matter, plant and animal. Interruption of this recycling seems to result in an irreversible elimination of the rainforest. Peasants who had, by the sweat of their brow, cleared the primary forest along the Transamazon Highway were compelled to abandon their fields after a single year, as they could not even grow a decent crop of manioc. Nevertheless, in the south of the State of Bahia, the cacao plantations around Itabuna are located on the Archaean basement, but in a rather intensely dissected area, where, during the last dry climatic oscillation, some 18,000 years ago, instability resulting from an open vegetal cover permitted a considerable stripping of the infertile regolith. Cocoa yields are high on slopes where the topographic surface coincides approximately with the weathering front, so that the roots of the trees are able to penetrate into the softened granite and gneiss, where incompletely weathered minerals still yield the necessary nutriments. In contrast, the plateau remnants, where stability continued uninterrupted for lack of slope, remain forested, as their thick regolith is unsuitable for any crops. Exceptional conditions, worth researching, are therefore necessary for commercial agriculture to get established in topostable areas of the humid tropics that are not favoured by volcanic rocks (including ashes), limestone, 'young' sediments, and a few less common parent materials.

In general, then, in environments that are not so favoured, the destruction of the rainforest is an ecological crime. Too frequently the Brazilian government has paid high subsidies to companies to level this 'lung of the world'. Pairs of tractors linked with steel chains destroy the forest, which in some cases is burnt, the profit resulting from the difference between the cost of deforestation and the subsidy.

Problems in recently stabilized environments

What characterizes environments that have become stable recently, at the dawn of the Holocene or even later, say less than 10,000 years ago, is the importance of palaeoclimatic legacies in the form of surficial formations and landforms. Occasionally relict phenomena are preserved in soils, such as truncated or buried horizons, or pedogenic products distinct from recent ones. The preservation of relict features requires special conditions, which are unequally realized even over short distances. Soil mosaics predominate: a juxtaposition of different types of pedogenesis frequently makes them both heterogeneous and heterochronic, that is formed during different periods of time; polyphased soils may even be part of them. The complexity is great. Adjustment of agronomic solutions to the edaphic factor is particularly delicate; it should rely on a carefully differentiated experimentation to be truly representative, a problem that will be treated in Chapter 7.

To develop such environments not only must its present characters and evolutive tendency be correctly understood, but also its genesis and the conditions in which the relict features have been formed and preserved. Reconstruction of the entire kinematics over thousands, even hundreds of thousands of years must be undertaken. The succession of the different environmental dynamics must be placed in the perspective of the Quaternary epoch. This may require participation of specialists dealing with very specific matters, such as the identification of fossil molluscs, diatoms, or pollen, and the dating of radioactive materials.

Certain legacies are very favourable from the point of view of agriculture, improving the ecological conditions. This is the case of well-drained, friable and porous **loess**, rich in particles setting free valuable mineral elements, or of, sometimes vast, **alluvial deposits** accumulated during recent periods of instability, but now slightly incised, preserving them from floods and hydromorphic conditions. Such low, only slightly weathered alluvial terraces, not yet mineralogically or chemically impoverished, frequently constitute ideal sites for irrigation. But their sedimentological origin should be known to prevent their degradation by salinization (see pp. 172–4).

Unfortunately such valuable legacies, which should be carefully preserved, are frequently fragile. Indeed, loess, which is friable and surficially decarbonized, is quite vulnerable to rillwash and easily entrained in cultivated land. Repeated ploughing, however, will eradicate gullying, as long as it is minor, thus maintaining a generalized ablation. This has been demonstrated in the vicinity of Strasbourg by Lemée and Wey (1950), who determined the content of calcium carbonate at a constant depth below the level disturbed by ploughing. A largely decarbonized 'lehm' was encountered in areas of little ablation, whereas the loess is not pedogenized and rich in carbonate in areas of much ablation. Comparisons, however, should be made only over short distances, as the initial content of calcium carbonate varies over a few kilometres only. In harsher climates, such as of the steppes of southern Russia, runoff is more intense and gullying more rapid. Between the 1860s and 1940s the surface affected by gullying increased at the rate of 5 per cent per year, which demonstrates the degree of instability of poorly managed land. The loess was stable before cultivation began, as shown by the formation at its surface of a thick chernozem rich in highly polymerized organic matter. The agricultural vulnerability of loess is easily explained: an aeolian deposit, it is composed of silt particles whose dimension is close to minimum for entrainment on Hjulstrom's curve. Some volcanic ashes pose similar problems.

The **forms** of the inherited relief may also increase the risks of degradation. If presently stable, owing to the biostatic effect of the vegetation, they can easily be reactivated by the very processes that originated them; in fact, they would reinforce these processes through a positive feedback effect. Such runaway mechanisms cause the multiplication of gullies and result in induced badlands, in which the threshold of surface runoff is lower. Some areas of Amazonia enter into this category of environment, as, for example, the Tertiary formations in the area of Obidos and Santarem, where airborne radar imagery shows a highly dissected relief with relatively steep slopes, frequently of the order of 10°, and a high density of talwegs. This relief was formed during the last marine regression (low sea level) in a dry climate with a discontinuous plant cover. A number of tributary valleys were then barred by the natural levees of the Amazon, which grew higher with the rising post-glacial sea level. But not a single delta developed in the newly flooded valley mouths (rias) as the land, newly covered by rainforest, did not provide any sediments. If the present forest is slashed to make room for highways or pastures, or is simply exploited for the immediate profit of its timber, the processes that formed the inherited

relief will again start to function, but at an accelerated rate owing to a wetter climate. Runoff will quickly entrain the soils, swamps will form by deposition of regolithic materials in present standing bodies of water or behind the alluvial fans of the most newly active affluents. Sanitary conditions will worsen.

Mass wasted materials have different effects and affect smaller areas. Even when stabilized, they are prone for a long time to renewed activity, as the affected material has lost cohesion and is now more permeable. The liquid limit then is easily reached and a new movement triggered. Any kind of land use, therefore, should at least not favour, preferably counteract, infiltration and, therefore, not make use of unsealed irrigation canals, channel terraces, or highway drains spilling into slid materials. Such geomorphic units should neither be cut nor filled for the construction of highways, railways or a canal, as any change in the static pressures will trigger instability and not only destroy the structure but also render unstable a much larger area. The highway between Trujillo and Bocono, in Venezuela, offers a typical example of such a catastrophic activation of mass movements. It became motile as soon as it was opened and its use, permanently precarious, requires enormous expense. The large quantity of debris that reached the river below completely changed its regime to one of instability, threatening settlements and other roads and becoming unsuitable as a source for domestic water and irrigation. Detailed geomorphological studies are necessary prior to any intervention in order to try to prevent future catastrophes.

Other inherited phenomena, too, are responsible for serious limitations to the ecologic utilization of the environment. A good example is the Pampa Deprimida of Argentina. (J. Tricart was assigned by FAO to INTA, an Argentine organization concerned with problems of agricultural and pastoral development, to study this region from the pedologic and agronomic points of view. The mission involved five months of work in 1968. Thanks to UNESCO he went twice more and kept in contact with the Argentine team. Agronomists had already developed an experimental approach for resolving the problem by 1972. Unfortunately, in 1985, just before the end of the military dictatorship, the experimented methods had not been applied for complete lack of financial support.) This region, situated between Buenos Aires and Mar del Plata, along the lower course of the Río Salado, covers an area that has been subsiding until the present. Gradients are extraordinarily low, as indicated by the topographic maps which have a contour interval of only 25 cm! Runoff is therefore most inefficient, although the climate actually is humid, with 800–1,000 mm of annual precipitation. Many streams coming down from the Sierra de Tandil, to the south, disappear by evaporation before being able to reach the Río Salado or the Atlantic. During heavy rains the waters spread and flood vast areas of the depression. Several attempts to develop the lowland have failed since the end of the nineteenth century.

Two factors compromise the development of the Pampa Deprimida. First, the water regime with its catastrophic floods, which prevent the cattle from feeding, as no hay is made, and also drought, for as soon as it does not rain for two weeks, the quality of the pasture plummets and the feeding of the animals again falls short. This vulnerability is caused by the superficial implantation of the grass, frequently not deeper than 10 cm, itself controlled by the edaphic factor. Second, the edaphic conditions, characterized by widespread development of alkaline soils, paradoxical in a humid climate.

The origin of the salt, its emplacement, and subsequent evolution had to be researched in order to understand and map the soils and seek agricultural solutions. This meant that all the dynamics of the environment since the early Quaternary had to be reconstructed.

During the early Quaternary, while the region was still subsiding, large quantities of fine volcanic ash, ejected by Andean volcanoes, were deposited. They are responsible for the introduction of the salt. Certain minerals then liberated soluble ions, which remained in the region in spite of several reworkings and were incorporated into the soils and certain surficial formations. During humid periods the minor gradients, as today, impeded the evacuation of the salt toward the Atlantic. A certain amount of leaching reduced its proportion in marginal zones, while a large quantity remained in the most depressed areas. During the Mindel-Riss interglacial (the Yarmouth) brown soils with an indurated B argillic horizon formed in part of the Pampa Deprimida. They have since been truncated, generally down to the top of the more resistant B horizon, during the succeeding dry period, corresponding to the Riss (Illinoian). During this period and during the pre-Flandrian regression (i.e. the Würm or Wisconsin), semi-arid climates prevented the evacuation of the salt toward the ocean. Aeolian action then built dune fields blocking runoff in the western part of the

region. The wind also produced hydro-aeolian deflation depressions down to below the present 0 m contour line. The saline silts deflated from them were spread over the argillic horizon of the brown soils, which by then had been truncated to that level. Since then a moderate leaching of the salt has occurred with a return to a humid climate at the beginning of the Holocene. This resulted in the formation of solods, that is in an alkalinization that penetrated into and transformed the old argillic B horizon. Both because of mechanical resistance and chemical composition the roots of the herbs hardly penetrate this horizon at the contact of the aeolian silts, so that their implantation is particularly shallow when the aeolian materials are thin. The soils, then, are easily waterlogged as their substratum is quite impermeable; all that is needed are somewhat protracted rains, as the surface gradient is almost nil. Floods, therefore, are not caused by input from the neighbouring hills, whose extent is rather limited. An expensive system of peripheral drainage channels built to catch the upland runoff does not have the least effect. Thus hydrologic and edaphic problems are closely related, both depending on the general evolution of the natural system that we have summarized (Tricart 1969b; 1969/70a; 1973c; Durán 1987).

Knowledge of the environmental dynamics and their successive changes is part of the realm of geomorphology, but in this case it would not be complete without taking into account their pedologic aspects. These, too, are closely related to the geomorphic evolution and are basic to an understanding of the soils themselves and their distribution. Their mapping, based on geomorphic indices, greatly benefited from air photo interpretation.

Agronomic research began soon after the beginning of the pedologic work. Problems can be posed and experiments begun in representative sites as soon as the characteristics of the ecologic environments are sufficiently known. Experiments, begun in 1970, raised high hopes; they include the following techniques aimed at increasing the thickness of the soil penetrated by roots.

1 Ploughing gradually deeper to lower the level inhibiting root penetration, thus destroying the compactness of the top of the indurated argillic B horizon. This simultaneously increases the water retention capacity, which reduces the harmful effect of rainless periods.
2 Using minor relief features to organize a surficial water regime, including bulldozer excavated

ponds behind earth dams, and a system of desalinization ditches. A better internal drainage by increased leaching and a means of lowering flood crests is thus taken care of. By themselves the ditches would accelerate runoff, but together with the ponds not only is runoff slowed, but also water is stored that can serve as drinking places for livestock.

At the same time attention is given to a better selection of existing forage crops and introduction of new ones to make the most of the modified environment. When faced with unfavourable inherited conditions, as is the case here, relatively high investments should be approved to correct them. Indeed, if the development is well conceived, its effect may be durable, even definitive. The resulting increase in production then can sustain levies that amortize the investments. In this example, the Argentine government intended to make use of a loan from the World Bank that would have been repaid thanks to increased income from taxes on production, export, and from other levies. Regrettably, for internal political reasons, no improvement in crops has been made. Actually a financial scheme of this sort is not applicable in a case of a correction of certain limiting factors of the present environmental dynamics. In such a case, when the dynamics cannot be changed, a continuous action is necessary: the costs incurred are not figured then as capital expenses but as costs of production. Unfortunately, such reflections have insufficiently held the attention of planners and economists, whose unfamiliarity with the environment sometimes causes them to reject rational development projects on the pretext of not being sufficiently profitable. But how to calculate profitability properly with a poor knowledge of natural mechanisms? Too many planners and economists still classify land and water as renewable resources. They forget that the resources are maintained, even increased, only thanks to adequate developments and rational management. In the opposite case they are destructible and non-renewable, exactly as a mineral deposit. The expression 'agricultural mining', occasionally used by geographers, is often justified, especially in presently stable but fragile environments. Such management is ominous on certain terrains inherited from a relatively recent period of instability. The area of Santarem and Obidos in Amazonia (noted above) falls into this category. The opposite is true in the case of the cacao plantations of the Itabuna area of Bahia, where recent conditions of instability destroyed most of

the unfertile regolith formed during a long period of stability. Theoretical generalizations are always dangerous and should be avoided in favour of ecodynamic reconstructions.

MORE OR LESS STABLE ENVIRONMENTS: SLOWING DOWN OF THE EVOLUTION, RESTORATION

In moderately unstable and very unstable environments, land development is confronted with dynamics that the least error in planning can intensify. The susceptibility of such environments is high, their margin of tolerance low. The present dynamics, whether natural or induced, are a limiting factor to their development, which must scrupulously avoid an intensification of the dynamics. In many cases the exploitation of the land should be such as to slow, even check, or reverse the evolutionary trend in order to initiate an *improvement*. A *restoration* may be in order if present harmful dynamics are, at least in part, the result of a process of degradation.

The mechanisms of degradation, generally, consist of the following sequence of events (Figure 22).

1 A modification of the plant cover, whose biostatic effect has been diminished. It may be the result of an ecologically unfavourable climatic change or a negative human intervention, such as unwise agricultural procedures or overgrazing, effects of urbanization or mining.

2 A degradation of the soil resulting from a change in plant cover, decreasing the organic input, therefore the organic activity, and, for instance, the process of nitrification. Changes in soil climate, such as excessive heating, drought or hydromorphism may also occur, caused by a change in atmospheric climate or a modification of the screening effect of the plants. Lastly, soil compaction by livestock or agricultural machinery may be a factor. Soil degradation, then, can result from biological, chemical or mechanical causes, as well as from a change in climate or from human actions.

3 Changes in the characteristics of the soil affect the flow of water. Leaching, a chemical process, and evolution of the organic matter, a biological

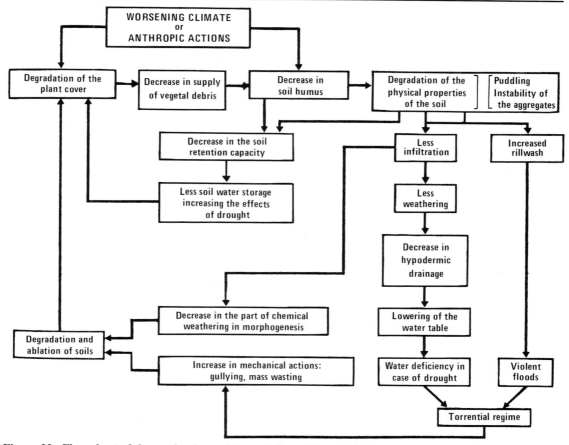

Figure 22. Flow chart of the mechanisms of degradation of the physical environment

process, decrease the stability of the aggregates. This, in turn, influences the morphogenic (splash erosion) and hydrologic rillwash/infiltration) processes, therefore the soil water regime and soil water reserve available to plant roots, which, when insufficient, slow plant growth. There is, therefore, a feedback which, by way of the plant cover, reinforces the processes of splash erosion and rillwash, while reducing the soil water content.

4 Rillwash becomes increasingly important in the water regime, amplifying the torrential regime of streams and their morphogenic activity. The flow of material increases: particles are entrained at the expense of the soil, which is beheaded or lacerated where dissection occurs, and reworked or buried in depositional areas. This instability is both indirectly, through the medium of the soil, and directly an unfavourable ecologic factor, reflecting a further, positive, feedback.

Recalling these well-known factors shows that the

initiation of degradational mechanisms may be caused by either a natural phenomenon, such as a climatic change, or by humans. Humans usually act much faster on the vegetal cover than a changing climate, in particular through fire or forest clearing. They can also increase and accelerate the effects of a climatic oscillation, such as happened to the biocoenoses of the northern Sahara during the Roman period, or to those of the Sahel, on the southern margin of the Sahara Desert, in recent times. The danger is increased when the vegetation is relict, that is, has survived from a former period to which it was adapted, but now has to struggle against less favourable conditions. This frequently seems to be the case of the Amazon rainforest or of the cedars of the mountains of North Africa.

Degradational mechanisms include a number of positive feedbacks, as we have seen; they cause an acceleration of the process. The rare, accurate, available quantitative data, such as those concerned with the expansion ratio of the area devastated by gullying in the southern Russian Plain, indicate that

Plates 41 & 42 Examples of catastrophic degradation of the environment
Ph. JT CLXXVI-32. Lower Rio S. Antonio, Bahia, Brazil. Upstream diamond placer mining overloads the stream with debris (background) and causes the destruction of the flood plain. Gravel and sand bars develop and sapping occurs. Spontaneous vegetation of thorn xeromorphic forest, a good phytostabilizer. This degradation annihilates any possibility of irrigated agriculture, urgently needed in this environment.

the phenomena accelerate according to an exponential curve. The momentum, it is true, would probably slow down and cease to be of an exponential character if no new intervention took place. In the case of the gullies this would occur when the friable materials are gradually being liquidated and the slopes of the ridge crests rounded off after the incision had been checked by a more resistant substratum. Our original exponential curve then would be only the lower part of a sigmoidal curve. As we have already noted, the most spectacular gullies are not those that produce the most sediments. But, as concerns economic development, the beginning of an exponential curve is of great significance. It points to the necessity of preventive measures and the need for very early remedial action. Powerful mechanisms, difficult to check, must be contained once the dynamics of degradation have been unleashed: the risks of failure are great, the costs high. In the Soummam Basin, in Algeria, whose degradation is relatively modest, the restoration of the watershed may be estimated at approximately five times the cost of the hydraulic structures on the river, which is 110 km long (CGA – Coyne & Bellier 1973).

Land development in unstable environments should pay highest attention to morphogenic processes, which must be viewed as important constraints restricting freedom of action. And this concerns not only the actual natural processes, but also those that could be induced.

When with the establishment of the Soil Conservation Service in the United States in 1935, a few years after the Dust Bowl, the decision was taken to implement rational modifications in land use to stem the wastage of soil and water, geomorphological knowledge was far less advanced than it is today. The Davisian framework of the field, mainly theoretical and academic, then in vogue paid no heed to the morphogenic processes. As a result, pedologists and agronomists devised the administrative rules of 'soil conservation', intervening into a domain marginal to theirs, and without the benefit of an interdisciplinary group of scientists. This explains a number of deficiencies in their approach.

First, there is exclusively talk of 'erosion', a

vague term, which should be banned from the scientific vocabulary, like 'laterite' and 'peneplain'. The origin of its widespread usage is attributable to G. K. Gilbert, whose definition included weathering and transport besides corrosion. An example of this is W. M. Davis's 'cycle of erosion' (see Baulig 1958). Etymologically, to erode means to gnaw (-*rod*) off (*e*-). The same root (*rod*) exists in corrode. On the geomorphological plane this means to wear away by mechanical action (abrasion, impact) or by chemical action (corrosion, dissolution). Aside weathering and transport, to apply 'erosion' to the entrainment of particles by hydraulic action or by wind is a misuse of the term. Respectively, this is ablation (to carry away, to entrain) and deflation. (Ablation results in a loss of material, as in the case of snow or glacial ablation, which results from melting or direct evaporation: 'sublimation'.) However, the expression 'splash erosion' is correct, as the impact of the raindrops breaks up the soil. The misuse of the term is serious from the practical point of view, as it allows the processes of weathering, of the

preparation of the material to be passed over in silence. As regards the latter, the study of the resistance of the aggregates to splash erosion was undertaken, mainly in France, and thanks to S. Hénin, only after the Second World War, some twenty years after the foundation of the US Soil Conservation Service, a disparity in time and in space worth noting.

Second, the misuse of the term 'erosion' is also characteristic from another point of view. Davis's concept of 'normal erosion' centred all its attention on dissection, while neglecting the depositional phenomena. To examine only those regions from which materials were removed is to have a truncated view of natural phenomena. At the present time, we must insist that geomorphology must be based on the study of *flows* of material. These, together with tectodynamics, produce the changes in the geometry of the Earth's surface. What is removed here is deposited there. Such flows are discontinuous in time and in space. Their interruptions produce more or less extensive and more or less durable deposits, ranging from in

Plate 42 Ph. JT CCCLXXXII-33. In the suburbs of Dakar, 'niayes' invaded by sand dunes at Pikine, Senegal. 'Niayes' are fresh water swamps dammed by coastal dunes. The dunes used to be fixed. Imprudent clearing by bulldozer of the vegetation for future urban development has caused the reactivation of the dunes. The degradation of the niayes, which had been accommodated to market gardening, causes them to turn into malarial swamps, a sanitary danger that is increased by low living standards and shanty development by Sahel drought refugees. A worthy ecological unit has been lost.

transit materials on slopes to oceanic sediments. The mobilization of material on a slope has the ineluctable consequence of a deposit accumulated further down. The ablation of soils on interfluves usually spreads on lowlands a less fertile material. Frequently, the economic effects of interfluve degradation is less damaging than the aggradation of valley bottoms. To focus one's attention on 'erosion' only tends to occlude this interdependence so important in land management.

Third, the pervading influence of Davis's cycle of normal erosion and the dearth of studies dealing with specific morphogenic processes led to an overemphasis of the role of slope and running water to explain the risks of degradation. Slope is easy to measure, being an elemental technical operation which can be entrusted to a worker with little professional training. The data obtained satisfy the formalities of the Soil Conservation Service and can be shown to respond to a concern for rationality, but that is more apparent than real. The value of slopes is only one parameter among others. To exaggerate its importance may be erroneous.

In Colombia, in the Repelón irrigated perimeter, where cotton is grown, slopes of 2° or less are gullied by surface runoff. The plant poorly covers the soil, which remains exposed, is puddled and gullied while 2° slopes are classified as being cultivable without restrictions. When they are occupied by citrus groves below which only moderate weeding takes place the same glacis do not suffer any degradation. Similarly, in many countries of western Africa (Senegal, Mali, Burkina Faso, Niger), the argillaceous or sandy soils of very gently sloping glacis are rapidly degraded when crop rotations and techniques of cultivation are ill-adapted. Millet–cotton and sorghum–cotton rotations, carelessly practised by traditional techniques in many areas, produce absurdly low yields, which heavy use of mineral fertilizers hardly increase. Higher yields are possible only through a change in cultivation methods allowing a slowing of the degradation of the fragile soils.

If the principle of a land-capability classification as a function of constraints engendered by risks of surface runoff is good, its application should be substantially modified. Making use of the considerable progress of geomorphology, we can state the following.

1 The ecogeographic environment should be considered as a system: this standpoint has been explained in Part I. It studies the interactions between different phenomena and defines flows of material, whose abundance, related to surface area, permits an estimate of the degree of environmental instability. Ablation and deposition are not dissociated: 'erosion' is not viewed unilaterally.

2 Gravitational energy is taken into account: it helps the functioning of the system and explains the degree of environmental instability; it never acts by itself; it is only one parameter among others. Feedbacks occur, producing threshold effects whose theoretical value is difficult to calculate. For example, in Belgium, Govers (1986) has determined that gully incision starts in a silty soil with less than 15 per cent clay if the content of organic matter reaches a threshold of 3 per cent. The existence of such thresholds is determined from field observations and measurements; they have only a regional, sometimes a local, value, as do the constraints that are determined from them.

3 Environmental instability means different things depending on the processes that act in Nature or that may act when certain changes are brought about. Running water is only one process among others. True, its role is sometimes predominant, but in certain cases only. To exaggerate it for lack of discernment may produce serious tactical errors. This is the case of ridge-type terraces (to impound water, in subhumid climates, until it infiltrates) on clay-rich soils, which trigger very dangerous mass movements, as occurred in the Wadi Chekrâne Basin of the eastern Rif Mountains of Morocco.

Rather than applying a series of routine practices, which satisfy administrative formalities, we call upon scientific acumen to discover the originality of each case and to apply to it the best adapted therapy. We shall discuss the methods we have elaborated to this effect in Chapters 7 and 8. But first, we shall examine a number of restraining techniques and see how they can be inserted into the environment.

Mass wasting processes pose the most difficult problems. The energy involved is considerable. To try to contain them with rigid structures is useless, even to protect well-defined sites, such as a road or other engineering works. The sagging of materials cracks and breaks the strongest walls. Walls actually increase the pressure that is exerted upon them, as they impede drainage in spite of the instalment of weep-holes. Gabions, which allow for drainage and are somewhat flexible, are preferable; they do not increase the phenomenon they are supposed to contain and can be rebuilt when mass wasting has seriously impaired them. Gabions, for one, are useful for the protection of river banks, especially in sites where current sapping threatens collapses of material. This type of intervention at the base of a slope is about the only one that can have any success, especially when it is preventive.

While some mass movements are caused by undermining at the base of a slope, others are triggered by the pull of gravity when the coefficient of internal friction of the material, containing clay, decreases owing to an increase in water content. This causes the plastic or, more frequently, the liquid limit to be reached. Theoretically, the triggering of the movement could be prevented by lowering the water content, that is by artificial drainage. But that is not only costly, but not very effective. Furthermore, water table levels sometimes vary with climatic cycles. But, most of all, drains must be installed at rather great depth: 10, 20 and even 30 m, which is a delicate enterprise. Moreover, the movement cannot be completely arrested, so that the drains are eventually damaged, their function impaired, enabling new mass movements. The few cases in which drains have been successful always involved restricted sites, usually in urban areas, where, unlike rural areas, water infiltration can be controlled.

Planting trees is not always effective either. Indeed, injured by mass movements their growth is stunted. Moreover, they overload the ground, assisting gravity. They favour the infiltration of light and moderate showers, therefore the entrapment of water in the materials, which is conducive to slumps (see Plate 40, p. 167). True, some species extract a lot of water from the soil, but that does not seem to compensate for the negative effects. A dense grass cover is preferable; it absorbs almost as much water as trees, while surface runoff proceeds without impunity. Indeed, fine materials, apt to mass wasting, are also apt to gully. Trying to prevent one process should not, of course, induce another. Unfortunately, in certain wet and dry seasonal climates such as the Mediterranean, gullying tends to occur at the beginning of the rainy season when the vegetative cover is open, while mass wasting processes take place near the end of that season when argillaceous soils are saturated. To control the two phenomena simultaneously is therefore difficult. Nevertheless, well-managed grazing practices or adoption of adequate cropping systems and techniques may prevent a degradation of the ecodynamic conditions.

Conditions in part similar to those that increase

hydraulic action also favour aeolian action. Entrainment of particles in both cases depends on the superficial cohesion of the soil (structural stability) and the biostatic effect of the vegetation. Instalment of plant screens or improvement of soil structure impede both degradation by wind and by rillwash. But the plant screens must have an adequate structure: they should include a low and dense plant cover, producing a combing effect on rillwash and on wind. A well-constituted plant screen protects a width of land fifteen times the height of the plants when blowing at right angles to it. Its efficacy not only reduces deflation but also the transpiration of plants, resulting in a net increase in production.

Mulching, too, protects the soil from deflation, splash erosion and surface runoff. It also decreases evaporation and improves the soil water regime and, with some delay, increases the organic content of the soil. The use of refuse, such as rice chaff or certain types of sawdust, permits the stabilization of certain highly degraded environments or the reduction of intense morphodynamics.

Other practices, on the other hand, have adverse effects and should be used only after a careful analysis of the natural dynamics. This, in particular, concerns the destruction of crusts caused by puddling, which break up the soil, permitting its deflation. The best solution is to improve the soil's structure or introduce mulching, which, together, reduce the negative effects of wind and rain. These examples demonstrate the necessity of an interdisciplinary approach which takes into account the environmental dynamics in order to find the best solutions to counteract the injurious dynamics and, at the same time, improve ecologic conditions and crop yields. Usually only yields, a very partial aspect of land use, are taken into account in an economic evaluation: an erroneous attitude, which should be reckoned with.

Problems are less complex when splash erosion and rillwash are predominant. In the worst case, the use of two different methods may be combined on condition they be carefully coordinated. The first method involves a modification of slopes in order to diminish rillwash and its effects. In some cases recourse may be had to *channel* or *ridge terraces* (see *Soil: 1957 Yearbook of Agriculture*, USDA: 299) on condition that they do not cause a risk of mass movements, which may be investigated by a geomorphological study, and that they are built and maintained in such a way that they do not overflow. This is difficult: it is an important reservation we have concerning this technique. Moreover, channel terraces, which are expensive to

Plate 43 Failure in conservation
Ph. CDXXI-7 cn. Disastrous failure of terracing, Ras el Ma catchment, Tunisia. Although lithology (interstratified marls and sandstones) is favourable, deep gullies have incised the terraces, twenty years old at the time of the photograph.

build, often result in a lesser harvest and are viewed as a negative investment. In India, at Bellary, in Mysore, a study made by the Indian government and the Ford Foundation has revealed a 30 per cent reduction of the cotton harvest and a 39 per cent of that of safflower cultivated during the rainy (monsoon) season. In Madhya Pradesh, channel terraces caused a drop in yield of 14 per cent in 1972, in areas where the earth to build them was extracted locally, and the total land surface lost to cultivation was 5–10 per cent. Moreover, by obstructing the passage of beasts of burden, they delayed certain cultivation procedures, which are then not carried out at the right time, further reducing yields. The result is that farmers are dissatisfied, refuse to maintain the terraces, which adds more problems. Generally preferable are *buffer strips*, formed by well-rooted plants that produce an effective combing effect at ground level. They permit a self-regulation of the water regime in the form of infiltration. A variable but never excessive proportion of running water infiltrates, while the surplus flows gently and abandons most of its solid load in the plant screen,

which slows it. Such buffer strips gradually produce lynchets, as their effect is progressive. Their use should be associated with good soil management that simultaneously augments production and infiltration. There is a positive feedback: an increased availability of water increases with yields and the variety of plants that can be grown, such as new, more productive, but also more demanding, varieties, or new species. The effects of this type of development are somewhat slow, but this extra time can be put to good use by instructing farmers and to develop the infrastructure.

The second method involves work on talwegs by usual correction techniques. The kinds of structures should be determined by interdisciplinary research, associating specialized geomorphologists and engineers. The harnessing of stream courses has two purposes: to prevent regressive processes that proceed from the talwegs and degrade the interfluves, and to reduce the dangers, especially from floods and wandering stream courses, that threaten stream valleys and their flood plains. Detailed study of the Soummam Basin (Algeria) by the Centre de Géographie Appliquée and Coyne &

Bellier (1973), has demonstrated that a more intensive use of the alluvial lowland, a priority object of the government, depends on remedial work in the watershed. The object here, to control stream flow, is to stop regressive gullying, which increasingly lacerates the slopes farmed by the peasants. Such action also, indirectly, reduces the torrential character of the runoff and decreases its solid load by leaving behind the coarsest materials and, above all, by stopping the worst sapping of stream banks also protected by gabion groynes and riprap. Construction of small barrages with cemented stone walls, old rails, or tree trunks, and in gullies with fascines, arrests regressive incision and slows down stream flow. Indirectly, they also permit the stabilization of the flanks of the incisions. The effects of the harnessing of stream courses are rapid, more so than that of the botanical treatment of the watershed. But their efficacy decreases with time, as small barrages on torrential streams are rapidly encumbered, which causes a renewed transit of materials. Lastly, all structures require maintenance, whose cost gradually increases with age.

The most rational solution is to begin with the harnessing of the stream beds themselves; this rapidly improves conditions. But the treatment of slopes, which takes more time, should not be delayed, as it may reduce and, in the most favourable case, eliminate the necessity for important structures on the streams.

When using plants to induce stabilization (phytostabilization), two concepts need to be intimately associated one with the other:

1 The morphodynamic concept, which aims at controlling the geomorphic processes that produce environmental instability.
2 The ecologic concept of 'seres', that is a succession of phytocoenoses from a simple pioneering plant association, consisting of a few resistant species, to more and more complex associations. Such a succession is possible only if it is programmed to harmonize with a decrease in geomorphic activity, that is can benefit from an increasing environmental stability.

Such a method has been applied in Mauritania in the project Ceinture Verte de Nouakchott, by Eng. Abby Ould Boulabatt. Tricart has observed it under the guidance of the engineer. The problems are acute. In the 1950s Nouakchott was surrounded by Sahelian pastures that fed transhumant cattle; now the landscape is one of Saharan ergs, that is active dune fields. The sand dunes, pushed from the NNE/NE, are assaulting the buildings of the capital. A conference centre under construction has been abandoned and high multi-flats buildings have been filled with sand up to the second floor before being finished. It is urgent to stop the sand. After several years of unsuccessful attempts Eng. Abby succeeded in elaborating an effective strategy consisting of the following steps:

1 To begin with, 'mechanical control', using 'structures' to stabilize the dunes in crucial areas, as means were too scanty to apply them to the entire area of active dunes. Wattles, made with Euphorbia stems, have been planted along a grid of rectangles whose long axes are perpendicular to the trade winds, which move most of the sand. Euphorbia have two useful properties in this regard: locusts do not eat their leaves, and, being succulents, they need very little rainfall. Furthermore, in 'good' years the wattles 'flower' and produce shoots.
2 Drought-resistant plants, among which *Zygophyllum*, an evergreen short grass, unpalatable to locusts (but excellent feed for camels), are planted in the rectangles. They fix the sand as they spread. The best techniques, periods and means of reproduction (seeds, slips) of the various indigenous plants, and how to use the least water for their sprouting and growth are tested in an experimental station outside of Nouakchott (see Plate 51, p. 213).
3 Besides trying to stabilize the sand, a simultaneous attempt can be made to make the enterprise at least partly profitable. To begin with one should aim at a maximum density of the plant cover, which ensures the phytostabilization of the sand. Furthermore, the phytocoenose should be as diversified as possible, which increases its stability and resistance to drought and blight. And, finally, preference should be given to plants that are useful as forage, fuel, handicraft material, and so on.

Relatively abundant rain in 1988 gave 100 mm in August and September. The surviving vegetation again became green and seeds germinated. There was hope. But, regrettably, a locust invasion on 9 October scraped all the green bark off the very few remaining trees and consumed all their leaves. During J. Tricart's visit in November 1988 acacias and Prosopis looked all but dead although all will probably survive, but they lost the ecological benefit of a 'rainy' year. This example was given for its methodological value, to demonstrate the need for integrated studies and action. From this theme we proceed to another taxonomic level, that of the development of heterogeneous regions.

DEVELOPMENT PROBLEMS AT THE REGIONAL LEVEL

We shall be concerned only with natural regions, leaving aside other types, such as administrative or economic regions centred on a city. Even with these restrictions, we have to deal with territories that possess two apparently contradictory characteristics: they are heterogeneous and, as such, should not be treated as a framework for land use planning, but they are also integrated, at least in part, into a single system, which creates a certain interdependence between them, which should be taken into consideration in planning. Such partial solidarities pose specific problems, which we shall now examine. We are obliged to face a dialectic contradiction: our position is quite different and more complicated than that of economists who, more comfortably, postulate 'homogeneous regions' in their view of planning. The difference is of the type that opposes, in the words of Pascal, '*l'esprit de finesse et l'esprit de géométrie*'.

Fluvial basins, for us, are the main natural regions. Their heterogeneity is the rule; they are divided into sub-basins, each with its own characters. Yet, a fluvial basin has a certain cohesion. It forms a system from the double point of view of the flow of materials (water and its load) and energy. The dynamics of the system are characterized by the diurnal and seasonal variations (regime) of stream flow (discharge), which depend on atmospheric conditions. The energy is provided by gravity and varies with the gradient, which is the result of the geomorphic evolution. It is used by power stations, but also does natural work in that, through the medium of the flowing water, it transports materials provided by the watershed and the stream beds themselves. Part of the energy is dispersed by friction against the stable part of the river bed and the loose materials that are beyond the tractive competence of the flowing water. The wetted perimeter, which produces the friction, increases little with increased discharge, so that there is a rapid increase in velocity and turbulence, and, therefore, in the tractive competence and erosive capacity of the stream. The energy inherent in streams varies considerably and is enormous

when rivers are in flood. When materials are available in sufficient quantity, the work performed by streams in flood increases not linearly but exponentially with discharge. Indeed a series of positive feedbacks come into play, the least of which is not the flood wave itself, which steepens the gradient of the advancing wave and therefore its velocity. Many of these phenomena and relationships have been known to civil engineers for well over a century and need to be taken into account in land use planning.

On the practical level, these mechanisms have important consequences.

The cost of structures to protect the land increases rapidly with the magnitude of the floods, therefore with decreasing occurrence. In general, what is most expensive is not to control the floods, but to prevent their morphogenic effects through the stabilization of river banks, the protection of dikes, and the channelization of the flow of coarse materials. But riverside residents also have to be taken into account. In France, this is a normal administrative practice with 'ten-year floods', while more exceptional ones fall into the category of special measures, such as aid to victims of catastrophes.

Floods are therefore a constraint to land use planning that, moreover, is all the more serious as they are frequent. They require measures to protect flood plains ever increasingly bought up or seized by urban sprawl, factories and major highways. There are, unfortunately, no positive aspects to floods, even power stations cannot profit from them as the rush of superabundant water exceeds the capacity of the plants. The only solution is the construction of dams to stock part of the water to reduce damage downstream and to use the water when there is a shortage. Dams must be all the larger and, for equal results, investments all the higher, the more variable the discharge. Moreover, dam sites should be available to begin with, which depends on the structural geomorphology; the larger the dams needed, the fewer the suitable sites.

The maintenance costs of a dam are low. Most of the financial burden comes from amortization, the annuities depending on the number of years to repay the loan, which in turn depend on the rate of siltation of the reservoir. This infilling can hardly be prevented at the present stage of technology. To flush out the sediments a current stronger than the one that deposited the material is needed. The difference is particularly high for particles less than 0.1 mm, mainly silts and clays, because of their cohesion, as is shown by Hjulstrom's diagram.

These sediments are particularly abundant in the deeper, downstream part of the reservoir where turbulence is least and settling of the finest materials easiest. As to dredging, its cost is generally prohibitive. Furthermore, the recovered materials must be disposed of. Barrages where gates remain open, or (even without any gate) cause little sedimentation, but do not retain the water, merely lowering flood crests. Intermediate solutions, such as provided by dams with low sill floodgates, allowing passage of the most heavily loaded part of a flood, as in open-gate barrages, and then to stock the rest, are of delicate operation, as the volume of material carried in relation to discharge varies greatly with each flood. When the time of amortization is calculated in relation to the rate of siltation, the sedimentary input acquires an economic value, albeit negative. A plan aiming to reduce siltation then appears 'profitable' to economists.

Inversely, low water stages create shortages.

Hydroelectric production decreases. If the equipment is designed to handle high discharges, most of the time it will run at limited capacity, which increases the cost price of the harnessed energy. It is therefore economically profitable to augment the discharge, which justifies regularization barrages. But it is usually also at low water stage that agriculture requires the most water, as irrigation becomes necessary during dry weather to prevent falling crop yields. Lastly, when low water occurs during a hot spell, as frequently happens, urban consumption, too, rises; it is then in conflict with rural needs. But the aspect is not merely quantitative, there is also a quality problem: while polluting products originating in urban areas and factories remain about the same, their concentration increases as there is less water to dilute them. Rotterdam, which is at the exit of the huge sewer that is the Rhine, then experiences serious problems, as water, even though treated, becomes dangerous to drink.

Plate 44 Destruction of a delta
Ph. JT CDX-87 cn. Head of the Maharivo Delta, south-west Madagascar. Degradation in the mountain catchment of the Maharivo River increasingly destabilizes its delta. At the time of the photograph (April 1972) extensive alluvial bars were being built in the river bed at high water. This aggradation increases the risk of sudden changes in the channel network during future floods. To reduce this risk requires conservation measures in the catchment before any work is done in the delta. Nevertheless, an expensive programme of rice cultivation had already been started.

The development of fluvial basins therefore has a double objective:

1 a reduction in the variation of discharge, in order to decrease the dangers of high water and to increase stream flow at low water, which simultaneously reduces pollution
2 a reduction of fluvial morphogenic work, thanks to the regularization of discharge, but which is also necessary in order to increase the longevity of the reservoirs and to improve the quality of the water used by the public and certain industries.

Such improvements more and more frequently have different goals: trying to satisfy different needs.

The cohesion of the system that constitutes a fluvial basin is the result of the interdependence of its parts. When taken into account, the development of the basin is said to be integrated, as we shall now illustrate.

The hydrological aspect concerns the interdependence of surface and subsurface waters. Much of the recharge of aquifers occurs during floods: the water then infiltrates the alluvial deposits. When it has replaced all the air waterlogging occurs. Unless the alluvium contains an abundant clay matrix, it constitutes a free aquifer in equilibrium with the river. However, there is a certain delay, which depends on the rate of water circulation in the materials; this lagging has a regulatory effect. During flood part of the discharge is withdrawn from the river by infiltration, which helps to lower flood crests. This mechanism often plays a more important role than the geometric effect of the water spreading over the floodplain, where its velocity is much reduced by friction. At low stage, the water stocked in the alluvial materials is returned to the river, maintaining its flow. In that way stream flow may have ceased upstream while it persists downstream, although not a single spring may be evident.

Such conditions have certain advantages. Besides a regularization of the discharge, they provide farmers with easily reached ground-water. Furthermore, the water has been filtered and is of better quality, which is important for domestic urban use. Such shallow aquifers frequently feed deeper ones through slow percolation, as, for instance, into a non-karstified limestone. This is the case of the Meuse River recharging the ground-water of the Jurassic limestones of the Paris Basin. But these mechanisms do not require the flooding of the alluvial plains, they function at all times because the aquifer is in equilibrium with the river.

Certain engineering works may disturb this situation. For example, the construction of the Blondel power station on the Rhône River has changed the hydrogeologic conditions of the Pierrelatte Plain. To increase the height of the waterfall, the tailrace was deeply embedded in the alluvial materials, which lowered the water table to such an extent that it fell out of reach of the plant roots over a large part of the plain, affecting agriculture. Similarly, in the Département du Haut-Rhin, hydraulic work related to the Rhine and beginning with the excavation of the planned Grand Canal d'Alsace, just after the Second World War, resulted in the lowering of the water table and the drying up of the Hardt wetland, used for pasture and making hay. This canal was built step-wise immediately parallel to the Rhine downstream from Kembs. Its main function (which was to be hydroelectric) was eventually supplanted by navigation, which led to the disuse of the old Canal du Rhône au Rhin to the west. At each of four steps were built a lock and a power station. But the flux of water between the partly concrete-lined Grand Canal and the alluvial ground-water was slow, so that the water table dropped along the lined reaches of the canal. To save the farmers, whose livelihood was threatened, the Ministry of Agriculture introduced a system of irrigation fed by the Rhine. But the water rapidly infiltrated the cobbly alluvial materials and leached the finer fractions, causing a further degradation and abandonment of the land. At a later date farmers introduced hybrid corn, which requires irrigation, but produced further problems. In the meantime, the former West Germany, having become a political partner, requested and finally succeeded in having the technical aspects of the project modified in order to avoid similar problems on its side of the Rhine. Thus, downstream from Neuf-Brisach and to Strasbourg, four short derivation canals with locks and power stations at artificial waterfalls were built, the used water being returned to the Rhine not to disturb the water table. There is therefore no continuous canal; the larger Grand Canal d'Alsace has rendered redundant a section of Canal du Rhône au Rhin since the construction of a branch connecting it to Mulhouse.

The introduction of irrigation or changes in land use or farming techniques also have their effects. Irrigation, especially by gravity, is one of the best methods to recharge ground-water. The creation of irrigation perimeters may therefore be beneficial to ground-water resources. However, there is a danger of pollution by pesticides and certain fertilizers. On the other hand, a reduction of the irrigated land can have opposite effects. For example, the growth of the city of Lima, Peru on the torrential alluvial fan of the Rimac at the expense of the irrigated land has reduced the recharge of the ground-water and lowered the water table, adversely affecting the city's water supply. The phenomenon, which had the city officials worried, was explained by Tricart. Inversely, the construction of a network of agricultural drains has the effect of increasing flood discharge. Depending on the conditions, they may increase the danger of floods downstream. In an arid climate, too, the artificial recharge of aquifers by irrigation may, through surficial waterlogging and intense evaporation, cause the salinization/alkalinization of the land. We have already given an example of this in the lower valleys of the Pacific coast of Peru. Huge areas have become uncultivable through salinization/alkalinization in the Middle East, including Egypt, and in Pakistan. These various effects should be considered in rational land use planning in order to prevent unpleasant surprises, which are always costly and sometimes dangerous.

The turbidity produced by the transport of solids in streams can be reduced by developments that improve a fluvial regime. The purity of the water goes hand in hand with the conservation of land. It depends on the good management of slopes and the rectification of stream courses, as we have seen. The reduction of the torrential character of small basins has beneficial effects on important developments downstream. The installation of dams pays off, as storage of the water and its steady release result in more regular stream flow. And a dam that previously could provide only seasonal compensations can, after treatment of the watershed, transfer surpluses from one year to another. But, most importantly, the transport of solids has been reduced, the longevity of the reservoirs lengthened, and their profitability increased. Several studies have shown, that even in such highly dissected regions as the Alps, a large proportion of the transported solids come from a small part of a particular basin. Not uncommonly 90 per cent of the material comes from only 10 per cent of the watershed. The conclusion is evident: it is profitable to concentrate much work on a critical but small section of a basin. Moreover, the constraints will affect only a small number of people, who will be more readily and fairly compensated.

To be rational such a development should be carefully programmed. The treatment of the watershed should begin as soon as all decisions

have been made, that is sufficiently in advance of the construction of dams, of irrigation channels, and of the rectification of stream courses. As mentioned, the effects of certain actions are felt with some delay and progressively. It is important to be aware of this. Unfortunately, too often work begins with the construction of a big dam, which is spectacular and lends itself to pompous inaugurations and grand speeches, which may verge on deception. Full account should be taken of natural mechanisms and less spectacular, more difficult but indispensable work should be started in time on the watershed. All the consequences that the major structures will have on the behaviour of the streams and on the hydrogeological conditions downstream should be foreseen. The operation of large dams may be subject to certain constraints to prevent the occurrence of destructive effects. A sufficient discharge in the natural bed should be maintained at all times to prevent a change in the regime of the alluvial ground-water, to dilute the polluting effluents, and to maintain satisfactory ecologic conditions. Indeed, when the alluvium is no longer moved by floods, it is colonized by plants, which increases its surface roughness. If high discharge has to be released, it flows more slowly, which increases the risk of flooding. If trees grow in the bed or on the banks, they may be toppled as a result of sapping and constitute dangerous obstacles that cause much turbulence. They may also be entrained and damage structures or even form obstructions at bridge sites and spillways. Part of the damage caused by the Guil River (French Alps) in June 1957 was caused by such phenomena. These dangers can be prevented by controlling the vegetation; for example, by periodically cutting the trees or by impeding plant growth by an appropriate hydrologic regime. Problems of this kind were raised at the time of the harnessing of the Durance River, of which the Guil is a tributary. (The problem is monitored in Strasbourg (CGA, CEREG and GSIS). See Trautmann 1989; 1991.)

Certain developments make use of a difference in elevation between two neighbouring rivers to obtain a greater 'fall' by diverting the water of the higher into that of the lower. The result is an important change in the dynamics of both rivers. The diverted flow is subtracted from the natural flow in one case and added to it in the other. On the reach of the river whose flow has been reduced, the bed is poorly maintained by natural processes. One should make certain, however, that it is nevertheless able to manage a serious flood downstream from the divergence. On the river

Plates 45–47 Efficient traditional land management
Ph. JT CDXVI-20 cn. Traditional Indian practice aimed at preventing any kind of trauma resulting from
the construction of the road to the Tuba radio and hertzian waves retransmission station under
construction in 1988. A pavement of a hand-laid mosaic of irregular stones and wisely designed drains
disperse the running water energy when discharged into the open forest. Mexico.

receiving the diversion, discharge is increased and
its activity during floods is larger than it was before.
The instability of alluvial bars and the undermining
of banks are bound to increase. To avoid problems
it is well advised to take preventive measures,
mainly by protecting the stream banks.

Perhaps the most caricatural example of
cascading errors and mistakes is given in a book
published by a group of experts from various UN
agencies (Ives 1988). In the Kingdom of Nepal, in
the Himalayas, a dam on the Kulekhani River was
planned in order to provide electricity for the
capital, Katmandu. A 600 m fall was created by the
diversion of the Kulekhani River into the Rapti
River through a tunnel immediately downstream
from the dam. The system, financed by
international agencies, went into operation in 1982.
The reservoir flooded 235 dwellings and obliged the
evacuation of some 1,200 persons, all of them
peasants. The catchment above the dam with an
area of 212 km^2 was inhabited, in 1982, by some
36,000 people, nearly all of them peasants living in
a non-monetary subsistence economy (170
inhab./km^2).

The people who were asked to move were
offered either to be relocated in the hot tropical
Siwalik foothills, where nothing was prepared for
their installation and their training in the
exploitation of a very different ecologic
environment, or to be indemnified by a sum of
money. More than 80 per cent chose the second
solution, which appeared the more acceptable one
because it was exempt of any hazardous
transplantation. It resulted, however, in a
catastrophic failure. Indemnities were delayed two
years, while the people became consumers of high-
priced food and amenities that had to be paid in
cash. They were obliged to borrow money at
usurious rates while inflation was rampant. When
they finally received their money, the most they
could do was repay usurers. No one succeeded in
re-establishing himself as a peasant. So they
became a lumpen proletariat, a new phenomenon
in Nepal!

But, unfortunately, this is not all. Ives (1988)
insists on the fact that the whole economy and
living conditions in the valley suffered a disruption.
Downstream of the diversion, the abandoned

Plate 46 JT CDLXXXIX-57. Upper Lobregat watershed, Catalonia, Spain, alt. 900–950 m. Cretaceous limestones. An excellent traditional land management is abandoned because of rural depopulation. Cultivation was safe on slopes with a mean gradient of 20° as a result of gathering stones used for terracing. A pioneer forest is colonizing the abandoned fields.

Kulekhani river bed became dry. Water mills there, which were a cornerstone of the traditional economy, being used for grinding grain and for a number of cottage industries, ran dry, causing another catastrophe. Upstream, similar problems occurred. Many water mills were flooded on the best land on the valley bottom, while overpopulation befell the remaining land, with serious problems of transportation across the reservoir. Misuse of the overexploited land induced gullying and mass-wasting processes, which materially increased the rate of sedimentation in the newly created reservoir. With some cruelty, Ives (1988) remarks that the Royal Government, aware of the unpreparedness, has paid 'some million of dollars to the tender' for preliminary investigations. Regretfully, this is not a unique case.

A fluvial basin, therefore, should be developed by taking into account the interactions that take place between the divers hydrological, geomorphological, and hydrogeological aspects that characterize it. The unity of natural phenomena should not be occluded by the division of research into various disciplines. This unity also creates common interests between different regions. Some regions can be developed in order to increase their production, which benefits from conditions that favour investments. They are *producing regions*. But the proper function of the developments and, as a consequence, the profitability of the investments they require, is often conditioned by the dynamics of other regions, which play a decisive role in the formation of the liquid and solid discharges. They are *collateral regions*. A direct intervention into them is not justified. Seen under this angle, conservation or restoration measures applies to them cannot be viewed as being profitable. But they do become profitable if, in the framework of the entire basin, their effects on the development of the downstream producing regions is recognized. The Mucuchies area (Venezuela) provides an example of such a regional association in planning (Figures 7(a) and (b), pp. 76–7).

CONCLUSION

The rational use of the natural environment presents great difficulties, even if we provisionally leave aside the relationships between humans and the environment, which will be discussed in Chapter 7. Every use of the land involves a modification in the dynamics of the natural environment and of the biocoenoses which it supports. It can be rational only in so far as we can evaluate in advance the various changes (desired or not) that it will occasion. We have made some progress in this matter during the 1980s but much work remains to be done. As we have shown in Part I, the first efforts of interdisciplinary studies were made from insufficient methodological prerequisites. They were based on a static attitude that avoided the posing of problems. It failed to come up with a methodological revision and remained caught up in its own routine, whether it was the CSIRO with its 'land systems' or the American Land-capability Classification, intended

Plate 47 Ph. JT CDXLIII-16. Traditional land and water management in a dry valley near Tarrega, western Catalonia, Spain. Oligocene marls with limestone interbeds. Hazardous environment. Here terracing is efficient as there is no risk of mass wasting. Walls built with the local limestone gathered in the fields and without the use of cement retain both water and the fine material moved by occasional runoff, but act in a cybernetic manner, letting any excess water pass through. With time, the small valley has been transformed into a staircase of good, flat arable plots, on which most of the intense rainfall that occurs from time to time in this sub-Mediterranean climate can infiltrate. The peasants of both the New and the Old World who invented these management practices were illiterate.

for soil conservation. Unfortunately, these methods led to a bureaucratic attitude, which assured their diffusion.

Ecology, for its part, for historic reasons, developed in a somewhat distorted fashion. Systematists and biologists had a large part in it, in so far as they favoured the study of the relationships between living beings over that of their relationships to the natural environment. This is understandable as botanists and zoologists have a basically biological education rather than one dealing with the environment, even though 'ecology', from the Greek root *oikos*, meaning house, originally meant the science of the environment of living beings. Ecologists therefore have been concerned mainly with the physiological adaptations of the living beings to the constraints imposed on them by the physical environment, and with food chains, now analysed in terms of the flow of energy and materials. The study of the natural

environment, however, was neglected, as systems theory was adopted by physical geographers only during the 1960s, and so was incapable of providing ecology with the material for a better balance of the field. Administrative structures, too, have played an obdurate role, as the specialized disciplines have hampered the development of interdisciplinary research. Strangely, the popular ecology movement, specifically concerned with the environment and its degradation, has helped to straighten the concept of ecology back to its etymological meaning.

Advanced research is presently capable of studying the interactions of the various elements of the natural environment. The kinds of interactions, however, must first be determined and their mechanisms understood. Hopefully we have given demonstrative examples of them, if not a full account. At the present time this is all that we can do, as we are in the qualitative stage, that is, the initial stage of scientific research. Given sufficient means, it should permit without too much delay the beginning of meaningful measurements; but the main difficulty is to know what to measure and to know the significance of the values obtained.

Quantification is indispensable in the rational development of the land. At the present time, however, it is nearly always premature; but economists insist on quantifying. Ignorant of natural phenomena, they pay little attention to qualitative warnings. In the most favourable case, like engineers, they introduce arbitrary numerical values into their calculations, which present a great danger. The lack of communication between naturalists, technicians and economists is a serious handicap to rational land development. It puts into doubt the politics of research and certain conceptions about the basic, as well as post-graduate, training of scholars.

7 PLANNING RATIONAL AGRICULTURAL DEVELOPMENTS

Having investigated the scientific problems posed by the development of the rural environment, we now broaden our outlook. Development or management is not a gratuitous act without definite object. If that were so, it would be better to organize integral natural reserves from which all human intervention is banished. Such reserves do exist and are justified, but they are more like museums. Their role is to preserve evidence of a landscape that has been transformed less than the surrounding country; their study may help understand the problems of development, but this will not be considered here.

Development of the natural environment has a human object: to preserve and improve our ecologic support in the face of the demographic explosion. In many cases this basic object has been neglected in favour of immediate profits. Nevertheless, doubts and objections are now clearly and forcefully voiced against policies of economic growth at all costs. Public opinion, at least in certain countries, has become aware of the 'quality of life'. Such preoccupations are possible only in so far as the security of life itself is assured, when a sufficiently high standard of living has been attained. Only well-to-do peoples can demand it. Rural development should take this into account: the necessity of assuring a sufficiently high production to improve standards of living, the desire, expressed by many in the industrialized countries, to see life become more pleasant and, above all, less subject to pollution of all kinds, the proliferation of which is the result of profit-hungry technological developments and unrestrained advertising for ever more consumption.

We shall examine how to harmonize problems of rural development with the preoccupations of society. We begin by investigating the degree of tolerance of the natural environment as regards competitive uses, followed by how a development study ought to be organized.

THE DEGREE OF TOLERANCE OF THE NATURAL ENVIRONMENT TO COMPETING USES

Technological development, even more than demographic pressure, generates a competition between different land uses and ecologic resources. Residential areas, transportation routes and industrial activities rapidly encroach upon areas that have an ecologic use. The total area devoted to agriculture in the Netherlands since 1930 has shrunk in spite of the reclamation, at enormous cost, of the IJssel Lake polders, which have added 160,000 ha of new land. California has lost 1.6 million ha of farmland between 1964 and 1985. An evolution of this sort is alarming: industry operates on fossil fuels and geologic ores, all of which are non-renewable resources, while vegetal production is dependent on practically ever-renewable amounts of solar energy. (Solar energy is the result of atomic structure rearrangements of solar matter. As such, it undergoes a decay. But this decay is spread over billions of years, so that it is completely beyond our scope. We are thus justified in writing 'practically' ever-renewable.) It is urgent to realize the full implications of this. In the mean time the competition for land is fierce: it cannot remain anarchic and devastating. A rational solution has to be found in order to arrive at an optimal use of land and its resources, which rapidly become increasingly scarce.

Mahler (1973) has proposed a land classification that may help solve this problem. It includes the following classes.

1 *Land suitable for intensive use*
   (a) without major initial investment
   (b) with major initial investment
2 *Land suitable for extensive use*   It cannot justify large investments except for the protection of highly productive cropland; if that is not the case, the use of the land should be improved.
3 *Land unsuitable for development*

Plate 48 Destabilization by earthquake
Ph. JT CCCXCI-10. A site dangerous for a settlement, just above Recuay, Peru. Photograph taken at the beginning of July, five weeks after the earthquake of 31 May 1970. The broad, flat-topped divide is suitable for agriculture and looks attractive at first sight for the relocation of Recuay, threatened by future slumps. There is no flooding risk, nevertheless it is unstable. Two twin-amphitheatres excavated by former landslides have been partly reactivated. Another, on the left, and a few others in the background were caused by the earthquake. Intense gullying, the result of bad land management, is another risk, which may cause mass movements in a future quake. Two houses at the lower edge of the photo are located in a dangerous area; their relocation has been recommended.

(a) left in reserve awaiting technological progress or a change in socio-economic conditions that change the situation
(b) intrinsically unusable, such as rock slopes, high mountains, deserts where irrigation is impossible, and so on.

This classification, according to Mahler (1973), should be combined with the greater or lesser need for protective measures. Mahler's attitude corresponds to ours. It is rather different from the one that is commonly adopted and seeks to define a land's *aptitude*. Perhaps it was inspired by the American Land-capability classification for conservation planning, which distinguishes more or less severe constraints. Indeed, Mahler's first category is subdivided into land unaffected by constraints other than those of everyday conservation (1a), and into land subject to certain constraints, but which may be remedied by adequate measures modifying the characteristics of the environment, as, for example, drainage or irrigation (1b). The second category groups together land subject to such constraints that high yields cannot be expected from it. In the third category constraints are presently excessive in relation to our present technological means and population pressure. This way of proceeding may be applied after a study of the natural environment has been made according to the method proposed in the preceding chapter, the principles of which have been published at about the same time as Mahler's work. Mahler's classification combined to that of the degree of stability of the environment may guide a rational land use to various competing schemes. Non-agricultural uses should be earmarked for land that is least apt for agricultural production, which is at the bottom of the list.

Nevertheless, Mahler's proposal remains rather general: in practice it is necessary to go into greater detail. The problem, for example, is posed for urban sprawl: thus the Agence d'Urbanisme de la Communauté Urbaine de Strasbourg has requested the Centre de Géographie Appliquée to make a study that would enable it to determine the best use of the land. The work, completed more than ten years ago with methods that have been improved since, included a map, on the scale of 1:25,000, of the various characteristics of the natural environment: surficial materials, present geomorphic processes, including those resulting from anthropic degradation, hydrologic conditions, and land use: residential, types of crops, forest, grassland. The confrontation of these factors has thrown light on certain decisions. For example, the cobbly sands of the Lower Low Terrace of the Rhine offer a good foundation, but the water table is high, which makes subterranean works prohibitive in cost. The agricultural value of the soils is mediocre. Adjacent to this zone, between dikes, is the modern floodplain of the Rhine, occupied by forest. The Lower Low Terrace, therefore, is suitable for low-density cottage-type residential housing with pleasant surroundings. This solution avoids expensive subterranean works such as multilevel crossroads or main sewers.

Engineers of the Société Nationale du Canal de Provence have also been confronted with this type of problem. The object of this organism is to help development of regional agriculture, especially by irrigation. The *Départements* have their representatives on its board of directors. Provence is subject to a very high pressure of urbanization, of tourism, and of secondary residences around Marseilles and the coastal cities. There are, therefore, serious problems of the use of space and of land development, which the Society of the Canal of Provence has been called upon to arbitrate. Falque (1972) has tentatively tried to apply the 'ecologic planning' approach of I. L. McHarg (1969) to guide decisions. It consists, first, of an ecologic 'inventory' of land use. This preliminary base may be criticized on the same grounds as the 'land systems' of the CSIRO. To use 'geomorphology' (whose nature does not seem to be well understood) to explain the 'physiography' is to reverse the order of things. More interesting are Falque's own ideas, although their basic premises limit their further development. They include the following steps.

1 'Interpretation of the inventorized data to arrive at the prospective land use for each zone of the entire area under study' (Falque 1972: 8), each aspect of the natural environment to be examined in relation to its aptitude with regard to each type of possible use. The result is put on 'maps of intrinsic aptitudes'.

2 'Establishment of a value system for each elementary zone in regard to all possible land uses' (Falque 1972: 8). Superposition of the maps of intrinsic aptitudes of the various aspects of the environment enables the selection of 'high value' areas, where aptitudes are many and profitable, and areas of more or less low value, with few and mainly mediocre aptitudes. To appreciate areas of 'high value', where several different uses are possible, the degree of compatibility of the various uses should be determined. Tables with double entries conceived as 'matrices' are created to this effect. Four degrees of compatibility have been determined: incompatible, not very compatible, rather compatible, and compatible, which can easily be substituted by conventional values, such as 0, 1, 2, 3. The more or less favourable character of the natural characteristics for each type of land use (second facet of the table) and the types of degradation they are apt to produce (third facet) are also evaluated. The results of this confrontation are then mapped on a 'synthetic map of aptitudes'. Thus is defined the natural aptitude or 'supply' of the land.

3 The economist, in parallel fashion, makes a 'growth model' to determine the demand for space. This demand is confronted with the supply or offer. By further including the landscape's aesthetic criteria, it becomes possible to propose a land use plan.

This procedure, as Falque (1972) remarks, is worthy of interest, as instead of considering the natural environment as an inexhaustible resource, whose use is subject, without limitation, to economic forces, the environment is made to appear as the result of a balance of equal importance to that of the social and economic demands. We are in full agreement with this view, which, moreover, satisfies a preoccupation of Mahler, who emphasizes that one of the main deficiencies of present studies is the gap between the knowledge of the natural environment and that of the socio-economic conditions. Mahler attributes it, in part, to a difference in methods. We succeeded in avoiding this serious difficulty by introducing the 'HUMAN ACTIVITIES' in our flow chart of the Earth's natural system (Figure 3, p. 21). By putting the problem at this level, we escape the cost–benefit discussions of economists and the intellectual complications of the human and social sciences. We consider only the *result*, not the way it is arrived at.

Nevertheless, Falque's approach, no matter how interesting its principles, encounters certain difficulties which limit its use. Two are particularly serious. First, the approach to the study of the natural environment remains that of an inventory, static, insufficiently integrated. Our own concept, which is based on the dynamics of a natural system and on its degree of stability, more readily reveals the nature of the constraints which oppose themselves to the use of the environment. It answers more directly the basic question: 'What are the limiting factors and the main present problems concerning the development of the area?', to quote Mahler (1973). Falque's approach can be integrated into ours, as it takes into account the same aspects, interposing them, however, in a different way.

Second, the matrix and the cartographic superposition are clumsy methods, difficult to manipulate. They may be seductive at first sight, producing a hoped-for quantification. In reality there is a big chance that this hope may not be fulfilled (see Chapter 8). The graphic superposition of different maps quickly results in a saturation, which is observed visually or photographically. We have ourselves experienced these difficulties when perfecting our hydromorphological maps, although we superimposed only three maps (hydromorphological, slope, and plant cover). To process the various parameters contained in the matrices with help of a computer also results, rapidly, in a saturation. All this limits the apparently rigorous character of the method.

All told, it is preferable to proceed with a systems analysis. Indeed, this helps in elucidating the dynamics in which there are many feedbacks. The transformation of the natural environment modifies these dynamics, therefore the environment on which they act. As Mahler emphasizes, a development policy requires 'a mutual process of adaptation of natural resources, technology, and of man himself' (1973: 257).

FLOW CHART OF STEPS LEADING TO AN AGRICULTURAL DEVELOPMENT

The main problem is that of the integration of natural environment studies with economic and social investigations. Among the traditional disciplines, geography is the only one that openly studies human–land relationships. Unfortunately certain geographers are insufficiently aware of the importance of this aspect of their field and, like economists or sociologists, whom they imitate, tend to ignore it, keeping their distance from the study of the natural environment. This attitude is regrettable and will, sooner or later, throw them into the camp of secondary economists or sociologists, above whom genuine economists or sociologists will always be preferred. Geographic thought, of course, has evolved considerably: from a rather coarse determinism, according to which humans were under the strict dependence of the environment, to more dialectic conceptions revealing complex interactions.

To help satisfy practical needs, we have given much thought to these concepts. Every intervention in Nature necessarily produces a modification of the relationships between humans and their environment. Because of it, George, for example, prefers to speak of 'voluntary geography'. Our approach leads to the formulation of a flow chart (Figure 23) consisting of three tiers:

1 On the upper tier are shown the successive steps in human intervention: initial knowledge of the problems, diagnostic, search for solutions, and application of the solutions.
2 On the lower tier are listed the types of organisms that should intervene in each of these steps.
3 On the intermediate tier are shown, in boxes, the kinds of interventions and the studies or operations they necessitate. They can be regarded as 'black boxes' from the point of view of data processing.

The chart is divided into two parts after step 3, when a *choice* of a political nature must be made, assuring the transition from informative studies to action. The three steps preceding this choice should permit the accumulation of ever increasing knowledge, so that the choice may be made with full knowledge of the facts.

Initial knowledge

The initial knowledge is based on the consideration of the relationships between the human group and the ecologic environment in which it lives, or in which it will eventually live in the event of a development by colonization resulting from a migration. This concept is not fundamentally different from the one that has inspired traditional geographical research: to know how to use existing material is always valuable. Many scholarly works carried out without a practical object may be put to use in this stage of operations. But a careful examination of their appropriateness to the pursued object is necessary. As to ecology, not every ecological study necessarily serves as a basis for a developmental programme, whatever the views on the matter of certain ecologists, who have the deplorable tendency to believe only in their own competency. Early work normally begins with the various existing scholarly works, but should not be limited to a mere reference list. Not only should outdated information be updated, but also an integrated viewpoint of the natural and the human components be strived for. In this way, the problem of the relationships between physical and human studies is resolved from the start. This is important. But an integrated viewpoint requires adequate information, which is not always available. We have given examples in so far as the natural environment is concerned. From the human point of view, ordinary demographic statistics are seldom sufficient: the latent underemployment of underdeveloped regions should be analysed. Many persons classified as 'active' are only partially so. For what reason? Does this situation equally affect all age groups or only some? Why? Does it occur throughout the year or only at certain periods? In answering these questions, the importance of real underemployment and its characteristics should be made clear. To be informed on these points is indispensable if a modification in professional activities is sought. The attitude of people to such problems, especially their perception of the natural environment on which they depend, of the resources it offers and the difficulties it confronts them with should also be known. This requires sociological inquiries while profiting from the advice of someone who is well acquainted with the natural environment and the problems of land development.

These interdependencies are evident from the arrows on the flow chart (Figure 23). One of them reflects the problem of the perception of the natural environment by the human group, the other the influence of the natural environment on the human group. This, among others, includes the hygienic conditions, endemic diseases, their negative effects on demographic, cultural and economic growth, and the problems of nutrition and their sanitary aspects. Lastly, the relationships between the human group and the natural environment are materialized in a certain agrarian system. They rely on certain techniques, which require detailed study. To understand this agrarian system the study team should be interdisciplinary and composed of members who are familiar with the natural environment, members familiar with the human group, and members acquainted with technical matters. This initial phase should take place in a regional framework. Which? Several solutions are possible: to be efficient a great deal of flexibility is necessary. It may be an administrative unit, a fluvial basin, a particular ecologic environment, or the territory of a tribe or village.

The diagnostic

To analyse the diagnostic it is necessary to understand what impedes a rational development and to ascertain the evolutive trend in a temporal and spatial framework. While each of these aspects has been illustrated separately in the form of a box, the determination of the diagnostic should be based on a comprehensive view of the whole.

The initial step is to make a clinical examination of the agrarian system to determine its deficiencies and seek their explanation. In general they are natural or human constraints that are too severe to be overcome. Hygienic conditions and nutrition have already been mentioned. The lack of technical means may be a factor; it may result in exploitation of poor-quality land, where input of labour is poorly compensated because of low productivity. Sometimes the peasants realize this, but their techniques do not usually enable them to cultivate potentially better land because it is poorly drained, has heavy soils or is insalubrious. In the Sudanese Zone of western Africa, for instance, many valley bottoms, which could support a relatively intensive agriculture, remain unexploited because of the ravages of onchocerciasis, for which there is no remedy. A complete mastery of the ecologic environment would be necessary to eliminate it.

Such problems of land use are then put in a temporal and spatial perspective. In time, to analyse its recent evolution in order to discover its present trend. Whether the trend is favourable or not is important to know, as the situation may slowly improve by itself or become progressively worse. The causes of this evolution should be determined in order to know which factors to favour, in the case of a positive evolution, or to counteract, in the case of a regressive evolution. The diagnostic should come up with a choice of remedies. Allowance should be made for the spatial heterogeneity of the phenomena, whether

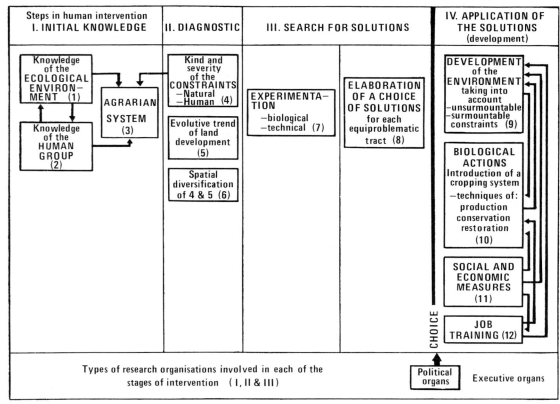

Figure 23. Flow chart for programming land use studies

Source: Made by J. Tricart from a document by J. Kilian in a collaborative programme between the CGA and IRAT.

The general concept

The flow chart shows four successive steps (I–IV) in human intervention. Their nature is briefly indicated in the form of 'black boxes', which are explained below.

The steps are organized from left to right. To execute the operations, indicated in columns, it is necessary to have available the results of the operations indicated in the preceding column. A thick line separates steps III and IV. This division marks an interruption in the technical aspects of the operation. It corresponds to a **choice**, to a **decision**, which is necessarily of a political nature and which, as such, is incumbent upon the political authorities. If the choice is made by the technicians, in lieu of the politicians, the latter may be accused of being ruled by technocrats; if these are foreign, a neo-colonial situation may be said to exist. This break is therefore important. The object of the operations situated to the left is to *prepare a choice*; they should lead to as large a number as possible of solutions that the objective conditions permit. To restrict their number means an encroachment upon the prerogatives of the authorities. The operations that precede the choice are incumbent upon specific *study organisms*. Their work should be objective and strictly apolitical. Once the choice is made (column IV), the decision of the public authorities must be put into action. The work is then the task of *executive organs* responsible to and under the control of the public organs.

Details concerning the various operations

Each of the 'black boxes' on the flow chart is numbered and referred to below.

1 **Knowledge of the ecologic environment** should stress constraints, some static (stoniness, soil heterogeneity, steep slopes, etc.) others dynamic (intense rillwash, beheading of soils, hydromorphism, etc.). It should be conceived in a systems framework, able to define the structure of the system, that is the hierarchy of the components. Study of the ecologic environment is based on physical geography and leads to ecology. Evaluation of the degree of morphodynamic stability is a valid approach, previously explained; it permits the integration of pedogenic, agronomic and conservation problems.

2 **Knowledge of the human group** presents qualitative as well as quantitative aspects. Social structure greatly influences the use of the ecologic environment by way of attitudes, cultural level, and investments. The main quantitative aspect is demographic. Its analysis cannot be exclusive, it should take note of ethnic groups and social classes in plural or stratified societies.

3 The **kind of agrarian system** constitutes a synthesis between (1) and (2). It should show the relationships between the human group and the ecologic environment. The solutions provided by ethnic, cultural or social groups that occupy the same territory may be quite different from one another. African societies, in Mali, for example, offer an excellent demonstration of it. Certain agrarian systems are senseless on the ecological plane, but meaningful on the human level. Analysis should make clear such factors, which explain the adopted solutions.

4 The **definition of constraints** includes their hierarchy (Duclos 1973). It is directly derived from study of the present agrarian system. This system, indeed, is narrowly dependent on the constraints inherent to the ecologic environment and those which are the consequence of the social structure of the human group. Both cause impediments that should be understood. Most are complex and have their origin in the relationships between the human group and the environment. It is therefore imperative that the two aspects 'natural environment' and 'human group' never be separated. These constraints, moreover, should be studied according to two axes of reference: a temporal axis (evolutive trend of the agrarian system) and a spatial axis (spatial diversification).

5 The **evolutive trend** of the agrarian system should take into account human–environment relationships, that is evaluate the changes to which the relationship is subjected, for example, as the result of demographic growth (increased pressure of humans on resources), land abandonment (degradation of fallow land, environmental consequences of reforestation, etc.), cultural or social changes (mutations in the use of resources), or economic factors. Furthermore, the impact of human intervention on the ecologic environment as a result of the agrarian system should be evaluated: improvements in the quality of the soil, of the hydrologic conditions and, unfortunately, more frequently, degradation, causing an increase in morphodynamic instability and, correlatively, an increase in ecologic constraints.

6 The mechanisms also have a **spatial distribution**. The natural as well as the human factors act in a diversified way, both qualitatively and quantitatively. The concept 'homogeneous region' is a pure abstraction, which may be misleading. From the point of view of rural management, which is a therapy as concerns the degradation of the ecologic environment, it is very important to take account of this diversification. One of the objects of the diagnostic study, therefore, is to define *equiproblematic tracts*, that is areas that pose the same development problems. This, on the one hand, entails an analysis of the nature of the problems and, on the other, a delimitation of tracts.

7 **Experimentation** should start with the delimitation of equiproblematic tracts, using them, to begin with, to establish a network of experiments that should be as representative as possible. In that regard, account should be taken of the nature of the problems posed, whether they are ecological and determined by the characteristics of the natural environment or human and consisting of the introduction of new practices and their acceptance by whatever social, ethnic, cultural, or other group. Experiments on specific parcels, which are not affected by the 'viscosity' of the human group, should be combined with experiments with various types of farmers or peasants, the object of which is to analyse these 'viscosities' and define steps to reduce them.

8 It is imperative that the **choice of solutions** to be presented be as wide as possible. It certainly should not be limited to those which might please the local authorities. These may soon be replaced. The study should serve regardless of the political fluctuations, as long as the initial conditions are not radically modified.

9, 10, 11 and 12 The **application of the solutions** is determined by the governing body and, therefore, has a definite orientation that is much more limited than what has been proposed. The arrows on the far right indicate the interdependence of the four aspects of the application of the chosen solution. This solution may determine a modification of certain natural constraints (*surmountable constraints*), for example, by irrigation, by protection from floods, etc. Other constraints, not to be modified, must be accounted for, however. Still others, lastly, such as pedological aspects, may be progressively reduced by agronomic practices (organic or mineral fertilizers, removal of stones, etc.). This, among others, is the object of *biological actions* (techniques of conservation restoration). To choose a cropping system that effectively protects the soil during critical periods is of the utmost importance. This choice should be made in accordance with the susceptibility of the natural environment to an increase in morphodynamic instability. The biological actions require *social and economic measures* favouring investments, technical progress, and *job training*.

natural or human. Differences in the characteristics of the environment or in those of the human group produce modifications in the agrarian system or in its evolutive trend. These matters should be determined as knowledge of them helps improve the diagnostic and determine the possible applications of solutions to be sought later.

At this point of the research, it becomes possible to define *equiproblematic tracts*, that is to map (on a medium scale) the different problem areas. These tracts may be subdivided according to the acuity of the problems. Depending on the case, they relate to natural or to human factors or sometimes to types of relationships between humans and their environment. The fundamental concepts of geography may, once again, be put to good profit here.

The search for solutions

Solutions appropriate to the kinds of problems posed in each equiproblematic tract as well as to its geographic characteristics, whether natural or human, must be found. They must depend on *agronomic research*, which can be divided into two steps forming a logical sequence.

General agronomic problems and those that are specifically posed by certain plants or certain crops must be examined. Research involving plants concerns the selection or improvement of plant varieties, the study of the behaviour and adaptation of plant varieties, the physiology of each species, and the defence against parasites, predators, diseases and weeds. Research can also determine conditions of acclimatization of exotic plants whose qualities have been recognized elsewhere, as the remarkable winged bean. Study of the spontaneous vegetation may be useful and reveal 'ecologic equivalents' of a cultivated plant.

On the agronomic plane, experimentation deals with everything that is not really specific to a plant: the study of the soil, its constraints, its preparation, the physical factors of fertility, the circulation of water, the role of organic matter, the dynamics of nitrogen, the study of fertilizers, of crop rotations and the maintenance of soil fertility in the framework of the cropping system.

Part of this research, helped by experimentation, is practised in enclosed parcels where the natural conditions of the environment are not always perfectly represented, even if the experiments are carried out on soils representative of the ecology. The parcels are situated, and this is to be expected, on the most favourable sites, which pose the least

'parasitic' problems. With time, however, the soil is modified while experiments are carried out, so that an artificial support is created, different from the original soil. It may be that, finally, only the climate remains the same. The available facilities justify the technique determined by the objective, which frequently and foremost, is to resolve the chemical constraints. In plant selection, varietal improvement or agronomy, the shortcomings are only minor. But problems of *environmental improvement* cannot be resolved that way. What is necessary are experiments realized under meaningful conditions, highly *representative* and *specific* of the various types of natural environment to be treated. But this step, no matter how necessary and indispensable, is only a preliminary step, exactly as the study of the physical and cultural geographic environment. It should be followed by another, that of *differentiated experimentation* as a function of the equiproblematic tracts. For example, in the Pampa Deprimida in Argentina a decision was taken to conduct several experiments aimed at improving the soil water regime on private *estancias*. The sites were chosen relative to the geomorphological investigations and soil types. Experiments were carried out on representative sites by competent agronomists in close collaboration with a geomorphologist and a senior soil scientist. Also a farmer, compensated for the damage incurred to his land, was associated with them. The results were promising, but unfortunately without sequel in the well-known disastrous political conditions suffered by Argentina.

Differentiated experimentation has two distinct objectives. First, to study the interactions between the plant cover and the ecologic environment. Research projects should be concerned with the agricultural land, including pastures and managed forests, specifically with processes of edaphic and geomorphic degradation, measurement of their intensity, experiments with techniques aimed at restricting them, such as methods of cultivation, modes of plantation, crop rotation, manures, mineral and organic fertilizers, structures in the framework of the parcel, such as hedges, wind breaks, buffer strips, channel or ridge type terraces. In Burkina Faso, for example, discontinuous rillwash is the major geomorphic process on the argillaceous vertisols of the long but gentle slopes of the Bittou area, underlain by granito-gneiss. This process quickly degrades the upper soil horizons after only a few years of traditional agriculture in a contrasted climate. The loss of organic material is considerable with, as a corollary, a degradation of soil structure, which breaks down. An earthy mulch develops, at first appreciated by the peasants and the experimenters, as it temporarily provides a good seed bed. However, the degradation quickly leads to a progressive drying up of the argillaceous underlying horizons. Desiccation cracks cease to form and the water runs off more than it infiltrates, thus accelerating the problem, which leads to lower crop yields. Agronomic research should investigate this specific problem and ponder themes of research integrating agricultural techniques (tilling methods, among others), crop rotations, stripcropping and ways to reconstitute the organic matter of the soil. It is futile to dissociate these treatments, which, if studied separately, would result in costly impasses. The object of research, here, is to improve the circulation of water on slopes in argillaceous soils by means of a series of closely associated treatments resulting in the elaboration of an agrarian system adapted to the land. This type of research, which may be called 'accompanying research', remains indispensable if we are to reach the farmer or peasant. Another example: attacks by parasites and diseases should be studied as well as their insertion into the biocoenose, their relationships with the ecogeographic environment, and techniques, including biological ones, on how to fight them.

Second, the other objective of differentiated experimentation is to adapt itself to the social environment. The farmer or peasant is not a laboratory or experimental farm technician. Experimentation, therefore, to provide the results demanded by it, to be sufficiently profitable, considering the cost, should situate itself at several *levels*, moreover highly imbricated, but which gradually make it more representative of the social and physical geographical conditions and, because of them, more expedient to a rational development.

Agronomic research should therefore be carried on at the following levels:

1 *A basic research level* whose object is genetics, varietal improvement and agronomy (fertilization, the nitrogen problem, the dynamics of the mineral elements, the preparation of the soil) in the major natural domains (humid temperate zone, dry tropical zone, high altitude tropical levels). This research is conducted on the major soil groups representative of each tested ecologic environment.
2 *An accompanying research level* whose goal is to resolve development problems; it should be

conducted on parcels highly representative of the types of natural environment. Its object is to study crop–environment relationships, *including* techniques of conservation down to the level of the parcel. Topics of research are specific to the crop land.
3 *A social level* which should be realized in reality and under conditions of responsibility, that is by the farmers or peasants themselves on certain of their parcels chosen with regard to both their natural and human representativity, together with the advice and under the responsibility of agronomists.

This last phase of experimentation directly prepares the *application of the solutions*, especially *job training*. It also permits the beginning of the last step of the preparatory studies, the *formulation of a series of solutions*.

It is very important that the public authorities who make the choice can make it from a reasonable number of solutions. To propose only one solution, or (which is hypocritical) two or more solutions but only one of which is plausible, is an abuse of confidence. It forces the hand of the political organ responsible for the choice or deprives it of its power, which amounts to dishonesty. Those in charge of the studies are consultants only, nothing more: it is their duty to provide honest information, not to make decisions. If they do, they act like technocrats, to which public opinion is generally hostile, especially when the consultants are foreigners, giving the operation a neo-colonial air. The ethics of scientists condemns such attitudes. For example, experimentation makes possible a series of different solutions for the rational land use of an alluvial plain along a perennially flowing river:

1 Preservation of an economy based on cattle-raising
   • with an improvement of open range (ranching)
   • with improved enclosed pastures
   • with sown pastures and stall-feeding.
2 Introduction of a cropping system
   • associated with cattle-raising through rotation with sown pastures
   • more or less intensive cropping associated with or without cattle-raising
   • development of an irrigation perimeter; intensive cropping associated cattle-raising.

For each of these agrarian solutions experimentation can calculate investment costs and profitability. It can also throw light on certain imperative conditions on the level of techniques, of individual or collective farming equipment, of credit, and of job training. It can provide information on environmental impacts in a perimeter larger than the one to be developed. Irrigation, for example, decreases downstream water resources. Are the higher profits superior to those that the same water would have provided elsewhere with other developments? Is there competition between the water consumers? What conditions should be fulfilled on the social level for the best use of the water? What will be the return on investments taking into account the natural and human constraints? What complementary actions should be taken to improve this profitability and what are the conditions of their success?

Here is an overview of the various points that should be discussed when a series of solutions is presented. The choice by a well-informed government should not produce unforeseen surprises. The interactions of the regional system, in its natural and human aspect, should be emphasized and guide the decision and its application. The authorities should be clearly informed about the implication of their decision so that they are able to make the necessary accompanying measures it requires: this is essential for the success of the operation.

The realization of the project

The application of the solution – the realization of the project itself – is incumbent upon the executive organs. It should be carefully controlled by government representatives invested with the necessary authority. The realization of the agricultural development includes four main aspects, which are illustrated each in a box, but which are interdependent, as shown by the arrows (Figure 23).

The **development of the geographic environment** (9) is based on the awareness of constraints. For simplification we have grouped these into surmountable and insurmountable. These two categories are distinguished by two kinds of criteria: technical and financial.

1 *Technical*   We cannot replace a mountain by a plain, but we must take into account constraints of climate, solar radiation, etc. Within certain limits, constraints are mainly felt in increased costs or lower profits. This is the case of crop production or the raising of dairy cattle in mountains like the Alps. Such points should be examined during the search for solutions.

2 *Financial*   A certain development eliminating a constraint could be realized technically, but its cost would be prohibitive, or it has been found preferable to use the money for other investments. A case in point is the Pantanal region of south-west Brazil, whose hydrological development was passed over in favour of huge investments in the mining of industry of Amazonia (Carajás Project).

Financial constraints vary with time; they are partly dependent on the general economic situation. Development projects should take this into consideration and avoid making more difficult or costly a certain type of intervention that is not recommended at the time of the decision, but which could be adopted later. We concur, here, with Mahler's (1973) concept of land put into reserve.

Decisions may also depend on the aptitude of the rural population, whose reorientation may take much time. For example, to transform a pastoral nomad into an irrigation farmer is extremely difficult, certainly a long-term undertaking. Nevertheless, the capacity for innovation of traditional rural populations should not be underestimated, as recent observations in Mali by Tricart have demonstrated. Not only the peasants of Office du Niger lands learned, on their own, the practice of cutting the natural vegetation to store it for emergency fodder in the absence of rain, but the formerly transhumant Fulani herdsmen, who were compelled by the destruction of their range to abandon their traditional activities, became in a year the best rice cultivators on the outskirts of the Office du Niger's irrigated lands. Completely ignorant of the practice of rice cultivation, they scrupulously followed the instructions of the technical advisers, which is more than can be said of the peasants of Office du Niger region itself. Besides, having fled from their tribes, these Fulani have been completely freed from their traditional feudal servitudes, which were heavy.

Social and economic measures (11) often condition the efficacy of a development. For example, near the end of the colonial period, a certain number of dams were built in Upper Volta (Burkino Faso) to irrigate valley bottoms. They were never put into use, as it was ignored that the alluvial plains grazed by cattle during the dry season belonged to herdsmen (nobles) who wield the traditional power. For them, to cultivate the soil would be demeaning; it would mean the abandonment of their entire system of traditional values. The engineering works were conditional upon a complete change in mentality of the herdsmen, very difficult to realize, or by a transfer of property requiring political conditions that did not exist.

The **biological actions** (10) entail a change in the crops being grown and in the system of cultivation. These actions depend not only on the characteristics of the natural environment and its constraints but also on human conditions: the social and economic constraints, and the aptitudes of the peasants. All this has been examined during the determination of the various solutions. At that time the measures to be taken to realize the biological actions intended to produce a certain economic result, while at the same time preventing environmental degradation, have been discussed. In some cases such measures may involve an agrarian reform, in others the introduction of extra labour or the use of a credit or marketing agency. **Job training** (12) has already been considered in the last phase of experimentation.

The manner of proceeding we have presented tries to harmonize a rational procedure, based on the scientific knowledge of the problems, and the administrative requirements with a professional ethic that categorically rejects a technocratic and a neo-colonial attitude. This stance is generally valid, independent of political regimes and social structures. It is compatible with liberal or state capitalism, as well as with a more or less authoritarian socialism. The type of social and political organization determines the kind of organism that has the power of decision: it may be, depending on the case, a government agency, a corporation, company, a bank developing an enormous domain or region, or a group of cooperatives.

An important point in the application of a solution, whatever the political or social regime, is the time of response, or hysteresis, between the interdependent components of the development system. For example, as a result of economic and financial planning, machines may be rapidly introduced to overcome certain limitations, but a certain amount of time is needed for the operators to use them correctly. Administrative rules should also be adapted. The introduction of machines causes new forms of undesirable degradation; for example, for a considerable period bonuses were given to those Soviet tractor operators who consumed the least fuel. Quickly, of course, many realized that it was profitable to plough in the downslope direction. The result was a serious soil ablation, particularly in the area of the middle Volga, before a rather rigid bureaucracy changed its policy.

As indicated by Mahler (1973), development problems change with *degrees of developments*.

1 In the least developed countries the most important thing is to allow the people to make better use of the natural resources without causing a degradation.
2 As development proceeds, new technical solutions are introduced, such as mechanization and hydraulic structures; hysteretic problems are most important and hazardous.
3 In developed countries people are increasingly hostile to pollutions of all kinds and conscious of the 'quality of life'. Public opinion is ever more critical of the destruction of the natural environment, even organizing into unprecedented political parties, such as the Ecologists and Greens. A struggle results, which is becoming ever more acute and will affect rural management and planning, opposed by powerful, economic interests.

There is partial overlap of these types of situation, both in time and in space. In the south of Venezuela, for example, there are initial development problems in practically uninhabited regions, while between Caracas and Valencia problems of competition in the use of an insufficient water supply and concerns about pollution must be resolved.

In conclusion, we agree with Mahler that there are solutions that are worse than the problems they are supposed to solve. A careful examination of all the factors is imperative. It should be remembered that solutions, too, have negative aspects.

8 HOW TO PROCEED?

We hesitated before giving this title to the chapter. During the course of this work, as well as during the course of our professional experience in several domains and under various skies, we have advocated a systems approach and much flexibility in attacking problems. Are we now going to renege all this and propose a recipe, a precept? This, of course, is out of the question. We remain faithful to the systems approach, which presently is the best logical instrument we possess. This approach indeed places sectoral studies and the integration of subsystems on which they bear into a more comprehensive system, which, as far as we are concerned, is the development or management of the rural environment. Part I included four specialized chapters devoted to the geomorphological and pedological approaches, to water resources, and to remote sensing. Examples given in each of them showed the necessity of overstepping sectoral bounds. However, we do not think these examples are sufficient. For this reason we shall now provide some guidance intended to help readers who wish to attempt studies of the kind we advocate. Our intention is to provide a general methodological orientation, to communicate, to transmit some of our own experience.

At the risk of repeating ourselves, let us recall that to manage the environment and, more, develop it, is to intervene into dynamics that are or have been in different ways, to a lesser or greater degree, influenced by humankind. Part of these past or present interventions are the result of more or less clear or rational individual choices that range from the short-term 'profit logic' of agribusiness to various cultural traditions and the immediate struggle for survival. Schematically, two extremes may be distinguished: the short term and the long (or secular) term. Their contrast and their incompatibility are aspects of the social crisis that characterizes the end of the twentieth century, as rich in victims of war with its chemical arms, scorched earth policies, massacres of prisoners and opponents, and disastrous assaults on our ecologic environment, the specific concern of the International Geosphere–Biosphere Programme, as the worst years of the Black Death and the wars of the end of the Middle Ages. The fundamental contrast is that which opposes the short term to the long term: it should be the main concern of any environmental policy.

The short term in *agribusiness* is almost that of the stock market, as one of its characteristics is to be based on capital, therefore, to be narrowly dependent on the *money market*. Through its medium junk bonds invade agriculture. Agriculture is deeply in debt in the United States, Canada and Europe; if it does not pay off its debt, the whole credit sandcastle crumbles. No government can accept this and, even less, give the appearance of accepting it, which results in a veiled and hypocritical struggle in which words cease to correspond to acts. A good illustration is the conflict between the United States and the EEC. The short term corresponds to the time-span of the metabolic cycle of annual plants such as wheat, maize and sorghum, the basic crops of agribusiness, food for people, feed for raising industrial livestock, the basic ingredients of the so-called 'surplus crops' destined to a humanity that suffers from a dearth of food or is literally starving. The developing countries too, or at least a small group of business people and influential politicians representing them, have embarked on programmes of agribusiness with the help of loans provided by the industrialized countries. A true *Raubwirtschaft*, in its full etymological meaning, is being practised, for example, in Brazil. The short, annual term is totally incompatible with the management of an ecologic environment in which the most rapid phenomena, such as a soil modification by hydromorphism, functions over a decennial time span. This time-span is most frequently realized owing to an induced degradation (e.g. hydromorphism in the El Cenizo irrigation perimeter of Venezuela; alkalinization of the soils in Mali – Office du Niger; gullying in Russia and the Ukraine since the nineteenth century).

The secular long term corresponds to traditions, to an empiricism developed over the generations.

Its main characteristic is time. The contrast between the pre-colonial forest fallow of African agrarian systems and the shifting agriculture of the black slaves of Latin America is a good illustration. The African tribe is closely associated within a specific culture sociopolitical organization, land status, and techniques of food production. The object was the perpetuation of the tribe and its culture, identified by reference to its ancestors and origin and, occasionally, to certain descendants who brought it to its present location at the end of the last migration. There is no comparison with the black slaves forcibly torn from their original tribal structure, transplanted by force, decimated by the conditions under which they suffered, and subject to the tyranny of their owners' wardens. The prisons of First World countries are paradises in comparison. These diminished, isolated individuals were caught up in insurrections, which, if they succeeded, allowed them to escape. To remain free, they had to remain isolated and rootless. How could they manage the ecologic environment that gave them sustenance? They had lost their traditional culture, the techniques of their ancient tribes. They were familiar only with the ways of the pre-capitalist *Raubwirtschaft* of their old masters and their caretakers. Their shifting agriculture, like the traditional, makes use of the forest fallow, the slash and burn, as its first step in the agricultural cycle. But that is all: the rest, all of it, is a veritable perversion of the forest fallow agrarian system. The land is simply abandoned, like an exhausted mine, at the end of the agricultural cycle. The resemblance between agribusiness and this type of shifting agriculture is striking: they are two expressions of *Raubwirtschaft*, of a *pillage economy*, which some Latin Americans call *economía de saqueo*. The diamond placers of Rio S. Antonio, Bahia, give an excellent example of it (Plate 41, p. 182). In both cases, the impediment that prevents the proper management of Nature is mental: the greed of speculative gain here, technical ignorance there. The pillage, in both cases, takes place owing to the political conditions, here owing to a compromise with conscience, there owing to the absence of a decent social structure.

So we again recognize what we noted in Chapter 7: the *importance of the political factor* in the development or management of the ecologic environment. In this connection there is another point, that in all countries, but in various degrees, political decisions are made under the double influence of the political technostructure and the pressure of public opinion, more or less efficiently organized to satisfy various material and existential interests. (We give 'existential' a special meaning: everything that deals with the quality of life, medial conditions of existence, recreation, and all kinds of amenities.) American lobbyists are a good example, which has the merit of frankness, but which is absolutely unofficial; the same becomes clearly visible in the USSR about the reform of the economy, to say nothing of Japan, the countries of western Europe and those of the Third World.

This foreword was necessary, as professionals who have to come up with rural development or management proposals have to avoid many pitfalls, make their way through a veritable minefield. They should be aware of it, if they want to stay alive and prevent the burial of their proposals. This situation has to be faced at the beginning of the work, that of the posing of problems.

POSING THE PROBLEMS

The trigger that puts into motion development or management studies of the ecologic environment is nearly always political, governmental or the pressure of a movement of public opinion. Although quite desirable, the initiative seldom comes from scientists; it is not that they necessarily lack the motivation, but their independence being generally suspect, their ambitions are carefully thwarted. Research is therefore determined in relation to an *objective*, which may vary a great deal depending upon the case. Those that concern us most frequently are first, the struggle against calamities that menace human life in a relatively large area; for example, the case of desertification in west-central Mauritania, where the growth and even the maintenance of the capital Nouakchott is threatened by an invasion of dunes that have been reactivated by a drought of almost thirty years. The second objective is a better utilization of certain natural resources: especially land and water. This requires the following considerations.

1 Improve the water resources in one or several river basins, such as of the Fouta Djalon, in Guinea, according to a decision of the Chiefs of State of the Organization of African Unity (OAU). The object of this programme, established under the aegis of the United Nations and with their financial support, was to permit, thanks to the construction of hydraulic

engineering works in the headwater area of the highland, a better utilization of the water of its rivers, especially in Mali and Senegal. It was the *first time ever* that politicians at the highest level had taken into account the interdependence of the various parts of a river basin and expressed their desire that the developments be profitable to the peoples upstream as well as downstream. Both the ethical and technical originality of this decision should be appreciated when we think back, for example, to the mechanism of salinization of the valleys of the desert coast of Peru. It may be worth recalling that the improvement of the water resources at a particular point of a river basin consists in regularizing the flow of water (decreasing flood crests, raising low water levels), reducing the transport of solids (thereby increasing the stability of the river bed) and of dissolved materials (to decrease the salinization or alkalinization of the land).

2 Augment the agro-sylvo-pastoral production by means of a land use that is closer to the optimum defined by agronomists (*sensu lato*: without forgetting animal specialists and foresters). It goes without saying that this increase in production should not be a short-lived forward leap, in the sense of the 'leap forward' of the 'Cultural Revolution' (Quotation marks are indispensable as long as these official expressions are untrue: they indicate that we do not answer for them, far from it . . .) or that of a glacial surge. It should be based on ingenious developments and management skills that assure it a durable character: a new, more highly performing, steady state should be introduced, which implies not only the preservation of the natural resources but also their improved exploitation. We have shown in previous chapters that this is not a simple matter because of the complexities of the interactions that determine the dynamics of the natural environment.

3 Determine the local conditions for the establishment of new, previously chosen, ways of using the natural resources. For example, it could be the introduction of cattle-raising using various regional resources, perhaps in the form of a more or less complex transhumance, such as existed in the western Sahel before the Drought (referring to the long, serious drought afflicting the Sahel since the late 1960s) or, what happens more frequently, the establishment of irrigated perimeters, which should be adjusted to their ecodynamic framework to optimize the utilization of the land and the water and assure a steady state excluding a degradation by hydromorphism, salinization, alkalinization, etc. Such operations represent one aspect of the optimization and utilization of land and water resources in the framework of a change in land use. They, may, however, be introduced independently of such a change or have only slight or very general ties to land use in a very much larger area.

Such planning precedes the *preliminary projects*. As there is in the technical-administrative vocabulary no specific term to designate it, we shall propose the expression *preliminary* or *orientation studies*. A very recent example will show the difference between the two. When Tricart was invited by the Mauritanian government in November 1988 to evaluate the methods being applied in the framework of the Green Belt Programme of Nouakchott, his hosts hoped that he would prepare a preliminary project to fight the desertification going on across the whole of the west-centre of Mauritania, from approximately the latitude of Cape Temeris to the capital, some 160 km. This was based on a mistaken appreciation of the methodology of ecodynamic studies as related to the management of the natural environment: it would have implied an approach proceeding from the particular to the general. But the very heterogeneity – anisotropy of physicists – of the region precluded such an approach. A generalization is made from a number of representative samples by interpolation, the same procedure that is used in remote sensing and which consists of selecting, from previous knowledge, a number of 'training sites' that are processed by trial and error until a procedure for each one is found that optimizes the objects that we seek to know. To infer from a single object, the Green Belt of Nouakchott, the action to be applied to the entire, much larger and more complex, area amounted to tracing a curve by extrapolation from a single point. It is not because some economists proceed that way, with a success familiar to everybody, that the method is to be recommended. The approach followed to create the Green Belt of Nouakchott was found to be excellent (as we have shown on p. 187). But even under very favourable circumstances (which are exceptional) such a methodological error was unthinkable. Not only would it have resulted in a very serious failure, but also the adviser would have been unworthy of the confidence of the government.

A field reconnaissance had been anticipated and

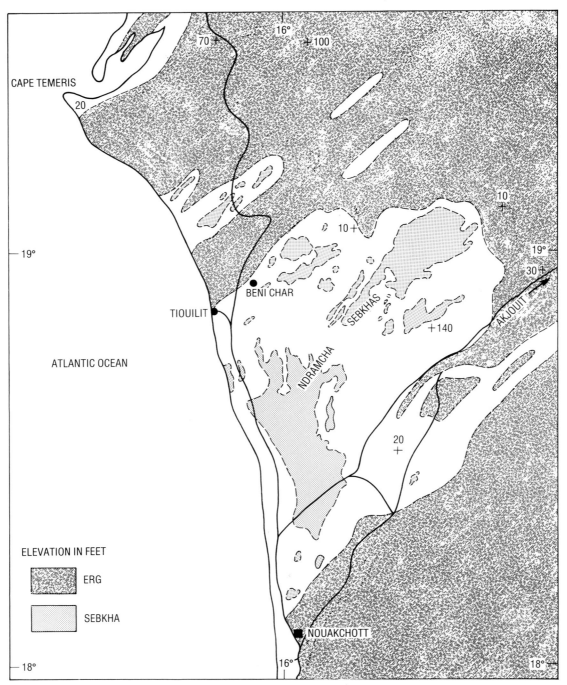

Figure 24. Mauritania, location map (base from Operational Navigation Chart, 1:1,000,000 1973, revised 1979).

Plates 49–52 The problem of the 'Green Belt' of Nouakchott
Ph. JT CDXIX-5 cn. Active 'elb' (alignment of barkhans) about 15 km north-east of Nouakchott (suburb
of Toujounine). The migrating sand comes from old, stabilized dunes that have been reactivated: the
sand, of different colours, appears in different tones of grey. In the foreground, coquina deposits of the
Nouakchottian Gulf (of about 5,000 BP). A small *Balanites aegyptiaca*, in the middle ground, is the only
surviving plant where in 1956 grew an open acacia woodland in a grassy pasture.

remarkably well prepared by Tricart's hosts,
proving that they were good field men. The
excursion revealed the area to be extraordinary
complex, practically uninhabited, difficult to cross,
totally devoid of water, and that the available
medium-scale map had only a 'purely accidental
resemblance' with reality, as the producers of
certain films take the precaution of warning the
public. The intellectual integrity and honesty of his
partners enabled Tricart, with supporting
arguments to convince them that to immediately
start with a preliminary project was out of the
question; a painful reality that was nevertheless
accepted. The well-conceived Nouakchott Green
Belt had to be continued and extended but
necessitated funds, which can come only from
abroad.

   In 1954 Tricart had aired the idea of cutting a
channel through a sand bar that plugged an old
Senegal River outlet, in the north of its delta, to
flood a number of salt flats (sebkhas) with 'free'
Atlantic water in order to prevent the deflation of

tiny salt crystals that are transported aloft by the
trade wind to settle on the delta, salinizing its soils.
This idea, somehow, had reached the ears of the
Mauritanian workers, who were thinking of
applying it to the Ndramcha sebkhas NNE of
Nouakchott. The idea was appealing, as in 1954,
and even more so because of the complete
desertification caused by the drought. The fishing
village of Tiouilit has no water at all; it has to be
brought in from Nouakchott by truck across a dirt
road, a section of which crosses the clay surface of
a sebkha that floods when spring tides coincide with
a high, directly onshore swell. The backshore then
is under attack and the sea water streams into that
and other sebkhas. It is tempting to regularize
these inflows to keep the sebkhas flooded. But all
this is only an 'idea'. Honesty requires a listing of
the problems involved in the realization of such a
project and an examination of how they may be
overcome. Furthermore, what exactly are the
advantages of such a scheme? A confrontation, a
balance of the pros and cons would be the object of

a later stage, that of making a preliminary project and, later still, of a feasibility study based on cost–benefit calculations.

The adopted 'strategy' was first, to continue work on the Nouakchott Green Belt (detailed in Chapter 6) not only because of the immediate threat to the city, but also because the objective of the works planned to the north and north-east can only ease the realization of the Green Belt and speed up the task of establishing the plant succession planned by the experimental station. The second part was to develop as rapidly as possible a study programme, eventually leading to the preparation of a preliminary development project of the west-centre of Mauritania, the object of which is to counteract its desertification and develop its resources. But for an unexpected non-scientific problem, these studies should be finished within three years. Preparation of the preliminary project is to be started before their completion, and, given the availability of sufficient data, finished a few months later. Making the studies within the administrative framework of a board is

recommended, as it facilitates the raising of funds from various sources.

The acquisition of indispensable data

First, configuration and extent of the closed depressions. Recourse to remote sensing is indispensable in the absence of decent maps. Relief is minor, as confirmed by field reconnaissance. The recordings can therefore be assembled into uncontrolled mosaics, devoid of troublesome distortions. This speeds up and reduces the costs of the orientation studies. Later, during the preparation of the preliminary project, the use of the remote-sensing recordings must be improved through acquisition of more costly geometrically rectified data. at least in part numerically processed. In that way expenses are spread out, increasing toward the realization of the project. If for one reason or another the project has to be abandoned, expenses will have been minimal at the time of this decision. *The outlay will be as much as*

Plate 50 Ph. JT CDXVIII-6 cn. Assault of the moving sand on Nouakchott. In the background, invasion of an active erg forced the construction of the buildings of the staff of the SMAR (Société Mauritanienne d'Assurances et Réassurances) to be abandoned. In the foreground, along the side of an important street on the town's margin, moving sands compelled the abandonment of middle-class dwellings under construction. The garage roof in the picture was originally 3 m above ground.

Plate 51 Ph. JT CDXVIII-3 cn. First stage of dune stabilization on the outskirts of Nouakchott, 300 m from the newly built Centre des Congrès. Active dunes are planted with euphorb branches, which offer at least a mechanical obstacle to drifting sand. With sufficient rain they sprout and eventually will form a living hedge. Acacias are planted in the enclosed spaces to try to reconstitute the original vegetation, i.e. an open woodland of acacias with a ground cover of grasses (*Cenchrus biflorus* mostly), formerly used as pasture. Refer to the Engineer Abby Ould Boulabatt for scale.

possible proportional to the expenses during the various steps of the project. *This is in general a desirable procedure.* A planimetric sketch of the configuration and extent of the closed depressions thus is made by using SPOT recordings, enlarged to the scale of 1:50,000. The sketch will be completed with other data (to be indicated below).

Second, it is useless to try to extract altimetric data from SPOT panchromatic recordings by photogrammetrically exploiting their stereoscopic overlap, as differences in elevation are too small, slopes too gentle, and trigonometric bench-marks entirely wanting. Topographic mapping, therefore, must be considered. This slow, painstaking work requires time and funds. The importance of the data requires that they be undertaken as soon as possible. They can be integrated into the general geodetic programme of the Islamic Republic of Mauritania, which was about to get started. Already a precise levelling had been done during the execution, for mining purposes, of the Nouadhibou-F'Dérick railway project. To integrate the geodesic points of the railway into the country's

triangulation network, it is necessary to cross our region. That several north–south transects through the west-centre of Mauritania, especially through the Ndramcha sebkhas, be made was therefore requested during the orientation phase of our studies. One of them is to follow approximately the coastal road, the others to be located further inland, eventually to reach the Nouakchott–Akjoujt road, located well south of the sebkhas, on the coquinas of an ancient Nouakchottian gulf. (According to geological practice, this 'stage' carries the name of the locality where it was first observed: the Nouakchottian is dated approximately 5,000 years BP.) During the phase of the preliminary project these topographic profiles will enable the planimetric correction of the errors made in the making of the uncontrolled mosaic, thus producing a controlled mosaic, a good topographic base for the carrying out of the eventual engineering works. The profiles will permit the determination of the extent of the closed depressions whose bottom lies below the highest sea level and which can therefore be directly or indirectly flooded (by digging channels into the thresholds that separate them from basins situated below mean sea level). The configuration of the closed depressions will then be known with a precision sufficient for the elaboration of the preliminary project. The thresholds interrupting the continuity of the sebkha system will have been identified, their locations, extent and approximate elevation made known. These topographic characteristics are completed by complementary field-work, tied in with earlier field-work, during the elaboration of the *project*. In this case, too, the rule of proportionality between cost and the stakes involved is respected.

Third, topographic levelling is a 'burdensome' operation: it will take many, many weeks during which it will be necessary to organize shuttles of vehicles to supply the topographers with food, water and fuel. The corresponding costs must therefore be offset as much as possible by using the logistics to make observations of the natural environment, to systematically sample its different aspects: geomorphic phenomena, surficial formations, hydrological conditions, vegetation and climatic-ecologic observations (relative humidity, wind, actual temperature and wind speed at ground level, temperature in the surficial soil and at several levels above it, in the free air and in the vegetation, at least at the topographers' camp sites and at some points not to distant from them. Bore holes, several metres deep, will be made with manual or powered soil augers along the topographic profiles and, as much as possible, at some distance on either side. This will transform the profiles into *ecogeographic transects*. The bore holes and appurtenant observations will be made on as large a number of units of physiognomic types as possible. Work will centre on the following.

1 Determination of soil moisture (taking soil samples, protected from desiccation, and sent to the laboratory in Nouakchott) and, occasionally, of the level of appearance of water in the bore hole.

Plate 52 Ph. JT CDXVIII-8 cn. A higher stage of revegetalization at Ten Souelim Experimental Station, on the eastern edge of Nouakchott. Eng. Abby is guiding J. Tricart during a visit. *Arenaria pyrotecnica* (foreground) was planted in October 1987. Although appetizing to cattle, it is not eaten by locusts, so that it remained intact during the locust ravage of 10 October 1988 (photograph was taken in November 1988). A hedge of *Euphorbia balsamifera* near Eng. Abby has taken root as 1988 was rather humid. The dark colour of the sand in the foreground at the foot of well developed *Arenaria* sp. is caused by dead locusts.

2 Taking of water samples, on the surface or in bore holes, to determine, in the laboratory, the pH and the content and kind of dissolved ions.

3 Identification of active morphogenic processes at the time of observation and those that have recently 99 left recognizable traces; taking of samples for laboratory sedimentological study and to confirm the nature of the processes and their intensity, if possible.

4 Determination of the stratigraphic succession of the surficial formations in the various physiognomic units of the natural environment by means of the recordings of the bore hole sections and the taking of samples of each of the strata, to be studied in the laboratory.

5 Phytogeographic characterization of the various plant associations, identification of insects and other creatures parasitizing them, sheltering in them, or consuming them (determination of biocoenoses, later to be related to the environment, the 'biotope').

6 Recording of relict hydromorphological features produced by past climatic events: traces of flooding, desiccation, splash erosion, deflation/aeolian deposition (a proof of the absence or cessation of flooding), to be combined with sampling to determine past morphogenic processes.

7 Taking aerosol samples near base camps, separating, as much as is feasible, those deposited at night from those deposited during daytime. The climatic data should be recorded always in the same vicinity as these samples, so that they may be confronted with their characteristics.

The observations along transects are similar to those practised by the school of E. Neef in the former GDR. If they can be made under good conditions, it would be desirable to consider extending them over a period exceeding that required for the realization of the topographic surveys. The periodicity of visits to specific points will then have to be determined in the light of the acquired experience and as a function of their accessibility, ecogeographic importance, and, lastly, to what scientific, technical and financial extent certain stations can be equipped with recording instruments.

The acquired data will then serve as training sites for the exploitation of the remotely sensed recordings, those of SPOT as they correspond to what will be observed in the field and, later, by going back perhaps fifteen years, to a diachronic processing of SPOT and earlier LANDSAT

recordings. An ecogeographic synthesis, now possible, will be shown cartographically on SPOT mosaics. How much processing of the remotely sensed data will be necessary will be decided after the acquisition of the data gathered along the transects: if limited to optical methods, panchromatic or false colour, a combination of these, or various types of numerical processing. And, of course, we still apply the rule of the proportionality of what is at stake. The other types of data to be gathered or determined have a more sectoral character, but are not less important because of it.

Fourth, the determination of regional oceanologic and climatic data is indispensable for the preparation of the preliminary project and, later, the project, and, last but not least, the management of the developments that will have been realized – if everything goes well, of course.

Oceanographic observations should be made, also for the development of the fishing industry, at Tiouilit or near the breach of the backshore, some 20 km to the south: winds and swell (velocity and direction of both) and tidal ranges. (This development has been decided: a refrigerated warehouse was under construction at Tiouilit in November 1988.) Possibly part of these data are already available, established years ago. They should be verified and completed by new installations, so that they can be used for the preparation of the preliminary project.

Standard weather stations should be established at Tiouilit and elsewhere, where also wind, relative humidity, and evaporation on a free water surface (Colorado tank) can be determined for the preparation of the project; the sooner the better, in order to increase the length of the observations. Nevertheless, their distribution must be based on the principles set forth in connection with hydromorphological maps: the sites should be as representative as possible of the ecogeographic units, which will be determined only during the course of the development of the research programme. Particular attention should be paid, in this uninhabited region, to the logistic possibilities of periodic retrieval of data and fully automatic instrumentation. The data to be gathered to determine the balance of swinging water tables are important for the use and management of the depressions that would be artificially flooded.

Fifth, there are good indications that the Nouakchottian transgression which extended far inland in a NE direction N of Nouakchott was guided by the presence of a SW–NE tectonic trough that would have functioned at least until the

Nouakchottian. The determination of the stratigraphic sequence along the planned transects and topographic profiles should provide some information in this regard and, perhaps, indications of its continued subsidence. The practical importance of these phenomena is obvious. They will favour the submergence of the potentially floodable sebkhas located in it, reduce the costs per km^2 of the work to be performed, and help the maintenance of the artificial lagoons. On the other hand, these tectonics also pose a problem. On the northern fringe of the sebkhas, ENE of Tiouilit, a Mauritanian firm has discovered an aquifer of very pure water, which is bottled and distributed on the national market in spite of major transportation problems when, from time to time, the road is flooded and sea water streams into the sebkhas. The aquifer, given the aridity of the climate and the purity of the water, is almost certainly fossil, that is inherited from a more or less remote and humid past when fresh water was able to infiltrate into it. Such waters are known from many locations in the midst of the Sahara Desert (Hassi Messaoud, Algeria; Libya). Therefore, inquiries should be made at the water company: what is the extent of the aquifer, what stratigraphical and structural information is it willing to supply in connection with it? Indeed, an artificial flooding of the sebkhas should under no circumstances cause the pollution of the aquifer by infiltration of brackish or hypersaline water, destroying its usefulness.

Sixth, research should also direct its attention to a specific, key point: the possibility of developing a sluiceway to the Ndramcha sebkhas, some 20 km south of Tiouilit. A boring operation several metres deep is necessary to ascertain its feasibility. A first step is to make a dozen or so borings in the breach used by the last oceanic overflows immediately behind the backshore and up to 1 km inland. There is, apparently, no surficial evidence that might reveal the kind and disposition of the subsurface materials. Somewhat north of the breach there are scattered fragments of beach rock. Were they part of a continuous buried layer? What is its thickness? If such a layer exists, the conditions of excavating an eventual sluiceway will be affected. If it is extremely resistant, which is not uncommon, it will have to be dynamited. On the other hand, it may serve as a good base for engineering works such as a sluice gate or jetties. Depending on the results of exploratory drilling, a complementary drilling programme will have to be undertaken (number, depth and location of additional drill-holes). This work is already part of the preparation of the preliminary project. With the results the highest

and modal sea water admission level can be determined, which, with use of the topographic profiles and SPOT imagery, will give some idea as to the extent of the depressions that can be gravity flooded. In the case of a positive decision, the information can be completed to prepare a preliminary project or, better, a series of preliminary projects with a number of variants.

The carrying out of the study programme, if it is adopted, would associate specialized Mauritanian and foreign personnel. Mauritanian personnel should participate as much as possible in teamwork with foreigners working in specific domains in which they have international experience. The policy of the government is to train its own personnel so that it can rely as much as possible on its own people. We agree with this, as it corresponds to our own convictions. Experience has convinced us that development has a nationalistic flavour (rather than 'xenophobic': xenophobia, like racism, is impoverishing, paralysing and destructive, as is evident in Africa and the Middle East). Stages abroad are foreseen for this personnel to enable its individuals to complete their training and widen their vision of the problems. Unfortunately, Mauritania is a small and poor country, presently undergoing severe ethnic problems. It lacks sufficiently trained people to respond to urgently needed tasks: recruiting will be difficult and insufficient. In any case, regardless of the task, participants should not be overworked in crash courses.

Let us now examine what is at stake: what can be expected at the end of the development?

Benefits that can reasonably be expected from the planned development

The main result expected by the Mauritanian Government is the one J. Tricart had hoped for by proposing (in 1954) the artificial opening of an old mouth of the Senegal River (les 'Maringouins') in order to flood the contiguous sebkhas located at the latitude of Keur Macène, at the southern extremity of the Mauritanian Aftout es Sahéli: to eliminate the source of salt dust deflation by the trade wind and, as a result, the settling of the salt in areas situated downwind of the sebkhas. This objective, of course, is still valid and has a priority rating, as it was the initial idea of the whole plan, decided upon by the politicians. It has, however, been re-examined.

Effects on the regional ecologic conditions

We have noted, first in the field and later in discussions with our Mauritanian partners, that a permanent flooding of the sebkhas would have the following ecologic consequences.

First, it would stop deflation on flooded depressions and the formation of aerosols. To make certain this effect is maximum, a sluice-gate should be constructed in the sluiceway. At specified times, to be determined, it would be opened and closed, respectively, at incoming and outgoing tides. It thus would be closed at all oceanic levels below that of the water introduced into the system behind the sluice-gate, which would function like a thermometer with a maximum indicator. In so far as evaporation would lower the water level in the system, oceanic water would automatically be introduced as soon as sea level is high enough to permit it. In that way the surface of the depressions excluded from deflation would be maximal.

Second, the great distance the aerosols migrate when the wind blows strongly enough from a constant direction, as is the case of the trade wind during practically the entire period from November to May/June in the west-centre of Mauritania, allows the tiny salt crystals to be spread at least as far as Nouakchott. During the cool season the high daily thermal range of the dry air causes the particles to absorb moisture during the night, weighing them down and causing their sedimentation. Samples of the accumulated salt have been gathered by Saleh Ould Merzoug, professor at the University and one of our partners: an excellent initiative, which must be continued. If these aerosols, as is probable, contain sodium chloride, and even if they are mainly composed of gypsum, they are a high ecological constraint. (Gypsum, in abundance, was identified in Strasbourg by A. Gobert in all sebkha samples brought back by J. Tricart.) They limit the number of species that can be tested in the experimental station and eventually grown in the Green Belt. They also increase the plants' need for water, which, of course, is particularly important in this arid climate and the present drought. The object of a number of experiments carried out by Eng. Abby is to determine a plant's minimum water need. The salt also slows plant growth. All these things indicate that the elimination of salt migration, by submergence of the sebkhas, would have indirect beneficial effects on the Green Belt. Accordingly there is no reason to interrupt the well-conceived Green Belt programme while preliminary research is being carried on, for two or three years, in the west-centre of Mauritania.

Creation of new resources owing to the flooding of the sebkhas

Tamarisks, regardless of salinity, do well along sebkha shores that are either permanently or periodically flooded with short interruptions. (Specialized foresters have such data at their disposal, but they should be related to the climatic and hydrologic conditions characteristic of the region.) Their water uptake is of the phreatophytic type, so that the width of the fringe of friable materials on which they grow is all the wider as the slope is gentle and the circulation of ground water extensive. Planting tamarisks is no problem, all that is needed is supervised unskilled labour. Tamarisks have a threefold advantage: they humidify the air by transpiration, which is beneficial to other plants and may be the beginning of new biocoenoses; they rapidly produce a hardwood, excellent as firewood or for making charcoal, in demand at Nouakchott, easier to transport than wood, and which can be substituted for expensive imported bottled methane gas. Lastly, tamarisks, thickset at ground level and with a dense root system, are excellent phytostabilizers. The shores of flooded sebkhas can therefore become productive while at the same time extending the area subtracted from the action of the wind.

Another resource, aquaculture, could be created. A specialist in this matter should be called in, as the problem, like all ecological problems, is complex. Schematically, it may be conceived that, if the engineering works at the access channel are properly designed and operated, the waters immediately inland from them will have approximately the same salinity as the oceanic water on the other side. Temperature, however, will be different because of the confinement and shallow depth of the artificial water body. Edible fish, faced with disappearance because of the taste of the well-to-do public, could be raised here; giant shrimp would be a possibility. This would require special installations; investments may be high, with a recourse to specialized personnel, but these could eventually be trained locally, and export of the seafood would be a source of foreign currency. A technical study followed by an economic one are necessary before making a decision, which will have repercussions on the engineering works. Away from the sluiceway the combined effects of evaporation and dissolution of the salt floor by the water of the basins may be expected to increase the concentration of dissolved salts and the spectrum of their composition. This is all that can be said at the present time. The object of part of the proposed studies (nature of the sediments, composition and strength of the solutions soaking the sediments) is to improve our knowledge of these questions. The abundance of gypsum, mined at one location, suggests the water will be rich in that mineral, which (according to specialists) will severely limit the possibilities of aquaculture, as fish tolerating gypsum belong to low-rated, non-marketable species. They might, at the most, be raised on a family basis for regional consumption (Nouakchott).

Schemes conducive to economic and other activities

Aquaculture is also part of this rubric, which is proof of the artificial character of classifications: they should not be taken too literally. Other developments can be the object of technical studies prior to deciding whether they merit being considered during the preparation of preliminary projects.

The first development would be the construction of locks in the sluiceway. If prolonged by a dredged channel and jetties, they would permit the installation of a fishing port in the calm waters on the landward side of the locks. This might be an important event in the development of the fishing industry of the region. At present the fishing craft at Tiouilit are winched on to the beach upon returning from a fishing journey. Most fishermen at Tiouilit (in November 1988) were Senegalese Wolof, which does not help the political dimension of the problem, considering the recent ethnic conflicts between Senegal and Mauritania.

Second, salt evaporators could be developed further into the interior, where the salt content of the water would rise due to evaporation. They would permit to economies in foreign currency, which presently finances about 30,000–40,000 tons of imported salt. The saltworks would provide employment and inexpensive salt to Nouakchott and on location, which would favour a fishing industry.

Third, a bridge would have to be constructed across the sluiceway if the road to the south is improved, which would allow the transit of vehicles, including the water bottle trucks of Beni Char. A bridge is part of the problem of the entire coastal road between Nouakchott and Nouadhibou, the former Port Etienne. It is so bad that, for much of its length, light vehicles prefer to use the beach at low tide.

Fourth, H. Faure has drawn our attention to another possibility, that of flooding the Ndramcha sebkhas for mining purposes, to extract boron, magnesium and other elements from the brines: this idea should be pursued. Our plan considered using the most concentrated brines in areas furthest removed from the ocean to extract these elements and bromine and, also, rare earth metals, prized in the electronics industry and of high commercial value. To realize this idea, the planning of small hypersaline evaporation basins in emerged locations should be included in the preliminary project. Stepped basins into which the water would be pumped by windmills would be a possibility. Eng. Abby is already in charge of finding good, reliable windmills that can be maintained by local blacksmiths. This example is extremely complex in many respects, including the near absence of available data and accessibility problems presented by the terrain. Nevertheless, it is a good example in so far as earnest political backing and the presence of highly motivated, competent, if insufficient, local specialists are concerned. The project also benefits from a disinterested foreign aid, an important part of which, provided by the Lutheran Foundation and the Netherlands government, is exclusively reserved for financing the preliminary studies. The French government, for its part, has a CAMPUS programme which can be used to train research staff at an overseas university for a maximum of three years. It can be financed by the Ministère de la Coopération if a programme of investigation with French university help is proposed by the foreign partner and is deemed important by its government for the development of the country. There are other possibilities of funding. The French Ministries of Foreign Affairs and Coopération are associated with the Ministère de la Recherche et de la Technologie for funding remote sensing research of development programmes. Accordingly, a request has been made by the Centre de Géographie Appliquée (CGA) and the Centre d'Etudes et de Recherches Eco-géographiques (CEREG-UA 95 CNRS) for a research project in Mauritania. Complete mutual trust is another important matter, as J. Tricart experienced in Nouakchott, where his hosts, without any restrictions, made available to him all archival information, including manuscript notes. However, it is also fair to note that in spite of the methodical gathering of references on index cards over a period of 30 years and of financial aid to Nouakchott, certain references remained unknown to him during the development of the research programme. An exhaustive bibliography remains wishful thinking.

The most delicate task facing an expert planner, according to our experience, is posing the problems and preparing the preliminary study programme. For this reason, we have given it an important place in this book. We shall now, more briefly, examine the next steps in the application of the approach we are proposing.

PRELIMINARY PROJECTS, MULTIPLE OPTIONS

First, a problem of terminology. Traditionally, the French have distinguished three different levels of approach in country planning:

1 *Preliminary studies*, or orientation studies, as described above.
2 *Preliminary projects*, which, based upon a sufficient knowledge of the posed problems, present the possible solutions (alternatives).
3 The *projects*, which transform a preliminary project chosen by the decision-maker into a definite plan with exact estimation of costs.

At this point everything is ready for *carrying out* the work. The public organisms then launch their *call for bids*, to which contractors ready to undertake the assignments reply. Usually, the practice of financiers is to choose the one with the lowest, least specific bid. Of course, guarantees should be provided and one should be aware of certain cost revision clauses in the contract. In fact, a strict bureaucratic application of these principles not infrequently results in higher costs, the lowest bidder, using revision clauses, being, finally, more expensive than its eliminated competitors. Apparently advantageous to the state, the system, in fact, does not in the least prevent agreements between firms, which protect their interests and their profits. The business profession has its ways.

Although in 1989 the French celebrated the bicentenary of the Revolution, which theoretically abolished all privileges, some public servants continue to profit legally from such privileges: the paymasters of the Treasury, which handle the public funds, receive a percentage of the business transactions. The same is true of the engineers of the old 'Ponts et Chaussées', (now 'Equipement') and of the Heads of the Departmental services of the Génie Rural, who receive from the public funds they handle a certain percentage on the amount of work carried out under their responsibility. To ask

them to reduce costs is useless. Such feudal survivals discourage rational projects at minimum costs. The importance of these emoluments depends on the personality, ethics and personal ambition of each engineer. The work to be done is curtailed in proportion to the deductions, as the available credit is fixed. There is a direct relationship between the statutes of the administration and the environment to be developed.

Another irritant, although less consequential, is that the international organisms of the United Nations use the term 'project' to designate the series of operations ranging from the preliminary studies to the carrying out of the project, and even to the follow-up of the completed work. Each operation keeps the same coded identification, which includes the operation itself, the year of its inception, and the name of the country in which it is to be realized. This is convenient from the administrative point of view. But if, in English, a 'project' may be an undertaking (e.g. a housing project), the French 'projet' is *only* a proposal to do something in the future. It may be cancelled, but if adopted and its execution has become a reality, it becomes a 'programme', a word common to both languages. This distinction, sadly, is overlooked by UN translators, who (translating lazily) transcribe 'project' into 'projet'. An ironic person might conclude that these international organizations are incapable of finishing what they plan and only dream. Fortunately, of course, this is seldom the case. Conclusion: such bungling in UN reports is to be deplored. As for us, we shall use the term 'project' in its narrow sense, equivalent to the more precise French *projet*.

A clear distinction between the preliminary studies and the preliminary project is not possible. The posing of development problems as a function of a definite goal set by the decision-maker indeed imperceptibly leads to the creation of preliminary projects as the problems become clearer thanks to an ever increasing knowledge of the study area. The Mauritanian example makes this perfectly clear. Although, at the time of writing, we are still at the very beginning of this project, we had to proceed to matters to be dealt with in the preliminary project. This by no means reflects an intellectual unruliness, quite the opposite: it is the double consequence of the very nature of reality as we perceive it and of recourse to a systems approach, by essence dynamic. But to embark on a discussion of formal logic would be sterile at this juncture, perhaps even negative. More useful is to proceed to another, more fundamental, aspect.

We shall now consider how to realize the integration of the various aspects of the environment that a planned development is going to modify. We have already approached this problem previously, but its importance now requires a more systematic examination in order to clarify the operational aspect of the studies. We have explained the drawbacks of the 'ecologic' approach of McHarg and its French adaptation by Falque (Chapter 7). We have experienced them ourselves when we perfected the making of hydromorphological maps. These, however, deal with only one *component* of the environment, rather than with the environment itself, which is much more complex, or, in other words, with a specific subsystem to be integrated into the system 'natural environment'. McHarg's matrices are binary correlations, and that only. They can be multiplied, but the storage capacity of the computer is quickly saturated. Because of their very nature, the computer can no more than reproduce the binary correlations put into it, nothing more. As the Americans say: 'garbage in, garbage out' (GI/GO). Let us also recall the heterogeneous character of these correlations: to give them a value in points is necessarily subjective and, from a logical point of view, constitutes, a veritable *camouflage*, a fraudulent merchandise: the illusion, and only the illusion, of quantification of their numerical value. A perilous operation, as all swindles, whose victims are always honest people! All tinkering – the imagination can think of many and clever ones – is of no avail. This approach is a blind alley, to be avoided. *Integration should not follow research, it should be done during the course of it*, be an aspect, a primordial aspect, of it at all stages, but mainly during the posing of problems and the making of the preliminary projects. Its role diminishes with the making of the projects themselves, as the comparing of options, the making of choices, is over and the time of translating the ideas into actions has come.

The procedure is dialectical: from the particular to the general, and returning from the general to the particular. In either direction there are forks and more forks: they should be followed but not systematically to the end, for in that case one would be quickly lost in a maze of subdivisions dealing with lesser and lesser objects of increasingly doubtful significance. Intellectually, perfectionism is sterile in so far as it is not limited. But, of course, there is no, and there cannot be, a recipe that codifies the way, indicating where to stop. It depends on what is being studied, on the person studying it and on his or her intuition and flair, which comes with experience, contacts, and open and receptive exchanges of ideas.

Here is an example derived from our Mauritania study. Tricart is totally ignorant of aquaculture: his personal experience is limited to choosing between the artificially bred salmon of supermarkets and the equally good salmon of Pacific Ocean provenance, twice as expensive. The gastronomic cost–benefit ratio is much better for the locally bred. He has, in Mauritania itself, had the idea of a possible integration of aquaculture and a flooding of the Ndramcha: the idea grew owing to his previous training as a sedimentologist and Quaternarist. Indeed, the enormous quantity of Nouakchottian *Arca senilis* accumulated over some 2,000 years and now forming extensive shell banks, specifically in the ancient SW–NE gulf, the locus of the sebkhas, is an indication of an *extraordinary high biological productivity*. Let us not go overboard and attempt to reintroduce *Arca senilis* although these shell remains are a godsend for the construction of roads, air strips, concrete buildings, and all uses requiring gravel. But the multitude of *Arca senilis* poses a palaeo-ecological problem. There is no reason to believe that the climate then was very different from now; solar radiation was much the same. Then as now, the interior was formed by quartzose sandy materials poor in nutrients. The ocean, however, thanks to upwelling of cold water in association with the Canaries Current introduces important quantities of nutrients along the shore. This in all likelihood also occurred in the recent geological past. Furthermore, the *Arca senilis* of the palaeogulf indicate waters whose salinity was an ecologic constraint: had this not been the case, there would have been, according to ecological theory, a greater variety of species. From all this we can conclude that under conditions not very different from the present these molluscs were able to prosper in this tectonic gulf, which implies an important primary production of phytoplankton. It is reasonable to assume that a flooding of the sebkhas by oceanic water could permit an important development of phytoplankton, which could be used to feed introduced marine creatures and form the basis of an aquaculture. This is the extent of the personal competence of Tricart, who is also equipped with a knowledge of general ecology. It is necessary to find somebody who can fill the gap, who has connections with other specialists, and who also has the same methodological attitude, without which it is difficult to work together. This person is F. Doumenge, a colleague of the Editorial Board of the *Annales de Géographie*, former President of ORSTOM (Office de la Recherche Scientifique et Technique pour les Pays d'Outre-Mer), and recently nominated to the management of the Institut Océanographique of Monaco. He agreed to take part in the preparation of the preliminary projects at the call of the Mauritanian Government.

Integration is realized in the following form at the level of the preparation of the preliminary projects.

First, by a division of labour, for which aquaculture provides a good example. A specific subsystem of the development, it can be studied only by keen specialists. To apply their expertise they need a good knowledge of the ecologic environment. We should, therefore, proceed at two successive levels: the idea having appeared, here, at the earlier level of the posing of problems, is communicated to a person who has both a knowledge and a direct experience in this particular domain and, moreover, a sufficiently broad vision to integrate the specialized knowledge into the regional whole. This person is Doumenge, who also held the post of Chaire d'Ethologie du Museum d'Histoire Naturelle de Paris, and as President of ORSTOM guided and evaluated many research projects, some of which dealt with aquaculture in tropical lands. If Doumenge can perfectly fulfil this role of subintegrator (integrator of a subsystem), he owes it to his education, experience and intellectual openness. We have proceeded from logical methods (systems integration) to the level of individuals, by essence unique. To find them is not easy: it is a primordial task of the coordinator. It depends on the coordinator's own experience and connections: both increase with time, with age. As the late A. Cailleux once observed: a person becomes a mathematician at age 25, a physicist at 30, and a naturalist much later. We could add an ecologist, a genuine ecologist, even later, and they are finished only when their declining health limits their means.

Second, the composition of the water in the flooded basins determines the kind of sea-life to be raised. This ecological factor determines the economic and financial possibilities: sale price, marketing, therefore income permitting the amortization of the investments and the operation of the aquaculture enterprise. These interdependences of the elements of the subsystem operate on a world scale, on which a country like Mauritania has no influence. The determinants may be qualified as being *imperative*. However, there is a certain margin of flexibility; to situate it at the level of the lowest development costs in the framework of an appeal to international offers is illusory. This margin of freedom is situated at the level of the conception of the developments to be realized and should therefore be taken into account at the time of the making of the preliminary projects. The composition of the water and the surface area to be occupied by water of the best ecological properties for a certain type of aquaculture destined for export depend on not only the balance water input/evaporation but also the nature of the lake's bottom. With regard to the balance water input/evaporation, to modify evaporation is practically impossible, but water input is a function of the design and size of the sluice-gate or locks. Certainly the environment also matters, but if engineers have no power over the range and frequency of the tides, they do determine the dimensions and level of the sluice or locks. It is a matter of costs, which depend, up to a point, on the subsurface materials (foundation, extraction of materials). The ratio of seafood sale price (imperative variable) to the cost of production (as a function of amortization costs and the functioning of the installations) is a variable that can be managed and should be studied as a function of our ecological knowledge concerning the possibilities of aquaculture. With regard to the nature of the lake's bottom, its soluble elements will be dissolved in the water, whose composition and concentration of solutes will be altered. To some extent this parameter can be modified by facilitating the flooding of certain depressions by lowering the thresholds across which the water will penetrate if these depressions do not unfavourably modify the solutes, and, if they do, preventing their flooding by dikes. Also in that case, a cost–benefit study should be made beginning with the ecological requirements of aquaculture and certain environmental characteristics. This is complex, but feasible. Nevertheless, a high degree of precision in matters concerning the natural environment cannot be attained. But, this is no reason to worry: what of prices and their evolution over a period of ten to twenty years, a minimal duration for the amortization of the whole installation?

This short analysis of the aquaculture subsystem justifies that certain studies be made at an early date: the engineering problems of the construction of the sluiceway, the study of the surficial materials, especially of the sebkhas, the oceanology of the shore at the planned access channel, and the climatic measurements, especially evaporation, using Colorado tanks. The climatic and oceanologic measurements should be started as soon as the problems are posed in order to dispose of a minimal duration of observations that can be used in the preparation of preliminary projects. Integration is therefore not only descending – the idea of flooding, of aquaculture, the quality of the water (concentration and kind of solutes) – but also ascending, in opposite direction, concerning the studies to be made. A systems approach indeed is a more effective and elaborate form of the dialectical method.

Third, a final form of integration is necessary. It concerns the conduct of the research itself: integration is practised from the start. Patient bibliographical investigations, always incomplete, even when most conscientious, the processing and interpretation of remote sensing data and aerial photographs, and field observations should, in part, be made by teamwork and be the object of discussions. These range from informing others of references encountered outside of one's own field to the confrontation by all of the different facets of the same objects as each one perceives them. This is an aspect of the dialectic of integration. But because of the very use of the dialectic method, one aspect coexists with its opposite aspect, the other limb of the dialectical contradiction: which requires a sectoral deepening of the observations. This confrontation is approached differently depending upon the discipline, requiring different means and more or less time. The same logistical means (vehicles, camps) can be used and serve research carried on in different areas, as for making bore holes, obtaining climatic or oceanologic data, etc. The importance of logistics is all the greater as the region to be studied is difficult to reach, cross and subsist in. The west-centre of Mauritania is second to none in this regard.

An important point, however, is that the various specialists, when they can work in the same location, require different amounts of time to accomplish their tasks. Much more time is needed to make a phytosociologic survey than to note and sample the succession of strata in a bore hole. To be obliged to depend on the same vehicle causes a loss of time to some, while others work under pressure, which is unsatisfactory. As much as possible, everyone should have his or her own means of transportation, be it on foot, a horse, or a bicycle with broad tyres that can easily be carried over a short distance where it cannot be ridden. This independence in the acquisition of basic data should be combined with discussions in the field, as about documents, in order to realize a progressive, step-by-step integration.

Ideally integration should come about by itself. If it does, it was well done; if insurmountable obstacles arise during discussions, it failed. The process should be repeated by going back to the point of irreconcilability, which may explain the problem. Repeating the observations that caused the divergence, a new problem may be identified that should be resolved. A set-back is thus avoided, had the preliminary project been applied by passing over the difficulty. The difficulty may also result, less seriously, from imperfect observations caused by fatigue or fortuitous circumstances, for example. In that case, one should honestly accept the critique, without misplaced *amour propre* and, better still, make one's own critique. J. Tricart has seen examples in the archives in Nouakchott. This has aroused a profound admiration for the person who did it. It is proof of both honesty and strength of character, indispensable qualities for a group of people to transform itself into a real team – another form of integration, human integration.

SEQUEL AND END: PROJECTS AND FOLLOW-UP

Coordinators of the preliminary studies and the preliminary projects see their role diminish to that of consultant during the preparation of the projects. The transformation into project of what is kept of the preliminary project may be compared to that of a quantity surveyor in public works. The task is to draw plans and to calculate the costs of the corresponding engineering or other works. Intellectually and technically, the operations are similar, whether they concern a dike, a sluice, a plantation, or the establishment of salt evaporators: also reasons to have recourse to the technical vocabulary of public works. It may happen that during the course of this phase engineers responsible for the carrying out of the project raise a question concerning a particular point of the preliminary project. The coordinator must then be able to reply without hesitation, although it may be necessary to consult with a member of the team that elaborated the preliminary project. Meeting with the entire team would mean that the preliminary project was not properly conceived. Consultations should be possible, easy and rapid, and should be included in the cost estimate presented when the bid for carrying out the project is submitted. If not, the firm will do everything in its power to avoid the fees of such consultations, which would be imputed to its own profit margin. Unfortunately, such fees are hard to predict, as the need for consultations becomes apparent only at the time the project is being carried out, which explains why it is seldom included in the budget. Sometimes governments financing a project, aware of the problem, anticipate the fees of such consultations or they can decide to cover fees themselves.

Once the project is finished, an appeal for offers to realize it is made. The official organs of the state interested or of the international organization that finances the operation assume the responsibility for the wording of the appeal for offers and, later, to examine the various offers to retain only the most attractive one. This is an administrative procedure, but it would be regrettable if it were only so. In that case one runs the risk that an agreement between the bidders favours the one they have chosen by a common accord – a kind of criminal offence – as well as the risk of a readjustment of costs envisaged in the contract. Such administrative problems have a technical (as well as scientific) aspect, which should be checked by the technical services that rely on the firm that has readied the project. Frequently this firm helps in the formulation of the appeal for offers, and also intervenes in that of the contract. There is a danger that one of the firms that respond to the offer has financial links (direct or indirect) with the consulting engineers that have prepared the project and have added to it specifications that could favour a specific amical firm or even totally eliminate the competing firms. Here and in the evaluation of the technical guarantees presented by the bidding firms, the intervention of the studies' coordinator may be very useful to inform or advise the technical services, whose competence is different from the coordinator's. This is another reason why certain governments take the precaution of anticipating and taking to their charge the consultation fees of the coordinator.

Finally, once realized, it is wise for the coordinator to keep sight of the development. Unfortunately, this is seldom done. The coordinator can give advice on the *management* of the enterprise to help avoid errors that could reduce its usefulness, and can recommend measures to prevent a degradation that, if it becomes irreversible, could jeopardize the works. The French Ministry of Agriculture, in spite of the importance of the studies and their cost, did not anticipate any follow-up of the restoration of the Guil Valley after the flood of June 1957 once the studies had been finished. J. Tricart, with support

from the Centre de Géographie Appliquée, sketched out such a follow-up (Tricart 1974d). On the scientific level, such follow-ups are seldom carried out in spite of the fundamental interest of knowing how the natural dynamics are modified and the scars healed. (Doctors and surgeons have a similar interest in their patients.) On the practical level of the development of restoration, there is a gain in experience, an emancipation of the tyranny of the short term, of the annual budgetary exercise by accountants, which are no more than bookkeepers, stingy to the last penny, but blind to millions of dollars that vanish with a premature degradation of developments that are not followed up.

GENERAL CONCLUSION

The old saying 'You can't see the wood for the trees' applies here. *Re*forestation is part of rural management. One reads about *re*forestation, never about *af*forestation, even when it is not at all certain that a forest previously existed. This *re* is an ideological affirmation, that of the successors of the great caretakers of Nature, such as N. Brémontier and the foresters of the Défence et Restauration des Terrains en Montagne in the nineteenth century. An ideological affirmation that is also a Freudian avowal, that of an inferiority complex, for, in France, the 'liberal' race for profits in which the Office National des Forêts has engaged has estranged this Office from its great predecessors. Fast-growing conifers, easily cut and quickly sold, have been substituted for the original hardwood forest, when they were not prematurely blown down by the wind. In that case, the same species, subject to the same fate, is replanted in the same location! The antithesis of good rural management, a short-sighted action, the inevitable result of the inexorable advance of progress.

Well, no, a thousand times no, this is not progress. The systems concept is gradually penetrating into more and more disciplines. J. Tricart had discovered it empirically at the time L. von Bertalanffy popularized it in 1969. He made it his own. The trees should not cloud the forest, but the forest should not mask the trees either. The systems approach is a superior form of dialectics. It is practised in two directions: an ascending one, of the objects (parts), even the smallest, studied by the most in-depth analyses, toward ever vaster ensembles, and a descending one, of ensembles of a certain taxonomic level, toward the objects that compose it, their components, and so on. Its upper limit is the Universe, its lowest the elementary particle of matter, ever more difficult and costly to track down. A rational development or management of nature, especially of rural activities, which take place in less artificial environments than factories or subways, makes use of this double procedure of ascending integration and descending analysis. What characterizes a systems analysis is the association of the two procedures, attributing to each, in each particular case, the place its merits, in this case, to devise management or development solutions for the rural environment. The electron has the same reality as the galaxy. Osmosis at the extremity of a rootlet is as much a medial reality as an Amazon flood. In that sense, either is of interest to land development, as both are dynamic realities, components of the functioning of Nature. The object of each development is to modify the functioning of the natural environment, to eliminate the restraints on biological productivity, and to remove the constraints opposing it whenever possible. But the systems approach, by centring the attention on the interdependences of the components, the nested subsystems that structure Nature, frees us from imitating the legendary sorcerer's apprentice. It helps understand the complexity of Nature and the web of interactions that manifest themselves in its dynamics. To develop the rural environment rationally, to manage it correctly, that is by assuring the non-degradation of its resources, are imperatives that impose themselves all the more forcibly on the eve of the twenty-first century as the world situation is characterized by

1 an ungovernable increase in population, which in one generation has passed from 4 billion to 5 billion people and shortly will reach 6 billion.
2 a vast majority of these people (between two-thirds and three-quarters) are poorly or insufficiently nourished to grow into healthy individuals
3 an industry whose quest for profit causes immeasurable deleterious effects on the ecologic environment – the reason why eminent scientists came together to formulate the International Geosphere–Biosphere Programme in September 1986.

But rural activities are not stagnant, they imitate industry, enter into competition with it as gravediggers of our ecologic environment in the form of agribusiness.

The situation, obviously, is serious and tragic: only the force of public opinion can avert a catastrophe. But part of this force resides in those who have been fortunate enough to receive a better education than others. This book is addressed to them. Its ambition is to help create an increased awareness of the problems, which is the object of the International Geosphere–Biosphere Programme.

BIBLIOGRAPHY

Note: Owing to unpredictable delays independent of the authors in the publication of the manuscript, the list of references had to be updated by works published in 1989 and 1990 available in Strasbourg at the beginning of December 1990.

Agron. Trop.: L'Agronomie Tropicale
Ann. Agron.: Annales Agronomiques
Ann. de Géogr.: Annales de Géographie
Berliner Geogr. Abh.: Berliner Geographische Abhandlungen
Bull. Assoc. des géogr. fr.: Bulletin de l'Association des géographes français
Bull. Assoc. Fr. pour l'Et. du Quat.: Bulletin de l'Association française pour l'étude du Quaternaire, now 'Quaternaire'
Cah. de Géogr. phys.: Cahiers de géographie physique
Cah. ORSTOM, sér Pédol.: Cahiers ORSTOM, série Pédologie
Doc. B.R.G.M.: Document Bureau de Recherches Géologiques et Minières
Geogr. Ber.: Geographische Berichte
Göttinger Geogr. Abh.: Göttinger Geographische Abhandlungen
IASH: International Association of Scientific Hydrology
Münchener Geogr. Abh.: Münchener Geographische Abhandlungen
Peterm. Geogr. Mitt.: Petermanns Geographische Mitteilungen
Rech. Géogr. à Strasbourg: Recherches Géographiques à Strasbourg
Rev. de Géom. Dyn.: Revue de Géomorphologie Dynamique
Rev. Géogr. des Pyr. et du SO: Revue Géographique des Pyrénées et du Sud-Ouest
Rev. Géogr. Phys. et Géol. Dyn.: Revue de Géographie Physique et Géologie Dynamique
Soc. Géol. de Fr.: Bulletin de la Société Géologique de France
Soil Sc.: Soil Science
Springer-V.: Springer-Verlag
Zeit. für Geom. Suppl.-Bd.: Zeitschrift für Geomorphologie – Supplement-Band

Acheampong, B. K. (1986) Evaluation of potential evapo-transpiration methods for Ghana. *Geo. Journal* 12(4): 409–15.
Concludes that Penman method gives more exact results for Ghana than other methods.
Ackleson, S., Klemab, V., McKim, H., Merry, C. (1985) A comparison of SPOT simulated data with LANDSAT MSS imagery for delineating water masses in Delaware Bay, Broadkill River and adjacent wetlands. *Photogram. Eng. & Remote Sensing*, 51(8): 1123–9.
Acot, P. (1988) *Histoire de l'écologie.* PUF, Paris, 285 pp.
Basic work: the historical approach allows us to situate in the general framework of the evolution of scientific thought the various concepts and their modifications.
Adam L. (1969) Geomorphological research and mapping in strongly eroded areas. *Res. Problems in Applied Geogr.* Ak. Kiadó, Budapest: 41–71.
Adam, L. (1979) Complex physical–geographical mapping in the service of agriculture. *Abstracts* 21. Hung. Ac. Sc., Geographical Res. Inst.: 27–32.
Attempts to add all useful parameters, without integration.
ADEBEM, Agence de Bassin Seine-Normandie (1979) *Influence de la forêt et du déboisement sue le débit des cours d'eau, étude bibliographique* Mme Roux: 21 + 44 pp.
AFES/INRA (1990) *Referentiel Pédologique Français*, 3e Proposition (April), 279 pp.
To be printed from 1991 onwards. New pedogenic conceptions of the French soil survey, which insert soils in the 'landscape' framework.
Ager, C. M., Milton, N. M. (1987) Spectral reflectance of lichens and their effects on the reflectance of rock substrates. *Geophysics* 52(7): 898–906.
A lichen cover of only 30 per cent eliminates the difference in reflectance between slates and hornfels.
Agnesini, S., Fouque, G., Papani, G. (1978) La carta delle forme di degradazione dei versanti dell'Appennino Parmanse. *Gruppo di Studio del Quat. padano* (Parma) 4: 163–81.

Relationships and ratio of mass wasting to gullying per basin.
Ahnert, F. (1977) Some comments on the quantitative formulation of geomorphological process in a theoretical model, *Earth Surface Processes* 2: 191–201.
Formulation of soil thickness/weathering/denudation rates.
Ahnert, F. (1981) Über die Beziehung zwischen quantitativen, semiquantitativen und qualitativen Methoden in der Geomorphologie. *Zeit. für Geom. Suppl.-Bd* 39: 1–28.
Aitchinson, G., Grant, K. (1967) The P.U.C.E. program of terrain description, evaluation and interpretation for engineering purposes. *Proceedings of the 4th regional conference for Africa on soil mechanics and foundation engineering.* Capetown 1: 1–8.
Alexander, D. (1987) The 1982 urban landslide disaster at Ancona, Italy. *Nat. Hazard Res. Working Paper* 57, 63 pp., 6 fig.
Alexander, R. W., Calvo, A. (1990) The influence of lichens on slope processes in some Spanish badlands. In: J. B. Thornes (Ed.) *Vegetation and erosion* pp. 385–98. J. Wiley & Sons, Chichester.
Allaire, G., Stoupy (1972) Analyse écologique et cartographique du paysage, doctoral diss., Paul Sabatier University, Toulouse.
Attempt to correlate land use with a number of parameters of the physical environment.
Amaral, G. (1985) Remote sensing systems comparisons for geological mapping in Brazil. *Doc. B.R.G.M.* 82: 91–106.
American Society of Photogrammetry and Remote Sensing (1983) *Manual of remote sensing* 2nd ed. Falls Church VA.
Annales de Géographie (1981) Aspects géographiques de la télédétection 90(499): 257–380. A symposium.
Ansseau, C. (1985) Les unités symphytosociologiques, bases de l'analyse du paysage. In: Berdoulay, V., Phipps, M. Coord. *Paysage et système* pp. 33–9. Univ. d'Ottawa.
Anthony E. (1985) Geomorphology, water table and soil relationships in Holocene beach ridges in southern Sierra Leone. *Catena* 12: 167–78.
Antrop, M. (1985) Télédétection et analyse du paysage. In: Berdoulay, V., Phipps, M. Coord. *Paysage et système* pp. 125–33. Univ. d'Ottawa.

Armand, A. D. (1985) Processus d'auto-organisation et d'autorégulation dans le paysage. In: Berdoulay V., Phipps M., Coord. *Paysage et système* pp. 75–86. Univ. d'Ottawa.

Armstrong, A. (1984) The hydrology and water quality of a drained clay catchment. In: Burt, T., Walling, D. E. (Ed.) *Catchment experiments in fluvial geomorphology* pp. 153–68. Geo Books, Norwich.

Arnett, R. (1978) Regional disparities in the denudation rate of organic sediments. *Zeit. für Geom. Suppl.-Bd* **29**: 169–79.

Arrignon, J. (1987) *Agro-écologie des zones arides et sub-humides*. Coll. Techn. Agric. & Prod. Trop., XXXIX, Maisonneuve & Larose. Agence de Coop. Cult. & Tech., Paris, 283 pp. 80 fig. *A good exposition about windbreaks and their efficiency.*

Atlas of interpretation of multispectral aerospace photographs. Methods and results (1982). Ak. Verlag, Berlin and Nauka. Moscow, 83 pp. *Trilingual: German, Russian and English. View of the USSR and GDR.*

Aubert, G. (1965) Classification des sols. Tableaux des classes, sous-classes, groupes et sous-groupes de sols utilisés par la section de pédologie de l'ORSTOM, *Cah. ORSTOM, sér. Pédol.* **3**(3): 269–88.

Aubert, G. (1984) Observations sur les caractéristiques, la dénomination et la classification des sols salés ou salsodiques. *Cah. ORSTOM. sér Pédol.* **20**(1): 73–8.

Aubert, G., Duchaufour Ph. (1956) Projet de classification des sols. *Sixth Intern. Soil Congr.*, Paris, **5**(97)E: 597–604.

Aubert, G., Fournier, F. (1955) Les cartes d'utilisation des terres. *Sols Africains* **3**(1): 89–109.

Aubert, G., Segalen, P. (1966) Projet de classification des sols ferrallitiques. *Cah. ORSTOM, sér. Pédol.* **4**(4): 97–112.

Aussenac, G. (1980) Le cycle hydrologique en forêt. In: Pesson, P. (Ed.) *Actualités d'écologie forestière*, Gauthiers-Villars, Paris 517 pp. 283–307.

Australian Ac. Sc. & CSIRO, Adelaide (1961) *Symposium on geochronology and land surfaces in relation to soils in Australasia*, Adelaide, Dec. 5–8, 223 pp.

Auzet, V. (1987) L'érosion des sols cultivés en France sous l'action du ruissellement. *Ann. de Géogr.* **96**(537): 529–56. *Useful references.*

Avenard, J. M. (1971) *La répartition des formations végétales en relation avec l'eau du sol dans la région de Man-Touba.* Trav. & Doc. ORSTOM, Paris, 159 pp.

Avenard, J. M. (1972) *Le régime hydrique des sols dans l'explication du contact forêt-savane dans l'Ouest de la Côte d'Ivoire.* ORSTOM, Adiopodoumé (Ivory Coast) 7 pp.

Avenard, J. M. (1977) *Cartographie géomorphologique dans l'Ouest de la Côte d'Ivoire.* Notice explicative 71, ORSTOM, Paris, 99 pp, 44 fig. *3 coloured folded maps.*

Avenard, J. M. (1989/90) Sensibilité aux mouvements de masse (solifluxion). *Cah. ORSTOM sér. Pédol.* **XXV**(1/2): 119–29.

Avenard, J. M., Bonvallot, J., Latham, M., Renard-Dugerdil, M., Richard, J. (1973) Le contact forêt-savane en moyenne Côte d'Ivoire. *Ann. de Géogr.*, **LXXXI**(453): 513–44. *Example of integration of major methodologic importance.*

Avery, B. (1985) Argilic horizons and their significance in England and Wales. In: Roadman, J. (Ed.) *Soils and Quaternary landscape evolution* pp. 69–86. J. Wiley & Sons, Chichester.

Axelsson, S., Edvardsson, O. (1971) Passive microwave radiometry and its potential applications to Earth resources surveys. *Basic physics and technology* ESRO CR-71, 96 pp, fig.

Axelsson, S., Klemas, V., McKim, H. (1985) A comparison of SPOT simulator data with LANDSAT MSS imagery for delineating water masses in Delaware Bay, Broadkill River and adjacent wetlands. *Photogram. Eng. & Remote Sensing* **51**(8): 1123–9.

Azzi, G. (1954) *Ecologie agricole* Baillière et fils, Paris, 428 pp, illustr., maps diagrs. Also Italian Ed.: Dante Alighieri, Genoa (1944) and Spanish Ed.: Elite, Caracas (1947).

Bagnouls, F., Gaussen, H. (1957) Les climats biologiques et leur classification. *Ann. de Géogr.* **66**(355): 193–220.

Bakker, J. P. (1959) Recherches néerlandaises de géomorphologie appliquée. *Rev. de Géom. Dyn.* 10: 67–84.

Baldwin, M., Kellogg, C. E., Thorp, J. (1938) Soil classification. In: *Soils & men* Yearbook of Agric. USDA pp. 979–1001.

Barat, C. A. (1963) La géomorphologie appliquée en République Populaire Roumaine, constatations et suggestions. *Rev. de Géom. Dyn.* **14**: 145–52.

Barat, C. A. (1966) Considérations de quelques problèmes actuels de la géomorphologie appliquée. *Rev. de Géom. Dyn.* **16**: 114–28.

Barde, J. P. (1970) Ecologie de économie. *Bull. Soc. Ecologie* **1**(3): 159–69.

Bardinet, C. (1978) Télédétection et géographie. Une ère nouvelle de l'observation de la Terre. *Hérodote* **12**: 127–48. *Good general overview, except for RADAMBRASIL (inaccuracies). Need for a 'global' vision.*

Bardinet, C. (1981) Télédétection des paysages africains par LANDSAT et METEOSAT. Les zones d'Afrique centrale de N'Djamena (Tchad) et d'Annaba (Algérie). *Ann. de Géogr.* **90**(499): 354–80.

Bardinet, C. (1987) *Télédétection, environnement et urbanisation.* Thèse Lettres, Paris VIII, 2 vol., 567 pp., published by the author, E.N.S. 45 rue d'Ulm Paris 75231 Cedex 05. Although this PhD research is entitled 'urbanisation', it covers many general aspects of remote sensing and environmental data.

Bardinet, C., Cabot, J. (1985) Télédétection de paysages tchadiens par Landsat. *Information Géographique* **49**: 45–52, folded images in colour, bibl.

Bardinet, C., Fosset, R., Monget, J. M. (1983) *Télédétection et géographie appliquée en zone aride et sud-méditerranéenne.* Coll. de l'Ecole Normale Supérieure de Jeunes Filles **19** (1982), 407 pp, fig. reproductions of imagery, coloured folded maps in pocket. *Studies of areas in Brazil, Algeria, Chad, Morocco, Mali, Sahel and Hopei.*

Bariou, R. (1978) *Manuel de télédétection*, Paris, SODIPE, 349, 100 fig. *Review of basic concepts of physics and technology, followed by interpretation of the recordings. Examples relating to the geographical environment.*

Bariou, R., Lecamus, D. (1981) Télédétection: méthodes et problématique de l'interprétation. Part 1. *Photo Interprétation*: 81–4, 6.1 to 6.20. *Bibliography according to themes, not analytic.*

Barnett, D., Edlung, D., Dredge, L., Thomas, D., Prevett, L. (1975) *Terrain classification and evaluation, Eastern Melville Island, N.W.T.* Geol. Survey Canada, 1318 pp, 11 maps, 3 legends. *Canadian application of the CSIRO approach to the Arctic.*

Barrett, E. C., Curtis, L. F., Coord. (1974) *Environmental remote sensing: application and achievements.* Bristol Symp. Oct. 2 (1972), London, Arnold, 309 pp. illustr. *A series of communications dealing either with techniques or with their application to the geographical environment.*

Barrett, E. C., Curtis, L. F. (1982) *Introduction to environmental remote sensing*, 2nd ed., Halsted Press, Wiley, New York. *Same type of contents as the preceeding reference, but presented systematically in the form of a textbook.*

Barrue-Pastor, M. (1985) *Alibi paysager et législations montagnardes d'aménagement rural (XIXe–XXe siècles).* Ass. Ruralistes Fr., Coll. de Strasbourg, 25 pp. *Shows clearly the aspect 'struggle of classes' of the 'reforestation' policy, in French mountains during the period beginning in the middle of the nineteenth century.*

Barry, R. G., Chorley, R. G. (1987) *Atmosphere, weather and climate.* 5th ed., Methuen, London, New York, 460 pp.

Barsch, D., Fränzle, O., Leser, H., Liedtke, H., Stäblein, G. (1978) Geomorphologische Karte der Bundesrepublik Deutschland 1:25 000 (GMK 25), herausgegeben von der Koordination-kommission des GMK-Schwerpunktprogramms der Deutschen Forschungsgemeinschaft, Karten und Erläuterungen, Berlin, Auslieferung Geocenter, Stuttgart.

Barsch, D., Liedtke, H. (1980) Principles, scientific value and practical applicability of the geomorphological map of the Federal Republic of Germany at the scale of 1:25 000 (GMK 25) and 1:100 000 (GMK 100) with 6 fig. & 2 tables. *Zeit. für Geom. Suppl.-Bd* **36**: 296–313.

Barsch, D., Mäusbacher (1979) Geomorphological and ecological mapping. *Geojournal*, Wiesbaden **3/4**: 361–70.

Barsch, D., Stäblein, G. (1982) Erträge und Fortschritte der geomorphologischen Detail-kartierung. *Berliner Geogr. Abh.* **35**, 134 pp. 5 folded maps.

Barsch, H. (1978) Landschaftskundliche Aspekte des Geosystem-Konzepts. *Wissenschaftliche Zeitschrift, Pädagogische Hochschule Karl Liebknecht* Potsdam **22**(3): 335–41.

Barsch, H., Richter, H. (1975) Grundzüge einer naturräumlichen Gliederung der DDR auf der Basis typisierter Naturräume in der chorischen Dimension. *Peterm. Geogr. Mitt.* **119**: 173–9.

Barsch, H., Wirth, H. (1983) Methodische Untersuchungen zur Auswertung multispektraler Fernerkundungsdaten für Flächennützungskartierungen in der DDR. *Peterm. Geogr. Mitt.* **127**: 191–202.

Bartkowski, T. (1968) Les méthodes de division du pays en microrégions pour les besoins de l'évaluation du milieu géographique. *Geographica Polonica* **14**: 217–21.

Bartowski, T. (1971) Upon methods of evaluation of geographic environment. *Przeglad Geograficzny* **43**: 263–81.
Proceeds in two steps: 1. Inventory of the characteristics of the environment, 2. Assessment of the environment according to land use criteria (which is necessarily subjective).

Bartkowski, T. (1972) Upon the notion of resources of geographical environment and upon methods of their measurement. *Przeglad Geograficzny* **44**: 31–61.

Bartkowski, T. (1984) L'essai de l'évaluation du milieu géographique à quelques exemples choisis de la plaine de la Grande Pologne. *Zeszyty Naukowe, PAM Georg.* **4**: 76 pp.
An example of excessively parametric methods and the rare procedures they suggest.

Battiau-Queney, Y. (1988) L'évolution géomorphologique du Piedmont appalachien et de la Plaine Côtière du New-Jersey à la Géorgie (U.S.A.). *Cah. de géogr. phys.*, Univ. Sc. & Techn. Lille **6**: 82 pp.
Application of plate tectonics to megamorphology. Another paper on the same topic is forthcoming in Rev. de Géom. Dyn. (1989) **38**(1): 1–15.

Battiau-Queney, Y. (1989) Constraint from deep-crustal structure on long-term landform development of the British Isles and Eastern United States. *Geomorphology* **2**: 53–70.

Baudière, A., Somson, P. (1984) Modes de perception de l'éboulis par les botanistes. *Actes Colloque du 8 janvier 1983*, Paris, Eboulis . . ., Univ. de Paris X: 41–49.
The botanist authors make very careful studies of the ecological effects of scree slopes.

Baudoin, A., Decae, A., Demathieu, P. (1972) La détection à distance à l'IGN. *Bull. Inform. IGN*, **19**: 1–16.

Baulig, H. (1958) La leçon de Karl Grover Gilbert. *Ann. de Geogr.* **67**(362): 289–307.

Bavel van, C. H. M., Kirkham, D. (1948) Field measurement of soil permeability using auger holes. *Soil Sc. Soc. Amer. Proc.* **13**: 90–6.

Bawden, M. (1965) A reconnaissance of the land resources of eastern Bechuanaland. *Journal of Applied Ecology* **2**: 357–65.

Bawden, M. (1967) Applications of aerial photography in land system mapping. *Photogrammetric Record* **5**: 461–73.

Beaudet, G., Dufaure, J. J., Godard, A. (1982) La géographie physique existe. *Hérodote* **24**: 136–56.
General overview, open to applications and to the interdependence of phenomena.

Becht, M. (1989) Suspended sediment yield of a small drainage basin in Upper Bavaria. *Catena Suppl.* **15**: 329–42.
Excellent observations confirming our own model of discontinuous transport from the divides to the rivers and along the streams themselves.

Becht, M., Wetzel, K. F. (1989) Die Einfluss von Muren, Schneeschmelze und Regenniederschläge auf den Sedimentbilanz eines randalpinen Wildbachgebietes. *Die Erde* **120**: 189–202.
Suggestive and precise observations and measurements of general application.

Becker, F. (1978) Bases physiques de la télédétection et sa problématique. *La Houille Blanche* 7/8: 491–98.

Beckett, P., Burrough, P. (1971) The cost effectiveness of different soil survey procedures. *J. Soil Sc.* **22**: 481–9.
Prior to the publication of the morpho-pedological approach, which is much less expensive.

Beckett, P. H. (1974) The statistical assessment of resource surveys by remote sensors. *Environmental Remote Sensing, Bristol Symp.* 2 Oct. (1972) Arnold, London pp. 9–27.
Calibration problems of spectral signatures.

Belaïd, R., Belkhodja, K. (1967) *Essai de synthèse de l'évolution géormorphologique et pédologique du Quaternaire en Tunisie.* Colloque de Géographie Maghrebine, Tunis, 5–10 Oct, 53 pp.

Belaïd, R., Belkhodja, K. (1970) Essai de synthèse de l'évolution géomorphologique et pédologique du Quaternaire en Tunisie. *Sols de Tunisie* **2**: 23–64.
Attempt, advanced for its time, to associate the evolution of landforms and soils with Quaternary climatic oscillations. Established a tradition in Tunisia. It is applicable elsewhere.

Bell, F. C. (1969) Generalised rainfall–duration–frequency relationships. *Proc. Am. Assoc. Civil Eng.* **95** (HYL): 311–27.
Deals mainly with rainfalls of less than two hours.

Bell, J. P., McCulloch, J. S. G. (1966) Soil moisture estimation by neutron scattering method in Britain. *J. Hydrology* **4**(3): 254–266; a further report in **7**: 415–33.

Belosel'skaja, G. A. (1956) Essai de subdivision physico-geographique du désert Mouïunkuom. *Voprosy Geografii* **39**: 168–78.
Bases the natural units on an evolutive community.

Ben-Zishai, R., Burton, S., Vandelinde, M. (1990) The last, precious drops. *Time* **45**, Nov. 5: 34–40.
Some dramatic examples of the shortage of potable water and of its misuse.

Berdoulay, V. (1985) Convergences des analyses sémiotiques et écologiques du paysage. In: Berdoulay, V., Phipps, M. Coord. *Paysage et système* pp. 141–53. Univ. d'Ottawa.

Berdoulay, V., Phipps, M. Coord. (1985) *Paysage et système.* Editions Univ. d'Ottawa, 195 pp.
A collective publication exploring different aspects of the landscape concept.

Berg, J. A. van den (1989) Variability of parameters for modelling soil moisture conditions. *Nederlandse Geogr. Studies* **93**: 207 pp.

Berlin, G., Tarabzouni, M., Al-Nasser, A., Sheiko, K., Larson, W. (1986) SIR-B sub-surface imaging in a sand-buried landscape: Al Labbash Plateau, Saudi Arabia. *IEEE Trans. Geosc. & Remote Sensing* **G-24**(4): 595–602.

Berton, R. (1989) *La mémoire du sol.* Presses Univ. Nancy, 176 pp.
An exposition of some very wise techniques of aerial photography in order to enhance the visibility of near surface objects. Archaeological examples.

Bertrand, G. (1968) Paysage et géographie physique globale. Esquisse méthodologique. *Rev. Géogr. des Pyr. et du SO* **39**(3): 249–72.
Basic paper.

Bertrand, G. (1970) Ecologie de l'espace géographique. Recherches pour une science du paysage. *Société de Biogéographie.* Comptes rendus, séance du 19 décembre 1969: 195–205.

Bertrand, G. (1972) Ecologie d'un espace géographique. Les écosystèmes du Valle de Prioro (Espagne du Nord-Ouest). In *Espace Géographique* **2**: 113–28.

Bertrand, G. (1972) Les structures naturelles de l'espace géographique. L'exemple des montagnes cantabriques centrales (nord-ouest de l'Espagne). *Rev. Géogr. des Pyr. et du SO* **43**: 175–206.

Bertrand, G. (1982) Construire la géographie physique. *Hérodote* **26**: 90–116.

Bertrand, G. (1984) Les géographes français et leurs paysages. *Ann. de Géogr.* **93**(516): 218–29.

Bertrand, G., Dollfus, O. (1973a) Essai d'analyse écologique de l'espace montagnard. *L'Espace Géographique* **3**: 165–70.

Bertrand, G., Dollfus, O. (1973b) Les paysages du Népal central et leur organisation. *Bull. Assoc. des géogr. fr.* **404–405**: 383–99.

Bertrand, G., Taillefer, F., Viers, G., Hubschmann, J., Delpoux, M. (1972) Colloque interdisciplinaire de la 'Science du paysage et ses applications'. *Rev. Géogr. des Pyr. et du SO* **43**: 127–74.

Bertrand, R. (1972) Morphopédologie et orientations culturales des régions soudaniennes du Siné Saloum (Sénégal). *Agron. Trop.* **27**(12): 115–90.

Bertrand, R. (1973) Contributions à l'étude hydrologique, pédologique et agronomique des sols gris sableux hydromorphes de Casamance (Sénégal). *Agron. Trop.* **28**(12): 145–92.

Bertrand, R. (1974) Les systèmes de paysages des plaines inondables du delta vif du Niger (Mali). Une application de la cartographie morphopédologique en vue de l'aménagement hydroagricole. *Agron. Trop.* **29**: 154–210, 2 maps in colour.

Bertrand, R. (1975) Les écotopes des plaines inondables du Delta Intérieur du Moyen Niger (Rép. du Mali). *Rev. de Géom. Dyn.* **24**: 123–49.

Bertrand, R., Bourgeon, G., Angepe, A. (1980) Conception des études pédologiques nécessaires à la création d'un complexe agro-industriel sucrier. Exposé critique d'un cas concret en Côte d'Ivoire. *Agron. Trop.* **35**(1): 9–19.
An outstanding methodological analysis, among the very few achievements of the IRAT which have been published.

Bertrand, R., Feau, C. (1979) Etude morphologique, micromorphologique et hydrologique des sols des vallées du haut bassin du Noun (N'Dop, Cameroun). *Rev. de Géom. Dyn.* **23**(3): 97–112.

Bertrand, R., Valenza, J. (1979) Méthode de cartographie des milieux naturels du Sénégal oriental. Evaluation des possibilités agro-sylvo-pastorales. *Agron. Trop.* **37**(4): 329–39.
Proposes a taxonomy fulfilling the needs of preliminary development studies.

Bethemont, J. (1977) *De l'eau et des hommes. Essai géographique sur l'utilisation des eaux continentales.* Paris, Bordas, 280 pp.

Bethemont, J., Cretin, C. Coord. (1988) *La Loire et l'aménagement du bassin ligérien.* Coll. Univ. St Etienne, 19–20 Oct., St Etienne, 252 pp.

Bezkowska, G. (1986) The structure and types of geocomplexes in the central part of the South Great Poland Lowland. *Acta Geogr. Lodziensia,* **54**, 130 pp. (in Polish with an extensive English abstract).

Billard, A. (1987) *Analyse critique des stratotypes quaternaires.* Editions CNRS, Centre Régional de Publication, Meudon, 143 pp, 42 fig.

Billwitz, K. (1963) Die sowjetische Landschaftsökologie. *Peterm. Geogr. Mitt.* **107**: 74–9.
Handy concise summary, many references; of historical interest; easier to examine than the original Soviet publications.

Bird, E. C. F. (1979) Coastal processes. In: Gregory K. J., Walling, D. E. (Ed.) *Man and environmental processes* pp. 82–101. Dawson, Folkestone.

Birkeland, P. W. (1984) *Soils and geomorphology,* Oxford Univ. Press, Oxford, New York, 372 pp. Revised ed. of *Pedology, weathering and geomorphological research* (1974)
Written from the perspective of the use of soils in Quaternary geological research.

Birot, P. (1959 1965) *Précis de géographie physique générale.* Colin, Paris, 403 pp., 82 fig., 22 pl.
Geomorphology is summarily treated, but refers to dynamic and climatic aspects.

Birot, P. (1979) Evolution des climats et transformation des paysages. *Le Courrier du CNRS* **34**: 75–9.
Deals, in part, with the approach proposed by J. Tricart.

Birot, P. (1981) *Les Processus d'érosion à la surface des continents.* Masson, Paris, 607 pp., 54 fig., 21 ph.
Completes the preceding references.

Bisset, J., Parkinson, D. (1980) Long-term effects of fire on the composition and activity of the soil microflora of a subalpine coniferous forest. *Canadian J. Botany* **58**(15): 1704–21.
Six years after a natural fire, the biomass ratio fungi/bacteria is still lower, than in soil which did not suffer burning, as a result of a higher pH.

Biswas, A. (1983) Role of geosciences in water resources development. In: Symp. *Role of geosciences in development,* Oct. 1981, pp. 22–30. Tokyo Geogr. Soc.

Biswas, A., Dakang, Z., Nickum, J., Changming, L. (Eds) *Long distance water transfer.* Tycooly, Dublin, 417 pp.

Blackburn, G. (1962) The uses of soil classification and mapping in Australia. *Trans. intern. social and soil sciences comm.* IV & V, New Zealand pp. 284–90.

Blake, D. H., Paijmans, K., McAlpine, J. R., Saunders, J. C. (1973) *Landform types and vegetation of Eastern Papua.* CSIRO. Land Res. Series, 32, 140 pp., 7 fig., 24 pl. phot.
Shows the slight evolution undergone by the Land Survey approach: relationships between physiography and vegetation are presented instead of 'Land Systems'.

Blanck, J. P. (1968) *La boucle du Niger (Mali), cartes géomorphologiques et notice. Projet d'aménagement.* C.G.A., Univ. Louis Pasteur, Strasbourg, 31 pp., 27 fig., 12 phot., portfolio of 12 maps in colour, scale 1:100 000.

Blanck, J. P. (1969) Investigación geomorphológica aplicada a proyectos de aprovechamento hidro-agricola del valle medio del Rio Niger (Rep. of Mali). *Revista Geografica,* Mérida **10**(22–23): 5–30.

Blanck, J. P. (1979) Comportement de l'eau dans les sols de la vallée alluviale du Rio Orituco (Etat Guárico, Venezuela) au début de la saison des pluies. *Recherches Géographiques à Strasbourg* **10**: 5–34.
Basic ecologic significance of pF values.

Blanck, J. P. (1986) Etude écodynamique de la région de Maradi (Niger), un exemple d'application à la lutte contre la sécheresse. *Géo-Eco-Trop* **6**(4): 249–78.
Precise example of the increase in instability resulting from drought.

Blanck, J. P., Cloots-Hirsch, A. R. (1977) *Unité écologique expérimentale, région de Maradi, Etude écodynamique.* DGRST, ACC, Lutte contre l'aridité en milieu tropical. C.G.A. LA 95 au CNRS, Strasbourg; 67 pp., 29 fig., 9 phot., coloured ecodynamic map.
Study made in co-operation with IRAT.

Blanck, J. P., Gobert A. (1982) Un aspect du milieu naturel: le régime hydrique des sols, l'exemple de la région de Maradi (Niger). *Ann. de Géogr.* **91**(505): 305–39.

Blanc-Pamard, C. (1978) *Concepts et méthodes pour une analyse écologique des petits espaces ruraux.* CNRS, Ec. Hautes Et. Sc. Soc., Labo. Sociol. et Géogr. Africaines (Paris), 40 pp.
Contains a bibliography.

Blanc-Pamard, C., Peltre, P. (1984) Dynamique des paysages préforestiers et pratiques culturales en Afrique de l'Ouest (Côte d'Ivoire centrale). ORSTOM, *Mém.* **106**: 55–71.

Blandin, P., Lamotte, M. (1984) Ecologie des systèmes et aménagement: fondements théoriques et principes méthodologiques. In: Lamotte M, Coord. *Fondements rationnels de l'aménagement d'un territoire,* 139–62 pp. Masson, Paris.

Bloom, A. L. (1978) *Geomorphology, a systematic analysis of late Cenozoic landforms.* Prentice-Hall, Englewood Cliffs, N.J.: 510 pp., 248 fig.
Standard American text.

Blum, W. E. R. (1988) *Problems of soil conservation.* CDPE, Council of Europe, Strasbourg, 46 pp., 10 fig.
Important information about biological aspects of pedogenesis, soil conservation and management problems.

Boardman, J. (Ed.) (1985) *Soils and Quaternary landscape evolution,* J. Wiley & Sons, Chichester.
This assemblage of 16 papers demonstrates the broad perspective and leading position of pedologists of the British school.

Bobek, H., Schmithüsen, J. (1949) Die Landschaft im logischen System der Geographie. *Erdkunde* **3**: 112–20. Also in Werner Storkebaum (Ed.) (1967) *Zum Gegenstand und zur Methode der Geographie.* Wissenschaftliche Buchgesellschaft, Darmstadt, 257–75 pp.

Bodechtel, J. (1973) *Spacelab application in geology, geography, hydrology,* ESRO Summer School 1973, IV: Earth Resources, 17 pp.

Boels, D. (1982) Physical soil degradation in the Netherlands. *ICW Techn. Bull.,* NS **12**: 47–65.

Bollman, J. (1984) Geomorphologische Daten und kartographische Darstellung. *Berliner Geogr. Abh.* **36**: 27–36.
Inventory of data to be digitalized in order to be entered in a data bank. Mostly topographic data.

Bonell, M., Gilmour, D., Cassells, D. (1983) Preliminary survey of the hydraulic properties of rainforest soils in tropical North-East Queensland and their implications for runoff processes. *Catena,* (suppl.) **4**: 57–78.

Bonneau, M. (1983) Conséquences des enrésinements massifs sur les écosystèmes. *Le Courrier du CNRS* **52** (suppl.), 85–91 pp.

A good analysis of the noxious effects, in France, of artificial coniferous forests.

Bonneau, M., Souchiez, B. (1979) Vol. 2. Constituants et propriétés du sol. In: Duchaufour P., Souchiez B. *Pédologie*, 480 pp., 140 fig. Masson, Paris.

Bornand, L., Icole, M. (1984) Les relations pédologie–géomorphologie–géologie du Quaternaire, rapports réciproques. Association Française de l'Etude du Sol, *Livre Jubilaire du Cinquantenaire*, 141–52 pp.

Bottner, P. (1972) Evolution des sols en milieu carbonaté. La pédogénèse sur roches calcaires dans une séquence bioclimatique méditerranéene alpine du sud de la France. *Soc. Géol. de Fr. Mém.* **37**, 156 pp., 41 fig.

Boulet, R. (1970) La géomorphologie et les principaux types de sol en Haute-Volta septentrionale. *Cah. ORSTOM sér. Pédol.* **8**(3): 245–71.

Boulet, R. (1975): Toposéquences de sols tropicaux en Haute-Volta. Equilibres dynamiques et bioclimats. *Cah. ORSTOM sér. Pédol.* **13**(1): 3–6.

Boulet, R., Bocquier, G., Millot, G. (1977) Déséquilibre pédoclimatique dans les couvertures pédologiques de l'Afrique tropicale de l'Ouest et son rôle dans l'aplanissement des reliefs. *Soc. Géol. de Fr. Bull.* **30**: 235–43.

Boulet, R., Chauvel, A., Humbel, F. X., Lucas, Y. (1982) Analyse structurale et cartographie en pédologie. *Cah. ORSTOM sér. Pédol.* **19**(4): 309–51.

Boulet, R., Godon, P., Lucas, Y., Worou, S. (1984/5) Analyse structurale de la couverture pédologique et expérimentation agronomique en Guyane Française. *Cah. ORSTOM sér. Pédol.* **21**(1): 21–31.

Boulvert, Y. (1971) Un type de modelé cuirassé: série métamorphique de Kouki en République Centrafricaine. Sols et géomorphologie. *Cah. ORSTOM sér. Pédol.* **9**(4): 399–460.

Bourgeat, F. (1964) Etude de la basse vallée du Kamoro, Tananarive, ORSTOM, 101 pp., fig., miméogr.

Bourgeat, F. (1972) Sols sur socle ancien à Madagascar. *Types de différenciation chronologique au cours du Quaternaire*, Mém. ORSTOM 57, 335 pp., 26 fig., 18 phot.

Bourgeat, F., Aubert, G. (1972) Les sols ferrallitiques à Madagascar. *Madagascar* **20**: 1–23.

Bourgeat, F., Balas, B., Revel, J. C. (1980) Influence de la morphogénèse et de la pédogénèse sur l'opposition des versants en moyenne montagne. Etude de la vallée de la Ballongue (Pyrénées ariégeoises). *Rev. de Géom. Dyn.* **29**(2): 66–78.
Good example of the application of the morphogenic–pedogenic balance.

Bourgeat, F., Sourdat, M., Tricart, J. (1979) Pédogénèse et morphogénèse d'après des exemples à Madagascar. *Madagascar Rev. de Géogr.* **35**: 9–53.

Bourgeat, F., Zebrowski, C. (1969) Les vallées alluviales de l'ouest et du nord-ouest de Madagascar. Caractérisation de certains sols pour les cultures de décrue. *Terre Malgache. Tany Malagasy*, Tananarive, **5**: 115–32.

Bourrier, J. (1954) Remarques sur l'évolution de la vitesse de filtration par unité de pente d'un sol au cours d'une période d'irrigation. *Annales techniques Génie Rural, Documents*, 74 d, 27 pp.
Microbial development causes a gradual decrease in the rate of filtration, especially in argillaceous soils.

Bourykine, A. M. (1959) Le rôle de la forêt et des espèces buissonnantes dans la lutte contre l'érosion. *Pochvodenie* **8**: 104–12.
Demonstrates the high degree of water retention of the litter in broad-leaved forests.

Bouyoucous, G. J. (1929) A new simple and rapid method for determining the moisture equivalent of soil and the role of soil colloids on this moisture equivalent. *Soil Sc.* **27**(1): 233–41.

Bouyoucous, G. J. (1949) Nylon electrical resistance unit for continuous measurement of soil moisture in field. *Soil Sc.* **67**: 319–30.

Bouyoucous, G. J., Mick, A. H. (1940) An electrical resistance method for the continuous measurement of soil moisture under field conditions. *Mich. Agro. Exp. Sta Techn. Bull.* **172**, East Lansing, Mich., 38 pp.

Boyer, L. (1981) Generalisation in semi-detailed geomorphological mapping. *ITC Journal* **1**: 98–123.
Application of the ITC system and legend to various landforms and scales.

Brabb, E. E., Harrod, B. L. (Eds) (1989) *Landslides, extent and economic significance*. Balkema, Rotterdam & Brookfield, 385 pp.
Numerous numerical data about damage. Collection of regional monographs.

Braque, R. (1982) *La forêt et ses problèmes dans le sud du Bassin Parisien (Berry, Nivernais) étude de géographie physique*, thèse Etat, Clermont II, 2 juin 1978. Univ. of Paris VIII, Vincennes-St Denis, 3 vol., 943 pp. 1 vol. of fig. & tables.
Remarkable monograph, of general methodological value. Important bibliography. Measurements and critiques of them.

Braukämper, K. (1989) Zur Gliederung der Lösse und Böden am Nordrand des Rheinischen Schiefergebirges in der Umgebung von Bochum. *Frankfurter Geowiss. Arb.* D **10**: 96–105.
The various soils are included in a geomorphosequence which gives their genetic and chronological explanation.

Braune, E., Looser, U. (1989) Cost impact of sediments in South Africa rivers. *IAHS Public.* **184**: 131–143.
General and regional assessment of the sedimentation problem.

Bravard, J. P. (1987) Le Rhône du Léman à Lyon. *La Manufacture*, Lyon, 412 pp.
Remarkable work, showing how fluvial dynamics are the main factor, first of the vegetation, in the evolution of the environment.

Bravard, J. P., Amoros, C., Pautou, G. (1986) Impact of civil engineering works on the successions of communities in a fluvial system. *Oikos* **47**: 92–111.

Bret, B. (Ed.) (1989) Les hommes face aux sécheresses, IHEAL-EST, Paris, 422 pp.
Communications to a symposium, treating most of the human aspects of Brazil and West Africa.

Briggs, D., Courtney, F. (1989) *Agriculture and environment.* Longman, Harlow, 442 pp.
A broad and deep overview, with detailed information.

Briggs, D., Shishira, E. (1985) Soil variability in geomorphologically defined survey units in the Albudeite area of Muria Province, Spain. *Catena* Suppl. **6**: 69–84.

Brimblecombe, P., Pfister, C. (Eds) (1990) *The silent countdown.* Springer-V., Berlin.
Various examples of pollution are given in the different chapters of this collective book.

Brookfield, H. (1981) Man, environment and development in the Outer Islands of Fidji. *Ambio* **10**(2/3): 59–67.
A study of environmental sensibility.

Brosius, C., Gervin, J., Ragusa, J. (1977) *Remote sensing of the Earth*, NASA, J. F. Kennedy Space Center, Cocoa Beach, Florida; NASA-TM-79444, 497 pp.
A general text for the utilization of LANDSAT.

Brouwers, M., Latrille, E. (1974) Etude des terres cultivées de l'Ile d'Anjouan (Archipel des Comores). *Agron. Trop.* **29**(2–3): 212–57.

Brown, A. C., Baeber, K. E. (1985) Late holocene palaeocology and sedimentary history of a small lowland catchment in Central England. *Quat. Res.* **24**: 87–102.

Brown, L. R. (1971) Human food production as a process in the biosphere. In: *Man and the Ecosphere*, Freeman, San Francisco, pp. 75–83.
Convenient panorama of technical development.

Brown, W. M., III et al. (1979) A synoptic approach for analyzing erosion as a guide to land-use planning. *USGS Circ.* 715-L, 43 pp., 25 fig. with folded map.

Bruce, R. R., Flach, K. W., Taylor, H. M. (eds.) (1973) *Field soil water regime* (a symposium), SSSA Special Publ. Ser. n° 5, Madison, Wisc., 212 pp.

Bruneau, M., Kilian, J. (1983) Inventaires agro-écologiques, paysages et télédétection en milieu tropical. *CNES/CNRS, ATP. Télédétection.* Coll. de Chantilly, 18–19 Oct., 26 pp.

Bruneau, M., Kilian, J. (1984) *Approche des milieux agricoles du Tung Kula Ronghaï (Thaïlande) à partir de données satellitaires (LANDSAT).* Programme de coopération France-Université de Khon Kaen et Conseil National de la Recherche (Thaïlande), 24 pp., 2 fig., coloured map, also English text.

Bruneau, M., Rogala, J. P. (1982/3) Recherches sur la morphologie des paysages à partir d'une classification multitemporelle sur une image de Thaïlande. *Bull. de la Société Franc. de Photogrammétrie et de Télédétection* (87): 55–66.

Bryssine, G. (1954) Contribution à l'étude des propriétés physiques du sol. Note sur l'appréciation de la structure du sol. *Soc. des Sc. Natur. et Phys. du Maroc, Trav. Sect. Pédologie* **8** & **9**: 33–71.

Buckingham, E. (1907) Studies of the movement of soil moisture. *USDA, Bur. of Soil Bull.* **38**: 29–61.

Budkyo, M. I. (1956) *The heat balance of the Earth's surface.* Transl. by N. I. Stepanova. U.S. Weather Bureau, Washington.

Budkyo, M. I. (1974) *Climate and life.* Transl. by Miller, D. H., Academic Press, New York, 508 pp.

Burchard, J. (1980) Circulation of water in the Bobrza Basin. *Acta Geogr. Lodziensis* **40**: 135 pp., 45 fig., 15 phot. (in Polish, with substantial French summary).

Bureau de Recherches Géologiques et Minières (1986) *La première image SPOT de la Baie du Mont-St-Michel.* Coloured map, 1 pp. account, Orléans.
A spectacular example of SPOT imagery in infrared at ebb tide with different tones showing the types of material on the slikke, tidal channels, accumulation of shells and turbid water of some channels.

Burt, Walling, D. (Eds) (1984) *Catchment experiments in fluvial geomorphology.* Geo Books, Norwich, 543 pp.

Burton, I., Kates, R. W., White, G. F. (1978) *The environment as hazard.* Oxford Univ. Press, New York, 240 pp.

Butler, B. E. (1958) *Depositional systems of the Riverina Plain of south-east Australia in relation to soils,* CSIRO, Soil Publ. 10, 35 pp., 4 phot. pl.

Butler, B. E. (1959) *Periodic phenomena in landscapes as a basis for soil studies,* CSIRO, Soil Publ. 14, Melbourne, 20 pp., 3 fig. *Contrasts periods of stability and instability, the first favouring pedogenesis, the second soil ablation.*

Butler, B. E. (1962) Soil classification and mapping in Australia. *Trans. Intern. Social & Soil Science Communication,* IV & V, New Zealand, pp. 278–83.

Butler, B. E. (1963) The place of soils in studies of Quaternary chronology in southern Australia. *Rev. de Géom. Dyn.,* **14**: 160–5.

Butler, B. E. (1967) Soil periodicity in relation to landform development in south-eastern Australia. In: Jennings, J. N., Mabbutt, J. A. (Ed.) *Landform studies from Australia and New Guinea.* Cambridge Univ. Press, 231–55 pp.

Byers, H. G. et al. (1938) *Yearbook of Agriculture.* USDA.

Cabaussel, G. (1967) Photo-interprétation et synthèse écologique, essai d'application à la feuille de Grenoble (1:100 000). *Document pour la carte de la végétation des Alpes* **5**: 127–72.

Cadiot, B., Delauney, J., Humbert, M., Vogt, J. (1989) Inventaire et étude des risques géologiques en France au Service Géologique National. *L'Espace Géogr.*: 49–56.

Cailleux, A., Tricart, J. (1956) Le problème de la classification des faites géomorphologiques. *Ann. de Géogr.* **65**(349): 162–86.

Calder, I. R. (1990) *Evaporation in the uplands.* J. Wiley & Sons, Chichester, 148 pp.
Influence of landuse on the water budget.

Campbell J. B. (1987) *Introduction to remote sensing.* Guilford Press, New York, London, 551 pp.

Campos-Lopez, E., Anderson, R. (Eds) (1983) *Natural resources and development in arid regions.* Westview, Boulder, 363 pp.

Carbiener, R. (1976) Un exemple de prairie hydrophile primaire juvénile: l'Oenantho lachenalii-Molinetum de la zonation d'atterrissement rhénane résultant des endiguements du 19e siècle en Moyenne Alsace. *Coll. Phytosociol.,* Lille: 13–42.

Carbiener, R. (1980a) L'écologie, science de l'économie de la nature et ses implications Trav. du CERIT. *La Nature a t'elle un sens ?* Strasbourg: 89–111.

Carbiener, R. (1980b) Résumé de quelques aspects de l'écologie des complexes forestiers alluviaux d'Europe. *Coll. Phytosociol.,* Strasbourg: 7 pp.

Carbiener, R., Schnitzler, A., Walter, J. M. (1985) Problèmes de dynamique forestière et de définition de stations en milieu alluvial. *Coll. Phytosociol.,* Nancy: 655–86.

Carson, M. A., Petley, D. J. (1970) The existence of threshold hillslopes in the denudation of the landscape. *Trans. Inst. Brit. Geogr.* **49**: 71–95.
Demonstrates the influence of geomorphic on pedogenic processes.

Carter, V. (1983) *Wetland hyrology in the United States.* Col. Intern. Hydrol. Grandes Llanuras, 11–20 April, Olavarria (Argentine), 49 pp.

Casabianca, F. de (1968) *Méthode suivie sur les baibos du nord-ouest de Madagascar pour l'étude de la nutrition hydrique. Résultats obtenus en 1966.* Colloque sur la fertilité des sols tropicaux, IRAT, vol. 1, Tananarive, 51–68 pp.

Casas, R. R., Pittaluga, A. (1989) Amegamiento y salinización de los sueles en el Nordeste de la Provincia de Buenos Aires. *Com. al Seminario Internac. Hidrologia de Grandes Llanures,* CONAPHI, UNESCO, 20–24 Nov. N° 50.
To be published by UNESCO in 1991.

Cassanet, J. (1984) *Satellites et capteurs.* SAT, 1, Paradigme, Caen, 128 pp.

Castensson, R. (1985) Water resources conflicts in integrated river basin development. In: Lundquist, J. et al. (Ed.) *Strategies for river basin development,* pp. 245–54. Reidel, Dordrecht.

Cate, J. A. M. ten, Maarleveld, G. C. (1977) *Geomorphologische kaart van Nederland, schaal 1:50 000.* Toelichting op de legenda. Stichting voor bodemkartering, Wageningens Rijks Geologische Dienst, Haarlem, 91 pp.

Catinaud, H. (1990): Les milieux naturels du karst dans les environs de Villard-de-Lans (Vercors septentrional, France). *Zeit. für Geom. Suppl.-Bd* **77**: 85–105.
A pedagogical demonstration of the dramatic results to which anyone arrives when lacking the basic criteria and methodology.

Catt, J. A. (1986) *Soils and Quaternary geology: a handbook for field scientists.* Oxford, Clarendon Press, 267 pp.
Relates Quaternary geology to palaeosols and analyses the effect of cold climates on soils. Restricted to England, NW Europe and American Mid-West.

Catt, J. A. (1987) Palaeosols in Quaternary research. *Episodes* **10**(1): 35–7.
A kind of stratigraphic reference of Quaternary palaeosols and their modification after their development.

Cattizone, M. (1980) La carta del Land System delle Val d'Agri. Centro Studio Genesi, Clasific. et Cartogr. Suolo, CNR, Firenze. Publ. 60, 35 pp., 1 folded map.
A research organisation, the CSG demonstrates that the land systems are 30 years behind the time.

Centre National d'Etudes Spatiales (1969) *Principes de la détection à distance et application à l'étude des resources terrestres,* CNES, Paris: 554 pp., fig. Nov. 4–6.
Presentation of the physical principles of remote sensing, various techniques and documents (not commented). Applications to the study of the geographical environment.

Cerceau, D., et al. (1972) *Analyse des besoins géoscientifiques.* Rapport de contractant ESTEC N 1517/71, Nov. 122 + 19 pp., fig.

Cervelle, B. (1989) *SPOT: des yeux braqués sur la Terre.* Presses du CNRS, Paris, 214 pp.
Technical information about the various SPOT programmes for the next 15 years.

La Chambre Photogrammétrique: une des grandes premières du vol SPACELAB-1. Observation de la Terre (ESA, ASE) (1984) 5:7 pp.
Catalogue of problems per discipline and indications on techniques permitting their study. Bibliogr.

Chaminade, R. (1964) Etude des carences minérales du sol par l'expérimentation en petits vases de végétation. *Science du Sol,* numéro semestriel, 2nd sem.: 157–67.

Chapman, T. G. (1969) *CSIRO Symposium on land evaluation. Presentation and discussion of papers.* CSIRO, Canberra, August 26–31, 1968, 98 pp.

Chapman, T. G. (1969) Evaluation des terres: un colloque international *Nature et Resources.* UNESCO, Paris **5**(1): 2–9.
Review of the proceeding colloquium.

Chaptal, J. A. C., Count of Chanteloup (1823) Treatise on the culture of the vine and the art of making wine and vinegar.

Charreau, C. (1972) Problèmes posés par l'utilisation agricole des sols tropicaux par des cultures annuelles. *Agron. Trop.* **27**(9): 905–29.

Charreau, C., Nicou, R. (1971) L'amélioration du profil cultural dans les sols sableux et argilo-sableux de la zone tropicale sèche ouest-africaine et ses incidences agronomiques (d'après les travaux des chercheurs de l'IRAT en Afrique de l'Ouest. *Agron. Trop.* **26**(2): 209–55.

Chartres, C. J. (1983) The micromorphology of desert loam soils and implications for Quaternary studies in western New South Wales. In: Bullock, P. & Murphy, C. (Ed.) *Soil micromorphology* vol. 1: 273–79; Academic Press, London.

Chauvel, A., Bocquier, C., Pedro, G. (1977) Les mécanismes de la disposition des constituants des couvertures ferrallitiques et l'origine de la zonalité des couvertures sableuses dans les régions intertropicales de l'Afrique de L'Ouest. *Soc. Géol. de Fr. Bull.* **30**(4): 255–63.

Childs, E. C. (1967) Soil moisture theory. *Advances in Hydroscience* **4**: 73–117.

Childs, E. C. (1969) *An introduction to the physical basis of soil water phenomena.* Wiley-Interscience, London, New York, Sydney, Toronto, 493 pp.
A British textbook addressed to a broad spectrum of students but mainly to students of agriculture.

Childs, E. C., Poulovassilis, A. (1962) The moisture profile above a moving water table. *J. Soil Sc.* **13**: 272–85.

Cholley, A. (1950) Morphologie structurale et morphologie climatique. *Ann. de Géogr.* **59**(317): 321–35.
Excellent methodological overall view.

Chorley, R. J. (1962) Geomorphology and general systems theory. *U.S. Geological Survey, Prof. Paper* 500-B, 10 pp.

Chorley, R. J. (1963) Diastrophic background to twentieth century geomorphological thought. *Geological Society of America Bulletin* **74**: 953–70.

Chorley, R. J., Dunn, A. J., Beckinsale, R. P. *The history of the study of landforms or the development of geomorphology.* Methuen and Wiley, London, New York, vol. 1. *Geomorphology before Davis* (1964), 678 pp. Vol. 2 *The life and work of William Morris Davis* (1973), 847 pp.

Chorley, R. J., Kennedy, R. A. (1971) *Physical geography: a systems approach.* Prentice-Hall International, London, 370 pp.
Does not live up to what it promises.

Chorley, R. J., Schumm, S. A., Sugden, D. E. (1984) *Geomorphology.* Methuen, London, New York, 605 pp., 555 fig., 78 tabl. 33 pl.
Comprehensive summation of present state of knowledge, but ignores detailed geomorphological mapping.

Christian, C. S. (1952) Regional land surveys. *Journal of the Australian Institute of Agricultural Sciences* **18**: 140–6.

Christian, C. S. (1958) The concept of land units and land systems. *Proceedings of the 9th Pacific Science Congress* pp. 74–81.

Christian, C. S., Stewart, G. A. (1953) General report on survey of Katherine-Darwin region 1946. CSIRO. *Land Res. Ser.* n° 1, 156 pp., 21 pl. phot., colour maps, h.t.
As the serial number indicates, the first publication to follow the Land Surveys approach.

Christian, C. S., Stewart, G. A. (1968) Methodology of integrated surveys. Aerial surveys and integrated studies. *Proc. of Toulouse Conf.*, UNESCO pp. 233–80.
Added nothing new at the time.

Cihlar, J. (1987) Environmental factors influencing daytime and nighttime satellite thermal infrared images. *Can. J. Remote Sensing* **13**(1): 31–9.
During daytime, without cloud cover, land use is predominant information received.

Clague, J. (1982) The role of geomorphology in the identification of natural hazards. In Craig, R., Craft, J., ed. *Applied geomorphology*: 16–43. Allen & Unwin, London.

Clayden, B. (1982) Soil classification. In: Bridges, E., Davidson, D. (Eds) *Principles and applications of soil geography* pp. 58–96. Longman, Harlow.

Clement, P. (1990) Evolution géomorphologique d'un secteur nord-appalachien (Québec, Canada): approche dynamique. *Zeit. für Geom.* **34**(3): 283–99.
Present dynamics are weak. Glacial and interglacial geomorphogenesis is explored from an original standpoint.

Cline, A. J., Johnson, D. D. (1963) Threads of genesis in the Seventh Approximation. *Soil Sc. Soc. Amer. Proc.* **27**: 220–3. Madison, Wisc.

Cloots-Hirsch, A. R., Maire, G. (1980) *Recherches méthodologiques sur le réseau hydrographique de la Gartempe, études préalables aux aménagements de rivières, sectorisation et hiérarchisation d'objectifs,* Min. de l'Agric. Direction de l'Aménagement, Service Hydraulique, C.G.A. (LA 95 au CNRS), Univ. Louis Pasteur, Strasbourg, 78 pp, porfolio with 8 colour maps.

Cloots-Hirsch, A. R., Tricart, J. (1978) L'eau facteur écologique de l'aménagement: l'exemple de l'Alsace. *Revue de Géographie de Lyon* **4**: 339–54.

CNRS Centre d'études phytosociologiques et écologiques (1967) *Ecologie végétale et développement du territoire,* Montpellier, 32 pp.

CNRS (1973) Cartes des formations superficielles et cartes géomorphologiques de Basse-Normandie au 1/50 000 (feuille de Bayeux-Courseulles). *Centre Géom. CNRS Caen Bull.* **17**: 48 pp.

Coates, D. R. (1981) *Environmental geology and landscape conservation.* J. Wiley & Sons Inc. New York, 701 pp. annexes.

Coates, D. R., Vitek, J. D. (Eds) (1980) *Thresholds in geomorphology.* Allen & Unwin, London, 498 pp.
Collection of papers, some of which merit detailed study.

Cochran, A. (1972) *A selected bibliography on natural hazards.* Natural Hazard Research Group, Working Paper 22, 86 pp.

Cole, M. M. (1985) Geobotany in geological mapping and mineral exploration. *Doc B.R.G.M.*, Orléans **82**: 267–86.

Colloque de Lyon, B.R.G.M. (1979) 2 vol. Doc. 8, 1093 pp.
Symposium devoted to the geomorphological and geological conditions of settlements. Numerous examples of constraints and some recommendations for stabilizing the site.

Colman, E. A. (1953) *Vegetation and watershed management.* Roland, New York, 412 pp.
An appraisal of vegetation management in relation to water supply, flood control and soil erosion.

Combeau, A., Chaume, R. (1986) Quelques aspects de l'interaction sol-végétation en télédétection. *Cah. ORSTOM sér. Pédol.* **22**(3): 301–17.

Combeau, A., Monnier, G. (1961) Méthode d'étude de la stabilité structurale. Application aux sols tropicaux. *Sols Africains* **6**(1): 4–32.

Combeau, N., Oblat, C., Quantin, P. (1961) Observations sur certaines caractéristiques des sols ferrallitiques. Relations entre rendements et résultats d'analyse de sols. *Fertilité* **13**: 27–40.

Commission Interministérielle d'Etude de la Nappe Phréatique de la Plaine d'Alsace (1986) Programme d'actions pour la nappe phréatique de la Plaine d'Alsace. vi + 24 + 3 pp.

Common, R., Walker, T. (1963) Three samples of hydrographic mapping in Northern Ireland. *J. Inst. Water Eng.* **17**: 395–403.

Conacher, A. J. (1975) Throughflow as a mechanism responsible for excessive soil salinization in non-irrigated, previously arable lands in the Western Australian wheatbelt: a field study. *Catena* **2**: 31–68.

Conacher, A. J., Dalrymple, J. B. (1977) The nine-unit landsurface model. An approach to pedogeomorphic research. *Geoderma* **18**(1/2 s c. issue): 1–154.
The authors present, explain and justify a model which integrates contemporary pedogeomorphic processes and their responses within a landsurface catena framework.

Conacher, A. J., Dalrymple, J. B. (1978) Identification, measurement and interpretation of some pedogeomorphic processes. *Zeit. für Geom. Suppl.-Bd* **29**: 1–9.
Examples from GB. Changes in some soils by geomorphic processes after their development. Concurrent pedogenic/morphogenic interactions are ignored.

Conseil International de la Langue Française (1979) *Vocabulaire de la géomorphologie, index allemand et anglais.* Hachette (La Maison des Dictionnaires), Paris, 219 pp.
Indispensable; each term is defined in French and its English and German equivalents are given.

Cooke, H., Verstappen, H. Coord. (1981) *A drought susceptibility pilot survey in Northern Botswana.* Final report. ITC, Enschede, 237 pp.

Cooke, R. U. (1984) Geomorphological hazards in Los Angeles. *London Res. Ser. in Geogr.* **7**: 206 pp. Allen & Unwin, London.

Cooke, R. U., Doornkamp, J. C. (1974) *Geomorphology in environmental management.* Clarendon Press, Oxford, 413 pp., 149 fig., 39 tables.
Stress processes, their physical mechanisms and methods of study. Deficient bibliography.

Coote, D. (1984) Dégradation des terres par suite d'une utilisation agricole intensive. Simpson-Lewis, W. et al, Ed. Les terres du Canada, stress et impacts. *Dir. Gén. Terres et Environnement,* Ottawa: 246–78.

Coplanarh (1973) *Metodologías utilizadas por Coplanarh en el inventario nacional de tierras,* Coplanarh, Caracas, publ. **36**: 93 pp.

Coque, R. (1977) *Géomorphologie.* A. Colin, Coll. U, Paris, 430 pp.
Reflects the state of geomorphology in France to date.

Cosandey, C. M. (1980) Calcul a posteriori de la réserve d'eau du sol utilisée par la végétation durant l'été: une approche de l'ETR. *Rech. Géogr. à Strasbourg* **13/14**: 115–19.

Cosandey, C. M. (1983) Recherches sur les bilans de l'eau dans l'Ouest du Massif Armoricain, thèse Etat, Paris-Sorbonne, 515 pp., 196 fig.
Remarkable study of the various aspects of water circulation in a small forested basin. Account and critique of concepts and study methods.

Coster, M., Chermant, J. L. (1989) *Précis d'analyse d'images.* Presses du CNRS, Paris, 560 pp.
An excellent textbook.

Coudoux, J. (1982) Structures paysagiques en Cambrésis, analyse spectrale et multidate d'images LANDSAT. *Hommes & Terres du Nord:* 1–13.

Coudoux, J. (1986) Spécificité de la région boulonnaise à partir de l'analyse d'images LANDSAT. *Bull. Assoc. des géogr. fr.:* 107–13.

Coural, M. F. (1985) *Etude sur l'évolution récente des milieux sahéliens à partir des mesures fournies par les satellites.* Thèse Etat, Paris I, 20 June 1984, 407 pp. + appendices, 164 fig., 25 images, phot., maps.

Courtney, F. M. (1981) Developments in forest hydrology. *Prog. Phys. Geogr.* **5**(2): 218–41.

Courtney, F. M., Trudgill, S. R. (1984) *An introduction to soil study.* Edward Arnold, London, 2nd ed., 122 pp.
Includes an outline of the British 1980 classification.

Coyne & Bellier (1973) Etude de la regularisation de la Soummam: Géomorphologie Algeria, Secrétariat d'Etat à l'Hydraulique, programme spécial de la Wilaya de sétif.

Crechkine, D. (1990) La Mer d'Aral menacée de disparition. *La Recherche* **21**(226): 1380–8.
A disastrous example of environmental destruction as a result of 'socialist' and 'planified' economy.

Croft, A. R., Monninger, L. V. (1953) Evapotranspiration and other water losses on some aspen forest types in relation to water available for stream flow. *Trans. Am. Geophys. Union* **34**: 563–74.
Comparison of streamflow in relation to vegetal cover. Forest clearing substituted by grassland produces an additional runoff of 100 mm without increase in solid load with an annual precipitation of 1140 mm.

Crouch, R. J., Blong, R. J. (1989) Gully sidewall classification: methods and applications. *Zeit. für Geom.* **33**(3): 291–305.

Crozier, M. (1986) *Landslides.* Croom Helm, London, 252 pp. (pp. 195–212).

CSIRO (1983) *Soils, an Australian viewpoint,* Melbourne and Academic Press, London, 928 pp.

Culler, R., Hanson, R., Myrick, M., Turner, R., Kipple, F. (1982) *Evapotranspiration before and after clearing phreatophytes, Gila River flood plain, Graham County, Arizona.* USGS, Prof. Paper 655-P, 67 pp.

Cumuzzio, J. Casas, J. (1988) Accumulations of soluble salts and gypsum in soils of the central region, Spain. *Cah. ORSTOM sér. Pédol.* **XXIV**(3): 215–26.
Processes and aspects of the phenomenon.

Curran, P. J. (1985) *Principles of remote sensing.* Longman, Harlow, 282 pp., fig.
Excellent textbook.

Czarnecki, R. (1973) Über die Typologie der Terrains. Okochoren. *Przeglad Geograficzny* **45**: 101–8.
In Polish, with German summary.

Dacharry, M. (1990) Parade aux effets des inondations. *Bull. Assoc. des géogr. fr.* **67**(1): 5–12.
Casualties and destruction by floods increase steadily and quickly. Some prevention measures are discussed.

Damour, M. (1971) *Etude pour la mise en valeur des Baiboho du nord-ouest de Madagascar,* Tananarive, IRAM, n° 230, 46 pp, maps, 2 graph, 11 tabl., bibl.

Damour, M., Bouchard, L., Dobelmann, J. P. (1971) *Contribution à l'étude de la mise en valeur des plaines de Marovoay (Madagascar).* Le problème de la salinité. Institut de Recherches Agronomiques de Madagascar, Tananarive.

Damour, M., Dobelmann, J. P., Oliver, R. (1971) *Contribution à la mise en valeur des plaines de Marovoay (Madagascar). Un exemple de dessalage des sols sodiques.* Institut de Recherches Agronomiques de Madagascar, Tananarive.

Dan J., Yaalon, D. (1986) Pedomorphic forms and pedomorphic surfaces. *9th Intern. Congr. Soil Sc., Trans.,* vol. 4, Paper 60, Adelaide: 577–84.

Dansereau, P. (1976) *Le cadre d'une recherche écologique interdisciplinaire.* EZAIM. Presses Univ. Montréal, 343 pp. 31 fig.
More phytosociologic than interdisciplinary.

Dansereau, P. (1985) *Essai de classification et de cartographie écologique des espaces.* Et. Ecol., Univ. Laval, Québec, 10, 146 p., 8 fig., 38 phot., 15 separate maps.
Not always clear.

Darlot, A., Darves-Bornoz, R. (1958) Evaluation et utilisation rationnelle des quantités d'eau nécessaires aux irrigations. *Etudes et Travaux du Centre de Recherche du Génie Rural* **43**(3): 29 pp.
Critical examination of various evapotranspiration formulae. Detailed bibliography.

Darves-Bornoz, R. (1957) Recherches et connaissances sur les besoins en eau des sols cultivés. *Etudes et Travaux du Centre de Recherche du Génie Rural* **31**: 44 pp.

Davidson, D. (1980) *Soils and land use planning.* Topics in Applied Geography, xii + 129 pp. Longman, Harlow.
Inventory of soil cartography on the globe. Standards for pedologic surveys.

Davidson, D. (1982) Soils and man in the past. In: Bridges, E., Davidson, D. (Eds) *Principles and application of soil geography* pp. 1–27. Longman, Harlow.

Decourt, N. (1979) *Bases écologiques du développement des ressources sylvicoles.* Journées Scient. Ecologie & Développement du CNRS, Paris, 19–20 Sept. 34 + 5 pp.

Deffontaines, J. P. (1973) Analyse du paysage et étude régionale des systèmes de production agricole. *Economie rurale* **98**: 3–13.

Deffontaines, J. P. (1982) Activité agricole et paysage. *INRAP,* Doc. 29: 3–24.

Deju, R. A. (1971) *Regional hydrology fundamentals,* Gordon and Breach Science publ. New York, London, Paris, 204 pp.
The main concern is a mathematical approach to hydrologic phenomena at and above the Earth's surface and below the groundwater table at the level of the drainage basin.

Delaunay, A. (1983a) Notion de matériel parental: application de la relation de matériau parental/faciès forestier à la cartographie morpho-pédologique des forêts de plaines en zone tempérée. *Rev. de Géom. Dyn.* **32**(3): 89–92.
Good example of the fruitful application of the principles of morpho-pedologic mapping.

Delaunay, J. (1983b) *Carte des zones exposées à des glissements, écroulements, effondrements et affaissements de terrain en France.* Scale 1/1 000 000. Mém. BRGM (Orléans), 124, 18 pp., 3 fig., separate coloured map.

Delpoux, M. (1972) Ecosystème et paysage. *Rev. Géogr. des Pyr. et du SO* **43**(2): 157–74.
More concerned with ecosystems than with landscapes.

Delvaux, J., Galoux, A. (1962) *Les Territoires écologiques du Sud-Est belge.* Centre d'Ecologie Générale, travaux hors série, Services écologiques régionaux. Brussels, Part I, 147 pp.
Definition of an ecological station and a presentation of a taxonomy of spatial units.

Demangeot, J. (1967) Les tendances de la géomorphologique française. *Acta Geographica* **65–66**: 8–18.

Stresses the post-war period. Singles out major trends.

Demolon, A. (1952) Principes d'agronomie, 5th ed., vol. 1: *Dynamique du sol*, Masson, Paris, 520 pp.

Demolon, A. (1968) Principes d'agronomie, 6th ed., vol. 2: *Croissance des végétaux cultivés*, Masson, Paris, 590 pp.

Demoulin, A. (1990) Les silicifications tertiaires de la bordure Nord de l'Ardenne et du Limbourg méridional (Europe NW). *Zeit. für Geom.* **34**(2): 179–97.
Interesting reconstruction of the formation of cenozoic silcretes and of its interrelationship with geomorphic evolution.

Derruau, M. (1988) *Précis de géomorphologie*, 7th ed., 536 pp., 235 fig., Masson, Paris.
An old fashion ed., still Davisian, elementary textbook, with some good illustrations but too many obsolete, unsustainable positions.

De Santo, P. (1978) *Concepts of applied ecology.* Springer-V., New York, Heidelberg, Berlin, 130 pp.
A very useful textbook.

Dewolf, Y. (1978) Contribution à l'étude des marges occidentales du Bassin de Paris. Problèmes de Géomorphologie. Thèse Etat, Paris VII, Jan 14, 589 pp.

Dewolf, Y. (1985) De la représentation des formes de relief . . . ou les avatars de la cartographie géomorphologique. *Pour Fernand Joly*, CERCG, Paris: 339–45.
A history of concepts of geomorphological mapping in France, very far from being objective.

Dezert, B., Frecaut, R. (1978) *L'économie des eaux continentales. Aménagement et environnement.* SEDES, Paris, 185 pp., 33 fig.
Basic, clearly written, easy to read.

D'Hoore, J. L. (1976) *Soil diagnosis through remote sensing.* NATO Advanced Res. Inst. on Earth Observ. and Inform Systems for Resource Management and Environmental Control, Bermuda, Nov. 14–20: 11 pp.

Dietz, K. R. (1989) Fernerkundung und Erkennung von geologisch-geomorphologischen Strukturen am Beispiel von Testgebieten aus den USA, *Frankfurter geowissen Arb.* D 10: 79–190.
Ground truth for different remote-sensing test areas in the USA.

Dijk, D. C. van (1959) *Soil features in relation to erosional history in the vicinity of Canberra.* CSIRO, Soil Publ. 13, 41 pp., 19 fig.

Dixon, R. M. (1966) Water infiltration responses to soil management. PhD thesis, Univ. of Wisconsin, 175 pp. (Univ. microfilms, Ann Arbor, Mich.)

Dorywalski, M. (1958) An example of a morphodynamic map. *Acta Geographica Lodziensia* **2**: 68–99 (in Polish with English summary).

Dorywalski, M. (1968) Maps on natural geographical environment. *Geographica Polonica* **14**: 211–16.
Is limited to the mapping of certain types of landforms.

Dosso, H., Guillaumet, J. P., Hadley, J. (1981) The Tai Project: land use problems in a tropical rain forest. *Ambio* **10**(2/3): 120–5.
Monograph of general interest on the transformation of an uninhabited area of rain forest into an agricultural region, westernmost Ivory Coast.

Doyle, F. J. (1984a) The economics of mapping with space data. *ITC Journal* (1): 1–9.

Doyle, F. J. (1984b) Surveying and mapping with space data. *ITC Journal* (4): 314–21.

Drevon, J. J., Thery, D. (1977) Ecodéveloppement et industrialisation. Renouvellabilité et nouveaux usages de la biomasse. *Cahiers de l'Ecodéveloppement* (Paris), 9 126 + 16, 4 pp.

Dreybrodt, W. (1988) *Processes in karst systems.* Springer-V, Berlin, 288 pp, 184 fig.
A specialized textbook.

Drozdoy, A. V. (1986) Aquatic terrestrial natural systems and pollution of coastal regions. *Proc. VII Symp. UGI Comm. on Environmental Problems.* Palma de Mallorca, Sept. 1983: 88–99.
Proposes an integration of the environment based on water flow.

Dubucq, M. (1986) Télédétection spatiale et érosion des sols, étude bibliographique. *Cah. ORSTOM sér. Pédol.* **XXII**(2): 247–58.

Duchaufour, P. (1963) Soil classification: a comparison of the American and French systems. *J. Soil Sc.* **14**: 149–55.

Duchaufour, P. (1982) *Pedology, pedogenesis and classification*,

transl. by Paton, T. R. Allen & Unwin, London, Boston, Sydney, 448 pp.
Duchaufour's work is characteristic of a school of pedology that neglects interactions between morphogenesis and pedogenesis, focusing almost exclusively on the organic matter of soils, a theory contrary to that which has led to the conception of morphopedological maps.

Duchaufour, P. (1983) Pédogénèse et classification. In: Duchaufour, P., Souchier, B. *Pédologie*, Paris, Masson, 2nd ed. 491 pp., 101 fig.

Duchaufour, P. (1988) *Pédologie Coll. Abrégés* Paris, Masson, 224 pp., 71 fig.

Duclos, G. (1973) Appréciation de l'aptitude à la mise en valeur des sols de Provence. *L'irrigant* **60**: 16–32.
Hierarchical ordering of constraining phenomena.

Ducrocq, A. (1986) L'eau et l'énergie. *Total Information* **104**: 23–7.

Dufour, J., Gravier, J., Larue, J. P. (1990) Fortes pluies et érosion des sols. L'orage de mai 1988 dans la Sarthe. *Bull. Assoc. des géogr. fr.* **67**(2): 159–70.
Analyses the effects of the concentration of fields accompanied by the destruction of hedges.

Duggin, M. J. (1974) *On the limitations of target differentiation by means of spectral discrimination technique.* 9th Intern. Symp. Remote Sensing of Environment, April 15–19, Ann. Arbor, Michigan. Summaries p. 52.
Variation of reflected radiation as a function of atmospheric transmissivity and the MS bands of LANDSAT.

Dumas, B., Gueremy, P., Lhenaff, R., Raffy, J. (1984) Risques de mouvements de terrain dans une région sismique: la façade calabraise du Détroit de Missine aux abords de Villa San Giovanni (Italie). *Méditerranée* **51**(1/2): 99–106.

Dunne, T. (1978) Field studies of hillslope flow processes. In: Kirkby *Hillslope hydrology*, J. Wiley & Sons, Chichester, 227–93.
Excellent study by a naturalist.

Dunne, T., Dietrich, W. (1980) Experimental study of Horton oberland flow on tropical hillslopes. *Zeit. für Geom. Suppl.-Bd* **35**: 40–59.

Dunne, T., Leopold, L. (1978) *Water in environmental planning.* Freeman, San Francisco, 818 pp, 403 fig.
General concepts and some interesting examples (especially pp. 6–9).

Duran, D. (1987) *Sequías e inundaciones, propuestas*, OIKOS, Buenos Aires, 198 pp., 15 fig.

Durand, J. H. (1983) *Les sols irrigables*, ACCT & PUF, Paris, 339 pp., 14 fig., 19 phot.
Describes the circulation of water in the soil: agronomic problems.

Durand, J. H. (1989) *Arrêter le désert*, ACCT & PUF, Paris, 416 pp. 11 fig., 32 phot.
Important information about the quality and use of water in arid regions.

Durand, R. (1979) La pédogénèse en pays calcaire dans le Nord-Est de la France. *Soc. Géol. France Mém.* **55**: 198 pp., 62 fig., 5 phot. pl.

Durand-Dastes, F. (1977) *Les systèmes d'utilisation de l'eau dans le monde* CDU-SEDES, Paris, 182 pp, 22 fig., 2 cartes h.t.

Duvigneaud, P. (1974) *La synthèse écologique.* Doin, Paris, 296 pp., fig.
Excellent example of the difficulty ecologists have in apprehending the environment and to raise themselves to the level of a real synthesis.

Dury, G. H. (1972) Some current trends in geomorphology. *Earth-Science Review* **8**: 45–72.
Useful overview of the last 15 years, bibliography.

Dury, G. H. (1986) *The face of the earth.* Allen & Unwin, London, 5th ed., 242 pp.

Duthil, J. (1971) *Eléments d'écologie et d'agronomie*, vol. 1: *Connaissance du milieu*, Baillière et Fils, Paris, 585 pp.

Dylik, J. (1957) Dynamical geomorphology its nature and methods. *Bulletin de la société des sciences et des lettres de Lodz. Class III Sciences mathématiques et naturelles* **8**(12): 1–42.
First major paper announcing a new approach to geomorphology away from Davisian concepts.

Dylik, J. (1964) Some remarks on the development of modern geomorphology in Poland. *Czasopismo Geograficzne* **35**: 259–77.

Good historical review, stresses the importance of recent methodological changes.

Eden, M. J., Parry, J. T. (Eds) (1986) *Remote sensing and tropical land management*, J. Wiley & Sons, Chichester, 365 pp. *16 contributors deal with land classification and evaluation, land use survey, monitoring agricultural resources and land cover.*

Edmons, D., Painter, R., Ashley, G. (1970) A semi-quantitative hydrological classification of soils in North-East England. *J. Soil Sc.* 21(2): 256–64.

Eeles, C. W. O. (1969) *Installation of access tubes and calibration of neutron moisture probes*, Inst. of Hydrology, Rept. 7, Wallingford, England.

Ehrard-Cassegrain, A., Margat, J. (1982) *Introduction à l'économie générale de l'eau*. Masson, Paris, 361 pp., 48 fig. *Clear and accurate work on an important theme on which publications are few; the result of the cooperation of an economist and a well-known hydrologist.*

Eimberck, M. (1989/90) Facteurs d'érodibilité des sols limoneux: réflexions à partir du cas du Pays de Caux. *Cah. ORSTOM sér. Pédol.* XXV(1/2): 81–94. *The USLE is not so 'universal' as it pretends to be.*

Einsele, G. (1982) Limestone-marl cycles (peridotites): diagnosis, significance, causes. A review. In: Einsele, G., Steilacher, A. (Ed.) *Cyclic and event stratification*, pp. 8–59. Springer-V, Berlin, 536 pp., 380 fig. *World balance and budget of CO_2. Each year, photosynthesis extracts 10% of the atmospheric CO_2. There is the same total mass of CO_2 in the biosphere on one side and in the atmosphere on the other.*

Ellertson, B. W. (1968) Forest hydrologic research conducted by the Tennessee Valley Authority. *Water Res. Bull.* 4(2): 25–63.

Ellis, D. (1989) *Environments at risk. Case histories of impact assessment.* Springer-V., Berlin, 329 pp., 99 fig. *A fundamental book, with excellent examples.*

Embleton, C., Thornes, J. (1979) *Process in geomorphology.* Edward Arnold, London, 436 pp.

E.P.E., Min. Agric., D.R.N., SUDENE (1972) *Levantamento exploratorio-reconhecimento de solos do Estado da Paraiba.* Bol. Tecn. 15, Ser. Pedol., 683 pp., 114 fig., 2 separate maps. *This regional pedologic survey places soils in their geomorphologic context with regard to the physiography and present processes, the Quaternary evolution, the vegetation, and the climate. Uses the American classification. Maps on a scale of 1:500 000 on the one hand of the aptitudes of traditional agriculture, on the other of modern, mechanical agriculture, a distinction also adopted by RADAMBRASIL.*

Erhart, H. (1967) *La Genèse des sols en tant que phénomène géologique: esquisse d'une théorie géologique et géochimique – biostasie et rhexistasie*, 2nd edn. Coll. Evolution des Sciences 8 (1st edn 1956). Paris, Masson.

Ernsberger, H., Sokollek, V. (1985) Effects of land use on the hydrology of small basins in Hessen (Federal Republic of Germany). *AIHS Public.* 148: 147–57.

ERTS-1 (1976) *A new window on our planet.* Washington, Superintendent of Documents, US Gov. Printing Office, 362 pp., 256 fig. *Series of articles grouped by themes showing what Landsat-1 can contribute to the knowledge of the geographical environment.*

Essadiki, M. (1987) A combination of panchromatic and multispectral SPOT images for topographic mapping. *ITC Journal* 1: 59–66.

Estes, J. E., Senger, W. L. (Eds) (1974) *Remote sensing. Techniques for environmental analysis*, Hamilton, Santa Barbara, Calif., 340 pp. *Review of technical data, applications to the natural environment, geology, vegetation, agriculture, cities, regional aspects and conservation.*

Evans, R. (1980) Mechanics of water erosion and their spatial and temporal controls: an empirical viewpoint. In: Kirkby, M. J., Morgan, R. P. C. (Eds) *Soil erosion*, pp. 109–28, J. Wiley & Sons, Chichester, New York.

Evans, R., Carroll, D. (1986) Radar images for soil survey in England and Wales. *ITC Journal* 1: 88–93. *Expérience ARZOTU, Rapport final 1975–78. Contribution à l'analyse écologique des zones arides de Tunisie avec l'aide des données de télédétection spatiale.* CNRS, CEPE, Montpellier et CNES (1978): 222 pp., fig. phot.

Eyre, S. R. (1968) *Vegetation and soils. A world picture.* 2nd ed., reprinted (1973), 328 pp. 30 fig., 10 maps, 32 phot., Edward Arnold, London. *Various types of vegetation are presented with their relationships to soils in the perspective of geological evolution.*

Fabre, G. (1989) Les karsts du Languedoc méditerranéen (S.E. de la France). *Zeit. für Geom. Suppl.-Bd* 75: 49–81. *A good regional monograph.*

Fabre, G. (1990) La catastrophe hydrologique éclair de Nîmes (3 Octobre 1988). *Bull Assoc. géogr. fr.* 67(2): 113–22. *Another example of insufficient management of the environment. Description of the catastrophe, discussion for planning a better management.*

Fagot, P., Gadiolet, P., Magne, M., Bravard, J. P. (1989) Une étude dendrochronologique dans le lit majeur de l'Ain: la forêt alluviale comme descripteur d'une 'métamorphose fluviale'. *Rev. Géogr. Lyon* 64(54): 213–23. *Various tree species and their age allow the precise reconstruction of the change of their ecological environment, which result from fluvial dynamic alteration.*

Fairbridge, R. W. (Eds) (1968) *The encyclopedia of geomorphology*, Reinhold Book Corp., New York, 1295 pp. *Monographs on diverse subjects presented in alphabetical order. Useful.*

Faktorovitch, M. E. (1967) Transformation de lits à l'aval des usines hydroélectriques de grande puissance de l'URSS. *UGGI, Ass. Gén. Berne. Coll. Morphol. Rivières*: 401–3.

Falque, M. (1972) Pour une planification écologique. *L'irrigant* 59: 3–22.

Falque, M., Portier, Duclos G. (1973) Pédologie et planification écologique. *L'irrigant* 60: 1–15.

Fanthou, T., Kaiser, R. (1990) Evaluation des risques naturels dans les Hautes-Alpes et en Savoie. *Bull. Ass. des géogr. fr.* 67(4): 323–41. *A good analysis of the problem of natural risks in two French 'departments' in the Alps. Interesting methodology.*

FAO/UNEP (1977) *Assessing soil degradation.* FAO/UNEP expert consultation, Rome, 18–20 January, FAO Soil Bull. **34**: 83 pp.

FAO/UNESCO (1954) *Multilingual vocabulary of soil science.* Paris, Rome.

FAO/UNESCO (1974) *Soil map of the world*, vol. 1, legend, Paris, Rome, 59 pp.

FAO/UNESCO (1982) Document D: *Draft definitions of soil units at high level*, Rome, 7 pp.

Farr, T. (1985) Recent advances in geological mapping by radar. *Doc. B.R.G.M.* 82: 199–215.

Fauck, R., Lamoureux, M., Perraud, A., Quantin, P., Roederer, P., Vieillefon, J., Segalen, P. (1979) *Projet de classification des sols*, Paris, ORSTOM, 301 pp.

Faugères, L. (1980) Présentation du colloque sur les paysages méditerranéens. *Bull. Assoc. des géogr. fr.* **466**: 3–12. *General discussion of the 'landscape' concept.*

Faugères, L. (1990) Géographie physique et risques naturels. *Bull. Assoc. des géogr. fr.* 67(2): 89–98. *An overview, with statistics of casualties resulting from the various types of hazards, on a world basis.*

Faure, H. (1988) Le cycle global de l'eau modifié et corrigé par l'Homme. *Géochronique*, **28**: 10. *Effect of dams on the global water cycle.*

Feau, C. (1976) Unité écologique expérimentale de Maradi. Etude morpho pédologique. GERDAT-IRAT, 33 pp., appendices, 1 folded map.

Feau, C. (1977) Unité écologique expérimentale de Maradi. Etude morpho–pédologique au 1/20 000, GERDAT-IRAT, 28 pp., appendixes, 1 folded map. **Feau, C.** (1976/1977): this study of soils is supported by geomorphic and ecodynamic investigations by Blanck, J. P., Cloots-Hirsch, A. R.

Fedina, A. E. (1963) Systems of taxonomic units of physical–geographical regionalisation. *Izvestia akademia Nauk. SSSR. géogr. ser.* 2: 91–8. In Russian.

Fedina, A. E. (1965) *Fiziko geograficeskoe rajonirovanie* Izd. M.G.U., Moscow, 142 pp.

Feodoroff, A. (1960) Evaluation de la stabilité structurale d'un sol (indices). Nouvelles normes d'emploi pour l'appareil à tamiser. *Ann. Agron.* **11**: 651–9.

Feodoroff, A. (1961) Capacité de rétention pour l'eau et structure du sol. *Comptes rendus de l'Académie des Sciences*, Paris, **252**: 591–3.

Feodoroff, A. (1962) Ressuyage du sol et capacité de rétention pour l'eau. *Ann. Agron.* **13**(6): 523–47.

Feodoroff, A. (1965) Etude expérimentale de l'infiltration de l'eau non saturante. Cas d'un sol initialement sec et d'un arrosage sans formation de plan d'eau en surface. *Ann. Agron.* **16**(2): 127–75, (3): 231–63.

Feodoroff, A., Betremieux, R. (1964) Une méthode de laboratoire pour la détermination de la capacité au champ. *Science du sol* 2nd semester, Versailles: 109–18.

Feodoroff, A., Rafi, M. (1963) Evaporation de l'eau à partir du sol nu. *Ann. de Géogr.* **14**(4): 601–13.

Finkl, C. W. (1980) Stratigraphic principles and practices as related to soil mantles. *Catena* 7: 169–94.

Finson, K., Mellis, M. D. (1986) Remote sensing of natural resources with radar. *Progr. Phys. Géogr.* **10**(7): 185–93.

Firman, J. B. (1969a) Palaeosols. A stratigraphic definition. *8th Congr. INQUA*, Paris, sect. IIIb: 420–25.

Firman, J. B. (1969b) Stratigraphic analysis of soils near Adelaide, South Australia. *Trans. Royal Soc. South Australia*, **93**: 39–54.

Fitzgerald, E. (Ed.) (1974) *Multispectral scanning systems and their potential application to Earth resources surveys. Spectral properties of materials.* ESRO Contractor Report 232, 231 pp.

Fitzpatrick, E. A. (1980) *Soils, their formation, classification and distribution*, Longman, Harlow, 353 pp., 181 fig., 73 tabl., 4 pl. *Good on the classification of parent materials and the various soil classifications, including the author's own. FAO system used in description of world soils.*

Fitzpatrick, E. A. (1985) Relic periglacial features in the soils of north-east Scotland. *International Geomorphology 1985. Abstracts of Papers for the First Intern. Conf. on Geomorph.* T. Spencer (Ed.) 183 pp.

Flageollet, J. C. (1989) *Les mouvements de terrain et leur prévention.* Coll. Géographie, Masson, Paris, 224 pp., 119 fig. *A specialized textbook on mass-movement: processes, damage, preventive measures.*

Flores, A. L., Carlson, N. T. (1987) Estimation of surface moisture availability from remote temperature measurements. *J. Geophys. Res.* **92**(D8): 9581–5.

Floret, C., Fontanier, R. (1984) *L'aridité en Tunisie présaharienne.* Mém. ORSTOM, **150**: 544 pp. *Water needs compared on different soils, amount of rain necessary to replenish water reserves of different types of soil (in fact, surface layers).*

Flugel, W. A. (1979) Untersuchungen zum Problem des Interflow. *Heidelberger Géogr. Abh.* **56**: 170 pp., 27 fig., 3 maps.

Foin, T. H. C. Jr. (1976) *Ecological systems and the environment.* Houghton Mifflin, Boston: 591 pp., fig. *A valuable effort, a benchmark for the evolution of concepts.*

Fookes, P., Sweeney, M., Manby, C., Martin, R. (1985) Geological and geotechnical engineering aspects of low-cost roads in mountainous terrain. *Engineering Geol.* 21: 1–152.

Fori, C., Higgins, G., Purnell, M. (1986) Criteria for choice of land suitable for agricultural production. In: Lal R., Lal, A. (Eds) *Land clearing and development in the tropics.* Balkema, Rotterdam, pp. 19–28.

Forman, R. (1982) Interaction among landscape elements: a core of landscape ecology. *Perspectives in Landscape Ecology.* Intern. Congress, Veldhoven, April 19–27 (1981), pp. 35–48.

Fotografische Fernerkundung der Erde. Experimente auf der Orbitalstation 'Saliut-6'. Akademic Verlag, Berlin (1983), 219 pp.

Fournier, F. (1960) *Climat et érosion.* Paris PUF, 201 pp., 15 graphiques. *World perspective on suspended matter.*

Fournier, F. (1970) *Aspects de la conservation des sols dans les différentes régions climatiques et pédologiques de l'Europe.* Cons.

de l'Europe, Com. Eur. Sauvegarde de la Nat. et Ress. Nat., Strasbourg, 156 pp.

FRALIT (Equipe) (1977) *Télédétection du littoral océanique de la France.* Coll. Ecole Normale Supérieure de Jeunes Filles, Montrouge, **11**: 310 pp.

Francou, B. (1987) *L'éboulisation en haute montagne.* Thèse Etat, Paris VII et Centre de Géom. CNRS Caen: 689 pp.

Fränzle, O. (1982) Das Blatt 1826 Bordeshol als Beispiel der Möglichkeiten und Grenzen einer Bodenkundlichen sowie unwelt-chemischen Interpretation eines Flachlandes Blattes der GMK 25. *Berliner Geogr. Abh.* **25**: 102–12.

Frecaut, R. (1978) Les bilans de consommation d'eau dans les pays industrialisés. *Ann. de Géogr.* LXXXVII(482): 385–97. *Critical examination of statistical sources of the most important countries, evaluating their various uses.*

Frecaut, R. (1982) *Eléments d'hydrologie et de dynamique fluviales.* Vol. I, 147 pp., 11 fig. Univ. de Nancy II. *The death of the author has prevented the publication of Vol. 2. Much accurate data.*

Fritsch, E., Bocquier, G., Boulet, R., Dosso, M., Humbel, F. X. (1986) Les systèmes transformants d'une couverture ferrallitique en Guyane française. Analyse structurale d'une formation supergène et mode de représentation cartographique. *Cah. ORSTOM sér. Pédol.* **22**(54): 361–95.

Fujita, T., Suwa, H., Okuda, S. (1989) Chapter 3, Mass movement. *Trans. Japanese Geom. Un.* 10 A: 23–34. *Seismic generated mass movements in a volcanic region.*

Fulton, A. R., Jones, D. K., Lazzari, S. (1987) The role of geomorphology in post-disaster reconstruction. The case of Basilicata, Southern Italy. In: Gardiner, V. (Ed.) *International geomorphology*, pp. 241–62. J. Wiley & Sons, Chichester.

Furley, P. (1985) Radar surveys for resources evaluation in Brazil: an illustration from Rondônia. In: Eden, M. J., Parry, G. T. (Eds) *Remote sensing and tropical land management*, pp. 79–90. J. Wiley & Sons, Chichester.

Furley, P., Newey, W. (1983) *Geography of the biosphere.* Butterworth, London, 413 pp. *Excellent presentation of the US taxonomy and of its terms.*

Gadd, N., Peddle, T. (1984) Landslide. *Geos* **13**: 18–21.

Galay, V. J. (1988) Causes of river bed degradation. *Water Res.* **19**: 1057–90. *Includes a list of the depth of incisions downstream of US dams.*

Gallais, J. (1967) *Le Delta intérieur du Niger. Etude de géographie régionale.* IFAN, Dakar, 2 vols, 680 pp., 5 maps.

Galloway, R. W., Gunn, R. H., Story, R. (1970) *Lands of the Mitchell–Normandy Area, Queensland*, Land Research Series 26, CSIRO, Australia, 101 pp., 7 fig., 32 pl., 10 tabl., 2 folded coloured maps.

Galon, R. (1964) Hydrological research for the needs of the regional economy. *Geographia Polonica* 3: 239–50. *Extract of the 1:50 000 map.*

Galon, R. (1965) Sur les méthodes d'évaluation du milieu géographique en vue de l'aménagement planifié. *Mémoires et Documents du Service de documentation cartographique et géographique du CNRS* **10**(2): 20–8.

Gamez, P., Sari, M. (1979) Morphogénèse et karstogénèse en Woevre septentrionale, l'interfluve Loison-Othain. *Mosella* 9(1): 3–76.

Garcia, G. J. (1988) O impacto do Prodalcool na região Oeste do Estado de São Paulo. *Geografia* 13(26): 105–18. *Disastrous effects of the cultivation of sugar cane for alcohol production as a substitute for petrol, on social and environmental areas.*

García Novo, E., Ramírez Díaz, L., Torres Martínez, A. (1975) El sistema de dunas de Doñana. *Naturalia Hispanica*, **5**: 56 pp., 10 fig. 13 phot. *Shows the vulnerability of certain landscape units.*

Garcynski, F. (1980) Influence du taux de boisement sur le régime hydrologique dans trois régions des USA (corrélations multiples). Intern. Symp. on *Influence of Man on the Hydrol. Regime with special reference to representative and experimental basins.* UNESCO/IASH publ. Helsinki 23–26 June, **130**: 61–6.

Gardner, R. (1989) Late quaternary loess and paleosols; Kashmir Valley, India. *Zeit. für Geom. Suppl.-Bd* 76: 225–45.

Gardner, W. R., Kirkham, D. (1952) Determination of soil moisture by neutron scattering. *Soil Sc.* **73**: 391–401.

Gardner, W. R., Widstone, J. A. (1921) The movement of soil moisture. *Soil Sc.* **11**: 215–32.

Garescu, P., Zavoianu, I., Driga, B. (1967) Légende des cartes hydrogéographiques. *Revue Roumaine de Géologie, Géophysique et Géographie* sér. Géographie, **11**: 149–54.

Gates, D. (1962) *Energy exchange in the biosphere.* Harper, New York, 151 pp.

Gaucher, G. (1967) Les conditions de la pédogénèse dans la partie septentrionale du littoral sénégalais. *Pédologie* 17(2).

Gaucher, G. (1968) *Traité de pédologie agricole* (1) *Le sol et ses caractéristiques agronomiques.* Paris, Dunod, 578 pp., 140 fig., (2) (1981) *Les facteurs de la pédogénèse.* Dison (Belgium), Lelotte, 730 pp., 195 fig.
Excellent treatise, written by a researcher of vast experience and with a naturalistic outlook. Cf. in particular vol. **2**(6).
Relief et géomorphologie and (7) *L'érosion, facteur de pédogénèse.*

Gaucher, G. (1972) Contribution de la géomorphologie à la prospection pédologique. *Ann. de Géogr.* **81**(448): 697–710.

Gaucher, G., Burdin, S. (1974) *Géologie-géomorphologie et hydrologie des terrains salés.* Coll. Techniques Vivantes, PUF, Paris, 234 pp., 35 fig.

Gedroiz, K. (1929) Der absorbierende Bodencomplex und die adsorbierten Bodenkationen als Grundlage der genetischen Bodenklassifikation. *Kollodchem. Beihefte*: 1–112.

Gellert, J. (1968) Wesen der angewandten Geomorphologie. *Petermanns geographische Mitteilungen* **112**: 256–64.
Good concise account, bibliography.

Gellert, J. F. (1969) Thematische Karten, wichtige Hilfsmittel für die Territorialplannung. *Die Wirtschaft* 51/52, Dez. 18, p. 15.

Gellert, J. E. (1984) Neue Aktivitäten der geomorphologische Forschung und Kartierung in der VR China. *Peterm. Geogr. Mitt.* **128**: 293–7.

Gellert, J. E. (1985) Die geomorphologische Detailkartierung (GMK 25) der Bundesrepublik Deutschland, eine analytische Betrachtung. *Peterm. Geogr. Mitt.* (1): 63–8.
A very good summary with numerous bibliographical references.

Gellert, J. F. (1989) Zur Typisierung geomorphologischer General-bzw. Regionalkarten in den Massstäben von 1:1 Mio bis 1:5 Mio. *Peterm. Geogr. Mitt.* **133**(4): 291–301.

Geoabstracts *Remote sensing, photogrammetry and cartography.* Norwich, England.
Bimonthly references, but listing of non-English publications is far from complete.

Gerasimov, T. P. (1962) Application of soil survey data to agriculture and principles of soil classification and survey in the USSR. *Trans. Intern. Society of Soil Science. Comm 4&5, New Zealand:* 536–9.

Gerlach, T. (1976) Present day slope development in the Polish flysch Carpathians. *Prace Geograficzne* **122**: 116 pp., 22 fig. (in Polish, Engl. summ.).

Gerrard, A. J. (1981) *Soils and landforms, an integration of geomorphology and pedology.* Allen & Unwin, London: 219 pp.
Intends to demonstrate the importance of morphogenic processes to pedology, but deals more with morphogenic processes as such and with relationship rather than with dynamic interactions. Includes a thorough account of catenas.

Gerrard, J. (1990) *Mountain environments: an examination of the physical geography of mountains.* Belhaven Press, London, 317 pp.
Among others, rates of ablation in various mountains in the world.

Gierloff-Emden, H. G. (1976) Manual of interpretation of orbital remote sensing satellite photography and imagery for coastal and offshore environmental features (including lagoons, estuaries and bays). *Münchener Geogr. Abh.* **20**: 176 pp. fig.
Review of physical conditions by which light waves penetrate water. Littoral studies made with satellite photography and LANDSAT MSS recordings.

Gierloff-Emden, H. G. (1987) Fernerkundung mit SEASAT-Altimeter als Innovation zur Morphologie des Meeresbodens. *Münchener Geogr. Abh.,* Reihe B (**4**): 139–95.

Gierloff-Emden, H. G. (1989) *Fernerkundungskartographie mit Satellitenaufnahmen.* F. Deuticke, Vienna, 588 pp., fig.
An unrivalled specialized textbook of general interest.

Gierloff-Emden, H. G., Dietz, K. R., Klam, K. (1985) Geographische Bildanalysen von Metric-Camera Aufnahmen des Space Shuttle-Fluges STS-9, *Münchener Geogr. Abh.* **33**: 163 pp.

Gierloff-Emden, H. G., Wienecke, F. (1979) Geographische Fernerkundung. *42nd Deutscher Geographentag* Göttingen, pp. 145–66.
Excellent review of diverse satellites, their sensors, the types of information provided by LANDSAT and other programmes.

Gieseking, J. (Ed.) (1975) *Soil components* Vol. 2 *Inorganic components.* Springer-V., Berlin, Heidelberg, New York, 684 pp., 212 fig.

Giesshübel, S. (1989) Rezente geomorphologische Prozesse im Waldgrenzbereich Skandinaviens. *Frankfurter Geowiss. Arb.* D **10**: 107–17.
Degradation resulting from skiing and protection measures taken in Scandinavia.

Gigo, M. (1982) Les échelles spatio-temporelles en géographie physique. *Analyse Spatiale,* Nice, **12**: 21 pp.
Is mainly concerned with watersheds. Thorough methodological study demonstrating the problems that result from the complexity of the phenomena and their different spatial and temporal attributes.

Gigon, A. (1983) Typology and principles of ecological stability and instability. In: Messerli, B., Ives, J. (Ed.) Mountain Ecosystems, stability and instability. *Mountain Res. & Development* **3**(2): 95–102.

Gilbert, H., Payette, S. (1982) Ecologie des populations d'aulne vert (Alnus crispa Ait. Pursh) à la limite des forêts, Québec nordique. *Géogr. Phys. et Quat.* **36**(1/2): 109–24.
Effects of instability caused by periglacial phenomena on the wooded tundra.

Gillet, N. (1970) Les problèmes de l'utilisation de l'eau. *L'Agriculture tropicale* (10/11): 896–901.

Gilluly, J. (1963) The scientific philosophy of Gilbert G. K. In: Albritton Cl C. (Ed.) *The fabric of geology* Addison-Wesley, pp. 218–24.

Girard, C. M., Girard, M. C. (1975) *Applications de la télédétection à l'étude de la biosphère.* Coll. Sciences Agronomiques, Masson, Paris, 186 pp., 70 fig., 15 phot., 2 pl. in colour.
Review of physical aspects, types of sensors and their use for the study of soils, vegetation and crops.

Girard, M. C. (1986) Interprétation pédologique des photographies prises par SPACELAB-1. *ITC Journal* (1): 14–18.

Glangeaud, L. (1970) La méthode géodynamique des ensembles naturels bornés (nods), ses applications à l'évolution des grands ensembles mégamétriques terrestres. *Rev. Géogr. Phys. et Géol. Dyn.* **12**: 465–92.

Glaser, G. (1983) Unstable and vulnerable ecosystems, a comment on MAB research on island ecosystems. In: Messerli, B., Ives, J. (Ed.) Mountain ecosystems, stability and instability. *Mountain Res. and Dev.* **3**(2): 121–3.

Glooschenko, W. (1980) Coastal ecosystems of the James–Hudson Bay area of Ontario, Canada. *Zeit. für Geom. Suppl.-Bd* 34: 214–24.
Indirectly, the continuing glacio-isostatic uplift since deglaciation maintains the ecosystems in a permanent state of youth.

Gobert, A., Trautmann, J. (1979) Problèmes d'érosion et de sédimentation liés à l'implantation d'un lac de retenue hydroélectrique dans le bassin du Rio Bata (Colombie). *Rech. Géogr. à Strasbourg* **10**: 35–53.

Godefroy, P., Humbert, M. (1982) Procédure d'établissement des plans d'exposition aux risques naturels. BRGM, Serv. Géol. Nat., *Rés. Sc. et Techn.* 2e partie: 73–4.

Godron, M., Poissonet, J. (1972) Quatre thèmes complémentaires pour la cartographie de la végétation et du milieu. *Bull. de la Société Languedocienne de Géographie* **6**(3): 329–56.
Shows the greater or lesser aptitude of vegetation to heal wounds inflicted on the plant cover. Calculates the rate of recolonization based on pioneering successions.

Gorecki, A., Klementowski, J. (1989) Geomorpholoical effects of torrential rainfall in Ksiegienice Wilkie. *Czasopismo Geogr.* **LX** (3): 290–313. In Polish, English summary.
A detailed description of the dramatic effects of heavy rainfall in the Sudetes.

Goudie, A. (1982) *The human impact.* Blackwell, Oxford, 326 pp.

Treats some aspects of water resources and water balance.

Goudie, A. S. (Ed.) (1990) *Techniques for desert reclamation.* J. Wiley & Sons, Chichester, 281 pp.
Among other problems, salinization–alkalinization of soils.

Govers, G. (1986) Mechanismen van akkererosie op lemige bodems. Doct. diss. Royal Univ. of Leuven, labo. voor Experimentele Geomorphologie, Royal Univ. Leuven, 392 pp. + appendices.

Graf, W. L. (1988) *Fluvial processes in dryland rivers.* Springer-V., Berlin, 346 pp., 143 fig.

Gras, R., Monnier, G. (1963) Contribution de certains éléments grossiers du sol à l'alimentation en eau des végétaux. *Science du Sol.* 1(special n°): 13–20.

Greenland, D. J., Lal, R. (Eds) (1975) *Soil conservation and management in the humid tropics.* Proc. Intern. Conf. Soil Cons. & Management in the Humid Tropics, Ibadan, June 1975. J. Wiley & Sons, Interscience, Chichester, 283 pp.

Griend A., van der, Engman, E. T. (1985) Partial area hydrology and remote sensing. *J. Hydrology* 81: 211–51.

Grumazescu, H. (1966) The geographical region and the land use. *Revue Roumaine de Géologie, Géophysique et Géographie, série Géographie* 10: 167–75.

Guan-Soon, Lim (1974) Integrated pest control in developing countries of Asia. *SCOPE*, Misc. Publ., Indianapolis: 47–76.
A good general vision.

Gueremy, P., Vogt, J. (1987) Géomorphologie et risques naturels. (Actes du 1er Forum Franç. de Géom., Meudon-Bellevue, 26/27 Nov. *Rev. de Géom. Dyn.* 36(3/4): 97–122.

Guerini, M. C., Muxart, T. (1986) *Des difficultés liées à l'approche interdisciplinaire de l'analyse de l'interface Homme/ Milieu Naturel.* Ass. Ruralistes Fr., Coll. de Strasbourg, 16 pp.

Guigo, M. (1979) Hydrologie et érosion dans l'Apennin septentrional. Thèse Etat, Aix-Marseille II, 5 Oct., vol. 1, 501 pp.
Remarkable monograph describing the water balance of several basins.

Guillaume, M. (1960) Les aménagements hydro-agricoles de riziculture et de culture de décrue dans la vallée du Niger. *Agron. Trop.* 15(1): 73–91.

Guillobez, S. (1974) *Etude des sols gris de Casamance. Campagne de 1972–73*, IRAT, Paris.

Guitelson, A., Nikanoroy, A., Szabo, Gy, Szilagyi, F. (1986) Etude de la qualité des eaux de surface par télédétection. *Proc. Budapest Symp., IAHS Publ.* 157: 111–21.

Gunn, R. H., Nix, H. A. (1977) Land units of the Fitzroy Region, Queensland, CSIRO, *Land Res. Ser.* 39: 228 pp.
A survey 30 years after the first one, for comparison.

Gupta, A. (1987) Urban geomorphology in the humid tropics: the Singapore case. In: Gardiner, V. (Ed.) *International geomorphology 1986*, Part I, pp. 303–17. J. Wiley & Sons, Chichester.

Haark, R. (1983) A comparison of visual and numerical analyses of LANDSAT data for grassland and forest inventories in Swaziland, *ITC Journal* (1): 6–12.

Haanjes, H. (1965) Practical aspects of the Land System Surveys in New Guinea. *Journal of Tropical Geography* 21: 13–20.
Good account of the method. Bibliographic references.

Haase, G. (1964) Landschaftsökologische Detailuntersuchung und naturräumliche Gliederung. *Peterm. Geogr. Mitt.* 108: 8–30.

Haase, G. (1967) Zur Methodik grossmassstäbiger Landschaftsökologischer Erkundung. In: *Probleme der Landschaftsökologischer Erkundung.* Edited by E. Neef, Geographische Gesellschaft der DDR, Leipzig, pp. 35–128.

Haase, G. (1968) Inhalt und Methodik einer umfassenden landwirtschaftlichen Standortkartierung auf Grundlage Landschaftsökologischer Erkundung. In *Wissenschaftliche Veröffentlichungen des Deutschen Institut für Länderkunde.* (Ed.) E. Lehman, pp. 25–6. Bibliographisches Institut Leipzig, pp. 309–49.
With large scale maps in colour.

Haase, G. (1976) The chorical structure of the natural landscape. 23rd Intern. Geogr. Congress, Moscow 6: 14–8. Also in *Peterm. Geogr. Mitt. Die Arealstruktur chorischer Naturräume* 120: 130–5.

Haase, G. (1977) Ziele und Aufgabe der geographischen Landschaftsforschung in der DDR. *Geogr. Ber.* 82: 1–19.

Haase, G. (1979) Entwicklungstendenzen in der geotopologischen und geochorologischen Naturraumerkundung. *Peterm. Geogr. Mitt.* 123: 7–18.

Haase, G., Mannsfeld, K., Schmidt, R. (1986) Typen der Anordnungsmusters zur Kennzeichnung der Arealstruktur von Mikrogeochoren. *Peterm. Geogr. Mitt.* 130: 31–9.

Haase, G., Richter, H. (1983) Current trends in landscape research. *Geojournal*, Wiesbaden : 7(2): 107–19.

Haase, G., Schlüter, H. (1980) Zur inhaltlichen Konzeption einer Naturraumtypenkarte der DDR im mittleren Massstab. *Peterm. Geogr. Mitt.* 124: 139–51.

Haase, G., Schmidt, R. (1973) Zur Ermittlung des Ertragspotentials landschaftlich genutzter Flächen auf der Grundlage geoökologischer Erkundungen. *Quaestiones Geobiologicae* 11, Bratislava: 91–126.

Haase, G. et al. (1982) Kennzeichnung und Kartierung von Naturraumtypen im mittleren massstabsbereich, Leipzig. *Wissenschaftliche Mitteilungen des Institute für Geographie und Geoökologie der Akademie der Wissenschaften der DDR* Sonderheft 1.

Hadas, A., Swartzendruber, D., Rijtema, P. E., Fuchs, M., Varon, B. (Eds) (1973) *Physical aspects of soil water and salts in ecosystems.* Springer-V., New York, Berlin, 460 pp.

Hagedorn, H., Thomas, M. (Eds) (1980) Perspectives in geomorphology. *Zeit. für Geom. Suppl.-Bd* 36: 313 pp.
The promise of the title is not entirely fulfilled, yet certain papers merit study.

Haines-Young, R. H., Petch, J. R. (1980) The challenge of critical rationalism for methodology in physical geography. *Progress in Physical Geography* 4(1): 63–77.
Show that the inductive method results in reasoning in vicious circles. Recommend resource to the deductive method checked by constant observations.

Hallaire, M. (1953) *Diffusion capillaire de l'eau dans le sol et répartition de l'humidité en profondeur sous sols nus et cultivés* thèseo, Inst. Nat. de la Recherche Agronomique, Paris.

Hallaire, M. (1957) Le rôle de la végétation dans l'épuisement des réserves en eau du sol. UGGI. Intern. Assoc. Scientific Hydrology, Toronto meeting 2: 412–22.

Hallaire, M. (1960) Le problème du potentiel de l'eau dans le sol et la disponibilité de l'eau pour la végétation. *Annales de Physiologie Végétale*, Paris: 119–30.

Hallsworth, E., Beattie, J., Darley, W. (1982) Formation of soils in an aridic environment. Western New South Wales, Australia. *Catena Suppl.* 1: 83–102.
Interesting monograph of general interest.

Halm, K. (1986) Photographische Weltaufnahmen und ihre Eignung zur thematischen und topographischen Kartierung, zur Umweltverträglichkeitsprüfung (UVP) . . . *Münchener Geogr. Abh.* 35: 123 pp., 127 fig.

Hamilton, L., King, P. (1983) *Tropical forested watersheds: hydrologic and soil response to major uses or conversions.* Westview: 168 pp.

Hamza, A. (1984) Contribution à l'étude de la morphogénèse historique en Tunisie centrale. *Rech. Géogr. à Strasbourg* 22/23: 55–68.

Hanks, R. J. (1984) Prediction of crop yield and water consumption under saline conditions: 272–83. In: Shainberg, I., Shalhevet, J., *Soil salinity under irrigation, processes and management.* Springer-V., Berlin, New York, 349 pp.

Harden, J. (1982) A quantitative index of soil development from field descriptions: example from a chronosequence in central California. *Geoderma* 28: 1–28.

Harlin, J. M., Berardi, G. M. (1987) *Agricultural soil loss. Processes, policies and prospects.* Boulder & London, Westview, 369 pp.
A comprehensive work including the socio-economic aspects, limited to the US.

Harp, E., Wilbon, R., Wieczorek, G. (1981) *Landslides from the February 4, 1976, Guatemala earthquake.* USGS Prof. Paper 1204–A, 35 pp., 50 fig., 2 maps.

Harper, D. (1984) *Terre, mer et satellites. Introduction à la télédétection.* Ministry of Supply and Services, Ottawa, 2nd. (Ed.), 282 pp., 62 fig.

Harris, R. (1986) Satellite remote sensing: high spatial resolution. *Prog. Phys. Geog.* **10**(4): 579–86.

Harris, R. (1987) *Satellite remote sensing, an introduction.* Routledge, London, New York, 220 pp., 69 fig. *Excellent overall textbook, well informed, well illustrated.*

Harris, S. A. (1986) *The permafrost environment.* Croom Helm, London & Sydney, 276 pp.

Hashizume, M. (1989) The present state of natural hazard identification and international cooperation. *ITC Journal* (3/4): 166–8. *A second hand statistic of disasters.*

Hayward, M. (1985) Soil development in flandrian floodplains: River Severn case-study. In: J. Boardman (Ed.) *Soils and quaternary landscape evolution*, pp. 281–99. J. Wiley & Sons, Chichester.

Hearn, G., Jones, D. K. C. (1987) Geomorphology and mountain highway design: some lessons from the Dharan-Dhankuta Highway, East Nepal. In: Gardiner, V. (Ed.) *International geomorphology* (1985), Part I, pp. 203–19. J. Wiley & Sons, Chichester.

Heathcote, R. L., Thom, B. G. (Eds) (1979) *Natural hazards in Australia.* Aust. Ac. Sc. (Canberra), 531 pp.

Hempenius, S. (1975) Infrared thermography at the ITC. Part I, the radiation laws. *ITC Journal* (1): 1–52.

Hempenius, S., Marwaha, B., Murialdo, A., Ren-Xiang, W. (1983) Characteristics of the second generation earth observation satellites. *ITC Journal* (1): 21–33.

Hénin, S. (1976) *Cours de physique du sol.* I. *Texture, structure, aération.* ORSTOM. Initiations, Documents Techniques, Paris, 159 pp., 21 fig.; II. *L'eau et le sol, les propriétés mécaniques, la chaleur et le sol.* ORSTOM, Paris, EDITEST, Brussels, 222 pp., 72 fig. *Presently one of the best available works.*

Hénin, S., Feodoroff, A., Gras, R., Monnier, G. (1960) *Le profil cultural. Principes de physique du sol.* Société d'Editions des Ingénieurs Agricoles, Paris, 320 pp.

Hénin, S., Gras, R., Monnier, G. (1969) *Le profil cultural, l'état physique du sol et ses conséquences agronomiques*, 2nd ed. Masson, Paris, 332 pp.

Herbs, K., et al. (1975) *Einführung in die landschaftsanalyse Lehrmaterial zur Ausbildung von Diplom-lehrer.* Potsdam.

Hervieu, J. (1963) Les plaines de la Zomandao et de Ranotsara. Recherches sur l'aménagement du relief et l'évolution des sols à Madagascar sue le cadre d'unités géomorphologiques. *Cah. ORSTOM sér. Pédol.* **1**(3): 75–114, 9 fig., 16 phot.

Hervieu, J. (1967) Géographie des sols malgaches, essai synthétique. *Cah. ORSTOM sér. Pédol.* **5**(1): 39–82.

Hervieu, J. (1970) Le Quaternaire au Nord-Cameroun. Schéma d'évolution géomorphologique et relation avec la pédogénèse. *Cah. ORSTOM sér. Pédol.* **8**(3): 295–317.

Heuseler, H., Coord. (1976) *Die Erde aus dem All. Satellitengeographie unseres Planeten.* Deutsche Verlags-Anstalt G. Westermann, Stuttgart & Braunschweig, 180 pp. *Interesting collection of satellite images, but disappointing commentaries.*

Hewitt, K. (Ed.) (1973) *Interpretation of calamity. The risks and hazards.* Series I, 304 pp.

Hewlett, J., Hibbert, A. (1961) Increases in water yield after several types of forest cutting. *Bull. AIHS* **6**(3): 5–17.

Heyse, J. (1979) Geomorphological mapping of flat regions in Flanders (Belgium) and morphology and evolution of the coversands in the Flemish Lowland. *IGU Comm. Geom. Surv.*, *Proceedings.* 15th Plenary Meeting, 55–67 pp. *Interesting representation of slopes.*

Hiernaux, P. H., Justice, C. O. (1986) Suivi du développement végétal au cours de l'été 1984 dans le Sahel Malien. *Internat. J. Remote Sensing* **7**(11): 1515–31.

Higham, A. D. (1973) *The application of multispectral sensing to the European Spacelab Project*, ESRO Summer School, IV: Earth Resources, 22 pp. *General, lucid review, with useful figures, on the MSS. Response of the vegetation.*

Higham, A. D. et al. (1974) *Multispectral scanning systems and their potential application to earth-resources surveys.* Summary volume. ESRO-236, 206 pp. 46 fig.

Complete, detailed, well illustrated summary on the entire electromagnetic spectrum and sensors, airborne and orbital recording systems. Properties of terrestrial materials. Data processing.

Higham, A. D., Wilkinson, B., Kahn, D. (1973) *Multispectral scanning systems and their potential application to earth-resources surveys. Basic physics and technology.* ESRO Contractor Report CR-231, 186 pp., 74 fig.

Hiward, A. D., Kochel, R. G., Holt, H. E. (Eds) (1988) *Sapping features of the Colorado Plateau. A comparative planetary geology field guide.* NASA SP-491, 108 pp. *Piping processes and description of this regional example.*

Holeis, G. E. (Ed.) (1979) *Man's impact on the hydrological cycle in the United Kingdom.* Geo Abstracts, Norwich, 278 pp.

Holeman, J. (1981) The national erosion inventory of the Soil Conservation Service, US Department of Agriculture, 1977–78. *AIHS, Proc. Florence Symp., Public.* **133**: 315–9.

Holy, M. (1980) *Erosion and environment.* Pergamon, Oxford, 225 pp., 150 fig.

Holzer, T. I. (1989) State and local response to damaging land subsidence in United States urban areas. *Engineer. Geol.* **27**: 449–66.

Horton, J. H., Hawkins, R. H. (1965) Flow path of rain from the soils surface to the water table. *Soil Science* **100**: 377–83. *The authors 'show that the percolation of rain water through the soil to the water table is accomplished throughout most of the flow path by downward displacement of water previously retained by the soil at field capacity'.*

Houzard, G. (1984) Vers une typologie et une cartographie des sylvofaciès. *Mélanges Journaux*, Univ. de Caen: 33–48.

Howard, A. D., Remson, I. (1978) *Geology in environmental planning.* New York, McGraw-Hill, 478 pp. *Elementary. Gives useful criteria for the identification of present morphogenic dynamics. Good photographs.*

Howard, J. A. (1976) Phyto-geomorphic classification of land units. *UN/FAO seminar on the applications of remote sensing for natural resources survey, planning and development* Univ. of Reading. *Proposes a taxonomy of units.*

Howard, J. A., Mitchell, C. (1980) Phyto-geomorphic classification of the landscape. *Geoforum* **11**: 85–106. *Formulation of the 'land system' concept to date.*

Howard, J. A., Mitchell, C. W. (1985) *Phytogeomorphology.* J. Wiley & Sons, Interscience, New York: 226 pp.

Howe, R. H. L. (1960) The application of aerial photographic interpretation to the investigation of hydrologic problems. *Photogrammetric engineering* **26**: 85–95.

Hsü, K. J. (1989) *Physical principles of sedimentology.* Springer-V., Berlin, 233 pp., 64 fig. *An excellent textbook, with very sound methodological expositions.*

Hubrich, H. (1954) Typisierung von topischen Geokomplexen. *Géogr. Ber.* **29**(2): 119–27.

Hubrich, H. (1967) Die Landschaftsökologische Catena in reliefarmen Gebieten dargestellt an Beispielen aus den nordwestsächsichen Flachland. *Peterm. Geogr. Mitt.* **69**: 13–8. *The type of catena characterizes a michrochore. The water balance determined by the regolith is the determinant ecologic factor.*

Hubrich, H. (1984) Typisierung von tonischen Geokomplexen. *Geogr. Ber.* **111**: 119–27.

Hubschmann, J. (1972) Sols et paysages: quelques problèmes d'écologie du sol. *Rev. Géogr. des Pyr. et du SO* **43**: 147–56. *Morphogenic processes are not considered at all.*

Huggett, R. (1985) *Earth surface systems.* Springer, Ser. in Phys. Env., 1 xii, 270 pp., 162 fig. Springer-V., Berlin.

Humbert, J. (1982) Cinq années de bilans hydrologiques mensuels sur un petit bassin-versant des Hautes-Vosges (1976–80): le bassin du Ringelbach. *Rech. Géogr. à Strasbourg* **19/20**: 105–22. *The area of this catchment is only a few hundred ha. It consists of weathered granite and receives heavy snowfall.*

Humbert, M., Vogt, J. (1983) *Le fichier d'information sur les mouvements de terrain en France et ses applications.* BRGM, Serv. Geol. Nat., Note Techn. 16/83: 25 pp., 4 fig.

Hurault, J. (1969) Application de la photo-interprétation aux projets de développement régional en Afrique tropicale. *Bull. d'Inform. de l'Institut Géographique National* Déc. 9: 24–38.

Used a special aerial survey on 1/15 000 in southern Benin (Dahomey). Integrates land use aspects and human factors in oil palm plantations.

Hurault, J. (1971) L'érodibilité des sols surpâturés des hauts plateaux de l'Adamaoua (Cameroun), essai de caractérisation par des mesures d'infiltration. *Bull. Ass. Fr. Et. du Sol* (1): 23–56.

Hurault, J. (1978) Contribution des vues ERTS-LANDSAT à l'Etude des terres hautes de l'Adamaoua (Cameroun), *GDTA*, Toulouse, *Journées de Télédétection*, 21–23 Sept. 1977, St Mandé, 255–76 pp.

Hutter, N., Minning, C., Netterville, J. (1972) *Terrain maps, Mackenzie Valley*, Canada Geological Survey, Open File Report 93.

Hyde, R., Vespar, N. (1983) Some effects of resolution cell size on image quality. *LANDSAT DATA Users Notes*: 9–12.

Ibrahim, M., Rapp, M. (1979) Variations temporo-spatiales de la salinité du sol d'un peuplement de pins pignons (*Pinus pinea L*) du littoral méditerranéen. *Ecologia Mediterranea* **4**: 49–60.

IEEE Transactions Geoscience and Remote Sensing (1986) GE-24 (4).
This issue contains numerous important contributions on various sensor capacities and methodological experiments.

IGU (1968) The unified key to the detailed geomorphological map of the world 1/25 000–1/50 000, and a collection of figures under separate cover. Committee of Applied Geomorphology, sub-comm. Geomorphological Maps. *Folia geogr.* Krakow, II, 40 pp.
In fact this legend is the Polish one.

Ihemadu, S. O. (1987) The problems and prospects of remote sensing applications in developing countries. *ITC Journal* (4): 285–91.

Imeson, A., Jungerius, P. (1974) Landscape stability in the Luxemburg Ardennes as exemplified by a hydrological and micropaleontological investigation of a catena in an experimental watershed. *Catena* **I**: 273–95.

Inst. Geol. si Geogr., Acad. Rep. Soc. Românîa (1969) Geografia vali Bunarii Romanesti. Anexa de hart: Ed. Acad. Rep. Soc. Românîa, Bucuresti: 761–77, 26 pl. h. t.
Maps covering the valley of the Romanian Danube, with a legend like that of the CGA maps.

Institut National de la Recherche Agronomique (1979) *L'eau et la production agricole*, Paris & Versailles, 269 pp., fig.

Institut de Recherches Agronomiques Tropicales et des Cultures Vivrières: Rapports annuels 1962–73.

Irmay, S. (1956) Extension of Darcy's law to unsteady, unsaturated flow through porous media. *Sympos. Darcy Intern. Assoc. Sci. Hydrol.*, Dijon, **2**: 57–66.

Isachenko, A. G. (1973) *Principles of landscape science and physical-geographic regionalisation*, transl. from the Russian edition (1965) by Zatorski, R. J. (Ed.) by Massey, J. S., Rosengren, Melbourne Univ. Press: 311 pp.

Ives, J. D. (1988) Development in the face of uncertainty. In: Ives, J. D., Pitt, D. C. (Eds) *Deforestation: social dynamics in watersheds and mountain ecology*. Routledge, London, 247 pp.

Ives, J., Hansen-Bristow, K. (1983) Stability and instability of natural and modified timberline landscapes in the Colorado Front Range. *Mountain Res. & Dev.* **3**(2): 149–55.

Ives, J., Pitt, D. C. (Ed.) (1988) *Deforestation, social dynamics in watersheds and mountain ecology*. Routledge, London and New York, 247 pp.
This very general title in fact includes monographs mainly devoted to the Himalayas.

Jacquinet, J. C. (1969) *Etude écologique intégrée de l'unité régionale de développement de Soliman (Tunisie)*, CEPE, Montpellier, 250 pp.
The study of the ecological framework is deficient and not integrated.

Jager, W., Riecke, G. (1966) Landschaftsökologische Talstudien in den Diedrichshäger Bergen. *Wissenschaftliche Zeitschrift der Universität Rostock*, 15, Math.–Naturwiss. Reihe 7–8: 943–60.

Jahn, A. (1963) Importance of soil erosion for the evolution of slopes in Poland. *Nachr. Ak. Wiss. Göttingen. II. Math. Phys. Kl.* **15**: 229–37.

Jahn, A. (1968) Denudational balance of slopes. *Geographica Polonica* **13**: 9–29.

Jamagne, M. (1967) Bases et techniques d'une cartographie des sols. Paris, *Inst. Nat. Rech. Agron.*, 142 pp. *Ann. Agron.* 18, n° hors série.

Jeffery, S. (1981) *Our usual landslide, ubiquitous hazard and socioeconomic causes of natural disasters in Indonesia.* Natural Hazard Res., Working Paper 40, 53 pp., 2 fig.

Jenny, H. (1941) *Factors of soil formation: a system of quantitative pedology.* McGraw-Hill, New York, 281 pp.

Jespersen, M. M., Rasmussen, E. (1989) Margrethe-Koog Landgewinnung und Küstenschutz im südlichen Teil des dänischen Wattenmeeres. *Die Küste* **50**: 97–154.
Techniques of stabilizing and winning land on coastal marshes, combining geomorphology and plant ecology with a minimum of embankments and ditches.

Johnson, D. L. (1985) Soil thickness processes. *Catena Suppl.* **6**: 28–40.

Johnson, D. L. (1989) Subsurface stone lines, stone zones, artifact-manuport layers and biomantles produced by bioturbation via pocket gophers (*Thomemys bottae*). *American Antiquity* **54**: 370–89.

Johnson, D. L. (1990) Biomantle evolution and the distribution of earth materials and artifacts. *Soil Sc.* **149**(2): 84–102.
Important aspect of pedogenesis.

Johnson, D. L., Keller, E. A., Rockwell, T. K. (1990) Dynamic pedogenesis: new views on some key soil concepts, and a model for interpreting Quaternary soils. *Quaternary Res.* **33**: 306–19.
A very interesting appraisal.

Johnson, D. L., Watson-Stegner, D. (1987) Evolution model of pedogenesis. *Soil Sc.* **143**(3): 349–66.

Johnson, D. L., Watson-Stegner, D. (1990): Chapter 31, the soil-evolution model as a framework for evaluating pedoturbation in archaeological site formation. *Geol. Soc. America*, Centennial Spec. Pub. **4**: 541–60.
A general overview.

Johnson, D. L., Watson-Stegner, D., Johnson, D. N., Schaetzl, R. J. (1987) Preisotropic and proanisotropic processes of pedoturbation. *Soil Sc.* **143**(4): 278–92.
Completes the former reference.

Joly, G. (1984) *Les données-images* SAT, 2, Paradigme, Caen, 133 pp.
Different types of data obtainable from LANDSAT, how to obtain them in Europe.

Joly, F., Bessac-Giraudet, J., Vuillegot, C. (1987) *Carte géomorphologique de la France au 1:1 000 000 (Quart Nord-Ouest).* Coll. Reclus, Modes d'Emploi (Montpellier), **11**: 39 pp.

Jones, D. (1980) British applied geomorphology: an appraisal. *Zeit. für Geom. Suppl.-Bd* **36**: 48–73.

Jordan, C., Heuveldop, J. (1981) The water budget of an Amazonian forest. *Acta Amazonica* **11**(1): 87–92.

Journaux, A. (1977) Morphogénèse quaternaire et pédogénèse dans l'Etat de São Paulo. Recherches françaises sur le Quaternaire, INQUA 1977. *Suppl. Bull. Assoc. Fr. pour l'Et. du Quat.* (50): 295–301.

Julian, M., Nicod, J. (1989) Les karsts des Alpes du Sud et de Provence. *Zeit. für Geom. Suppl.-Bd* **75**: 1–48.
Good exposition on the altitudinal distribution of the various karstic features.

Jungerius, P., van Zon, H. (1964) Sources of variation of soil erodibility in drainage basins in Luxembourg. In: Burt, T., Walling, D., (Ed.) *Catchment experiments in fluvial geomorphology*, 235–46. Geo. Books, Norwich.

Jungerius, P. D. (Ed.) (1985) *Soils and geomorphology*, Cremlingen, Catena Verlag, Catena Suppl. **6**: 174 pp.
A collection of 12 research papers dealing with response of soils to erosion, soils and relief, age of soils and landforms, and weathering, including karst.

Jurdant, M., Dionne, J. C., Beaubien, J., Belair, J. L., Geradin, B. (1972) An ecological survey of the Saguenay-Lac Saint-Jean region, Québec, Canada. *International Geography* **1**: 259–61.

Kadomura, H. (1980) Erosion by human activities in Japan. *Geo Journal* **4**(2): 133–44.
Catalogue of all forms of degradation including those caused by quarries, housing developments, etc.

Kadomura, H., Yamamoto, H., Imagawa, T., Rivière, A. (1983) Environmental implications of the 1977/78 Usu eruption. Symp. *Environments and man's control of them*, Spec. Public. Univ. of Hiroshima, 207–24.
Phytocoenoses are maintained in a pioneer stadium by repeated eruptions.

Kahn, F. (1982) *La reconstitution de la forêt tropicale humide. Sud-Ouest de la Côte d'Ivoire.* Mém. ORSTOM, 97, 150 pp., 38 fig.
To be compared with H. Dosso & Alii.

Kalesnik, S. V. (1962) Landscape science, *Soviet Geography*, American Geographical Society, Occasional publication n° 1: 201–4.

Kalms, J. M. (1972) *Esquisse morphopédologique de la zone de rénovation des Beni Slimane (Algérie).* IRAT, SODETEG, Paris.

Kaloga, B. (1966) Etude pédologique des bassins-versants des Volta Blanche et Rouge en Haute-Volta. *Cah. ORSTOM sér. Pédol.* 4(1): 23–62.

Kaloga, B. (1977) Contribution de l'étude de la composition granulométrique des sables à la connaissance des mouvements de matière dans les sols ferrugineux tropicaux du Centre-Sud de la Haute-Volta. *Cah. ORSTOM sér. Pédol.* 15(3): 217–38.

Kalpage, F. (1976) *Tropical soils. Classification, fertility and management.* Macmillan, London, 283 pp., 7 fig., 8 maps.

Kaminska, R., Konecka-Betley, K., Mycielska-Dowgiallo, E. (1986) The Liszyno dune in the Vistula Valley (east of Plock), *Biuletyn Peryglacjalny* 31: 141–62.

Kayser, K., Manshard, W., Mensching, H., Schultze, J. (1966) Das Africa-Kartenwerk. Ein Schwerpunkt-Program der deutschen Forschungsgemeinschaft. *Die Erde* 46: 85–95.
Mapping programme of 18 different phenomena with a synthesis of the natural and another of the human environment of sample-regions at the scale of 1:1 000 000.

Keen, B. A. (1931) *Physical properties of soils.* Longman, Harlow, 380 pp.

Kemmerling, G. L. L. (1921) De uitbarsting van den G. Ketoeb in den nacht van den 19 den op den 20sten Mei 1919. Dienst van het Mijnwezen in Nederlandsch Oost-Indie. *Vulkanologische Mededeelingen* 2: 6–37.

Kemp, D. D. (1990) *Global environment issues. A climatological approach.* Routledge, London, New York, 220 pp.
An original exposition, written by a Canadian climatologist. Many interesting examples of environmental degradation, and some of successful rehabilitation.

Kemp, R. A. (1985) Pedogenic, environmental and stratigraphic implications of a complex Quaternary soil at Stebbing, Essex, England. *International Geomorphology 1985. Abstracts of Papers for the First Intern. Conf. on Geomorphology.* T. Spencer (Ed.), n° 318.

Kemper, B. (1987) Erosionprobleme in Lateinamerika. Beispiele aus Südbrasilien und Bolivien. *Tübinger Geogr. St.* 96: 143–55.

Kesik, A. (1982) Flood affected areas in Canada: inventory, assessment and cartographic presentation, synopsis. *IGU Working Group on Geom. of River and Coastal Plains* 3: 23–120.

Keydel, W. (1989) Fernerkundung mit Mikrovelle zur Beobachtung von Land- und Seeoberflächen. *Münchener Geogr. Abh.* A 41: 23–35.
Radar technics and potential for the investigation of both continental and marine areas.

Kienholz, H. (1977) Kombinierte geomorphologische Gefahrenkarte 1/10 000 von Grindelwald. *Geogr. Oerhensia.* G, 4.204 pp., 26 fig., 4 coloured folded maps.

Kienholz, H. (1986) Slope stability and erosion in the Nepalese middle mountains and in the Khumbu area. In Kuhle, ed. Internat. Symp. Tibet-Hochasien, Göttingen, 1985. *Göttinger Geogr. Abh.* 81: 127–40.

Kienholz, H., Hafner, H., Schneider, G., Zimmermann, M. (1984) Methods for assessment of mountain hazards and slope stability in Nepal. *Erdwissenschaftliche Forsch.* 18: 147–60.
Well conceived study programme including types of investigations, legend of geomorphological maps, etc.

KiewietdeJonge, C. (1984) Büdel's geomorphology. *Progress in Physical Geography* 8: 218–48 & 365–97.

Kilian, J. (1964) Etude pédologique des baibos de la Bamarivo (Madagascar). *Agron. Trop.* 19(11): 996–1017.

Kilian, J. (1969) Les formations marines sableuses de la côte Est de Madagascar entre Mahanoro et Foul-Pointe (Madagascar). *Agron. Trop.* 24(2): 161–73.

Kilian, J. (1970) Etude des sols tourbeux et semi-tourbeux utilisés en culture bananière dans la région de Tamatave. *Fruits* (Fruits d'Outremer) 25(1): 35–45.

Kilian, J. (1972) Contribution à l'étude des aptitudes des sols à la riziculture des bas-fonds sans aménagements dans le nord-Dahomey. *Agron. Trop.* 27(3): 321–57.

Kilian, J. (1973) *Aménagement des vallées des Volta (Haute-Volta). Etudes pédologiques. Conceptions de travail. Application au terroir de Moqtedo.* IRAT, Paris.

Kilian, J. (1974) Etude du milieu physique en vue de son aménagement. Conceptions de travail. Méthodes cartographiques. *Agron. Trop.* 29(2/3): 141–53.
Methodological study on soil mapping: shows its artificial character.

Kilian, J., Tessier, J. (1973) Méthodes d'investigation pour l'analyse et le classement des bas-fonds dans quelques régions de l'Afrique de l'Ouest. Propositions de classification d'aptitudes des terres à la riziculture. *Agron. Trop.* 28(2): 156–72.

Kilian, J., Tricart, J., Tessier, J. (1977) Ecodynamique et recherche agronomique dans le bassin supérieur de la Volta Blanche (Haute-Volta). *Bull. IFAN*, 38-A (4): 737–76.

Kilian, J., Velly, J. (1964) Diagnostic des carences minérales en vases de végétation sur quelques sols de Madagascar. *Agron. Trop.* 19(5): 413–43.

Killmayer, A., Epp, H. (1983) Use of small format aerial photography for land use mapping and resource monitoring. *ITC Journal* (4): 285–90.

King, C. (1986) Etude des sols et des formations superficielles par télédétection. *Doc. B.R.G.M.* Orléans, 96: 174 + 26 pp., 65 fig., 7 pp. of coloured images.
A textbook on how to interpret satellite sensed data for soils and surficial materials.

King, R. B. (1970) A parametric approach of land system classification. *Geoderma*: 37–47.

King, R. B. (1982) Rapid rural appraisal with LANDSAT imagery: a Tanzanian experience. *Zeit. für Geom. Suppl.-Bd* 44: 5–20.
Deals mainly with land use.

King, R. B. (1987) Review of geomorphic description and classification in land resource surveys. In: Gardiner, V. (Ed.) *International geomorphology* (1986) Part II, pp. 383–403. J. Wiley & Sons, Chichester.
The most recent exposition of the land surveys approach.

Kirkby, M. J. (Ed.) (1978) *Hillslope Hydrology*, J. Wiley & Sons, Interscience, Chichester. Publ.: 389 pp.

Kirkby, M. J. (1987) Papers on theoretical geomorphology: introduction. In: Gardiner, V. (Ed.) *International geomorphology* (1986), Part II, pp. 1–2. J. Wiley & Sons, Chichester.

Kirkby, M. J., Morgan, R. P. C. (1980) *Soil erosion* in Landscape systems, a series in geomorphology by the B.G.R.G., J. Wiley & Sons, Interscience, Chichester: 312 pp.
In general excessively statistical and mathematical with little reference to natural phenomena. Excellent study by J. de Ploey & D. Gabriels on 'Measuring soil loss and experimental studies': 63–108, ref.

Kirkham, D., van Bavel, C. H. M. (1948) Theory of seepage into auger holes. *Soil. Sci. Soc. Am. Proc.* 13: 75–82.

Kleiss, H. (1970) Hillslope sedimentation and soil formation in northeastern Iowa. *Proc. Soil Sci. Soc. Amer.* 34: 287–90.

Klimazewski, M. (1968) La carte hydrographique détaillée et son importance scientifique et pratique. *Mélanges M. Pardé*, Ophrys, Paris: 341–50.
Account of the Polish concepts.

Klimazewski, M. (1979) The importance of geomorphological, hydrographical and climatological mapping for the development of physical geography and precise knowledge of the geographical environment. *Folia Geographica.* Phys. Geogr. Ser., 12: 5–35.

Klimazewski, M. (1983) A detailed geomorphological map. In: Sharma, H. S. (Ed.) *Perspectives in geomorphology*. Concept, New Delhi, pp. 191–220.

Klink, H. J. (1969) *Das naturräumlichen Gefüge des Ith-Hils-*

Berglandes, Forschungen zur Deutschen Landeskunde, 58 pp., 3 coloured maps.

Klug, H., Lang, R. (1983) Einführung in die Geosystemlehre, Wissenschaftliche Buchgesellschaft, Darmstadt: 187 pp., 44 fig. *Continues with more clarity the taxonomy of the GDR.*

Knapp, B. J. (1973) A system for field measurement of soil water movement. *Brit. Geomorph. Res. Group. Tech. Bull.* **9**: 26 pp.

Knighton, A. D. (1984) *Fluvial forms and processes.* Edward Arnold, London: 218 pp.

Knox, J. C. (1989) Long and short-term episodic storage and removal of sediment in watersheds of southwestern Wisconsin and northwestern Illinois. *IASH Publ.* **184**: 157–64. *Rediscovers, with interesting observations and arguments the discontinuity in the terrestrial detritic fluxes discussed more than 20 years ago by J. Tricart. Effects of land use changes in Mississippi watershed.*

Kohl, H. (1964) Erfahrungen aus Arbeiten zur naturräumlichen Gliederung in Oesterreich. *Mitteilungen der österreichische geographische Gesellschaft* **56**: 291–303. *Parts played by geomorphology and hydrology as dominant integrating factors.*

Kohlhepp, G. (1986) Problems of agriculture in Latin America: production of food-crops versus production of energy-plants and export. *Applied Geogr. and Development* **27**: 60–92. *Excellent analysis of the deep crisis of Latin American agriculture, with a generous social objective: equally good treatment of the ecodevelopment concept.*

Kohlhepp, G. (1987) Ecological and socioeconomic problems of the expansion of human settlement and agricultural activities in tropical rain forest regions. *C. R. Conf. Internat. Inst. de la Vie,* Fort de France 15–18 (1985): 122–131.

Kondraki, J. (1960) Types of natural landscapes (geographical environment) in Poland. *Przeglad Geograficzny,* **33** suppl.: 29–39.

Kondraki, J. (1964) Problems of physical geography and physico-geography regionalization of Poland. *Geographia Polonica* **1**: 61–77. *Results in a determination of landscapes.*

Kondracki, J. (1966) Geographical studies on the Pinczowe District. *Prace Geograficzny* **47**: 190 pp., 8 maps. *Results in a classification of units as a function of dominant factors.*

Kondracki, J. (1967) Landschaftsökologische Studien in Polen. *Wissenschaftliche Abhandlungen der Geographische Gesellschaft der DDR* **5**: 216–31. *Review of Polish research, bibliography.*

Kovacs, G. (1981) *Hydrology of the soil moisture zone.* Vituki Közlemények (Budapest) **33**: 130 pp.

Kovacs, G. (1981) Hydrological investigation of the soil water zone: 207–242. In: G. Kovacs & Assoc. *Subterranean hydrology,* Water Res. Publ., Littleton, Colo, 978 pp. *A real treatise, very complete, basic.*

Kovda, V. A., Szabolcs (I) (1979) Modelling of soil salinization and alkalinization. *Agrokémia és Talajtan* **28** Suppl.: 208 pp.

Kowalska, A. (1965) Attempt of showing on a map hydrological conditions occurring in soils developed from Quaternary deposits. *Przeglad Geograficzny* **37**(2): 369–86. *Legend of the 1:25 000 maps.*

Kozlowski, T. T. (1964) *Water metabolism in plants.* Harper & Row, New York, 227 pp.

Kozlowski, T. T. (Ed.) (1968) *Water deficits and plant growth,* 6 vol. Academic Press, New York. *Most comprehensive and detailed, extensive bibliographies. Cf. especially vol. 1–4.*

Kramer, P. J. (1969) *Plant and soil water relationships: a modern synthesis.* McGraw-Hill, New York, 482 pp.

Krebs, C. (1984) *Ecology. The experimental analysis of distribution and abundance.* Harper & Row, New York, 678 pp. *A reference book.*

Kubiena, W. L. (1953) *The soils of Europe,* Th. Murby, 317 pp. *Also editions in Spanish and German.*

Kugler, H. (1974) Geomorphologische Karten als Beispiele thematisch-kartographischer Modellierung territorialer Phänomene. *Wiss. Z.,* Univ. Halle **23** M (5): 65–71.

Kunicyn, L. F., Retejum, A. J. (1973) Wechselwirkungen zwischen Naturkomplexen und technischen Systemen. *Geographische Berichte* **68**: 161–7.

Kwaad, F. J. (1977) Measurements of rainsplash erosion and the formation of colluvium beneath deciduous woodland in the Luxembourg Ardennes. *Earth Surface Processes* **2**(2/3): 161–74. *Excellent example of morphogenic–pedogenic interaction.*

Labeyrie, V. (1975) La crise de l'environnement, l'économie de la nature et l'économie humaine. *Mondes en Développement*: 527–65.

Labeyrie, V. (1980) Combustibles fossiles, biomasse et énergie (suite). *SEPANT,* Nov.: 5–17. *A contribution on the sensitivity of spontaneous phytocoenoses.*

Lacoste, Y. (1980) *Unité et diversité du tiers-monde,* I: Des représentations planétaires aux stratégies sur le terrain, Paris. *Hérodote,* Maspéro, 203 pp; fig. (159–76). *General review of the different methodological approaches.*

Lambert, R. (1975) Recherches hydrologiques dans le Sud-Est du bassin garonnais. Thèse Etat, Toulouse–Le Mirail, 2 vol.: 750 pp., 247 fig. *The author's concept of hydrologic farmland (*terroirs hydrologiques*) is close to that of hydromorphic units and can be mapped.*

Lambert, R. (1977) Geographie et budget hydrologique. *Ann. de Géogr.* **86**(477): 513–21.

Lamotte, M. (1983) Structure et fonctionnement d'un écosystème de savane. *Le Courrier du CNRS. Suppl.* **52**: 71–9.

Lamouroux, M., Quantin, P., Segalen, P. (1983) Les principes du projet de classification des sols présenté par un groupe de travail de l'ORSTOM, animé par Segalen P. (1979). *Cah. ORSTOM sér. Pédol.* **20**(2): 169–79.

Lancaster, N. (1989) *The Namib sand sea. Dune forms, processes and sediments.* Balkema, Rotterdam, 180 pp., 88 fig. *A very detailed monograph, some elements of it of general application.*

Landmann, M. (1989) Reliefgenerationen und Formengenese in Gebiet des Lluidas Valle-Poljes/Jamaica. *Tübinger Geogr. St.,* **101**: 213 pp., 41 fig., 8 maps.

LANDSAT (1986) Brief LANDSAT program history. *LANDSAT Data Users Notes* **35**: 1–9.

Landsat Data Users Notes (1978–86), quarterly originally published by NASA, then by NOAA, 1–35, continued by EOSAT, LANDSAT Application Notes (4300 Forbes Blvd., Lanham, MD 20706).

Lang, R. (1982) Quantitative Untersuchungen zum Landschaftshaushalt im südostlichen Frankenalb. *Regensburger Geogr. Schr.* **18**: 277 pp., 64 fig., 8 phot.

Larsson, R., Hanson, G. (1985) *Applied visual LANDSAT inventories for water resources development.* UNGI Rap, 61, Uppsala: 33 pp. + Annexes, colour plates.

Laugenie, C. (1982) La région des lacs, Chili méridional. Thèse Etat, Bordeaux III, 2 vol; 822 pp., 150 fig., 33 pl. phot., 4 maps in pocket.

Le Bissonnais, Y., Bruand, A., Jamagne, M. (1989/90) Etude expérimentale sous pluie simulée de la formation des croûtes superficielles. Apport à la notion d'érodibilité des sols. *Cah. ORSTOM sér. Pédol.* **25**(1/2): 31–40. *Influence of the hydric condition of soils on sealing by raindrops.*

Lecarpentier, C. (1975) L'évapotranspiration potentielle et ses applications. *Ann. de Géogr.* **84**(463–4): 257–74 & 385–414. *Account, comparison, and significance of various formulas: basic critical study.*

Lecordix, P. Y. (1985) Thematic investigations in France based on metric camera imagery. *Metric Camera Workshop, Proc.* ESA–ASE SP-209, April: 135–7.

Le Houerou, H. N. (1986) The desert and arid zones of Northern Africa. In Venari, M. et al. (Eds) *Hot desert and arid shrublands.* Chap. 4. 101–47. Elsevier, Amsterdam.

Lelong, F., Wedraogo-Dumazet, B. (1987) Influence de la végétation sur la mobilisation chimique des éléments dans les bassins-versants granitiques du Mont-Lozère (France). In: Godard, A., Rapp, A., Coord. *Processus et mesure de l'érosion,* pp. 299–311, 25e Congr. Intern. Géogr., Paris (1984), Ed. CNRS (Paris).

Lemée, G., Wey, R. (1950) Observations pédologiques sur les sols actuels de loess aux environs de Strasbourg. *Ann. Agronomiques* **1**(2): 1–12.

Lemieux, G. H., Labonte, M., Perron, S., Verrault, R., Vachon, G. (1988) Comment parer au gel dans les bleuetières de la Sagamie? *GEOS* **2**: 22–6.

Lenco, M., Heymann, Y., Ferrault, P. (1978) *Expérience de télédétection aérienne sur la vallée de la Garonne et la région de Montauban.* Ministère de l'Environnement et du Cadre de Vie, Documentation Française, Paris, 104 pp., 15 pl.
Good general review on basic data. Definition of technical terms.

Leopold, L. B., Langbein, W. (1963) Association and indeterminacy in geomorphology. In: Albritton, Cl. C. (Ed.) *The fabric of geology*, pp. 184–92. Addison-Wesley, New York.

Leopold, L. B., Wolman, M. G., Miller, J. P. (1964) *Fluvial processes in geomorphology.* Freeman, San Francisco, London. 522 pp., 128 fig., 48 tabl.
Excellent work, extending into problems of dissection and fashioning of slopes.

Leopoldo, P., Franken, W., Matsui, E., Salati, E. (1982) Estimativa de evapotranspiraçâo de floresta mazônica de terra firme. *Acta Amazônica* **12**(3 suppl.): 23–8.
Of a total annual rainfall of 2.089 mm., only 541 mm flow into the river, 534 mm being intercepted and 1.014 mm evapo-transpired.

Leow, K., Smith, B. (1981) Soil pH and textural variation in the eluviated A horizon on basement complex slopes under a savanna climate. Northern Nigeria. *Zeit. für Geom.* **25**(1): 73–98.

Leroux, P., Roussel, P. (1978) Procédé de quantification et déplanification du paysage rural français. GDTA, Toulouse. *Journée Télédét.* 21–23 Sept. (1977): 367–79. IGN, St Mandé.

Leser, H. (1976) *Landschaftskölogie.* Stuttgart, Eugen Ulmer, 432 pp., 49 fig.

Leser, H. (1981) *Die geomorphologische Kartierung in der Schweiz*, Basel, 25 pp.

Leser, H. (1982) Probleme der geomorphographischen Darstellung auf Blatt Wehr (GMK Blatt 4, 8313 Wehr). *Berliner Geogr. Abh.* **35**: 87–95.
A sample.

Leser, H. (1985) Perspektivprobleme geomorphologischer Detailkarten. *Peterm. Geogr. Mitt.* **129**: 279–88.
cf. references.

Leser, H. (1986) Bodenerosion-Erforschung eines geoökologischen Prozesses. *Hall. Jb. für Geowissenschaften* **11**: 1–17.

Leser, H. (1987a) Zum Stand zur Entwicklung grossmasstäbiger geomorphologischer Karten. *Mitt. Geogr. Ges. Munchen* **72**: 183–201.

Leser, H. (1987b) Geomorphologische Prozessforschung als Mittel zur Erfassung des Landschaftshaushaltes. *Verhandl. Dtschen Geographentages* 45, Stuttgart, 110–20.

Leser, H., Stählein, G. (1978) Legende der geomorphologische Karte 1:25 000 (GMK25), 3, Fassung im GMK-Schwerpunktprogramm. *Berliner Geogr. Abh.* **30**: 79–90.

Lesourd, M. (1986) Permanence de la sécheresse aux Iles du Cap Vert: l'aménagement rural ou la lutte contre l'irréversibilité; *Et. Sahéliennes* (Rouen), pp. 109–28.
A well documented analysis of the consequences of drought in an unpopulated semi-arid country and of how an agrarian reform and a remodelling of land use intend to achieve a better use of scanty resources.

L'Espace Géographique (1984) Géographie et télédétection : **13**(3): 169–304.
Numerous contributions on land use, vegetation and digitalized data processing.

Lichtfield, W. (1969) *Soil surfaces and sedimentary history near the Macdonnels Ranges.* N.T., Soil Publ. CSIRO, 44 pp., 24 fig., 4 pl.

Liedtke, H. (1989) West Germany's natural regions and their potential. *Geogr. Rundschau* Spec. N°, 12–9 pp.
Uses LANDSAT MSS scenes, which have an effect on the vegetal cover and the relief.

Lieth, F. H., Box, E. (1972) Evaporation and primary productivity, Thornthwaite Memorial Model. *Publ. in Climatology*, Laboratory of Climatology **25**(3): 37–46.

Lillesand, T. M., Kiefer, R. W. (1987) *Remote sensing and images interpretation.* 2nd ed. J. Wiley & Sons, Inc., New York, 721 pp.
Excellent, very complete text, copious bibliography.

Liu Tung-sheng, Guo Xu-dong, Dong Guang-rong (1987) The periglacial phenomena on Loess Plateau, China. In: Pecsi, M.,

French, H. T. (Eds) *Loess and periglacial phenomena.* Akad. Kiado, Budapest, pp. 141–9.
Rediscovers what has already been discussed by Tricart, J. (1985) and adds some mistakes of their own.

Lluvias torenciales e inundaciones en Alicante (1983). Inst. de Geogr., Univ. Alicante, Serv. de Publ. Univ. de Alicante, 129 pp.
A cascading feedback system exaggerated the damage and casualties.

Lobert, A., Cormary, Y. (1964) Variabilités des mesures de caractéristiques hydrodynamiques. *Cah. ORSTOM, sér. Pédol.* **2**(2): 23–50.
Shows the high variability of K on small surfaces, such as a wall of a soil pit.

Lockwood, J. (1983) Modelling climatic change: 25–50. In: Gregory, K. (Ed.) *Background to paleohydrology*, J. Wiley & Sons, Chichester, pp. 486.

Löffler, E., Haantjes, H. et al. (1972) *Land resources of the Vanimo area, Papua, New Guinea*, Land Research Series **31**: 126 pp., 10 fig., 20 phot. pl., 4 unfolding coloured maps.
A good example of the method.

Long, G. (1969) Ecologie végétale et aménagement du territoire. *Science-Progrès, La Nature* **3412**: 281–8.
Exclusive position: only an ecologic study permits a comprehensive, integrated approach of the major facts of the biophysical environment, which in the end, begs the question.

de Loor, G. P. (1973) *General aspects on the technology of remote sensing. An introduction*, ESRO Summer School, IV: Earth Resources, 24 pp.

Louis, H. (1979) *Allgemeine Geomorphologie*, 4th ed., Auflage unter Mitarbeit von Fischer K, de Gruyter, Berlin, New York.
Standard text in the Federal Republic since 1st edition in 1959.

Luthin, J. N. (Ed.) (1957) *Drainage of agricultural lands*, Am. Soc. Agron., Madison, Wisconsin, 620 pp., extensive bibliography.

Lutz, G., Trautmann, J., Tricart, J. (1982) Bibliographie analytique des publications de télédétection du GTS (Groupe de recherche en télédétection radiométrique de Strasbourg) relatives au milieu naturel. *Ann. de Géogr.* **91**(505): 356–63.

Lvovich, M. I. (1954a) Influence of soils on streamflow. *Izvestia Akademia Nauk SSSR, ser. Geogr.* **5**: 40–8 (in Russian).
Experimental data from the area of Saratov.

Lvovich, M. I. (1954b) Agriculture and fluvial regimes. *Priroda* **10**: 43–53 (in Russian).
Excellent study of the kinds of streamflow on the Russian Plain.

Lvovich, M. I. (1979) *World water resources and their future.* English translation. In: Nace, R. L. (Ed.) Amer. Geophys. Union, Washington, 415 pp.

Lynn, D. (1986) Timely thermal infrared data acquisition for soil survey in humid temperate environments. *ITC Journal* (1): 68–76.

Lynne, G., Taylor, G. (1986) Geological assessment of SIR-B imagery of the Amadeus Basin, NT, Australia, *IEEE Trans. Geosc. and Remote Sensing*, GE-24(4): 575–81.

Maarleveld, G. C., de Lange, G. W. (1972) Een globale geomorfologische en landschappelijke kartering en waardering van de uitwaarden van de nederlandse Grote Rivieren. *Landbouwkundig Tijdschrift* **84**(8): 273–88.
Coloured landscape map on 1:50 000 looks much like facing geomorphological map.

Mabbutt, J. A. (1968) Review of concepts of land classification. In: Steward, G. A. (Ed.) *Land evaluation.* Macmillan, Melbourne.

Mabbutt, J. A., Steward, G. A. (1963) The application of geomorphology in resources surveys in Australia and New Guinea. *Rev. de Géom.* **14**: 97–109.

MacCown, R. I. (1973) An evaluation of the influence of available soil water storage capacity on growing season length and yield of tropical pastures using simple water balance models. *Agricultural Meteorology* **11**: 53–63.

McHarg, I. L. (1969) *Design with nature.* The Natural History Press, New York.

MacIsaac, G. F., Hirschi, M. C. (1989) Nitrogen and phosphorus in eroded sediment from corn and soybean tillage systems. *IAHS Public.* **184**: 3–10.
An excellent example of the influence of agriculture on pollution and of the losses resulting from soil erosion.

McMahon, T. A. (1977) The relief and land form map of Australia: does it show rock types and land forms of hydrologic significance? *Catena* **4**(1/2): 189–99.
Example of intellectual endemism: vaguely rediscovers the principle of hydromorphologic mapping through the use of a 1:2 000 000 map.

McPherson, B., Hendrix, G., Klein, H., Tyus, H. (1976) *The environment of South Florida. A summary report.* USGS, Prof. Paper 1011, 82 pp., 27 fig.

McQueen, I., Miller, R. (1972) *Soil moisture and energy relationships associated with riparian vegetation near San Carlos, Arizona,* USGS, Prof. Paper 655-E, 50 pp, 47 fig.
Detailed study of the water balance of an alluvial plain in a semiarid climate.

McRoy, M. L., Keiser, A. F., Kite, S. J. (1989) The 'catastrophic' storm and flood of November 1985 in a Central Appalachian river basin, USA. *Second Intern. Conf. Geom.* Frankfurt/Main, Sept. 3–9, Abstracts: 190–1.
This flood resulted from Hurricane Juan.

Maertens, C. (1964) Influence des propriétés physiques des sols sur le développement radiculaire et conséquences sur l'alimentation hydrique et azotée des cultures. *Science du sol,* 1st semester **2**: 31–41.

Mahaney, W. C. (Ed.) (1989) *Quaternary and environmental research in East African mountains.* Balkema, Rotterdam & Brookfield, 483 pp.
Periglacial and glacial features, various environmental monographs.

Mahler, P. J. (1973) Integrated surveys and environmental problems associated with land development in developing countries. *ITC Journal,* Special issue, Symp. Enschede, 16–20 Oct. (1972) (2): 256–71.

Maignien, R. (1960) *Les sols du delta vif du Niger. Région de Mopti.* ORSTOM, Dakar.

Mainguet, M. (1990) La désertification: une crise autant socio-économique que climatique. *Sécheresse* **1**(3): 187–95.
An excellent evaluation of the desertification problem, by an author who has a broad experience.

Mainguet, M., Chemin, M. C. (1988) Wind system and sand dunes in the Taklamakan Desert. *Chinese Journal of Arid Land Res.* **L** (2): 135–142.
Description of the various aeolian landforms. Morphometry and genesis. Aridity is quite ancient.

Mainguet, M., Chemin, M. C. (1989) The concept of sandy-aeolian sediment budget applied to the sand deposits of the Sahara and the Sahel. *Selected Papers of the ISEUNRAA, Science Press,* Beijing, pp. 1061–121.
A general model for dynamics and forms of wind action.

Mainguet, M., Chemin, M. C. (1990) Le massif du Tibesti dans le système éolien du Sahara. *Berliner Geogr. St.* **30**: 261–76.
An excellent overview in a well-known series.

Maksymiuk, Z. (1980) Les formes d'alimentation des rivières et leur rôle dans le bilan d'eau sur l'exemple du bassin de la Widawka. *Acta Geogr. Lodziensia* **42**: 119 pp., 31 fig., 12 photos.
Excellent monograph based on measurements enabling the determination of variations in water balance.

Marek, K. H., John, K. H., Jähn, S. (1987) L'utilisation de la photographie multispectrale métrique pour l'étude de l'environnement et des ressources. *Rev. d'Iéna* **4**:160–3.

Margaleff, R. (1969) Diversity and stability: practical proposal and a model of interdependence. *Brookhaven Symp. in Biology,* n° **22**: 264 pp. (pp. 25–37).

Manikowska, B. (1983) Etudes paléopédologiques dans les régions des dunes de la Pologne centrale. *Rech. Géogr. à Strasbourg,* **22/23**: 227–35, illus.
English summary.

Manikowska, B. (1986) Sol fossile de la phase de transition Pléistocène-Holocène dans les dunes continentales de la Pologne centrale. *Biuletyn Peryglacjalny* **31**: 199–211.

Manil, G. (1959) Climax et pédoclimax. I – discussion des notions de base. *Bull. Soc. Royale de Botanique de Belgique* **91**(2): 217–37.
Fundamental.

Marbut, C. F. (1927) A scheme for soil classification. *Proc. & Papers, First Intern. Congr. Soil Sc* **4**: 1–34.

Margat, J. (1986) L'eau et les hommes. *TOTAL-Inform.* **104**: 3–12.
Well illustrated.

Margat, J. (1990) Les gisements d'eau souterraine. *La Recherche,* **221** (May).
Interesting data on the age of 'fossil' water and underground water resources and their use.

Margat, J., Ricour, J. (1963) Présentation des maquettes de la première carte hydrogéologique normalisée à grande échelle réalisée en France: feuille de Douai au 1/50 000. *Bull. Soc. Géol. de France* **5**(7): 47–51.
Two reduced examples in colour corresponding to two different concepts.

Markham, B. L., Barker, J. L. (1983) Spectral characterization of the Landsat-4 MSS sensors. *Photogramm. Eng. & Remote Sensing* **49**(6): 811–33.

Markham, B. L., Barker, J. L. (1985) Spectral characterization of the Landsat thematic mapper sensors. *Int. J. Remote Sensing* **6**(5): 697–716.

Markov, K. K., Dobrojedow, O. P., Orlow, I. A., Sudakov, N. G. Sujetowa, J. A. (1971) *Einführung in die allgemeine physische Geographie,* German transl., H. Haack, Gotha-Leipzig, 164 pp., 31 fig., 1 coloured map.
Representative of Soviet geography, very concise, valuable for its methodological approach.

Marosi, S., Szilard, J. (1964) Landscape evaluation as an applied discipline of geography. *Applied Geography in Hungary,* Akad. Kiado, Budapest, pp. 20–35.
Excellent concise account.

Marre, A. (1981) Dynamique des versants sur le Djebel Sidi Driss (Tell nord-constantinois, Algérie). *Trav. Inst. Géogr. Reims* **45/46**: 107–15.

Marron, D. C. (1989) The transport of mine tailings as suspended sediment in the Belle Fouche River, west-central South Dakota. *AISH Public.* **184**: 19–26.
An excellent example of long-lasting damage to environment.

Martin, C. (1989) Pertes en terres par ruissellement des sols défrichés sur gneiss à la station Lambert (Massif des Maures, Var, France). *Rev. de Géom. Dyn.* **XXXVIII**(1): 17–29.
Detailed observations, statistical calculations. An excellent example.

Martin, D. (1967) Géomorphologie et sols ferrallitiques dans le centre Cameroun. *Cah. ORSTOM, sér. Pédol.* **5**(2): 189–218.

Marty, R. J. (1970) Les méthodes d'évaluation du bilan de l'eau en agriculture. *Bull. Ass. franc. pour l'ét. du sol* **1**: 31–40.

Massonie, J., Mathieu, D., Wieber, J. (1971) Application de l'analyse factorielle à l'étude des paysages. *Séminaires et Notes de recherche,* n° 4, Cahiers de géographie de Besançon: 51 pp.

Mather, J. R. (Ed.) (1954) The measurement of potential evapotranspiration *Publ. in Climatology,* Laboratory of Climatology **7**(1): 225 pp.

Mather, J. R. (1968) Irrigation agriculture in humid areas. In: Court, A. (Ed.) Eclectic Climatology. *Yearbook, Assoc. Pacific Coast Geographers* **30**, Oregon State Univ. Press, Corballis, pp. 107–22.

Mäusbacher, R. (1983) Die geomorphologische Detailkarte der Bundesrepublik Deutschland (GMK 25) – ein nutzbarer Informationsträger auch für Nicht-Geomorphologen, *Materialen zur Physiogeographie* **5**: 15–28.

Mäusbacher, R. (1985) Die Verwendbarkeit der geomorphologischen Karte. *Berliner Geogr. Abh.* **40**: 97 pp., 15 fig., 16 appended maps.

Meadows, M. E., Sugden, J. M. (1988) Late Quaternary environmental changes in the Karoo, South Africa. In: Dardis, G. F., Moon, B. P. (Eds) *Geomorphological studies in southern Africa,* pp. 337–59. Balkema, Rotterdam.

Meentenmeyer, V., Fox, E. O. (1987) '2. Scale effects in landscape studies' *Ecol. Studies* **64**: 15–34, Springer V., New York.
Africa, pp. 337–59, Balkema, Rotterdam.

Meentenmeyer, V., Fox, E. O. (1987) 2. Scale effects in landscape studies, *Ecol. Studies* **64**: 15–34, Springer V., New York.

Megnien, C. (1970) *Atlas des nappes aquifères de la région parisienne* Portefeuille de 59 cartes et notice. BRGM (Paris).

Meijerink, A. M. J. (1978) On the nature of base flood and groundwater occurrences in the Serayu River basin. *ITC Journal* (3): 503–13.

Meijerink, A. M. J. (1990) Hydrologic cycles and aerospace surveys. *ITC Journal* (2): 152–61.
Flow chart of the various planning operations for water resources.

Mensching, H. (1968) Bericht über Stand und Aufgaben des 'Africa-Kartenwerkes'. *Die Erde* **99**: 14–41.

Messerli, B., Ives, J. (1983) Mountain ecosystems, stability and instability. *Mountain Res. and Dev.* **3**(2): 193 pp.

Metric Camera Workshop (1985) Proceedings of a joint DFVRL-ESA workshop held at Oberpfaffenhofen, 11–13 Feb. *ESA-ASE SP-209*, April 1985, 210 pp.

Meyer, L. D. (1986) Erosion processes and sediment properties for agricultural cropland. In: Abrahams, A. D. (Ed.) *Hillslope Processes* (16th Annual Geomorph. Symp., Binghampton, N. Y.) pp. 55–76.

Meyers, J. D., Rickert, D. A., Hines, W. G., Vickers, S. D. (1979) Erosional problems related to land-use activities in the Willamette River basin, Oregon, *USGS Misc. Investig. Series Maps*, I 0921-B.
Application of a parametric approach.

Michel, P. (1966) Les applications des recherches géomorphologiques en Afrique occidentale. *Rev. de Géogr. de l'Afrique occidentale* **3**: 37–60.
Excellent regional overview.

Michel, P. (1968) Morphogenèse et pédogenèse. Exemples d'Afrique occidentale. *Sols Africains* **13**(2): 171–94.

Michel, P. (1983) Les formations de la vallée du Sénégal (Afrique de l'Ouest). Rapports géomorphologie-sols-latitudes culturales, leur cartographie au 1/50 000. Coll. *Est. e Cartogr. Form. Superf.* 27 Aug.–7 Sept. 1978, Univ. S. Paulo (Brazil), **1**: 403–18.
Excellent monograph. Recent big dams have completely altered the use of the environment by the peasant communities.

Michel, P. (1984) Les variations du climat au Quaternaire récent dans le Sahel d'Afrique occidentale et leurs conséquences sur les formations superficielles, l'hydrographie et la pédogenèse. *Bull. de la Soc. Languedocienne de Géogr.* **18**(3–4): 125–37.
Good example of an integrated study.

Middleton, N. J. (1989) Desert dust. In: Thomas, D. S. G. (Ed.) *Arid zone geomorphology* pp. 263–83. Belhaven Press, London.

Mietton, M. (1988) Dynamique de l'interface lithosphère-atmosphère au Burkina Faso: l'érosion en zone de savane. Thèse Grenoble I: 511 pp.
Measurements of soil loss using various traditional conservative practices. Overall environmental dynamics of a tropical climate based on microclimatic measurements by the author.

Milhous, R. (1982) Effect of sediment transport and flow regulation on the ecology of gravel-bed rivers. In: Hey, R., Bathurst, J., Thorne, C. (Eds) *Gravel-bed rivers*. J. Wiley & Sons, Chichester, pp. 919–42.

Miller, D. E. (1973) Water retention and flow in layered profiles. In: Bruce, R. R. et al. (Eds) *Field soil water regime*. SSSA Special Publ. Ser. no 5, Madison, Wisc., pp. 107–17.

Millington, A. C., Townshend, J. R. (1987) The potential of satellite remote sensing for geomorphological investigations. An overview. In: Gardiner, V. (Ed.) *Internat. geomorphology* (1986) Part II, pp. 331–42. J. Wiley & Sons, Chichester.

Ministère de l'Environnement, Mission des Etudes et de la Recherche (1979) Troisièmes Journées Scientifiques et Techniques. *L'eau, la recherche, l'environnement*, Limoges 10, 11, 12, Oct. (1979), Paris, 596 pp.

Ministère de la Qualité de la Vie. Etabl. Public. Régional Alsace (1978) *Ressources naturelles et aménagement de la Région Alsace. Atlas des contraintes eaux et nuisances.* Univ. Louis Pasteur. Centre de Géogr. Appl. et Serve. Géol. d'Alsace et de Lorraine, cartes au 1:100 000.

Ministère de la Qualité de la Vie, Secrétariat d'Etat à l'Environnement (1976) Abrégé sur une nouvelle source d'information: la télédétection. *Documentation Française*, Paris, 128 pp.
Excellent review of the physical basis, sensors and use of recordings. Numerous curves and tables. Reproduction of images of the 10 bands of the Daedalus system. Infrared false colour and coloured equidensities.

Ministry of Overseas Development (1975) *The land's potential.* Work of the Land Resources Division, London, 20 pp.

Adopted with minor changes, the CSIRO Land Surveys approach.

Mitchell, C. W. (1973) *Terrain evaluation. An introductory handbook to the history, principles and methods of practical terrain assessment.* Longman, Harlow, 221 pp.

Mitchell, G. (1971) Carte géomorphologique et description du milieu naturel: la montagne de la Clape. *Mémoires et Documents du Service de documentation cartographique et géographique du CNRS* **12**(1972): 165–80.
Application of the CSIRO's method. Comparison with a detailed geomorphological map of the same region.

Mitscherlich, E. A. (1920) *Bodenkunde für Land und Forstwirte*, 3 rd. ed., Paul Parey, Berlin (4th ed., 1923): 339 pp.

Modenese, M. C. (1980) Intemperismo e morfogênese no Planalto de Campos de Jordão (S.P.). *Rev. Brasil. Geociências* **10**: 213–25.

Molinier, R. R. (1971) La cartographie écologique au service de l'aménagement du territoire. *Bull. Museum d'histoire naturelle de Marseille* **31**: 77–84.
Has made maps, covering Provence, showing plant assemblies in equilibrium, where equilibrium has been disturbed, or has been degraded. His approach, like ours, is to determine degrees of stability.

Molinier, R. R. (1972) Carte écologique. L'exemple de la région Provence-Côte d'Azur au service de l'aménagement du territoire. *Aménagement et Nature* **26**: 26–7.
Illustrates the delicate balance and the sensitivity of the natural environment.

Monget, J. M. et al. (1985) Geological cartography of Gabon using side-looking radar imagery: an example of an integrated mapping project. *Doc. B.R.G.M.* **82**: 107–28.

Mooneyhan, D. W. (1975) *All you ever wanted to know about remote sensing*, NASA Earth Res. Symp., Houston, Texas; June 1975, vol. IIa: 11–28.
Good technical review of LANDSAT sensors and recordings.

Moor, G. de, Dapper, M. de (1979) *Phases initiales d'érosion par ruissellement sur les plateaux à couverture sableuse aux environs de Kolwezi (Shaba, Zaire)* Coll. 'Erosion Agricole en Milieux Tempérés'. Strasbourg-Colmar 20–23 Sept. 1978. ULP, Strasbourg: 63–68.

Moore, J. W. (1989) *Balancing the needs of water use*. Springer-V., New York, 287 pp.

Moore, R. K. (1973) *Physics of remote sensing*. ESRO Summer School, IV: Earth Res., 36 pp.

Morariu, T., Mihailescu, V., Sayu, A., Iancu, M. (1960) Méthodes appliquées à la division en régions naturelles du territoire de la République populaire roumaine. *Recherches et Etudes Géographiques*, Ac. Popular Rep. of Rumania: 117–27.

Morariu, T., Tufescu, V. (1965) Problèmes de géographie appliquée en Roumanie. *Rev. de Géom. Dyn.* **15**: 34–9.

More, R. J. (1969) Water and crops: 197–208. In: Chorley, R. J. *Water, earth, and man, a synthesis of hydrology, geomorphology and socio-economic geography*. Methuen, 588 pp.

Morello, J., Adamolli, I. (1968) Las grandes unidades de vegetación y ambiente del Chaco Argentino. INTA, Serie *Fitogeográfica*, **10**: 125 pp, 17 phot.
Poses the problem of delimitation of units (types, coincidence between the limits of different factors).

Morgan, R. P. C. (1979) *Soil erosion. Topics in applied geography*. Longman, Harlow, 113 pp.
Account of W. H. Wischmeier's conceptions and methods of calculating soil loss.

Morgan, R. P. C. (1985) Soil erosion measurement and soil conservation research in cultivated areas of the UK. *Geo. Journal* **151**: 11–20.
Points out how little is known about soil erosion in the UK. Ref.

Morgan, R. P. C., Hatch, T., Sulaiman, W. (1982) A simple procedure for assessing soil erosion risk: a case study for Malaysia. *Zeit. für Geom. Suppl.-Bd.* **44**: 69–89.

Morgan, R. P. C., Morgan, D. D. V., Finney, H. J. (1984) A predicative model of the assessment of soil erosion risk. *J. Agric. Engineering Res.* **30**: 245–53.
A more comprehensive model than the USLE.

Mormont, M. (1987) Définir l'environnement: obstacles sociaux et pédagogie. 1° Sessions Carrefour Environnement-Pédagogie-

Evaluation, 7, 8, 9 April. Strasbourg, Actes Préliminaires. Comm. SP I, 24 pp.

Moros, C., Richardot-Coulet, M., Pautou, G. (1982) Les ensembles fonctionnels des entités écologiques qui traduisent l'évolution de l'hydrosystème . . . *Rev. de Géogr. de Lyon* **57**(1): 49–62.
Excellent example of the influence of river-bed dynamics on various biocoenoses.

Morrison, R. B. (1967) Principles of Quaternary stratigraphy. In: Morrison, R. B., Wright, H. E. (Eds) *Quaternary soils.* International Association of Quaternary Research, Seventh Congress Proceedings, Vol. 9.

Moscatelli, C., Scoppa, C. (1983) *Características hidroedáficas de la Pampa Deprimida*, Coloquio Intern. Hidrol. Grandes Llanuras, Olavarría, Apr. 11–20, 16 pp., 1 fig.

Mosley, M. P., Zimpfer, G. L. (1976) Explanation in geomorphology. *Zeit. Für Geom.* **20**(4): 381–90.
Useful overview.

Moss, M. (1983) Landscape synthesis, landscape process and land classification, some theoretical and methodological issues. *Geo. Journal* **7**(2): 145–52.
A meaningful criticism which attempts to integrate with the landscape concept as a basis. Unfortunately, what the author proposes on its own is quite restricted and is limited to the plant productivity aspect.

Moss, R. P. (1977) Deductive strategies in geographical generalization. *Prog. Phys. Geogr.* **I**(1): 23–39.

Moss, R. P (1981) Ecological constraints on an agricultural development in Africa. *African Research & Documentation* **25**: 1–12.
A strong and firmly argued criticism of the Land systems. Compare to R. B. King (1982).

Mückenhausen, E. (1962) The soil classification system of the Federal Republic of Germany. *Trans. Intern. Society of Soil Sc. Communication* 4 & 5, New Zealand: 377–87. Also in *Pédologie*, Ghent, spec. nº 3 (1965): 57–74.

Muckleston, K. (1982) Attempts to reconcile conflicting demands over Columbia River outputs. *IASH Publ.* **135**: 395–403.

Mulcahy, M. J. (1961) Soil classification in relation to landscape development. *Zeit. für Geom.* **5**: 211–25.
Good example of the concept of the Australian pedological school of B. E. Butler.

Mulcahy, M. J. (1967) Landscapes, laterites and soils in southwestern Australia. In: Jennings, J. N., Mabbutt, J. A. (Eds) *Landform studies from Australia and New Guinea.* Cambridge Univ. Press, Cambridge, pp. 211–230.

Mulcahy, M. J., Churchward, H., Dimmock, G. (1972) Landforms and soils on an uplifted peneplain in the Darling Ranges, Western Australia. *Australian J. Soil Res.* **10**: 1–14.
Excellent example, characteristic of the approach of the Australian school of thought.

Mulders, M. A. (1987) *Remote sensing in soil science.* Elsevier, Amsterdam (Dev. in Soil Sc., 15), 379 pp., fig.; 5 col. plates.

Muntz, A., Faure, C., Laine, E. (1905) Etude sur la perméabilité des terres, faite en vue de l'irrigation. *Annales de la Direction de l'hydraulique.*

Musy, A., Meylan, P., Morzier, C. (1978) Etude des composantes du bilan hydrique d'un sol par télédétection. *La Houille Blanche*, **7/8**: 541–7.

Myette, C. (1980) Hydrologic budget of Eagle Lake in Central Minnesota. *USGS, Geol. Surv., Res.*, 1980, Prof. Paper 1175: 121.
Hydrologic balance for year 1972.

Naert, B., Jamagne, M., Kilian, J, Leneuf, N., Servat, E. (1979), Inventaire, cartographie et évaluation des potentiels agricoles des sols. Etat des recherches et des besoins en télédétection. *3° Coll. Intern. GDTA*, Toulouse (1980): 6–13.

Nanson, G. C., Erskine, W. D. (1988) Episodic changes of channels and floodplains on coastal rivers in New South Wales. In: Walter, R. F. (Ed.) *Fluvial geomorphology of Australia*, Academic Press, Australia, pp. 201–21.
Important contribution to the problem of frequency/intensity of geomorphogenetic phenomena.

NASA (1976) *Mission to Earth: LANDSAT views the world.* NASA.

NASA (1987) *HIRIS, High resolution imaging spectrometer: science opportunities for the 1990s.* EOS, Instrument Panel Report IIc, XV + 74 pp., 38 fig.

NASA (1990) *EOS, a mission to Planet Earth.* NASA, Washington, 36 pp. photos.

NASA (n.d.) *SAR, Synthetic Aperture Radar.* EOS, Instrument Panel Report IIf, XXVII + 233 pp.

NASA (n.d.) *From pattern to process: the strategy of the Earth Observing System.* EOS Science Steering Committee Report, vol II, XIII + 140 pp., 79 fig.

Naumann-Tümpfel, H. (1977) Bemerkungen zum geographischen Aspekt der ökosystemforschung. *Geogr. Ber.* **83**: 57–63.

Naveh, F., Liebermann, A. (1984) *Landscape ecology, theory and application*, Springer-V., New York, 356 pp., 77 fig.
Some useful reviews.

Neboit, R. (1983) *L'homme et l'érosion.* Fac. Lettres et Sc. Hum., Clermont-Ferrand II, **17**: 183 pp.

Neboit-Guilhot, R. (1990a) Les mouvements de terrain en Basilicate (Italie méridionale). *Bull. Assoc. des géogr. fr.* **67**(2): 123–31.
Occurrence of various types of mass-movements in a tectonically unstable region.

Neboit-Guilhot, R. (1990b) Les contraintes physiques et la fragilité du milieu méditerranéen. *Ann. de Géogr.* **XCIX**(551): 1–20.
Analysis of a good example in South Italy, in a seismic region, and mass-movements in the Apennines.

Neef, E. (1962) Die Stellung der Landschaftsökologie in der physische Geographie. *Geogr. Ber.* **25**: 349–56.

Neef, E. (1963) Topologische und chorologische Arbeitsweisen in der Landschaftsgenese. *Peterm. Geogr. Mitt.* **107**: 249–59.

Neef, E. (1964a) Zur grossmasstäbigen landschaftsökologische Forschung. *Peterm. Geogr. Mitt.* **108**: 1–7.

Neef, E. (1964b) Topologische und chorologische Arbeitsweise in der Landschaftsforschung. *Peterm. Geogr. Mitt.* **108**.
A historical benchmark.

Neef, E. (Ed.) (1967a) *Probleme der Landschaftsökologischen Erkundung und Naturräumliche Gliederung.* Symposium Sept. 27–Oct. 2 (1965), Leipzig, Wissenschaftliche Abhandlungen der Geographischen Gesellschaft der DDR, Leipzig 5, 300 pp. (with papers by Haase, G., Richter, H., Uhlig, H.).

Neef, E. (1967b) Entwicklung und Stand der Landschaftsökologischen Forschung in der DDR, in preceding reference: 22–34.

Neef, E. (1972) Geographie und Umweltwissenschaft. *Peterm. Geogr. Mitt.* **116**: 81–8.

Neef, E. (1982) Naturhaushalt und Gebietscharakter. 15 Jahre landschaftsökologischer Forschung durch die Sächsische Akademie der Wissenschaften. *Geogr. Ber.* **102**: 19–32.

Neef, E. et al. (1973) *Beiträge zur Klärung der Terminologie in der Landschaftsforschung.* Geogr. Inst. Akad. Wiss. DDR, Leipzig, 38 pp.

Negre, R. (1968) La végétation du bassin de l'One (Pyrénées centrales). *Portugaliae Acta Biol.* B, **9**: 196–290.
Monograph showing the influence of climate, exposure, geomorphology and palaeoclimatic relicts.

Neto, J., Pereira de Queiroz (1984) De la carte géomorphologique de détail à l'étude de l'environnement à São Paulo (Brésil). *Mélanges A. Journaux*, Univ. of Caen, pp. 99–107.

Neumeister, H. (1971) Das System Landschaft und die Landschaftsgenese. *Geogr. Ber.* **59**: 119–33.

Neumeister, H. (1977) Theoretische Fragen zur Landschaftsgenese. *Geogr. Ber.* **82**: 20–32.

Nicod, J. (1989) Formes d'aplanissement et de régularisation des versants dans les roches carbonatées. *Travaux de l'UA 903 au CNRS* (Aix), **XXVIII**: 19–34.
Definition of the various karstic landforms.

Nilsen, T. H. (1986) Relative slope-stability mapping and land-use planning in the San Francisco Bay region, California. In: Abrahams, A. O. (Ed.) *Hillslope processes.* (16th Annual Geomorph. Symp., Binghampton, N.Y.).
Is concerned with widespread landsliding evidence.

Nimpuno, K. (1989) Disasters and social response. *ITC Journal* (3/4): 175–82.
Psychological aspects. Responsibility of media in giving a distorted, in some cases completely wrong evaluation of the situation.

Nir, D. (1987) Regional geography considered from the systems approach. *Geoforum* **18**(2): 187–202.

Nir, D., Klein, M. (1974) Gully erosion indicated by changes in land-use in a semi-arid terrain (Nahal Shiqma, Israel). *Zeit. für Geom. Suppl.-Bd.* **21**: 191–201.

Nix, H. A., Fitzpatrick, E. A. (1969) An index of crop water stress related to wheat and grain sorghum yields. *Agricultural Meteorology* **6**(5): 321–37.

Nouvelles de SPOT, published by SPOT IMAGE, Toulouse. In the US: SPOTLIGHT, quarterly since 1987 (SPOT Image Corp., 1897 Preston White, Dr., Reston, VA 22091–4326).
Both publications are free and may be obtained by writing to SPOT IMAGE.

Ofomata, G. E. K. (1987) *Soil erosion in Nigeria: the views of a geomorphologist.* Univ. of Nigeria, Inaugural Lectures Series, 7, 43 pp., 10 fig., 4 phot.

Ohlsson, E. (1972) *Summary report on a study of passive microwave radiometry and its potential applications to Earth Resources Surveys*, ESRO, CR-116, Sept. (1972): 79 pp.

Okunishi, K., Okuda, S. (1982) Refuge from large scale landslides. A case study: Nishiyoshino landslide, Nara prefecture, *Japan. J. of Disaster* (2): 79–85.

Oliva, P., Salomon, J. N. (1984) Le delta du Mangoky et sa Région (Madagascar), cartographie par télédétection spatiale. *Trauvaux et Documents de Géographie Tropicale*, CEGET, Bordeaux **51**: 169–97.
Useful methodological aspects.

Olivry, J. C. (1987) Méthode simplifiée de prédétermination des crues sur de petits bassins-versants en milieu intertropical, l'exemple du Cameroun. *J. d'Hydrol. de Strasbourg, Crues et Inondations* 16, 17, 18 Oct. (1986) C.G.A., Strasbourg pp. 77–91.
Inspired by the hydromorphological mapping methods of the CGA.

Olson, G. (1981) *Soils and the environment.* Chapman & Hall, New York, London, 178 pp. 84 fig.

Olsson, K. (1985) *Remote sensing for fuelwood resources and land degradation studies in Kordofan, the Sudan.* Medd. Lunds Univ. Geogr. Inst. Avhandlingar, **100**: 182 pp.
Sophisticated ground techniques for evaluating and calibrating remotely sensed data.

OPIT (1977) *Etat de l'art en télédétection*, 2e partie: chap. I, Télédétection et aménagement. 77/463, Nov., 214 pp.

Opp, C. (1985) Bemerkungen zur Catena-Konzeption unter besonderer Berücksichtigung der eine Catena ausbildenden Prozesse. *Peterm. Geogr. Mitt.* **129**: 25–32.

Orlov, V. I. (1965) The development of the West Siberian Plain by man. The map of Nature's dynamics. *Priroda* **5**: 79–85 (in Russian).

Ormsby, J., Blanchard, B., Blanchard, A. (1985) Detection of lowland flooding using active microwave systems. *Photogramm. Engin. & Remote Sensing* **51**(3): 317–28.

ORSTOM (1972) Proposition de classification des andosols. Groupe de travail sur les andosols. *Cah. ORSTOM, sér. Pédol.* **10**(3): 303–4.

Ovenden, L. (1989) Les tourbières, un réservoir de carbone qui fuit. *GEOS* (3): 19–24. Bilingual, French/English.
A reconstruction of ecodynamics in the Canadian Arctic during the Holocene.

Ozenda, P. (1971) La cartographe de la végétation dans les Alpes occidentales: état actuel et projets en cours. Actes Coll. 'Flore et Végét, chaînes alpine et jurassienne'. *Ann. Littér. Univ. Besançon*: 9–15.
Historical benchmark. This botanist is particularly open to the spatial aspects of his discipline.

Ozenda, P. (1977) La cartographie écologique. *Le courrier du CNRS* **24**: 2–10.

Ozenda, P. (1985) *La végétation de la chaîne alpine dans l'espace montagnard européen.* Paris, Masson, 352 pp, 323 fig., one unfolding coloured map.

Pachoud, A. (1975) *Carte de zones exposées à des risques liés aux mouvements du sol au 1/20 000 (carte ZERMOS)*, avec notice explicative. BRGM (Paris), 41 pp.

Paffen, K. (1948) Ökologische Landschaftsgliederung. *Erdkunde* **2**: 167–74.

Paffiloy, D. V. (1976) *Natural historic classification of natural ecosystems.* 23rd Internat. Geogr. Congr., Moscow. Vol. 4, pp. 96–100.
A clear orientation of ecology towards the natural environment, and one of the few scientific works of Soviet scientists in a western language.

Pagney, P. (1988) *Climats et cours d'eau de France.* Coll. Géogr., Masson, Paris, 256 pp., 93 fig.

Paijmans, K. (1970) Land evaluation by air photo interpretation and field sampling in Australian New Guinea. *Photogrammetria* **26**: 77–100.
CSIRO Land Surveys approach.

Painter, R., Ashley, G. (1970) A semiquantitative hydrological classification of soils in North-East England. *J. Soil Sc.* **21**(2): 256–64.

Palacio Prieto, J. L. (1988) Destruccion de tierra en el flanco oriental del Nevado de Toluca, el caso de la cuenca del Arroyo del Zaguan. *Bol. Inst. Geogr. UNAM (Mexico)* **18**: 9–29.
A very suggestive monograph of a system of gullies: dynamics, tentatives of stabilization.

Pallmann, H. (1947) Pédologie et phytosociologie. *Congr. Inter. de pédologie méditerranéenne*, Montpellier, May, pp. 1–36.

P.A.N., Instytut Geografii (1964) *Key and explanation of the hydrographic map of Poland on the scale of 1/50 000.* Warszaw: 48 pp., 1 carte.

Panizza, M. (1978) Analysis and mapping of geomorphological processes in environmental management. *Geoforum* **9**(1): 1–15.

Panizza, M. (1981), Coord. Studio coordinato interdisciplinare sulla stabilita e gli interventi di difesa nell'area del Monte Santa Giulia (Val Rosenna, Appennino Modenese) *Atti Soc. Naturalisti e Matematici Modena*, **CXI**, Vol. 2, Parte 1° (1980): 126 pp.

Panizza, M. (1987) Geomorphological hazard assessment and the analysis of geomorphological risk. In Gardiner, V. (Ed.) *International Geomorphology* 1986, Part I: 225–9. J. Wiley & Sons, Chichester.

Papadakis, J. S. (1938) *Ecologie agricole*, Librairie agricole de la Maison rustique. Paris, 306 pp.

Papadakis, J. (1975) *Climates of the world and their potentialities.* Publ. by the Author, Buenos Aires, 200 pp.
An original approach to climates, oriented towards ecological regionalization and management.

Park, C. C. (1980) *Ecology and environmental management.* Longman, Harlow, Coll. Studies in Physical Geogr., 272 pp.
A reference book.

Parlange, J. Y. (1971) Theory of water movement in soils: 2. one-dimensional infiltration. *Soil Science* **111**: 170–4.
A mathematical formulation.

Parry, J. T (1985) Background, perspective and issues for remote sensing in the Tropics. In: Eden, M. J., Parry, J. T. (Eds) *Remote sensing and tropical land management*, pp. 337–60, J. Wiley & Sons, Chichester.

Parry, J. T., Williams, M. G. (1985) LANDSAT and the detectability of Land Systems in Northern Kenya. In: Eden, M. J., Parry, J. T. (Eds) *Remote sensing and tropical land management*, pp. 101–130, J. Wiley & Sons, Chichester.

Passarge, S. (1913) Physiogeographie und vergleichende Landschaftsgeographie. *Mitt. Geogr. Ges. Hamburg* **27**.

Pavich, M., Markewich, H. (1979) Soil stratigraphy on fluvial terraces of the Potomac and Rappahannock rivers. *U.S. Geol. Surv. Research* (1980). *USGS Prof. Paper* **1175**: 73–4.

Pavlovsky, R., Saint Ours, J. de (1953) *Etude géologique de l'archipel des Comores.* Trav. du Bureau géologique 51, Tananarive, 55 pp., 8 pl. geol. map in colour.

Pédologie (1965) (Revue belge de pédologie) special n° 3. International symposium on the classification of soils.

Pedro, G. (1987) Géochimie, minéralogie et organisation des sols. Aspects coordonnés des problèmes pédogénétiques. *Cah. ORSTOM, sér. Pédol.* **XXIII**(3): 169–86 (1988).

Pedroli, B. (1983) Landscape concept and landscape and rangeland surveys in the Soviet Union. *ITC Journal* (4): 307–21.

Peguy, C. P. (1988) *Jeux et enjeux du climat.* Coll. 'Pratiques de la Géographie'. Masson, Paris, 255 pp, 14 fig.
A vividly written book, for a non-specialized public, which sweeps

away many traditional opinions. Examples of climatic and hydrologic constraints are considered for environmental management.

Pelletier, J. (1982) Types et zones d'écoulement des eaux dans les plaines et collines de la région de Morestel, Brégnier-Cordon. *Rev. Géogr. Lyon* **57**(1): 25–38.
Uses certain concepts from legend of hydromorphological maps of the CGA.

Penck, W. (1924) *Die morphologische Analyse.* Geogr. Abh. 2, Stuttgart, Engelhom. Engl. transl. by H. Czech & K. C. Boswell, Macmillan & Co., London, 1953.

Penman, H. L. (1948) Natural evaporation from open water, bare soil, and grass. *Proc. Roy. Soc. London*, ser. A193: 120–45.

Penman, H. L. (1963) *Vegetation and hydrology*, Techn. Commun. **53**: 124 pp., Commonwealth Bur. of Soils, Harpenden, England.

Pereira, H. C. (1973) *Land use and water resources in temperate and tropical climates*, Cambridge Univ. Press, Cambridge, 246 pp.
Gives historical account of methods developed for measuring hydrological effects of land use changes.

Perrusset, A. C. (1978) L'aménagement du territorire au Gabon et l'évolution des paysages équatoriaux. *Ann. Univ. du Gabon* (2): 117–22.

Perry, A. H. (1981) *Environmental hazards in the British Isles*, 191 pp., Allen & Unwin, London.

Pessl, F., Langer, W., Ryder, R. (1972) *Geologic and hydrologic map for land-use planning in the Connecticut Valley, with examples from the folio of the Hartford North Quadrangle.* USGS, Circular 674: 12 pp.

Pewé, T. L. (1955) Origin of the upland silt near Fairbanks, Alaska. *Geological Society America Bull* **66**: 699–724.

Phipps, M. (1969) Recherches sur la distribution géographique et l'utilisation du sol. Structure locale, modelé biogéographique, structure régionale, doct. diss., Toulouse: 122 pp.
Uses multivariate analysis in order to define the units, but is limited to static parameters.

Pieri, C. (1989) *Fertilité des terres de savanes.* Min. Coopération/CIRAD/IRAT, 444 pp.
Unfortunately, ignores the morpho-pedological approach of the IRAT.

Pinto Peixoto, J., Oort, A. M. (1990) Le cycle de l'eau et le climat. *La Recherche*, 22 L (May): 570–9.
Some maps are 'exciting' at first sight, but unfortunately, lack precision and the reader must be cautious, for mistakes in the paper.

Pissart, A., Bollinne, A. (1978) L'érosion des sols limoneux cultivés de la Hesbaye. *Pédologie* **98**: 161–82.

Pitty, A. F. (1971) *Introduction to geomorphology*, Methuen, London, 526 pp., 134 fig., 20 tables.
Excellent text, very modern conception.

Pitty, A. F. (1979) *Geography and soil properties*, Methuen, London, 287 pp.

Pitty, A. F. (1982) *The nature of geomorphology*, Methuen, London, 161 pp.

Ploey, De J. (1985) The origin of modern and old colluvium in the light of a colluviation model. *Recents Trends in Phys. Geogr.*, Study Ser. Univ. Brussels, **20**: 157–71.

Ploey, De J. (1986) *Bodeneorosie in de lage landen, een europees milieu problem.* ACCO, Leuven en Amersfoort, 108 pp.

Polska Akademia Nauk, Instytut Geografii (1964) *Key and explanation of the hydrographic map of Poland on the scale of 1/50 000*, Warsaw, 48 pp., map.

Posey, D. A. (1987) Etnobiologia e ciencia do folk: sua importância para Amazônia. *Tübinger Geographische Studien* **95**: 95–108.
A very subtle analysis of how the Indians have acquired an integrated knowledge of the ecological environment and practise an applied ecology based on keen observations.

Poss, R. (1978) La dynamique de l'eau saturante dans les sols de la périphérie d'un inselberg en milieu ferrallitique de transition (N Côte d'Ivoire). *Cah. ORSTOM sér. Pédol.* **16**(2): 131–54.

Pouquet, J. (1969) Géomorphologie et ère spatiale. *Zeit. für Geom.* **13**: 414–71.
Emphasis on HRIR aboard Nimbus II. Identification of fracture

zones, rocky surfaces, regolith moisture, palaeohydrography, and types of valleys in Pacific SW and Egypt.

Pouquet, J. (1971) *Les sciences de la terre à l'heure des satellites*, Coll. Sup., 'Le Physicien', PUF, Paris, 259 pp, 33 fig., 4 photo pl.
Basic principle, types of satellites, their instrumentation, data processing and application to earth sciences.

Pouyllau, D., Seurin, M., Pouyllau, M. (1990) Piémont et accumulations alluviales dans la région Guanare-Masparro. *Trav. & Doc. Géogr. Trop.* (Bordeaux) **63**:77–135.
A Venezuelan example of the different soils formed on a terrace sequence.

Prat, C. (1989/90) Relation entre érosion et systèmes de production dans le bassin-versant sud du lac de Managua (Nicaragua). *Cah. ORSTOM, sér. Pédol.* **XXV**(1/2): 71–182.

Prego, A. (1989) *El aqua pluvial y su real aprovechamiento en la Llanuras.* Sem. Internac. Hidrol. Grandes Llanuras, Buenos Aires, 20–24 Nov. (1989) CONAPHI/UNESCO, com. n° 56. To be published by UNESCO in 1992.
Application of the management techniques experimented in the Pampa Deprimida following J. Tricart's investigations.

Price, M. (1986) Analysis of vegetation change by remote sensing. *Prog. Phys, Geogr.* **10**(4): 473–91.

Probleme des Physisch-geographischen Gliederung (1966) Materialen des Symposium über naturräumliche Gliederung. Sept. 16–24 *Prace Geograficzny* 69: 112 pp., one map.
Useful bibliographies.

Proctor, J. (1986) Tropical rain forest: structure and function. *Prog. Phys. Geogr.* **10**(3): 383–400.
Instability due to typhoons.

Prokaev, V. I. (1967) *Fundamentals of the methodology of physical geographical regionalisation*, Leningrad, 248 pp. (in Russian).

Puech, J. (1969) Etude expérimentale de la circulation de l'eau non saturante de différents sols vers une zone d'absorption. *Ann. Agron.* **20**(5): 245–61.

Pujos, A., Raynal, R. (1959) La Géomorphologie appliqué au Maroc. *Rev. de Géom. Dyn.* **10**: 103–5.

Pullan, R. A. (1970) *The soils, soil landscapes and geomorphological evolution of a metasedimentary area in northern Nigeria*, Univ. of Liverpool, Dept. of Geogr., Research Paper 6, 144 pp., 17 fig.
Applies C. G. Stephens' 'pedologic landscapes' concept. Adds description of present degradational processes to the usual physiographic descriptions and describes soils using their physiographic units.

Pye, K. (1988) *Aeolian dust and dust deposits.* Academic Press, London, 338 pp.
A good general exposition.

Quantin, P. (1972a) Les andosols. Revue bibliographique des connaissances actuelles. *Cah. ORSTOM sér. Pédol.* **10**(3): 273–301.

Quantin, P. (1972b) Note sur la nature et la fertilité des sols sur cendres volcaniques provenant d'éruptions récentes dans l'archipel des Nouvelles-Hébrides. *Cah. ORSTOM sér. Pédol.* **10**(3): 207–17.

Rabchevsky, G. (n.d.) *Remote sensing of the Earth's surface*, A.R.A. Concord. MA, 32 pp.

Rabotnov, T. A. (1976) *On the organization of biogeoceonosis.* 23rd Internat. Geogr. Congr., Moscow. Vol. 4, 105–9.
Presents Sukachev concepts, which are insufficiently known in the West.

Ramann, E. (1917) *The evolution and classification of soils* (trans. 1928 Whittles, C. L.).

Raudkivi, A. J. (1979) *Hydrology, an advanced introduction to hydrological processes and modelling*, Pergamon, Oxford, New York, 479 pp.
A quantitative, essentially theoretical, approach addressed to engineers. Does not include methods of river gauging, field measurements, and hydrological mapping.

Raunet, M. (1973) Contribution à l'étude pédo-agronomique des 'terre du barre' du Dahomey et du Togo. *Agron. Trop.* **28** (11), 1049–69.

Raunet, M. (1974) Etude morpho-pédologique dans la région des

Béni-Slimane (Algérie). Contraintes pour la mise en valeur. *Agron. Trop.* **29**(2/3): 258–99.

Raunet, M. (1979) Importance et interactions des processus géochimiques, hydrologiques et biologiques (termitières) sur les surfaces d'aplanissement tropicales granito-gneissiques. Exemple du Kenya occidental. *Agron. Trop.* **34**(1): 40–53.

Raveneau, J. (1972) Eléments d'une cartographie globale de l'habitat rural. Quelques exemples appliqués au comté de Bellechasse, Québec. *Revue de géogr. de Montréal* **26**: 35–49.
Method of superposition applied to the main components of the physical environment.

Raynal, R. (1962) Pédologie et géomorphologie au Maroc. *Revue de géogr. du Maroc*, Rabat (1/2): 19–21.

Raynal, R. (1970) Géomorphologie et vocation des sols dans les pays du bassin occidental de la Méditerranée. *An. Univ. Bucuresti, Geogr.* **19**: 21–33.
Relationships between geomorphology, soils and land use.

Reason, C. J. C., Steyn, D. G. (1990) Water erosion in British farmers fields – some causes, impacts, predictions. *Progress in Physical Geography* **14**(2): 199–219.

Rebillard, P., Ballais, J. L. (1984) Surficial deposits of two Algerian playas as seen on SIR-A, SEASAT, and LANDSAT co-registered data. *Zeit. für Geom.* **28**(4): 483–98.

Rebillard, P., Dixon, T. (1985) Geologic interpretation of SEASAT SAR imagery near the Rio Lecantur, Mexico. *Doc. B.R.G.M.* **82**:129–41.

Rebillard, P., Pascaud, P. N., Sarrat, D. (1985) Complémentarité des superpositions d'images spatiales multispectrales et multitemporelles, un cas d'application à la Tunisie. *Photo-Interprét.* (2): 15–24.

Rees, J. (1990) *Natural resources, allocation, economics and policy.* 2° ed., Routledge, London, New York, 499 pp.
An overview, mostly devoted to mineral resources.

Referentiel Pedologique Francais (1990) 3° approximation, proposition. INRA, Service de Cartographie des Sols. Olivet. To be published from 1991 onwards in the form of successive booklets beginning with the soils of cold regions and followed by those of temperate and warm regions.

Regrain, R. (1980) Géographie physique et télédétection des marais charentais. Thèse Etat, Univ. Bretagne Occ., Brest, 9 June (1979), 512 pp., 272 fig.
A magnificently illustrated, regional monograph of exceptional interest from the point of view of method and 'global' approach.

Regrain, R. (1981) Données de télédétection et données de références. *Ann. de Géogr.* **90**(499): 260–83.
About remote sensing and 'ground truth'.

Regrain, R. (1982) Bibliographie analytique des publications de télédétection des équipes FRALIT (France Atlantic Littoral) et LANDSCHAD (Landsat Chad) et associées. *Ann. de Géogr.* **91**(505): 340–55.

Reid, J., Parkinson, R., Twomlow, S., Clark, A. (1990) The impact of agricultural landuse changes on soil conditions and drainage. In: Thornes, B. (Ed.) *Vegetation and erosion*, pp. 199–215. J. Wiley & Sons, Chichester.
Very good examples and acute description of some processes.

Reineck, H. E. et al. (1990) Microbial modification of sedimentary surface structures. In: Heling, D. (Eds) *Sediments and environmental geochemistry*, pp. 254–78. Springer-V., Berlin.
Biological processes of evaporites concentration, crystallization and deposition. Interference with calcium carbonate precipitation.

Remote Sensing of the Environment Univ. of Michigan. Intern. symp. on remote sensing of the environment held annually at Ann Arbor, Michigan.

Rendell, H. E. et al. (1989) Chronology and stratigraphy of Kashmir loess. *Zeit. für Geom. Suppl.-Bd.* **76**: 213–23.
Confirms R. Gardner (1989) same volume.

Revue de Géomorphologie Dynamique, since 1984 (2) 'Chronique de Télédétection', about progress in remote sensing concerning the natural environment, its use and methodological aspects.

Rhind, D., Ray, H. (1989) *Land use.* Methuen, London, 272 pp.
Makes use of remote sensing techniques to collect data.

Ribeyrol, Y. (1988) La 'machine océan'. *Le Monde*, 28 Dec., 13660, p. 9.

Ribeyrol, Y. (1989) Ozone: cap sur l'Arctique. *Le Monde*, 11 Jan., 13672, p. 18.

Rice, R. J. (1977) *Fundamentals of geomorphology*, Longman, Harlow, New York, 387 pp., 163 fig., 8 tabl.
Text deals with certain aspects of geomorphology only, but in a useful way.

Richard L., Vartanian, M. de (1978) Carte écologique des Alpes au 100 000e. Feuillez de Chamonix et Thonon-les-Bains. *Doc. Cartogr. Ecol.* (Grenoble), **XX**: 1–39.
'Ecology' in fact, is limited to series of vegetation!

Richards, K. S., Arnett, R. R., Ellis, S. (1985) *Geomorphology and soils*, Allen & Unwin, London, 441 pp.
A collection of 21 invited review and overview papers in a multidisciplinary approach by 35 authors, mainly centred on the UK. Includes papers on soil degradation caused by agricultural practices, trafficability of soils, radiocarbon dating and duricrusts.

Richards, L. A., Wadleigh, C. H. (1952) Soil water and plant growth. In: Shaw, B. T. (Ed.) *Soil physical conditions and plant growth*. Academic Press, New York, 508 pp.

Richards, L. A., Weaver, L. R. (1943) Fifteen atmosphere percentage as related to the permanent wilting percentage. *Soil Science* **56**: 331–9.

Richardson, J. (1982) Some implications of tropical forest replacement in Jamaica. *Zeit. für Geom. Suppl.-Bd.* **44**: 107–18.
A study of sensitivity.

Richter, G. (1976) *Bodenerosion in Mitteleuropa.* Wiss. Buchgesellschaft Darmstadt. Wege der Forschung 330, 559 pp.

Richter, G., Sperling, W. (1976) *Bodenerosion in Mitteleuropa*, Wege der Forschung vol. 430. Wissenschaftliche Buchgesellschaft, Darmstadt, 559 pp.
Historical review; basic concept; methods of research, approach, measurement and mapping; effects in central Europe; soil erosion in Fed. Rep., GDR, Czechoslovakia; preventive measures, planning and implementation.

Richter, H. (1978) Eine naturräumliche Gliederung der DDR auf der Grundlage von Naturraumtypen. *Beitrage zur Geographie*, N.F. **29**: 323–40.

Richter, H. (1981) Die inhaltliche Konzeption der Karte Flächenutzung und naturräumliche Ausstattung 1:750 000 in 'Atlas DDR'. *Peterm. Geogr. Mitt.* **125**: 207–12, with unfolding coloured map of natural units and land-use.

Richter, M. (1978) *Landschaftsökologische Standortanalysen zur Ermittelung des natürlichen potentials vom Weinbergbrachen am Drachenfels.* Arb. zur Rheinl. Landeskunde 45, 70 pp., 21 fig., 8 maps.

Riezebos, P., Slotboom, R. (1974) Palynology in the study of present-day hillslope development. *Geologie en Mijnbouw* **55**(6): 436–48.

Rijtema, P. E. (1965) An analysis of actual evapotranspiration, Wageningen, PhD Thesis, VLO 659.

Riou, G. (1990) *L'eau et les sols dans les géosystèmes tropicaux.* Masson, Paris, 221 pp., 51 fig., 29 phot.
A French textbook, in which some basic concepts and techniques are described.

Riquier, J. (1953) *Les sols d'Anjouan et de Mayotte*, Mémoires Institut de Recherche Scientifique de Madagascar, Tananarive, Ser. D 5: 1–62.

Riquier, J. (1978) *World assessment of soil degradation. A methodology to assess soil degradation.* FAO/UNEP Project, AGL Div., FAO, Rome.

Risler, Ch. E. (1884–87) *Géologie agricola*, 4 vol. Berger-Levrault, Paris.

Risser, P. G. (1987) 1. Landscape ecology: state of the art. *Ecol. Studies* **64**: 3–14.

Robelin, M. (1960) La transpiration des plantes. *Bull. de l'Assoc. franç. pour l'Etude du Sol* (6/7): 320–6.

Robelin, M. (1962) L'évaporation réelle de différents couverts végétaux bien alimentés en eau et évapotranspiration potentielle. Détermination expérimentale. *Ann. Agron.* **13**: 493–522.

Robineau, Cl. (1966) *Société et économie d'Anjouan.* Mémoires ORSTOM **21**: 264 pp., figures.

Robinove, C. (1979) *Integrated terrain mapping with digital LANDSAT images in Queensland, Australia.* USGS, Prof. Paper 1102, 39 pp.

Robinson, D. A., Kukla, C. J. (1985) Anthropogenic increase of winter surface albedo. *Catena* **12**(2/3): 215–25.

Roche, M. A. (1963) *Hydrologie de surface*, Gauthiers-Villars, Paris, 430 pp.
Work of an engineer with a vast experience in applied hydraulics and techniques of irrigation in deserts and the tropics.
Roche, P. (1970) Les problèmes de fertilité des sols. *Agron. Trop.* **25**(10/11): 875–95.
Rode, A. A. (1969) *Theory of soil moisture*, vol. 1. *Moisture properties of soils and movement of soil moisture*, transl. from the Russian by Schmorak, J., Israel Program for Scientific Translations, Jerusalem, IPST Press, 560 pp.
Romani, L. (1989) *Structure des grandeurs physiques*. Libr. Scient. & Techn. Albert Blanchard, Paris, 210 pp.
Original and personal views on general methodological problems.
Roose, E. (1977) Erosion et ruissellement en Afrique de l'Ouest. *ORSTOM, Travaux et Documents* **78**(1978): 108 pp., 8 fig., 7 phot.
Abstract from the author's Dr./Eng. diss. Abundant data on soil loss and overland flow derived from experiments on parcels at Adiopodoumé, the Ivory Coast, using a rain simulator. Basic, indispensable work with application of the Wischmeier–Smith formula.
Roose, E. (1980) Dynamique actuelle de sols ferrallitiques et ferrugineux tropicaux d'Afrique occidentale. Thèse sciences, Univ. d'Orléans, 587 pp.
Roose, E., Sarrailh, J. M. (1989/90) Erodibilité de quelques sols tropicaux. Vingt années de mesures en parcelles d'érosion sous pluies naturelles. *Cah. ORSTOM, sér. Pédol.* **XXV**(1/2): 7–30.
A very useful summary of the extensive research conducted by E. Roose in Africa.
Rosenbaum, E. (1976) Shoreline structures as a cause of shoreline erosion: a review. In: Tank, R. (Ed.) *Focus on environmental geology*, 2d ed. pp. 166–79. Oxford Univ. Press, New York, London, Toronto.
Rosenberg, N. J., Hart, H. E., Brown, K. W. (1968) *Evapotranspiration: review and research*, Publ. 20, Univ. of Nebraska, College of Agric. and Home Ec. and Nebraska Water Res. Research Inst., Lincoln, 78 pp., many ref.
Ross, P. P (1977) *Arability map of the Tucson area*, Arizona. USGS, 1:250 000.
Rouse, C. (1990) The mechanics of small tropical flowslides in Dominica, West Indies. *Engineer. Geol.* **29**: 227–59.
Lixiviation and clay neogenesis vary with mean rainfall amounts and influence directly the types of mass movements, principally during hurricanes.
Rouse, W. R. (1960) *The moisture balance of Barbados and its influence on sugar cane yield. Part A of Two studies in Barbadian climatology*, by W. R. Rouse & David Watts, Montreal, McGill Univ. (1966), 65 pp.
Roussel, I. (1990) Les inondations en milieu urbain et la gestion du risque: l'exemple de l'agglomération nancéienne. *Bull. Ass. Géogr. Fr.* **67**(1): 13–22.
Bad management of the black waters in the agglomeration enhance the damage resulting from the floods.
Roux, A. L. Coord. (1986) Recherches interdisciplinaires sur les écosystèmes de la basse-plaine de l'Ain (France). Potentialités évolutives et gestion. *Doc. Cartogr. Ecol.* **29**: 166 pp.
1 folded coloured map. Interesting attempt at integration.
Rozov, N. N., Ivanova, E. N. (1968) Approaches to soil classification. *World Soil Resources Report* **32**, Rome, FAO, pp. 53–77.
Ru, Jinwen et al. (1984) Application of thermal remote sensing to study of geology in vicinity of Guilin. *Carsologia Sinica* (Guilin, China) **3**(1): 77–86.
Rudberg, S. (1979) An attempt at large scale geomorphological mapping in Fennoscandia landscapes. *IGU Comm. Geom. Surv., Proceedings*, 15th Plenary Meeting Modena-Catania, pp. 75–81.
Ruellan, A. (1983) Morphologie et fonctionnement des sols: quelques réflexions pour l'avenir de la pédologie. *Cah. ORSTOM sér. Pédol.* **20**(4): 265–70.
Ruellan, A. (1984/5) Les sols dans le paysage. *Cah. ORSTOM sér. Pédol.* **21**(2/3): 198–207.
Ruhe, R. V. (1956) Geomorphic surfaces and the nature of soils. *Soil Sc.* **82**: 441–55.
Ruhe, R. V. (1965) Relation of fluctuations of sea-level to soil genesis in the Quaternary. *Soil Sc.* **99**: 23–9.

Ruhe, R. V. (1969) Application of pedology to Quaternary research. In: Pawlak, S. (Ed.) *Pedology and Quaternary research*, pp. 1–23. Univ. of Alberta Press, Edmonton.
Illustrates Ruhe's work concerning the use of palaeosols as stratigraphic markers.
Ruhe, R. V. (1975) *Geomorphology, geomorphic processes and surficial geology*, Atlanta, Houghton Mifflin, 246 pp.
Emphasizes Quaternary studies in close association with soil science.
Ruhe, R. V., Dabiels, R., Cady, J. (1967) *Landscape evolution and soil formation in southwestern Iowa*, USDA Techn. Bull. 1349, 242 pp., 86 fig.
Ruhe, R. V., Walker, P. (1968) *Hillslope models and soil formation in open systems*, Paper J-5736, Iowa Agric. & Home Econ. Experimental Station, Ames, Iowa, Project n° 1250.
Rutter, N. Faure, H. (1987) Glacial change and the Quaternary. *Episodes* **10**(1): 3–4.
Ryerson, B., Game, J. (1988) SPOT: a new window on Canada. *GEOS* (1): 14–7.

Sabins, F. F. (1987) *Remote sensing: principles and interpretations*, Freeman, New York, 2nd ed., 449 pp.
Good general text, applications mainly geological, coloured plates.
Sachs, I., Bergeret, A., Schiray, M., Sigal, S., Thery, D., Vinaver, K. (1981) *Initiation à l'écodéveloppement*. Privat, Toulouse, 365 pp.
Proposes a new attitude for resolving development problems, which is based on the preservation of natural resources and social consciousness.
Salomé, A. I., van Dorsser, H. J. (1985) Some reflections on geomorphological mapping systems. *Zeit. für Geom.* **29**: 375–80.
Salomé, A. I., van Dorsser, H. J., Rieff, P. L. (1983) A comparison of geomorphological mapping systems. *ITC Journal*, Enschede: 272–4.
Salomon, J. N. (1987) Le Sud-Ouest de Madagascar. Thèse Etat, Aix, 2 vol., 998 pp., 238 fig., 68 phot., 4 h.t.
Elaborate monograph describing the factors of a regionalization of the environment and the vegetation.
Sarmiento, G., Monasterio, M. (1971) Ecología de las sabanas de América tropical. Analisis macroecológico de los Llanos de Calabozo, Venezuela. *Cuadernos Geográficos*, Mérida 4: 127 pp.
Hampered by its static approach in the application of the 'land system' method.
Sartz, R. S. (1970) *Effect of land use on the hydrology of small watersheds in southeastern Wisconsin*, Symposium on the results of research on representative and experimental basins, IASH-Unesco Publ. **96**: 286–95.
Satterwhite, M., Ehlan, J. (1982) Landform-vegetation relationships in the northern Chihuahuan Desert, *Catena*, Suppl. **1**: 195–209.
Interpretation of Landsat scenes using a combination of geomorphology, vegetal cover and soils to define natural units.
Sauvage, C. (1974) L'Homme et la Biosphère. *Le Courrier du CNRS*, **13**: 26–30.
Schaber, G. G., McGauley, J. F., Breed, C., Olthoeft, G. (1986) Shuttle imaging radar: physical control on signal penetration and subsurface scattering in eastern Sahara. *IEEE Trans. Geosc. & Remote Sensing*, G-24 (4): 603–23.
Schanda, E., Coord. (1976) *Remote sensing for environmental sciences*, Springer-V., Berlin, 367 pp., 178 fig.
Interesting, especially on microwaves.
Schick, A. (1974) Alluvial fans and desert roads. A problem in applied geomorphology. Ak. Wiss. Göttingen. *Symp. Geomorphologische Prozess*, pp. 418–25.
Schieber, M. (1983) Bodenerosion in Südafrika. Vergleichende Untersuchungen zur Erodierbarkeit subtropischer Böden und zur Erositivät der Niederschläge in Sommerregengebiet Südafrikas. *Giessener Geogr. Schr.*, **51**: 139 pp., 65 fig.
Schiesser, W., Giovannini, P. (1989) *Environmental protection. A safeguard to life*. Swiss-Re, Zürich, 63 pp.
Schmidt, G. (1964) Zur landschaftsökologischen Kartierung im norddeutschen Jungmoränenland. *Peterm. Geogr. Mitt.* **108**: 193–200.
Makes a comprehensive map from maps of nivation, soil erosion, microclimates and soil series.

Schmidt, K. H. (1978) Gleichgewichtzustände in geomorphologischen Systemen. *Geogr. Zeitschr.* **66**(3): 183–96.

Schmiedecken, W., Stiehl, E. (1983) Wald und Wasserhaushalt, Klimatologische und hydrologische Untersuchungen in der Ruhreifel. *Studia Geogr.* **16**: 165–95.
Detailed study of the water balance in a small basin of 2.66 km^2 for a period of 3$^{1/2}$ years.

Schmithüsen, J. (1963) Der wissenschaftliche Landschaftsbegriff. *Mitt. flor-soziol. Arbeitsgem.* **10**: 9–19.

Schmithüsen, J. (1973a) Die ökologischen Aspekte der Landschaftsforschung in *Referate des III Internationalen Symposium über Inhalt und Objekt der Komplexen Landschaftsforschung*, Bratislava.

Schmithüsen, J. (1973b) Was verstehen wir unter Landschaftsökologie?. *Tagungsbericht und wissenschaftliche Abhandlungen, Deutscher Geographentag*, pp. 409–17.

Schneider, G. (1979) Die ökologische Kartierung der Europäischen Gemeinschaft: EG-Aktien im Rahmen einer Politik der vorbeugenden und integrierten Umweltplanung. *Raumforschung und Raumordnung* **37**(1): 15–23.
The title is long . . . the contents somewhat disappointing.

Schneider, S. (1974) *Luftbild und Luftbildinterpretation*. Lehrbuch der allgemeinen Geographie, XI, De Gruyter, Berlin & New York, 530 pp., 181 fig., 216 phot.
Mainly about airphoto interpretation, but also remote sensing, especially thermography. Important bibliography.

Schofield, R. K. (1935) The pF of the water in soil. *Trans. 3rd Intern. Congr. Soil Sc.* **2**: 37–48.

Schofield, R. K., Botelho da Costa, J. V. (1935) The determination of the pF at permanent wilting and the moisture equivalent by the freezing point method. *Trans. 3rd Intern. Congr. Soil Sc.* **1**: 6–10.

Scholz, E. (1974) Zur Klassifikation geomorphologischer Karten nach Massstab und Inhalt. *Wiss. Z. Pädagogischen Hochschule Potsdam* **18**(3): 393–402.

Schoneich, R. (1970) Physiotope und ihre räumliche Ordnung im Bereich der östlichen Randzertalung des Hagenower Altenmoränenlandes. *Geogr. Ber.* **54**: 42–59.
Geomorphology is the determinant factor.

Schramm, G., Warford, J. J. (Eds) (1989) *Environmental management and economic development World Bank*. J. Hopkins Univ. Press, Baltimore, London, 208 pp.
Some contributions are of interest for instance that of J. J. Warford, pp. 7–22.

Schulze, R. E., McGee, O. S. (1978) Climatic indices and classifications in relation to biogeography of southern Africa. In: Werger, M. J. W. (Ed.) *Biogeography and ecology of southern Africa*, pp. 19–52. Junk, The Hague.

Schumm, S. A. (1977) *The fluvial system*. J. Wiley & Sons Inc., Interscience, New York, 338 pp.

Schwartz, D. (1986) Les podzols tropicaux, témoins de l'évolution des paysages. Symp. Internat. de Dakar, April. *Trav. & Doc. ORSTOM*, **197**: 435–8.

Schwartz, D. (1987) Les podzols tropicaux sur Sables Batéké en Rép. Pop. du Congo. Description caractéristiques, genèse. In: Righi, D., Chauvel, A., Coord. *Podzols et podzolisation*. INRA/AFES, pp. 25–36.
Pedogenesis, in these two works by D. Schwartz is studied in close association with the geomorphic evolution, both being a function of environmental change resulting from climate and the regional geomorphic evolution which throw light upon each other.

Scott, R., Healy, P., Humphreys, G. (1985) *Land units of Chimby Province, Papua, New Guinea*. CSIRO, Div. of Water and Land Res., Natural Res. Series 5, 162 pp.

Sebly, M. J. (1985) *Earth's changing surface*, Clarendon Press, Oxford, 607 pp.
Comprehensive advanced modern text.

Ségalen, P. (1967) Les sols et la géomorphologie au Cameroun. *Cah. ORSTOM, sér. Pédol.* **5**(2): 137–88.

Segersom, K. (1980) *Erosion studies at Paricutin, state of Michoacán, Mexico*. USGS, Bull. 965-A, 164 pp.

Selleron. G. (1985) *Télédétection et forêt. Dynamique de la forêt landaise de 1975 à 1980 (LANDSAT and SPOT simulation)*. CNRS, Centre Régional de Publ. de Toulouse, 371 pp., 81 fig., 12 coloured photographic pl.

Seyhan, E. (1972) *Potential use of remote sensing techniques in hydrology*. NIWARS, Publ. 3, 46 pp + annexes.

Shaw, C. F. (1927) The normal moisture capacity of soils. *Soil Sc.* **23**: 303–17.

Shilts, W. W., Kettles, I. M. (1989) Geology and acid rainfalls in Eastern Canada. *GEOS* (3): 25–32.
Acid soils and subsoils enhance the acidification and the damage resulting from acid rains.

Short, N. M. (1982) *The Landsat tutorial workbook, basics of satellite remote sensing*, NASA Ref. Publ. 1078, NASA, Washington D.C., 553 pp.
Comprehensive manual, full of enclosures.

Short, N. M., Blair, R. W. (1986) *Geomorphology from space. A global overview of regional landforms*, NASA Sp., 486: 717 pp.
Unfortunately insufficient information caused too many mistakes that render the commentaries of the magnificent images unusable.

Short, N. M., Lowman, P. D., Finch, W. A. (1976) *Mission to Earth: Landsat views the World*, NASA, Washington D.C., 359 pp, 400 plates, most in colour.
Magnificent atlas, scenes from all over the world.

Sieffermann, R. G. (1988) Le système des grandes tourbières équatoriales. *Ann. de Géogr.* **97**(544): 642–66.
The accumulation of peat in Borneo takes place within the framework of the geomorphic evolution, but when the author discusses Amazonia, he makes serious mistakes owing to insufficient bibliographic research: his good intentions produce only partial results, which is a pity.

Simmons, I. G. (1974) *The ecology of natural resources*. Edward Arnold, London, 424 pp.

Simmons, I. G. (1979) *Biogeography: natural and cultural*. Edward Arnold, London, 400 pp., fig.
Excellent text on ecology issuing into biogeography.

Simonson, R. W. (1971) Soil association maps and proposed nomenclature. *Soil Sc. Soc. Amer. Proc.* **35**: 959–64.

Sinson, E. A. (1982) The protection of water quality within the European Economic Community. *IASH Publ.* **139**: 3–11.

Sioli, H. (1985) The effects of deforestation in Amazonia. *Geo. Journal*, **151**: 197–203.

Slater, C. S., Bryant, J. C. (1946) Comparison of four methods of soil moisture measurement. *Soil Sc.* **61**: 131–55.

Slaymaker, O., Balteanu, D. (Eds) (1986) Geomorphology and land management, *Zeit. für Geom. Suppl.-Bd.* **58**: 190 pp., 79 fig., 13 phot., 43 tabl.

Smith, G. D. (1963) Objectives and basic assumptions of the new soil classification system. *Soil Sc.* **96**: 6–16.

Smith, G. D. (1965) Lectures on soil classification. 12e conférence, Science du Sol, *Pédologie*, spécial n° 4, Ghent (Belgium), 134 pp.

Smith, G. W. (1966) The relation between rainfall, soil water and yield of copra on a coconut estate in Trinidad. *J. Applied Ecology* **3**(1): 117–24.

Snytko, W. A. (1976) Raum-Zeit-Modelle von natürlichen Regimen der Geosysteme, dargestellt an geochemischen Prozessen im Transbaikalgebiet. *Geogr. Ber.* **79**: 111–7.

Sobolev, L. N., Utexhin, V. B. (1973) *Russian (Ramansky) approaches to community systematization*. In: Tüxen, Gen. Ed. Handbook of vegetation science, V: 75–103. Junk, The Hague.
Interesting as it concerns the evolution of concepts.

Sochava, V. B. (1970) Plant communities and the dynamics of natural systems. *Soviet Geography, Review and Translation* **11**: 605–16.

Sochava, V. B. (1971) Geography and ecology. *Soviet Geography, Review and Translation* **12**: 277–93; also in *Peterm. Geogr. Mitt.* **116**: 89–98 (1972).
Brief description of the taxonomic hierarchy of biogeographic units. Flow chart of the steppe ecosystem.

Sochava, V. B. (1972a) Geographie und ökologie. *Peterm. Geogr. Mitt.* **116**: 89–98.

Sochava, V. B. (1972b) The study of geosystems: the current stage in complex physical geography. *International Geography* **1**: 298–301.

Sochava, V. B. (1974a) Das Systemparadigma in der Geographie. *Peterm. Geogr. Mitt.* **118**:, 161–6.

Sochava, V. B. (1974b) Geotopology as part of the study of geosystems. In: *Tropical aspects of the study of geosystems*, Novosibirsk, pp. 3–86 (in Russian).

Sochava, V. B. (1976) The study of geosystems. *Reports of the Institute of Geography and the Far East*. Ac. of Sc. USSR Siberian Branch, Special (51) Issue for the XXIII Intern. Geogr. Congr., Irkutsk, pp. 3–40 (in English).

Sochava, V. B. (1977) Konzeptionelle Grundlagen und Leitlinien der klassifikatorischen Ordnung von Geosystemen. *Geogr. Ber.* **84**: 161–75. Preface by Haase.
A useful overview of the Soviet approach.

Sochava, V. B., Krauklis, A. A., Snytko, V. A. (1975) Toward a unification of concepts and terms used in integral landscape investigations. *Soviet Geography, Review and Translation* **16**: 616–22.

Sokolov, V., Chernov, Y. (1983) Les écosystèmes arctiques: conservation et développement dans un milieu extrême. *Nat. & Ress. (UNESCO)* **19**(3): 2–9. Exists in English, French, Spanish, Arab, Russian.
Extreme conditions offer more demonstrative examples.

Solntsey, V. N (1976) Spatial and temporal structure of the geosystem. 23rd *Intern. Geogr. Congr.*, Moscow, **5**: 30–4.

Sorensen, J. (1981) Emergency response to Mt St Helens' eruption, March 20 to April 10 (1980). *Natural Hazard Res.*, Working Paper **43**: 63 pp., 7 fig.

Sorre, M. (1947) *Les Fondements de la géographie humaine*, vol. 1 *Les Fondements biologiques: essai d'une écologie de l'homme*, 2nd edn. Colin, Paris.

Sourbes, I., Waldteufel, P. (Eds) (1987) *L'espace, une nouvelle frontière. Habiter l'espace?* ADEMAST, Paris, 170 pp.
Information about orbits, sensors and progammes of various satellites.

Soutadé, G. (1980) Modelé et dynamique actuelle des versants supraforestiers des Pyrénées orientales. Thèse Etat, Bordeaux III, 1978, Albi, 442 pp., 121 fig., 63 phot.

Soutadé, G. (1984) Pyrénées. *Rech. Fr. sur les Phén. Périglac.* 25° Congr. Intern. Géogr. Paris, pp. 79–91.
Influence of morphogenic processes on the content and profile of organic materials in soils.

Sparks, B. W. (1986) *Geomorphology*, 3rd. ed. Longman, Harlow, 561 pp., 283 fig.
Traditional, small scale, partly Davisian oriented, elementary text.

Spécial télédétection (1982) *Bull. Inform.*, Institut Géographique National **44**(1): 70 pp.
Presentation of the various remote sensing activities of the IGN (numerous colour reproductions from data processing) of SPOT and its future use, and of thermographs.

Speight, J. G. (1977) Landform pattern description from aerial photographs. *Photogrammetria* **32**: 161–82.

Spencer, T, Douglas, I. (1985) The significance of environmental change: diversity, disturbance and tropical ecosystems. In: Douglas, I, Spencer, T. (Eds) *Environmental change and tropical geomorphology*, pp. 13–33. Allen and Unwin, London.

SPOT: User Handbook (1986) 2 vol.: 1. References, 2. SPOT User Handbook, CNES, SPOT, Toulouse, 1987 (*Guide des utilisateurs de données SPOT/IMAGE*).
These 2 volumes are composed of separately paged dossiers in a ring-binder so that new pages can be added or specific documents extracted. They include a description of the system, how to order recordings, describes their characteristics and diverse stages of processing and gives typical examples of their uses.

SPOT (Nouvelles de. News) A serial published by SPOT-Image, a French and English version. Delivered free in any country.
Please address yourself to the SPOT-Image agency of your own country.

Staring, W. C. H. (1856–1860) *De bodem van Nederland. De samenstelling en het ontstaan der gronden in Nederland ten behoeve van het algemeen beschreven*, 2 vol., Haarlem, A. C. Kruseman.

Stead, D. (1990) Engineering geology in Papua-New Guinea, a review. *Engineer. Geol.* **29**(1): 1–29.
An excellent regional monograph of a country where hazards are serious and varied.

Stephens, C. G. (1953) *A manual of Australian soils*, CSIRO, Melbourne.

Stephens, C. G. (1961) *The soil landscapes of Australia*, Soil Publ. 18, CSIRO, Melbourne.
Heralds the idea that morphopedologic units are more satisfactory than the old 'land units'.

Stephens, C. G. (1963) The 7th Approximation, its application in Australia. *Soil Sc.* **96**: 40–48.

Stephens, C. G. (1965) Climate as a factor of soil formation through the Quaternary. *Soil Sc.* **99**(1): 9–14.

Stephens, C. G. (1967) Soil stratigraphy and its applications to correlation of Quaternary deposits and landforms and to soil science. A review of an Australian experience. *Proc. 7th Congr. INQUA*, **9**: 282–91.

Steuer, M. (1979) Wahrnehmung und Bewertung von Naturrisiken. *Münchener Geogr. Hefte* **43**: 234 pp., 44 fig.

Stiller, H., Sagdejew, R. (1980) *Sojus-22 erforscht die Erde*. Akademisch Verlag, Berlin (DDR), 283 pp., 182 fig.

Stocking, M. (1980) Soil loss estimation for rural development: a position for geomorphology. *Zeit. für Geom. Suppl.-Bd* **36**: 264–73.

Stoddard. D. R. (1965) Geography and the ecological approach. The ecosystem as a geographical principle and method. *Geography* **50**(228): 242–51.

Strahler, A. N., Strahler, A. H. (1983) *Modern physical geography*, J. Wiley & Sons, Inc., New York, 2nd ed., 532 pp., 705 fig., 34 tables, 55 plates.
Excellent basic text on the natural environment considered as the support of living beings, in the framework of systems theory.

Streif, H. (1990) *Das ostfriesische Küstengebiet*, 2d ed., 376 pp., 48 fig., Borntraeger, Berlin, Stuttgart.
Excellent regional example of the constraints imposed by the sea to the inhabitants of coastal lowlands, different types of protection planned through time.

Suisse de Réassurances (1989) *Les périls de la nature et les sinistres catastrophiques*. Zürich, 32 pp., 12 fig. There are versions in various other languages (English, German).
Very accurate evaluation of the financial consequences of natural disasters.

Swain, P. H. (1986) Remote sensing. In: Young, T. Y., Fu, K. S. (Eds) *Handbook of pattern recognition and image processing*, pp. 613–23. Academic Press, New York.

Swartzendruber, D. (1969) The flow of water in unsaturated soils. In: De Wiest, R. J. M. (Ed.) *Flow through porous media*, pp. 215–92. Academic Press, New York, London.

Sweeting, M. M. (1990) The Guilin karst. *Zeit. für Geom. Suppl.-Bd* **77**: 47–65.

Szangolies, K. (1983) Télédétection de la Terre avec un nouveau système d'appareils. *Revue d'Iéna* **4**: 160–3.
Also published in English, German and Russian. East-German metric camera equipment, characteristics, and products.

Szollosi-Nagy, A., Kundzewicz, Z. W., Cordova-Rodriguez, J. (1987) Surface water hydrology. In: Kundzewicz, Z. W., Gottschalk, L., Webb, B. *Hydrology 2000*, pp. 9–15. IASH 171, Wallingford, UK.
The challenge of the future in surface water hydrology.

Szupryczynski, J. (1971) Scrutiny and appraisal of the geographic environment on a regional base. *Przeglad Geograficzny*, 43 pp: 311–21.
Historical review of the hydromorphological map of Poland: by 1968 already 58 970 km² had been surveyed and published on 41 sheets at a scale 1:50 000.

Tada, F., Oya, M. (1968) Geomorphological survey map of the Yoshino river basin, Shikoku, in the Western part of Japan, showing classification of flood-stricken areas. *Przeglac Geogr.* **40**: 289–92.
One of the few Japanese maps of this kind published outside Japan.

Tank, R. (Ed.) (1976) *Focus on environmental geology*. Oxford Univ. Press, New York, 2° ed., 538 pp.

Tarlet, J. (1977) Milieu naturel et aménagement. Les méthodes de planification écologique. *Ann. de Géogr.* **86**(474): 104–200.
An exposition of McHarg's approach.

Tarlet, J., Walleix, F. (1972) Un cas d'application de la planification écologique: l'étude de Toulon-Ouest. *L'Irrigant* **59**: 23–52.

Tarpley, J., McGinnis, D. (1984) Vegetation cover mapping from satellites. *LANDSAT Data Users Notes* 30 March: 9–12.

Tavernier, R. (1963) The 7th Approximation: its application in western Europe. *Soil Sc.* **96**: 35–9.

Tazieff, H., Derruau, M. (1990) *Le volcanisme et sa prévention.* Masson, Paris, 256 pp., 39 fig.
A useful summary of the volcanological research of H. Tazieff, with a description of several eruptions and the means used to contain them or save the people at risk.

Télédétection des milieux naturels et urbains (1987) Rech. Géogr. à Strasbourg **27**: 88 pp.
Contains papers on application programmes and monographs about results obtained in geomorphology–geology and climate (haze and fog).

Tessier, J. (1974) Terroir de Mogtedo (Haute-Volta). Etude morpo-pédologique en vue de la mise en valeur des terres. *Agron. Trop.* **29**(2/3): 312–69.

Thibout, F. (1974) Interactions morphogénèse–pédogénèse. Example d'application dans la région de Be'chloul (Algérie). *Agron. Trop.* **29**(2/3): 300–11.

Thomas, D. S. G. (1988) Analysis of linear dune sediment-form relationships in the Kalahari dune desert. *Earth Surf. Proc. & Landforms* **13**: 545–53.

Thomas, D. S. G. (1989) *Arid zone geomorphology.* Belhaven Press, London, 372 pp.

Thomas, M. F. (1989a) The role of etch processes in landform development. I, Etching concepts and their applications. *Zeit. für Geom.* **33**(2): 129–42.

Thomas, M. F. (1989b) The role of etch processes in landform development. II, Etching and the formation of relief. *Zeit. für Geom.* **33**(3): 257–74.

Thomas, S. (1982) *Trends and developments in global natural disasters*, 1947–1981. Nat. Hazard Res., Working Paper **45**: 22 pp.

Thornes, J. B. (1985) The ecology of erosion. *Geography* **70**: 222–35.

Thornthwaite, C. W. (1948) An approach towards a rational classification of climate. *Geogr. Review* **38**: 55–94.

Thornthwaite, C. W., Mather, J. B. (1955) The water balance. *Publ. in Climatology* **8**(1): 104 pp.

Thouret, J. C. (1990) Les risques volcaniques et volcano-glaciaires dans les montagnes peuplées: identification, cartographie, évaluation. *Bull. Assoc. des Géogr. Fr.* **67**(2): 133–48.
General methodological aspects are discussed before a well documented monograph of the various volcanic hazards.

Tiedemann, H. (n.d.) The force of water. *Swiss.-Re* Zürich: 85 pp., 81 fig. There are also German and French versions.
A very well documented and illustrated monograph about the hazards resulting from floods.

Tihay, J-P. (1976) Dynamique des versants de milieux montagnards dans la vallée de la Soummam (Algérie). *Ann. de Géogr.* **85**(469): 257–80.

Tihay, J-P. (1981) L'approche géomorphologique dans l'analyse des milieux naturels de la zone tropicale humide. L'exemple d'un front de colonisation agricole dans le nord de la Colombie. *Travaux de l'Institut de Géogr. de Reims* **45/46**: 89–106.
Major work discussing general methodological concepts and a research method on the natural environment and man–environment relationship.

Tihay, J-P., Tricart, J. (1984) assisted by Ortiz, J., Pérez Preciado, A. *Manual de percepción remota en geografía física*, IGAC, Bogotá, 2 vol. 315 & 204 pp.
General information about techniques and documentation available. Colombian examples.

Tison, J., Dubertret, L., Castany, G. (1962) Une légende pour les cartes hydrogéologiques. *Bull. Int. Ass. Sc. Hydr.* **7**(3): 18–32.

Torres, C. (1975) L'utilisation de la thermographie et enregistrements infrarouges thermiques pour la télédétection des formations superficielles et l'étude du milieu naturel. Thèse 3e cycle, UER de Géogr., Univ. de PARIS I, July 2nd, 324 pp.

Townshend, J. (1981) The spatial resolving power of Earth Resources Satellites. *Prog. Phys. Geogr.* **5**(1): 32–55.

Toy, T. J. (1979) Potential evapotranspiration and surface-mine rehabilitation in the Powder River basin, Wyoming and Montana. *J. of Range Management* **32**(4): 312–7.

Trafas, K. (1981) Remote sensing on research on industrial air pollution in Cracow area. *Folia Geogr. Phys.* **14**: 121–7, in Polish, with English abstract p. 127.

Trautmann, J. (1981) L'utilisation de la télédétection aérienne infra-rouge pour l'étude de la dynamique fluviale du Rhin. *Ann. de Géogr.* **90**: 284–310.

Trautmann, J. (1984) Surveillance de la pollution thermique par thermographie. L'exemple de la centrale nucléaire de Fessenheim en Alsace. *Rev. Géogr. de l'Est*, Nancy, **24**(2/3): 215–36.
Extensive exposition of the approach, combining calibrated measurements on the Earth's surface and aerial sensing.

Trautmann, J. (1987) ATP Télédétection Spatiale. Lits fluviaux et paysage riverains, organisation et évolution. *Rev. de Géom. Dyn.* **36**(4): 140–1.

Trautmann, J. (1989) Actes de la table ronde télédétection du milieu naturel, 11–13 September.

Trautmann, J. (1991) Forthcoming paper. *Rev. de Géom. Dyn.*

Tricart, J. (1952) La geomorphologie et la notion d'échelle. *Rev. de Géom. Dyn.* **3**: 213–18.

Tricart, J. (1955) Un complément des cartes géologiques: les cartes géomorphologiques. *Bull. Société Géologique de France*, 6e sér. **4**: 739–50.

Tricart, J. (1956) Aspects géomorphologiques du Delta du Sénégal. *Rev. de Géom. Dyn.* **7**(5/6): 65–86.

Tricart, J. (1958) Etude de la crue de la mi-juin 1957 dans les vallées du Guil de l'Ubaye et de la Cerveynette. *Revue de Géographie Alpine*, 565–627.

Tricart, J. (1959a) Présentation d'une feuille de la carte géomorphologique du Delta du Sénégal au 1/50 000. *Rev. de Géom. Dyn.* **10**: 106–16.

Tricart, J. (1959b) Enquête sur les organismes faisant des recherches de géomorphologie appliquée: le Centre de géographie appliquée (Université de Strasbourg). *Rev. de Géom. Dyn.* **10**: 85–96.
This number of the Revue *(May–Dec.) is entirely concerned with applied geomorphology.*

Tricart, J. (1960) Etude géomorphologique du projet d'aménagement du Lac Faguibine (République du Mali). *Sols Africains* **5**(3): 207–89 (bilingual: French and English).

Tricart, J. (1961a) Mecanismes normaux et phénomènes catastrophiques dans l'évolution des versants du bassin du Guil (Hautes Alpes, France) *Zeit. für Geom.* **5**(4): 277–301.

Tricart, J. (1961b) L'aménagement du Lac Faguibine (République du Mali). *Tiers-Monde, Etudes*, pp. 39–78.

Tricart, J. (1961c) Note explicative de la carte géomorphologique du Delta du Sénégal. *Mémoires du Bureau de Recherches Géologiques et Minières* 8.

Tricart, J. (1962a) *Problèmes de développement dans les Andes vénézuéliennes*, SEDES-CDU, Paris, 96 pp., 9 fig., 4 phot. pl.

Tricart, J. (1962b) Panorama et problèmes de la géomorphologie appliquée dans le monde. *Revue de Géogr. du Maroc* **1–2**: 11–18.

Tricart, J. (1962c) *L'Epiderme de la terre. Esquisse d'une géomorphologie appliquée.* Coll. Evolution des Sciences, Masson, Paris, 167 pp., 35 fig.
Concise account, easy to read.

Tricart, J. (1962d) Les discontinuités dans les phénomènes d'erosion. *Intern. Assoc. Scientific, Hydrol.*, 59. Commission Control Erosion: 233–43. English transl. In: Labonne, J. B., Mosley, M. P. (Eds) (1982) Erosion and sediment yield. *Benchmark Papers in Geology* **63**, Hutchinson Ross, Stroudsburg, PA: 34–43.

Tricart, J. (1963a) La cartographie hydrologique détaillée et son intérêt pour l'étude des régimes fluviaux. *Mémoires et Travaux de la Société Hydrotechnique de France* **I**: 51–56.

Tricart, J. (1963b) Cartes géomorphologiques et géomorphologie appliquée: l'expérience du Centre de Géomorphologie Appliquée. *Prace Geor., Probl. Geom. Mapping* **46**: 113–20.
This volume contains numerous papers on geomorphological mapping.

Tricart, J. (1964) Geomorphologie et aménagement rural (exemple du Venezuela). *Coopération Technique* (Institut d'Etude du Développement économique et social), Paris **44–45**: 69–81.
Mainly about geomorphological maps: with extract in colour of Mucuchies.

Tricart, J. (1965a) Morphogénèse et pédogénèse, I: Approche méthodologique: géomorphologie et pédologie. *Science du Sol* **1**: 69–85.

Tricart, J. (1965b) *Principes et Méthodes de la géomorphologie*, Masson, Paris, 496 pp., 36 fig., 8 pl., one coloured map. *Systematic presentation, discussion of various methodological problems. Important bibliographies.*

Tricart, J. (1965c) Rapport de la mission de reconnaissance géomorphologique de la moyenne vallée du Niger. *Mém. IFAN* **72** Dakar: 196 pp.

Tricart, J. (1966) Géomorphologie et aménagement rural, exemple du Vénézuéla. *Coopération Technique* **44/55**: 69–81.

Tricart, J. (1968a) Aspects méthodologiques des études de ressources pour le développement. *Mélanges O. Tulippe*, Duculot, Gembloux, pp. 345–61.

Tricart, J. (1968b) Facteurs physiques et régionalisation. *Regionalisation et Développement.* Colloques Internationaux du CNRS, Sciences Humaines, Strasbourg, June 26–30 (1967), pp. 41–63.

Tricart, J. (1968c) Méthode de cartographie au 1:1 000 000 du contexte hydrologique élaborée au Centre de Géographie Appliquée, Univ. de Strasbourg, *Mélanges Maurice Pardé*, Ophrys, Paris, pp. 671–82.

Tricart, J. (1968d) *Précis de géomorphologie*, SEDES, Paris, vol. 1 *Géomorphologie structurale*, 322 pp., 114 fig.; vol. 2 *Géomorphologie dynamique générale* (1977a) 345 pp., 153 fig.; vol. 3 *Géomorphologie climatique* (1981a), 313 pp., 78 fig. *A modern view of geomorphology, focusing on the interdependence of geomorphology and other aspects of the environment.*

Tricart, J. (1969a) Cartographic aspects of geomorphological surveys in relation to development programmes. *World Cartography* (UN Dept of Social Affairs), New York, **9**: 75–83.

Tricart, J. (1969b) Oscillations du niveau marin et changements climatiques dans la Pampa Deprimida (Pampa Argentine). *Bull. Assoc. Fr. pour l'Et. du Quat.* (4): 243–68.

Tricart, J. (1969/70a) Actions éoliennes dans la Pampa Deprimida. *Rev. de Géom. Dyn.* **19**(4): 178–89.

Tricart, J. (1969/70b) Le Salar del Huasco (étude géomorphologique). *Rev. de Géom. Dyn.* **19**(2): 49–84. *With detailed geomorphological map on a scale of 1:46 000.*

Tricart, J. (1970) Place du géographe dans l'étude des problèmes d'aménagement régional et de développement. *Cah. de Géogr. de Québec* **31**: 63–77.

Tricart, J. (1971) Les études géomorphologiques pour la conservation des terres et des eaux. *Options méditerranéennes*, Oct. **9**: 94–99.

Tricart, J. (1972a) *La Terre, planète vivante*, Paris, Coll. Sup., PUF, 183 pp.

Tricart, J. (1972b) Influence de la géomorphologie sur les sols dans la Pampa Deprimida (Argentine). *Cah. ORSTOM sér. Pédol.* **10**(2): 153–68.

Tricart, J. (1972c) Reconnaisance géomorphologique de l'île d'Anjouan. *Madagascar, Revue de Géographie* **21**: 79–98, 10 phot.

Tricart, J. (1972d) Quelques aspects de l'énergie dans le milieu physico-géographique. Hans-Poser-Festschr. *Göttinger Geogr. Abh.* **60**: 27–37. *An early attempt at systemic integration based on energy flows.*

Tricart, J. (1973a) La géomorphologie dans les études intégrées d'aménagement du milieu naturel. *Ann. de Géogr.* **82**(452): 421–53.

Tricart, J. (1973b) Etude de l'évolution morphogénique récente d'un secteur de l'Amazonie sur mosaïques de radar latéral (W. d'Obidos, Brésil). *Photo-Interpretation* **73–5**(5–6): 30–41.

Tricart, J. (1973c) Geomorfologia de la Pampa Deprimidao, base para los estudios edafológicos y agronómicos, INTA, Buenos Aires, Col. Científica nº 12, 202 pp., 15 fig., 15 tabl., folded maps.

Tricart, J. (1973d) Un problème de géomorphologie appliquée: le choix des sites d'habitat dans une région sismique (Andes centrales, Pérou). *Ann. de Géogr.* **82**(449): 8–27.

Tricart, J. (1974a) De la géomorphologie à l'étude écographique intégrée. *Agron. Trop.* **29**(2/3): 122–32.

Tricart, J. (1974b) Existence de périodes sèches au Quaternaire en Amazonie et dans les régions voisines. *Rev. de Géom. Dyn.* **23** (4): 145–58.

Tricart, J. (1974c) Apports de ERTS-1 à notre connaissance écogénétique des Llanos de l'Orénoque (Colombia et Vénézuéla).

Symposium on European Resources Satellite Experiments, Frascati, Jan. 28–Feb. 1 (1974). *ESRO* SP-100, pp. 317–24.

Tricart, J. (1974d) Phénomènes démesurés et régime permanent dans les bassins montagnards (Queyras et Ubayeo, Alpes françaises). *Rev. de Géom. Dyn.* **23**(4): 99–114.

Tricart, J. (1975a) Variations de l'environnement écologique. *Rev. Géogr. Lyon* **50**(1): 5–17.

Tricart, J. (1975b) L'inventaire des resources naturelles du Brésil dans le cadre du Projeto RADAM. *Ann. de Géogr.* **84**(46): 97–103.

Tricart, J. (1975c) Les Vosges et la Plaine d'Alsace vue du satellite ERTS-1. *Ann. de Géogr.* **84**(462): 129–73.

Tricart, J. (1976a) Ecodynamique et aménagement. *Rev. de Géom. Dyn.* **25**(1): 19–32. *With ecodynamic map of Sainte-Maxime on scale of 1:25 000.*

Tricart, J. (1976b) Quelques aspects des rapports entre la pédogènèse et la morphogenèse dans la Rift Valley d'Ethiopie. *Ann. de Géogr.* **85**(470): 499–502.

Tricart, J. (1976c) Quelques aspects de l'utilisation des images multispectrales du satellite LANDSAT-1 (ex-ERTS) dans l'étude écologique des pays tropicaux (Mali, Colombia, Venezuela). *Travaux et Documents de Géographie Tropicale*, CEGET, Bordeaux **25**: 79–119. (Réunion d'Information des 18–19 April 1975).

Tricart, J. (1976d) La région d'Obidos (Amazonie brésilienne) sur les images LANDSAT. Comparaison avec les mosaïques-radar. *Photo-Interprétation* **76–2**(4–5): 22–35. *This, and Tricart (1973b) complement each other. Their ecodynamic significance is demonstrated.*

Tricart, J. (1977a) Types de lits fluviaux en Amazonie brésilienne. *Ann. de Géogr.* **86**(473): 1–54.

Tricart, J. (1977b) in *Apports de la télédétection à l'étude des régions arides et subarides.* 1) Informations fournies par les satellites de resources terrestres LANDSAT, pp. 3–9. 2) Les effets de la sécheresse au Mali: région au Nord du Lac Débo, pp. 51–67: *Publ. Centre Perfect., Aménagement du Milieu Naturel*, Univ. Louis Pasteur, Strasbourg.

Tricart, J. (1977c) Existe-t-il des resources naturelles renouvelables? *L'Homme et l'Humanité* **59**: 17–20.

Tricart, J. (1978a) *Géomorphologie applicable*, Masson, Paris, 204 pp., 7 fig., 16 pl. *Methodological studies, presentation of specific cases. Bibliography.*

Tricart, J. (1978b) Développement agricole et étude intégrée du milieu naturel. *Etudes Géographiques L. Papy*, Maison Sciences de l'Homme d'Aquitaine, pp. 209–18.

Tricart, J. (1978c) Le sol dans l'environnement écologique. *Rev. de Géom. Dyn.* **27**(4): 113–28.

Tricart, J. (1978d) Ecologie et développement: l'exemple amazonien. *Ann. de Géogr.* **87**(481): 257–93.

Tricart, J. (1978e) Les enregistrements de télédétection, source d'information pour l'étude de l'environnement écologique. *Rev. de Géom. Dyn.* **27**(1): 29–41. *For aerial photographs and various types of sensors; comparative tables of types of information provided by photographs and imagery.*

Tricart, J. (1978f) Degrés de stabilité en forêt ombrophile: Amazonie et Nouvelle-Guinée. A propos de l'article de E. Löffler. *Zeit. für Geom.* **23**(3): 357–9.

Tricart, J. (1978g) Vocations de terres, resources ou contraintes et développement rural. *Hérodote* **12**: 65–76.

Tricart, J. (1979a) Comparaison des informations 'écographiques' fournies par trois types de radar. *ITC Journal* (4): 35–47.

Tricart, J. (1979b) Inventaire du milieu naturel et banque de données. *Ann. de Géogr.* **88**(489): 605–13. *A review of a CSIRO study of Environments of South Australia (1977) 7 vol.*

Tricart, J. (1979c) Paysage, écologie et approche systémique. *Bull. Assoc. de géogr. fr.* **465**: 377–82.

Tricart, J. (1979d) L'analyse de système et l'étude intégrée du milieu naturel. *Ann. de Géogr.* **88**(490): 705–14.

Tricart, J. (1979e) Paysage et écologie. *Rev. de Géom. Dyn.* **28**: 81–95.

Tricart, J. (1979f) Types de lits fluviaux en Amazonie brésilienne. *Ann. de Géogr.* **86**(473): 1–54.

Tricart, J. (1981a) Géomorphologie et Quaternaire d'après une image RBV: la vallée du Sénégal entre Bogué et Podor (Sénégal, Mauritanie). *Ann. de Géogr.* **90**(499): 311–26.

Tricart, J. (1981b) L'Amazonie: raisons écologiques d'un paradoxe historique. *Bull. de liaison des prof. d'Hist. et géogr. de l'Acad. de Strasbourg*, CNDP **22**: 34–50.

Tricart, J. (1981c) Ecologie & géographie. *Bull. de liaison de prof. d'hist. et de géogr. de l'Acad. de Strasbourg.*, CNDP **22**: 6–17.

Tricart, J. (1981d) Ecologie & géographie. In: 'Terrains vagues et terres promises'. *Cah. de l'Inst. d'Et. du Dév.* Genève. PUF, Paris, pp. 255–79.

Tricart, J. (1982a) Climatic influence on geomorphology. In: Sharma, H. S. (Ed.) *Perspectives in Geomorphology. Recent Trends*, vol. 1, New Delhi, Concept, pp. 21–36.

Tricart, J. (1982b) L'Homme et les cataclysmes. *Hérodote* **74**: 12–39.

Tricart, J. (1982c) Régimes hydriques et géographie. *Ann. de Géogr.* **91**(505): 301–39.

References on the Maradi experimental area of Niger.

Tricart, J. (1982d) El Pantanal: un ejemplo del impacto de la geomorfología sobre el medio ambiente. *Geografia, Rio Claro* **7**(13–14): 37–50.

Tricart, J. (1982e) Taxonomical aspects of the integrated study of the natural environment. *ITC Journal* (3): 344–7.

Tricart, J. (1982f) Géographie/écologie. *Hérodote* **26**: 47–66.

Tricart, J. (1983) L'éruption du volcan El Chichón (Mexique) mars–avril 1982. *Ann. de Géogr.* **92**(515): 385–402.

Tricart, J. (1984a) L'apport de la géomorphologie à l'aménagement d'un territoire. In: Lamotte, M., Coord. *Fondements rationnels de l'aménagement d'un territoire* pp. 98–113. Masson, Paris.

Tricart, J. (1984b) L'Ecogéographie, approche systémique et aménagement. *Hérodote* **33/34**: 230–50.

Tricart, J. (1985a) Paysage et télédétection. In: Berdoulay, V., Phipps, M. (Eds) *Paysage et système*. chap. 9 pp. 114–123. Univ. d'Ottawa.

Tricart, J. (1985b) Cartographie hydromorphologique et aménagement du Fouta Djallon (Guinée). In: *Pour Fernand Joly* CERCG, Paris, pp. 547–555.

For the first time hydromorphological mapping is included in a UNDP financed programme.

Tricart, J. (1985c) Les loess de la Chine du Nord-Est, leur contexte paléogéomorphologique. *Ann. de Géogr.* **94**(524): 411–31.

Tricart, J. (1986a) Geomorphology for the future: Geomorphology for development and development for geomorphology. In: V. Gardiner (Ed.) *International Geomorphology* Part I, pp. 35–44, J. Wiley & Sons, Chichester.

Tricart, J. (1986b) Problèmes de développement en Amazonie et en Guyane. *Ann. de Géogr.* **95**(532): 715–37.

Tricart, J. (1987a) Le milieu naturel terrestre, intégration systémique. *Rev. de Géom. Dyn.* **36**(1): 3–16.

Tricart, J. (1987b) Qu'apporte la télédétection en géomorphologie? Actes du Premier Forum Français de Géomorphologie, Meudon, 26–27 Nov. *Rev. de Géom. Dyn.* **36**(4): 132–7.

Methodological problems, examples by different French investigators, discussions.

Tricart, J. (1987c) Algunos aspectos de las relaciones entre el Hombre y los ecosistemas. *Divulgación*, Inst. Geogr. Univ. Nac. A. México **7**: 15–30.

Tricart, J. (1988a) L'Amazonie, milieu naturel, mise en valeur. *Ann. de Géogr.* **47**(544): 667–80.

Tricart, J. (1988b) Une menace pour notre milieu: l'effet de serre. *Rev. de Géom. Dyn.* **37**(1): 19–24.

A general presentation of the problem with critical assessment of some US publications.

Tricart, J. (1989a) Système expert pour l'étude, l'évaluation, la gestion et l'aménagement des ressources en eau. *Rev. de Géom. Dyn.* **38**(4): 129–44.

The only presently existing attempt at competent system devoted to water resource research, evaluation, conservation and management.

Tricart, J. (1989b) Earth natural system. A contribution to the

Geosphere–Biosphere Program. *Geoökodynamik* **10**(2/4): 159–76.

Tricart, J. (1989c) Rôle du volcanisme explosif et du vent dans la formation des précipités calcaires quaternaires ('tosca' de la Pampa Argentine). *Bull. AFEQ* **26**(37): 45–54.

A complementation of the former papers of the author about the Pampa Deprimida. Calcrete results, in an area where there is no calcium carbonate in the rocks, from the reworking of aeolian dust produced by volcanic explosions.

Tricart, J. (Ed.) (1990) *Actes de la Table-Ronde Télédétection du Milieu Naturel*, Strasbourg 11–13 Sept. (1988). Bilingual, French and English. Centre de Géographie Appliquée, Strasbourg.

Tricart, J., Blumenroeder, D. (1979) Télédétection dans le Sud Bahianais (Brésil). *Rech. Géogr. à Strasbourg* **10**: 63–85.

Tricart, J., Blumenroeder, D. (1981) Essais de compositions colorées pour l'étude des paysages (images LANDSAT Sud-Bahia, Brésil). *Photo-Interprétation* **81–6**(2–3): 8 pp.

Tricart, J., Bravard, J. P. (1991) L'aménagement des trois plus grands fleuves européens: Rhin, Rhône, Danube. Problèmes et méfaits. *Ann. de Géogr.* forthcoming.

Tricart, J., Cailleux, A. (1962–69) *Traité de géomorphologie*, SEDES, Paris, 5 vol., 2120 pp., 425 fig., 51 pl.

The most complete treatise of climatic geomorphology in existence, without equivalent. Contains abundant analytical and critical bibliographies at the end of each chapter. Two volumes have been translated into English by C. KiewietdeJonge.

Tricart, J., Cailleux, A. (1972) *Introduction to climatic geomorphology*. (Engl. translation by C. KiewietdeJonge), London, Harlow, 295 pp.

Tricart, J., Govea de Carpio, D. (1974) *Muestrario geomorfológica de Venezuela*, M.O.P., Cartografía Nac., Dep. de Géogr. e Historia y de Cultura y Publ. del Inst. Pedagógico de Caracas, 150 pp., 55 air phot., stereotriplets, 2 radar mosaics.

All documents are discussed.

Tricart, J., Guerra de Macedo, N., Cardoso da Silva, T., Brochu, M., Avenard, J. M. (1965) *Rapport de la mission de reconnaissance géomorphologique de la vallée moyenne du Niger (Janv.–Apr., 1957).* Mém. IFAN 72, 196 pp., maps, fig.

Tricart, J., Hirsch, A. R., Griesbach, J. C. (1965) La géomorphologie et les eaux souterraines dans le bassin de Santiago du Chili. *TILAS* (Fac. des Lettres de Strasbourg), V, pp. 605–614.

Tricart, J., Hirsch, A. R., Griesbach, J. C. (1966) La géomorphologie du bassin du Touch (Haute-Garonne), ses implications pédologiques et hydrologiques. *Rev. Géogr. des Pyr. et du SO.* **37**: 5–46.

First large scale hydromorphological map published in France.

Tricart, J., Lopez Recendez, R., Cervantes Borga, J. (1983) L'éruption du volcan El Chichon (Mexique), mars–avril 1982. *Ann. de Géogr.* **92**(512): 385–402.

Tricart, J., Maine, G., Cloots-Hirsch, A.-R. (1981) L'Hypodermisme. In: Livre jubilaire offert à Ch.-P. Pequy. Grenoble, Institut de Géographie Alpine, pp. 525–47.

Tricart, J., Michel, M. (1965) Monographie et carte géomorphologique de la région de Lagunillas (Andes vénézuéliennes). *Rev. de Géom. Dyn.* **15**(1/3): 133.

Tricart, J., Pagney, P., Frécaut, R. (1984) *La Pantanal (Brésil) étude écogéographique.* Trav. & Doc. de Géogr. Trop., CEGET, 52, 4th trimester, 92 pp., maps, fig.

Tricart, J., Rimbert, S., Lutz, G. (1979) *Introduction à l'utilisation des photographies aériennes en géographie, géologie, écologie, aménagement du territoire.* SEDES, Paris, vol. 1. *Notions générales, données structurales, géomorphologie*, 247 pp., 68 pl.

Includes statements on principles and on qualitative and quantitative procedures of photo-interpretation. Graded exercises with explanations.

Tricart, J., Trautmann, J., Gomes, A. et al. (1984) *Etude écodynamique de la plaine côtière méridionale du Rio Grande do*

Sul (Réserve écologique de Taim et son cadre), Rech. Géogr. à Strasbourg, special n°, 63 pp., fig., 8 loose leaf pl.

Tricart, J. et al. (1982) Télédétection des paysages, quelques réflexions méthodologiques. In: *Télédétection et géographie appliquée en zone aride et sud-méditerranéenne* pp. 59–84. Coll de l'Ecole Normale Sup. de Jeunes Filles, Montrouge N° 19.

Troll, C. (1950) Die geographische Landschaft und ihre Forschung. *Studium Generale*, Bonn **4/5**: 163–81.

Troll, C. (1963) Landscape ecology and land development with special reference to the tropics. *J. Tropical Geography* **17**: 1–11.

Troll, C. (1966) *Landscape ecology*. Publ. of the ITC–UNESCO Centre for Integrated Surveys, Delft, 23 pp.

Trustrum, N. A., De Rose, R. C. (1988) Soil depth–age relationship of landslides on deforested hillslopes, Taranaki, New Zealand. *Geomorphology* **I**(2): 143–60.
Rate of reconstitution of the soils on fresh material outcropping after a landslide.

Turc, L. (1950) Le bilan d'eau des sols. Relations entre les précipitations, l'évaporation et l'écoulement. *Ann. Agron.* **1**(5): 5–131.

Turc, L. (1961) Evaluations des besoins en eau d'irrigation. Evapotranspiration potentielle, formule simplifiée et mise à jour. *Ann. Agron.* **12**(1): 13–49.

Turc, L. (with techn. collab. of Lecerf, H.) (1972) Indice climatique de potentialité agricole. *Science du Sol* 2 (special n°), pp. 81–102.
Mathematical approach and comparison with other indices.

Turner, M. G. (Ed.) (1987) Landscape heterogeneity and disturbance. *Ecol. Studies* **64**: 239 pp. Springer-V., New York.

Twidale, C. R. (1976) *Analysis of Landforms*. Wiley, Sydney, 572 pp., 336 fig., 293 pl., 13 tables.
The best illustrated of all texts. Frequently presents multiple working hypotheses in the explanation of landforms.

Tyurin, L. V., Gerasimov, I. P., Ivanova, E. N. (1965) *Soil survey. A guide to field investigation and mapping of soils*. Israel Progr. Sci. Transl., Jerusalem 4, 356 pp.

UNEP (1983) *Rain and stormwater harvesting in rural areas*. Tycooly, Dublin, 238 pp.

UNESCO (1962) Les échanges hydriques de la plante en milieu aride et semi-aride. *Proc. Madrid colloquium*, Paris.

UNESCO (1973) Réponse des plantes aux facteurs climatiques. *Proc. Upsala colloquium.*, Paris.

UNESCO (Progr. MAB) (1975) Groupe de travail international sur le Projet 3 *Impact des activités humaines et méthodes d'utilisation des terres à paturages: savanes, prairies (des régions tempérées aux régions arides)*. Rapports MAB, 25, 100 pp., 14 fig.

UNESCO–UNEP (1988) *Evaluation environnementale intégrée du développement des resources en eau: directives méthodologiques*. Rapport du Groupe de Travail présidé par L. Hartmann. UNESCO, Paris, 196 pp.

UNESCO, UNEP, UNDP (1980) Desertification in the Oglat Merteba region, Tunisia. Case study presented by the Government of Tunisia. *Nat. Ress. Res.* **18**: 11–51.

UNESCO, PNUG, FAO (1981) Ecosystems pâturés tropicaux. Rech. sur lem Ress. Nat. **16**, 675 pp.

USDA (1957) *Soil, the 1957 Yearbook of Agric*. US Government Printing Office, Wash. D.C., 784 pp.

USDA (1967) *Manual on conservation of soil and water*, Agricultural handbook n° 61, Washington, DC.

USDA, Soil Survey Staff, SCS (1960) *Soil classification, a comprehensive system. 7th Approximation*, Washington, DC, 265 pp.

USDA, Soil Survey Staff, SCS (1975) *Soil taxonomy. A basic system of soil classification for making and interpreting soil surveys*. Agricultural handbook n° 436, Washington, DC.

USGS (1980) *Costs of landslide damage*. Geological Survey Research. Prof. Paper 1175, pp. 267.

USGS (1983) *Goals and tasks of the landslide part of a ground-failure hazards reduction program*. Circular 880, 2⁰ ed., 48 pp., 19 fig.

Usselmann, P. (1971) Carte géomorphologique et carte hydromorphologique au 1/50 000: le bassin du Lebrija

(Colombie), extrait 1/4 SW. *Mémoires et Documents* du Service de Documentation Cartographique et Géographique du CNRS, Paris, 12 (1972): 181–92. Included: two coloured maps.

Vaughan, R. A. (Ed.) *Remote sensing applications in meteorology and climatology*. Proc. NATO/ASI, Dundee. Reidel, NATO/ASI ser. C, 201.
Includes information about remote sensing of aerosols and air pollution.

Veihmeyer, F. J., Hendrickson, A. H. (1955) Does transpiration decrease as soil moisture decreases? *Trans. Am. Geophys. Union* **36**(3): 425–48.
The rate of soil moisture extraction is not influenced by the water of the soil as long as the water is above the permanent wilting percentage.

Veraguse, J. (1973) L'arénisation du massif d'Athis de l'Orne (Basse-Normandie), Bull. Centre de Géomorphologie, CNRS, Caen 16, 59 pp., 23 fig.

Verdin, J. (1983) Corrected vs. uncorrected LANDSAT-4 MSS data. *LANDSAT Data Users Notes* **27**, June: 4–7.

Verger, F. (1956) Les conquêtes sur la mer, de la Zélande au Jutland. *Ann. de Géogr.* **65**: 270–87.
An excellent example of management founded on a combination of 'structures' and guidance of vegetation growth based on the same philosophy as the Mauritanian example presented in the book.

Verger, F. (1982) *L'observation de la Terre par les satellites*. Coll. Que sais-je? PUF, Paris, 128 pp., 32 fig.
Updates J. Pouquet (1971), more succinct. Complete, clear, well documented.

Verger, F. (1984) La télédétection spatiale, outil géographique. *L'Espace Géographique* **13**(3): 169–72.
Compares remote sensing of coasts by LANDSAT MSS and TM and SPOT (simulated).

Verger, F. (1985) SPOT instrument de la géographie. *L'Information Géographique* **49**(1): 17–25.

Verger, F. (1989) L'intérêt d'observer la Terre depuis l'espace. *La Vie des Sc.*, Sér. Gén. **6**(2): 93–112.

Verigo, S. A., Razumova, L. A. (1961) *Soil moisture and its significance in agriculture*. Part I, transl. from the Russian by D. M. Keane, Nat. Lending Library for Sc. & Techn, 448 pp.
See especially chapter 2: Mechanism of the movement of soil moisture, pp. 23–41.

Verstappen, H. T. (1982) Applied geomorphological survey and mapping: three approaches. *Proc. Latin Amer. Reg. Conf. IGU*, Rio Claro, 9–14 Aug.: 14–22.

Verstappen, H. T. (1983) *Applied geomorphology, geomorphological surveys for environmental development*, Amsterdam, Oxford, New York, Elsevier, 437 pp.
Comprehensive, magnificently illustrated work: detailed references.

Verstappen, H. T. (1987a) Remote sensing applications of the Earth's surface, an outlook into the future. *Photogrammetria* **41**: 59–71.

Verstappen, H. T. (1987b) Methodische Probleme der geomorphologischen Kartierung mittels Fernerkundung. *Mitteilungen Basler Afrika Bibliogr.* **19**: 19–43.

Verstappen, H. T., Zuidam, R. van (1968) *ITC system of geomorphological survey*. ITC textbook of photo-interpretation, VII-2, ITC, Delft, 49 pp.
Based almost exclusively on photointerpretation. The system is most suitable for countries where scientific knowledge is scant and for students of intermediate level in geomorphology. Trilingual: English, French and Spanish.

Viers, G. (1967) *Eléments de géomorphologie*. Nathan, Paris, 208 pp., 119 fig.
Short elementary presentation but with interesting ideas.

Vincent, C. (1989) Le bouclier de la Vie. *Le Monde*, 11 Jan. n° 13, 672.

Vincent, P. (1990) *Biogeography of the British Isles. An introduction*. Routledge, London & New York, 315 pp.
Good examples of changes of land-use and of their consequences on ecodynamics.

Vink, A. P. A. (1968) The role of physical geography in integrated surveys of developing countries. *Tijdschrift voor Economische en Sociale Geografie* **59**: 294–312.
Concise account of the method of 'land systems'.

Vink, A. P. A. (1975) *Land use in advancing agriculture*, Springer-V., New York, 394 pp., 94 fig., 115 tables.
A major work of truly international scope.
Vink, A. P. A. (1982) Landscape ecological mapping. *ITC Journal* (3): 338–43.
Vink, A. P. A. (1983) *Landscape ecology and land use*. London, Harlow, 264 pp., transl. from the Dutch by author, an agronomist: Edited by Davidson, D. A.
Vision, T. M. (1987) Vision en perspective avec des images composites TM, *Observation de la Terre* 18 June: 4–5.
Viville, D., Ambroise, B. (1987) Spatial variability of soil hydric properties in the Ringelbach catchment (granite, Vosges, France). In: Gardiner, V. (Ed.) *International geomorphology* (1986), Part II, pp. 405–10. J. Wiley & Sons, Chichester.
Vliet-Lanoe, B. van (1988) Le rôle des ségrégations de glace dans les formations superficielles de l'Europe de l'Ouest. Processus et héritages. Thèse Etat, Paris I. Centre de Géom. du CNRS (Caen), 2 vol., 854 pp., 349 fig.
A huge quantity of observations, micro and macroscopic, about the occurrence of ice in non-consolidated deposits, its origin, its effects.
Vogt, H. (1979) Méthode d'étude complexe de l'érosion agricole des sols à l'exemple du vignoble alsacien. Coll. *Erosion agric.* Milieu Tempéré Strasbourg-Colmar 20–23 Sept. (1978). Strasbourg, ULP, pp. 199–201.
Vogt, H. Coord. (1978) *Erosion agricole des sols, problèmes de méthode, applications en Alsace*. Rech, Géogr. à Strasbourg **9**: 150 pp.
Vogt, T. (1989) Quelques éléments de discussion au sujet des croûtes calcaires. *Ann. de Géogr.* **98**(545): 71–9.
An interesting overview about calcrete formation.
Vogt, T., Schneider, C. (1987) Repérage et classification de formations superficielles en milieu subaride à partir de données LANDSAT MSS. L'exemple de Goulimine (Anti-Atlas Occidental, Maroc). *Rech. Géogr. à Strasbourg* **27**: 43–52.
Voute, C. (1982a) Remote sensing. *ITC Journal* (1): 37–44.
Good historical review: future development of platforms and sensors.
Voute, C. (1982b) Space for whom. *Futures* Oct.: 448–61.
Voute, C. (1983) *Essential elements of educational programmes on space science and technology and their applications including those that could be developed at/for local institutions in the developing countries*. ECA–ECWA Un. Nations Seminar on Space Applications, Addis Ababa, 4–8 July, ITC, Enschede (Netherlands), 36 pp.
Voute, C. (1986) The future generation of resources satellites. *ITC Journal* (4): 307–17.
Voute, C. (1987) Using outer space for managing matters on Earth: a dream come true or a nightmare in the making. *ITC Journal* (4): 292–9.

Waananen, A. et al. (1977) *Flood-prone areas and land use planning. Selected examples from the San Francisco Bay region, California*. USGS, Prof. Paper 942, 75 pp., 28 fig.
Wahrstom, E., Nichols, T. (1969) The morphology and chronology of a landslide near Dillon Dam, Dillon, Colorado. *Engineering Geol.* **2**: 149–74.
Waibel, L. (1933) Was verstehen wir unter Landschaftskunde? *Geogr. Anzeiger.* **34**: 197–207.
Waldron, H. (1967) *Debris flows and erosion control problems caused by the ash eruption of Irazu volcano, Costa Rica*. USGS, Bull. 1241-I, 37 pp., 1 map.
Walker, A., Robinove, C. (1981) *Annotated bibliography of remote sensing methods for monitoring desertification*, USGS Circular 851, 25 pp.
Walker, H. J. (1987) Potentials for international collaboration in geomorphological research. In: Gardiner, V. (Ed.) *International geomorphology*, 1986, Part I, pp. 11–24. J. Wiley & Sons, Chichester.
Walker, P. H., Hall, G. F., Protz, R. (1969) Soil trends and variability across selected landscapes in Iowa. *Proc. Soil Sc. Soc. Amer.* **32**: 97–101.
Wall, J. R. D. (1964) Topography–soil relationships in lowland Sarawak. *J. of Trop. Géogr.* **18**: 192–9.
Walling, D. E. (1979) Hydrological processes. In: Gregory, K. J., Walling, D. E. (Eds) *Man and environment*. Dawson, Folkestone, pp. 57–81.
Walling, D. E. (1980) Physical hydrology. *Progr. Phys. Géogr.* **4**(1): 107–117.
Walter, H. (1954) Le facteur eau dans les régions arides et sa signification pour l'organisation de la végétation dans les contrées subtropicales. CNRS. *Colloque international 'Division écologique du monde'*, pp. 271–83.
Walter, J. M. (1972/4) Arbres et forêts alluviales du Rhin. *Bull. Société d'Histoire Naturelle.* Colmar **55**: 37–88.
Remarkable study showing the interactions between fluvial dynamics and a riparian forest in process of dying out as a result of industrial development along the Rhine.
Ward, J. V., Stanford, J. A. (1979) Ecological factors controlling stream zoobenthes. In: Ward, J. V., Stanford, J. A. (Eds) *The ecology of regulated streams*, pp. 35–56. Plenum Press, New York, xi + 398 pp.
Ward, R. C. (1975) *Principles of Hydrology*, 2nd ed., McGraw-Hill, London, 367 pp.
A non-mathematical, non-applied, systematic geographical approach with a chapter on the drainage basin, useful for chapter 6. References on soil moisture chapter 6 complete those of the reference list.
Wasson, R. J., Clark, R. L. (1985) Environmental history for explanation and prediction. *Search* **16**(9/12): 258–63.
Weber, C. (1985) Geological remote sensing: Quo Vadis? *ITC Journal* (4): 221–7.
Weischem, W. (1977) *Die ökologische Benachteiligung der Tropen*. Teubner, Stuttgart, 127 pp., 39 fig.
Weise, R., Barsch, H. (1979) Geomorphologische Kennzeichnung chorischer Naturraumtypen im glazial bestimmten Tiefland der DDR, Martin-Luther Univ., Halle Wittenberg, *Wissenschaftliche Beiträge* **45**(Q5): 34–42.
Welch, R., Ehlers, M. (1987) Merging multiresolution SPOT HRV and LANDSAT TM data. *Photogrammetric Eng. & Remote Sensing* **53**(3): 301–3.
Welsch, E. B. (1980) *Ecological effects of waste water*. Cambridge Univ. Press, Cambridge.
West, E. A. (1978) The equilibrium of natural streams. *Geo-Abstracts*, Norwich, 205 pp., 30 fig.
Methodological discussions of general interest, especially in the introduction.
White, R. L. (1973) An examination of the value of site analysis in field studies in tropical Australia. *Zeit. für Geom.* **17**: 156–84.
Whittow, J. (1980) *Disasters: the anatomy of environmental hazards*. Allen Lane, London, 411 pp.
Wieber, J. C. (1985) *Cartographier le paysage*. 'Pour Fernand Joly', Centre d'Etudes et de Réalisations cartographiques géographiques, 431–4 pp.
Wieder, M., Yaalon, D. (1985) Catenary soil differentiation on opposite-facing slopes related to erosion-deposition and restricted leaching processes, northern Negev, Israel. *J. of Arid Env.* **9**: 119–36.
Wieneke, F. (1987) Der Einfluss der räumlichen Dimension der Daten auf die Einsatzmöglichkeit photographischer fernerkundung landschaftsökologischer Untersuchungen. *Geomethodica* (Basel) **12**, pp. 579.
Wieneke, F., Rust, U. (1976) Methodischer Ansatz, Techniken und Ergebnisse geomorphologischer Untersuchungen in der Zentralen Namib. 1^0 *Basler Geomethodischen Colloquiums*, 107–50 pp.
Wiesker, K. P. (1986) Programme zur Erfassung von Landschaftsdaten, eine Bodenerosionsgleichung und ein Modell der Kaltluftentstehung. *Heidelberger Geogr. Abh.* **79**: 83 pp., 14 fig.
The author prefers using a collection of limiting factors to the adoption of a 'potential' for constructing a data bank.
Wilbert, J. (1962) Deux exemples de relations entre pédologie et géomorphologie au Maroc. *Rev. de Géogr. du Maroc* (1/2): 31–5.
Wilding, L., Smeck, N., Hall, G. (Eds) (1983) *Pedogenesis and soil taxonomy*, I, *concepts and interactions*. Elsevier, Amsterdam.
Wilgat, T. (1968) The compilation of a general hydrogeographical map with Lublin Voivodship as an example. *Geographia Polonica* **13**: 151–8.
Williams, A. R., Morgan, R. P. (1976) Geomorphological mapping applied to soil erosion evaluation. *J. Soil & Water Conserv.* **31**: 164–9.

Williams, P. J. (1979) *Pipelines and permafrost: physical geography and development in the circumpolar North.* Longman, Harlow, 98 pp.

Williams, P. J. (1982) *The surface of the Earth. An introduction to geotechnical science.* Longman, Harlow, 212 pp.

Williams, P. J. (1986) *Pipelines and permafrost.* Carleton Univ. Press, Don Mills (Ontario), 129 pp. 19 phot.

Wilmen, J. (1978) Interprétation des images des satellites LANDSAT en vue d'études urbaines et régionales. *Bull. Soc. Fr. Photogramm.* **70**: 13–23.

Wilshire, M. (1980) Human causes of accelerated wind erosion in California's deserts. In: Coaches, O., Vitek, J. (Eds) *Three holds in geomorphology*, Allen & Unwin, London, pp. 415–33.

Winiger, M. (1983) Stability and instability of mountain ecosystems. Definitions for evaluation of human systems. In: Messerli, B., Ives, J. (Eds) *Mountain ecosystems, stability and instability*, pp. 103–11. *Mountain Res and Dev.,* **3** (2).

Wischmeier, A. M. (1972) A rainfall erosion index for a universal soil-loss equation. *Soil Science of America Proc.* **23**: 246–9.

Wischmeier, W. H. (1975) Estimating the soil loss equation's cover and management factor for undisturbed areas in: *Present and prospective technology for predicting sediment yields and sources.* USDA Agricultural Research Service Rpt. n° ARS-S-40: 118–24.

Wischmeier, W. H., Smith, D. D. (1962) Soil loss estimation as a tool in soil water management planning. *Int. Assoc. Scient. Hydrol. Publ.* **59**: 148–59.

Wischmeier, W. H., Smith, D. D. (1978) *Predicting rainfall erosion losses*, USDA, Agricultural Research Service Handbook 537.

Wisler, C. O., Brater, E. F. (1959) *Hydrology*, 2nd ed., J. Wiley & Sons, Inc., New York, 408 pp.

Wit, K., Ziemonska, Z. (1960) Hydrography of the western Tatra Mts. Explanation to the map 'Tatry Zachodnie' 1:50 000. *Polska Ak. Nauk.*, Institute of Geography, Krakow, 99 pp., 7 pl., map (in Polish with English summary).

Wit-Jozwik, K. (1968) Examples of hydrographical maps of southern Poland (showing regions with different systems of water circulation). *Przeglad Geograficzny* **40**(2): 271–83.

Witkin, I. (1972) Map showing seiche, rockslide, rockfall and earthflow hazards in the Henrys Lake quadrangle, Idaho and Montana, USGS, 1 map, scale 1/62 500.
Cited as an example of a series of quadrangles prepared by the USGS as surveys of the various types of geomorphic hazards. Scales vary.

W.M.O. (1975) *Drought and agriculture.* Techn. Note **138**: 127 pp., 16 fig.

Wolman, M. G., Gerson, R. (1978) Relative scales of time and effectiveness of climate in watershed geomorphology. *Earth Surface Processes* **3**(2): 189–208.
Well-considered general concepts.

Woodwell, G. M., Houghton, R. A., Stone, T. A., Nelson, R. F., Kowalick, W. (1987) Deforestation in the tropics: new measurements in the Amazon basin using LANDSAT and NOAA Advanced. Very High Resolution Radiometer. *J. Geophys. Res.* **92**(D2): 2157–63.

Wright, R. L. (1972) Principles in a geomorphological approach to land classification. *Zeit. für Geom.* **16**: 351–73.

Yaalon, D. (1960) Some implications of fundamental concepts of pedology in soil classifications. 7th Internat. Congr. Soils Sc., Madison. *Transactions*, IV,V,**16**: 119–23.

Yaalon, D. (1986) Palaeozols in the mainstream pedological literature: a review of some recent texts. *Prog. Phys. Geogr.* **10**(4): 587–93.

Yankovitch, L. (1956) Résultats de 22 années d'expériences dans les cases lysimétriques et cases de végétation du service botanique et agronomique de Tunisie. *Annales du Service Botanique et Agronomique de Tunisie*, 29, Tunis.

Young, A. (1968) Natural resources surveys for land development in the tropics. *Geography* **53**(240): 229–48.

Young, A. (1972) The soil catena: a systematic approach. *Internat. Géogr.* I: 287–9.
An attempt to include some dynamic aspects in the catena concept. Nevertheless, it remains somewhat obsolete if compared with the pedogenic/morphogenic balance proposed seven years earlier.

Zilliox, L. (1982) L'action de recherche interdisciplinaire du groupe 'PIREN Eau' en Alsace. *Rech. Géogr. à Strasbourg* **19/21**: 241–7.

Zinck, A. (1970) *Aplicación de la geomorfología al levantamiento de suelos en zonas aluviales*, MOP, Div. Edafología, Barcelona (Venezuela), 79 pp.

Zonneveld, J. I. S. (1974) On abstract and concrete boundaries, arranging and classification. *Tatsachen und Probleme der Grenzen in der Vegetation.* Intern. Symp. Inst. Verein Vegetationskunde, Rintels Cramer Verlag: 17–42.

Zonneveld, J. I. S. (1977) Stability and dynamics of ecosystems. *Ned. L.W.O.* **4**(1): 16–28.

Zonneveld, J. I. S. (1979) Land evaluation and landscape science. In: *ITC textbook of photo-interpretation* 2nd ed., VII-4: 134, pp. 6 fig.
Comparison of the land surveys, Vinogradov and Neef approaches (21–28), problems of cartographic legend (29–35) and of the minimum area necessary for defining landscape units (33, 36).

Zuidam, R. van (1982) Considerations on systematic medium-scale geomorphological mapping. *Zeit. für Geom.* **26**(4): 473–80.

Zuidam, R. van (1985/6) *Aerial photo-interpretation in terrain analysis and geomorphologic mapping.* Smits, The Hague, pp. 442, photos.

Zuidam, R. van, Zuidam-Cancelado, F. I. van (1978/9) In: *ITC textbook of photo-interpretation*, vol. VII, Chapter 6. Terrain analysis and classification using aerial photographs. vol A geomorphological approach. ITC, Enschede 310 + 23 pp., 93 phot., 18 pl.
This work, like the CSIRO Land Surveys, is based on photo interpretation. The authors follow the same approach, such that, in reality, geomorphology remains physiography.

Zvonkova, T. V. (1959) *Landform studies for practical purposes.* Geografguiz, Moscow, 304 pp., 59 fig. (in Russian–French transl. by SIG, BRGM 3188).
Overview of Soviet research and methods used in the USSR.

Zvonkova, T. V. (1960) Applications pratiques de la géomorphologie en U.R.S.S. *Rev. de Géom. Dyn.* **11**: 122–4.

Zvonkova, T., Salichtchev, K. (1970) *Small scale maps for assessment of natural environmental conditions.* Univ. Ed., Moscow (in Russian).

ORGANIZATIONS INDEX

SUBJECT INDEX

AUTHOR INDEX

PLACE NAMES INDEX